THE CASE AGAINST MIRACLES

Edited by John W. Loftus

Copyright © 2019 Hypatia Press

All rights reserved. No part of this publication may be reproduced, stored in or introduced into a retrieval system or transmitted in any form or by any means, electronic, mechanical, photocopying, recording or otherwise without prior written permission from the publisher.

Published by Hypatia Press in the United States in 2019

ISBN: 978-1-83919-306-4

Cover design by Claire Wood

www.hypatiapress.org

This volume is dedicated to the legacy of David Hume, considered to be the greatest English-speaking philosopher who ever lived.

I flatter myself, that I have discovered an argument...which, if just, will, with the wise and learned, be an everlasting check to all kinds of superstitious delusion, and consequently, will be useful as long as the world endures.
– From *Of Miracles* by David Hume (1711-1776).

What made Hume's argument in *Of Miracles* particularly influential is due to the arrogance of statements like the one above. For a defense of the power of ridicule see, "Was David Hume's Argument *Of Miracles* Original? The Role of Ridicule" at my blog: http://www.debunking-christianity.com/2019/11/was-david-humes-argument-of-miracles.html

ADVANCE PRAISE

The Case against Miracles is the most important anthology to ever be written about miracles.
— Peter Boghossian, author of *A Manual for Creating Atheists* and *How to Have Impossible Conversations*.

While some entries are stronger than others, *The Case against Miracles* represents a powerful critique of the miraculous. Its central arguments demand the attention of any serious defender of the Christian faith.
— Trent Horn, a Christian apologist who earned three master's degrees in theology, philosophy, and bioethics, and author of nine books, including *Answering Atheism*.

This book is a secular miracle! An extremely rare event. For gathering this well-reasoned material into such an accessible volume, John Loftus should be canonized.
— Dan Barker, author of *Godless, Free Will Explained*, and *GOD: The Most Unpleasant Character in All Fiction*.

Christians need be aware of what non-Christian scholars are saying. In this thoughtful and stimulating volume, editor John Loftus brings together a number of the most accomplished atheists and other skeptics to deal with the crucial topic of miracles, an issue that is important on all sides.

— Gary R. Habermas, Distinguished Research Scholar & Chair, Dept. of Philosophy, Liberty University

In this book Loftus has marshaled all the key arguments to prove that people should seriously doubt all religious miracle claims. It should be required reading in all seminaries.
– Karen L. Garst, PhD, editor of *Women Beyond Belief* and *Women v. Religion.*

Every John W. Loftus book is a must-read; he continues to assemble some of the finest and most insightful minds in contemporary counter-apologetics. Putting biblical miracle claims under the magnifying lens, it weighs the evidence and finds them wanting. *The Case against Miracles* is a superb resource and a handy field guide for anyone forced to traipse through the treacherous jungles of the miraculous.
– David Fitzgerald, author of *Nailed, Jesus: Mything in Action,* and *The Complete Heretic's Guide to Western Religion.*

John Loftus' *The Case against Miracles* is a must read for anyone who truly and honestly wonders whether a miracle has ever occurred. Especially useful is its treatment of Craig Keener and his reports of the miraculous. Not only is the speciousness of Keener's stories exposed, and the myriad faults of his investigate approach laid bare, but the details of how investigation into the miraculous must be approached is clearly articulated.
– David Kyle Johnson, Ph.D, author of The Great Courses' "*The Big Questions of Philosophy*"

The Case against Miracles is a must read go-to book for showing the key flaws in the arguments Christian apologists use to convince people that miracles are real. It's the best book ever written on miracles.
– Mark W. Gura, president of Atheist Alliance of America, author, and atheist activist.

CONTENTS

Foreword: On Miracles and Truth   1
    By Michael Shermer

Introduction   9

Part 1: Miracles and the Abject Failure of Christian Apologetics

1| Miracles and the Challenge of Apologetics   29
    By David Corner

2| God Would Not Perform Miracles   58
    By Matthew McCormick

3| Extraordinary Claims Require Extraordinary Evidence   79
    By John W. Loftus

4| Properly Investigating Miracle Claims   114
    By Darren M. Slade

5| Assessing Keener's Miracles   148
    By Edward T. Babinski

6| The Abject Failure of Christian Apologetics   171
    By John W. Loftus

7| Why Do Christians Believe in Miracles?   202
    By Valerie Tarico

Part 2: Properly Investigating the Miracle of Biblical Revelation

8| Why the Romans Believed the Gospels   231
    By R. G. Price

9| How New Testament Writers Helped Jesus Fulfill Prophecy   255

By Robert J. Miller

10| The Prophetic Failure of Christ's Return   278

By Robert Conner

11| Five Inconvenient Truths that Falsify Biblical Revelation   302

By David Madison

Part 3: Properly Investigating Key Biblical Miracles

12| Evolution is a Fact!   331

By Abby Hafer

13| Old Testament Miracle Genres as Folklore and Legend   377

By Randall Heskett

14| Science, Miracles and Noah's Flood   403

By Clay Farris Naff

15| Jesus Christ: Docetic Demigod   423

By Robert M. Price

16| Miracles of the Christian Magicians   446

By Robert Conner

17| Credulity At Cana?   467

By Evan Fales

18| The Resurrection of Jesus Never Took Place   491

By John W. Loftus

19| Paul's Christianity   519

By Robert Conner

Epilogue   546

Appendix: Hume On Proof and Mathematical Probability 551
By John W. Loftus

About the contributing Authors 561

FOREWORD

ON MIRACLES AND TRUTH

BY MICHAEL SHERMER

Have you ever gone to the phone to call a friend, only to have the phone ring first and find your friend on the line? What are the odds of that? Not high, to be sure, but the sum of all probabilities equals one. How many times did you phone your friend and he or she didn't call? How many times did your friend phone and you weren't thinking of him or her? Multiply that by a couple hundred million people in the U.S. alone making dozens of calls a day, and it becomes almost inevitable that this seemingly miraculous connection—which many people attribute to synchronicity or Karma or a supernatural force or God or whatever—is fully explained by probabilities. Given enough opportunities, outlier anomalies—even apparent miracles—will happen. And thanks to the confirmation bias in which we look for and find confirming evidence for what we already believe and ignore or rationalize away disconfirming evidence, we will remember the hits and forget the misses.

A miracle may be defined in many ways, so let's start with this colloquial meaning of a highly unusual event, as when someone exclaims "it's a miracle!" when winning the lottery, or "it was miraculous" when recovering from a serious illness, or most famously at the end of the 1980 Olympic hockey game when the underdog U.S. team defeated the mighty Russian juggernaut and the ABC TV sports commentator Al

Michaels exclaimed "Do you believe in miracles?!" Let us quantify this intuitive sense of a highly unlikely event as one with million-to-one odds of occurring. Now let's apply some back-of-the-envelope calculations along the lines of the apparently miraculous phone call above. Assuming we're awake and alert for 12 hours a day and that, say, one bit of information flows into our brains through our senses per second, that generates 43,200 bits of data per day, or 1,296,000 per month. Even assuming that 99.999 percent of these bits are totally meaningless (and so we filter them out or forget them entirely), that still leaves 1.3 "miracles" per month, or 15.5 miracles per year. That is, with enough data accumulating from the world there's bound to be highly unusual occurrences that we notice. How unusual? One in a million.

I once employed a similar back-of-the-envelope calculation to explain death premonition dreams, you know, the type where someone has a dream about a loved one dying and the next day they find out that a grandparent or parent or close family member or friend passed away in the middle of the night, maybe even around the time of the dream. How unusual is that? Well, the average person has about five dreams per night, or 1,825 dreams per year. If we remember only a tenth of our dreams, then we recall 182.5 dreams per year. Let's say that there are 300 million adult dreaming Americans who thus produce 54.7 billion remembered dreams per year. Sociologists tell us that each of us knows about 150 people fairly well (the so-called Dunbar number named after Robin Dunbar who discovered this in his research on human social networking), thus producing a network social grid of 45 billion personal relationship connections. With an average annual death rate of 2.4 million Americans per year (all causes, all ages), it is inevitable that some of those 54.7 billion remembered dreams will be about some of these 2.4 million deaths among the 300 million Americans and their 45 billion relationship connections. In fact, it would be a *miracle* if some death premonition dreams did *not* come true! Here's an announcement you'll never hear on television:

Next on Oprah: a woman who has had numerous death premonition dreams not one of which has come true yet, but stay tuned because you won't want to miss her incredible story.

But this is not what most Christians, theologians, and religious apologists mean by the word *miracle*. They mean something more than a highly improbable event within the natural laws of nature. They mean something divine has happened, and to make this case Christian apologists go deep into the weeds of philosophy and theology (and sometimes even science) to make their case, for example Lee Strobel's 2018 book *The Case for Miracles*, which includes a chapter on my own journey from religious belief accepting miracles to scientific skepticism rejecting miracles.

It is vital that we have a viable response to the claims of Christians and others that miracles are real, and John Loftus has done just that in this, the most comprehensive work ever compiled for, as it is aptly titled, *The Case against Miracles*. The chapters span the range of miracle claims, including the philosophical arguments of Christian apologists, biblical miracles from the Old Testament to the New, the miracle of creation, the miracle of life, the miracle of Noah's Flood, the miracle of the virgin birth of Jesus, the miracles Jesus' allegedly performed such as turning water into wine (I've seen Penn & Teller perform this one!) and raising the dead, and of course the biggest miracle of them all (for Christians anyway), Jesus' resurrection from the dead and ascendency into heaven. I thought I knew a lot on these topics—inasmuch as I was once a born-again Christian myself and made these arguments, then became a born-again Skeptic debating believers—but I learned more from reading this one book than all other works combined. *The Case against Miracles* belongs in every library and personal bookcase of both believers and skeptics.

Let's start with how the word "miracle" is defined. In John Loftus's introduction to *The Case against Miracles* he notes that the pre-scientific biblical "signs and wonders" definition applied to just about everything that happened in the world, from the ordinary to the extraordinary—

from normal births to virgin births, from rain to deluges, and from famines to feasts. Clearly this will not suffice. If everything is a miracle then nothing is a miracle. And as Loftus notes, as science developed over the centuries more and more of these signs and wonders were explained by natural law, leaving fewer and fewer divine miracles.

Enter the Enlightenment philosopher David Hume, who, in his 1758 *An Enquiry Concerning Human Understanding* famously defined a miracle as "a violation of a law of nature," and less famously as "a transgression of a law of nature by a particular volition of the Deity, or by the interposition of some invisible agent." In fact, his Section X, "Of Miracles," provides a generalized, when-all-else-fails analysis of miraculous claims. That is, when one is confronted by a true believer whose apparently supernatural or paranormal claim has no immediately apparent natural explanation, Hume gives us an argument that even he thought was so important (and Hume was not a modest man) that he placed his own words in quotes and called it a maxim. I think it is so useful an argument that I have called it (in my 1997 book *Why People Believe Weird Things*) *Hume's Maxim*:

> The plain consequence is (and it is a general maxim worthy of our attention), "That no testimony is sufficient to establish a miracle, unless the testimony be of such a kind, that its falsehood would be more miraculous than the fact which it endeavours to establish." When anyone tells me that he saw a dead man restored to life, I immediately consider with myself whether it be more probable, that this person should either deceive or be deceived, or that the fact, which he relates, should really have happened. I weigh the one miracle against the other; and according to the superiority, which I discover, I pronounce my decision, and always reject the greater miracle. If the falsehood of his testimony would be more miraculous than the event which he relates; then, and not till then, can he pretend to command my belief or opinion.

In the two and a half centuries since Hume wrote this passage we have learned much about deception and self-deception from the study of human perception, memory, and cognition, especially the plethora of cognitive biases that distort our picture of reality, so *Hume's Maxim* is even more supported today than it was in his time. People are routinely deceived by others, they deceive themselves, and they misperceive how the world works. When someone tells us of a miracle they witnessed, or of a miracle someone told them about, it is far more likely that they "either deceive or be deceived, or that the fact, which he relates, should really have happened."

When we are thinking about miracles, as with anything else that happens in the world, what we are after is a causal explanation, and here John Loftus cuts to the chase when he cites my friend and colleague David Kyle Johnson's definition of a miracle—winnowed-down from Hume—as "A miracle is simply an event caused by God." As Johnson explains, "For any given event, if we knew that God took special care to cause it, we would (and should) call that event a miracle—regardless of whether it involved the violation of natural law." However, it is important to distinguish this from something that *appears* divinely caused but was, in fact, simply a highly improbable natural occurrence, along the lines of my million-to-one odds analysis above. We want to distinguish between a natural and a supernatural event when considering miracle claims. This is why I agree with Loftus' definition:

A miracle is a supernaturally caused extraordinary event of the highest kind, one that's unexplainable and even impossible by means of natural processes alone.

Pulling back to look at an even bigger picture of what we're after here in thinking about miracles is the question *What is truth?* This is the question I have been trying to answer my entire professional life. I am, professionally speaking, a skeptic, inasmuch as I publish a magazine called *Skeptic* and penned a monthly column in *Scientific American* called "Skeptic". According to the *Oxford English Dictionary*, a *skeptic* is "One who holds that there are no adequate grounds for certainty as to the truth of any proposition whatever." This is too solipsistic. Etymologically, its Latin derivative is *scepticus*, for "inquiring" or "reflective." Further variations in the ancient Greek include "a seeker after truth; an inquirer who has not yet arrived at definite convictions." So skepticism is *reflective inquiry into the truth*, and in many cases we have adequate grounds for certainty as to the truth of many propositions. For example:

There are over 500 pages in this book, *The Case against Miracles*. True by observation.

Dinosaurs went extinct around 65 million years ago. True by verification and replication of radiometric dating techniques for volcanic eruptions above and below dinosaur fossils.

The universe began with a Big Bang. True by a convergence of evidence from a wide range of phenomena such as the cosmic microwave background, the abundance of light elements like hydrogen and helium, the distribution of galaxies and the large-scale structure of the cosmos, the redshift of most galaxies, and the expansion of space.

These propositions are "true" in the sense that the evidence is so substantial it would be unreasonable to withhold one's provisional assent. It's not impossible that the dinosaurs died recently, just after the creation of the universe 10,000 years ago (as Young Earth Creationists believe), but it is so unlikely we need not waste our time considering it.

Then there are negative truths, such as the null hypothesis in science that the nonexistence of something is the truth. You claim that you have a cure for AIDS, a drug that can eliminate 100% of HIV in a body. Before the FDA will approve your drug for sale to the public you must provide substantial evidence that your claim is true in the scientific sense, that is, to reject the null hypothesis that you do not have such a drug. More simply, when people tell me Big Foot is real, I say "show me the body and I'll believe, otherwise I remain skeptical." The null hypothesis in this example is that Big Foot does not exist. Finally, it is telling that among the tens of thousands of government emails, documents, and files leaked in recent years through Wikileaks, there is not one mention of a UFO cover up, a faked moon landing, or that 9/11 was an inside job by the Bush administration. Here the *absence of evidence is evidence of absence*. This has implications for miracle claims.

The null hypothesis is that your claim of a miracle is not true until you prove otherwise. Here we say that the *burden of proof* is on the miracle claimant, not the skeptic or scientist to disprove the miracle claim. Let's consider the biggest religious miracle claim of all—that Jesus was resurrected. Now, the proposition that Jesus was crucified may be true by historical validation, inasmuch as a man named Jesus of Nazareth probably existed, the Romans routinely crucified people for even petty crimes, and most biblical scholars—even those who are atheists, such as the renowned University of North Carolina at Chapel Hill Religious Studies professor Bart Ehrman—assent to this fact. The proposition that Jesus died for our sins, by contrast, is a faith-based truth claim with no purchase on valid knowledge. It cannot be tested or falsified. It cannot be confirmed. It can only be believed or disbelieved based on faith or the lack thereof. In between these propositions is Jesus's resurrection, which is not impossible but would be a miracle if it were true. Is it?

Here we turn to Section XII of David Hume's *Philosophical Essays Concerning the Human Understanding*, "Of the Academical or Sceptical Philosophy," in which the Scottish philosopher distinguishes between "antecedent skepticism", such as Descartes's method of doubting everything, that has no "antecedent" infallible criterion for belief; and "consequent skepticism," the method Hume employed that recognizes the "consequences" of our fallible senses, but corrects them through reason: "A wise man proportions his belief to the evidence."

The *principle of proportionality* demands *extraordinary evidence for extraordinary claims*, as Carl Sagan famously said (quoting the lesser known sociologist of science Marcello Truzzi, thereby confirming the observation that pithy and oft-quoted statements migrate up to the most famous person who said them). Of the approximately 100 billion people who lived before us, all have died and none returned, so the claim that one of them rose from the dead is about as extraordinary as one will ever find. Is the evidence commensurate with the conviction? According to the University of Wisconsin-Madison philosopher Larry Shapiro in his 2016 book *The Miracle Myth*, "evidence for the resurrection is nowhere near as complete or convincing as the evidence on which historians rely to justify belief in other historical events such as the destruction of Pompeii." Because miracles are far less probable than ordinary historical occurrences like volcanic eruptions, "the evidence necessary to justify beliefs about them must be many times better than that which would justify our beliefs in run-of-the-mill historical events. *But it isn't.*"

What about the eyewitnesses? Maybe they "were superstitious or credulous" and saw what they wanted to see, Shapiro suggests. "Maybe they reported only feeling Jesus 'in spirit,' and over the decades their testimony was altered to suggest that they saw Jesus in the flesh. Maybe accounts of the resurrection never appeared in the original gospels and were added in later centuries. Any of these explanations for the gospel descriptions of Jesus's resurrection are far more likely than the possibility that Jesus actually returned to life after being dead for three days."

The principle of proportionally also means we should prefer the more probable explanation over the less, which these alternatives surely are. In *The Case against Miracles* John Loftus devotes a chapter to this greatest of all miracles—the resurrection—and it is the best analysis I've ever read. In time, all of these "god-of-the-gaps" type arguments for miracles will fall, and with them the last epistemological justification for religious belief beyond blind faith. Perhaps this is why Jesus was silent when Pilate asked him (John 18:38) "What is truth?"

Michael Shermer, publisher of *Skeptic* magazine (www.skeptic.com). For nearly 18 years, he was the monthly "Skeptic" columnist for Scientific American. He is the author of numerous books including W*hy People Believe Weird Things* and *The Believing Brain*.

INTRODUCTION

This anthology is about miracles and why there isn't enough objective evidence to believe in them. In the pre-scientific biblical past, miracles were described as "signs and wonders." This biblical phrase referred to the actions of god in his created world. In the Bible, everything that happened was due to god's action in the world. The only conceptual difference that mattered was whether events were ordinary (that is, they occurred frequently, or frequently enough), or extraordinary (that is, they didn't happen much, or not at all), or miraculous (that is, they were extraordinary events of the highest kind). Ordinary events were the result of divine actions no less than extraordinary events and miraculous events. Whether it was the birth of a baby or a virgin birth, rain or a deluge, the sun moving in the sky or standing still, millions being fed on manna or a famine, they were all the result of divine deeds. For people living in this pre-scientific superstitious era anything was possible.[1] They were even told they could pray for a mountain to be uprooted and cast into the sea and god would do it,[2,3,4] although such a prayer was never instantaneously answered!

One of the most accurate definitions was stated by David Hume in his ground-breaking chapter of arguments against miracles. A miracle may be accurately defined as "*a transgression of a law of nature by a*

---

[1] On this, see Chapter 13 of *Why I Became an Atheist*, "The Strange and Superstitious World of the Bible."
[2] Mark 11:23.
[3] Matthew 21:21.
[4] Luke 17:6.

particular volition of the Deity, or by the interposition of some invisible agent."⁵ His most famous definition simply says a miracle is "a violation of a law of nature."⁶ This expresses the same idea. Violation or transgression? It's the same difference.

A miracle must be an event caused by a supernatural force or being, a god. Such an event could not take place on its own in the natural world without the action of a god. It must be an event which involves the interfering, or suspension, or transgressing, or breaching, or contravening, or violating of natural law. Such an event could not be explainable by science because it would be an event impossible to occur by natural processes alone. A miracle is therefore an extraordinary event of the highest kind.

Consequently a miracle is not merely an extremely rare event within the natural world, or something that just happened "at the right time." We know from statistics that extremely rare events take place regularly in our lives. How many times have you heard believers say their god did a miracle, or answered a prayer, based on a very unlikely set of circumstances? You hear this from Mennonites, Methodists, Moonies, Mormons, and Muslims, and every other believer who possesses a prayer-answering god. [If there aren't a plethora of different gods answering these prayers then one god answers them all, thus creating conflict and wars between believers over who possesses the right god.] Believers will quote their *believing* doctors who say the odds of being healed were "one in a million," as evidence of a miracle healing. Listen, a one in a million healing is not equivalent to a miracle. The reason is because of the statistics of large numbers.

Statistician David Hand shows us this in his book, *The Improbability Principle: Why Coincidences, Miracles, and Rare Events Happen Every Day*. He convincingly shows that "extraordinarily rare events are

---

⁵ David Hume, *An Enquiry Concerning Human Understanding*, Section X "Of Miracles," footnote 21, online at: https://www3.nd.edu/~afreddos/courses/43811/hume-on-miracles.htm. Italics are his, presumably for emphasis.
⁶ Ibid Section X "Of Miracles" Part 1 #90

anything but. In fact, they're commonplace. Not only that, we should all expect to experience a miracle roughly once every month." He is not a believer in supernatural miracles though. "No mystical or supernatural explanation is necessary to understand why someone is lucky enough to win the lottery twice, or is destined to be hit by lightning three times and still survive. All we need is a firm grounding in a powerful set of laws: the laws of inevitability, of truly large numbers, of selection, of the probability lever, and of near enough."[7] There is a growing list of books making this same point.[8] *Extremely rare events within the natural world are not miracles*. Period. We should expect extremely rare events in our lives many times over. No gods made these events happen.

A miracle doesn't need to be limited to just a temporary suspension of natural laws by a god either. Richard L. Purtill's definition for an anthology on miracles edited by leading evangelical apologists R. Douglas Geivett and Gary Habermas, is that a miracle "is an event in which God *temporarily* makes an exception to the natural order of things, to show God is acting."[9] But why must a miracle be limited to temporary exceptions? As far as the Christian theist knows, the whole world operates by perpetual or permanent miracles. An omnipotent god who created the universe, and the laws of nature with it, should be able to do perpetual miracles to alleviate the most horrendous instances of suffering in the world. Such a god could have stopped the 2004 Indian Ocean tsunami

---

[7] David J. Hand is an emeritus professor of mathematics, a senior research investigator at Imperial College London, and former president of the Royal Statistical Society. His book is published by Scientific American/Farrar, Straus and Giroux, 2014.

[8] Other important books are as follows: Jeffrey S. Rosenthal, *Knock on Wood: Luck, Chance, and the Meaning of Everything* (HarperCollins Publishers, 2018), and his earlier book, *Struck by Lightning: The Curious World of Probabilities* (Joseph Henry Press, 2006). Rosenthal is a professor of statistics at the University of Toronto, having received his PhD in mathematics from Harvard. Joseph Mazur, *Fluke: The Math and Myth of Coincidence*, (Basic Books, 2016). Mazur is an emeritus professor of mathematics at Marlboro College in Vermont. Leonard Mlodinow, *The Drunkard's Walk: How Randomness Rules Our Lives* (Vintage; Reprint, 2019). Mlodinow co-wrote with Stephen Hawking *The Grand Design*, and previously earned his PhD in theoretical physics from the University of California at Berkeley. John Allen Paulos, *Innumeracy: Mathematical Illiteracy and its Consequences*, (Holt-McDougal, 2001). Paulos is a professor of mathematics at Temple University.

[9] Richard L. Purtill, *"Defining Miracles," In Defense of Miracles: A Comprehensive Case for God's Action in History*, (Downers Grove: InterVarsity Press, 1997), p. 64. Italics mine.

by a snap of his omnipotent fingers. He could have stopped the underwater earthquake *before it happened*, thus saving a quarter of a million lives. Then he could make sure the earthquake would never take place in the future either, with a perpetual or permanent miracle. The divine hiddenness advantage here is that none of us would ever know he did it, because it never would have happened. So, he could have done it and remained hidden if he wanted to, for some hidden reason. In fact, he could stop all horrendous naturally caused suffering in this manner, and none of us would be the wiser. We would just conclude this is how the natural world works, with much less suffering.

Since there are clear instances where a perfectly good, omnipotent god should have intervened with a perpetual miracle but didn't, like stopping the 2004 Indian Ocean tsunami, we can reasonably conclude he doesn't do them at all. But the possibility of perpetual miracles supports philosopher David Kyle Johnson's contention that "a miracle is simply an event caused by God."[10] This holds true whether we can attribute a perpetual miracle to god or not. It also holds true whether a miracle violates nature's laws or not. Johnson says, "if we knew a god caused an event in the world we would (and should) call that event a miracle—regardless of whether it involved the violation of natural law." Johnson makes the point that David Hume "simply equated the definition of miracle with the conditions under which one is justified in believing in a miracle."[11] Okay, got it. However, the crucial question for Hume—and this present anthology—is whether we can *know* that any miracles have taken place. Hume's case against miracles depends on an accurate description of the conditions under which people are justified in believing in a miracle. And on this point Johnson agrees with Hume, that the criterion for knowing a miracle occurred is whether an event "violates natural law." On this crucial point Johnson goes on to argue that, "if an event does not violate natural law, then it will have a natural

---

[10] David Kyle Johnson, *"Justified Belief in Miracles is Impossible,"* in Science Religion and Culture, (May 2015), Vol. 2, Issue 2, p. 62. In an email he said it's "roughly a worldly event caused by God."
[11] Ibid.

explanation—and available natural explanations will always be more adequate than supernatural ones."[12]

Given the above considerations here's my definition: *A miracle is a supernaturally caused extraordinary event of the highest kind, one that's unexplainable and even impossible by means of natural processes alone.* I use the word "extraordinary" here thoughtfully, and I defend its use in chapter 3. No lower standard than this is worthy of being recognized as a miracle. Even if it's remotely possible there's a god who does miracles, s/he should know that reasonable people should not accept anything less. Otherwise, credulous people with lower standards for recognizing miracles as mere coincidental events could be swindled by any two-bit nefarious street preaching huckster, or famous TV personality, or faith healer, or priest, who desires their money, their kids or their lives.

Apologists, philosophers, theologians, bishops and pastors who lower these standards in order to allow for timing coincidences as miracles, as does Craig Keener,[13] J.P. Moreland,[14] and Lee Strobel[15] to name just three of thousands, are doing their parishioners and students a disservice. Most all the miracle cases described by their apologetical books are based on rare coincidences that can be explained by chance. The others are probably exaggerations, undocumented tales, wishful thinking and even lies, akin to hucksters who claim to have discovered Noah's nonexistent ark. The reason believers see evidence of miracles in rare coincidences is simply because they're ignorant about statistics and the probabilities built on them. There can be no reasonable doubt about this.

---

[12] Ibid, p. 63.
[13] Craig S. Keener, Miracles: *The Credibility of the New Testament Accounts* (Grand Rapids, Michigan: Baker Academic, 2011), 2 volumes.
[14] J.P. Moreland, *Kingdom Triangle: Recover the Christian Mind, Renovate the Soul, Restore the Spirit's Power* (Grand Rapids, MI: Zondervan, 2007).
[15] Lee Strobel, *The Case for Miracles: A Journalist Investigates Evidence for the Supernatural* (Grand Rapids, MI: Zondervan, 2018).

Hume's famous definition in its wider context is quite powerful as a way to know whether a miracle has ever occurred and why mere testimony alone doesn't justify believing one took place:

A miracle is a violation of the laws of nature; and as a firm and unalterable experience has established these laws, the proof against a miracle, from the very nature of the fact, is as entire as any argument from experience can possibly be imagined. Why is it more than probable, that all men must die; that lead cannot, of itself, remain suspended in the air; that fire consumes wood, and is extinguished by water; unless it be, that these events are found agreeable to the laws of nature, and there is required a violation of these laws, or in other words, a miracle to prevent them? Nothing is esteemed a miracle, if it ever happens in the common course of nature. It is no miracle that a man, seemingly in good health, should die on a sudden: because such a kind of death, though more unusual than any other, has yet been frequently observed to happen. But it is a miracle, that a dead man should come to life; because that has never been observed in any age or country. There must, therefore, be a uniform experience against every miraculous event, otherwise the event would not merit that appellation. And as a uniform experience amounts to a proof, there is here a direct and full proof, from the nature of the fact, against the existence of any miracle; nor can such a proof be destroyed, or the miracle rendered credible, but by an opposite proof, which is superior.

The plain consequence is (and it is a general maxim worthy of our attention), 'That no testimony is sufficient to establish a miracle, unless the testimony be of such a kind, that its falsehood would be more miraculous, than the fact, which it endeavours to establish; and even in that case there is a mutual destruction of arguments, and the superior only gives us an assurance suitable to that degree of force, which remains, after deducting the inferior.' When anyone tells me, that he saw a dead man restored to life, I immediately consider with myself, whether it be more probable, that this person should either deceive or be deceived, or that the fact, which he relates, should really have happened. I weigh the one miracle against the other; and according to the superiority, which I discover, I pronounce my decision, and always reject the greater miracle. If the falsehood of his testimony would be more miraculous, than the event which he relates; then, and not till then, can he pretend to command my belief or opinion.[16]

Hume makes it clear that miracles are extraordinary events of the highest kind, events that are impossible to take place in the natural world by natural processes alone. He also offers a general maxim for how reasonable people should evaluate miracle claims. Is there any better way to treat them? I think not, not when we consider the specific examples he offered. Elsewhere he mentioned two other examples: "the raising of a house or ship into the air."[17] I too focus on concrete examples, like the claim of a virgin birthed god in the ancient superstitious past. It's the best way to examine miracle claims.

Atheist philosopher Michael Levine agrees in his chapter for an anthology on miracles edited by one of the leading experts on the subject, Graham H. Twelftree.[18] He finds little interest in the kinds of questions others love to quibble about, briefly discussing three of them:

There are basically three philosophical questions of interest about miracles. The first is whether miracles are possible. The second is whether anyone can ever be justified, epistemologically speaking, in believing that a miracle has occurred. *With regard to this question it is important to note that the fact one can imagine conditions in which belief in a miracle would be justified does absolutely nothing to show that anyone has been so justified.* The third question is whether anyone is or has been so justified…The first two

---

[16] David Hume, *An Enquiry Concerning Human Understanding*, Section X "Of Miracles" Part 1, #90-91, online at: https://www3.nd.edu/~afreddos/courses/43811/hume-on-miracles.htm
[17] Hume "Of Miracles" footnote 21.
[18] Michael Levine, "Philosophers On Miracles" in Graham H. Twelftree, ed., *The Cambridge Companion to Miracles* (Cambridge University Press, 2011), pp. 291-308.

questions have sheltered philosophers from dealing with the only philosophically significant question about miracles *per se*—the third question. The first two questions...may be worth pursuing in their own right, but they are of little consequence when it comes to the important third question about miracles. Is anyone epistemologically justified in believing in a miracle—for example, on the basis of Scripture and historical evidence?

Philosophical discussion about miracles frequently ignores the question of whether there exists historical evidence, testimony—including testimony in the form of Scripture—or first-hand experience, that justifies belief in the miraculous. Those who wish to champion miracles either argue that such evidence exists or else they merely assume it. But the question of whether such evidence does exist, by itself, is the crucial question about justified belief in miracles.[19]

The focus of this anthology agrees with what I quoted from Levine.

As the author of the book *Unapologetic: Why Philosophy of Religion Must End* (Pitchstone Press, 2016) I should preemptively ward off any critics, since that book is a call to end the philosophy of religion as unworthy of thinking adults. I never once said we should stop thinking and arguing about religion or religious doctrines. It was actually the opposite. We should do so until such time as religions no longer exist, if that should ever happen. My requirement is that philosophers of religion should put up the requisite evidence for their respective faiths, or proverbially shut up.

In *Unapologetic* I started with what most philosophers of religion already recognize, that the philosophy of religion discipline is in crisis. There is a current debate on how to teach it in the university classrooms, and with it, several different proposals for doing it right. *My book is an atheist proposal for how atheist philosophers should teach the philosophy of*

---

[19] Ibid., pp. pp. 291-294. Italics mine since this point needs to be acknowledged. Levine purposely left out the possible fourth question, "What is a miracle?" and explains in a footnote, "I do not, however, think that there is much of philosophical interest attached to this question."

religion correctly—italicized for emphasis since some people just don't get it.

My call was to stop giving any specific religion more credence in the classrooms than others around the globe. I called on atheists to treat all faith-based doctrines the same, favoring none, to the extent this is possible. I even suggested that ridiculing religious beliefs was a fair response to ridiculous religious beliefs. We already do it to many religious beliefs. It's just that all religious beliefs are ridiculous to some degree. That doesn't mean we should *just* ridicule ridiculous religions and paranormal beliefs. This book is evidence against that misinterpretation. But the more we ridicule religion then the more we marginalize religious faith-based claims. I further argued that the best way to treat religions isn't to do so philosophically by treating some religious doctrines more seriously than others, but by treating religion and its doctrines according to the already existing parent discipline of *Religious Studies* and its subsidiaries, *Comparative Religion*, and *Anthropology of Religion*, along with *Biblical Studies, Koran Studies*, and so on, if done correctly as I explain, by eschewing faith in the classroom just as surely as we should do in other disciplines of learning. Faith in any specific religion shouldn't get special treatment in the university. The doctrines of religions and their miracle stories should be understood according to the standards of historical research and science whenever applicable, without any special pleading.

In this present anthology I've divided chapters into three parts. Part 1 *Miracles and the Abject Failure of Christian Apologetics*, has to do with the unreasonableness of believing in and defending miracle tales. Chapters 1-3, written by David Corner, Matthew McCormick and myself, have a philosophy of religion orientation, with a bit of unavoidable overlap. They are more than sufficient to introduce the philosophical issues this book must address. Both Corner and I argue Hume's arguments succeed, and we defend them against his detractors. McCormick objects to Hume by saying, "it would be a mistake" to rule out miraculous claims "*a priori* or virtually so with Hume's global standards." I hope he re-considers what Hume actually said by considering what Corner and I have written. Hume's focus is whether we can believe in miracles based exclusively on the *testimony of others without personally having seeing one*. Miracles may have occurred. It's just that with testimonial evidence alone no miracle claim has ever overcome the staggering consistent evidence from the uniformity of nature, and it's extremely unlikely any miracle claim will ever do so. That aside, McCormick starts out by forcing believers into a dilemma, arguing that if the god of theism exists, he would not do miracles. So either give up the miracle stories in the Bible, or show why McCormick's philosophical arguments are wrong. The way these three chapters are written is how philosophers should teach the discipline in their classrooms. Atheist philosophers should teach what they think in the classroom to the best they can, that's all. Allow room for discussion, yes of course, but they should not back down from controversy, as much as possible. They should argue against faith-based conclusions because faith-based conclusions are unworthy of university graduates.

One thing noteworthy is that the kinds of things people have considered possible has changed over the centuries, with the advances of science. So the Christian god—along with other ancient deities—are doing less and less as science progresses. Yet the plausibility of us accepting the miracle claims in the ancient superstitious past depends, to a large degree, on experiencing verifiable miracles in today's world. That is, if miracles don't take place today, why should we believe they took place in the past? If in our world miracles do not happen, they probably did not happen in first century Palestine either, and that should be the end of it.

Chapters 4–5, written by Darren Slade and Edward Babinski, show us how to properly investigate miracles by focusing on Christian apologist Craig Keener's assertions, which are found to be empty. We could do the same kinds of investigations of Catholic healing claims at Lourdes, France, where it's believed the virgin Mary appeared in a cave, or of Hindu healing claims from bathing in the Ganges River, or Muslim healing claims from visiting Mecca and/or the Imam Reza shrine, as one shrine of many. My informed opinion is that we would get the same exact results.

My chapter 6 on the abject failure of Christian apologetics forces Christians to think about what could have been different. What if there really were sufficient objective evidence for the miracles of the Christian faith? Then there would never be any different apologetics method to defend the Christian faith other than evidentialism—which claims to have sufficient objective evidence for these miracles. The fact that eighty percent of Christian apologists reject evidentialism in favor of four different methods is proof, all on its own, that even Christian apologists don't think there is sufficient objective evidence for their miracle claims. Then in chapter 7 Valerie Tarico more than adequately explains why people still believe in miracles, despite the fact that there aren't any good reasons based on enough evidence to do so.

In Part 2, *Properly Investigating the Miracle of Biblical Revelation*, authors investigate the miracle of biblical revelation with a focus on prophecy. Revelation doesn't always predict the future, but revelation which is perceived to do so is considered a particularly forceful miracle. It's often said that prophecy and miracles provide twin independent supports for Christianity. The truth is that prophecy is as much of a miracle claim as other biblical miracles. David Hume understood this and explained: "all prophecies are real miracles...If it did not exceed the capacity of human nature to foretell future events, it would be absurd to employ any prophecy as an argument for a divine mission or authority from heaven." Hume, having already offered some very strong arguments against miracles, went on to say, "What we have said of miracles may be applied, without any variation, to prophecies."[20]

In chapter 8 R.G. Price expertly shows the crucial role that faked prophecy had in spreading the gospel message to the Romans. He credits the spread of Christianity in the Roman world to the perception that it fulfilled prophecy. To see this at the outset, let me introduce it with a

---

[20] Hume *Of Miracles* #101.

few obviously faked Old Testament prophecies. One concerned King Josiah, who ruled over Judah in the South from about 640 to 609 BCE. Both Josiah's name and his specific reforms were "prophesied" to king Jeroboam three hundred years before Josiah was born. Jeroboam was the very first king of the northern tribes, who reigned from about 922 to 901 BCE.[21] Later, at the end of the kingly "history," a king named Josiah does exactly what Jeroboam had reported three centuries earlier![22] The question here is not whether a god could predict Josiah and his specific reforms three hundred years in advance. It's whether an ancient king like Josiah would demand that his scribes write faked prophetic propaganda to support his current reforms! We have plenty of examples of the latter. We have no other examples of the former. That scribes inserted lies into the Hebrew sacred texts is confirmed by the prophet Jeremiah (Jer. 8:8). Since this faked prophecy can still be found in our texts means there are probably other lies in them. So a skeptical attitude is required when reading the texts of the Bible.

In one of the most ridiculous examples of faked prophecy, prefaced by a condemnation of false prophets and containing a promise that god will fulfill his prophecies, the prophet Isaiah "predicted" (in 689-86 BCE) that a yet-to-be-born Persian King named Cyrus would restore the Jews to Jerusalem from captivity, and that they would rebuild their city and their temple (Isaiah 44:23-28). Isaiah's "prophecy" was uttered a century before Jerusalem was destroyed in 589-87 BCE, and about 150 years before Cyrus would restore the Jews to Jerusalem (c. 539 BCE). But such a prediction would make no sense to the Jews of Isaiah's day, who could still see Jerusalem standing, and wouldn't have a reason to think their god would destroy it given his promises (2 Samuel 7). Most significantly, there isn't a good explanation for why the "weeping" prophet Jeremiah didn't refer to Isaiah's prophecy eight decades afterward in 606 BCE, when he was being tormented as a traitor for

---

[21] See 1 Kings 13:1–2.
[22] See 2 Kings 23:15–20.

predicting, as Isaiah's prophecy assumed, the destruction of Jerusalem and the Babylonian captivity of its inhabitants (Jer. 25:11; 38:1-28).

There are also a series of faked prophecies in the book of Daniel, purportedly made during King Nebuchadnezzar's reign over Babylon, from about 605 – 562 BCE (see both Daniel 2 & 7). These prophecies were about the futures of four centuries of kingdoms, beginning with Babylon and including Medo-Persia, Greece, and Rome. Even evangelical scholar Kenton Sparks argues that these prophecies are faked. They are "amazingly accurate and precise" up until a certain point where they "fail." He wrote: "Scholars believe that this evidence makes it very easy to date Daniel's apocalypses. One merely follows the amazingly accurate prophecies until they fail. Because the predictions of the Jewish persecutions in 167 BCE are correct, and because the final destiny of Antiochus in 164 BCE is not, it follows that the visions and their interpretations can be dated sometime between 167 and 164 BCE."[23] Daniel predicted that Antiochus would die in a location between Jerusalem and the Mediterranean Sea (Daniel 11:45), but he died instead in Persia by falling out of his chariot as it was rushing along (2 Maccabees 9:5-9).

In chapter 9 Robert Miller explains why Old Testament prophecy is anything but a miracle. New Testament writers misread it to produce a faked sense of prophetic fulfillment. His concluding paragraphs are strong. Robert Conner effectively argues in chapter 10 that the New Testament prophecy of Christ's return was a failure, and along with it Christianity. Then David Madison in chapter 11 argues decisively for five inconvenient truths that undercut any hope of thinking the revelation in the Bible as a whole is from an intelligent, perfectly good, omnipotent god.

In Part 3, *Properly Investigating Key Biblical Miracles*, there are eight chapters discussing key miracle claims in the Bible. The first and foremost miracle is the supposed miracle of creation. It's the one miracle every theist uses to confirm their sect-specific faith. Even deists use it.

---

[23] Kenton L. Sparks, *God's Word in Human Words: An Evangelical Appropriation of Critical Biblical Scholarship* (Grand Rapids, MI: Baker Academic, 2008), pp. 116–18.

But despite all their claims it doesn't *confirm* any of their faiths. It's merely *consistent* with them. A creation miracle doesn't show any of them to be the one true faith, for none of them follow exclusively from it. The creation miracle is, however, a *necessary condition* of these differing religious faiths. So against all these faiths Abby Hafer in chapter 12 deals what I consider a death blow to creationism, and with it every religious faith where this belief is a necessary one. One of the biggest scientific revolutions has been evolution by natural selection's successful and complete explanation of the origins of humans and nature, and Hafer expertly presents the evidence showing why evolution is a fact. It's probably the single best chapter on it in print. Then Randall Heskett in chapter 13 deals a devastating hit to the miracle stories in the Old Testament. He conclusively shows these miracle stories are nothing more than folklore and legend, just as Hafer did with regard to creation stories. These tales should not be taken seriously.

Clay Farris Naff's chapter 14 is an interesting one. Using the Flood tale of Noah in Genesis he forces believers into a dilemma. In his words, "If a miracle is an event that defies normal explanation, then why attempt to use science to explain it?" But "if science can provide a plausible explanation for an event, then it's not truly a miracle." Believers cannot have it both ways!

Robert Price's panoramic and educational 15th chapter shows us that Christians themselves don't know what they mean when they say Jesus was God incarnate. His main point is that there has to be some intelligible meaning to the incarnation before we can judge if that claim is even possibly true. But they can't do it since no theologian has ever made sense of a being who is 100% god and 100% man with nothing essential excluded.

I am happy to have Robert Conner write three chapters. His work needs to be better known. In chapter 16 he argues that Jesus and the earliest Christians were magicians, not miracle workers. In chapter 19 Conner provocatively argues from what we know about the apostle Paul, that there's reason to think he was crazy. If so, and if he was the original

Christian, then the credibility of Christianity is seriously damaged. While I'm not so sanguine as to think Christians will accept this, Paul's personality is the issue if we're to think he's a credible witness on behalf of Christianity.[24]

Chapter 17 is written by Evan Fales, on the Cana of Galilee story of Jesus turning water into wine. He argues this story didn't happen. We know the tales in the Old Testament were originated, borrowed, edited, and compiled in later centuries for social/political purposes, and/or had metaphorical meanings for people of that day. Why not the tales in the New Testament? Could it be that neither the authors of these New Testament stories nor the original readers actually believed they took place? That's the point of his chapter.

What Fales argues finds support from R.G. Price's book, *Deciphering the Gospels*.[25] Price argues the earliest gospel named Mark "was written as a fictional allegory invented in the mind of the original author, in which essentially every scene is a fabricated literary allusion."[26] Price tells us:

> In reaction to the First Jewish–Roman War and the sacking of Jerusalem, some follower of a Pauline sect wrote a fictional story,

---

[24] David Madison makes a great case against Paul's credibility himself in his post, "When a Nasty Piece of Work Writes Scripture." http://www.debunking-christianity.com/2019/03/when-nasty-piece-of-work-writes.html In it he quotes classical scholar Michael Grant, saying that Paul's letters "display a startling mixture of conciliatory friendliness and harsh, bitter, inexorable bullying." Paul "...is the very opposite of a tranquil, serene personality. Always pursuing, always pursued, he is the victim of violent, manic-depressive alternations of moods" (Saint Paul, pp. 22-23). He also quotes A. N. Wilson, who adds, "To say that the apostle Paul was self-contradictory is an understatement. He was a man who was fighting himself and quarreling with himself all the time; and he managed to project the warfare in his own breast on to the Cosmos itself" (Jesus, p. 23).

His deficiencies emerge so clearly from his letters; he displayed no interest whatever in philosophy, art, architecture, education; he ridiculed 'earthly wisdom.' His gaze was always on the clouds, awaiting Jesus' arrival. That error poisoned everything. It's no surprise that this religious fanatic was wrong about marriage, about angels being judged by cult members who got into the Jesus kingdom, and about governments being ordained by God. His goofy beliefs emerged from his hallucinations—in which he was sure he heard personally from the dead Jesus.

So, we're entitled to ask: How can Paul's central theological certainties—let's be honest: his flashes of magical thinking—be trusted even a tiny bit?

[25] *Deciphering the Gospels: Proves Jesus Never Existed* (Copyright R.G. Price, revised edition, 2018).
[26] p. 81.

casting Paul's Jesus as the protagonist in a narrative that was meant to show that the Jews had brought the war upon themselves and that the destruction of the temple by the Romans was a punishment from their own god for not having heeded Paul's message of harmony between Jews and Gentiles. This story is what we now call the Gospel of Mark. This story is what introduced the idea that Jesus was a real person who had lived on earth.[27]

Chapter 18 is mine on the resurrection miracle of Jesus, which is the most important miracle specific to Christianity, next to prophecy. I've written a lot on this topic. Reason and the woeful lack of objective evidence demand that we conclude the resurrection never took place.

I conclude this book with an Epilogue containing a challenge for believers to be honest about their faith. Then I close it out with an Appendix where I discuss and defend William L. Vanderburgh's important book defending David Hume against his critics, especially John Earman in his 73-page essay included in his anthology on miracles titled, *Hume's Abject Failure: The Argument Against Miracles* (Oxford University Press, 2000).

I've now had one book published per year beginning in 2008 with my magnum opus, *Why I Became an Atheist*. That's eleven books if we count the 2012 revision to my first one. While there are miracle claims

---

[27] Ibid., pp. xx-xxii. Price goes on to argue:

The Gospel of Mark is a polemic against the leaders of the Jerusalem cult - James, John and Peter. The Gospel of Mark essentially portrays the movement as a failure. In the Gospel of Mark all the disciples fail to understand Jesus. All of the disciples abandon Jesus. Peter fully betrays Jesus; Peter is not being cast as a leader of the Jesus movement; he is being cast as a failure who should be seen as a discredited figure with no right to authority at all. This is all because the Gospel of Mark is a story written from a Pauline perspective, and the apostle Paul was in conflict with Peter and the other leaders of the Jerusalem church. The Gospel of Mark is all about actually promoting Paul's vision and Paul's leadership.

In the story of Mark what we are told is that the disciples all totally fail to understand Jesus, they all abandon him, they all fail to receive the mystery - the revelation. It is the women who receive the mystery of Christ but, "They said nothing to anyone, because they were afraid." This is the final line of the original ending of the Gospel of Mark. The women receive the revelation and they tell no one. Now again, The Gospel of Mark is a story written by a Pauline follower, from a Pauline perspective. The women tell no one, so who is the person that reveals the revelation to the rest of the world? It is Paul. This is the "secret mystery" of the Gospel of Mark. Source: "Jesus: His Life - The Crucifixion" at Debunking Christianity: http://www.debunkingchristianity.com/2019/04/jesus-his-life-crucifixion.html

we didn't deal with in this present anthology, my four other anthologies and monographs discuss many of them, like the miracle claims of the *Exodus* by Cambridge-trained archeologist Dr. Rebecca Bradley, the *Bethlehem Star* by physics instructor Dr. Aaron Adair, the *Shroud of Turin* by paranormal detective Joe Nickell, *life after death* claims by physicist Victor Stenger, *faith healings* by physician Harriet Hall, MD, *petitionary prayers* by psychologist Valerie Tarico, and so on.

I never expected I would write one book much less this many. One might think of them as containing a small encyclopedia of arguments against the Christian faith and religious faith in general. I don't claim to be anything special. I'm just doing the best I can based on what I know with an intense passion as great as any good athlete. With such a passion I have offended a few people online that I wish I hadn't. I blame myself for having a single-minded purpose to free people who were deceived by their childhood indoctrination into believing and acting on absurdities. I haven't always treated people who got in my way very well, especially atheists and agnostics who were supposed to be on my side in this war of ideas. No, this is not an apology in many cases. This is an explanation. But maybe if I had just been more like I am in person...or in my books...things would be different.

I thank my readers, no matter how many books of mine they've read. I also thank each and every contributor for helping to bring believers to their senses about religion and miracles, especially Valerie Tarico, for her valuable contributions to all five of my anthologies. Yes, what we do matters, one person at a time. All I can hope for at this point is that these works gain a wider and wider audience.

Hopefully,
John W. Loftus

PART 1

MIRACLES AND THE ABJECT FAILURE OF CHRISTIAN APOLOGETICS

1| MIRACLES AND THE CHALLENGE OF APOLOGETICS

By David Corner

Proponents of theistic religions have historically pointed to scriptural reports of miracles as evidence for the existence of their God. This appeal to miracles is related to other appeals that are often made in support of theistic religious belief, such as the appeal to the appearance of design in the universe, or arguments for a first cause in the context of the Cosmological Argument for the existence of God. The particular charm of an appeal to miracles is that, unlike design or cosmological arguments, miracles appear to take place under circumstances that might recommend one adopting a particular religion. If, for example, we were to become persuaded that Jesus worked miracles, and that these miracles were made possible only through the power of God—the all-powerful, omniscient, and wholly benevolent creator of the universe—it would make the occurrence of these miracles evidence not just for the existence of God, but for the veracity of the Christian revelation generally.

Thus, the reports of miracles in Christian scriptures may serve an apologetical appeal. We may broadly understand "apologetics" as referring to any attempt to defend belief in a god or gods as reasonable; our focus here will be on apologetics for the Christian God. A persuasive case for the existence of God is one that it is irrational to reject. We might call such a case an instance of *strong* apologetics. Weak apologetics seeks to defend one's belief against the claim that it is irrational to believe in God. Strong apologetics mounts an offensive, while weak apologetics is defensive in orientation.

In what follows, "apologetics" will refer to strong apologetics, and "apologist," to one who would attempt to show that it is unreasonable to refuse to accept scriptural reports of miracles as reliable. Such an apologist seeks to show that there is strong evidence in favor of the miracles reported in the Christian bible, and that, since miracles cannot be done except by God, they are evidence for the existence of God and for the authority of the Christian revelation.

I will argue that such an appeal to miracles, in order to succeed, must overcome three hurdles. It must first show (1) that the testimonial reports of an event the apologist wishes to identify as a miracle are strong enough to force us to acknowledge the event really did occur. If this can be done the apologist has the additional burden of showing (2) that this exceptional event cannot be explained by natural causes. Should the apologist succeed in surmounting these two obstacles, she will have shown that we must adopt a picture of nature by which not every event has a natural cause. But this leaves open the possibility that a putative miracle really represents what we might refer to as a "natural anomaly." A natural anomaly would be an event that is not consistent with natural law, but which provides no grounds for asserting divine intervention. Thus, the third hurdle for the apologist (3) is to show that the event in question is not a natural anomaly, but something that could only be brought about by God.

My focus will be to argue here that the apologist cannot surmount any of these three hurdles, much less all of them at once, and that the apologetical appeal is doomed to fail. Let us begin by considering how we might best define "miracle."

1. The Definition of "Miracle"

In sketching out a brief philosophical discussion of miracles, it would be desirable to begin with a definition of "miracle." Unfortunately, part of the controversy in regard to miracles is over just what is involved in a proper conception of the miraculous. As a rough beginning, it must be in some way extraordinary, unusual, or contrary to our expectations. Disagreement arises, however, as to what makes a miracle something worth wondering about. In what sense must a miracle be extraordinary? One of the earliest accounts is given by St. Augustine, who held[1] that a miracle is not contrary to nature, but only to our knowledge of nature; miracles are made possible by hidden potentialities in nature that are placed there by God. In *Summa Contra Gentiles* III:101,[2] St. Thomas Aquinas, expanding upon Augustine's conception, said that a miracle must go beyond the order usually observed in nature, though he insisted that a miracle is not contrary to nature in any absolute sense, since it is in the nature of all created things to be responsive to God's will.

In his *Enquiries Concerning Human Understanding*,[3] David Hume offered two definitions of "miracle;" first, as a violation of natural law;[4] shortly afterward he offers a more complex definition when he says a miracle is "a transgression of a law of nature by a particular volition of the Deity, or by the interposition of some invisible agent."[5] This second definition offers two important criteria that an event must satisfy in order to qualify as a miracle: It must be a violation of natural law, but this by itself is not enough; a miracle must also be an expression of the divine will. This means that a miracle must express divine agency; if we have no reason to think that an event is something done by God, we will have no reason to call it a miracle.

2. MIRACLES AND WORLDVIEW

The outcome of any discussion of miracles seems to depend greatly on our worldview. The usual theistic view of the world is one that presumes the existence of an omnipotent God who, while transcending nature, is

---

[1] Augustine, *The City of God*, XXI:8.
[2] Aquinas, Thomas, *Summa Contra Gentiles*, III:100-103.
[3] David Hume, *Enquiries Concerning Human Understanding*, (Ed. L.A. Selby-Bigge 3rd ed. Oxford: Oxford University Press, 1975).
[4] Hume, *Enquiries*, 114.
[5] Hume, *Enquiries*, 115n.

nevertheless able to act, or to express his will, within the natural world. Clearly belief in miracles is already plausible if our enquiry may presume this view of things. The usual way of making this out might be described as *supernaturalistic*. The apologetical appeal to miracles is typically a supernaturalistic one. For this reason, the cogency of this appeal depends on the cogency of supernaturalism.

Those who would defend supernaturalism sometimes do this through a commitment to an ontology of entities that exist in some sense outside of nature, where by "nature" is meant the totality of things that can be known by means of observation and experiment, or more generally, through the methods proper to the natural sciences.

Defenses of supernaturalism may also take a methodological turn by insisting the natural sciences are incapable of revealing the totality of all that there is. Methodological supernaturalism is committed as well to the view that our knowledge of God must be supplemented by revelation, for example, supersensory religious experience, or a direct communication by God in scripture, such as the Bible or the Qur'an.

There is also an ontological and a methodological naturalism. Ontological naturalism denies the existence of anything beyond nature; methodological naturalism holds that observation and experiment—or generally speaking, the methods of the empirical sciences—are sufficient to provide us with all of the knowledge that it is possible for us to have. Naturalism is sometimes further characterized as holding that nature is uniform, which is to say that all events in nature conform to generalizations (e.g. laws) which can be verified by means of observation. Naturalists do commonly hold this view—confidence in the uniformity of nature is an important part of the scientific enterprise—but strictly speaking this represents an additional metaphysical commitment regarding the nature of the universe and its susceptibility to human understanding. If nature turns out not to be fully lawlike, this would not require the rejection of naturalism. A failure of uniformity, or what a believer in miracles might refer to as a violation of natural law, would imply only that there are limits to our ability to understand and predict natural phenomena. So, the metaphysical naturalist may still be able to reject attempts by theists to explain a particular natural phenomenon by appeal to the supernatural. Where the supernaturalistic worldview is quite open to the possibility of miracles, naturalism is much less sympathetic, and many naturalists even rule out the possibility of miracles altogether; see Lewis,[6] Martin,[7] and Davis.[8]

Historically, apologists have pointed to the occurrence of miracles as evidence for theism. Such an apologetical interest puts important constraints on an account of miracles. If they wish to point to a miracle as supporting belief in a supernatural deity, obviously they cannot begin by assuming the supernaturalistic worldview; this would beg the question. If they are trying to persuade a skeptic of a particular god's existence, they are trying to demonstrate there is something beyond or transcending nature, and she will demand to be persuaded on her own terms; they must make use of no assumptions beyond those that are already acknowledged by the naturalistic worldview.

3. THE FIRST HURDLE: ON ESTABLISHING THE CREDIBILITY OF TESTIMONY

A major concern with the rationality of belief in miracles is with whether we can be justified in believing that a miracle has occurred on the basis of testimony. And testimony—scriptural testimony in particular—is crucial to the apologetical appeal. The first hurdle that the apologist must overcome is to establish the credibility of this testimony.

To determine whether the report of a miracle is credible, we need to consider the reliability of the source. Suppose subject S reports some state of affairs (or event) E. Are S's reports generally true? Clearly if she is known to lie, or to utter falsehoods as jokes, we should be reluctant to

---

[6] C.S. Lewis, *Miracles*, (New York: Macmillan, 1947).
[7] Michael Martin, *Atheism: A Philosophical Justification*, (Philadelphia, Temple University Press, 1992), 192.
[8] Stephen Davis, "*Beardsmore on Hume on Miracles*," Religions and Hume's Legacy, ed. Phillips, D.Z. and Tessin Timothy, Claremont Studies in the Philosophy of Religion, (New York: St. Martin's Press, 1999), 131.

believe her. Also, if she has any special interest in getting us to believe that E has occurred—if, for example, she stands to benefit financially—this would give us reason for skepticism. It is also possible that S may be reporting a falsehood without intending to do so; she may sincerely believe that E occurred even though it did not, or her report may be subject to unconscious exaggeration or distortion. Aside from the possibility that she may be influenced by some tangible self-interest, such as a financial one, her report may also be influenced by emotional factors—by her fears, perhaps, or by wishful thinking. We should also consider whether other reliable and independent witnesses are available to corroborate her report.

We must also ask whether S is herself a witness to E, or is passing on information that was reported to her. If she witnessed the event personally, we may ask a number of questions about her observational powers and the physical circumstances of her observation. There are quite a few things that can go wrong here; for example, S may sincerely report an event as she believed it to occur, but in fact her report is based on a misperception. Thus, she may report having seen a man walk across the surface of a lake; this may be her understanding of what happened, when in fact he was walking alongside the lake or on a sand bar. If it was dark, and the weather was bad, this would have made it difficult for S to have a good view of what was happening. And of course, we should not neglect the influence of S's own attitudes on how she interprets what she sees; if she is already inclined to think of the man she reports as walking on water as being someone who is capable of performing such an extraordinary feat, this may color how she understands what she has seen. By the same token, if we are already inclined to agree with her about this person's remarkable abilities, we will be all the more likely to believe her report.

If S is merely passing on the testimony of someone else to the occurrence of E, we may question whether she has properly understood what she was told. She may not be repeating the testimony exactly as it was given to her. And here, too, her own biases may color her understanding of the report. The possibility of distortions entering into testimony grows with each re-telling of the story.

4. HUME'S ARGUMENT

In Section X of his *Enquiry Concerning Human Understanding*, Hume tells us that it is not reasonable to subscribe to any "system of religion" unless that system is validated by the occurrence of miracles; he then argues that we cannot be justified in believing that a miracle has occurred, at least when our belief is based on testimony—as when, for example, it is based on the reports of miracles that are given in scripture. His stated aim is to show that belief in miracle reports is not rational, but that "our most holy religion is founded on Faith, not on reason."[9] Hume surely intends some irony here, however, since he concludes by saying that anyone who embraces a belief in miracles based on faith is conscious of "a continued miracle in his own person, which subverts all the principles of his understanding";[10] this is very far from an endorsement of a faith-based belief in miracles.

There is some dispute as to the nature of Hume's argument against miracles, and *Enquiries* seems to contain more than one such argument. The most compelling of these is the one I will call the Balance of Probabilities Argument. Hume tells us that we ought to proportion our certainty regarding any matter of fact to the strength of the evidence. When we examine some of the considerations that go into assessing the strength of testimony, there is no denying that testimony may be very strong indeed when, for example, it may be given by numerous highly reliable and independent witnesses.

Nevertheless, Hume tells us that *no* testimony can be adequate to establish the occurrence of a miracle. The problem that arises is not so much with the reliability of the witnesses as with the nature of what is being reported. A miracle is, according to Hume, a violation of natural

---

[9] Hume, *Enquiries*, 130.
[10] Hume, *Enquiries*, 131.

law. We suppose that a law of nature obtains only when we have an extensive, and exceptionless, experience of a certain kind of phenomenon. For example, we know that it is a matter of natural law that a human being cannot walk on the surface of water while it is in its liquid state; this fact is based on the weight of an enormous body of experience gained from our familiarity with what happens in seas, lakes, kitchen sinks, and bathtubs. Given that experience, we always have the best possible evidence that in any particular case, an object with a sufficiently great average density, having been placed onto the surface of a body of water, will sink. According to Hume, the evidence in favor of a miracle, even when that is provided by the strongest possible testimony, will always be outweighed by the evidence for the law of nature which is supposed to have been violated.

Considerable controversy surrounds the notion of a violation of natural law. However, it would appear that all Hume needs in order to make his argument is that a miracle is an exception to the course of nature as we have previously observed it. Thus, given that we have a very great amount of experience regarding dense objects being placed onto water, and given that in every one of these cases that object has sunk, we have the strongest possible evidence that any object that is placed onto water is one that will sink. Accordingly, we have the best possible reasons for thinking that any report of someone walking on water is false—and this no matter how reliable the witness.

While objections are frequently made against Hume's conception of natural law, no particularly sophisticated account of natural law seems to be necessary here, and Hume's examples are quite commonsensical: All human beings must die, lead cannot remain suspended in the air, fire consumes wood and is extinguished by water.[11] So regardless, it is still true that we can only assign a negligible probability to the occurrence of a counterinstance to any of these generalizations.

---

[11] Hume, *Enquiries*, 114.

At times Hume sounds as though he thinks the probability of such an event is zero, given its unprecedented nature. However, regardless of Hume's original intent, this is a more extravagant claim than his argument requires. He is free to admit that some small probability may be attached to the prospect that a dense object might remain on the surface of a lake; it is sufficient for his purposes that it will always be *more* likely that any witness who reports such an event is attempting to deceive us, or is himself deceived. After all, there is no precedent for any human being walking on water, but there is ample precedent for the falsehood of testimony even under the best of circumstances.

Accordingly, Hume says[12] that "no testimony is sufficient to establish a miracle, unless the testimony be of such a kind, that its falsehood would be more miraculous, than the fact, which it endeavors to establish." We must always decide in favor of the lesser miracle. We must ask ourselves, which would be more of a miracle: That Jesus walked on water, or that the scriptural reports of this event are false? While we may occasionally encounter testimony that is so strong that its falsehood would be very surprising indeed, we never come across any report, the falsehood of which would be downright miraculous. And even if there were such a report, the best an apologist can hope for is a suspension of judgment; that the probability of the miracle occurring, and the probability of the testimony being false, are equal. Accordingly, the reasonable conclusion will always be that the testimony is false or, at the very best, requires the suspension of judgment.

Thus concerning Paul's report of Jesus' resurrection in 1 Corinthians 15: It may be *unlikely* the witnesses were wrong about whether they saw Jesus; and it may also be *unlikely* the testimony of these witnesses may have been distorted before reaching Paul; it may additionally be *unlikely* Paul incorrectly reported what he heard about the event, and it may be *unlikely* Paul's original letter to the Christian community in Corinth has not been accurately preserved in our modern translations of the

---

[12] Hume, *Enquiries*, 115ff.

New Testament. Suppose the apologist can successfully argue that a failure in the transmission of testimonies to the resurrection at any of these points would be entirely without precedent in human experience.

It is very difficult to see how any such historical argument might be made. But the physical resurrection of a human being is also without precedent, so that the very best the apologist can hope for is that both alternatives—the testimony is false, versus Jesus returning to life—are *equally* unlikely, which seems only to call for a suspension of judgment, and is not sufficient to command a belief that the miracle really occurred.

Having said all this, it may strike us as odd that Hume seems not to want to rule out the possibility, in principle, that very strong testimony might establish the occurrence of an unprecedented event. He imagines a hypothetical story[13] where the sun had gone dark for eight days a century and a half earlier beginning on January 1, 1600, in which the testimony to this fact continued to be received from all over the world and without any variation. Hume suggests we should believe it—and *then look for the cause*. Hume, speaking as a historian, is well aware that nothing like this has ever occurred. But even if we were convinced that such an event really did take place—and the evidence in this hypothetical case would be considerably stronger than the evidence for any of the miracles of the Bible—we should suppose that the event in question really had a natural cause after all. In this case, the event would not be a violation of natural law, and thus according to Hume's definition, would not be a miracle.

---

[13] Hume, *Enquiries*, 127.

5. THE SECOND HURDLE: SHOWING THE ESTABLISHED EXCEPTIONAL EVENT CANNOT BE EXPLAINED BY NATURAL CAUSES

This marks an additional hurdle for the apologist. Not only must the apologist meet the very high burden of showing that it is likely an exceptional event has occurred; should the apologist be successful in doing this, she must go on to show this implies that a violation of natural law has occurred, and not that our previous understanding of natural law was incorrect. The occurrence of the purported miracle might be understood as evidence for the existence of God, but it is at least as reasonable to suppose that it is evidence that our understanding of natural law is not complete. The apologist must argue that the latter interpretation of things is not only incorrect, but unreasonable—i.e. that any skeptic who denied that our understanding of natural law was complete, after accepting the report that such an exceptional event really did occur, is being unreasonable.

Despite the possibility that a putative miracle might actually have a natural explanation, Hume wants to say that the quality of a miracle report is never high enough to establish the occurrence of such an unlikely event, at least when the report is given in the interest of establishing a religion, as such reports typically are. People in such circumstances are likely to be operating under any number of passional influences, such as enthusiasm, wishful thinking, or a sense of mission driven by good intentions; these influences may be expected to undermine their critical faculties. Given the importance to religion of a sense of mystery and wonder, those very qualities which would otherwise tend to make a report incredible seem to become qualities that convince believers. In a religious context, believers may irrationally accept such a report not so much *in spite of* its absurdity but *because* of it.

6. PROBLEMS WITH HUME'S ARGUMENT

There is something clearly right about Hume's argument. The principle he cites surely resembles the one that we properly use when we discredit reports in tabloid newspapers about alien visitors to the White House, or tiny mermaids being found in sardine cans. Nevertheless, the argument has prompted some criticisms.

Some of these criticisms make use of Bayesian probabilistic analysis; John Earman, for example, argues that when the principles of Hume's arguments "are made explicit and examined under the lens of Bayesianism, they are found to be either vapid, specious, or at variance with actual scientific practice."[14] The Bayesian literature will not be discussed here, though Earman's discussion of the power of multiple witnessing deserves mention. Earman argues that even if the prior probability of a miracle occurring is very low, if there are enough independent witnesses, and each is sufficiently reliable, its occurrence may be established as probable. Thus, if Hume's concern is to show that we cannot *in principle* ever have good reason to believe testimony to a miracle, he would appear to be wrong about this.[15] Of course, the number of reliable witnesses required might be very large, and it may be that none of the miracles reported in any scripture will qualify, as this present volume of authors argue. It is true that some of the miracles of the Bible are reported to have occurred in the presence of a good number of witnesses. But it must be emphasized that the testimony of one person, or even of four, that some event was witnessed by a multitude is not the same as having the testimony of the multitude itself.

First of all, the report that a miracle was witnessed by several hundred people may simply be untrue; it is possible that the number was exaggerated over time, as the story was passed from person to person. Also, the fact that we have only the hearsay testimony of a few writers,

---

[14] John Earman, *Hume's Abject Failure: The Argument Against Miracles*, (New York: Oxford University Press, 2000).
[15] Earman, *The Argument Against Miracles*, Ch. 18.

and not the direct testimony of a much larger number of first-hand witnesses, makes it impossible for us to assess the credibility of that larger group. We don't know enough about them to determine their individual credibility, nor do we know if their individual testimonies were self-consistent. Without being able to cross-examine them, we don't even know whether their testimonies were consistent with one another, nor do we know if any of these supposed witnesses later recanted. So this kind of hearsay testimony could be concealing a good number of problems for the apologist.[16]

Another objection against Hume's argument is that it makes use of a method that is unreliable; that is, it may have us reject reports that are true or accept those that are false. Consider the fact that a particular combination of lottery numbers will generally be chosen against very great odds. If the odds of the particular combination chosen in the California Lottery last week were 40 million to 1, the probability of that combination being chosen is very low. So we wouldn't have any good reason, per Hume, to accept the *Los Angeles Times* report of which ticket is the winner.

The unreliability objection, made out in this particular way, seems to have a fairly easy response. There is no skeptical challenge to our being justified in believing the report of a lottery drawing; that is, reports of lottery drawings are reports of ordinary, rather than extraordinary or miraculous events, akin to reports of rainstorms and presidential press conferences. They do not require particularly strong testimony to be credible, and in fact we may be justified in believing the report of a lottery drawing even if it came from an otherwise unreliable source, such as a tabloid newspaper. This is surely because we know in advance that while the odds against any particular combination are very great, all of the other particular outcomes are equally unlikely; thus, we have no prejudice against any particular combination. We know people are going to

---

[16] See John Loftus' chapter on the resurrection, in this volume, for more.

win the lottery from time to time; we have no comparable assurance that anyone will ever be raised from the dead.

Does Hume's Argument Beg the Question?

Some commentators have suggested that Hume's argument begs the question against miracles.[17,18] Suppose I am considering whether it is possible for a human being to walk on water. I consider my past experience with dense objects, such as human bodies, and their behavior in water. I consider the testimonies of everyone that I have personally known who has ever waded in water. I may even conduct a series of experiments to see what will happen when a human body is placed without support on the surface of a body of water. I always observe these bodies to sink. I now consider what is likely to occur, or likely to have occurred, in some unknown case. My past experience with water gives me very good reason to think that this is what will happen. But of course, in this case, I am not asking whether nature will be following its usual course. Indeed, I am assuming that it will be, since otherwise I would not refer to my past experience to judge what was likely in this particular case; my past experience of what happens with dense bodies in water is relevant only in those cases in which the uniformity of nature is not in question. But this means that to assume that our past experience is relevant in deciding what has happened in the case of a reported miracle, as Hume would have us do, is to assume that nature was following its usual course—it is to assume that there has been no break in the uniformity of nature. It is, in short, to assume that no miracle has occurred. In order to take seriously the possibility that a miracle has occurred, we must take seriously the possibility that there has been a breach in the uniformity of nature, which means that we cannot assume, without begging the question, that our ordinary observations are relevant. For it may turn out that nature is not uniform after all.

---

[17] Lewis, *Miracles*, 103.
[18] J. Houston, *Reported Miracles*, (Cambridge: Cambridge University Press, 1994), 133.

It would be a mistake, however, to suppose that this criticism represents a victory for apologetics. While the apologist may wish to proceed by asking the skeptic to abandon her assumption that ordinary experience is relevant to assessing the truth of miracle reports, this seems to beg the question in the opposite direction. Ordinary experience will only fail to be relevant in those cases in which there was in fact a break in the uniformity of nature, i.e. in those cases in which a miracle has occurred, and this is precisely what the skeptic requires to be shown. It is tempting to suppose that there is a middle ground; perhaps the skeptic need only admit that it is *possible* that ordinary experience is not relevant in this case. However, it is difficult to determine just what sort of possibility this would be. The mere *logical* possibility that an exceptional event may have occurred is not something that the skeptic has ever questioned; when I infer that I will sink in the waters of Silver Lake, I do so in full recognition of the fact that it is logically possible that I will not.

If the apologist is asking for any greater concession than this, the skeptic may be forgiven for demanding that she be given some justification for granting it. She may be forgiven, too, for demanding that she be persuaded of the occurrence of a miracle on her own terms—i.e. on purely naturalistic grounds, without requiring her to adopt any of the assumptions of supernaturalism. It would appear that the question of whether miracle reports are credible turns on a larger question, namely, whether we ought to hold the supernaturalistic worldview, or the naturalistic one. One thing seems certain, however, and that is that the apologist cannot depend on miracle reports to establish the supernaturalistic worldview if the credibility of such reports depends on our presumption that the supernaturalistic worldview is correct.

7. Conceptual Difficulties

Recent criticisms of belief in miracles have focused on the concept of a miracle. In particular, it has been held that the notion of a violation of natural law is self-contradictory. No one, of course, thinks that the report of an event that might be taken as a miracle—such as a resurrection or a walking on water—is logically self-contradictory. Nevertheless, some philosophers have argued that it is paradoxical to suggest both that such an event has occurred, *and* that it is a violation of natural law. This argument dates back at least as far as T.H. Huxley.[19] Should an apparent miracle take place, such as a suspension in the air of a piece of lead, scientific methodology forbids us from supposing that any law of nature has been violated; on the contrary, Huxley tells us (in a thoroughly Humean vein) that "the scientist would simply set to work to investigate the conditions under which so highly unexpected an occurrence took place; and modify his, hitherto, unduly narrow conception of the laws of nature."[20] More recently this view has been defended by Antony Flew[21,22,23] and Alastair McKinnon.[24] McKinnon has argued that in formulating the laws of nature, the scientist is merely trying to codify what actually happens; thus, to claim that some event is a miracle, where this is taken to imply that it is a violation of natural law, is to claim both that it actually occurred, but also, paradoxically, that its occurrence was contrary to the normal course of events.

Let us say that a statement of natural law is a generalization of the form "All As are Bs;" for example, all objects made of lead (A) are also objects that will fall when we let go of them (B). A violation would be represented by the occurrence of an A that is not a B, or in this case, an object made of lead that does not fall when we let go of it. So, to assert a violation of natural law has occurred is to say both that all As are Bs, and also to say there exists some A that is not a B. It is to say, paradoxically, that all objects made of lead will fall when left unsupported, but that there was one object made of lead that did not fall when left

---

[19] T.H. Huxley, *Collected Essays*, Vol. VI, Hume: With Helps to the Study of Berkeley, (New York: D. Appleton and Company, 1894), 157.
[20] Huxley, *Collected Essays*, 156.
[21] Antony Flew, *God and Philosophy*, (New York: Harcourt, Brace and World, 1966).
[22] Antony Flew, "Miracles," *Encyclopedia of Philosophy*, Vol. 5, (New York: Macmillan and Free, 1967), 346-353.
[23] Antony Flew, *Hume's Philosophy of Belief*, (Bristol: Thoemmes Press, 1997).
[24] Alastair McKinnon, "*Miracle and Paradox*," (American Philosophical Quarterly, 1967), 4:308-314.

unsupported. Clearly, we cannot have it both ways; should we encounter a piece of lead that does not fall, we will be forced to admit that not all objects made of lead will fall. McKinnon argues that a counterinstance to natural law shows that our understanding of natural law is incorrect and must be modified—which implies that no violation has occurred after all.

This criticism does not undermine the Christian belief that miraculous events really did occur.[25] But if Antony Flew is correct,[26] for the apologist to point to any of these events as providing evidence for the existence of a transcendent God or the truth of a particular religious doctrine, we must not only have good reason to believe that they occurred, but also that they represent an overriding of natural law—an overriding that originates from outside of nature. To have any apologetic value, then, a miracle must be a violation of natural law, which means that we must (*per impossibile*) have both the law and a real exception rather than merely a supposed one.

a. Violations as Nonrepeatable Counterinstances to Natural Law

This opens up the need for the apologist to overcome the second hurdle we have identified, by showing that a putative miracle really is inconsistent with natural law. Suppose we take it to be a law of nature that a human being cannot walk on water; subsequently, however, we become convinced that on one particular occasion (O)—say for example, April 18th, 1910—someone was actually able to do this. Further let's suppose that after the occurrence of O, water goes back to behaving exactly as it normally does. In such a case our formulation of natural law would continue to have its usual predictive value, and surely, we would neither abandon it nor revise it. The only revision possible in this case would be to say "Human beings cannot walk on water, except on occasion O." In this case O is what might be called a *nonrepeatable counterinstance* to

---

[25] George L. Mavrodes, "*Miracles and the Laws of Nature,*" Faith and Philosophy, Vol. 2 No. 4, October 1985.
[26] Flew, "*Miracles,*" 148.

natural law. Faced with such an event we would retain our old formulation of the law, which is to say that the exceptional event O does not negate that formulation. This means that there is no contradiction implied by affirming the law together with its exception.

But to escape from being an entirely ad hoc hypothesis, it is necessary to identify some natural feature (F) of the circumstances in which O occurred that will explain why O occurred in this one case, when normally it would not. F might be some force operating to counteract the usual tendency of a dense object, such as a human body, to sink in water. In this case, on discovery of F we are in a position to reformulate the law in a fruitful way, saying that human beings cannot walk on water except when F is present. Since the exception in this case expresses the proposition that human beings can walk on water whenever F is present, our reformulation has the kind of generality that a statement of natural law must have. But while it explains the past interaction of dense bodies with water as well as the original formulation did, it doesn't precisely explain why the feature F allowed someone to walk on water on occasion O but not on any other occasions. Finally, feature F doesn't have any predictive capabilities. It doesn't serve to predict what can happen in the future, since we cannot know when F will be present and when it is absent.

Following Ninian Smart[27] and Richard Swinburne,[28] we might now understand a violation as a nonrepeatable counterinstance to natural law. We encounter a nonrepeatable counterinstance when someone walks on water, as in case O, and having identified all of the causally relevant factors at work in O, and reproducing these, no one is able to walk on water. Since a statement of natural law is falsified only by the occurrence of a repeatable counterinstance, it is paradoxical to assert a particular statement of law and at the same time insist that a *repeatable* counterinstance to it has occurred. But there is no paradox in asserting the existence of the law together with the occurrence of a counterinstance that is not repeatable.

---

[27] Ninian Smart, *Philosophers and Religious Truth*, (New York: Macmillan, 1964), 37.
[28] Richard Swinburne, *The Concept of Miracle*, (London: Macmillan, 1970), 26.

b. Miracles as Outside the Scope of Natural Laws

The force of this line of reasoning is to deny that natural laws must describe the actual course of events. Natural laws do not describe absolutely the limits of what can and cannot happen in nature. They only describe nature to the extent that it operates according to laws. To put the matter differently, we might say that natural laws only describe what can happen as a result of natural causes; they do not tell us what can happen if a supernatural cause is present. As Michael Levine[29] has put the point:

> Suppose the laws of nature are regarded as non-universal or incomplete in the sense that while they cover natural events, they do not cover, and are not intended to cover, non-natural events such as supernaturally caused events if there are or could be any. A physically impossible occurrence would not violate a law of nature because it would not be covered by (i.e. would not fall within the scope of) such a law.

On this understanding, a physically impossible event would be one that could not occur given only physical, or natural, causes. But what is physically impossible is not absolutely impossible, since such an event might occur as the result of a supernatural cause. One way to make this out is to say that all laws must ultimately be understood as disjunctions, of the form "All As are Bs unless some supernatural cause is operating." If this is correct, then it turns out that strictly speaking, a miracle is not a violation of natural law after all, since it is something that occurs by means of a supernatural intervention. Furthermore, since statements of natural law are only intended to describe what happens in the absence of supernatural intrusions, the occurrence of a miracle does not negate any formulation of natural law.

It is difficult, however, to see how this possibility can be useful to the apologist. The apologist wishes to appeal to testimony in order to

---

[29] Michael P. Levine, *Hume and the Problem of Miracles: A Solution*, (Dordrecht: Kluwer Publishers, 1989), 67.

establish the occurrence of a supernaturally caused event. As we have seen, there is no existing scriptural testimony that is strong enough to accomplish this, given the minimal probability that the event really did occur. Now we are imagining the apologist as claiming that the skeptic has underestimated the probability of the event's occurrence, because the skeptic has assumed that there was no supernatural force operating at the time. 'Not so,' says the apologist; there was indeed a supernatural force at work, which means our ordinary calculations of probability must be set aside. Now, she says, the testimony is strong enough to establish that the event really did occur.

Of course, in making this argument that we should set aside the probabilities, the apologist is now asking the skeptic to assume that the event was the result of supernatural intervention. But this is what her appeal to probabilities was supposed to show in the first place. Thus, in asking the skeptic to grant this assumption, she begs the question. That there is a supernatural force in operation is something she must prove based on the probabilities; she cannot ask the skeptic to grant this as an assumption. Indeed, if the skeptic was to grant what the apologists asks, the testimony would become superfluous; the skeptic would have already granted what the testimony was supposed to prove.

8. THE THIRD HURDLE: SHOWING THE EXCEPTIONAL EVENT COULD ONLY BE BROUGHT ABOUT BY GOD.

We have seen two ways in which the concept of a miracle, described as an event that nature cannot produce on its own, may be defended as coherent. We can say that a miracle is a violation of natural law and appeal to the conception of a violation as a nonrepeatable counterinstance, or we may deny that miracles are violations of natural law since, having supernatural causes, they fall outside the scope of these laws. Neither of these descriptions can help apologists.

Nevertheless, conceptual difficulties remain. Antony Flew[30,31,32] has argued that if a miracle is to serve any apologetic purpose, as evidence for the truth of some revelation, then it must be possible to identify it as a miracle without appealing to criteria given by that revelation; in particular, there must be natural, or observable, criteria by which an event can be determined to be one which nature cannot produce on its own. Flew refers to this as the Problem of Identifying Miracles.

Let us see how this problem arises in connection with these two conceptions of the miraculous. Are there natural criteria by which we can distinguish a repeatable from a nonrepeatable counterinstance to some natural law? Suppose some formulation of natural law (All As are Bs) and some event that is a counterinstance to that formulation (an A that is not a B). The counterinstance will be repeatable just in case there is some natural force F present in the circumstances that is causally responsible for the counterinstance, such that every time F is present, a similar counterinstance will occur. But suppose we do our best to reproduce the circumstances of the event and are unable to do so. We cannot assume that the event is nonrepeatable, for we have no way to eliminate the possibility that we have failed to identify all of the natural forces that were operating to produce the original counterinstance. The exceptional event may have been produced by a natural force that is unknown to us. No observable distinction can be made between a case in which an exception is repeatable, having been produced by some as-yet undiscovered natural force, and one that is not. Worse yet, the naturalist will argue that the very occurrence of the exception is evidence that there is in fact some previously unknown natural force at work; where there is a difference in effects, there must be a difference in causes—which for the naturalist means, of course, *natural* causes. It is important to bear in mind that the apologist must meet the skeptic on her own (naturalistic) terms. Thus, she must show that it is unreasonable to suppose that the

---

[30] Flew, *God and Philosophy*.
[31] Flew, *"Miracles."*
[32] Flew, *Hume's Philosophy*.

occurrence of an apparent exception to natural law is not an exception at all; she must show that the occurrence of this apparent exception is better evidence for a divine intervention than it is for the existence of a previously unknown natural law. She must show that this is a non-repeatable exception to natural law.

If we were confronted with an apparent exception to natural law, we would no doubt continue to operate with our previous understanding of the law until we discovered the circumstances under which the exception might be repeated. But this does not make it unreasonable to suppose that we will someday discover what these are, and this is what is demanded of the apologist. So, it is exceedingly difficult to see how an appeal to non-repeatability will help the apologist to overcome the second of our hurdles, and show that a putative miracle has no natural explanation.

Nor does the difficulty go away if we adopt the supernaturalistic view of natural law. On this view, natural laws only describe what happens when supernatural forces are absent; a genuine miracle would not violate natural law because it is the effect of a supernatural cause. Suppose an extraordinary event occurs, which the apologist would like to attribute to a supernatural cause. The following two states of affairs appear to be empirically indistinguishable:

1) The event is the result of a natural cause that we are as yet unable to identify.
2) The event is the result of a supernatural cause.

This, of course, is due to the fact that we do not observe the cause of the event in either of these cases—in the first, it is because the cause is unknown to us, and in the second, because supernatural causes are unobservable *ex hypothesi*. Thus, the issue here is whether we should suppose that our failure to observe any cause for the event is due to our (perhaps temporary) inability to fully identify all of the natural forces that were operating to produce it, or whether it is because the cause, being supernatural, is in principle unobservable. If Flew is right, then in order to identify the event as a miracle, we must find some way to rule out the possibility of ever finding a natural cause for it; furthermore, if the identification of this event as a miracle is to serve any apologetic purpose, we must find some empirical grounds for doing this.

And so the third hurdle appears for the apologist. Not only do apologists have to overcome the first hurdle by showing some testimony to a miracle is true, and overcome the second hurdle by showing the alleged miraculous event can't be explained under natural law, they must also overcome the third hurdle, which is showing that the miraculous event did not occur spontaneously. Thus, there remains a third possibility, which is that:

3) The event has no cause at all.

That is, it is possible that the event is simply uncaused or has occurred spontaneously. It is clear that there can be no observable difference between an event that has a supernatural cause, since such a cause is in principle unobservable, and one that fails to have any cause at all. The challenge for an account of miracles as supernaturally caused is to show what the difference is between an event that has a supernatural cause, and an event that simply *lacks* any cause. And this represents the third hurdle that the miracle apologist must clear. The problem is this: If the apologist succeeds in showing (a) that an event reported by scripture is likely to have occurred, and (b) that it cannot be explained by our current, or *any future,* understanding of natural law, then we can conclude not every event that occurs in nature has a natural explanation. It is tempting to infer from this that the event has a supernatural cause, but this inference is not warranted. All that has been shown so far is that events in nature do not always fall under the scope of natural law. Not one, but two options remain: One (a) is that some events have supernatural causes, but importantly, there is also the possibility that (b) events in nature do not always have causes. An event without any cause at all may be described as a *"lusus naturae,"* or *sport of nature.* And a sport of nature is not a miracle. The occurrence of such an event does not permit any inference that divine activity is at work.

The implications of this are quite significant: Even if the naturalist were forced to admit that an event had no natural cause, and that nature is, therefore, not fully lawlike, this still does not commit her to supernaturalism. It is possible that nature undergoes spontaneous lapses in its uniformity. Such events would be nonrepeatable counterinstances to natural law, but they would not be miracles. They would fall within the unaided potentialities of nature; the naturalist need not admit the necessity of supernatural intervention to produce such events, because their occurrence requires no appeal to any transcendent reality. Indeed, should we become persuaded that an event has occurred that has no natural cause, the naturalist may argue that simplicity dictates we forgo any appeal to the supernatural, since this would involve the introduction of an additional entity (God) without any corresponding benefit in explanatory power.

9. Supernatural Causes and Supernatural Explanations

Apologists, however, will insist that this is precisely the point. Describing an extraordinary event as the effect of a supernatural cause, and attributing it to divine intervention, is justified by the fact that it offers them a chance to explain it where no natural explanation is available.

The notion of a supernatural explanation deserves careful attention. The naturalist will surely argue that the conception of a supernatural explanation—together with its cognate, the notion of a supernatural cause—is confused.

First, as regards the conception of a cause: Paradigmatically, causation is a relation between two entities, a cause (or some set of causal circumstances) and an effect. Now there are many cases in which we witness the effect of a cause that is not seen; I might for example hear the sound of a gunshot, and not see the gun that produced it. So, I can infer there is a gun somewhere nearby that produced that sound. This is an inference from effect to cause, and is similar to what the apologist would like to do with a miracle, inferring the existence of God (as cause) from the occurrence of the miracle (as effect). But what makes my inference possible in this case is, as Hume would point out, the fact that I have observed a regular conjunction of similar causes with similar effects. This is precisely what is lacking when it comes to supernatural causes. I cannot ever experience the conjunction of a supernatural cause with its effect, since supernatural causes are unobservable and non-detectable (by definition)—nor can I make an inference from any phenomenon in nature to its supernatural cause *without* such an experience. Indeed, given the very uniqueness of God's putative interventions into nature, it is difficult to see how the notion of divine causation could draw on any kind of regularity at all, as empirical causes do.

It is true that science often appeals to invisible entities such as electrons, magnetic fields, and black holes; perhaps the apologist conceives her own appeal as having a similar character.[33] These things, one may argue, are known only through their observable effects. But the causal properties of such natural entities as electrons and magnetic fields are analogous to those of entities that *are* observable; this is what warrants us to refer to them as *natural* entities. Furthermore, these properties may be described in terms of observable regularities, which means that entities like electrons and magnetic fields may play a role in theories that have predictive power. Thus, for example, an appeal to electrons can help us predict what will happen when we turn on a light switch. God is not a theoretical entity of this kind. Far from being able to play a role in any empirical regularities, God's supposed miraculous interventions into nature, as these are conceived by the supernaturalist, are remarkable for their uniqueness.

Another reason for doubting that God can possess causal powers analogous to those enjoyed by natural objects arises from the fact that God is typically conceived as lacking any location in space—and on the view of some philosophers, as being outside of time as well. Causal relationships among natural entities play out against a spatiotemporal

---

[33] Douglas R. Geivett, "The Evidential Value of Miracles," in Douglas R. Geivett and Gary R. eds, *In Defense of Miracles: A Comprehensive Case for God's Action in History*, (Downers Grove: Intervarsity Press, 1997), 183.

background. Indeed, it would seem that to speak of God as the cause of events in nature encounters something similar to the Problem of Mind-Body Interaction. All of the cases of causal interaction of which we are aware occur between physical entities that are fundamentally similar to one another in terms of possessing physical properties such as mass, electrical charge, location in space, etc. Thus, we know for example how one billiard ball may move another by virtue of the transfer of momentum. But God, as normally conceived by theistic religion, possesses none of these qualities, and cannot therefore interact with physical objects in any way that we can understand. God cannot, for example, transfer momentum to a physical object if God does not possess mass.

It may be argued that the conception of an explanation is inextricably intertwined with that of causation, so that if the conception of a supernatural cause is an empty one, the notion of a supernatural explanation can hardly be expected to get off the ground. The apologist may respond by distinguishing the sort of explanation she intends to give, when she attributes a miracle to divine agency, from the sort of explanation that is common to the natural sciences. In particular, she might characterize them as *personal* explanations, which work to explain a phenomenon by reference to the intentions of an agent—in this case God. Now, it is true that personal explanations of God's actions do not have quite the same empirical basis as do scientific ones; nevertheless, like scientific explanations, personal explanations do typically have empirical consequences. For example, if I explain Bertrand's running a red light by saying that he wanted to be on time to his meeting, I have given a personal explanation for Bertrand's behavior, but it is one that is testable. Furthermore, this explanation also serves as a basis for rough predictions about other actions that Bertrand might be expected to perform, e.g. he will likely take other steps in order to make it to his meeting on time.

The most obvious way in which appeals to divine agency fail to be analogous to the usual sort of personal explanation is in their failure to yield even the vaguest of predictions.[34] Suppose, for example, that we attribute walking on water to divine intervention. From this description, nothing follows about what we can expect to happen in the future. Unless we can introduce additional information provided by revelation, we have no grounds for inferring that God will bring it about that additional miracles will occur; he may, or he may not. Indeed, as far as this kind of predictive expansion is concerned, we seem no better off saying that some event came about because God willed it to occur than we would be if we said of it simply that it had no cause, or that it occurred spontaneously. (Indeed, often when someone says, "It was God's will," they are calling attention to the inscrutability of events.) In light of this fact, there is no reason why the naturalist should find such a supernatural explanation compelling; on the contrary, faced with a putative miracle, if her concern was to explain the event, she would be justified in following Hume's advice and continuing to hold out for a natural cause and a natural explanation—one that possesses predictive power—or in the worst case, to simply shrug off the incident as inexplicable, while denying that this inexplicability warrants any appeal to the divine. In fact, given that an appeal to divine intervention carries no explanatory weight, the Principle of Parsimony seems to demand that God be removed from the picture. The Third Hurdle under discussion here places a responsibility on the apologist to spell out just exactly why it is that saying, "God caused it to happen" is any better than saying "It had no cause."

Undoubtedly the word "cause" is used in a very diverse number of ways, and the apologist will surely say it's wrong to claim no sense can ever be attached to a statement of the form "God caused x to occur." The same may be said regarding the notion of an explanation. But the apologist cannot have it both ways. It is the apologist who claims to understand supernatural causes as analogous to the sort of causes that are of interest to natural science. If supernatural causes are not sufficiently

---

[34] See Patrick Nowell-Smith, *"Miracles,"* in New Essays in Philosophical Theology, ed. Antony Flew and Alastair MacIntyre, (New York: Macmillan, 1955).

similar to natural ones, they cannot be expected to fill the gap when natural causes are found to be lacking.

The point here is worth emphasizing. The most fundamental challenge to someone who wishes to appeal to the existence of supernatural causes is to make it clear just what the difference is between saying that an event has a supernatural cause, and saying that it has no cause at all. Similarly, when it comes to the prospect of giving a supernatural explanation: If we are unable to find any natural explanation for an event, what warrants our saying that such an event has a supernatural explanation, as opposed to saying that it is inexplicable and being done with it?

10. COINCIDENCE MIRACLES

Given the difficulties that arise in connection with the suggestion that God causes a miracle to occur, a non-causal account deserves consideration. R.F. Holland[35] has suggested that a religiously significant coincidence may qualify as a miracle. Suppose a child who is riding a toy motorcar gets stuck on the track at a train crossing. A train is approaching from around a curve, and the engineer who is driving it will not be able to see the child until it is too late to stop. By coincidence, the engineer faints at just the right moment, releasing his hand on the control lever, which causes the train to stop automatically. The child, against all expectations, is saved, and his mother thanks God for his providence; she continues to insist that a miracle has occurred even after hearing the explanation of how the train came to stop when it did. Interestingly, when the mother attributes the stopping of the train to God, she is not identifying God as its cause; the cause of the train's stopping is the engineer's fainting. Nor is she, in any obvious way, offering an explanation for the event—at least none that is intended to compete with the naturalistic explanation made possible by reference to the engineer's medical

---

[35] R.F. Holland, *"The Miraculous,"* (American Philosophical Quarterly, 1965), 2:43-51.

condition. What makes this event a miracle, if it is, is its significance, which is given at least in part by its being an apparent response to a human need.

Like a violation miracle, such a coincidence occurs contrary to our expectations, yet it does this without standing in opposition to our understanding of natural law. To conceive of such an event as a miracle does seem to satisfy the notion of a miracle as an event that elicits wonder, though the object of our wonder seems not so much to be *how* the train came to stop as the simple fact *that* it stopped when it did, when we had every reason to think it would not.

But now a new problem emerges: If the question of whether an event is a miracle lies in its significance, and if its significance is a matter of how we understand it, then it is hard to see how the determination that some event is a miracle can avoid being an entirely subjective matter. In this case, whether or not a miracle has occurred depends on how the witnesses *see* it, and so (arguably) is more a fact about the witnesses, and their response to the event, than it is to the event itself.[36] But in all other cases we do not typically think in this way; whether or not Caesar crossed the Rubicon is not a matter of how anyone experiences things. The question of whether Caesar crossed the Rubicon is an objective one. Surely the apologist wishes to say the question of whether God has acted in the world, in the occurrence of a miracle, is objective as well. And surely any dispute over the cause of a putative miracle is a dispute over the facts, not a dispute about how people *view* the facts.

A non-causal account of miracles, like Holland's, manages to avoid some of the conceptual problems that attend the traditional attempt to understand a miracle as a violation of natural law. Unfortunately, such an account pays a substantial price. In acknowledging that miracles can be completely consistent with natural law, one loses the ability to appeal to the occurrence of one as objective evidence for the existence of God.

---

[36] Smart, *Philosophers and Religious Truth*, 35.

2| GOD WOULD NOT PERFORM MIRACLES

BY MATTHEW MCCORMICK

I. INTRODUCTION

As debates over whether any miracles such as the resurrection have raged on, little thought has been given to two questions: first, if a miracle occurs, could we derive support for the claim that God exists from it? And second, if God were going to act, would he act by means of miracles? That is, is a miracle the sort of thing he would do? I will argue that the answers to these two questions are no, thus upending any further argument about whether or not some miracles have occurred. Even if a full-blown violation of the laws of nature occurs, we have compelling reasons to reject the hypothesis that the all-powerful, omniscient creator of the universe was responsible for it. A being of infinite power and knowledge wouldn't act by means of miracles.

II. MIRACLES AS EVIDENCE FOR GOD

Traditionally, miracles have been understood as violations of the laws of nature.[1] And attention has mostly been focused on whether we could

---

[1] There have been a number of arguments contesting the "violation of the laws of nature" definition. Collier says, for example, "The impossibility of a complete explanation in terms of natural laws is not itself sufficient for an event to be a miracle, as the fundamental indeterminacy postulated by the standard interpretation of quantum theory shows." Collier, John. "Against Miracles," Dialogue, vol. 25, (1986), pgs. 349-352. See also: Holland, R.F. "The Miraculous," American Philosophical Quarterly, 2 (1965), 43-51. Reprinted and revised in *Logical Analysis and Contemporary Theism*, ed. J. Donnelly. New York: Fordham University Press, 1972. 218-235. Hughes, C. 'Miracles, laws of nature and causation', *Proceedings of the Aristotelian Society*,

have sufficient evidence to believe that such an event has occurred. Let us suppose, for the sake of argument, that such an interruption of the natural order occurred. What could we then infer? Many have either implicitly or explicitly assumed that if a miracle occurs, then proof or at least substantial support for the existence of God is in hand. Many of us, both skeptics and believers, appear to take it for granted that if there really were a Jesus, for example, who did and said all the things he is purported to, then we'd have compelling reasons to think that the God of Christianity is real. If Jesus was resurrected from the dead, then it would seem that Christianity would be vindicated from skeptical arguments against God.

Many atheists and non-believers have been just as guilty of buying into these assumptions when arguing that there really was no Jesus, or that the virgin birth motif was common among various first century religious sects, or that the Bible contains internal inconsistencies, or that there was no intelligent designer of life on Earth. The presumption seems to be that if there really was a Jesus, or if his mother was a virgin, or if the Bible is consistent, or if there were a non-natural cause of life on Earth, then we would be forced to accept that we have compelling

---

supplementary volume 66 (1992), 179–205.Larmer, Robert, "Miracles, Evidence, and God," *Dialogue: Canadian Philosophical Review*, vol. 42, no. 1, pp. 107-122, Winter 2003. Mawson, T. J. "Miracles and Laws of Nature," *Religious Studies: An International Journal for the Philosophy of Religion*, vol. 37, no. 1, pp. 33-58, March 2001. Mavrodes, George, "Miracles and the Laws of Nature," *Faith and Philosophy*, vol. 2, No. 4, Oct. 1985. pgs. 333-346.

In cases where miracles are defined more broadly to include events that can be accounted for according to natural law (such as a bus driver falling asleep at the wheel and coming to a stop before hitting a child), the argument from the occurrence of a miracle of this sort to the existence of God will be much more difficult to make since an obvious natural explanation is readily available. And in cases where miracles are defined to be acts of God, then the debate over inferring the existence of God from the evidence becomes a debate about whether or not an event is a miracle. I am electing to frame that discussion in terms of whether or not naturally inexplicable events provide evidence for the existence of God.

On accounts where the laws of nature are conceived of fundamentally as probabilistic, like Swinburne's (and indeed, according to modern physics textbooks) a miracle may be defined as an exceedingly unlikely event given the laws of nature, rather than a violation of them. I take it that as the likelihood of an event increases according to the laws of nature, the extent to which that event can be employed to prove the existence of God diminishes. I believe it will be possible to adapt the arguments I am making to accommodate many of these different accounts of what a miracle is, and we can proceed with the simpler definition.

evidence that theism is true, or that Christianity has been proven. Evan Fales, for example, an avowed skeptic, has said that were an undeniable miracle to occur such as the stars in the sky suddenly realigning to spell "Mene Mene Tekel Upharsin" thus making headlines all over the world and sending astronomers into a frenzy, then "that would convince me of theism (or polytheism); no other explanation is remotely plausible."[2] It appears that the reason that so many skeptics go to battle with such tenacity over whether Jesus was real, or whether we have sufficient reason to believe in miracles, is that if those claims are corroborated, then the debate is lost.

The problem, I will argue, is that miracles, even the most robust ones, do not show the existence of an all-powerful, all-knowing, all-good being (the omni-God), and the gap of proof for the more specific and articulated Christian God is even wider. Even more importantly, I will argue that God would not perform miracles, so if one occurred, we could be sure that God did not do it. Therefore, miracles don't lend any support to the God hypothesis.

The debate about miracles since Hume has largely focused on whether or not such events ever occured or whether or not it is ever reasonable to believe that they have.[3] In the end, I am more epistemologically open to the prospect of having sufficient miracle evidence than Hume; I think we should remain open to the possibility that a person equipped with good tools, adequate concepts, and sufficient means of investigation could be in an epistemic position, albeit rarely, where believing a miracle occurred is reasonable. That puts me in a different camp than the hordes of skeptics following Hume who appear to believe that only the most extraordinary amount of evidence could be sufficient to

---

[2] Fales, Evan. "Successful Defense? A Review of In Defense of Miracles" Philosophia Christi, Vol. 3, no. 1. Series 2. 2001. 13.
[3] See, for instance, J.L. Mackie, *The Miracle of Theism: Arguments For and Against the Existence of God* (Oxford: Clarendon Press, 1982); Steve Clarke, "When to Believe in Miracles," *American Philosophical Quarterly*, vol. 34, no. 1, pp. 95-102, January 1997; Mavrodes, "David Hume and the Probability of Miracles, *International Journal for Philosophy of Religion*, vol. 43, no. 3, pp. 167-182, June 1998; and Wesley Salmon, "Religion and Science: A New Look at Hume's Dialogues," reprinted in *The Improbability of God*, eds. Michael Martin and Ricki Monnier. Amherst, NY: Prometheus Press, 2006.

prove a miracle. It would be a mistake, I believe, to rule such a claim out *a priori* or virtually so with Hume's global standards. Surely the all-powerful creator of all of reality would have sufficient power at its disposal to generate evidence that would be compelling; and I'd rather be prepared to revise all of my beliefs and the convictions I attach to them proportionally to the evidence. I won't explore an account of what would be sufficient evidence here, however. I have argued extensively, though, that the evidence we have concerning miracles like the resurrection fall painfully short of this standard.[4] For my purposes, let us assume that it is possible for miracles, conceived as violations of the law of nature, to occur. And let us also suppose that we had sufficient evidence in hand to justify believing that it occurred leaving aside what that evidence might look like. Now what can or should we infer?

I will focus my argument around several questions: To what extent can the occurrence of a miracle be construed as evidence for the existence of the sort of God that is traditionally envisioned? Let us separate some properties: would it be reasonable to take a miracle as an indicator that a single, supernatural, and personal being of infinite power, knowledge, and goodness is responsible? Even in the best-case scenario, the argument to the God conclusion is vastly underdetermined. But it gets even worse; if a miracle occurred, I will argue that we could be sure that an omni-being *did not* do it.[5]

III. WHAT WOULD A MIRACLE SHOW?

What seems to have infused much of our thinking about miracles is some slipping between necessary and sufficient conditions. One might assume that if, in order to perform a miracle, a being must be omnipotent,

---

[4] McCormick, Matt. *Atheism and the Case Against Christ*. Prometheus Press, 2012.
[5] Unless otherwise noted, I will use "God," and "omni-being," interchangeably and to mean a being that is all-powerful, all-knowing, and all-good. There is a significant literature concerning the best way to understand those terms and there are several rival definitions for each. As far as I can see, the points I will make can be applied with equal effect to the different definitions, so I will just use "omnipotent," "omniscient," and "omni-benevolent," without elaboration.

omniscient, and infinitely good, and if we had compelling grounds to believe that a miracle had occurred, then we would have compelling evidence that God exists. The problem, however, is that while these divine properties appear to be sufficient to perform miracles, they are not necessary.

Since Christianity is the predominant religion in the west, and since the resurrection of Jesus is the miracle upon which is it founded, I am going to focus my attention there. However, to the extent that other religious traditions are founded on miracles, my arguments can all be expanded to apply to them. So first I'll say a few words about God and Jesus. According to the Christian faith, the relationship between Jesus and God is complicated. The Christian God is, by all accounts, an omni-god. He is the all-powerful, all-knowing, singular, personal and infinitely good creator of the universe. Jesus is alleged to have been his son, who was divine, but he was also a man, by Christian doctrine. The extent to which he was a man and lacked the status of a fully omni-being is a point of some controversy, even between believers. God, we will assume, could have resurrected or not resurrected Jesus if he chose, and the miracles of Jesus were, either directly or indirectly God's doing by most believers' lights. We can, I believe, speak of God's performing the miracles that are attributed to Jesus without disruption of this argument. There were other alleged miraculous events, more often in the Old Testament, such as the burning bush or the destruction of Sodom and Gomorrah, that have been directly attributed to God. It is God's acts, such as these, that we are interested in here. Now we can turn to the central questions.

Is omnipotence required to violate the laws of nature? Consider these two events, both violations of the laws of nature: First, someone walks on water. Second, all of the nuclear fusion reactions that drive the burning of every star in the universe are stopped and all of those stars are instantly rendered cold and inert. It is reasonable to think that walking on water takes less power than it would take to stop all of the fusion reactions for all stars. In part, it seems that the former would take less power if we were to try to accomplish it by acting within the framework of natural law. Using physical means to try to bring the former event about in some natural fashion would, I think, be less difficult than the latter.

Admittedly, it could be a poor analogy to draw conclusions about how much supernatural power is required for different acts from how much natural power would be required. But other reasoning is convincing: a being could have the power to perform one violation of the laws of nature and not another. Imagine two supernatural entities, one who could do all and only those miraculous feats that Jesus is said to have performed, and another who could do all of the Jesus miracles and infinitely many others as well. Surely the latter would be more powerful on any reasonable account of power, than the former. Or we could imagine that some force is able to make a human walk on water or stop the sun's burning only once and only for a moment, but never again. The laws of nature would be violated in these cases with less power than omnipotence because, presumably, omnipotence would include the power to perform such acts as well as many others at any time. An agent that could enable someone to walk on water, but that could not reverse time, could not stop the nuclear reaction of the sun, or could not perform any other miracles would not be omnipotent. This reasoning shows that, at the least, omnipotence appears to be merely consistent with miracles but it is not required. Were we to come across compelling evidence that a miracle occurred it might suggest to us that there *could* be an omnipotent force that was responsible, but not that it must be an omnipotent force. In Hume's famous comment in the *Enquiry*, he supposes that,

> ...all authors, in all languages, agree that, from the first of January, 1600, there was total darkness over the whole earth for eight days: suppose that the tradition of this extraordinary event is still strong and lively among the people: that all travelers, who return from foreign countries, bring us accounts of the same tradition, without the least variation or contradiction: it is evident, that our present philosophers, instead of doubting the fact, ought to receive it as

certain, and ought to search for the causes whence it might be derived.[6]

Perhaps an omnipotent supernatural being did it, but perhaps it was a force that was only capable of doing that and nothing else. Suppose I told you that I can deadlift 1,000 pounds, and to demonstrate, I deadlift 100 pounds. You respond with skepticism, so I say, "Well, if I could deadlift 1,000 pounds, I'd be able to lift 100 pounds, so what you saw is *consistent* with my being able to lift 1,000 pounds. Therefore, this is evidence that I can deadlift 1,000 pounds."

What about infinite knowledge? Is omniscience necessary in order to violate the laws of nature? No. You could have an unintelligent, but very powerful being who actually violates the laws of nature to burn the image of a face on a fish stick because he thought that would make people believe in him.[7] There have been a few times when something on my car wasn't working, and foolishly, I tinkered around with the components that I reasoned were responsible without really knowing what they do or very much about how they work. And then, after messing around with the settings on the carburetor, or taking some fuses out of the fuse box and putting them back in, or checking the oil, inexplicably and much to my surprise, the car started working properly again. So there are times when I have managed to fix my car, but I was largely in the dark about how I did it, what I did, or what was wrong in the first place. There's no reason in principle to deny that this same sort of thing could be going on with a being who intervenes in nature to bring about miracles. Perhaps he sort of faked it, tinkered blindly a bit, and the results seem to have come out the way he wanted or perhaps not. In fact, this sort of God hypothesis might make much more sense of the examples of miracles that we often hear about: statues bleeding from the eyes, statues drinking milk, and fish sticks bearing the image of Jesus. Omniscience appears to be consistent with miracles, but it is not necessary, and cannot

---

[6] Hume, David. *Enquiry Concerning Human Understanding*. Oxford University Press, 99.
[7] Recently an Ontario man found an allegedly miraculous burn pattern on a fish stick he had cooked that resembles Jesus.

be inferred. Suppose I told you my I.Q. was 200, and I took a high school algebra test to prove it and I scored a perfect 100: "Well, my having an I.Q. of 200 is consistent with my perfect math score. If I was that smart, I could score perfectly. Therefore, the evidence indicates that my I.Q. is 200."

Is omni-benevolence necessary to bring about a miracle? Again, the answer is no.[8] Typically, we think that miracles are fortuitous events. But Satan's torturing Job at God's behest was clearly a violation of the ordinary course of nature. Presumably, if Satan hadn't engaged in his challenge with God, then Job would not have miraculously lost all of his livestock, had his wife and children die, developed boils all over his body, and so on. Left to the normal course of natural laws, Job's life would have been much less unpleasant. Perhaps the misfortunes that befell Job were God's actions and an indispensable part of an infinitely good plan in the grand scheme of things. We also presume, for example, that Satan's appearance to Jesus in the desert was miraculous. So we can agree that there's nothing intrinsically good, and nothing intrinsically infinitely good about a violation of the laws of nature. Therefore, miraculous events need not arise from good sources. And therefore, miracles don't entail the existence of a good source or sources.

Miracles that appear to accomplish good ends might seem to be consistent with infinite goodness but omni-benevolence is not necessary.[9] Many of the miracles that we have been told about seem to reflect good will—Jesus heals the sick, raises the dead, cures blindness, or feeds

---

[8] By some accounts, see T.J. Mawson, "Miracles and Laws of Nature," *Religious Studies: An International Journal for the Philosophy of Religion*, vol. 37, no. 1, pp. 33-58, March 2001, and Robert Larmer, "Miracles and Overall: An Apology for Atheism?" *Dialogue: Canadian Philosophical Review*, vol. 43, no. 3, pp. 555-568, Summer 2004, for example, a miracle is, by definition, a good thing. Mawson says, "there would be something odd about calling an event a miracle if one did not think it was for the good." (37) Perhaps so, although for our argument what is relevant is that supernatural interventions in the course of nature perpetrated by good agents and by evil agents are alike in this central respect: they both produce a violation of the laws of nature. So, were we to encounter one of those, the question is, what could we infer about its source? That the cause is good cannot be assumed a priori in an argument that seeks to show that an infinitely good supernatural being exists.

[9] In the next section we will consider an argument that a being's performing miracles is incompatible with that being possessing omni-benevolence.

the hungry. But are any of these acts indicative of infinite goodness? Infinite justice? Moral perfection? Again, not by themselves. Would any single, finitely measurable miracle indicate infinite goodness in the author? No. I have some degree of goodwill, and sometimes I act on that basis and do kind or loving things for others. But for much of the rest of the time, apathy, distraction, selfishness, or indifference set in and my actions don't reflect much goodness at all. So singular, or even multiple miracles that seem to have good results may be consistent with infinite goodness, but they are not sufficient to entail it. Like the omnipotence examples above, a good miracle could be the result of a momentary lapse into goodness by a being who is otherwise indifferent or even malevolent. The full list of Jesus' miracles: turning water to wine, raising Lazarus from the dead, feeding some starving people, withering a fruitless tree, and so on, is indicative of just as much goodness as might be required to do those acts, but no more. Suppose I tell you that I am the kindest, most charitable, most loving, most compassionate human being in history. Then to illustrate, I give a homeless man $5. You are skeptical, but I insist, "that act is consistent with my being the morally best person in history, therefore, it indicates that I am." Miracles are consistent with a range of goodness, or even no goodness at all, so a miracle can't be sufficient evidence for an infinitely good cause.

IV. WOULD GOD PERFORM MIRACLES?

Now, having seen that we cannot infer infinite divine properties from real miracles, what of the stronger thesis that God would not perform them? Let us consider omni-benevolence first. There are compelling reasons to think that an infinitely good being would not do miracles, even ones that do vast but finite good; if one were to occur, we should infer that the responsible party is *not* omnibenevolent.

Many miracles are presented as good: Jesus is alleged to have healed a crippled man so that he could walk again, he also cured a group of lepers, and miraculously fed thousands of hungry people. Many people are alleged to have been miraculously healed by drinking or bathing in the spring waters at Lourdes, France. Mohammed is said to have multiplied food and drink supernaturally on several occasions in order to feed hungry masses. God is reported to have parted the Red Sea to save the Israelites, all toward purportedly good ends.

The problem is that at any given moment on the planet, now and when these miracles are alleged to have happened, there are millions or even billions of other people who are not being cured, healed, or benefitted by a miracle. A miracle that we attribute to an infinitely good God is problematic because of what it omits; it is alleged that it indicates that God is there, and under some circumstances, he will intervene in the course of nature to achieve some good end. But there are all of these other cases, many of which appear to be perfectly parallel, or even more desperately in need of divine intervention, yet none occurs. While Jesus turns water into wine at one party, thousands or millions of other parties go dry. Even worse, millions of people suffer horribly from disease, famine, cruelty, torture, genocide, and death. The occurrence of a finite miracle, in the midst of so many instances of unabated suffering, suggests that the being who is responsible doesn't know about, doesn't care about, or doesn't have the power to address the others. If a doctor travels to a village with enough polio vaccine to inoculate 1,000 children, but only gives it to ten of them, and withholds it from the rest, and then watches the rest get sick, be crippled, or die, we would conclude that doctor was a monster, not a saint. That doctor had the power, the knowledge, the wherewithal to alleviate more suffering, but did not. That doctor must be lacking in some regard.

Christine Overall makes a step towards the same conclusion, "If Jesus was the Son of God, I want to know why he was hanging out at a party, making it go better [turning water into wine], when he could have been healing lepers, for example."[10] We can press the point further. Suppose a miraculous event suddenly heals all the suffering in the world

---

[10] Overall, Christine, "Miracles, Evidence, Evil, and God: A Twenty-Year Debate," Dialogue: Canadian Philosophical Review, vol. 45, no. 2, pp. 358.

today. An omnibenevolent being would have done it sooner. Why not yesterday? And why not in Auschwitz or Dachau in 1945, and why not when the bubonic plague was ravaging and killing millions in Europe during the 1300s?[11] We are left with this question: There are vast amounts of comparable suffering in the history of sentience that were not or are not being alleviated by miracles. How could we possibly infer infinite goodness, love, or kindness in some supernatural source that has shown the ability and the willingness to fix a select few and knowingly ignore the rest? Overall has the correct answer, "a being that engages in events that are trivial, capricious, and biased cannot be a morally perfect God."[12]

V. KNOWLEDGE AND GOODNESS MUST BE ACTUALIZED.

A useful distinction here is to see that knowledge and goodness must be fully actualized, whereas power can be merely potential. With goodness, to act below capacity is to fail to be good. Being good entails actually doing those things within one's capacity, and to the fullest extent of one's capacity that goodness recommends. To leave off doing some good that is within one's capacity actually diminishes one's goodness in a way exerting less power than one's full capacity does not. Goodness that is

---

[11] Overall and I are essentially in agreement on this point. She says, "As those who would defend the argument from evil point out, there is a huge amount of evil in the world—psychological and physical suffering, malnutrition, starvation, pandemics, cruelty, torture, poverty, racism, lynching, sexism, child abuse, assault, war, sudden deaths from natural disasters—the list in appalling.... Instead of using miracles to feed a smaller number, to transform water into wine, or to convert a few people, God could very well be performing miracles that have a much larger effect, especially on the lives of the millions of children whose suffering is particularly incomprehensible to anyone with a sense of justice. The question is why a good God would be concerned with details like the need for wine at a wedding, and yet apparently not be concerned with huge tragedies like the holocaust of six million Jews." Ibid, pg. 360. My claim is that even if some force were to enact some vast reparation like miraculously preventing the holocaust, we still would not have sufficient evidence for omni-benevolence as long as any other events remain. An omnibenevolent being would not have allowed any such horrors to occur at all if they had been worthy of repair, so a miracle, in principle, would neither be consistent with, nor evidence for omni-benevolence.
[12] Ibid, pg. 359

restrained where there is no internal or external limitation that is limiting it is not goodness at all.

Consider the contrary position. Suppose that being good to a particular extent only requires that one has the potential to be that good. Suppose a being warrants the label "good," not for the actual good acts that it engages in, but for the good acts it could potentially do but does not. How many more good acts are there that I could do that are not outside the range of my power and knowledge? How much more good could I have done with my actions with no significant external obstacles than the ones I've done? There are vastly more good acts that I could have easily done than what I have actually done. Do I deserve the label "good," or praise as being virtuous on the basis of those potential goods, or on the basis of the actual goods I've done? Potentially, I'm a moral Martin Luther King, or Ghandi, or Buddha. But surely I do not deserve to be labeled as good as Martin Luther King on the grounds that potentially I could have performed good acts on the scale that he did. I deserve to be morally praised for the good I've actually done. So, being good must mean acting at full capacity, not below. And being infinitely good must mean acting at full infinite capacity. Miracles then, even good but finite ones, are not the means by which an infinitely good being would act.

Of course, there are good actions that I failed or will fail to accomplish in my life because I lack power or knowledge to achieve them, and I may not deserve moral blame for those. Or we would not diminish the goodness we attribute to me as a result of my failure to achieve those. I lack the power and the knowledge to cure cancer, as did Martin Luther King, but we are not therefore less good as a result. We are absolved from credit or blame for those actions that are beyond our capacity. But God will not lack the power or the knowledge to accomplish any action that is good. So, God's failure to do those acts cannot be similarly absolved.

Similarly, knowledge must be actualized, not merely potential. Traditionally, omniscience entails God's knowing all and only truths. There are no truths that escape him. His merely having the potential to know all of the truths is insufficient to warrant the label omniscience. My potential to acquire the knowledge for performing brain surgery, or being a nuclear physicist doesn't warrant claiming that I have that knowledge. So the limited scope of miracles cannot be attributed to God's not knowing more. Miracles, as confined, local events solving local problems, such as getting Lazarus back on his feet, aren't the sort of expansive, world spanning events befitting an omniscient being. An omniscient God doesn't forget to get enough wine for the party in the first place. Local problems needing local solutions won't pop up for a being that knows everything and has the power to do anything. Miracles, as finite, local adjustments to achieve narrowly framed goals, are incoherent as actions of a being whose knowledge and power encompass all of reality.

The question we began with is whether or not we can infer God's infinite goodness from a good miracle. But now we have considerations suggesting that an infinitely good being will not act below its good capacity. Infinite goodness, knowledge, and power in a being would preclude it doing only part of the good job. If some being saw fit to fix one evil in the world, then there are evils worth fixing from its perspective. In the inductive problem of evil discussion, William Rowe has called these, "instances of intense suffering which an omnipotent, omniscient being could have prevented without thereby losing some greater good or permitting some evil equally bad or worse."[13] In a good miracle, then, it would appear that the being responsible has found a case to be one where it could prevent suffering without losing a greater good, or allowing an equal or worse evil. The defender of God's infinite goodness is put in the unfortunate and unreasonable position of having to argue that only the miracles of Jesus, for instance, were instances of intense suffering which God could have prevented without losing a greater good or permitting some equally bad or worse evil. The defender will have to argue that there were no other instances in all of the history of sentience except the raising of Lazarus, the withering of the fig tree, the turning of water into

---

[13] Rowe, William. "Friendly Atheism, Skeptical Theism, and the Problem of Evil," *International Journal for Philosophy of Religion* (2006) 59:79–92

wine, and so on where God could have and should have acted miraculously. They are committed to the view that only the exact list of Jesus' miracles constitutes the complete list of all the good, miraculous acts that an infinite God could accomplish; that list and no more is God acting at full capacity. That position strikes me as unreasonable. If those instances warrant a miraculous intervention, then there are more. There are many others that look just like it, and there are many cases that appear to be worse. But those other interventions did not occur. An infinitely good, knowing, and powerful God would have performed those too. So, whatever the source of those miracles may be, it is not infinitely good. An infinitely good God wouldn't leave the job partially done.

James Keller develops this point into a moral argument against God's performing miracles on the ground. "The claim that God has worked a miracle implies that God has singled out certain persons for some benefit which many others do not receive," Keller argues, "implies that God is unfair." "More specifically," he continues, "there may be two cases which are similar in all ways that seem relevant, yet in one case there will be a recovery (which some deem a miracle) and in the other case no recovery."[14] For one person to receive miraculous assistance while someone else whose situation resembles the first case in every important respect does not is unjust. An infinitely good being would not be responsible for such injustices. So a miraculous event of this sort would not be brought about by a just God.

A person confronted with a miracle is in this situation: Here's a case of the laws of nature being violated, possibly in order to rectify a case of what appears to be pointless evil. There are many other cases of what appear to be pointless evils now and in the past that were not rectified. Lots of them resemble this one in all the relevant respects that I can think of. And many of them are far worse and appear to be even more worthy of being repaired. What is reasonable to conclude about the possible goodness of the source behind the miracle I am considering? If it is

---

[14] Keller, James. "A Moral Argument against Miracles," *Faith and Philosophy*. vol. 12, no. 1. Jan 1995. 54-78.

omnibenevolent, then it would have fixed those too. So, if this event arose from some supernatural source or sources, it is reasonable to conclude that they or it are not omnibenevolent.

Ironically, the challenge to God's existence presented by inexplicable suffering is *made worse* for the theist who alleges that God performs miracles. Every case where someone claims that their prayers led to their rapid recovery from terminal cancer, or that their piety helped bring back a loved one safe from the fighting in a war zone shines a light on all the other cases of suffering that went unabated despite heartfelt prayers, decent lives, and fervent piety. Miracles, if they occur, point to a decidedly less than infinitely good cause.

For the Christian, it would strain credulity less to argue that God is all good and loving without the complications that miracles introduce. That is, the theist in these cases would have less explaining to do, and could possibly make more sense of the compatibility of a world that does not have these local, capricious miracles, than a world where one person wins the lottery, or has a cancer tumor vanish, or is the sole survivor of horrible accident, while wars, famine, plagues, and drought kill millions elsewhere. If an omni-God performed no miracles, one might offer up some generalized account of gratuitous suffering like Hick's soul-making theodicy wherein the inflexibility of the laws of nature builds moral and intellectual virtue in us. A good God wouldn't alter the course of nature, according to this popular view, because it gives us the opportunity to help others, show generosity and love, and to acquire knowledge of the world.[15] But the occurrence of miracles suggests a being who is at best arbitrary and capricious.

---

[15] John Hick says, "Suppose, contrary to fact, that this world were a paradise from which all possibility of pain and suffering were excluded. The consequences would be very far-reaching... No one would ever be injured by accident: the mountain-climber, steeple-jack, or playing child falling from a great height would float unharmed to the ground; the reckless driver would never meet with disaster... There would be no call to be concerned for others in time of need or danger, for in such a world there could be no real needs or dangers.

To make possible this continual series of individual adjustments, nature would have to work by "special providences" instead of running according to general laws which men must learn to respect on penalty of pain or death. The laws of nature would have to be extremely flexible: sometimes gravity would operate, sometimes not; sometimes an object would be hard and solid, sometimes soft. There could be no sciences,

1) Knowledge and goodness must be actualized properties.
2) God is alleged to be infinitely knowledgeable and good.
3) Miracles are not consistent with infinite knowledge and goodness.
4) Therefore, an infinitely knowing and good God would not perform miracles.

VI. GOD WOULDN'T DO MIRACLES; GOD ISN'T AN UNDERACHIEVER

Now let me expand the argument that God would not perform miracles. Consider the question now from the other side. Assume that there is an all-powerful, all-knowing, all-good, singular, and personal divine being. What sort of acts would it engage in? That being's actions will perfectly and completely achieve that agent's purposes. Its acts will achieve their ends as fully as they can be fulfilled. The resulting state of affairs will be the perfect manifestation of that agent's will. There won't be any restraint from some external force. There won't be any knowable solution or knowable fact or knowable outcome that such a being wouldn't be aware of. There will be nothing beyond its power. The results of its actions will not dissatisfy that being because it still desires something that cannot be had, or because it cannot obtain its goals.

So generally, we should assume that if some anomalous event occurs, and that event is the result of the exercise of an omni-being's will, then the state of affairs produced through that event will be completely and exactly what that being sought to achieve. The results will be as perfect a fulfillment of that being's will as can possibly be achieved. There are cases where finite beings like ourselves seek to accomplish some goal that is beyond our power, or out of ignorance, we employ the wrong means to accomplish our ends. So our results may or may not reflect good intentions, competence, knowledge, and ability. And our results

---

for there would be no enduring world structure to investigate." Hick, John. *Philosophy of Religion*. Englewood Cliffs, NJ: Prentice-Hall, 1963. 44-45.

may or may not succeed at getting what we wanted. But an omni-being will not fail to achieve its desired ends for lack of ability, incompetence, moral virtue, or ignorance.

Consider two computer programming students working on a homework project to produce some output Y from an input X using a programming language. Smith creates a circuitous, inefficient, clumsy, and unnecessarily complicated program that fulfills the required task with hundreds of lines of code. Smith's program produces the Y output from input X, but it takes lots of time, and the program contains lots of unused and unhelpful features. Jones is smarter than Smith and has a more powerful command of the means at her disposal. She finds a simple, elegant, efficient solution that achieves the same output with a few dozen lines of code with no wasted time, and no unnecessary features. The instructor would rightly give Jones the better grade; she has enacted a better solution to the problem. By extension, an omniscient, omnipotent, morally perfect being would achieve the most elegant, effective, and righteous means to achieve its ends. Omniscience would grasp that solution perfectly, omnipotence would enact it without any restraint, moral perfection would guide its goodness. We'd also expect, if that being is infinitely good, morally perfect, or omnibenevolent, then it would have only had the highest, most noble, most appropriate goals as targets for the exercise of its will, whatever those might be.

As a result, we shouldn't expect lesser, insufficient acts from such a being. *A priori*, we wouldn't expect to see minor gestures, insignificant events, or trivial results. Unhappy, incomplete outcomes only arise from the actions of a being who lacks foresight, ability, judgment, or virtue.

Since, as we have seen, the typical miracles that have been alleged in history could have been brought about by a force or forces that are not all-powerful, knowing, and good, God would be acting far below capacity if he had done them.

Even if we set aside my argument miracles are precluded for God by his goodness and knowledge, we can see that miracles are a more superficial, ineffective, and indirect means for achieving ends than an omni-

God would enact. Consider some of the purposes that have been attributed to miracles. If God has the goal of instilling belief, inspiring faith, fortifying resolve, discouraging misbehavior, or enforcing commandments, it takes very little imagination to conceive of more direct, effective, and sustained means of achieving those ends. As Ted Drange has argued, if these were God's goals, then it would have been a simple matter to directly implant belief into all people's minds, or perform more spectacular miracles that would convince more people. What would be more personal than if Jesus had reappeared to everyone, not just a handful of easily discredited zealots? Millions of angels, disguised as humans, could have spread out to preach the word behind the scenes. Or God could have protected the Bible from defects in writing, copying, and translation.[16] God, if he had been responsible, would have been vastly more effective at achieving these goals.

Walking on water, turning water into wine, and raising the dead are underpowered, inelegant, clumsy solutions to the various goals that are typically attributed to God when we reflect on what an omni-being is capable of. Jesus could have given a more conclusive demonstration of his divinity to more people than raising a single dead man, or destroying a fig tree that had no fruit in front of a handful of already converted witnesses. Jesus' resurrection as it has come to us was an isolated event. No one seems to have seen the stone being moved or the body being reanimated. Only a few people saw the tomb afterward. And only a tiny group of people had a close encounter with Jesus when he returned.

Without exception, the miracles that have been presented in Christianity as well as the rest of the world's religions have been ambiguous, under-documented, obscure, contentious, and divisive. It takes very little imagination to envision events that would have been vastly more appropriate and effective for a divine being. An infinitely powerful being could have just *saved* the Israelites instead of the prolonged conflicts with the Pharaoh of Egypt involving plagues, murdering children, parting the

---

[16] Drange, Ted. "The Argument from Nonbelief to Atheism," *Religious Studies* 29 (1993):417-32.

Red Sea, and so on. An omni-being could have simply achieved whatever ends for humanity he had in the entire Jesus saga. If some being's intention was to foster confusion, strife, and sectarianism, however, that end was accomplished quite effectively. When we consider the alleged miracles of history with a sufficiently broad conception of what divine power, knowledge, and goodness would be, no other goals seem to fit as well.

Consider the problem this way. For all of the alleged miracles in history, facsimiles that are undetectable to anyone but an expert can be performed naturally by even mediocre magicians and illusionists. David Copperfield makes the Statue of Liberty disappear on television. Penn and Teller catch bullets in their teeth. A Las Vegas magician appears to walk on water in a swimming pool and float in the air over the Luxor hotel. Imagine the social and religious impact these ingenious illusionists could have had amongst the superstitious, poor, and uneducated masses of New Testament Palestine. Religious leaders such as Billy Graham, Peter Popoff, Robert Tilton, Pat Robertson, and Jerry Falwell use cruder and more transparent trickery and deception to win the hearts of millions of people and acquire vast wealth from more educated, modern people. My point is not to suggest that Jesus was merely performing sleight of hand tricks, although that is certainly a possibility. My point is that surely an omni-God, were he to opt to manifest himself through miracles, would do better than feats that look just like sleight of hand tricks that are so easily faked. It is more reasonable to conclude that an infinitely powerful, knowledgeable, and good being would not perform miracles than to attribute acts to him that an ordinary illusionist could effectively fake.

The full list of alleged miracles and paranormal phenomena in history is full of fabrications, frauds, and confusions. Were God, the infinite creator of the universe to perform one that is real but that resembles the natural fakes, then it stands the same chance of exoneration as the one innocent man who is mistakenly jailed. He cries out for justice in a prison full of guilty criminals who all passionately insist that they are innocent too. Couldn't an omni-being do better than that? Would he allow himself to be so grossly mistaken, maligned, and misunderstood? Why would he bury the message?

When we consider the larger picture, miracles become unworthy of God. Whatever God was purportedly trying to accomplish, aren't there more effective ways to do it? Couldn't this act have been bigger? Smarter? More effective at that goal? And if so, then the fact that it isn't bigger, smarter, or better gives me convincing evidence that was not God who was responsible. If a reasonable person is confronted with a miracle, they should conclude: if God were attempting to demonstrate his existence to me there would be no obstacles. But this miracle is insufficient to that task. So a miracle is not the sort that would be performed by God. He would do much better than this if he was trying to demonstrate his existence, or whatever the purported goal.[17]

Similarly, if God were attempting to accomplish good in the world, then there would be no obstacle to his achieving much more of it than this miracle does. Suppose that thousands of the sick get healed, or the hungry get fed, or the Red Sea parts to save the Israelites. None of these miracles accomplishes nearly as much as God could. So it is a mistake to conclude that a miracle is a manifestation of his infinite power, or love.

In many examples, God punishes with miracles. Lot's wife gets turned into pillar of salt for watching the destruction of Sodom and Gomorrah when God commanded her not to. The view that Hurricane Katrina was sent by God to punish sinners in New Orleans has been popular among American evangelical preachers. If God were attempting to exact some punishment or retribution through a miracle, then it would be grossly inconsistent to arbitrarily single out some individual for lesser misdeeds while ignoring so many others, particularly when the misdeeds of others are so grievous. An omni-being would achieve vast,

---

[17] James Keller has argued that for God to put some people into a favorable situation with regard to having their faith fortified, or their body of evidence improved, while so many others are not provided with the same benefit is unfair. So bias or preferential treatment is yet another reason to conclude that God, if one exists, would not employ miracles in order to achieve some epistemic end. "A Moral Argument Against Miracles," *Faith and Philosophy: Journal of the Society of Christian Philosophers.* vol. 12, no. 1. Jan. 1995. pg. 62.

effective, balanced, just punishment. Miracles cannot be God's punishment.

If a reasonable person has thought through the implications of what it would be for an omni-being to act, the reaction should be something like, "That's it? That's the best you've got? How am I supposed to believe in an omni-being on the basis of *that*? Any old demigod could do *that*. And there are good reasons to think God would not do *that*." These considerations will plague all of the alleged purposes we devise for the results of a miracle. And if there does not appear to be any way that this could be God's act, then it is reasonable to conclude God did not do it.

We now have powerful reasons to accept this argument:

God wouldn't act in any ways that are below full capacity.

Performing a miracle would be acting below full capacity for God.

Therefore, God wouldn't perform miracles.

XIII. CONCLUSION

Our discussions of miracles, in focusing on whether we have enough evidence to believe that one has occurred, have often neglected a more fundamental problem that upends the miracle debate for God. Even if miracles are real, neither omnipotence, nor omniscience, nor omnibenevolence are necessary in order to perform them. In fact, an infinite God would not perform miracles because miracles are below full-capacity for God, and God wouldn't act in any ways that are below full-capacity. So even if one happens, we won't be able to infer God's existence from them because God would not perform miracles.

3| EXTRAORDINARY CLAIMS REQUIRE EXTRAORDINARY EVIDENCE

BY JOHN W. LOFTUS

In this chapter I'm going to defend the ECREE principle, or slogan, which is an acronym for *Extraordinary Claims Require Extraordinary Evidence*. Christian apologist William Lane Craig asserts the ECREE principle "is the argument that David Hume (1711–1776) basically offered against believing in miracles."[1] So my focus will be on David Hume's arguments against miracles in chapter ten of his *Enquiry Concerning Human Understanding*.[2]

Hume's chapter had two parts to it. In Part 1 he argued that in order to believe a miracle took place it must have a miraculous level of evidence to overcome the overwhelming evidence from the laws of nature that it didn't occur. The best that human testimony could possibility produce on behalf of a miraculous event is to equal or match the evidence from the laws of nature against it. So even if it's remotely possible this burden could be met, we should suspend judgment on whether or not a miracle took place.

In Part II Hume goes on to argue against this remote possibility. He offers four supplemental arguments that human testimony has never

---

[1] *Reasonable Faith: Christian Truth and Apologetics*, p. 273, and the Oct 18, 2013 interview on YouTube, "Don't Extraordinary Claims Need Extraordinary Evidence?" at
https://www.youtube.com/watch?v=5HgRWvqf-wM.
[2] David Hume, *An Inquiry Concerning Human Understanding*, Section X *Of Miracles* Part 1, #90-91, online at: https://www3.nd.edu/~afreddos/courses/43811/hume-on-miracles.htm #91

come close to requiring a suspension of judgment. Consequently, no one should believe any miracle actually took place, or religion having miracles as its foundation. In what follows we'll consider both parts and deal with a few objections.

To be clear, Hume consistently expressed himself in probabilistic terms, not certainties, so it's obvious he's not rejecting miracles *a priori* (before examining the facts) or arguing in a circle, or begging the question. See for yourselves:

> In our reasonings concerning ***matter of fact***, there are all imaginable degrees of assurance, from the highest certainty to the lowest species of moral evidence.
>
> A wise man, therefore, proportions his belief to the evidence. In such conclusions as are founded on an infallible experience, he expects the event with the last degree of assurance, and regards his past experience as a full proof of the future existence of that event. In other cases, he proceeds with more caution: He weighs the opposite experiments: He considers which side is supported by the greater number of experiments: to that side he inclines, with doubt and hesitation; and when at last he fixes his judgement, the evidence exceeds not what we properly call probability. All probability, then, supposes an opposition of experiments and observations, where the one side is found to overbalance the other, and to produce a degree of evidence, proportioned to the superiority. A hundred instances or experiments on one side, and fifty on another, afford a doubtful expectation of any event; though a hundred uniform experiments, with only one that is contradictory, reasonably beget a pretty strong degree of assurance. In all cases, we must balance the opposite experiments, where they are opposite, and deduct the smaller number from the greater, in order to know the exact force of the superior evidence.[3]

Hume expressed himself with this *general* maxim:

---

[3] Hume, *Of Miracles*, #87. Emphasis on "matter of fact" is mine. This phrase will be discussed in the Appendix.

That no testimony is sufficient to establish a miracle, unless the testimony be of such a kind, that its falsehood would be more miraculous, than the fact, which it endeavours to establish; and even in that case there is a mutual destruction of arguments, and the superior only gives us an assurance suitable to that degree of force, which remains, after deducting the inferior.[4]

William Lane Craig explains the connection between ECREE and Hume's general maxim in this manner:

It wouldn't take much evidence for someone to believe that, say, he saw [someone] walking across the parking lot to his church. We would accept somebody's testimony to that. But suppose somebody were to report to you they saw [that person] flapping his arms and flying across the parking lot to the church. You wouldn't believe that. You would believe either he was lying or he was mistaken or something else. Extraordinary events require extraordinary evidence. Therefore, you should never believe in miracles because you would never be able to have enough evidence to overcome the laws of nature contradicted by the miracle. You should always choose to believe that there has been some mistake made.[5]

Craig conveniently mischaracterizes Hume, since Hume's conclusion is that human testimony *alone* will never be enough to overcome the laws of nature. Regardless, Craig goes on to assert this "seemingly commonsensical slogan," as popularized by Carl Sagan and "beloved in the free thought subculture," is "demonstrably false."[6]

---

[4] David Hume, *An Inquiry Concerning Human Understanding*, Section X "Of Miracles" Part 1, #90-91, online at: https://www3.nd.edu/~afreddos/courses/43811/hume-on-miracles.htm #91
[5] *Reasonable Faith: Christian Truth and Apologetics*, p. 273, and the Oct 18, 2013 interview on YouTube, "Don't Extraordinary Claims Need Extraordinary Evidence?" at https://www.youtube.com/watch?v=5HgRWvqf-wM.
[6] Ibid.

THE ECREE PRINCIPLE

The ECREE principle—"extraordinary claims require extraordinary evidence"—is a subset of a larger principle having to do with claims made about the objective world of nature and its workings. All claims about the objective world require *sufficient corroborating objective evidence commensurate with the nature of the claim*. This applies to ordinary claims, extraordinary claims and miraculous claims. The amount and quality of the evidence required is dependent on the type of claim being made. To understand this better let me provide a brief description of each kind of claim, explain the kind of evidence required, then offer a couple of concrete examples.

First, an ordinary claim is one made about ordinary events that are commonplace within nature, which requires ordinary levels of evidence. Most all of these claims are accepted based on human testimony alone. Concerning what might cause us to doubt human testimony Hume offered a few suggestions:

We entertain a suspicion concerning any matter of fact, when the witnesses contradict each other; when they are but few, or of a doubtful character; when they have an interest in what they affirm; when they deliver their testimony with hesitation, or on the contrary, with too violent asseverations.[7]

If a trustworthy person tells us she saw a car accident on Main Street, we would believe her. If a trustworthy person tells us he just talked to his mother on the phone we would believe him. The corroborating objective evidence in these cases is the previous evidence establishing the trustworthiness of that person. Examples of these claims abound and are clear cut.

Second, an extraordinary claim is one made about extraordinary events that are extremely unusual, rare and even strange within the world of nature, which require extraordinary levels of evidence. For the record, David

---

[7] Hume, *Of Miracles*, #88.

Hume distinguished between extraordinary claims and miracle claims. When it comes to "extraordinary" claims Hume says "the evidence, resulting from the testimony, admits of a diminution, greater or less, in proportion as the fact is more or less unusual."[8] That is, the more unusual the extraordinary claim then the more extraordinary the objective evidence should be, since "here is a contest of two opposite experiences; of which the one destroys the other, as far as its force goes," leaving the force of what remains.[9]

Two interesting examples of these types of extraordinary claims have been suggested by atheist historian and philosopher Richard Carrier, in his debate with evangelical apologist Michael Licona. If Carrier claimed to own either a nuclear missile, or an interstellar spacecraft, it would take an extraordinary amount of objective corroborative evidence for reasonable people to accept it, because it's not very probable he could own either of them.[10]

Third, a miraculous claim is one made about miraculous events that are unexplainable and even impossible by natural processes alone, which requires miraculous levels of testimonial evidence.

What other *rhetorical* word besides *miraculous* best explains the level of testimonial evidence required, if the claim is about events that violate or transgress or break or breach or fracture nature, according to Hume? What kind of human testimony can overcome the extremely strong overwhelming evidence that no scientist has ever conducted an experiment under strict laboratory conditions who received different results than other scientists who conducted the same exact experiment under the same exact conditions? For Hume, *no other amount of human testimony but miraculous levels of human testimony are able to overcome the overwhelming evidence of the known laws of nature. At best, it can only equal it.*

---

[8] Hume, *Of Miracles,* #89.
[9] Hume, *Of Miracles,* #90.
[10] See "Mike Licona vs. Richard Carrier debate review" at *Common Sense Atheism*: http://commonsenseatheism.com/?p=9593

Believers have been hostile to Hume. They continue to believe in their sect-specific miracles despite his standards. But they duplicitously use his standards when assessing the miracles of the religions they reject. This double standard assessment must end. Either they should stop being skeptical of miracle claims in general, or be equally skeptical of their own miracle claims, the ones they were most likely indoctrinated to believe.

CRITICISMS AND MISUNDERSTANDINGS

For the purposes of discussing the ECREE principle we can think of a miracle as an extraordinary type of extraordinary claim requiring the very highest kind of objective evidence. One criticism of ECREE is that this principle is "logically self-defeating." According to Dean Meadows at *Apologia Institute*,

> The statement seems to collapse in on itself because the claim is asserted as a universal principle, meaning it applies independently and is binding on everyone in all spheres of life. Where is the extraordinary evidence that this particular universal principle is true? Given that there is no extraordinary evidence to prove that 'extraordinary claims require extraordinary evidence,' this claim is logically self-defeating.[11]

My response is threefold. First, since all claims about the objective world require *sufficient corroborating objective evidence commensurate with the nature of the claim*, it's clear that extraordinary types of extraordinary claims require more than mere ordinary testimonial evidence. They require a sufficient amount of objective evidence for them, that is, extraordinary evidence of the highest kind. Why would Meadows object to this reasonable requirement unless he tacitly admits his own beliefs don't have a sufficient amount of objective evidence for them?

---

[11] Apologia Institute: https://apologiainstitute.com/do-extraordinary-claims-really-require-extraordinary-evidence/.

Second, such an objection entails there must be exceptions to the ECREE principle. Which ones? Undoubtedly Meadows would claim his own miracle claims are the exceptions, which is special pleading, something I pointed out elsewhere.[12] He needs to put forth one such example and justify it. Of course, to do so would require producing extraordinary evidence which is what the ECREE is all about. Beyond this, he should show us how to evaluate other similar extraordinary claims made by the millions, especially coming from the religions he doesn't accept. Just tell us how to evaluate the claim that Joseph Smith was visited by an angel Moroni, who gave him some inspired golden plates, then go and do likewise to thy own claims.

Third, the answer to his objection is a simple one. What we say is that it's *almost certainly the case* the ECREE principle is true. By speaking exclusively in terms of the probabilities there's no self-defeating claim here, which is what those of us who think exclusively in terms of the probabilities say. Believers who think this grants them any victory at all are simply not thinking exclusively in terms of the probabilities by proportioning their beliefs based on the strength of the evidence.

When it comes to accepting a highly improbable extraordinary claim William Lane Craig argues we don't need "miraculous evidence" or "lots of evidence" or even "an enormous amount of evidence."[13] Craig offers an often-repeated analogy based on winning the lottery. He says that by showing us the winning lottery ticket a friend can convince us she overcame the staggering odds by winning it. Hence, "the evidence for the winning pick is, indeed, extraordinary," says he, even though it's not a lot of evidence, or an enormous amount of evidence or miraculous evidence."[14]

---

[12] See my chapter 7 on special pleading in *How to Defend the Christian Faith: Advice from an Atheist* (2015).
[13] "The Doctrine of Christ (part 16)" podcast on June 29, 2008: https://www.reasonablefaith.org/podcasts/defenders-podcast-series-1/s1-the-doctrine-of-christ/the-doctrine-of-christ-part-16/; the Oct 18, 2013 interview on YouTube, "Don't Extraordinary Claims Need Extraordinary Evidence?" at https://www.youtube.com/watch?v=5HgRWvqf-wM. See also his book, *Reasonable Faith: Christian Truth and Apologetics*, p. 273.
[14] Craig, *Reasonable Faith*, p. 273.

First off, Craig starts by stating the obvious, which misses the point. Extraordinary claims require extraordinary evidence, which entails *sufficient corroborating objective evidence commensurate with the nature of the extraordinary claim*. That means sufficient objective evidence should be sufficient, regardless of whether it's one piece of objective evidence like a lottery ticket, or a hundred pieces of objective evidence. It might mean a small amount of objective evidence, or a big amount of objective evidence, or some very strong objective evidence, or an enormous amount of very strong objective evidence.

Craig also fails to understand that every weekly lottery drawing finds a winner eventually. There are roughly 1600 ongoing lotteries each year, which means there are about that many unique winners per year too. There just doesn't seem to be much that's extraordinary about this, especially when compared to an extraordinary claim of a miracle, which by definition is something impossible by means of natural processes alone.[15] That's because winning the lottery isn't analogous to a unique miraculous claim.

Hume's general maxim is about the weight of human testimonial evidence to miracles given the natural world that precludes them. But what we find exclusively on behalf of miracles in the Bible is human testimony, ancient pre-scientific superstitious human testimony, second-third-fourth-hand human testimony, conflicting human testimony filtered by editors, redactors, and shaped by early Christian debates for decades and/or centuries in the ancient pre-scientific world, where miracle claims were abundant without the means to discredit them.

Let's take at face value the extraordinary miraculous tale that a virgin named Mary gave birth to the god/baby Jesus. There's no *objective evidence* to corroborate her story. None. We hear nothing about her wearing a misogynistic chastity belt to prove her virginity. No one checked for an intact hymen before she gave birth. Nor did she provide her

---

[15] On the occurrence of extremely rare events see David Hand's excellent book, *The Improbability Principle: Why Coincidences, Miracles, and Rare Events Happen Every Day*. Published by *Scientific American* / Farrar, Straus and Giroux, 2014.

bloodstained wedding garment from the night of her wedding that supposedly "proved" she was a virgin before giving birth (Deuteronomy 22:15–21). After Jesus was born Maury Povich wasn't there with a DNA test to verify Joseph was *not* the baby daddy. We don't even have firsthand *testimonial evidence* for it, since the story is related to us by others, not Mary, or Joseph. At best, all we have is the second-hand testimony of one person, Mary, or two if we include Joseph who was incredulously convinced Mary was a virgin because of a dream, *yes, a dream* (see Matthew 1:19–24), one that solved his dilemma of whether to "dismiss her quietly" or "disgrace" her publicly, which would have led her to be executed for dishonoring him.[16] We never get to independently cross-examine them, along with the people who knew them, which we would want to do, since they may have a very good reason for lying (pregnancy out of wedlock?).

Now one might simply trust the anonymous gospel writer(s) who wrote this extraordinary story down, but why? How is it possible *they* could find out that a virgin named Mary gave birth to a deity? Think about it. No reasonable investigation could take Mary and/or Joseph's word for it. With regard to Joseph's dream, Thomas Hobbes tell us, "For a man to say God hath spoken to him in a Dream, is no more than to say he dreamed that God spake to him; which is not of force to win belief from any man." [*Leviathan*, chap. 32.6] So it's down to Mary. Why should we believe her? On this point believers are faced with a serious

---

[16] Joseph's dream is used in The Gospel of Matthew's narrative to help explain why Mary was not put to death for dishonoring him because of adultery. There are five other dreams in this gospel account which were all intended to save someone's life. So, Joseph's dream was probably meant to save Mary's life too (Matthew 1:19-23; 2:12; 2:19-23; & 27:19). Matthew J. Marohl shows in *Joseph's Dilemma: "Honor Killing" in the Birth Narrative of Matthew* (Wipf & Stock Publisher, 2008), that "Joseph's dilemma involves the possibility of an honor killing. If Joseph reveals that Mary is pregnant, she will be killed. If Joseph conceals Mary's pregnancy, he will be opposing the law of the Lord. What is a 'righteous' man to do?" "Early Christ-followers understood Joseph's dilemma to involve an assumption of adultery and the subsequent possibility of the killing of Mary." This was part of their culture. Honor killings were justified in both the Old and New Testaments. Jesus even agreed with the Mosaic Law (Exodus 21:17; Leviticus 20:9) against his opponents on behalf of honor killings of children who dishonored their parents (Mark 7:8-13). The tale of the woman caught in adultery, where Jesus exposes the hypocrisy of her accusers, doesn't change what Jesus thinks of the law either (John 8; Matthew 5:18).

dilemma to their faith. For if this is the kind of research that went into writing the gospels, we shouldn't believe anything else they say without requiring corroborating objective evidence. But if research was unnecessary for writing their gospels—because they were divinely inspired—why do gospel writers give us the pretense of having researched into it (see Luke 1:1–4)? Why not simply say their stories are true due to divine inspiration and be done with the pretense? Then the gospel authors would be admitting their tales lack the required corroborating objective evidence, which in turn means there isn't a good reason to believe them.

But let's suppose these anonymous gospel authors were given the required objective evidence for the virgin birth. It doesn't change a thing, for they *don't produce it or tell us about it!* We'd still be forced to trust an anonymous gospel writer's testimony, which is the very thing we need corroborated. It would be akin to being asked to believe the Mormon founder Joseph Smith had really been given some sacred golden plates to translate, based merely on what we're told, except that accepting anonymous writers two thousand years ago is magnified by the hundreds. That kind of blind faith is something adults should jettison from their mental world.

The real problem apologists have with Hume's arguments is that there aren't any good reasons to believe miracles took place. For if they did, believers wouldn't be objecting to Hume. All Christians have to do is ask what they would be saying if there were sufficient objective evidence to believe in miracles. That this evidence doesn't exist is why believers must object to Hume. Otherwise they would agree with Hume's reasonable requirements then go on to present sufficient objective evidence showing the miracles of their religion occurred.

So Christians have a choice to make, either 1) Miracles did not take place, per Hume, because there's no reason to accept mere testimony to them; or 2) Even if miracles did take place, mere testimonial evidence for them is insufficient, per Hume, so there's still no good reason to accept them. Given that Christians only have, at best, second-handed human testimony in the Bible, this is the choice forced upon them. If their god had even a minimal amount of foresight, he could have provided this objective evidence, but he didn't.[17]

HUME PART I

Christian apologists unanimously think Hume's main argument in Part 1 fails, which is the controversial part.[18] C.S. Lewis claimed Hume was begging the question. He argued the only way Hume can know miracles have not happened is "if we know that all reports of them are false. And we know all the reports to be false only if we already know that miracles have never happened."[19] Robert J. Fogelin dismissed this objection as a gross misreading of Hume:

> Hume nowhere argues, either explicitly or implicitly, that we know that all reports of miracles are false because we know that all reports of miracles are false...Hume begins with a claim about testimony. On the one side we have wide and unproblematic testimony to the effect that when people step into the water they do not remain on its surface. On the other side we have isolated reports of people walking across the surface of the water. Given the testimony of the first kind, how are we to evaluate the testimony of the second sort? The testimony of the first sort does not show that the testimony of the second sort is false; it does, however, create a strong presumption—unless countered, a decisively strong presumption—in favor of its falsehood. That is Hume's

---

[17] See "What Would Convince Atheists To Become Christians?; The Definitive Answers!" posted on 4/04/2017 at my Debunking Christianity blog, http://www.debunking-christianity.com/2017/04/what-would-convince-atheists-to-become.html

[18] See Richard Swinburne, *The Concept of Miracle*, Macmillan, St. Martin's Press, London, U.K., 1970, Douglas Geivett and Gary R. Habermas, eds., *In Defense of Miracles—A Comprehensive Case of God's Action in History* (InterVarsity Press, Downers Grove, Illinois, 1997), books by C.S. Lewis, William Lane Craig, Norman Geisler, Craig Keener, Lee Strobel, and others too many to name.

[19] C.S. Lewis, *Miracles: A Preliminary Study* (New York: Macmillan, 1947), p. 105.

argument, and there is nothing circular or question begging about it.[20]

Others have criticized Hume as if he's saying it's impossible for miracles to occur because nature's laws preclude them from happening. This is not the case. Evan Fales argues that Hume could not have intended to say miracles are logically impossible, "for granting it would have made the path to his conclusion in 'Of Miracles' much easier—even trivial. And Hume clearly intended a much more substantive result."[21] Even the Christian apologist, Ronald Nash, agreed, saying,

Hume could not have been arguing that miracles are impossible. Instead of attacking miracles metaphysically (by arguing they are impossible), Hume's challenge turns out to be epistemological in nature. That is, he argues that even though miracles could occur, it is never rational to believe that any alleged miracle took place.[22]

Several atheist philosophers think Hume's argument in Part I succeeds, including Antony Flew, Evan Fales, Nicholas Everitt, Robert J. Fogelin,[23] and William L. Vanderburgh.[24] There are others.

Nicholas Everitt argues, "The real destructive power of Hume's critique lies in his philosophical argument" in Part 1, "that even in the most favorable circumstances possible (favorable, that is, to a belief in theism) it would not be rational to believe that a miracle occurred."[25] Everitt explains, that:

Since a miracle is by definition a violation of a law of nature, it is maximally improbable. So, if testimony in favour of a miracle is to be rationally credible...it must be hugely strong testimony—in fact, maximally strong. But even if the testimony were to achieve

---

[20] Robert J. Fogelin, *A Defense of Hume on Miracles* (Princeton, NJ: Princeton University Press, 2003), pp. 19–20.
[21] *Debating Christian Theism*, editors, J. P. Moreland, Khaldoun A. Sweis and Chad Meister (Oxford University Press, 2013), p. 299.
[22] Ronald Nash, *Faith & Reason*, (Grand Rapids, Zondervan, 1988), p. 228.
[23] Robert J. Fogelin, *A Defense of Hume on Miracles*, 2003.
[24] Vanderburgh, *Hume on Miracles, Evidence and Probability* (Lexington Books, 2019).
[25] Nicholas Everitt, *The Non-Existence of God* (Routledge, 2003), see pp. 114-117.

maximal strength, it would all be cancelled out by the antecedent improbability of anything which contravenes the laws of nature...and since the net evidence would be zero (maximal evidence for is cancelled by maximal evidence against), the rational response would be non-belief in the occurrence of the supposed miracle.

Antony Flew was another atheist who defended Hume, explaining him as follows:

> A strong notion of the truly miraculous can only be generated if there is first an equally strong conception of a natural order. Where there is as yet no strong conception of a natural order, there is little room for the idea of a genuinely miraculous event as distinct from the phenomenon of a prodigy, of a wonder, or of a divine sign. But once such a conception of a natural order has taken firm root, there is a great reluctance to allow that miracles have in fact occurred, or even to admit as legitimate a concept of the miraculous...Exceptions are logically dependent upon rules. Only in so far as it can be shown that there is an order does it begin to be possible to show that the order is occasionally overridden. The difficulty (perhaps an insoluble one) is to maintain simultaneously both the strong rules and the genuine exceptions to them.[26]

Let me put it this way: Believing in miracles demands a near impossible double burden of proof. What believers must show is that an alleged miracle could not have happened within the natural world because it was impossible on naturalistic grounds alone (or else it's not considered miraculous). Then they must turn around and claim such an impossible event probably took place. In other words, the probability that a miracle took place is inversely proportional to the probability that a miraculous event could take place within the natural world order (i.e., the less probable that a miracle could take place then the more probable it did not

---

[26] Antony Flew, 'Miracles,' in *The Encyclopedia of Philosophy*, ed. Paul Edwards et al. (New York: Macmillian, 1967), vol. 5, p. 347.

take place). In this way the improbability of an extraordinary miracle claim rises in proportion to the improbability that it could occur, and vice versa.

Is Hume right? A wise person, a reasonable person, should not believe nature was violated without sufficient corroborating objective evidence commensurate with the claim, and there is basically no good corroborating objective evidence for any miracle in the Bible. Now, it's true there is evidence *consistent* with some biblical miracles, such as the archaeological findings of the Pool of Siloam in Jerusalem, where Jesus supposedly told a blind man to go and be healed, and was healed. But archaeological findings like that are not considered to be corroborating evidence. At best what Christians have are archaeological findings that are *consistent* with what they believe, in the same way as the existence of the city of Bethlehem is consistent with the claim that Jesus was born of a virgin there, or as the existence of the city of Roswell, New Mexico, is consistent with the claim that aliens are real. This kind of evidence is negligible at best since what we're looking for is confirming evidence. What we have instead is plenty of disconfirming evidence. In my previous anthology, *Christianity in the Light of Science*, there are three chapters showing why archaeology disconfirms the Bible, including the tales of the Exodus from Egypt, and the existence of the town of Nazareth during the time Jesus was supposedly raised there.

What might surprise readers is that some atheist/agnostic philosophers think Hume's argument in Part I fails, like Michael Levine, Michael Martin, Graham Oppy, and John Earman.[27] Michael Levine for instance says "it fails" as an "unsuccessful" "superfluous" "misadventure."[28] Graham Oppy, who has been every fundamentalist apologist's friend for taking their beliefs seriously, strangely says "Hume's argument

---

[27] See Michael Martin, *Atheism: A Philosophical Justification*, pp. 194-196, Michael Levine, *The Cambridge Companion to Miracles*, ed., Graham H. Twelftree, (Cambridge University Press, 2011), pp. 291-308, and Graham Oppy *Arguing About Gods*, pp. 376-382. Agnostic/atheist John Earman thinks Hume's argument is an *Abject Failure* (as seen in his book by that title).

[28] In Graham H. Twelftree, ed., *The Cambridge Companion to Miracles*, "Philosophers On Miracles" (Cambridge: 2011), pp. 292, 302, 292 respectively.

against belief in miracle reports fails no less surely than do the various arguments from miracle reports to the existence of an orthodoxly conceived monotheistic god."[29] Surely he doesn't really mean that? Does he? J.L. Mackie defended Hume against some objections, although he thought Hume's main argument needed "improvement" due to "inaccuracies" even calling some of it "very unsatisfactory." But rather than rejecting it Mackie decided it just needed "tidied up and restated" as I'll share later.[30]

One of Michael Levine's criticisms is that Hume's argument against miracles comes directly from his empiricist epistemology, which requires a sense impression for something to be considered a matter of fact. As such, Levine says Hume's argument against miracles "is a gloss for understanding the underlying supposition that one cannot have an 'impression' of a supernatural event."[31] Hume's underlying empiricism is seen in several key arguments he makes. He argues we don't have sense impressions of *cause and effect* or of divine activity, or the self for that matter, which is nothing but a bundle of sensations. So, Levine says, "Given his view that divine activity is impossible to know, Hume's argument in Part I is in a sense superfluous."

Of course, I find Levine's criticism quite uncharitable, because drawing out the implications of a previously held epistemology is worthwhile, especially if no one had done so before. Had Hume not done so, someone else would. Most importantly, Hume's argument in Part 1 is an independent one irrespective of his underlying empiricist supposition. Hume could still have written that chapter regardless of his epistemology.

After we discuss Part II of Hume's arguments, we'll focus on three serious objections from John Earman, which are shared by some other critics.

---

[29] *Arguing About Gods*, pp. 376.
[30] *The Miracle of Theism*, pp. 25, 27, 23, 17 respectively.
[31] Twelftree, ed., *The Cambridge Companion to Miracles*, p. 302.

HUME PART II

David Hume backs up his main contention in Part I with four supplemental arguments in Part II. Hume could imagine a scenario where a huge amount of reliable testimonial evidence from an enormous number of disinterested people might convince us that an extraordinary miraculous event took place. He admitted such a possibility with regard to a hypothetical case in which testimonial evidence was overwhelming that on January 1, 1600 (about 150 years earlier), there was total darkness over the entire planet for one week of days.[32] But he goes on to argue we never have this kind of testimonial evidence.

This is my point and that of Michael Levine, who argues that in Part II Hume deals with the only significant philosophical question that matters: "Is anyone justified in believing in miracles—for example, on the basis of Scripture?" He says "This is the question that many philosophers on miracles either (1) ignore or postpone—while addressing questions about laws of nature instead; (2) affirm—despite what historical scholarship and sophisticated biblical (textual) criticism tell us; or (3) casually presuppose to be answered affirmatively." On this crucial question Levine argues Hume's argument that "no one is justified in believing that a miracle occurred, at least not on the basis of testimony, succeed."[33]

Hume's First Supplemental Argument

First, Hume argues there isn't to be found "in all history, any miracle attested by a sufficient number of men, who are of unquestioned good sense, education, and learning as to secure us against all delusion in themselves; of such undoubted integrity, as to place them beyond all suspicion of any design to deceive others . . . and at the same time,

---

[32] Hume, *Of Miracles*, #99.
[33] Twelftree, ed., The Cambridge Companion to Miracles, p. 296.

attesting facts performed in such a public manner and in so celebrated a part of the world, as to render the detection unavoidable."[34]

Christian apologist Michael Licona objects to this in his massive book defending the resurrection, saying that "If Hume's criteria for accepting testimony as true were employed outside of miracle-claims, we would probably have to dismiss the vast majority of what we believe we presently know about the past. Much of what we hold about the past was reported by a lone source and it is rarely 'beyond all suspicion.'"[35]

The ingenuity of Christian apologists to exploit good arguments in reverse never ceases to surprise me. Licona fails to understand the difference between the evidential requirements for ordinary claims from extraordinary miraculous claims. Ordinary claims about ordinary events can usually be taken at face value. But that doesn't mean we have to leave it there. Ordinary claims having ordinary evidence are backed up by a whole boat load of objective evidence presumed to be there *if we were to check*. If a close friend said she took an Amtrak Wolverine train ride from Detroit to Chicago and is considered trustworthy, there's no reason to require any objective evidence proving she did. But it exists just as surely as a boat load of evidence exists showing she is trustworthy. Perhaps it would be the train ticket itself, or a surveillance camera on the train, or the selfie she took with a person she met on the way. This is the kind of sufficient objective evidence required when it comes to any claim. It's just that we don't need to require it when it comes to ordinary claims, whereas, we must insist on sufficient objective evidence in addition to one's testimony when it comes to miracle claims that defy nature.

I wrote a whole chapter on the paucity of historical evidence titled, "The Poor Evidence of Historical Evidence,"[36] and I think Licona is correct about how little evidence there is for "much of the past." There is a good argument based on this agreement though, one that escapes him.

---

[34] Hume, *Of Miracles*, #92.
[35] Michael Licona, *The Resurrection of Jesus: A New Historiographical Approach*, (Downers Grove, IL: InterVarsity Press, 2010), pp. 138–39.
[36] See chapter 7 in my book, *Why I Became an Atheist*, 2nd edition.

A miracle claim is about an event where "there could be no natural cause," according to Licona's own definition.³⁷ So if historical evidence about ordinary claims in the past has such a poor quality to it, as Licona admits, then how much more does historical evidence of extraordinary miracle claims in the past? If the first is the case, then the second is magnified by thousands.

Hume's Second Supplemental Argument

Hume argues we should give preference to that which is "founded on the greatest number of past observations," and as a historian Hume knew many instances of forged miracles, which prove the strong propensity of mankind to believe a wondrous and extraordinary story and then exaggerate it when they retell it.

Michael Licona argues instead that miracle claims should be investigated on a case-by-case basis rather than by adopting the antecedent probabilities against them.³⁸ He suggests we should ignore or dismiss these antecedent probabilities and investigate miracle claims in isolation from each other without utilizing any background information that these other claims always turn out to be false (or, to be gracious, almost always). Since it would be impossible to investigate every miracle claim, Licona says Hume is wrong to suggest that uniform experience is against miracles. But to the contrary, it's precisely because we cannot investigate all miraculous claims we must come up with some sort of conclusion about the antecedent probabilities when assessing whether any given one of them took place. What Licona is trying to do is escape from shouldering the full burden of proof against the backdrop of the probabilities.

---

³⁷ Licona, *The Resurrection of Jesus*, p. 134.
³⁸ Ibid., pp. 139, 143, 180.

Hume's Third Supplemental Argument

Hume argues that miracle claims originate among tribes who are uncivilized, ignorant, and barbarous. Hume rhetorically asks, why is it that "such prodigious events never happen in our days?"[39]

Whether miracles are happening in our day is the subject of two chapters in this anthology by Darren Slade and Edward Babinski. Michael Licona argues however, that if we followed Hume, we would never be able to believe any improbable event took place even though improbable events do occur. Yes, it might be that some improbable extraordinary events took place, even though history leaves no trace of it for historians to conclude they happened. So what if it is? If that's the case, then that's the case. No one should expect there is sufficient evidence for everything that happened in the past. The point is that we can only accept the conclusions that can be reasonably justified. Aliens from space might have abducted someone, but without sufficient evidence commensurate with such a claim there is no reason why anyone should believe the person who asserts it. We can only believe what is probable. So Licona ends up objecting to the fact that miracles are improbable. If that's the case, then that's the case. It's not Hume's fault.

Hume's Fourth Supplemental Argument

Finally, Hume argues that competing religions support their beliefs by claims of miracles; thus, these claims and their religious systems cancel each other out. That is, any miracles that count for one religion cancel out the probability of the miracles of the other, and vice versa.

Christian apologist Ronald Nash admitted this was the strongest of Hume's four arguments.[40] Richard Swinburne however, countered that competing religious claims only cancel each other out if the proclaimed

---

[39] Hume, *Of Miracles*, #94.
[40] Ronald H. Nash, *Faith & Reason: Searching for a Rational Faith* (Grand Rapids, MI: Zondervan, 1988), p. 238.

miracles of each religion did in fact occur and if these purported miracles are used to establish the truth of each of these separate religions.[41] Claims of miracles are used by different religions to establish their contrary doctrines, so whether they took place is the main issue here. Hume argues his point "is not in reality different from the reasoning of a judge, who supposes that the credit of two witnesses, maintaining a crime against anyone, is destroyed by the testimony of two others, who affirm him to have been two hundred leagues distant, at the same instant when the crime is said to have been committed."[42] For Hume, this is a credibility problem. Hume questions how he can even know whether the miracles of two differing religions actually occurred, since the credibility of both is suspect. This becomes a particularly forceful point when it comes to the overwhelming numbers of Jews in the days of Jesus who did not believe in his resurrection, an issue I'll return to in a later chapter.

Hume sums up Part II in the past tense, after all is said and done:

Upon the whole, then, it appears, that no testimony for any kind of miracle *has ever amounted to a probability*, much less to a proof; and that, even supposing it amounted to a proof, it would be opposed by another proof; derived from the very nature of the fact, which it would endeavour to establish. It is experience only, which gives authority to human testimony; and it is the same experience, which assures us of the laws of nature. When, therefore, these two kinds of experience are contrary, we have nothing to do but substract the one from the other, and embrace an opinion, either on one side or the other, with that assurance which arises from the remainder. But according to the principle here explained, this substraction, with regard to all popular religions, amounts to an entire annihilation; and therefore we may establish it as a maxim, that no human testimony can have such force as to prove a miracle, and make it a just foundation for any such system of religion.[43]

---

[41] Swinburne, *The Concept of Miracle*, pp. 60–61.
[42] Hume, *Of Miracles*, #95.
[43] Hume, *Of Miracles*, #98-99.

The fact that a miracle requires extraordinary evidence over and above the fallibilities of ordinary human testimony is not an unreasonable demand on Hume's part. It's the nature of the beast. That human testimony to miracles is fallible is known with a great deal of assurance. A forensic television show I watch had a character say, "The evidence doesn't lie. People do." So we should follow the objective evidence wherever it leads, especially with the discovery of a great many cognitive biases showing we believe what we prefer to believe because our subconscious brains will lie to keep us within the comfort zone of our tribal relationships.[44] To overcome them we must be willing to leave our tribal comfort zone, if necessary. For most people this is unthinkable. Where the battle rages is how to best minimize our biases in weighing religious faiths, which Michael Licona admits. The only solution is to seek sufficient objective evidence for what we conclude, or withhold belief.

JOHN EARMAN'S OBJECTIONS TO HUME

I turn now to three major objections of agnostic philosopher John Earman, in his pejoratively titled book, *Hume's Abject Failure: The Argument Against Miracles*.[45] His first objection is explained and answered by Aron Lucas.[46] As we've seen, Hume's general maxim is "That no testimony is sufficient to establish a miracle, unless the testimony be of such a kind, that its falsehood would be more miraculous, than the fact, which it endeavours to establish." According to Earman, Hume's maxim is basically that no one should believe a miracle unless it is greater than 50% probable in light of the evidence. Lucas: "When interpreted in this way, Hume's maxim appears to be simple commonsense. Of course testimony can only establish a miracle if it makes that miracle probable! Who could possibly think otherwise?" So Earman faults Hume for stating the

---

[44] See the Wikipedia article on Cognitive Biases: https://en.wikipedia.org/wiki/Cognitive_bias.
[45] New York, NY: Oxford University Press, 2000.
[46] See "Hume's Maxim: How a 'Trivial Truth' is Too Strong for Christian Apologetics" (2017) https://infidels.org/library/modern/aron_lucas/hume.html, used with his permission. I'm editing it down for simplicity and brevity without significant loss.

obvious, that it's a trivial truth no apologist would dispute in the first place. It contributes nothing to the literature on miracles, and is unworthy of the praise it has received. But Lucas shows, with several good examples, that "while Hume's maxim may be an obvious banality to Earman, a quick reading of modern apologetic literature reveals that this is far from obvious to many of today's primary defenders of Christianity." Most of them believe, contrary to Hume's maxim, that mere testimony can establish a miracle. So Lucas says, "if Hume is to be faulted for stating the obvious, many of today's leading Christian thinkers should be faulted all the more for failing to see the obvious."

Take just one example from William Lane Craig, who inserts a different probabilistic standard than Hume's for accepting a miracle:

The successful Christian apologist need not show that the probability of the resurrection hypothesis is greater than 50 percent, or more probable than not. Rather, what he must show is that the probability of the resurrection is greater than any of its separate alternatives. Thus, even if the resurrection hypothesis has a probability of, say, only 30 percent, and none of its alternatives scores higher than, say, 10 percent, then it is far and away the best explanation.[47]

This is clearly at odds with Hume, but as Lucas explains, "the questions 'what is the best explanation' and 'what probably happened' address two separate issues, and it is the second question that we are interested in answering. The first question is only valuable insofar as it helps us answer the second." Lucas offers us an appropriate analogy:

Imagine a 20-sided die that is biased in favor of side 20. It lands on 20 1/5 of the time, and the other 19 sides are equally probable. If you had to bet on a single number, 20 would be the best bet. But if you had the bet on whether it will land on 20 or not land on 20, you should obviously bet against 20. Similarly, if the

---

[47] William Lane Craig, "Responses" in *Five Views on Apologetics* ed. Steven B. McGowan (Grand Rapids, MI: Zondervan, 1999), p. 126.

Resurrection is the best explanation, then the resurrection is the best individual option. But if we had to bet on whether the Resurrection is true or false, we should still bet against it.

A second major objection of Earman's is that Hume uses "the straight rule" of induction. He wrote:

> Hume is saying that when experience is uniform—when sufficiently many A's have been examined and all have been found to be B's—then we have 'proof' that all A's are B's...So here in a nutshell is Hume's first argument against miracles. A (per Hume) miracle is a violation of a presumptive law of nature. By Hume's straight rule of induction, experience confers a probability of 1 on a presumptive law. Hence, the probability of a miracle is flatly zero. Very simple. And very crude.[48]

The problem with "the straight rule" is that it's rejected in the scientific community. Atheist philosopher Elliot Sober explains why: "The fact that no counterexample to 'All A's are B' has yet been encountered hardly allows one to be absolutely certain that all A's are B, or that the next A will be B. Scientists are often open to the possibility that future observations will not resemble those made in the past."[49] But since Hume is constantly talking about probabilities, and even admits it's possible a miracle took place,[50] Sober argues Hume shouldn't be interpreted as using the straight rule.[51] Vanderburgh likewise disputes Earman's contention since Hume was offering epistemological arguments (i.e., why we can't reasonably conclude miracles have occurred) rather than ontological ones (i.e., whether miracles have ever in fact occurred):

> Contrary to what many of his critics have suggested, Hume does not think that his proof against miracles establishes the impossibility of the existence of miracles. Rather, Hume thinks the

---

[48] John Earman, *Hume's Abject Failure* (New York: Oxford University Press, 2000). pp. 22-23.
[49] Elliott Sober, "A Modest Proposal," *Philosophy and Phenomenological Research* 118 (2004): 489-96.
[50] See Hume, *Of Miracles*, #99, concerning the hypothetical possibility that on January 1, 1600 (about 150 years earlier), there was total darkness over the entire planet for one week of days.
[51] Elliott Sober, "A Modest Proposal."

available evidence gives such a high degree of probability to the laws of nature that belief in the existence of miracles can never be rational—that is, sufficiently well-grounded epistemologically.[52]

A third major objection of Earman's is that Hume failed to understand probability theory, specifically Bayes' Theorem.[53] William Lane Craig argues alongside of Earman the agnostic, that "Hume failed to appreciate this whole probability calculus. That is why his argument was an abject failure. He didn't take into account all of the factors." He says Hume "incorrectly assumes that miracles are intrinsically highly improbable." But they can be "highly probable relative to our background information," by which is meant the sum total of everything he and other theists believe.[54] So he uses pejorative rhetoric to say Hume's arguments are "mathematically fallacious."[55]

Michael Gleghorn chimes in: "Hume never actually establishes that a miracle is highly improbable in light of our general knowledge of the world," since a part of what's included in the Christian's general knowledge of the world is the belief that God exists. "Whether or not a miracle is considered highly improbable relative to our general knowledge of the world is largely going to depend on whether or not we believe in God." So "if the belief in God is part of our general knowledge of the world, then God can bring about miracles!"[56]

I have space for three responses. First let's ask what if Earman is correct? What then? Does belief have it easier? No, not at all. In the

---

[52] William L Vanderburgh, *David Hume on Miracles, Evidence, and Probability* (Lanham, MD: Lexington Books, 2019), p. 7.
[53] I don't have space to explain Bayes' Theorem adequately if you don't already understand it. Do a search for "Bayes' Theorem Problems, Definition and Examples": https://www.statisticshowto.datasciencecentral.com/bayes-theorem-problems/. I think my discussion of the points in question can be understood without understanding this excellent mathematical tool, and the reasoning behind it.
[54] Craig and Moreland, *Philosophical Foundations for a Christian Worldview*, p. 571.
[55] He said this in his debate with Bart Ehrman on March 28, 2006 at the College of the Holy Cross, on the question: "Is There Historical Evidence for the Resurrection of Jesus? https://ehrmanblog.org/ehrman-vs-craig-evidence-for-resurrection/
[56] Dr. Michael Gleghorn "Hume's Critique of Miracles" for Probe Ministries at https://probe.org/humes-critique-of-miracles/.

scientific, agnostic, atheist world we have no gods or superheroes, just geniuses in moments of time. So even if this particular argument by Earman does succeed against Hume, it doesn't grant Christian believers any relief from their burden of proof, or help in any other way. On Facebook Richard Carrier told us why:

> Earman didn't "refute" Hume, so much as he fixed Hume. Earman shows that reframing Hume's argument in a Bayesian framework fixes everything wrong with the original argument as worded. Hume's mistake is subtle, and arises from the imprecision of his wording and formulation. He hadn't quite known yet of the correct logical form of what he was trying to say, but it is remarkable he came very close to the same insight his contemporary Thomas Bayes did. Earman's fix rehabilitates Hume's argument.

Take for example the progress of science. As it progresses the science of yesterday was not false, just incomplete. Read Isaac Asimov' essay called *The Relativity of Wrong*.[57] It will forever change how you view science. He explains why the discredited science of the past is not to be considered wrong, but rather incomplete, by discussing the changing views of the shape of the earth, from flat to spherical to pear-shaped (it's now considered an oblate spheroid, or oblate ellipsoid). The same thing can be said about Newton's laws of motion as completed (not falsified) by Einstein's relativity equations. Newton's equations were not wrong, even though he didn't factor time into them, as Einstein did. They just don't work at or near the speed of light. In a like manner, Hume gave us the initial questioning paradigm to evaluate testimonies to miracles, which still holds true. But now with Bayes' Theorem we might now have a better way to think about miracles with a more complete paradigm.

Hume still said a lot of things that are true and beyond refutation. What is mathematically fallacious about saying the wise person must proportion his or her beliefs according to the strength of the evidence?

---

[57] Isaac Asimov, "The Relativity of Wrong" in *The Skeptical Inquirer*, Fall 1989, Vol. 14, No. 1, Pp. 35-44, http://chem.tufts.edu/answersinscience/relativityofwrong.htm

Hume said that. Hume is also credited with the ECREE principle, even though he didn't use the phrase, which still works even if he didn't frame it into a Bayesian framework. When the evidence isn't decisive, we must suspend judgment. Hume said that too. According to Hume we should think exclusively according to the probabilities. Who got so many people thinking and debating this issue? David Hume did. He's had a towering influence on philosophy and theology ever since.[58]

My second response is that Hume's argument succeeds despite the fact he didn't use Bayes' Theorem. Vanderburgh briefly addresses this issue in his article for *Hume Studies*.[59] He shows Hume was aware of Bayes' Theorem but didn't think he needed it to make his argument. Earman chastises Hume for being unaware of Bayesianism and of mathematical probability generally. This is unfair on two counts. First, Bayes's work on probability was not widely known in 1748 when Hume published the first edition of the *Enquiry*. Richard Price arranged the posthumous publication of Bayes's essay only in 1763, and it remained obscure even after its publication; Price's paper applying Bayesian methods to the evidence for miracles appeared in 1767. We know Hume read and admired that paper, but he neither addressed Bayesian arguments nor revised his account of miracles for the 1768 and 1777 editions of the *Enquiry*. This suggests that Hume ultimately did not view Bayes's work as relevant to the argument against miracles. Second, Hume's discussion of the probability of chances "shows without controversy that he was familiar with the basic concepts of probability based on the calculus of chances." Given Hume's familiarity with Pascalian probability in general, and his acquaintance (through Price) with Bayesian ideas, his non-numerical treatment of the evidential

---

[58] See my post, "Why Do We Need A Book Against Miracles After Hume?" http://www.debunking-christianity.com/2019/04/why-do-we-need-book-against-miracles.html
[59] *Hume Studies*, Volume 31, Number 1, April 2005, pp. 37–61.

probability of miracles must be seen as a deliberate philosophical position, not as a result of negligence or ignorance.[60]

What Hume is aiming at is seen in his general maxim: "Therefore we may establish it as a maxim, that no human testimony can have such force as to prove a miracle, and *make it a just foundation for any such system of religion*." His twofold contention is not only that mere testimonial evidence for a miracle is insufficient for believing in a miracle, but also that miracles cannot be an adequate foundation for a religion. Hume is undercutting miracles and any religion born of miracles in one fell swoop. Going for the jugular vein of miracles does all the work, for it also deals a death blow to the religion of any miracle working god.

If miracles are the foundation for a religion, then an apologist for that religion cannot bring up a miracle working god to establish his supposed miracles. For miracles are supposed to be the basis for the religion and its miracle working god. In the context of this present anthology, apologists must deal with the chapters in this book in an honest attempt to see if the god of the (whole) Bible exists and that Christianity is the true religion. One cannot reason backwards from the existence of their god to the miracle testimonies in the Bible. For the issue is whether the god of these miracles exists in the first place.

Apologists have only the testimonial evidence from ancient pre-scientific humans, without any relevant objective corroborating evidence. They cannot claim the Bible is divine testimony either, until they have established that the testimony in the Bible is good enough to establish its miracles. These are the kinds of problems Hume surely understood, which is why he didn't bother with Bayes' Theorem. And if this doesn't explain why he didn't use Bayes, it doesn't matter. These same reasons are why no one needs to adopt Bayes when debating impossible events in the natural world like miracles, which have no prior data to work from, and no prior miracle working god who would do them.[61]

---

[60] Ibid, p. 53.
[61] I don't object to using Bayes' Theorem when applied appropriately to questions for which we have prior data to determine their initial probability. I do have objections to the use of Bayes' Theorem when assessing

Apologists might start by first arguing for their god's existence, but very few of them say, "Here is the objective evidence that our god exists." They always seem to talk in terms of "presenting an argument" rather than "presenting the evidence," which is very telling. So, an unevidenced god will not help an unevidenced miracle, just as an unevidenced miracle will not help an unevidenced god. The only thing apologists can do is special plead to their God and his religion by assuming what needs to be proved.

Just consider what apologists William Lane Craig and J.P. Moreland say about the hypothesis, "Jesus rose naturally from the dead." They argue such a hypothesis is "fantastically, even unimaginably, improbable . . . given what we know about cell necrosis."[62] In other words, they admit the evidence is woefully lacking to believe Jesus rose up from the dead without a miracle, or without a miracle working god, or without a miracle working god who would do such a miracle—that is, a Christian god. Got it! They need a miracle to believe Jesus rose from the dead. So therefore, that's how they argue, backwards, from their prior belief in a miracle working god who would do such a miracle, to the miracle of the resurrection of Jesus. They do this because they realize that on natural grounds alone, they cannot make the case that a miracle like the resurrection took place. But if god comes first then whence comes god, the god of the resurrection? If the miracle of Jesus' resurrection cannot be reasonably accepted unless the Christian god exists and raised him up from the dead, then where is the evidence for the god who raises Jesus up from the dead? The best explanation is that they just presuppose such a God due to cultural and familial influences, for if they didn't already believe in the Christian god there would be no reason to think Jesus came back from the dead, because dead people stay dead.

---

miraculous events in the world which violate natural laws, where there is no prior data to work from. See my post, "Hypothesis: Since Bayes' Theorem Cannot Help Us It Should be Abandoned" along with the tag below it, "Bayes' Theorem." URL: http://www.debunking-christianity.com/2019/03/hypothesis-since-bayes-theorem-cannot.html. I know people disagree, that's why I'm not making a big deal of it here.

[62] J. P. Moreland and William Lane Craig, *Philosophical Foundations for a Christian Worldview* (Downers Grove, IL: InterVarsity Press, 2003), 571.

My third response to Earman's objection has to do with the whole notion of background information, background knowledge, and plausibility frameworks. Since they refuse to discuss the honest question of whether Jesus came back from the dead separately from their god, Craig and Moreland claim the hypothesis, "God raised Jesus from the dead" can be "highly probable relative to our background information."[63] By this, they mean the sum total of everything they were raised to believe inside their religious cultures. This cultural background information provides them with the justification for sidestepping the ECREE principle requiring objective corroborative evidence to confirm human testimonies to miracles, by trusting the ancient mariner's tales. At this point they're already assuming their Christian god exists and is the one who raised Jesus from the dead, for if the hypothesis was that "Allah raised Jesus from the dead," we already know the answer—of course not! Nor would it be the Hindu god, or any of the pantheistic gods and/or goddesses, a deistic god, or even the Jewish god, since overwhelming numbers of Jews don't believe in the Christian god.

Indeed, it's true that our general background information about how the world works plays a part in assessing whether a miracle has occurred. For when we talk about the probability of some event or hypothesis A, that probability is always relative to a body of background information B. So, we cannot merely speak of the probability of A without taking into consideration that background information, B, all of it. Got it! No one can evaluate miracle claims without using previously acquired background information. *But what shouldn't count as background information are unevidenced indoctrinated beliefs we inherited from parents, who in turn blindly accepted what they were told. Only background knowledge should count!* Previously acquired knowledge of how the world works should be based on sufficient objective evidence commensurate with the type of information being sought. Otherwise, culturally inherited indoctrinated background information can and will lead people to

---

[63] Ibid.

believe in delusions against any and all objective evidence to the contrary.

If Christians object then they should stop playing the hypocrite by allowing Muslims or Orthodox Jews, or Hindus, or Satanists to use their own specific background information to determine whether Jesus was raised from the dead. I've argued extensively for *The Outsider Test for Faith* to help establish a standard for how we should think of the *other guy's* miracles. It's a non-double standard based on the golden rule: to treat your own miracle claims the same way you treat others from the perspective of an outsider, a nonbeliever, with the same level of reasonable skepticism believers already use when examining the other religious faiths they reject.[64] Treat your own indoctrinated faith just as you treat the religions you reject. It's the only way to know which religion is true, if there is one. It's the only way to help eliminate a whole host of cognitive biases that keep believers inside their delusions. So when it comes to background beliefs, background information, or plausibility frameworks, the only ones that count are based on objective evidence which we would properly call background knowledge. Plenty of people have misinformed background beliefs that need to be subjected to the same objective standards as the outsider test for faith.

J. L. Mackie recognized this when he distinguished between the two different contexts for assessing miracles. He developed an important Neo-Humean argument against miracles:

> The defender of a miracle…must in effect concede to Hume that the antecedent improbability of this event is as high as it could be, hence that, apart from the testimony, we have the strongest possible grounds for believing that the alleged event did not occur. This event must, by the miracle advocate's own admission, be contrary to a genuine, not merely supposed, law of nature, and therefore maximally improbable. It is this maximal improbability that the weight of the testimony would have to overcome.

---

[64] See my book, *The Outsider Test for Faith* for more.

Where there is some plausible testimony about the occurrence of what would appear to be a miracle, those who accept this as a miracle have the double burden of showing both that the event took place and that it violated the laws of nature. But it will be very hard to sustain this double burden. For whatever tends to show that it would have been a violation of a natural law tends for that very reason to make it most unlikely that it actually happened.[65]

Mackie then distinguishes between two different contexts in which an alleged miracle might be considered a real one. First, there is the context where two parties "have shared background information or beliefs, that they have accepted some general theistic doctrines and the point at issue is, whether a miracle has occurred which would enhance the authority of a specific sect or teacher. In this context supernatural intervention, though prima facie ('on the surface') unlikely on any particular occasion is, generally speaking, on the cards: it is not altogether outside the range of reasonable expectation for these parties."

The second context is a very different matter, when "the context is that of fundamental debate about the truth of theism itself. Here one party to the debate is initially at least agnostic, and does not yet concede that there is a supernatural power at all. From this point of view the intrinsic improbability of a genuine miracle…is very great, and that one or other of the alternative explanations…will always be much more likely—that is, either that the alleged event is not miraculous, or that it did not occur, or that the testimony is faulty in some way…This entails that it is pretty well impossible that reported miracles should provide a worthwhile argument for theism addressed to those who are initially inclined to atheism or even to agnosticism."[66]

---

[65] J. L. Mackie, *The Miracle of Theism* (Oxford: Clarendon Press, 1982), pp. 25–26.
[66] Ibid., pp. 26–27.

PRIVATE SUBJECTIVE MIRACLES

There is a different type of miracle claim being touted by many Christian apologists in the face of Hume's arguments. When concluding his chapter on miracles Hume acknowledged this was their only way out. Since "reason is insufficient" to establish a miracle, Hume concluded the Christian religion "cannot be believed by any reasonable person" without one. So "whoever is moved by Faith to assent to it, is conscious of a continued miracle in his own person, which subverts all the principles of his understanding, and gives him a determination to believe what is most contrary to custom and experience." This kind of miracle is based in private subjective religious experiences and should be called *private subjective miracles*, because they cannot be adequately explained by the natural processes of the brain alone, just as biblical miracles cannot be adequately explained by the natural processes of nature alone.

There are two of them. One) Christians claim the gospel writers received private subjective messages from the spirit world who subsequently wrote down these messages known as the divinely inspired Scriptures. On this see David Madison's excellent chapter for a refutation. Two) Apologists also argue that Christians receive their own private subjective messages that lead them to trust the private subjective messages of the gospel writers. At this point it's private and subjective *all the way down without any foundation for their beliefs*. I call this what it is, paranormal activity, the giving and receiving of psychic messages from beyond. Christians would scoff at my description of these messages as psychic, but what else are they? Spirit communication would be coming from a god on this account. But there would be no difference as to the medium, or the reliability of these messages, when compared to others who claim to have psychic abilities.

Christians have these private subjective miracle experiences that prove with certainty their entire sect-specific religious faith is true down to the minute details. Conservative Christians, for instance, will come away feeling certain they had an experience with Jesus, who existed eternally as the second person of the trinity and was born of a virgin, and so on, and so on, what are described as the "great truths of the gospel" by Alvin Plantinga.[67] But even among Christians who claim the Bible is inspired there's an extensive amount of disagreement with the *content* of these divine messages. *How is that possible if these messages all come from the same divine source?* There are even five major Christian views of what it means to say the Bible is divinely inspired.[68]

Skirting the requirement for extraordinary evidence of the *objective* kind, J.A. Cover, claims his own private subjective miracle:

> The divine authority of Scripture seems to me not something that one could really establish at all. Some of us came to believe it at our parents' knee. (But then, how'd *they* come to know it?) To accept the authority of Scripture on the authority of my parents will work all right as an explanation of why I *do* believe it, but hardly works as a justification of the belief itself (why I *should* believe it). My own view is that no amount of historical scholarship can establish the inspiration and authority of scripture.

He asks,

> What sort of evidence could there be about God inspiring the Gospel writers (say) or the selection of the Canon that would underwrite belief in those? My suspicion is that [Alvin] Plantinga is right: our warrant in believing the Bible to be the authoritative Word of God owes to the work of the Holy Spirit. Full stop, pretty much.[69]

Cover admits the evidence can't even convince a theist who is a non-Christian saying: "We oughtn't expect too much from an apologetic of miracles: there's no *forcing* a theist to be a Christian."[70]

Cover's views are akin to what apologist Vincent Torley realized after reading Michael J. Alter's excellent skeptical book, *The Resurrection:*

---

[67] Alvin Plantinga, *Warranted Christian Belief,* pp. 245, 262.
[68] On this see my book *Why I Became an Atheist,* chapter 17 "Prophecy and Biblical Authority."
[69] Note 15, page 370, in *Reason for the Hope Within,* ed. Michael J. Murray.
[70] Ibid., Note 16, page 374.

A Critical Inquiry.[71] Before he read it he believed "a Christian could make a strong case for Jesus' having been raised from the dead, on purely historical grounds." Afterward he says, "I no longer espouse this view." And goes on to say "Whether one chooses to continue believing it (as I do) or not, one is forced to accept…that belief in the Resurrection cannot be built on the foundation of historical data, for it is a foundation of sand."[72]

As I'll show in chapter 6 on the abject failure of Christian apologetics, an overwhelming number of apologists have abandoned an apologetic of miracles, one that attempts to show Jesus arose from the dead purely on historical grounds. Gone from their cogitations is a god of the cosmos and history. Now all they have left is a god of the gaps and worse, a god of the guts. Apologists argue Christians are warranted in believing they experience private subjective miracles from their god, and that this provides all the proof they need for their sect-specific religion to be true, notwithstanding the fact that their god reveals himself *in the same exact private subjective way as the other Christian and non-Christian gods do.* These kinds of private subjective miracles are claimed by Muslims on behalf of Mohammed and the Koran, or Orthodox Jews and the Old Testament, or Hindus and the Bhagavad-Gita ("Song of God"), or Joseph Smith and the Mormon Scriptures.

Just look at it from a different perspective. Imagine apologists for Scientology honestly admitting there's no objective evidence that *body thetans* exist, or apologists for Mormonism honestly admitting there's no archaeological evidence that confirms the Book of Mormon. Imagine those apologists saying, as did Blaise Pascal, that "the heart has its reasons, of which reason knows nothing," or as the Protestant John Wesley said, that his heart was "strangely warmed." Imagine they continued believing even though they openly admitted no objective historical

---

[71] Xlibris, 2015.
[72] "Christian Apologist Vincent J. Torley Now Argues Michael Alter's Bombshell Book Demolishes Christian Apologists' Case for the Resurrection": http://www.debunking-christianity.com/2018/09/christian-apologist-vincent-j-torley.html

evidence or archeological evidence for the basis of their faith. Wouldn't we all think they were delusional? This is exactly what we're seeing from Christian apologists: the demise of the reasonableness of Christianity by the very intellectuals who are supposed to defend it.

4| PROPERLY INVESTIGATING MIRACLE CLAIMS

BY DARREN M. SLADE

INTRODUCTION

In his imposing two-volume work, *Miracles: The Credibility of the New Testament Accounts*, Craig Keener (1960–) documents contemporary miracle claims in order to demonstrate that there is a significant number of geographically widespread miracle reports today. The problem is that Keener's work is limited in its apologetic value, oftentimes proving only anecdotally that people continue to believe they have witnessed or experienced a miracle. The author not only admits these limitations, but he also declares that he avoided a thorough fact-finding investigation to authenticate the credibility and accuracy of these stories. Keener simply leaves the work of substantiating miracle claims to future investigators.[1] What is interesting is Keener's use of the term "credibility" in his subtitle when, in fact, neither the credibility, suitability, nor accuracy of his catalog of miracles (or the New Testament accounts) are corroborated with a forensic investigation or other fact-finding techniques. Indeed,

---

[1] Craig S. Keener, *Miracles: The Credibility of the New Testament Accounts*, vols. 1 & 2 (Grand Rapids, MI: Baker Academic, 2011), 1–17. For the myriad of eyewitness miracle accounts, see pp. 264–599. For the limitations of his research, see pp. 9–14, 249–57.

research from several thousand psychological studies and publications consistently reveals that eyewitness accounts are routinely inaccurate.[2]

The purpose of this chapter is to expose would-be paranormal investigators to the potential variables that could discredit or distort a claimant's reporting of a miracle. Likewise, this chapter will also identify some of the investigative practices needed to help substantiate or falsify a miracle claim. The thesis here is that stories of a fantastic nature ought to be thoroughly investigated according to the rigors implemented in judicial interviewing and interrogation tactics with an awareness of and attention to the possibility of deception, as well as the psychological variables known to affect the suitability and accuracy of eyewitness testimonials. Three main areas will support this thesis: 1) an analysis of claimant credibility; 2) a survey of claimant suitability; and 3) a discussion on claimant accuracy. First, it is important to understand the terms and definitions used in this brief review.

Definitions

For the purposes of a fact-finding paranormal investigation, "miracles" are here defined as anomalous and religiously noteworthy events that surpass the ability of physical nature to produce (naturally) under the particular circumstances in which it occurred. As such, they have a supernatural (or what Keener labels "extranormal") causation.[3] Likewise, claimants are considered "credible" about a specific miracle report if they are not deliberately attempting to promote a belief or perception in others (e.g. an investigator), without advanced and explicit warning, that the claimant considers to be inaccurate, insincere, false, untrue, or unfounded. In other words, claimants are credible if they are not lying. For investigators, credibility gauges a claimant's history of and proclivity for

---

[2] See Amina Memon, Aldert Vrij, and Ray Bull, *Psychology and Law: Truthfulness, Accuracy and Credibility*, 2nd ed., Wiley Series in Psychology of Crime, Policing, and Law (West Sussex, England: John Wiley & Sons, 2003), 107–10.
[3] Cf. Robert A. Larmer, *The Legitimacy of Miracle* (Lanham, MD: Lexington Books, 2014), 32–37 and Michael R. Licona, "Historians and Miracle Claims," *Journal for the Study of the Historical Jesus* 12, no. 1/2 (2014): 119.

telling the truth about miracles and, thus, assesses whether the claimant is engaging in deliberate falsifications, exaggerations, or minimizations that intentionally distort a testimony's correspondence to reality. Credibility also requires the absence of "subtle lies," which can include literal truths that are designed to mislead investigators. These lies also manifest in the form of evading questions and concealing or omitting relevant details that would potentially discredit the claimant's testimony.[4]

Similarly, in this chapter, "suitability" refers to the appropriateness of considering certain persons a legitimate "eyewitness" in the sense that they possess the minimal cognitive and affective characteristics at the time of the "miracle" event. To be considered suitable, these persons needed to be free from obstructive external and internal influences, such as poor visibility conditions or certain mental illnesses, while also being present in an optimal environment conducive for providing a detailed and accurate account of the incident.[5] Finally, the term "accuracy" here denotes a high degree of factual correspondence between an eyewitness's testimonial and the initial stimuli generated during the episode. Hence, a witness's account of the miracle must be both true and correct, to a high degree of relative certainty, in order to be considered "accurate."[6] As such, any miracle investigation that relies on personal testimony ought to scrutinize a claimant's credibility, suitability, and accuracy in order to eliminate reasonable suspicion of deceit, suboptimal settings, or psychological distortions. To do otherwise would be to approach miracle

---

[4] Günter Köhnken, "Behavioral Correlates of Statement Credibility: Theories, Paradigms, and Results," in *Criminal Behavior and the Justice System: Psychological Perspectives*, ed. Hermann Wegener, Friedrich Lösel, and Jochen Haisch, Research in Criminology (New York: Springer-Verlag, 1989), 271–72; Memon, Vrij, and Bull, *Psychology and Law*, 7–8.

[5] See, for example, Michael C. Bromby and Maria Jean J. Hall, "The Development and Rapid Evaluation of the Knowledge Model of ADVOKATE: An Advisory System to Assess the Credibility of Eyewitness Testimony," in *Legal Knowledge and Information System, JURIX 2002: The Fifteenth Annual Conference*, ed. Trevor J. M. Bench-Capon, Aspassia Daskalopulu, and Radbound G. F. Winkels (Amsterdam, Netherlands: IOS Press, 2002), 145–46.

[6] Cf. Judith C. S. Redman, "How Accurate Are Eyewitnesses? Bauckham and the Eyewitnesses in the Light of Psychological Research," *Journal of Biblical Literature* 129, no. 1 (Spring 2010): 178n8 and Köhnken, "Behavioral Correlates of Statement Credibility," 271.

claims credulously and naïvely without the critical methodology necessary for a proper fact-finding investigation.

METHODOLOGY AND SCOPE

This chapter was initially inspired by Keener's two-volume collection of modern-day stories about the occurrence of miraculous events where he argues, contra David Hume (1711–1776), that miracle reports are common (similar to those found in the New Testament) and that paranormal explanations for these reports should not be discounted completely.[7] What is surprising is that Keener does not assess the evidential value of these miracle reports, though he intends to use them as an apologetic in establishing "the *credibility* of the New Testament [miracle] accounts."[8] Rather than thoroughly investigate these contemporary miracle claims, Keener merely catalogues them "without asking questions of causation, since all of them illustrate the primary point that eyewitnesses can claim miracles. I do so even though I find some of the accounts more plausible and evidentially compelling for our secondary point than others....I thus take the accounts *mostly at face value* while recounting them."[9] Although Keener does concede that there exist natural explanations for many of

---

[7] Keener, *Miracles*, 1–4.
[8] Keener appears to use the term "credibility" as a synonym for *plausibility*, meaning the New Testament miracle reports are not immediately outlandish or otherwise fanciful in nature. "My concern is to focus instead on the more introductory question of the plausibility of eyewitness miracle reports" (Keener, *Miracles*, 9). Elsewhere, he writes, "What we tend to dismiss in [New Testament miracle reports] most readily is the credibility of those reports not easily susceptible to alternative (i.e., in our case, naturalistic) explanations" (p. 101). On the distinction between probability and plausibility, see Nicholas Rescher, *Plausible Reasoning: An Introduction to the Theory and Practice of Plausibilistic Inference* (Assen, Netherlands: Van Gorcum Ltd., 1976) and Douglas Walton, "Rules for Plausible Reasoning," *Informal Logic* 14, no. 1 (Winter 1992): 33–51.
[9] Keener, *Miracles*, 1–2; emphasis added. Keener writes elsewhere, "Many of these voices, in fact, can recount reports (including at times their own eyewitness testimony) of phenomena, both associated with Christianity and not associated with it, that seem difficult to explain, *if taken at face value*, without recourse to the activity of suprahuman entities" (p. 221; emphasis added). However, Keener acknowledges the difficulty of taking miracle claimants at face value without a proper investigation, remarking, "Claims do not by themselves constitute proof....While eyewitness claims do not constitute indisputable proof, they do constitute evidence that may be considered rather than a priori dismissed" (p. 2).

these "miracle" stories, he freely admits that a theistic worldview is guiding much of his assessment.[10]

Despite Keener's modest ambition and justifiably enthusiastic approach to the subject matter, he does suggest that a *bona fide* miracle is the best explanation for many of these stories, even personally certifying some of them himself.[11] The problem is that a theistic worldview (to the extent possible) should not play a determinative role in the explanation process when a thorough investigation of the evidence has yet to occur. Paranormal investigators ought to recognize that eyewitness testimonies, even their own, often represent the viewpoints and invested interests of those making the miracle claim. There is a significant potential for these stories to be fabricated, erroneous, misinterpreted, inconsistent, prejudicial, and fragmentary. Hence, investigators cannot simply take miracle claims at "face value."[12] Instead, a critical methodology for investigating miracle claims, as opposed to a hyperskeptical approach, allows researchers to admit the possibility of miracles without credulously or naïvely accepting unsubstantiated claims (a "naïve theist" approach). Here, a more critical attitude can still hypothesize, and even conclude, "extranormal" causation without hastily asserting a *bona fide* miracle prior to conducting a thorough investigation.[13] It is important to note that a critical methodology distinguishes between properly investigating a miracle claim (e.g. did the event actually occur) and judging whether the event is supernatural in origin. A "critical" methodology focuses on the former, not the latter, by employing fact-finding techniques designed to gauge a miracle claimant's credibility, suitability, and accuracy. Assessing whether a natural or supernatural explanation is the most plausible is

---

[10] Keener, *Miracles*, 14. For Keener's critique of natural explanations, see pp. 10–14, 603–759.
[11] Keener, *Miracles*, 712–59.
[12] Robert L. Webb, "The Rules of the Game: History and Historical Method in the Context of Faith: The *Via Media* of Methodological Naturalism," *Journal for the Study of the Historical Jesus* 9, no. 1 (2011): 60, 62–63, 65, 67–70.
[13] Cf. Licona, "Historians and Miracle Claims," 114–18 and Webb, "The Rules of the Game," 75–76 (esp. 76n34), 78.

subsequently left to individuals after examining the results of a thorough investigation.

This chapter responds to Keener's work in particular because Keener boasts, "I know how to ask necessary questions and am confident that my notes meet the standards traditionally used by many journalists."[14] Later, Keener suggests that eyewitness testimony from a personal associate is second only to observing the miracle directly. "I have a closer association with some of the sources, and I have good reason to trust the veracity of a number of the informants, in particular those whom I know well."[15] Keener's assumptions about having asked the right questions (like a journalist) and having received accurate depictions from acquaintances are precisely the same assumptions made by untrained and inexperienced investigators who are liable to make hasty and impulsive judgments. Journalists may know how to ask questions that expand a news story's narrative (e.g. detailing the basic who, what, when, where, why, and how of a person's recollection), but they do not always know how to assess a person's credibility, suitability, and accuracy like properly trained investigative journalists and law enforcement personnel.

As any good investigator will explain, friends, family, colleagues, and acquaintances are not immune from lying or embellishing their stories, and even well-intentioned eyewitnesses habitually misconstrue or misjudge dramatic events. In fact, Keener acknowledges that a person's religious fervor regularly results in fraudulent claims.[16] Hence, a thorough investigation is still needed before trusting "the veracity" of paranormal events. Keener appears to admit as much: "Because miracles are irregular events, we do not simply take miracle reports at face value without some evidence; the debate involves the level of evidence necessary to provide probability in a given case or whether the standard is too high to admit any evidence."[17]

---

[14] Keener, *Miracles*, 12.
[15] Keener, *Miracles*, 251.
[16] Keener, *Miracles*, 614–16.
[17] Keener, *Miracles*, 186n105.

The purpose of this chapter is to argue that Keener's "Proposed Explanations" section in *Miracles* is a bit premature without a thorough investigation. The biggest weakness of Keener's journalistic reporting is that he presumes he has been careful *enough* to warrant such pronouncements. Here, the purpose of this chapter is to fill in a particular gap of knowledge regarding miracle claims. Keener explains, "Further research might offer more controlled studies…more follow-up interviews with and consulting the medical records of persons claimed by various written sources to be healed; and so forth." He continues, "Further investigation may weaken the reliability of a few of my sources and my sources' sources."[18] In the event that future paranormal investigators wish to assess some of the miracle claims in Keener's work, or elsewhere, these investigators will need to know how to conduct a proper fact-finding investigation. Only then can someone make a reasonable judgment about an event's probable and possible supernatural origins, beginning first with assessing whether a claimant is credible or not.

CLAIMANT CREDIBILITY

To avoid a credulous or uncritical acceptance of a person's miracle claim, interviewers ought to possess several character traits shared among highly effective investigators, including being honest yet cautious, guarded against fraud, and overly inquisitive. Ideally, they should possess a sense of when things are unusual about someone's testimony, an attentiveness to details, and the capacity to control, minimize, or eliminate their own biases.[19] Unfortunately, research from several hundred studies indicates that people are poor lie detectors, averaging a 54% accuracy rate in identifying deception, which is only slightly better than mere guesswork.[20]

---

[18] Keener, *Miracles*, 12–13.
[19] James W. Osterburg and Richard H. Ward, *Criminal Investigation: A Method for Reconstructing the Past*, 5th ed. (Newark, NJ: Anderson Publishing, 2007), 12–13.
[20] Charles F. Bond Jr. and Bella M. DePaulo, "Accuracy of Deception Judgments," *Personality and Social Psychology Review* 10, no. 3 (2006): 214–34. See also, Köhnken, "Behavioral Correlates of Statement Credibility," 280–81.

Indeed, those who are more confident in their ability to detect lies in others are also more likely to be incorrect about their judgments.[21] In laboratory settings, even professionals whose vocation involves the detection of lies are not able to recognize deception significantly better than the general public.[22] Moreover, studies indicate that people have mistaken notions about how to detect lying, including the incorrect assumption that certain verbal and nonverbal cues such as body gestures, posture, fidgeting, speech disfluencies (e.g. stuttering and hesitations), and gaze aversion accurately indicate deception.[23]

In reality, however, liars do not consistently display verbal or nonverbal markers of dishonesty.[24] Thus, merely accepting people's reports without a thorough investigation of their credibility offers little to no apologetic value beyond the fact that some people claim to have witnessed a miracle. Considering that these stories are not likely to exhibit the same affective or behavioral signals as other high-stake scenarios (e.g. concealing a crime), it is unlikely that a mere interview can determine whether someone's report is fictitious or not.[25] Paranormal investigators

---

[21] Bella M. DePaulo et al., "The Accuracy-Confidence Correlation in the Detection of Deception," *Personality and Social Psychology Review* 1, no. 4 (1997): 346–57.

[22] Surprisingly, Secret Service personnel, CIA agents, sheriff's deputies, and police officers are unable to detect lies in one-quarter to one-third of low-stake situations (see Maria Hartwig, Pär Anders Granhag, and Timothy Luke, "Strategic Use of Evidence During Investigative Interviews: The State of Science," in *Credibility Assessment: Scientific Research and Applications*, ed. David C. Raskin, Charles R. Honts, and John C. Kircher [San Diego, CA: Academic Press, 2014], 5–6 and Memon, Vrij, and Bull, *Psychology and Law*, 9–11, 26–27).

[23] Hartwig, Granhag, and Luke, "Strategic Use of Evidence," 6; Memon, Vrij, and Bull, *Psychology and Law*, 30–33.

[24] Miron Zuckerman, Bella M. DePaulo, and Robert Rosenthal, "Verbal and Nonverbal Communication of Deception," in *Advances in Experimental Social Psychology*, ed. Leonard Berkowitz (New York: Academic Press, 1981), 14:1–59. However, these studies are limited in their approach to lying, making the application or elimination of verbal and nonverbal cues inconclusive. For an overview of these studies, see Memon, Vrij, and Bull, *Psychology and Law*, 14–20, 28–36. Likewise, according to some research, cognitive overload due to deception may, in fact, cause the impairment of speech (see Günter Köhnken, "Speech and Deception of Eyewitnesses: An Information Processing Approach," in *Social/ecological Psychology and the Psychology of Women: Proceedings of the XXIII International Congress of Psychology of the International Union of Psychological Science*, ed. Florence L. Denmark [Amsterdam, Netherlands: North-Holland, 1985], 7:117–39). For potential verbal and nonverbal cues to deception, see Memon, Vrij, and Bull, *Psychology and Law*, 11–18.

[25] Interestingly, people are more likely to perceive stories with an excessive amount of bizarre details as less believable than stories with fewer peculiarities (see the research findings in Kristine A. Peace, Krista L. Brower,

need to be aware that liars will attempt to convince people of their stories by strategizing beforehand. While testifying, deceivers will often avoid or deny details that could potentially expose their falsities by providing investigators with overly simplified and persuasive descriptions.[26] Thus, investigators ought to practice due diligence by verifying a claimant's credibility.

Verifying Credibility

A pre-interview background investigation into people's lifestyle, personal history, and propensity to lie about certain subjects will help assess their credibility by determining whether the claimant possesses a trustworthy character. This initial investigation should also explore possible conflicts of interest where claimants have already received or anticipate receiving some form of personal gain from their story (financial or otherwise). The investigator will also need to identify whether the claimant has ulterior motives for their report. While a history of truthtelling does not automatically solidify a person's credibility, paranormal investigators should be wary about accepting someone's testimony at face value if the claimant has a propensity for lying about religious subjects or personal experiences.[27] The rationale for this cautiousness is simple: investigators would have no assurance that the claimant is telling the truth without external corroborating evidence. Likewise, if an investigator discovers a deliberate falsehood in any part of the claimant's testimony, then the

---

and Alexandra Rocchio, "Is Truth Stranger Than Fiction? Bizarre Details and Credibility Assessment," *Journal of Police and Criminal Psychology* 30, no. 1 [March 2015]: 38–49).

[26] Hartwig, Granhag, and Luke, "Strategic Use of Evidence," 14–15.

[27] For example, Joseph Smith, founder of the Church of Jesus Christ of Latter-day Saints (i.e. Mormons), had been arrested, tried, and convicted of being "an impostor" on March 20, 1826 for attempting to deceive people into believing he could locate buried gold by placing a dark seer stone inside of a hat. Four years later, in 1830, Joseph Smith published the Book of Mormon based on his supposed discovery of buried golden plates, though Smith would later say he had actually unearthed them on September 22, 1823, almost thirty months *prior* to his conviction (see Fawn M. Brodie, *No Man Knows My History: The Life of Joseph Smith the Mormon Prophet*, 2nd ed. [1945; repr., New York: Alfred A. Knopf, 1978], 16–33, 427–29). These facts alone should cast significant suspicion on Smith's claim to have discovered buried golden plates, especially since the golden plates were never made public and have since been hidden away from further examination.

entire report becomes suspect and potentially unusable. Once claimants pass the initial background check, investigators will then need to concentrate on the content of their story, utilizing cognitive approaches to lie detection.[28]

For the initial interview, researchers need to allow claimants to report what they remember in its entirety without interruption or interrogation. However, investigators should still obtain basic information (if not voluntarily disclosed) about the people involved (including race, gender, physical descriptions, attire, relationships to other persons, etc.), actions done before, during, and after the incident, spatial elements about the location, and timeframes of the incident. Wherever possible, the investigator should audio and video record every interview. A claimant's credibility is questionable if they are unable to recall these basic details, although investigators will also need to differentiate between recognizable facts and details that are easily confused (e.g. a person having a beard vs. unshaven stubble). If anyone involved in the incident did something that could impede identification (e.g. wearing a disguise), then the testimony will likely be difficult to corroborate.[29] Descriptions of a relative nature where the individual has to estimate certain details, such as causal relationships, distances, numbers of people, height, weight, and age, are likely to be guesses and, therefore, less consistent or accurate.[30] In any case, interviewers must refrain from briefing claimants about the questions they will ask or even suggesting that others have corroborated their story. The reasoning is because these kinds of comments could increase a claimant's confidence level and appearance of sincerity, which will make credibility and accuracy harder to detect.[31]

---

[28] See Köhnken, "Behavioral Correlates of Statement Credibility," 272–75 and Bromby and Hall, "ADVOKATE," 146.
[29] Cf. Memon, Vrij, and Bull, *Psychology and Law*, 112–13.
[30] Elizabeth F. Loftus, *Eyewitness Testimony* (Cambridge, MA: Harvard University Press, 1979), 27–31.
[31] Gary L. Wells, Tamara J. Ferguson, and R. C. L. Lindsay, "The Tractability of Eyewitness Confidence and Its Implications for Triers of Fact," *Journal of Applied Psychology* 66, no. 6 (December 1981): 688–96; C. A. Elizabeth Luus and Gary L. Wells, "The Malleability of Eyewitness Confidence: Co-Witness and Perseverance Effects," *Journal of Applied Psychology* 79, no. 5 (October 1994): 714–23; Laura Smalarz and Gary L. Wells, "Eyewitness Certainty as a System Variable," in *Reform of Eyewitness Identification Procedures*, ed. Brian L.

For future investigators, it is important to know that liars tend to omit information while truthtellers tend to volunteer more details in their testimonies. In fact, "escape responses," where liars avoid or deny information, become more pronounced as they approach certain incriminating details in their story.[32] Investigators will eventually want to interview witnesses at least two or more times in order to identify any possible inconsistencies or contradictions in their narratives, in addition to obtaining further details or corrections to their previous statements.[33] In situations where there are two or more claimants, the investigator should implement the same interviewing processes for each person in order to detect inconsistencies and contradictions both with other claimants and with any empirical evidence obtained during the investigation.[34]

Once complete, investigators should then transcribe their initial interview and submit the transcript through the Criteria-Based Content Analysis (CBCA), which examines texts for the presence or absence of nineteen different content-related signals of truthtelling. Generally, reality-based statements are likely to contain more details and unusual phenomena than invented stories because fabrications derive mostly from a person's stock experience comprised of generalized scripts and schemas. These measures are also the underlying criteria for the Statement Validity Assessment (SVA), a test that is admissible as evidence in some Western European and American court systems.[35]

Cutler (Washington, DC: American Psychological Association, 2013), 172; Memon, Vrij, and Bull, *Psychology and Law*, 111–12. Attorneys with witnesses who are uncertain about their own testimonies are not likely to admit those witnesses as evidence into court cases (Smalarz and Wells, "Eyewitness Certainty," 162).

[32] Hartwig, Granhag, and Luke, "Strategic Use of Evidence," 18–21.
[33] Memon, Vrij, and Bull, *Psychology and Law*, 111.
[34] Cf. John C. Yuille and Judith Cutshall, "Analysis of the Statements of Victims, Witnesses and Suspects," in *Credibility Assessment*, ed. John C. Yuille, vol. 47, *Behavioural and Social Sciences*, Proceedings of the NATO Advanced Study Institute on Credibility Assessment (Maratea, Italy, 1988) (New York: Springer, 1989), 189.
[35] For details on the CBCA and SVA, including its procedures and research findings, see Aldert Vrij, *Detecting Lies and Deceit: The Psychology of Lying and the Implications for Professional Practice*, Wiley Series in the Psychology of Crime, Policing and Law (2000; repr., New York: John Wiley & Sons, 2001), 113–56 and Max Steller and Günter Köhnken, "Criteria-Based Content Analysis," in *Psychological Methods in Criminal Investigation and Evidence*, ed. David C. Raskin (New York: Springer Publishing Company, 1989), 217–45.

Part of the criteria that analysts use to determine a testimony's credibility are the following characteristics: the presence of a logical narrative structure, a sizable quantity of detail, contextual embeddings (e.g. portrayals of the environment), the spontaneous nature of narrative plotlines, descriptions of interactions, unusual and superfluous details, unexpected self-corrections or self-interruptions, and admitting a lack of memory about certain features. The more cues the CBCA and SVA detect, the more likely a claimant is telling the truth.[36] Credible eyewitnesses should be able to provide details of the location, people, and activities involved in the incident, both before and after its occurrence, which the investigator can then attempt to verify. However, while greater detail is a positive indicator of truthtelling, the more inaccuracies an investigator discovers in the testimony, the less reliable an eyewitness will be with accurately interpreting the incident.[37] Likewise, according to "Reality Monitoring" (RM), there is a qualitative difference between memories of actual events and reports based on fabricated or imagined stories. RM has demonstrated that authentic memories contain more contextual and sensory details, fewer references to the person's cognitive processes, and less eccentric or idiosyncratic information than false recollections.[38]

From this initial interview, investigators should be able to corroborate or falsify many of the claimant's details, such as descriptions of the event's location, the people involved, or anything else mentioned in the report. While researching these details, investigators should also note

---

[36] Content-related signs of deception, on the other hand, are often more incoherent and inconsistent, less detailed (especially regarding interactions, quotes of interactions, and unusual details), and less precise about chronological and spatial particulars ("contextual embeddings"). However, there is no single set of reliable cues to expose deception. These particular verbal cues are merely less likely to occur in deceptive testimonies. See Memon, Vrij, and Bull, *Psychology and Law*, 14, 19–20; Köhnken, "Behavioral Correlates of Statement Credibility," 273, 275–76; Peace, Brower, and Rocchio, "Is Truth Stranger Than Fiction," 38–39; and Yuille and Cutshall, "Analysis of the Statements," 186–88.
[37] Cf. Yuille and Cutshall, "Analysis of the Statements," 188.
[38] Marcia K. Johnson and Carol L. Raye, "Reality Monitoring," *Psychological Review* 80, no. 1 (January 1981): 67–85; Marcia K. Johnson, Shahin Hashtroudi, and D. Stephen Lindsay, "Source Monitoring," *Psychological Bulletin* 114, no. 1 (July 1993): 3–28.

other descriptions of the environment or situation (not initially provided by the claimant) before conducting subsequent interviews. This process will allow interrogators to utilize a fact-finding technique known as the "Strategic Use of Evidence" (SUE), which exposes falsehoods and signs of deception. Here, SUE employs a calculated strategy of asking *unexpected* questions about facts an eyewitness should know but had not previously disclosed to the investigator. For example, investigators might retrieve video footage of the claimant at a certain place and time, which was not mentioned during the interview. Investigators can also examine the location of the incident and the people involved for other factual details not described by the claimant. During subsequent interviews, the investigator can unexpectedly ask open-ended questions about these details, giving claimants an opportunity to lie in the process of answering (unaware that the investigator already knows the facts). The same strategy can be employed regarding information acquired during the initial background check, as well. This type of strategic questioning allows investigators to discern if claimants actually have experiential knowledge of the incident and to expose inconsistencies in their narration of the event.[39] The point is to ask questions about details an investigator already knows or can verify later.

The SUE method builds upon the assumption that there are cognitive disparities between deceivers and those telling the truth ("cognitive load hypothesis"). To lie is more mentally taxing than being honest because it requires greater brain activity and detail retention than authentic recall.[40] Because liars will attempt to avoid incriminating details, investigators need to think of questions that could potentially discredit their testimony. The goal is to identify "statement-evidence (in)consistencies," which reveal contradictions in a fabricated story. If a claimant is caught lying, the investigator can then ask further questions that would

---

[39] See Hartwig, Granhag, and Luke, "Strategic Use of Evidence," 1–10.
[40] Cf. Antonio L. Manzanero et al., "Evaluación de la credibilidad de relatos de personas con discapacidad intelectual," *Anales de Psicología* 31, no. 1 (January 2015): 338 and Köhnken, "Behavioral Correlates of Statement Credibility," 275.

require claimants to construct plausible sounding denials, alter their story, or proffer *ad hoc* explanations, further revealing their deception.[41] Ideally, an interrogator should insist on a polygraph test or Voice Stress Analysis (VSA) to detect lying, though this is not always practical or permissible by the claimant. Indeed, there are known problems with using polygraph and VSA equipment and, therefore, should not be the sole basis for assessing someone's credibility.[42]

It is important for investigators to be aware that minor inconsistencies in stories are not always an indication of untruthfulness, especially since discrepancies occur among actual witnesses during laboratory experiments.[43] Indeed, there exist four predominant reasons why eyewitnesses might report different details: 1) a person's point of view; 2) amount of attention given to the event; 3) focusing on different details; and 4) overall interpretation. To assess whether a discrepancy is inconsequential or not, the investigator should determine if the eyewitness had an adequate vantage point at an appropriate distance, as well as if the discrepancy is a result of elemental variables, such lighting and duration of the event.[44] Investigators should also seek to determine the witness's attention span during the incident, as well as whether they focused too

---

[41] Hartwig, Granhag, and Luke, "Strategic Use of Evidence," 16–21.

[42] See for example, Frank Horvath, "Detecting Deception: The Promise and the Reality of Voice Stress Analysis," *Journal of Forensic Sciences* 27, no. 2 (1982): 340–51; David C. Raskin, "Polygraph Techniques for the Detection of Deception," in *Psychological Methods in Criminal Investigation and Evidence*, ed. David C. Raskin (New York: Springer, 1989), 247–96; and Charles R. Honts, David C. Raskin, and John C. Kircher, "Mental and Physical Countermeasures Reduce the Accuracy of Polygraph Tests," *Journal of Applied Psychology* 79, no. 2 (1994): 252–59.

[43] Ronald P. Fisher and Brian L. Cutler, "The Relation between Consistency and Accuracy of Eyewitness Testimony," in *Psychology, Law, and Criminal Justice: International Developments in Research and Practice*, ed. Graham Davies et al. (New York: Walter de Gruyter, 1996), 21–28; Eric E. Jones, Phillip G. Palmer Jr., and Abby D. Bandy, "The Effect of Inconsistency on Evaluations of a Second Eyewitness: It Depends On Who Testifies First," *Psychiatry, Psychology and Law* 20, no. 6 (2015): 815. Researchers also need to be aware that in scenarios where there are two or more available witnesses, the testimony of the first witness will affect how the interviewer views the consistency and credibility of subsequent witnesses (Jones, Palmer, and Bandy, "The Effect of Inconsistency on Evaluations," 814–29).

[44] Interestingly, people tend to overestimate the length of events, especially when under stress (Irwin G. Sarason and Rick Stoops, "Test Anxiety and the Passage of Time," *Journal of Consulting and Clinical Psychology* 46, no. 1 [February 1978]: 102–9).

much or too little on certain details. Finally, investigators will need to evaluate whether these discrepancies are a result of misinterpreting the event due to preconceived expectations or biases.[45] Inconsistencies that are not easily explainable by these factors are likely to indicate more than just a superficial mistake of observation and can suggest a credibility problem with the claimant. Even more pertinent to a miracle claimant's credibility, however, is the presence of an overactive imagination and fantasy proneness.

OVERACTIVE IMAGINATIONS

Especially important to the study of miracles is the fact that a statistically significant portion of the general population *invent* past experiences simply because they *imagine* an event occurring ("imagination inflation"). Indeed, people are almost twice as likely to report false autobiographical memories simply because they have imagined a fictitious, hypothetical event, which is later reported as a genuine occurrence.[46] A similar issue involves people with "dissociation" problems, who are incapable of differentiating between actual memories and fantasies. While their everyday memories generally remain unblemished, dissociative people easily create false memories purely from their imaginative fancies. In fact, those who routinely fantasize in their daily life ("fantasy proneness") often create fictional memories that possess the same type of salience and lucidity as authentic memories. This proneness is especially characteristic among those who frequently spend time imagining

---

[45] Cf. Steven B. Duke, Ann Seung-Eun Lee, and Chet K. W. Pager, "A Picture's Worth a Thousand Words: Conversational Versus Eyewitness Testimony in Criminal Convictions," *American Criminal Law Review* 44, no. 1 (2007): 26–30.

[46] See Maryanne Garry and Devon L. L. Polascheck, "Imagination and Memory," *Current Directions in Psychological Science* 9, no. 1 (February 2000): 6–10; Giuliana Mazzoni and Amina Memon, "Imagination Can Create False Autobiographical Memories," *Psychological Science* 14, no. 2 (March 2003): 186–88; and Giuliana A. L. Mazzoni, Elizabeth F. Loftus, and Irving Kirsch, "Changing Beliefs about Implausible Autobiographical Events: A Little Plausibility Goes a Long Way," *Journal of Experimental Psychology: Applied* 7, no. 1 (March 2001): 51–59.

alternate realities, regularly hallucinate, and have intense religious, paranormal, or out-of-body experiences.[47]

While some studies suggest that reporting bizarre occurrences is actually a sign of credibility, these same unusual details could, in reality, be the result of imagination inflation, dissociation, and fantasy proneness. Thus, investigators (wherever possible) should account for this possibility by administering two specific tests in particular. The first is the Dissociative Experiences Scale (DES), which assesses whether a person is prone to confusing their own fantasies with actual memories. The second is the Creative Experiences Questionnaire (CEQ), which evaluates whether a person is prone to over-imaginative fantasies.[48] Afterwards, once a claimant's credibility is sufficiently established, investigators can then proceed to assess the person's suitability as an eyewitness.

CLAIMANT SUITABILITY

One of the first things investigators need to ascertain is "witness suitability" by examining whether eyewitnesses were even capable of accurately perceiving the event in the first place.[49] Helpfully outlined in the acronym ADVOKATE, investigators need details to the following categories: (A) the *amount* of time witnesses observed the event; (D) their *distance* from the event; (V) the *visibility* conditions at the time of the

---

[47] Memon, Vrij, and Bull, Psychology and Law, 142. On fantasy proneness, see Peter Hough and Paul Rogers, "Individuals Who Report being Abducted by Aliens: Investigating the Differences in Fantasy Proneness, Emotional Intelligence and the Big Five Personality Factors," Imagination, Cognition and Personality 27, no. 2 (2007–2008): 139–61; Harald Merckelbach, "Telling a Good Story: Fantasy Proneness and the Quality of Fabricated Memories," Personality and Individual Differences 37, no. 7 (November 2004): 1371–82; and André Aleman and Edward H. F. de Haan, "Fantasy Proneness, Mental Imagery and Reality Monitoring," *Personality and Individual Differences 36*, no. 8 (June 2004): 1747–54.

[48] Peace, Brower, and Rocchio, "Is Truth Stranger Than Fiction?," 43–44. For details on the DES, see Eve M. Bernstein and Frank W. Putnam, "Development, Reliability, and Validity of a Dissociation Scale," *The Journal of Nervous and Mental Disease* 174, no. 12 (December 1986): 727–35. For the CEQ, see Harald Merckelbach, Robert Horselenberg, and Peter Muris, "The Creative Experiences Questionnaire (CEQ): A Brief Self-Report Measure of Fantasy Proneness," *Personality and Individual Differences* 31, no. 6 (October 2001): 987–95.

[49] Bromby and Hall, "ADVOKATE," 145–46; Duke, Lee, and Pager, "A Picture's Worth a Thousand Words," 10–11.

event; (O) the degree to which their *observation* may have been obstructed; (K) their *knowledge* of (or familiarity with) the people, places, and objects involved; (A) were there *any* particular reasons for remembering the event; (T) the *time* elapsed since the event occurred; and (E) whether there are *errors* in the witnesses description of the event. These details help identify "defeating values" that would automatically disqualify a person as an accurate witness, such as being at a distance beyond fifteen meters from the event or making observations when the visibility level was below fifteen lux.[50]

Likewise, investigators need to assess people's physical and mental competency, as well, especially in terms of age and ability to comprehend the event. For instance, young children and seniors over the age of sixty are prone to mistaken remembrances and identifications.[51] Investigators should also establish whether the witnesses have frequent memory, visual, or auditory problems that might negatively affect their suitability. In terms of mental competency, investigators need to be cautious about relying solely on those with mental illnesses, developmental disabilities, or other cognitive handicaps that are known to affect the accuracy of their testimonies. Indeed, people with certain debilities are more likely to provide fewer details of an event, are more vulnerable to misleading questions, are more susceptible to misunderstanding requests for information, and are more likely to be inaccurate in their recall. Importantly, those with moderate intellectual or physical disabilities, while not being significantly less accurate than others, may be proficient at hiding their handicaps, which make investigators more vigilant about accepting testimonies without first assessing witness mental and perceptual competency.[52]

Finally, investigators ought to consider other non-optimal conditions, as well, such as inclement weather, interruptions, and distractions

---

[50] Cf. Elizabeth F. Loftus, "Reconstructing Memory: The Incredible Witness," *Psychology Today* 8 (December 1974): 116–19 and Bromby and Hall, "ADVOKATE," 146–47.
[51] Memon, Vrij, and Bull, *Psychology and Law*, 110.
[52] Cf. Memon, Vrij, and Bull, *Psychology and Law*, 100–1 and Manzanero et al., "Evaluación de la credibilidad," 338–44.

that might have affected a witness's observations. Investigators should also discover whether claimants were intoxicated or under the influence of any other substance that could potentially alter their perception of reality, including (but not limited to) alcohol, drugs, and prescription medication. Fatigue and other related factors, such as illness, dementia, fever, malnutrition, and dehydration can also create "malleable" witnesses whose perception and memory of the event are susceptible to distortion.[53] Once an investigator determines the eyewitnesses are suitable, they should then evaluate the accuracy of their testimonies.

CLAIMANT ACCURACY

In *Neil v. Biggers* (1972), the U.S. Supreme Court ruled that there are at least five variables required to determine the accuracy of eyewitnesses. The first involves an eyewitness's degree of certainty, stating that eyewitnesses must be certain about what they have witnessed. The second factor is whether the witness even had the capacity to view the event. Next is the attention given to the incident, suggesting that a fleeting glance is not sufficient. Fourth, they affirmed that eyewitnesses need to have quality descriptions of the occurrence. Lastly, there must not be a large gap of time between the event and its reporting.[54] Unfortunately, these guidelines are not adequate enough to establish the accuracy of an eyewitness's testimony.

As of March 1, 2019, the Innocence Project has exonerated 361 persons through DNA where over two-thirds (71%) were wrongfully convicted due to faulty eyewitness testimony.[55] As Gary Wells and

---

[53] Memon, Vrij, and Bull, *Psychology and Law*, 108–9, 111; Smalarz and Wells, "Eyewitness Certainty," 163, 167–68.
[54] Lauren O'Neill Shermer, Karen C. Rose, and Ashley Hoffman, "Perceptions and Credibility: Understanding the Nuances of Eyewitness Testimony," *Journal of Contemporary Criminal Justice* 27, no. 2 (May 2011): 187; R. Barry Ruback and Martin S. Greenberg, "Crime Victims as Witnesses: Their Accuracy and Credibility," *Victimology: An International Journal* 10, no. 1 (1985): 419; Smalarz and Wells, "Eyewitness Certainty," 162–63.
[55] See "The Cases," Innocence Project, accessed March 1, 2019, https://www.innocenceproject.org/all-cases/#exonerated-by-dna and "Eyewitness Identification Reform," Innocence Project, accessed March 1, 2019, https://www.innocenceproject.org/eyewitness-identification-reform.

Elizabeth Loftus remark, "Mistaken eyewitnesses account for more convictions of innocent persons than all other causes combined."[56] These numbers are not surprising considering there exist numerous psychological factors that notoriously affect a person's perception and memory of an event.[57] In fact, the consensus among surveyed experts on eyewitness testimony (by at least two-thirds majority) indicates that the following psychological variables impair the accuracy of an eyewitness's statement:[58]

1) the introduction of threatening objects, which worsens a person's capacity to observe other pertinent details ("weapon focus");
2) the length of time a witness observes an event where less time equates to less accuracy;
3) the rate of memory loss, which is highest immediately after an event ("forgetting curve");
4) the degree of witness confidence, which is not a reliable predictor of accuracy since outside factors can alter a person's assurance levels ("confidence malleability");
5) the wording of interview questions, which can adversely affect an eyewitness's memory;
6) the initial expectations of an eyewitness, which affect how they perceive events;
7) the accuracy of childhood memories, which is regularly mistaken or partially distorted and is typically less error-free than

---

[56] Gary L. Wells and Elizabeth F. Loftus, "Eyewitness Memory for People and Events," in *Handbook of Psychology*, ed. Alan M. Goldstein and Irving B. Weiner, vol. 11, *Forensic Psychology* (Hoboken, NJ: John Wiley & Sons, 2003), 149.
[57] These factors can be as simple as the age, gender, stereotype expectancies, and perceived distinctiveness of the people involved (see Shermer, Rose, and Hoffman, "Perceptions and Credibility," 186). Even a person being introverted makes them more susceptible to false memory suggestion, especially when coupled with an extroverted interviewer (Stephen Porter et al., "Negotiating False Memories: Interviewer and Rememberer Characteristics Relate to Memory Distortion," *Psychological Science* 11, no. 6 [November 2000]: 507–10).
[58] See Saul M. Kassin et al., "On the 'General Acceptance' of Eyewitness Testimony Research: A New Survey of the Experts," *American Psychologist* 56, no. 5 (May 2001): 405–16.

adults (being more vulnerable to interviewer suggestibility, peer pressure, and social influences);

8) and the habitual occurrence of "postevent information," where recollections often reflect material acquired only after the incident has occurred, which indicates that people cannot reliably discriminate between true and false memories.

With these variables in mind, investigators first need to consider the potential for memory bias when attempting to interview and, subsequently, corroborate miracle claims.

BIASED MEMORIES

There are three stages to memory: encoding, storage, and retrieval. Encoding is the process of transforming external stimuli into mental representations. However, exactly what aspects of an event become encoded depends on how much attention and focus is given to different details. This attention and focus similarly depends on the lucidity and salience of the stimuli at the time of encoding. Specifically, memorable details are those that stand out as unique or distinctive to the observer within the surrounding context and their preceding familiarity with the environment. Likewise, observers are more likely to remember details that are relevant or significant to them personally.[59] Indeed, incidents that have greater significance for an eyewitness are likely to be more accurate than insignificant events, though memory distortion is most prominent if the incident was unpleasant or displeasing to the observer.[60] Not surprisingly, people's personal interests and personalities will dictate which details they interpret as significant and salient. A person's culture, past

---

[59] See Susan T. Fiske and Shelley E. Taylor, *Social Cognition: From Brains to Culture*, 3rd ed. (Thousand Oaks, CA: SAGE Publications, 2017), 63–91.
[60] Richard E. Nisbett and Lee Ross, *Human Inference: Strategies and Shortcomings of Social Judgment* (Englewood Cliffs, NJ: Prentice-Hall, 1980), 45; Redman, "How Accurate Are Eyewitnesses?," 183. Cf. Ruback and Greenberg, "Crime Victims as Witnesses," 410–11.

experiences, preconceptions, prejudices, and preferences often dictate how people experience, remember, and interpret surprising events.[61]

Eyewitness testimony itself constitutes "autobiographical memory," meaning its sole source of information is the subjective perception of the individual who experiences and recalls past events. Its three primary components are verbal narrative, imagery, and emotion. Investigators need to realize that autobiographical memories assist people in making sense of the world and reflect how they have intuitively interpreted past events. Expectedly, people regularly recall and interpret details selectively in order to justify or rationalize their already held beliefs about reality. Thus, memory recall often appears in story form, which eyewitnesses then mold in order to captivate their audience and validate their actions and beliefs. The problem is that frequent retellings of a story tend to result in altering, adding, or omitting past details, which then become a solidified part of the autobiographical memory in future retellings.[62]

Finally, it is important to recognize that people are not just poor *eye*witnesses, but they are also consistently inaccurate *ear*witnesses, meaning people often provide inaccurate testimonies about conversations, words spoken, and intended meanings. Like other remembrances, conversational memory is vulnerable to the same biases and schema-driven errors as other memories.[63] In addition to the inherent bias of memory recall, investigators also need to be aware of other variables that can inadvertently distort a person's testimony.

OTHER POTENTIAL DISTORTIONS

One prominent variable that can affect the accuracy of miracle reports is the "source-confusion" or "source-monitoring" error where people misattribute the origin of their recollections to their own experiences.

---

[61] Redman, "How Accurate Are Eyewitnesses?," 182–83; Duke, Lee, and Pager, "A Picture's Worth a Thousand Words," 29–30; Ruback and Greenberg, "Crime Victims as Witnesses," 411–12.
[62] Redman, "How Accurate Are Eyewitnesses?," 180, 186, 189.
[63] See the numerous studies in Duke, Lee, and Pager, "A Picture's Worth a Thousand Words," 1–52.

For example, claimants may remember experiencing a miracle when, in reality, they only heard or read about the incident happening to someone else.[64] A thorough fact-finding investigation would identify whether the claimant was merely duplicating a local tale or whether the claimant has experiential knowledge of the incident in question. Similarly, people are susceptible to a postevent "misinformation effect," which occurs when outside people, including other witnesses, accidentally interject details into a person's memory, which then solidify as part of the eyewitness's storage and recall. Misinformation can also occur when people mistakenly remember or simply speculate about certain details, which also become part of the memory itself. Particularly during the interview process, witnesses unconsciously invent details to supply investigators with "what must have happened" for things they did not, in reality, observe. These factors are especially problematic for children because they are more susceptible to suggestibility, source confusion errors, and misinformation.[65] Thus, it is important that investigators not assume or inadvertently suggest unstated details about an event because of the potential for changing an eyewitness's memory.

Investigators also need to avoid an "interviewer bias" when asking questions. This bias occurs when an interviewer conveys details, stereotypes, or desired answers to the witnesses, which then (wittingly or unwittingly) prompts claimants to respond in a particular manner based on what they believe the investigator wants to hear. When conducting an

---

[64] Memon, Vrij, and Bull, *Psychology and Law*, 93–99; Johnson, Hashtroudi, and Lindsay, "Source Monitoring," 3–28.
[65] See Ira E. Hyman Jr., Troy H. Husband, and F. James Billings, "False Memories of Childhood Experiences," *Applied Cognitive Psychology* 9, no. 3 (June 1995): 181–97; Elizabeth F. Loftus and John C. Palmer, "Reconstruction of Automobile Destruction: An Example of the Interaction between Language and Memory," *Journal of Verbal Learning and Verbal Behavior* 13, no. 5 (October 1974): 585–89; Jo Saunders and Malcolm D. MacLeod, "New Evidence on the Suggestibility of Memory: The Role of Retrieval-Induced Forgetting in Misinformation Effects," *Journal of Experimental Psychology. Applied* 8, no. 2 (June 2002): 127–42; Michael McCloskey and Maria S. Zaragoza, "Misleading Postevent Information and Memory for Events: Arguments and Evidence Against Memory Impairment Hypotheses," *Journal of Experimental Psychology: General* 114, no. 1 (March 1985): 1–16; Redman, "How Accurate Are Eyewitnesses?," 186–87; Memon, Vrij, and Bull, *Psychology and Law*, 93–99; Duke, Lee, and Pager, "A Picture's Worth a Thousand Words," 34; Loftus, *Eyewitness Testimony*, 56–58.

interview, investigators must ask mainly open-ended questions that elicit free recall of the event while also avoiding the use of leading questions. Free recalls tend to be more accurate, whereas questions that are more specific, narrow, or leading tend to occasion inaccurate responses.[66]

This self-imposed limitation also extends to questions designed to arouse mental images of the event ("guided-imagery"). Although people may recall more information ("hypermnesia") during guided imagery, they are also predisposed to constructing false memories, which they then describe (with higher levels of confidence) as intensely vivid. As such, investigators must avoid asking claimants to speculate about details or to provide a definitive answer to their questions because witnesses will simply feel pressured to guess. Investigators need to allow witnesses to remain unsure, ambiguous, and even ambivalent about their memories without a compulsion to provide more details.[67] Known as a "system variable," interviewers can carelessly implant false memories into their subjects merely by the way they ask their questions. Indeed, indecisive eyewitnesses are particularly susceptible to a conformity pressure, being more likely to modify their accounts based on a perceived pressure from authority figures or their perception of what they believe the majority thinks about the event.[68]

An associated problem is known as a "confirming feedback effect" where people unconsciously suggest to eyewitnesses that their story is correct by displaying approval signals about the story's content, which can then distort their recall of the incident and artificially increase

---

[66] Cf. Gary L. Wells, R. C. L. Lindsay, and Tamara J. Ferguson, "Accuracy, Confidence, and Juror Perceptions in Eyewitness Identification," *Journal of Applied Psychology* 64, no. 4 (August 1979): 440–48; Jack P. Lipton, "On the Psychology of Eyewitness Testimony," *Journal of Applied Psychology* 62, no. 1 (February 1977): 90–95; Memon, Vrij, and Bull, *Psychology and Law*, 96–97, 101–6; and Yuille and Cutshall, "Analysis of the Statements," 176.

[67] Ira E. Hyman Jr. and Joel Pentland, "The Role of Mental Imagery in the Creation of False Childhood Memories," *Journal of Memory and Language* 35 (April 1996): 101–17; Redman, "How Accurate Are Eyewitnesses?," 187–88.

[68] Cf. Norman J. Bregman and Hunter A. McAllister, "Eyewitness Testimony: The Role of Commitment in Increasing Reliability," *Social Psychology Quarterly* 45, no. 3 (1982): 181–83; Hyman, Husband, and Billings, "False Memories," 181–97; Hyman and Pentland, "The Role of Mental Imagery," 101–17.

confidence levels. Simply expressing amazement or excitement about a miracle can increase people's sense of certainty about its authenticity. The feedback then results in distorting an investigator's perception of the testimony's truthfulness simply because humans are predisposed to believing that higher levels of confidence indicate higher levels of accuracy.[69] Hence, when Christian apologists (for example) exhibit an eagerness to corroborate miracle claims, particularly from friends and family, they may inadvertently compel claimants to fabricate, embellish, or omit details in response to the apologist's enthusiasm. The feedback loop ends up artificially heightening the sense of confidence and sincerity felt between interviewer and interviewee.[70] Indeed, witnesses who express a high level of confidence are just as likely to make mistakes as the general population, especially when considering that a witness's confidence and sincerity increases the more times they recount their testimony to others.[71] Therefore, prior to conducting an initial interview, researchers should determine approximately how many times eyewitnesses have recounted their testimony to others. Conversely, if people express honest doubt about their testimony, then investigators have reason to doubt it, as well.

Moreover, there exist certain biases that affect recall, as well. For instance, people have a tendency toward "retrospective biases" where people falsely superimpose their current experiences, feelings, attitudes,

---

[69] Smalarz and Wells, "Eyewitness Certainty," 163, 168–70. Interestingly, Keener appears to associate eyewitness confidence with a story's accuracy when he writes about people raising from the dead, "That the writers of the Gospels and Acts believed that the resuscitations they reported took place should no more be doubted than the *confidence* of many people later in history and today who believe that they have seen, and have offered eyewitness evidence for, analogous experiences" (Keener, *Miracles*, 537; emphasis added).

[70] Again, Keener appears to associate eyewitness sincerity with a story's accuracy, writing, "Given my knowledge of Elaine and the larger context of her life story ..., I have full confidence that she speaks with absolute sincerity" (Keener, *Miracles*, 570).

[71] Siegfried Ludwig Sporer et al., "Choosing, Confidence, and Accuracy: A Meta-Analysis of the Confidence-Accuracy Relation in Eyewitness Identification Studies," *Psychological Bulletin* 118, no. 3 (November 1995): 315–27; John S. Shaw III and Kimberley A. McClure, "Repeated Postevent Questioning Can Lead to Elevated Levels of Eyewitness Confidence," *Law and Human Behavior* 20, no. 6 (December 1996): 629–53; Köhnken, "Behavioral Correlates of Statement Credibility," 272; Smalarz and Wells, "Eyewitness Certainty," 165, 171–72; Shermer, Rose, and Hoffman, "Perceptions and Credibility," 185.

behaviors, and beliefs onto past events. The reverse is also true when people perceive and interpret a current event according to earlier experiences ("schema theory"). What people expect to see and hear affects their perception of reality. Once people assimilate a new interpretation about a past event, they are likely never to remember their previous beliefs about the episode. These errors then become established fact and will perpetuate through repeated retellings, even after individuals learn that their recall has, in fact, been wrong.[72] Investigators need to be mindful of these distortions by locating (where possible) the witness's previous statements to others in order to identify whether their interpretation of the memory has evolved or changed over time.

Researchers should also be cognizant of traumatic reports since these can result in memory repression, suppression, and partial amnesia of relevant details. Those events that are more salient due to surprise, heightened emotional arousal, and greater importance will sometimes become "flashbulb memories," which are especially intense in clarity and precision. However, higher stress levels actually impair and narrow a witness's perception of events. Though the individual believes their memory is acutely accurate, flashbulb memories are, in actuality, less accurate than normal memories and tend to deteriorate over time. Surprisingly, there is evidence that flashbulb memories do not even form immediately but begin the encoding process several days after having discussed the episode with others. This prolonged process suggests that flashbulb memories are just as susceptible to postevent misinformation as other memories.[73] When considering topics such as traumatic events, there is a lack of consistency during the encoding process. Emotional intensity appears to encode only certain memories in some circumstances, but not in all

---

[72] Daniel L. Schacter and Elaine Scarry, eds., *Memory, Brain, and Belief*, Pbk. ed. (2000; repr., Cambridge, MA: Harvard University Press, 2001), 3; Redman, "How Accurate Are Eyewitnesses?," 180–82, 185, 187–88.
[73] See Stephen Porter and Angela R. Birt, "Is Traumatic Memory Special? A Comparison of Traumatic Memory Characteristics with Memory for Other Emotional Life Experiences," *Applied Cognitive Psychology* 15, no. 7 (December 2001): 101–17; Memon, Vrij, and Bull, *Psychology and Law*, 128–35; Redman, "How Accurate Are Eyewitnesses?," 184–85; Shermer, Rose, and Hoffman, "Perceptions and Credibility," 186; Ruback and Greenberg, "Crime Victims as Witnesses," 411.

cases. Regardless, the evidence suggests that heightened arousal specifically reduces the accuracy of a person's recall.[74] Again, investigators need to be cautious with descriptions that are concomitant with flashbulb memories and conduct a thorough investigation to determine whether memory repression or suppression has occurred.

Another memory variable involves time delay. In general, memories are subject to rapid decay and postevent distortion where false memories actually increase over time. Hence, the longer the time between encoding, storage, and retrieval, the more difficult recall becomes for eyewitnesses.[75] Equally concerning is the chance of chronological displacement where people accurately remember the timeframe of an event but displace the date by several years.[76] Therefore, investigators need to identify how much time has lapsed since the event and whether their recollection is even in the right period of time. Spatial and experiential problems also arise from studies that indicate persons directly involved in an event are less accurate than bystanders. The presence of frightening objects and higher anxiety levels diminish an eyewitness's ability to recall important details since they tend to focus almost exclusively on alarming features. The same is true for situations where an unexpected item or an object that is inconsistent with the context appears in the situation, making

---

[74] Cf. Daniel B. Wright et al., "Field Studies of Eyewitness Memory," in *Reform of Eyewitness Identification Procedures*, ed. Brian L. Cutler (Washington, DC: American Psychological Association, 2013), 181–82 and Ken A. Deffenbacher, "The Influence of Arousal on Reliability of Testimony," in *Evaluating Witness Evidence: Recent Psychological Research and New Perspectives*, ed. Sally M. A. Lloyd-Bostock and Brian R. Clifford (New York: John Wiley, 1983), 235–51.

[75] See the research in Henry F. Fradella, "Why Judges Should Admit Expert Testimony on the Unreliability of Eyewitness Testimony," *Federal Courts Law Review* 2006, no. 3 (June 2006): 10; Craig R. Barclay, "Schematization of Autobiographical Memory," in *Autobiographical Memory*, ed. David C. Rubin (1986; repr., Cambridge, MA: Cambridge University Press, 1989), 82–99; Elizabeth F. Loftus, "Silence is Not Golden," *American Psychologist* 38 (May 1983): 564–72; Duke, Lee, and Pager, "A Picture's Worth a Thousand Words," 30–33; and Lipton, "On the Psychology of Eyewitness Testimony," 90–95.

[76] Steen F. Larsen, Charles P. Thompson, and Tia Hansen, "Time in Autobiographical Memory," in *Remembering Our Past: Studies in Autobiographical Memory*, Pbk. ed., ed. David C. Rubin (1995; repr., New York: Cambridge University Press, 1999), 129–56.

eyewitnesses succumb to an object-focus effect.[77] This attentional funneling, which narrows people's focus, unavoidably means a lack of or diminished awareness to other (potentially disconfirming) details.[78] Hence, investigators should note whether bystanders, unaffected by heightened emotional arousal, were also present and whether there were alarming features that could have distorted a witness's perception of the event.[79] It is important to recognize, however, that being aware of these variables is not, in fact, an endorsement of hyperskepticism about miracle claims.

UNDUE HYPERSKEPTICISM

In light of the potential for credibility issues and psychological distortions, two questions immediately present themselves: 1) should critical investigators possess a "presumption of truthtelling" with regards to a claimant's credibility, suitability, and accuracy until proven otherwise; and 2) who has the burden of proof when proposing a causal explanation (natural or supernatural) for a "miraculous" event?

First, in his book, *Scaling the Secular City*, J. P. Moreland argues that eyewitnesses ought to have the benefit of the doubt with a "presumption of truthtelling." For him, a presumption of lying is simply self-refuting, further implying that skeptics are unduly selective in which kinds of witnesses they believe.[80] In reality, Moreland is presenting a false dichotomy by suggesting there are only two options: either a presumption of truthtelling or a presumption of lying, both of which are equally

---

[77] See for example, Anne Maass and Günter Köhnken, "Eyewitness Identification: Simulating the 'Weapon Effect'," *Law and Human Behavior* 13, no. 4 (December 1989): 397–408 and Kerri Pickel, "The Influence of Context on the 'Weapon Focus' Effect," *Law and Human Behavior* 23, no. 3 (June 1999): 299–311.
[78] Peace, Brower, and Rocchio, "Is Truth Stranger Than Fiction," 42; Ruback and Greenberg, "Crime Victims as Witnesses," 416–19.
[79] Cf. Memon, Vrij, and Bull, *Psychology and Law*, 87–106, 110, 113–18.
[80] J. P. Moreland, *Scaling the Secular City: A Defense of Christianity* (Grand Rapids, MI: Baker Academic, 1987), 137–38.

unreasonable.[81] This mischaracterization is, in fact, a false dilemma. Rather than presume *anything*, it is possible (and more judicious) for people to withhold judgment until a thorough investigation is completed and all available data has been collected. Regardless, as any skilled investigator will explain and as Moreland partially admits, a presumption of truthtelling is only rational if the following elements are present:

1) claimants are mentally capable of expressing the truth;
2) they explicitly claim to be telling the truth, as opposed to engaging in (for example) irony or sarcasm;
3) they are willing to provide factual information that can be independently corroborated;
4) they lack a strong motivation for deception;
5) and they do not have a propensity for transmitting falsehoods about the subject matter under consideration.[82]

In this sense, critical investigators are not obligated to presume a claimant is either (in)credible, (un)suitable, or (in)accurate, especially with regard to fantastical stories such as miracles. This critical approach is especially relevant when considering that even honest witnesses, who are legally liable for some aspect of the event, may resort to distorting their accounts in order to hide embarrassing or incriminating details.[83] More innocently, people will also attempt harmonizing, ignoring, or discarding information from their testimony in order to alleviate the cognitive dissonance that occurs when other witnesses or details conflict with their version of the event.[84]

Second, the question about burden of proof is easy to address. The burden of proof rests on the person proposing an explanation for the

---

[81] Louis Gottschalk, *Understanding History: A Primer of Historical Method*, 2nd ed. (New York: Alfred A. Knopf, 1969), 150.
[82] These criteria, however, do not endorse an overly skeptical (and irrational) position of "poisoning the well." Just because someone has a criminal history, improper motives, or has falsified information in the past does not mean they are falsifying information in the present (though these factors should not be ignored, either).
[83] Cf. Ruback and Greenberg, "Crime Victims as Witnesses," 421.
[84] Redman, "How Accurate Are Eyewitnesses?," 187.

cause of a "miraculous" event.[85] Because this chapter argues that Keener's work has not engaged in a thorough fact-finding investigation, something he himself admits, it is practical to point out that his periodic endorsement of supernatural causation has not met the burden of proof and is, thus, premature and unfounded. There exists ample evidence, as presented in this chapter, that even honest, competent, confident, and sincere people can be mistaken about the facts and, therefore, require a thorough investigation before passing judgment about their claims to have witnessed a miracle.

Keener argues that many skeptics merely presume an antisupernatural stance, rather than a critical one, which automatically dismisses a miracle claim *a priori*. These hyperskeptics may offer *ad hoc* rationalizations for why a *bona fide* miracle could not have occurred, even resorting to implausible explanations, moving the goal posts, or promoting an as-yet unknown naturalistic explanation (a kind of "nature-of-the gaps" approach). No amount of evidence will likely convince hyperskeptics, and it may even be possible that academics are too inflexible in what they consider "evidence."[86] Of course, the criticisms go both ways. While this chapter is not advocating for hyperskepticism, there appear to be instances where Keener was simply not skeptical *enough* about the stories he catalogues. In any case, to withhold judgment because a thorough fact-finding investigation has not been established is not an example of hyperskepticism nor is it a confusion of probability with logical possibility. It is, rather, an example of critical thinking.

Besides, there are times when Keener falls into the same trap as his hyperskeptical counterparts. Oftentimes, Keener's "extranormal" explanations rely on the *lack* of falsifying evidence, which is simply an argument from ignorance. It is not the case that Keener is merely engaging in abductive inference-building, either, where his training and experience results in educated guesswork. Instead, his "God-of-the-gaps"

---

[85] T. Edward Damer, *Attacking Faulty Reasoning: A Practical Guide to Fallacy-Free Arguments*, 7th ed. (Boston, ma: Wadsworth, Cengage Learning, 2013), 7, 16–18.
[86] See the entire discussion in Keener, *Miracles*, 645–711, 739–59.

tendencies, where he believes a supernatural agent plausibly instigated a miracle, engages in causal oversimplification. He is right that a naturalistic explanation, such as the placebo effect or psychoneuroimmunology, does not preclude God's involvement. However, is God really a necessary or even sufficient explanation for the event in question? Or does an "extranormal" hypothesis create more questions than it answers, too severely restricting the number of other possibilities, such as those derived from the variables introduced in this chapter? Moreover, implying that a friend's sincerity and religious interpretation is enough to convince him of a miracle's legitimacy does nothing but associate the cause of an event with its religious effects.[87] Keener must know that a miracle claimant's *confidence* and *sincerity* does not make the claim credible, suitable, or accurate. These characteristics are malleable and can be artificially amplified. Finally, simply because one event (e.g. bodily healing) follows a separate event in time (e.g. prayer) is not sufficient to believe the one caused the other. A thorough investigation is still needed.

Ultimately, critical investigators should not only review the relevant data surrounding miracle claims, but they should try to falsify them, as well, by exploring alternative explanations and subjecting all sources to critical inspection. At the very least, investigators ought to provide publicly identifiable and scrutable evidence before suggesting an "extranormal" explanation.[88] Future miracle investigators would do well to remember the counsel of Judith Redman:

> Although trustworthy witnesses would have no desire to deceive their audience, their particular interests, experiences, and personalities would result in testimonies that were more likely to be accurate at some points than at others. This is especially the case when we are presented with information from someone who is known to have a vested interest in or bias toward a particular position or outcome. If it is the only information we can access, we

---

[87] Keener declares, "After all, I know these people and believe I have good reason for confidence in their testimony" (Keener, *Miracles*, 758).
[88] Webb, "The Rules of the Game," 70–74.

must rely on it, but we should certainly not trust it to the point where we accept it uncritically. We should still question those aspects of the testimonies of trustworthy witnesses that strike us as unusual. They are reliable in that they tell us *what they believe to be true*. This does not necessarily make it true.[89]

Otherwise, the desire to corroborate miracle claims lends itself to a "confirmation bias" by interpreting unexplainable events as validation of their already held religious beliefs.[90]

Conclusion

Craig Keener declares, "The collection [of miracle reports] would not prove that any given claims to miracles in the past were authentic (we have evidence and other reasons to affirm that many claims, in fact, have been inauthentic)."[91] This chapter concurs. What is problematic is that Keener still offers judgments (both natural and supernatural) without a thorough fact-finding investigation, suggesting that his work is far more apologetic in nature than he admits to his readers. His attempts at tempering the results of these miracle claims comes off as disingenuous, paying only lip service to the fact that far too many miracle claims have been falsified, far too many claimants discredited, and far too many naturalistic explanations prove just as satisfying (if not more so) than appeals to invisible, spiritual entities. While Keener acknowledges that a nonsupernatural explanation can account for many contemporary "miracle" claims, he also freely admits that he has an invested interest in demonstrating the authenticity of the New Testament. Of course, establishing

---

[89] Redman, "How Accurate Are Eyewitnesses?," 196; italics in original.
[90] Cf. Peter C. Wason, "On the Failure to Eliminate Hypothesis in a Conceptual Task," *Quarterly Journal of Experimental Psychology* 12, no. 3 (July 1960): 129–40; Margit E. Oswald and Stefan Grosjean, "Confirmation Bias," in *Cognitive Illusions: A Handbook on Fallacies and Biases in Thinking, Judgement and Memory*, Pbk. ed., ed. Rüdiger F. Pohl (2004; repr., New York: Psychology Press, 2012), 79–96; and Yoshifumi Harada and Murray Hunter, "'Walking Under a Ladder': Superstition and Ritual as a Cognitive Bias in Management Decision Making," *Economics, Management, and Financial Markets* 7, no. 4 (December 2012): 34–41.
[91] Keener, *Miracles*, 251.

that miracles are still *reported* today proves very little other than the fact that miracles are still reported; but so are ghost sightings, hauntings, and witch doctor healings just like they were in the ancient world. The truth is that Keener never once corroborated New Testament miracle stories (an implausible task) and never once conducted a thorough fact-finding investigation to corroborate modern-day miracle reports, either. His catalogue of miracles is often tantamount to accepting the word of his friends and acquaintances without any follow-up, though he admits that true believers routinely embellish or concoct self-validating miracle stories. Accepting people's claims simply because they are otherwise good, honest, and sincere people ultimately borders on pure naiveté.

Regardless, even with journalistic skillfulness, readers know nothing of Keener's investigative or interviewing practices. Did Keener ever try to falsify the credibility of his subjects (even his own friends, family, and colleagues), or did he just take everyone at face value all the time? Did he ever assess whether his interview subjects are prone to overactive imaginations and fantasies, something that is not easily detectable? Did he attempt corroborating that his subjects were, in fact, present and in a position to observe the event without obstruction or impairment? Were his subjects even mentally or physically competent to act as witnesses?

Did Keener account for the possibility of source-confusion, postevent misinformation, or retrospective biases? Did his questions rule out the effects of attentional funneling and object-focus effects? Did he take steps to avoid an interviewer bias or other system variables that implant false memories? Did Keener unintentionally cause a confirming feedback effect by showing signs of confidence and enthusiasm in the truthfulness of his subject's claims? Did Keener ever ask how many times a claimant has rehearsed the miracle story, which artificially heightens their sense of sincerity and confidence in the story's accuracy? How long before they first reported the miracle to others? Did Keener's interviews, or the interviews he cites of others, influence these claimants into accepting certain ideas or beliefs through suggestion? Indeed, was Keener even aware of these potential distortions enough to avoid them like a skilled interviewer would when conducting a fact-finding investigation?

The point of this chapter is not to accuse Keener of being wholly credulous. On the contrary, his two-volume work is a masterful catalogue that unquestionably proves his main point: people today still claim to have experienced miraculous events similar to those found in the New Testament, a point he admits was never really in contention.[92] In fact, given what is known about cognitive illusions, the high number of miraculous claims actually makes sense. The propensity for individuals to distort reality and misinterpret personal experiences, however unintentional, suggests that the number of people who believe they have witnessed a *bona fide* miracle would be high, indeed. Nevertheless, this is where Keener's work should have ended. After confessing he was unable to conduct a thorough investigation, is it really appropriate to offer a "Proposed Explanations" section without first acquiring all the data? What is being advocated in this chapter is not hyperskepticism but, rather, the refusal to pronounce judgment on a miracle claim until sufficient data has been collected to warrant such a verdict.

One of Keener's statements proves illustrative on this point: "Although in much of the Majority World medical documentation is hard to come by, a research team in which I have confidence *confirmed* a number of cases of extraordinarily significant improvements in hearing and vision after prayer."[93] Who *confirmed* these cases? What methods did they use to *confirm* the reports? Was a thorough investigation conducted? Was even an *adequate* one done? Readers are left only with Keener's "confidence," which has no bearing on the miracle claim. Unfortunately, Keener's work remains predominantly anecdotal and should not be viewed as providing sufficient case studies about the reality of *bona fide* miracles until these reports have been publicly and independently authenticated. Indeed, there is a good chance that his enthusiasm for using miracle stories to corroborate his already held religious beliefs

---

[92] Keener, *Miracles*, 2–3.
[93] Keener, *Miracles*, 716; emphasis added.

inadvertently generated the very results he desired. While Keener may be an adequate *interviewer*, he is not a trained or skilled *investigator*, which makes his pronouncement on causation quite premature. Thus, the research presented in this chapter will help future paranormal investigators satisfactorily and thoroughly substantiate the events described by miracle claimants. Though a supernatural explanation is possible, no miracle report can reasonably be considered "confirmed" without first corroborating the report's credibility, suitability, and accuracy.

5| ASSESSING KEENER'S MIRACLES

BY EDWARD T. BABINSKI

Dr. Keener in his work on Miracles cites claims of miracles past and present, especially those that resemble stories in the Gospels, adding that today there are "a massive number of miracle claims proliferating around the world."[1] He also boasts elsewhere of "a tidal wave of examples."[2] But he tones down such language in his conclusion: "Of course, many recoveries claimed as miracles have ready natural explanations...[but] even if cases as surely extra-normal as those just mentioned are a small proportion of the total claims, I believe that they are cumulatively too numerous to be simply dismissed."[3] He further diminishes such claims when he admits, "vast numbers of people in the world—probably the majority—who need healing...do not have it."[4] So, Keener's own caveats may reduce his "tidal wave" to a trickle after natural explanations and failed prayers (recalling the few hits, forgetting all the misses) are taken into consideration.

Keener himself admits, "I prayed [for my in-laws to be healed of failing health including arthritis, and prayed for a little girl to be healed

---

[1] Keener, Craig S., Miracles: The Credibility of the New Testament Accounts. (Grand Rapids, Michigan: Baker Academic, 2011), 2 volumes, v. 1. p. 1.
[2] Strobel, Lee, The Case for Miracles: A Journalist Investigates Evidence for the Supernatural (Zondervan, 2018), p.97
[3] Keener, Miracles, v. 2. p. 762.
[4] Keener, Miracles, v. 2. p. 767.

of deafness] but did not see any immediate changes,"[5] and, "my wife and I have suffered…eight miscarriages"[6] (though he cites claims in which women were able to bear children via "miracles," and even his mother-in-law knew a pastor whose prayers allegedly enabled "a woman whose uterus had been removed" to have a baby).[7]

Another story in Keener's book that comes from his in-laws, and which he repeats often in interviews[8] and lectures, he titles, "Raising of My Wife's Sister,"[9] in which his wife's sister at age two was outside playing when she suddenly screamed "Snake!" and began crying within earshot of her mother who strapped the crying toddler to her back and began running through the mountains to an evangelist, but "quickly discovered that the child had stopped breathing." About three hours later, per the mother's estimate, she reached the evangelist, they prayed, and the child began breathing. But no snake was seen by the mother hence its species was unknown as well as the toxicity of its bite. And how can one determine conclusively whether a two-year-old has totally ceased breathing, especially when the toddler is strapped to one's back and one is running in panic mode?

Compare this parallel story from Australia, "Lucky Escape for Snake Bite Toddler": A one-year-four-month-old toddler was bit by what may have been a deadly brown snake, "Through piercing screams of her son she phoned an emergency number, and tried to calm him down. The toddler then fell asleep. The doctor told her it was actually the initial shock of the event which probably caused the short loss of consciousness…But luckily…it was a dry bite. Although brown snakes are the second most venomous snakes in Australia, they often give a warning 'dry bite' without venom first…The doctors said there had been similar cases…four in the last week…[The toddler] was released from hospital

---

[5] Keener, *Miracles*, v. 2. p. 767.
[6] Keener, *Miracles*, v. 1. p. 10.
[7] Keener, *Miracles*, v. 1, p. 333-334.
[8] Stafford, Tim, "Expect a Miracle: Scholar Craig Keener Rediscovers the Reality of Divine Intervention," *Christianity Today*, December 2011, p. 34-37.
[9] Keener, *Miracles*, v. 1, p. 557.

a day later."[10] "A good percentage of venomous snake bites in humans occur without venom injection. This phenomenon is termed 'Dry' bite."[11] Though even a bite from a non-poisonous snake can cause an allergic reaction in young children and affect their breathing (without necessarily stopping it completely).

What is missing from Keener's story is how difficult it is to tell sometimes if a toddler is breathing—especially one that has fainted after experiencing a shock. Because their nostrils are small, they often breathe more quietly. Parents of even healthy toddlers are sometimes puzzled by how quiet and motionless they remain in their cribs. Since the mother was in panic mode and the toddler was strapped to her back, one suspects that only after the mother had reached her destination would the time be ideal to check more carefully for vitals and for the toddler to breathe more deeply. Nor was any mention made in the story of the status of the toddler's skin which would have begun to fill with stagnant blood that would have settled in certain regions if her heart had indeed ceased for as long as the story assumes, nor any mention of the condition of the toddler's skin where the snake bit her.

Speaking of alleged raisings from the dead, Keener mentions that an extraordinary number of them, "fourteen," are attributed to "one of the most famous healing evangelists,"[12] a Pentecostal preacher from the U.K., named Smith Wigglesworth (1859–1947). Keener adds that "Wigglesworth claimed that the greatest test of his obedience was when he called his just-deceased wife back to life but God told him to stop."[13] (Really? The same God whose power allegedly raised her, also told him to stop? God should make up his mind.)

Contra the melodramatic tales of miracles that Wigglesworth shared in his sermons, one should note the evidence Sandra Anne Carp

---

[10] Chillingworth, Breanna, "Lucky Escape for Snake Bite Toddler." http://www.essentialbaby.com.au/toddler/toddler-health/lucky-escape-for-snake-bite-toddler-20130811-2rpuj
[11] Naik, B.S., "'Dry bite' In Venomous Snakes: A Review." *Toxicon*, 2017, p. 63.
[12] Keener, *Miracles*, v.1, p. 421.
[13] Keener, *Miracles*, v. 1, p. 422 n.547.

uncovered concerning this Pentecostal legend.[14] Via extensive research she determined that "considerable diversity" exists "with regard to the exact number Wigglesworth raised," and those who claimed larger numbers either were unable to provide reliable sources or retracted their claim. Moreover, during the many decades Wigglesworth preached he only reported four cases in which he raised the dead. And he only claimed he had raised someone five years after Pentecostal newspapers had already begun to report rare claims by others. And the first time Wigglesworth reported each of his own four raisings it was to audiences on continents other than the ones where the raising allegedly took place, and only years after it allegedly took place, "in most cases it was over a decade later."[15]

Carp concluded that "Wiggleworth's raising from the dead stories appear to be intentionally deceptive claims." Wigglesworth's dramatic sermons in which he spoke of having raised people, including a close friend from his childhood and his own wife, "placed him in a legendary class of his own." Carp mentions self-aggrandizing stories Wigglesworth told compared with the lack of faith of fellow Pentecostals, including his wife. Wigglesworth inflated his mission reports concerning the number of people saved and healed. "He may have felt it was necessary to include an element of fiction, possibly in an attempt to defend himself and his ministry from critics," and gain more souls for what he was certain was his soon-coming Lord, i.e., Smith lived into his 80s and continued to preach that "We are in the last days, and before the Lord comes we trust to see the mightiest Revival the world has ever seen."[16]

He placed himself on a spiritual pedestal...unwilling to admit to imperfect faith with regard to his need for glasses...as this would

---

[14] Carp, Sandra Anne, A Pentecostal 'Legend': A Reinterpretation of the Life and Legacy of Smith Wigglesworth. M.Phil. thesis (University of Birmingham, 2016). http://etheses.bham.ac.uk/6538/
[15] For the details in each case see, "Smith Wigglesworth Raised the Dead?" https://edward-t-babinski.blogspot.com/2019/03/miracles-by-craig-s-keener-smith.html
[16] Carp, p.157.

have contradicted his 'Apostle of Faith' status [he preached that health was granted those with faith].[17]

On one occasion Wigglesworth declared to the sick "I'll only pray for you once, to pray twice is unbelief." The second night, a man approached the altar to receive prayer again and Wigglesworth, recognizing him, said "Didn't I pray for you last night? You are full of unbelief, get off this platform!" And on a number of occasions his approach to persons suffering from stomach complaints was to punch them in the stomach, sometimes with such force that it propelled them across the room because he believed he was dealing with satanic forces binding the afflicted. He even described cancer as "a living evil spirit."[18]

But despite his belief in complete healing via faith, he suffered the loss of wife and son, the lifelong deafness of his daughter, and his own battles with kidney stones and sciatica. Carp concluded, "As a result of this investigation, I believe the mythology surrounding Wigglesworth has been created by Wigglesworth himself; biographers and later authors continued to further develop these myths."[19]

Keener mentions in his book (and often repeats in lectures and interviews) that two famous skeptics dismissed claims of miracles regardless of what Keener claims was good evidence:

1) The philosopher David Hume (1711–1776) "dismissed...reports" of the healing of Marguerite Perier, the niece of Blaise Pascal on March 24, 1656, at the Jansenist Port-Royal monastery. Marguerite's "severe, long term fistula in her eye disappeared during the touch of a consecrated relic...The repulsive odor from her wound...and her apparent bone deterioration vanished immediately."[20] Keener reiterated this claim in an interview in Christianity Today,

---

[17] Carp, p.159-160.
[18] Wilson, Julian, Wigglesworth: The Complete Story: A New Biography on the Apostle of Faith Smith Wigglesworth. (Tyrone, Georgia: Authentic Media, 2004), p. 82-83,120.
[19] Carp, p. 85-100, 159-167.
[20] Keener, *Miracles*, v.1, p. 164.

"Pascal's niece was instantly and publicly healed of a running eye sore...most people would say the documentation for that was pretty good [but] Hume dismisses it."[21]

2) New Testament scholar, David F. Strauss (1808–1874), author of The Life of Jesus Critically Examined (a classic study of Gospel contradictions), "explained early Christian miracle stories as myths depicted as history." But "Strauss heard of contemporary miracle claims involving Lutheran pastor Johann Christoph Blumhardt, and a friend of Strauss [Eduard Morike] found himself cured of his inability to walk after visiting Blumhardt."[22]

Looking at Keener's first case, the healing of Marguerite, Pascal's niece, he does not cite a crucial primary source, a letter from one of Pascal's sisters at Port-Royal to Marguerite's mother (Jacqueline Pascal to Gilberte Pascal Perier, March 29, 1656). The letter is dated five days after Sister Flavie, Marguerite's caretaker, reported the girl's healing. And it states, "that evening" Sister Flavie overhead Marguerite telling another girl, "My eye is cured; it does not hurt me now."[23] Therefore, contra Keener, the healing was not noticed the instant the reliquary was applied in public.

Keener also fails to mention that the "fistula" was not literally "in the eye" which sounds like it was in the eyeball itself. The reports call it a "lacrimal fistula," having to do with a swollen tear sac—a small chamber near the nose into which excess lubrication of the eye drains, the duct from that sac to the nose was obstructed.

And the "bone deterioration" he mentions would have been internal and involved the creation of a tiny channel either through thin nasal bones, or cartilage, or through a malformed membrane (a not uncommon congenital defect), or some other obstruction of the duct that

---

[21] Stafford, p.36.
[22] Keener, *Miracles*, v.1, p. 176-177.
[23] Pascal, Jacqueline, *A Rule for Children and Other Writings*. Edited and translated by John J. Conley. (Chicago: University of Chicago Press, 2003), p.142.

normally channels excess eye moisture from the tear sac to the nose. Therefore, the "deterioration," coupled with a little pressure on the swollen sac may have facilitated the opening of a wider channel—enough to empty the sac and drain its contents into her nose as it normally does, leading to her cure.[24]

In other words, Sister Flavie told others that Marguerite's eye had ceased "watering" and the swelling between her eye and nose was gone,

---

[24] That was the assessment of two major historians of Port-Royal monastery, Sainte Beuve and Charles Beard, see the latter's work, Port Royal: A Contribution to the History of Religion and Literature in France. (London: Williams and Norgate, 1873). 2 volumes. v.1 p.314-315.

According to Dr. Sanford R. Gifford, Professor of Ophthalmology, "This girl undoubtedly had dacryocystitis," an infection of the lacrimal tear sac—a small chamber near the nose into which excess lubrication of the eye drains—the sac also has a duct that transfers lubrication into the nose. But some people are born with a thin membrane that blocks that duct, causing their eye to continually shed tears because the lacrimal sac can't empty into the nasal pharynx. This watery eye syndrome may continue for years "until at the age of five to ten years the contents of the lacrimal sac become infected." [Marguerite was six-and-a-half when hers became infected.] The lacrimal sac then swells with watery pus, and "when the infecting organism is a colon bacillus, or certain other organisms, such as proteus vulgaris, there is sometimes a bad odor. The enlargement of the sac sometimes produces a necrosis of the nasal wall, so that the secretion sometimes discharges in the nasal pharynx, but the opening is not large enough to drain all the secretion, so the swelling persists. Pressure on the lacrimal sac will drive the secretion either into the nose, or back into the [eye's] conjunctival sac [which was also described in Marguerite's case when pressure was applied to the swelling]...In some children I have succeeded by pressing hard on the sac in rupturing the membrane separating the duct from the nose, resulting in cure of the condition entirely. This is a recognized procedure which is usually tried on babies suffering from the condition...It may be that necrosis [of the nasal wall facilitated the cure in Marguerite's case, creating sufficient drainage]. It is certainly true that once a large enough opening appears in the nose to drain the secretion, the swelling disappears completely." Bishop, Morris, Pascal: A Life of Genius. (New York: Reynal & Hitchcock, 1936), p. 376 n. 19.

An article in a French medical journal examined the data concerning "The Miracle of the Holy Thorn" and its authors noted that Jacqueline Pascal wrote (in her letter mentioned earlier) that "two days" before Marguerite was healed, "she was starting to smell bad/feel ill again," but the use of the word "again" implies that some improvement in her condition prior to that time had occurred. And, "discharges of pus from the nose or other orbits eventually ends up drying up," so they "find it permissible to admit that the disease was coming to a normal end, and even an eighteen-month treatment [that Marguerite had undergone, which included applying pressure to the lacrimal sac] had not been without [some positive] effect on her." The healing might even have coincided with pressure from the reliquary expelling an obstruction in the duct or opening a sufficiently wide channel to drain her tear sac. Also, a "rapid occlusion of a fistula, whether lacrimal or osteitic are rather ordinary phenomena." (An "occlusion" = a closure; and, "osteitic" = inflammation of a bone as a consequence of infection.) Furthermore, the surgeon did not examine the insides of Marguerite's nose or mouth till a week of further healing had occurred. Targowla, Rene and Monique, "Le Miracle de la Sainte Epine de Port-Royal" [Miracle of the Holy Thorn of Port-Royal; Medico-Legal Aspects], Annales Medico Psychologiques, Vol. 115, Issue 4, April 1957, p. 635-658.

or at least much diminished. It had also been two months since the surgeon last saw the child, and it would be a week after Flavie's story that the surgeon would arrive to examine the child again, leaving time for further healing.

And it wasn't until after Sister Flavie told her version of the story that included the holy thorn reliquary that the surgeon declared it a miracle and began to promote it as such. (Nor were seventeenth century surgeons masters of medical knowledge, "For a long time yet, there would be no surgery academy: barbers and barber surgeons both shaved faces and were members of a worker's guild, i.e., humble artisans compelled to set up shops and work with their hands. To become a doctor required learning Latin, obtaining a degree, and signing a notarized commitment not to operate anymore.")[25]

A list of doctors and surgeons would later declare the healing of Marguerite to be a miracle. However, Guy Patin, former dean of the Paris Faculty of Medicine, though he publicly feigned to believe in the miracle, privately disputed the testimony of these "approvers of miracles." He said that some were too closely associated with Port-Royal [and Jansenism] to avoid bias, and others were unqualified "barber-surgeons...laced and booted lackeys who have never studied," adding that "the very initiative of the case [to declare the healing a miracle] is based on the dark prediction [of Port-Royal's surgeon as to the incurable and grave danger the girl was in—he wanted to cauterize her!], and, when he noted the healing, declared it a miracle, then attached himself with a lot of zeal to publish it, particularly to the Court" (letter of Guy Patin, Nov. 7, 1656 to Charles Spon).[26]

After Marguerite's healing was officially declared a miracle people flocked to the holy thorn reliquary (no longer displayed at Port-Royal but elsewhere) to press their rosaries and holy medals against it, after which eighty further miracles were claimed, though there was a hostile

---

[25] Targowla.
[26] Bibliothèque nationale de France. "Ex-voto de Marguerite Perier." http://expositions.bnf.fr/pascal/grand/bla_159.htm , and, Targowla, p. 650.

contemporary assessment of those miracles.²⁷ And what of the holy thorn's power today? Or Jansenism? They have both declined mightily to say the least.²⁸

Keener's second case of a famous skeptic dismissing good evidence involves Edward Morike (friend of famous New Testament critic David F. Strauss) who was "cured of his inability to walk." Keener's statement in the text is incorrect, he could walk, with difficulty. Keener states correctly in a footnote that Morike merely developed an "improved ability to walk." But even then, Keener neglects to tell readers that, "Morike's improvement did not last," as admitted in Keener's primary source.²⁹ A

---

[27] Kreiser, Robert B., Miracles, Convulsions, and Ecclesiastical Politics in Early Eighteenth-Century Paris. (Princeton, N.J.: Princeton University Press, 1978), p. 71 n.3.

[28] Sister Flavie (Marguerite's caretaker and superintendent of the children at Port-Royal, whose report is central to the story) was one of the most notorious characters in the history of the monastery. Passart, Catherine de Sainte-Flavie, Un projet ambitieux : le Dictionnaire de Port-Royal au XVIIe siècle https://journals.openedition.org/ccibp/605#tocto2n16

She feigned a host of personal illnesses followed by miraculous cures via her personal collection of relics. She intentionally deceived the children under her care that a rose had bloomed in winter after she had placed it in front of a picture of a Jansenist hero. And she tried to convince the children that she had supernatural knowledge of their affairs (she held the keys to the children's desks that contained their personal journals and letters). Flavie also was ambitious; she was among the first of her Sisters to abandon Jansenism when pressure was put on the monastery to do so, she spied on her sisters for the archbishop and even betrayed Blaise Pascal, all in an attempt to get the archbishop to choose her as Port Royal's new director. Schimmelpenninck, Mary Anne, Selected Memoirs of Port Royal...Taken from Original Documents. (London: Hamilton, Adams, & Co. Paternoster-Row, 1835). Fourth Edition. Vol. 1., p. 264-266, 273-278.

As for Blaise Pascal, he spent his final years as a religious solitaire at Port-Royal employing ingenious self tortures (such as wearing an iron belt full of points aimed at his bare flesh, and would give himself a blow with an elbow to double the pain of the pricks whenever some spirit of vanity arose in him, or even when he felt himself touched by the pleasure of conversation). He worked on his Pensées = thoughts, an apologetic work. Along with his fellow Jansenists he believed he was part of a holy remnant elected to salvation while the rest of the world was likely damned. Pascal urged his intelligence to commit suicide at this time, writing, "Take holy water, have masses said. That will make you believe naturally and will stupefy you" (nor was he being sarcastic). The years before his death he suffered painful illnesses of body and mind, and the final six months he was unable to write or even read, but visited churches, prayed, and meditated on exposed relics. He died at the age of thirty-nine. Bishop, Morris, Pascal: A Life of Genius. (New York: Reynal & Hitchcock, 1936), p. 331-338.

For further details see, "Craig S. Keener—Sister Flavie, Jansenist Piety, and Pascal" https://edward-t-babinski.blogspot.com/2019/03/miracles-by-craig-s-keener-sister.html.

[29] Ising, Dieter, Johann Christoph Blumhardt, Life and Work: A New Biography. Translated by Monty Ledford. (Eugene, Ore.: Cascade, 2009). Translated from Johann Christoph Blumhardt: Leben und Werk. (Göttingen: Vandenhoeck & Ruprecht, 2002), p. 222.

biography of Morike adds, "His health never improved sufficiently to allow him more than a few hours of productivity for weeks or months at a time...His own illness caused him constant pain, and his death on June 4, 1875 was not unexpected."[30] Another point Keener fails to mention is that Morike's improvement coincided not only with his visit to Blumhardt's healing/evangelism center and mountain hot springs, but with Morike's engagement to a beautiful younger woman he adored, which is bound to pick up a man's spirits, if not his pace.[31]

Furthermore, Keener's source concerning the healing ministry of Lutheran minister Rev. Blumhardt admits that Blumhardt "did not cover up the fact that there were disappointments; not everybody experienced healing. Among these were people with 'black star' [cataracts], congenital blindness or deafness...his prayer also seemed ineffective for his mother-in-law...Among the people who in 'rather large' numbers appealed for help, the bulk were mentally ill and epileptic...also people suffering pain...shortness of breath...skin diseases, blindness, deafness, muteness...[Blumhardt] did little more than admonish them to repentance...[teaching that] only when they 'gave themselves wholly to God' would their prayer for healing win through."[32] But did it, even then, "win through"? Another scholar writes, "The cure stories at [Blumhardt's center] are not extraordinary for their pronouncement of miraculous causes, located as they are in a century of ecstatic camp meetings, urban revivals and Marian apparitions...[with] the majority never cured of anything."[33]

Before discussing the "miracle" of "speaking in tongues" which is mentioned in Keener's book, and a practice he personally advocates, it may interest readers to know that Keener and I both converted in our

---

[30] Slessarev, Helga, Eduard Morike. (New York: Twayne Publishers, 1970), p. 21, 25.
[31] Isling, p. 223. For more on Eduard Morike's alleged healing by Blumhardt see https://edward-t-babinski.blogspot.com/2016/01/miracles-by-craig-s-keener-book-review.html.
[32] Isling, p. 208-209.
[33] Kohler, Daniel J., "Pilgrimage of Protestants: Miracles and Religious Community in J. C. Blumhardt's Wurttemberg, 1840-1880" in Die Gegenwart Gottes in der Modernen Gesellschaft: Transzendenz und Religiose Vergemeinschaftung in Deutschland / The Presence of God in Modern Society: Transcendence and Religious Community in Germany. Michael Geyer and Lucian Holscher. (Wallstein Verlag, 2006), p. 72.

teens, and had an unspoken experience of God (or so I thought at the time), and we both can "speak in tongues" (or even "sing in tongues"), though Keener's wife cannot, and less than half of all Pentecostals polled worldwide admitted they could.[34] Meanwhile, Trinity-denying groups like Oneness Pentecostals, Mormons, and The Way International, have, or have had, members, who can speak in tongues. The lattermost group will even sell you a training session to learn how.[35] Nor do ex-Pentecostals/ex-Charismatics lose the ability to speak in tongues, though they find little use for it.[36]

Keener repeats claims that on rare occasions the words spoken by those who "speak in tongues" have been recognized by native speakers, though he admits alternate explanations exist in some cases.[37]

Early in the history of Pentecostalism a founding figure, Charles F. Parham, noticed at a service in 1901 a person speaking in tongues that sounded Chinese. Parham took that as a sign that Spirit-filled Christians were being gifted with the ability to speak in any language necessary for the world to be evangelized. He also believed the Anglo-Saxons of Britain were descended from the ten lost tribes of Israel—and due to their superior God-given racial qualities, they were divinely chosen to accomplish His end time goals. Parham also helped train the famous black Pentecostal preacher, William J. Seymour, but when Parham visited the Azusa Street Mission where he had sent Seymour to preach and saw white women interacting closely with black men, Parham was appalled. Parham even tried to take over the Mission but "Seymour's white leadership forced Parham to leave. Parham left, taking a few hundred white followers with him to his new church in Los Angeles. Parham was also incensed that Seymour had become the leader of a movement that

---

[34] Walsh, Arlene M. Sanchez, Pentecostals in America (New York: Columbia University Press, 2018), p. 3, 115 n.2.
[35] https://www.thewayinternational.com/why-i-speak-in-tongues/
[36] "The Miracle of Speaking in Tongues?"
https://edward-t-babinski.blogspot.com/2019/03/miracles-by-craig-s-keener-miracle-of.html
[37] Keener, Miracles, v. 1, p. 328 n.126.

Parham believed was his,"[38] and called Seymour "a big buck n-[word]."[39] As for Seymour, the only copy of his church's international Pentecostal mailing list wound up in the hands of former member, Florence Crawford, another major figure in the early movement. She chaffed under male leadership and decided to start a Pentecostal church of her own. (Florence had two dissolved marriages and thought African Americans should be "servants.")[40] As for Pentecostal missionaries, they soon learned that their ability to speak in tongues wasn't nearly as helpful in communicating with people in distant lands as Parham predicted.[41]

Keener cites one claim that appears to stun even him involving "a boy who is able to see through his artificial eye!" The exclamation is Keener's, though he admits one author considered the claim fraudulent, "but unfortunately he does not provide the reasons."[42] But the reasons are obvious.[43]

Keener's expectations were not only stunned but stymied by the lack of "solid reports" of one miracle in particular:

I have neither found nor expect to find any solid modern reports of ascensions, which pure invention might create perhaps to evoke very exceptional biblical narrative.[44]

Hume or Strauss couldn't have said it better. They viewed tales of "ascensions," including Jesus's, as "pure invention created to evoke very exceptional biblical narrative," which in Jesus's case evoked the narrative of Elijah's ascent to heaven via a whirlwind "which some texts regard as a cloud."[45] The author of the ascension scene in the book of Acts even

---

[38] Walsh, p. 20.
[39] Walsh, p. xx, 21-23, 118 n.21.
[40] Walsh, p. xxvi-xxix.
[41] Walsh, p. 4.
[42] Keener, *Miracles*, v. 2, p. 706.
[43] "Boy Sees Out of Empty Eye Socket?" https://edward-t-babinski.blogspot.com/2019/03/miracles-by-craig-s-keener-boy-sees-out.html
[44] Keener, *Miracles*, v. 1, p. 587.
[45] Keener, Craig, *Acts: An Exegetical Commentary*, Volume 1 (Baker Academic, 2012).

"employed many of the same Greek terms from the story of Elijah's ascent to heaven in the Greek Old Testament version of 2 Kings."[46]

Furthermore, "a paucity of ascension narratives in the Old Testament are replaced by an abundance in Second Temple Jewish and Greco–Roman literature."[47] In other words, increasing numbers of ascension narratives began to appear in Jewish and Hellenistic literature right before the New Testament was written.

The author of the Gospel of Luke and book of Acts (the same author) even patterned his story on the need to compete with Roman propaganda:

> [Ascension stories] seek to authenticate the authority of the one ascending into heaven and give legitimacy to his successors—either the next princeps [in the case of Roman propaganda] or the disciples in the case of [Christian propaganda in] Luke-Acts. The reaction to Jesus's ascension establishes a connection with Roman ideology. For after Jesus ascends, the disciples worship him (Luke 24:52) [just as] Roman Emperors were worshiped [only] after their translation to heaven/apotheosis…This interpretation also receives support from some of the earliest readers of Luke-Acts, such as Justin Martyr, Minucius Felix, and Origen, who point out the comparison between the ascension of Jesus and the apotheosis of the Roman emperor…[which] validates placing the account of Jesus's ascension in Luke-Acts within the political context of its day…Unique among early Christian writings, the writer of Luke-Acts [even] claims for Jesus and the church the same titles and achievements commonly associated with Rome: 'savior,' 'bringer of peace,' 'ascension into heaven,' and 'ruler of the world.'[48]

---

[46] K. Giles, article on "Ascension," Dictionary of Jesus and the Gospels: The IVP Bible Dictionary Series, ed. by Joel B. Green, Scot McKnight, I. Howard Marshall (1992), p. 48.
[47] Bryan, David K. and Pao, David W., Ascent into Heaven in Luke-Acts: New Explorations of Luke's Narrative Hinge (Minneapolis: Fortress Press, 2016), p. 3.
[48] Gilbert, Gary, "Roman Propaganda and Christian Identity in the Worldview of Luke-Acts" in Contextualizing Acts: Lukan Narrative and Greco-Roman Discourse. (Society of Biblical Literature, 2003), p. 245-247.

Returning to Keener's statement about not even "expecting" to find "solid modern reports" of ascensions, it sounds puzzling coming from someone like himself who expects miracles more often than not. Besides, the world is flooded with iPhones, drones and satellite imagery, so if there are any Elijahs out there, why wouldn't one expect solid modern reports of ascensions? Does Keener imagine we have solid ancient reports of ascensions?

Another embarrassing fact about "ascensions" that Keener fails to mention is that people in the first century believed the most direct way to heaven was literally through the clouds as New Testament scholar James D. G. Dunn points out:

It is undeniable that the [ascension] narrative in [the New Testament's book of] Acts presupposes that 'heaven' is 'up there,' that is, physically above the earth, and that Jesus's being 'taken up' was a going up 'into the heaven' (the quadruple repetition of the Greek phrase for 'into/toward heaven' in Acts 1:10–11 is striking).[49]

The Judeo–Christian cosmology reflected in the Bible consists of variations of the basic idea of what can be called 'the cosmic building'—the underworld below, the earth in the middle, the heaven above...God has made the 'upper story' his dwelling place...he sits enthroned in heaven...and rides on clouds through his domain. Particularly interesting are the passages which seem to envisage a plurality of heavens (Deuteronomy 10:14; 1 Kings 8:27; Psalm 148:4). As we enter the New Testament era there were speculations as to how many heavens there were. Some thought one (1 Enoch, IV Ezra), others, three or five (Testament of Levi), still others seven (Testament of Abraham, Ascension of Isaiah, rabbinic tradition). So we are not surprised at the frequency with which New Testament writers speak of the 'heavens' (plural),

---

[49] Dunn, James D. G., "The Ascension of Jesus: A Test Case for Hermeneutics," Auferstehung - Resurrection: The Fourth Durham-Tubingen Research Symposium: Resurrection, Transfiguration and Exaltation... (Mohr Siebeck, 2004), p.312.

including several passages that speak of Christ's ascension as an ascending 'into,' 'above,' or 'through' the heavens (Acts 2:34; Ephesians 4:10; Hebrews 4:14; 7:26). Nor are we surprised that Paul thinks in terms of at least three heavens, with paradise identified as the third heaven. (2 Corinthians 12:2–3).[50]

So if Jesus "ascended" to heaven, and heaven is not literally "up there," then did God arrange an Indian Rope Trick in which Jesus vanished into another dimension only after he was out of sight of those on the ground? The author of Acts even added a cloud as an apocalyptic stage prop to lift Jesus skyward thus reinforcing the idea that one could get to heaven via vertical ascent.[51] Such a tale helped reinforce the ancient

---

[50] Dunn, James D. G., "Demythologizing the Ascension—A Reply to Professor Gooding" (1981), p. 24. And see, "The Holy Heavens of the Hebrews" http://edward-t-babinski.blogspot.com/2011/11/holy-heavens-of-hebrews.html. Also see, "The Cosmology of the Bible" in The Christian Delusion, ed., John Loftus (New York: Prometheus Books, 1995).

[51] "a cloud took him out of their sight." Acts 1:9 (International Standard Version)
Craig Keener cites Ernst Haenchen's claim that "Luke does not mention the cloud lifting Jesus." (Keener, Acts: An Exegetical Commentary, Volume 1). True, Haenchen claimed that "no earthly element (a whirlwind or the cloud itself) bears the exalted one aloft." But a study of the passage demonstrates the cloud was indeed Jesus's mode of transport:

"In Acts 1:9...the compound verb used [in Greek] cannot satisfactorily be rendered as 'received him out of their sight' (KJV translation); its literal sense is 'took up by getting under,' and thus depicts the cloud as a mode of transport...Still more misleading is the NIV translation, 'a cloud "hid" him from their sight' which appears to be a highly tendentious translation." James D. G. Dunn, "The Ascension of Jesus: A Test Case for Hermeneutics" in Resurrection: Wissenschafftliche Untersuchungen Zum Neuen Testament (2001), p. 310, 310 n.38.

"The verb is an aorist of 'take up by getting under,' 'take from below'...The Lord is thus caught up from below by the cloud." Maria Ð Thi Yn, The Lucan Journey: A Study of Luke 9:28-36 and Acts 1:6-11 as an Architectural Pair... (Peter Lang AG, Internationaler Verlag der Wissenschaften; New edition, 2010), p. 169.

"The verb is used in Acts 1:9 in the sense of 'to cause to ascend, take up.'" A Greek-English Lexicon of the New Testament and Other Early Christian Literature, 3rd edition (2000), p. 1038.

"The compound verb [in the Greek of Acts 1:9], with its idea of 'taking up in support' placed alongside the mention of the cloud, suggests that the cloud enveloped him from underneath and took him away (Dan 7:13)." Darrel L. Bock, Acts (Baker Exegetical Commentary on the New Testament) (Grand Rapids, Michigan: Baker Academic, 2007), p. 67.

"'He was lifted up, and a cloud took him out of their sight'...One should not press the text to mean that Jesus was first taken up and then later enveloped in the cloud. The event is not divided into separate acts, and the cloud is simply a vehicle." Hans Conzelmann, Acts of the Apostles: A Commentary on the Acts of the Apostles (Philadelphia: Fortress Press, 1987), p. 5,7.

error that we live in a storied cosmos and the heavens above are "holy." And this big screen theatrical illusion was staged for a restricted number of eyes (Luke 24:33; Acts 1:2)?

Also, there are only two narrative depictions of Jesus's ascent into heaven in the New Testament, and both come from the same author. They are found at the end of the Gospel of Luke and beginning of the book of Acts (hereafter referred to as Luke-Acts):

1) Luke 24:50–51 "...[a resurrected Jesus] led them out [of Jerusalem] as far as Bethany, lifted up his hands, and blessed them. While he was blessing them, he left them and was taken up to heaven." [International Standard Version]

2) Acts 1:9–1 "Jesus was taken up while those who had gathered together were watching, and a cloud took him [the cloud was Jesus's mode of transport, an apocalyptic stage prop—see endnote 51] out of their sight. While he was going and they were gazing [intently, straining to see, etc., the emphasis is in the Greek] up toward heaven, two men in white robes stood right beside them. They asked, "Men of Galilee, why do you stand looking up toward heaven? This same Jesus, who has been taken up from you into heaven, will come back in the same way you saw him go up into heaven."[52] [International Standard Version]

"The cloud is an apocalyptic stage prop employed by the author...Manuscript D (Codex Bezae) reads, 'a cloud took him up, and he was taken from them.'" Joseph A. Fitzmyer, The Acts of the Apostles (The Anchor Yale Bible Commentaries, 1998), p. 209, 210.

[52] "When the author of Luke-Acts makes the angels say: 'This same Jesus, who has been taken up from you into heaven, will come back in the same way you saw him go up into heaven' (Acts 1:11): we need only consider the reverse of this declaration in order to have before us the origin of the idea for the story of Jesus's ascension, i.e., just as Jesus will return from heaven with clouds, so he must surely have departed for heaven in a similar manner." D. F. Strauss, The Life of Jesus Critically Examined.

Also, comparing the author's ascension scene in Acts with his earlier empty tomb scene in Luke (an empty tomb scene not identical with such scenes in other Gospels), one notes how closely the author has simply mirrored his own creative work, as Keener admits:[53]

Luke 24: 4–9 Resurrection Story	Acts 1:10–12 Bodily Ascension Story
Suddenly two men in clothes that gleamed like lightning stood beside them…	Suddenly two men dressed in white stood beside them…
Question: "Why do you look for the living among the dead?" [Luke is the only Gospel in which the figures at the empty tomb ask a question.]	Question: "Men of Galilee, why do you stand here looking into the sky?" [Again, the dual figures ask a question.]
Explanation of Jesus's absence: "He is not here, but instead rose and is alive."	Explanation of Jesus's absence: "Jesus has been taken from you into heaven, but will return."
They return to the city. (24:9)	They return to the city. (1:12)

Angels in the ascension story speak like the author of Luke-Acts. They use the phrase, "Men of Galilee," just as the author used similar phrases such as, "Men of Judea," "Men of Israel," "Men of Athens," "Men of Ephesus" (Acts 2:14,22; 3:12; 5:35; 13:16; 17:22; 19:35; 21:28).

The phrase, "They were gazing intently" in the ascension scene (Acts 1:10), is used frequently by the author of Luke-Acts (Luke 4:20; 22:56,

---

[53] Keener, Craig, Acts: An Exegetical Commentary: Introduction and 1:1-2:47 (Baker Academic, 2012).

Acts 3:4,12; 6:15; 7:55; 10:4; 11:6; 13:9; 14:9; 23:1), but is found only twice in the New Testament outside of Luke-Acts.

The ascension scene is just one of several in Luke-Acts in which beings return to heaven. There is Luke 1:38 ("Then the angel left her."); 2:15 ("When the [multitude of] angels had left them and gone back to heaven"); 9:33 ("as Moses and Elijah were leaving"); 24:51 ("he [Jesus] left them and was taken up to heaven"). Such scenes are common to that author.

The author of Luke-Acts was plainly willing to alter stories in earlier Gospels to make them fit his new theological agenda, his new sacred history, which had its "…beginning at Jerusalem" (Luke 24:47) including resurrection and ascension scenes in or near Jerusalem. Therefore when Jesus is resurrected in the Gospel of Luke he first appears to disciples in or near Jerusalem and commands them, "Do not leave Jerusalem…" (Acts 1:4), unlike the message delivered at Jesus's tomb in the earliest Gospel, Mark, which was to meet the resurrected Jesus in Galilee: "Go and tell his disciples—especially Peter—that Jesus is going ahead of you to Galilee. There you will see him" (Mark 16:7). The Gospel of Matthew repeats that message and even has Jesus repeat it to the women leaving the tomb, "Go and tell my brothers to leave for Galilee, and they will see me there" (Matthew 28:10). The author of Luke-Acts alters the message that was repeated five times in the earlier Gospels of Mark and Matthew (the three times discussed above plus Mark 14:28 & Matthew 26:32). That the author of Luke-Acts had knowledge of the earlier message and creatively altered it to suit his new sacred history "starting at Jerusalem" is obvious, his message at the tomb reads, "Remember what he told you while he was still in Galilee…" (Luke 24:6). Galilee is no longer where the resurrected Jesus was "going on ahead" to be seen by his disciples, it is now a mere recollection of the past.

The evidence above favors the idea that the "Jerusalem-based" post-resurrection appearances and ascension narratives in Luke-Acts were primarily invented by the author.[54] He knew he had to compete with ascension narratives told by ideologues of the Roman Empire. He also had to combat embarrassing questions raised as to why Jesus, allegedly resurrected in Jerusalem, chose to wander off immediately into the hinterlands of Galilee to be seen.[55]

Keener admits he did not have the time or resources to vet more than a small number of the miraculous claims in his book (many of course are not even capable of being vetted due to the passage of time, lack of medical data, or their anecdotal nature). But his enthusiasm apparently got the best of him, hence his choice of quantity over quality.

Such enthusiasm even extends to Craig Keener's ability to hear God's voice, as recorded in the dual autobiography he wrote with his second wife, Medine.[56] The words from God that Craig hears often begin with the phrase, "My child," and consist of God reminding him how much he is loved, or, when Craig feels down, God reminds him how much his sufferings resemble those of Jesus, Elijah, Hosea, or other Bible characters who suffered (Craig of course knows such stories by heart being a biblical scholar). For instance, when Craig found out his first wife had been unfaithful, God empathized that He also suffered due to the Israelites being unfaithful to Him. Or God reminds Craig that He

---

[54] The use of isolated terms like "ascended" or "ascension" by other New Testament authors does not constitute multiple attestation of the narrative scenes found only in Luke-Acts. It merely attests to the belief that heroes wound up in the divine realm, and the divine realm lay literally above the earth, therefore an "ascension" (whether depicted as having been seen or merely implied) was how one got there. That was how and why people spoke about the "ascensions" of a wide variety of heroes, including that of the emperors Julius and Augustus Caesar before the New Testament was written.

On the other hand, the author of the Gospel of John could have known the Gospel of Luke. Prof. Mark Goodacre will be publishing a book on "John's Knowledge of the Synoptics." For instance, the Gospel of John adopts the "Jerusalem first resurrection appearances" motif found in Luke-Acts rather than Mark and Matthew's earlier view that "He has gone before you to Galilee, there you will see him." There is also intertextual evidence that the author of John drew upon names and stories from Luke and Mark, conflating such tales to create new ones. See my blog posts related to Gospel Trajectories https://edward-t-babinski.blogspot.com/search/label/gospel%20trajectories.

[55] Also see, "How Impressive Were Jesus's Miracles?"
https://edward-t-babinski.blogspot.com/2019/03/miracles-by-craig-s-keener-how_3.html

[56] Keener, Craig S., and Keener, Medine Moussounga, Impossible Love: The True Story of an African Civil War, Miracles and Hope Against All Odds (Minneapolis, Minnesota: Chosen Books, 2016)

is "with him." And when Craig thinks of how lonely he is and how much he wants to remarry, God says he will do what's best for him and Medine, the woman on Craig's mind. Sometimes God assures Craig everything will work out, He will protect the woman Craig loves and they will minister together, which, no surprise, was Craig's fondest hope as well.[57] But such words "from God" sound very much like a loving pep talk one gives one's self. I have known others who claimed similar divine communications of a benign and vague kind.

In their story Craig's future wife, Medine, eventually emerges from very real trials in revolutionary Africa, having suffered malaria, malnourishment, a taxi accident involving her foot, and PTSD (including doubts and disillusionment concerning whether Craig was the one, even whether she had made a mistake in deciding to return to the Congo after obtaining a Ph.D. in France). I guess that's how God works. She did not hear God's voice as Craig did, but there seemed no lack of African "prophets" delivering messages to her from God. But once one looks past the "spiritualizing" of her story, she appears to have survived mostly due to her determination, dogged persistence and intelligence. And of course she kept up communications with Craig and he with her as best they could during such trials. Meanwhile, Craig—trying to sort out his feelings for Medine and second guess hers—prayed, fasted, overworked himself, felt lonely and isolated, experienced his own case of PTSD, and finally suffered dehydration so severe he might have died. He wound up in the emergency room twice. Again, I guess that's how God works. Even when Medine and Craig were finally going to be reunited, their union was delayed an extra eight months due to travel restrictions put in place after the tragic attack on New York city's Twin Towers.

Was their meeting and reunion divinely guided? Keener sounds like someone who was quite lonely, a scholar stuck in a room with his books. Medine and he shared deeply held religious beliefs, concern for improved race relations, and an appreciation of each other's intelligence

---

[57] Keener, Impossible Love, p. 22, 23, 38, 43, 119, 120, 214.

(they both have Ph.Ds.). It doesn't seem far-fetched to imagine them getting together. They originally met at a religious event.

Was their story more remarkable than similar tales of lovers separated by long distances and danger? Such episodes have repeated themselves since time immemorial with I daresay narrower escapes. As for those couples who failed to reunite, their books, which will never be written, would have reminded us of all the times prayers or providence failed.

For both of them this is their second marriage, which is often less stressful and happier in many ways than their first. People are older, wiser, and closer to knowing what they want in a relationship. So I wish the Keeners the best, but I find their story fits the category of what folklorist Elaine Lawless calls "spiritual life stories."[58] And I wonder what messages from God or African prophets were simply forgotten by Keener or Medine because they didn't fit the profile of their story? Or if any of the original messages were vaguer and only later recalled as being more specific?[59]

Speaking of how one constructs one's "spiritual life story," Keener once mentioned in an article in Christianity Today that "God" provided him money he needed on two occasions. He even assured his readers (all of them, regardless of how different their situations and number of social connections might be compared with his) that his experience of having received money from "God" helps demonstrate that "God cares about us more than he cares about birds and flowers, yet he provides for them, Jesus says. How much more, then, will he provide for us."[60] Which seems trite coming from someone who admits that the majority of those who need healing do not receive it.

Does Keener really believe that God provides "for us" as Jesus says? The "us" refers to humanity in general since this was before everyone

---

[58] Walsh, p. 1, 115n. 1.
[59] Walsh, p. 11, mentions examples of prophetic misses from her own experience among Pentecostals.
[60] Keener, Craig, "When Jesus Wanted All My Money: And Everything Else. How I Learned He's An All-Or-Nothing Lord," Christianity Today, May 2016, p. 46-50.

had to believe Jesus was a messiah. Has God truly been that great a provider? Humans have to wrestle food from the ground by the sweat of their brows. But Jesus makes it sound like we are all living in a garden of Eden where God provides for birds, and humans even more so. Not a very comforting comparison since millions of birds are slaughtered in factories each month (or sacrificed in Old Testament days). Another way they perish is starvation. A third of adult birds and four-fifths of their offspring die of starvation every year.[61] Not surprising considering that birds have to eat from one-quarter to one-half their body weight daily to survive. Other studies reveal that birds die of everything from parasites and pathogens to predators, developmental defects, extreme weather, and collisions with windows. The cuckoo lays her eggs in the nests of other birds, it hatches early, then the cuckoo chick tosses the other eggs or chicks out of the nest. On the "Hunting and Escaping" video in the Trials of Life series one sees baby birds dragged from their nests by a rival species in order to feed the predator's own hungry chicks. I guess that's how God works. So when Jesus says that God cares about us more than birds, he isn't saying much—but it does make me more sympathetic toward birds.

So, Keener's "spiritual life story" often consists of focusing on the hits, viewing them as providential, and forgetting the misses. For instance, many with an advanced degree in theology, or with a seminary degree, wind up having to switch to a different profession. A large percentage of ministers who remain in the profession also suffer chronic depression.[62] Even in Keener's case, his success is a "miss" compared to yet rarer "hits" such as that of Edir Macedo—holder of a Ph.D. in Theology and Christian philosophy per his website and whose books have sold ten million copies. (Keener might not like to know that Edir also wrote an article opposing interracial marriage.)

---

[61] Lack, David, "Of Birds and Men," New Scientist, January 1996.
[62] See, "Christians Or Non-Christians Who Suffer Depression or Attempt Suicide. What We All Have in Common" https://edward-t-babinski.blogspot.com/2015/08/christians-or-non-christians-who-suffer.html. And, "Divine Providence or Mixed Messages? A Collection of News Items Showing How Christians Suffer Just Like the Rest of Us" https://edwardtbabinski.us/scrivenings/2015/divine-providence-or-mixed-messages.html

Macedo preaches a Gospel of miracles, deliverance, and prosperity (Keener agrees with the first two). Similar preachers have become so plentiful in South America, southern Asia, and Africa that a common joke is, "If your business fails, open a church." But Macedo practically has his own denomination. After decades spent as cofounder of a growing religious organization in Brazil he now owns twenty-three TV stations, forty radio stations, two major daily newspapers, a real estate agency, a health insurance company, and 49% of a bank, and helped a new President of Brazil get elected (one who advocates torture and promised to bulldoze the rain forest). I guess that's how God works.

Macedo even had a replica of Solomon's Temple built in Sao Paulo (with a conveyor belt system designed to carry tithes and offerings from the altar directly into a safe room). It seats ten thousand and is far larger than the Temple built by king Herod in Jesus's day—Macedo's is 18 stories tall with its floor and walls covered in $8 million worth of "Jerusalem stone" brought from Israel. And now that the Temple has been rebuilt perhaps Jesus will finally "descend from heaven" on an elevator cloud?[63]

---

[63] See footnote 51.

6| THE ABJECT FAILURE OF CHRISTIAN APOLOGETICS

BY JOHN W. LOFTUS

This chapter concerns itself with the diversity that exists among Christian defenders of their faith, known as apologists. There are five major methods, or strategies, of apologetics in defense of the Christian faith. It was my expertise when I was a student. I studied under leading defenders of five methods, as I wrote about in a previous book.[1] What can we learn from this fact? Plenty.

My three main contentions are that, 1) the use of reasoning to defend Christianity based on sufficient objective evidence has historically led to a rejection of Christianity; 2) most Christian apologists today, perhaps up to 80% of them, reject the use of reasoning to defend Christianity based on sufficient objective evidence; and 3) the best explanation for the above two contentions is that Christian apologists themselves admit their faith cannot be reasonably defended based on sufficient objective evidence. A few of them admit this blatantly, while others do so tacitly. And since it's unreasonable to believe in a particular religion—or anything else about the objective world—without reasoning based on sufficient objective evidence, it's unreasonable to believe in Christianity.

---

[1] This chapter is a better version of chapter five in my book, *How to Defend the Christian Faith: Advice from an Atheist* (2015), with a part of it coming from chapter 3 of my book *Unapologetic: Why Philosophy of Religion Must End* (2016), both published by Pitchstone Publishing. In the Introduction I tell of my pedigree. As I've said before, I might be wrong, but no one can say I'm ignorant.

All we have to do is ask what we would expect to find if there were sufficient objective evidence for the Christian faith. If it existed, then the use of reasoning to defend Christianity based primarily on the requirement for sufficient objective evidence would not have led to a rejection of Christianity, or led Christian apologists to reject it, or invent other ways to defend their faith.

Of course, the Christian rejection of evidence-based reasoning in favor of faith has a theological history stretching back to the New Testament, so it shouldn't be a surprise in and of itself. Jesus purportedly said, "I praise you, Father, Lord of heaven and earth, because you have hidden these things from the wise and learned, and revealed them to little children. Yes, Father, for this was your good pleasure." (Luke 10:21). Paul also wrote, "The message of the cross is foolishness to those who are perishing, but to us who are being saved it is the power of God. For it is written: 'I will destroy the wisdom of the wise; the intelligence of the intelligent I will frustrate.' Where is the wise man? Where is the scholar? Where is the philosopher of this age? Has not God made foolish the wisdom of the world? . . . For the foolishness of God is wiser than man's wisdom" (1 Cor. 1:18–25). Tertullian (160–220 CE) asked: "What has Athens [the seat of philosophical reasoning] to do with Jerusalem [the seat of religious faith and theology]?" Tertullian wrote of the absurdity of the incarnation of Jesus by saying, "Just because it is absurd, it is to be believed . . . it is certain because it is impossible." Martin Luther called reason "the Devil's Whore." As such, reason "can do nothing but slander and harm all that God says and does." Immanuel Kant said that he "found it necessary to deny knowledge of God…in order to find a place for faith." Søren Kierkegaard spoke of a "leap of faith" and argued faith in his god is based in a decision, a commitment, reserved for things that lacked sufficient objective evidence. William Lane Craig agrees by asserting "reason is a tool to help us better understand our faith. Should faith and reason conflict, it is reason that must submit to faith, not vice versa."[2]

Listen, there is something wrong with a religious faith where its best defenders say these kinds of things. If that's what they say, why should we think otherwise? Why should anyone? I see no reason to not do so. You'll never see a true intellectual say such things, and that should say something important to honest seekers of truth.

A VARIETY OF APOLOGETICAL METHODS

In 1953 Bernard Ramm was probably the first to call attention to apologetic differences in his book, *Types of Apologetic Systems*.[3] The value of Ramm's important work was in categorizing three systems of apologetics. His list included apologetics that stressed Christian experience (i.e., Blaise Pascal, Soren Kierkegaard and Emil Brunner), apologetics that stressed human reason (i.e., Thomas Aquinas, Joseph Butler, and F.R. Tennant), and apologetics that stressed revelation from their Christian god above (i.e., Augustine, Cornelius Van Til, and Edward John Carnell). In so doing Ramm highlighted ten major questions for Christian apologetics.

Ramm asked the following questions: 1) "What is the relationship between philosophy and Christianity?" 2) "What is the value of theistic proofs?" 3) "Must the apologist work with some theory of truth?" 4) "What is the importance of the doctrine of sin for apologetics?" 5) "What is the character of revelation?" 6) "What kind of certainty does Christianity offer?" 7) "Is there a common ground between believer and unbeliever which forms a point of contact for conversation and argumentation?" 8) "What is the character of faith?" 9) "What is the status

---

[2] William Lane Craig, *Apologetics: An Introduction* (Chicago: Moody Press, 1984), p. 21. This quote is left out of the third edition of this book, titled *Reasonable Faith: Christian Truth and Apologetics* (Wheaton, IL: Crossway Books, 2008). I'm sure he edited it out not because he changed his mind, but rather because he no longer wants to reveal what he really believes.
[3] Bernard Ramm, *Types of Apologetic Systems: An Introductory Study to the Christian Philosophy of Religion* (Wheaton, Ill.: Van Kampen Press, 1953).

of Christian evidences?" and 10) "What is the relationship between faith and reason?"[4] As Ramm explained, every single question he asked was answered differently by Christian apologists. Ramm brought these types of problems to the attention of a larger number of Christians, especially evangelicals.

Apologist James Beilby recently added an eleventh question to Ramm's list, "What is the task of apologetics?"[5] Apologists cannot even agree on their main task. I would argue the actual task of apologetics is to help Christian believers who are already in the fold. Based on Anselm's "faith seeking understanding" dictum, the task of apologetics has really been to validate what Christians already believe.

In recent books of mine I've added two other questions to Ramm's list. The first one is, "What if Christians were to go on strike?" This strike would be against having to do all of the evangelistic and apologetic work themselves. What if they stopped praying for others to be saved? What if they stopped telling others about Jesus? What if Christians stopped evangelizing and arguing on behalf of Christianity? What if all evangelists, missionaries, and apologists went on strike and instead let the Holy Spirit do the work? I know this will never happen of course, as it's a thought experiment with a purpose:

If Christians all went on strike, then Christianity would go out of existence. That's my prediction. You know it. I know it. Everyone who is not a Christian knows it. The Christian faith needs people of faith who proselytize. This is true of every religion. Without people of faith any given religion would die out because there is no deity behind any of them. That's what Christians think of other faiths. That's what they should think of Christian faith as well.

---

[4] In 1962 Ramm revised and re-titled his book to *Varieties of Christian Apologetics: An Introduction to the Christian Philosophy of Religion* (Grand Rapids: Baker Books, 1962). In the revised edition Ramm replaced Van Til and Carnell as representatives of systems stressing God's redemptive word of special revelation with John Calvin and Abraham Kuyper.

[5] James K. Beilby, "Varieties of Apologetics" in Khaldoun A. Sweis and Chad V. Meister, *Christian Apologetics: An Anthology of Primary Sources* (Grand Rapids, Zondervan, 2012), p. 30.

What's your prediction?

In order to suppose that the Christian faith would not die out Christians need to provide some objective evidence that God is doing something now that would help convert people even if Christians stopped sharing the Gospel. So, what, objectively, is God doing now? [*The Outsider Test for Faith*, Chapter 9, pp. 187–191]

My second question for apologists follows on its heels, "Why is it necessary to defend the Christian faith at all?" I offered four different scenarios where their Christian god could've done this work alone with much better results. I wrote:

If God supposedly gave up Jesus to die on the cross for our sins, which is the greater deed by far, then why has he failed (and continues to fail) to do enough to reach nonbelievers, which represents the lesser deeds? I mean really, if God did the greater deed then why doesn't he also commit himself to doing the lesser deeds? Isn't that backassward for an intelligent being?

Compared with an all-knowing God, even the best Christian defenders are bumbling idiots and incompetent fools. Compared with an all-loving God, even the best Christian defenders are utterly self-centered and completely unconcerned that people are going to hell. Compared with an all-powerful God, even the best Christian defenders are totally lacking any energy to help people believe...This doesn't make any sense at all, especially if there's a flaming hell to pay for those who are not convinced to believe and be saved. Surely a God like the one Christians believe in could have been more concerned for the lost than hiring the church to do this most important job. If Christians have been incompetent with this task, then God was incompetent in hiring them to do it. God should have cared for the lost more than that. As the CEO of his corporation his hiring practices are a failure. God should fire them and do the work himself. [*How to Defend the Christian*

Faith: Advice from an Atheist (Pitchstone Publishing, 2015), Chapter 1, pp., 22–22].

There have been plenty of books dealing with these types of questions, which have shown a great diversity of disagreement.[6] James Beilby informs us that after decades of debate, "None of the traditional apologetic systems has received the endorsement of a substantial majority of Christian apologists."[7] This is extremely important, for as Cardinal Avery Dulles noted in his magisterial history of apologetics, "The 20th century has seen more clearly than previous periods that *apologetics stands or falls with the question of method.*"[8] It's not just that Christian apologists disagree with each other on how to defend their faith. The problem is deeper than that. The whole enterprise of Christian apologetics depends on having a justifiable method for defending their faith. Without an

---

[6] Listed in order of date published: Gordon R. Lewis, *Testing Christianity's Truth Claims: Approaches to Christian Apologetics* (Chicago: Moody Bible Institute of Chicago, 1976, 1980). Lewis updated the book in 1990 which was published by University Press of America. Norman Geisler, *Christian Apologetics* (Grand Rapids: Baker Book House, 1976); Mark M. Hanna, *Crucial Questions in Apologetics* (Grand Rapids: Baker, 1981). John H. Gerstner, Arthur W. Lindsley, R.C. Sproul, *Classical Apologetics: A Rational Defense of the Christian Faith and a Critique of Presuppositional Apologetics* (Grand Rapids: Zondervan, 1984); Ronald B. Mayers, *Both/And: A Balanced Apologetic* (Chicago: Moody Press, 1984), revised by Mayers as *Balanced Apologetics: Using Evidences and Presuppositions in Defense of the Faith* (Grand Rapids: Kregel Academic & Professional, 1996); Norman L. Geisler, *Baker Encyclopedia of Christian Apologetics* (Grand Rapids: Baker Academic, 1998); Steven B. Cowan, ed., *Five Views of Apologetics* (Grand Rapids, Zondervan, 2000); Kenneth Boa and Robert M. Bowman Jr., *Faith Has Its Reasons: Integrative Approaches to Defending the Christian Faith* (Downers Grove: IVP Books; 2 ed., 2006); and John S. Feinberg, *Can You Believe it's True?: Christian Apologetics in a Postmodern Era* (Wheaton IL.: Crossway, 2013).

[7] James K. Beilby, *Thinking About Christian Apologetics: What It Is and Why We Do It (Downers Grove:* IVP Academic, 2011), p. 102.

[8] Emphasis is mine. Dulles, *A History of Apologetics* (New York: Corpus Books, 1971), (1st ed.), p. 246. This might be the earliest work detailing the history of Christian apologetics. The second 2005 edition of this book (Modern Apologetics Library, San Francisco: Ignatius Press) just adds six pages on twentieth-century evangelical apologetics (pp. 353-59). For primary source material see the two-volume set compiled by William Edgar and K. Scott Oliphint. eds., *Christian Apologetics Past and Present (Volume 1, To 1500): A Primary Source Reader* (Wheaton, Il, Crossway, 2009), and *Christian Apologetics Past and Present (Volume 2, From 1500): A Primary Source Reader* (Wheaton, Il, Crossway, 2011). Also consult the books edited by Khaldoun A. Sweis and Chad V. Meister, *Christian Apologetics: An Anthology of Primary Sources* (Grand Rapids, Zondervan, 2012); W. C. Campbell-Jack, Gavin J. McGrath, and C. Stephen Evans, eds., *New Dictionary of Christian Apologetics* (Downers Grove: IVP Academic, 2006).

agreed upon defensible method, their faith is doomed. Apologetics is in crisis with no hope of a solution.

Several Christian apologists have offered differing classifications, or taxonomies, of apologetics methods.[9] In what follows I'll offer my own classification from my perspective as an atheist, based on their primary approach in defending Christianity, using five headings: 1) Apologetics Based On Reasoning from Sufficient Objective Evidence; 2) Apologetics Based On Special Pleading; 3) Apologetics Based On Assuming What Needs to Be Proved; 4) Apologetics Based On Private Subjective Experiences; and 5) Eclectic Apologetics Based On Prior Conclusions. The only method that has any merit at all is the first one. It's the one that proponents of subsequent methods reject or degrade to second class status at best. Christians should find this very troublesome. After all, we're talking about apologetics, defending the truth of Christianity. And we're talking about their intellectuals, the educated ones who should know how to defend their faith the best.

1. APOLOGETICS BASED ON REASONING FROM SUFFICIENT OBJECTIVE EVIDENCE

The first method of apologetics is the use of reasoning to defend Christianity based primarily on the requirement for sufficient objective evidence. It is supposed to lead reasonable people to accept the truth of Christianity. This approach is called *Evidentialism* by apologists. When I first became a Christian believer, I was an evidentialist. I had read Josh McDowell's evidentialist book, *Evidence That Demands a Verdict,* which confirmed my faith for me. There can never be enough evidence for something. The more the better. And I thought I had plenty of evidence to believe based on his book. Other noteworthy evidentialist apologists of the past and present are William Paley (1743–1805), Joseph Butler

---

[9] For a short overview of the various apologetic systems and why they exist see James K. Beilby, "Varieties of Apologetics" in Khaldoun A. Sweis and Chad V. Meister, *Christian Apologetics: An Anthology of Primary Sources*, pp. 29-38.

(1692–1752), Clark Pinnock (1937–2010), Wolfhart Pannenberg (1928–2014), John Warwick Montgomery, Gary Habermas and John Feinberg (who disingenuously claims he's an evidentialist). In Montgomery's words, the task of evidentialists, like himself, consists "of marshalling the full panoply of factual evidence to show that Christianity is true and its rivals false."[10] According to Gary Habermas evidentialism "can be characterized as a 'one step' approach" to apologetics "in that historical evidences can serve as a species of argument for God. Instead of having to prove God's existence before moving to the specific evidences (the 'two step method'), the evidentialist treats one or more historical arguments as being able both to indicate God's existence and activity and to indicate which variety of theism is true."[11] John Feinberg claims to accept this "one step" evidentialist approach in his apologetics book when explaining why he didn't include a chapter on the existence of God: "I don't hold a methodology that requires one to prove God's existence before anything else can be addressed."[12]

Given Montgomery's claim for the need of evidence in general, and Habermas's claim for the need of historical evidence in specific, all of which should lead reasonable people to accept Christianity, then what could possibly be wrong with this? Nothing. That's what I think. Nothing. Sufficient objective evidence must be there for Christianity, or else reasonable people should not accept it. Period. It supposedly convinced the early disciples so it should convince us too. What if Muslims or Mormons or Orthodox Jews or any other religious people of faith admitted their respective faiths did not have sufficient objective evidence for them? Well, I think we should all just take them at their word, and look

---

[10] John Warwick Montgomery, "A Short History of Apologetics" in Khaldoun A. Sweis and Chad V. Meister, *Christian Apologetics: An Anthology of Primary Sources*, p. 27.
[11] Gary Habermas, "Evidential Apologetics" in Steven B. Cowan, ed., *Five Views of Apologetics* (Grand Rapids: Zondervan, 2000), p. 92.
[12] Feinberg, *Can You Believe It's True?: Christian Apologetics in a Postmodern Era* (Wheaton IL: Crossway, 2013), p. 34. He does think however, that an apologist in today's world must first argue that truth is objective and knowable, given that he deals with this in Part One of his book, covering 194 pages.

elsewhere for truth. That should be the end of any inquiry into the truth of their claims.

Historically with the Enlightenment and the rise of modern science, people began to adopt the use of reasoning to understand Christianity based primarily on the requirement for sufficient objective evidence. So, the Bible began to be subjected to these same requirements. As a consequence the Bible gradually lost its place among them as a blind authority. Some of the first evidentialists were the deists, who are largely left out of this discussion of apologetics, but they need to be included.

Deism is a method that began with Herbert Cherbury (1583–1648) in England. People like Voltaire, Immanuel Kant, Baruch Spinoza (a deist in method but a pantheist in conclusion), Thomas Paine, Ben Franklin, George Washington and Thomas Jefferson (just consider *The Jeffersonian Bible*) were known as deists.[13] Deism is not a conclusion, as most people think, but rather a method for correct religious understanding based on the light of natural reason, by which they meant reasoning based on objective evidence. Deism is thus the rightful child of natural theology, since it historically led to the natural religion of deism, as opposed to biblical or "revealed" religion. Deism passed through several different stages in several different countries. With each successive stage deists began whittling away what they could accept by the light of natural reason. Initially deists believed in a Christian god, but it steadily lost many of its key doctrines due to a lack of evidence, based on sound reasoning. They agreed on a creator god who worked providentially in the world and provided a source for good morals, and that there was an afterlife. But as time went on more and more deists didn't see the evidence of providence or the afterlife. The final stage of deism is largely of French origin, where their god was seen merely as the creator of the universe. God was viewed as an absent landlord who doesn't intervene in the

---

[13] See Kerry Walters, *Revolutionary Deists: Early America's Rational Infidels*, (Amherst, NY: Prometheus Books, 2011).

world.[14] The analogy for deists was the technological marvel of their time—the pocket watch. What should we think, deists would ask, if a watchmaker had to constantly repair the watch he made? The watch would have been made by an inferior watchmaker. So, if God created the world and had to regularly intervene with miracles then he didn't do a good job of creating it in the first place. Modern science has progressed past the original deist understanding of the Newtonian view of the world as a machine. But this scientific revolution didn't change the fact that deists didn't accept miracles due to a lack of sufficient evidence. After the 1859 publication of Darwin's magisterial work, *Origin of Species*, which accounted for the evolution of human beings from a common ancestor through natural selection, many deists became atheists, for that's what happens when reasoning based on the evidence. This also explains why so many Christians are anti-intellectual.[15]

Evidentialist apologists who argue based on sufficient objective evidence have gotten their method correct. It's not that a few of the alternative methods outright deny the value of evidence. It's just that they are based on other things as having a higher priority than the evidence, as we'll see. But why should any apologetics method not assign the highest priority to the evidence itself? That's very telling. It's because it can and rightfully does lead to unbelief.

2. APOLOGETICS BASED ON SPECIAL PLEADING

This type of apologetics is known as *Classical Apologetics* (or *Natural Theology*). It's named as such because it's assumed to be the method used by most theologians in earlier centuries, especially Thomas Aquinas. Evangelical apologist Norman Geisler was the first evangelical to see the

---

[14] J. O'Higgins distinguished between four types of Deism in "Hume and the Desists: A Contrast in Religious Approaches," *Journal of Theological Studies* 23, no. 2 (October 1971): 479, 480, which is summarized in Norman L. Geisler and William D. Watkins, *Worlds Apart: A Handbook on Worldviews* (Grand Rapids, MI: Baker Book House, 1989), pp. 148–49.
[15] See Susan Jacoby *The Age of American Unreason* (Vintage Books, 2009).

failure of evidentialism, as argued best in his book, *Christian Apologetics*.[16] With the demise of evidentialism apologists should have abandoned their attempts to defend Christianity. But they didn't! As we'll see next, Christian defenders just changed their approach. Geisler argued apologists should revert to the old-time abandoned (for the most part) Catholic type of apologetics, stemming from the classical theists, especially Thomas Aquinas. Modern representatives have included R.C. Sproul, John Gerstner, Peter Kreeft, J.P. Moreland, Edward Feser, and most notably William Lane Craig.

Unlike the evidentialist method which has only one step based in the evidence, this classical method has two-steps. The first step is to defend the theistic proofs for the existence of God. The second step is to provide the evidence that Christianity is true. Apologists must first effectively argue for the existence of God of theism, generally speaking, who created the universe. Then after successfully doing so, they must provide sufficient objective evidence that Christianity is the true theistic religion. If the first step cannot be done effectively their whole apologetic fails. Steven B. Cowan explains:

> Before one can meaningfully discuss historical evidences, one has to have established God's existence because one's worldview is a framework through which miracles, historical facts, and other empirical data are interpreted. Without a theistic context, no historical event could ever be shown to be a divine miracle. The flipside of this claim is that one cannot appeal to alleged miracles in order to prove God's existence."[17]

The reason why one cannot appeal to evidences for a miracle as evidence for God is explained by Norman Geisler: "The mere fact of the resurrection [of Jesus] cannot be used to establish the truth that there is a God. For the resurrection cannot even be a miracle unless there already is a God."[18]

---

[16] Norman Geisler, *Christian Apologetics* (Grand Rapids: Baker Book House, 1976).
[17] Steven B. Cowan, ed., *Five Views of Apologetics* (Grand Rapids: Zondervan, 2000), p. 16.
[18] Norman Geisler, *Christian Apologetics*, p. 95.

Both of these steps are essential to defend Christianity. If the first step isn't successful then neither is the second step, for the second step cannot be successful on its own. So, if theistic proofs are shown to fail then classical apologists cannot show Christianity is true. This isn't just me saying this. Classical apologists themselves say this. Other apologists dispute the force of the first step. John Feinberg doesn't think the first step is successful, saying, "I wouldn't try to prove God's existence first, if at all, in that I am not convinced that any of the traditional arguments succeeds."[19] Richard Swinburne, one of the great Christian apologists of our generation, rejects the force of two specific theistic arguments in particular:

> I think ontological arguments for the existence of God are very much mere philosophers' arguments and do not codify any of the reasons which ordinary men have for believing that there is a God. The greatest theistic philosophers have on the whole rejected ontological arguments and relied on *a posteriori* ones.[20]

Regarding the highly esteemed and often used Moral Argument to God's existence, Swinburne is emphatic: "I cannot see any force in an argument to the existence of God from the existence of morality."[21] He explains:

> I cannot however, see that, given that there are conscious men acquiring knowledge of the world, that man's awareness of moral truth is something especially difficult to explain by normal scientific processes. Men living in close proximity and needing fellowship might well be expected to grasp concepts of fairness and justice, especially when it would be of advantage to one group to bring home to other groups their moral obligations. A long

---

[19] John S. Feinberg, *Can You Believe It's True: Christian Apologetics in a Modern & Postmodern Era* (Wheaton, IL: Crossway, 2013), p. 321. This is not to mischaracterize Feinberg as saying these arguments don't have some evidential weight to them. He favors the argument from design, but none of them serves as a deductive proof, so they "don't offer the degree of objective certainty many believers, let alone non-believers would require" he continued.

[20] Swinburne, *The Existence of God*, 2nd, ed., (Oxford University Press, 2004), pp. 9-10.

[21] Richard Swinburne, *The Existence of God,* 2nd, ed. (Oxford University Press, 2004), p. 215.

tradition of writing on human evolution beginning with Darwin's *The Descent of Man* showed how man's moral awareness might be expected to develop by evolutionary processes, as man evolved from lower animals.[22]

If Christian apologists don't accept them why should we? Why should anyone?

Highly lauded Christian philosopher/apologist Alvin Plantinga says something everyone should take note of, since he rejects the force of theistic arguments in general:

I don't know of an argument for Christian belief that seems very likely to convince one who doesn't already accept its conclusion. That is nothing against Christian belief, however, and indeed I shall argue that if Christian beliefs are true, then the standard and most satisfactory way to hold them will not be as the conclusions of argument.[23]

Plantinga says this because he believes human beings are fallen creatures. Due to sin we cannot be convinced his god exists by arguments because fallen people cannot respond positively to his god. Sinners, nonbelievers, can only be saved directly by his god. So in turn, Plantinga doesn't think these arguments can convince *reasonable* outsiders, nonbelievers, because there are no reasonable non-believers. But just think how Plantinga first came to his conclusion. It didn't come from the Bible since so many other Christians dispute the relevant passages. The real reason he believes this is because so many people are non-Christians, non-believers. He must account for this fact. Surely it isn't due to the lack of sufficient evidence that so many people don't believe. Oh no! It must be due to the consequences of human sin. It could never be due to his god or the lack of evidence. All we have to do is ask what he would believe if 80–90 percent of the world's population were Christians. Could he continue to believe in the disastrous effects of sin for reasoning

---

[22] Ibid.
[23] Alvin Plantinga, *Warranted Christian Belief*, p. 201.

to his god? Christians lack an imagination at what could have resulted if things had turned out differently.

More importantly, even if the first step is successful it doesn't show much of anything. A lot more work needs to be done to show a specific god exists. Even if theistic arguments succeed to some small degree, the remaining question is which god do these arguments point to? A wide diversity of theists found in the different sects of Islam, Judaism, and Christianity all argue to the existence of a deity using the same exact theistic proofs. These arguments are mistakenly believed to show their own particular god exists. For instance, I once skimmed through a massive intelligent design book that argued for Allah's existence. A Christian or a Jew could lap up those volumes and use them to defend Christianity.

In other words, the theistic arguments to a deity do not grant a particular theist any relevant background information, or "priors," prior to examining the historical evidence for their own particular religious faith. Believers must still look at the evidence from the raw uninterpreted data to determine if a miracle took place, without using a potentially false presumption that their particular god performed the particular miracle under investigation. For even if there is a god of some kind, believers still have no reason to think their particular god did the miracle under investigation. So, when investigating a supposed miracle claim it cannot be treated with any special pleading. At their very best theistic proofs can only show there is a supernatural being or force; a deity who *could* do miracles. It doesn't show anything further, such as whether this deity does any miracles (for which see Mathew McCormick's chapter). This line of reasoning, suggested by David Hume in his *Dialogues Concerning Natural Religion,* destroys *Classical Apologetics* in one fell swoop as nothing more than special pleading.

Believers respond that theistic arguments open up the possibility of miracles. But which ones? I'm pretty sure Muslims and Jews, even as theists themselves, are no more open to Christian miracle claims than I am as a non-believer. Theism itself does not entail that the particular miracles in one's religious tradition have any more probability to them than others. For the record, even now I am open to this possibility, although given my present age of 65 and my studies throughout life—even as a former believer—I've become much less open to them. One would think I've given a god plenty of chances, yes?

Classical apologists depend on special pleading to the conclusion that if theistic arguments work then their miracle tales have been granted a higher, better status than others. But given that there is nothing in these arguments that lead a reasonable person to accept a specific sect's god out of the many other supernatural beings and/or forces, they open one's mind up to almost any possibility. They cannot reasonably favor any religious tradition's miracle claims. Every supernatural claim would be, strictly speaking, on the boards without any way to determine which god is actually doing them, if they're being done at all.

Classical apologists who reject evidentialism because evidentialism cannot convince non-believing outsiders, end up falling back into the laps of the evidentialists. They now face the same problems evidentialists face. They must still present sufficient objective evidence for the existence of the god who supposedly raised Jesus from the dead. They must do this by looking for the historical evidence apart from any given deity. The classical approach ends up being nothing more than a dressed up evidentialism. Unwittingly they have ended up back where they started from, embracing the evidentialist position from which they had previously rejected.

3) APOLOGETICS BASED ON ASSUMING WHAT NEEDS TO BE PROVED

This method for doing apologetics is known by the standard nomenclature of *Presuppositionalism*. It's a relatively new apologetical approach most associated with Cornelius Van Til (1895–1987), Gordon Clark (1902–1985), Francis Schaeffer (1912–1984), Greg Bahnsen (1948–1995), and John Frame. It's also a response to the demise of evidentialism. With its demise apologists didn't abandon their attempts to defend

Christianity. They offered a much different strategy that actually openly admits what I think describes most apologetics. Christian defenders simply presupposed their god exists (or even their type of Christianity as a whole), without objective evidence or arguments to the existence of God. Thus they end up begging the whole question. I'll include a very brief discussion of *Reformed Epistemology* in this section, since it also presupposes its own conclusion despite protestations to the contrary.

The presuppositionalist approach considers Christianity as a whole worldview and pits the rationality of its presuppositions against other worldviews. Presuppositions are defined as beliefs people presuppose prior to any argument or evidence. It's argued we all have them. A consistent set of presuppositions makes for a whole worldview. The goal of the presuppositionalist is to show the non-believer's worldview is inconsistent and/or self-defeating within itself. The presuppositionalist argues that non-believers who use reason and logic to defend their worldview cannot do so without assuming the Christian worldview. Only Christianity can justify the use of reason and logic. So, it's argued non-believers must therefore presuppose Christianity even as they argue against it.[24]

This apologetic strategy is reasoning by presupposition. It's admittedly circular reasoning because presuppositions are not inductively known by evidential reasoning, nor arrived at by deduction from premises to a conclusion. They are assumed to be true from the start without evidence. For instance, presuppositionalist John Frame wrote:

[A]re we not still forced to say, 'God exists (presupposition), therefore God exists (conclusion),' and isn't that argument clearly circular? Yes, in a way. But that is unavoidable for any system, any

---

[24] I've briefly argued against these contentions. See chapter 9 and 13 in the co-written book (with Randal Rauser) *God or Godless* (Grand Rapids, Baker Books, 2013). To assert God is the basis of logic is to fall within the same trap of the Euthyphro dilemma with regard to moral truth. Is something reasonable merely because God proclaims it so, or does God proclaim something reasonable because it is? Reason has shown itself trustworthy pragmatically–it just works. Of course, the brain doesn't reason as well as the presuppositionalist proclaims. Oriental philosophers may reject logic outright as *maya* because it's based on a rationalistic worldview they reject. So how presuppositional apologetics can make a dent in Oriental beliefs is a puzzle to me.

worldview. One cannot argue for an ultimate standard by appealing to a different standard. That would be inconsistent.[25]

Presuppositionalists, just like classical apologists, reject the evidentialist method. They admit there isn't sufficient evidence to convince non-believing outsiders for Christianity. In the presuppositionalist's mind unless the evidence is viewed through Christian presuppositions it's not considered evidence at all. The task of the Christian apologist is to destroy false presuppositions so non-believers can adopt the presuppositions of Christianity and believe.

According to presuppositionalists the evidence for the resurrection of Jesus can only be seen as supportive of what they already believe through the lens of Christian assumptions, not before. And then it's not the evidence that convinces them Jesus arose from the dead. It's the presuppositions that make the evidence for the resurrection seen for what it is. It's no wonder William Lane Craig accused presuppositionalists of committing a very serious informal fallacy, in these words:

> Presuppositionalism commits the informal fallacy of begging the question, for it advocates presupposing the truth of Christian theism in order to prove Christian theism. It is difficult to imagine how anyone could with a straight face think to show theism to be true by reasoning, 'God exists; therefore, God exists.' A Christian theist himself will deny that question-begging arguments prove anything."[26]

Gary Habermas accuses presuppositionalist John Frame of committing another serious informal fallacy. Says Habermas:

> He argues that rationalists must accept reason as an ultimate starting point, just as empiricists assume sense experience, and so on. So, the Christian may begin with Scripture as a legitimate starting point. But these are not analogous bases. While the rationalist uses reason and the empiricist uses sense experience as tools from

---

[25] Steven B. Coven, ed. *Five Views on Apologetics*, p. 217.
[26] *Five Views on Apologetics*, p. 233.

which to construct their systems, Frame assumes both the tool of special revelation and the system of Scripture, from which he develops his Christian theism. In other words, he assumes the reality of God's existence, his personal interaction with humans, plus a specific product: Scripture. Does Frame not realize that, in the name of everyone needing a presupposition, he has imported an entire worldview when others have only asked for tools?[27]

Where does evidence come into play for presuppositionalists if evidence is seen in light of circular presuppositions? Well, the evidence comes into play when presuppositionalists need it to come into play, not before. It's used in an ad hoc way, thus highlighting a third informal fallacy, the fallacy of ad hoc rationalization. This occurs when someone grabs some type of explanation, no matter how improbable, to save an argument from being refuted. The result is an explanation that may not be very coherent, does not explain much at all, and probably has no way of being tested. To the contrary, reasonable people need evidence from the very beginning. One simply cannot presuppose the truths of disputable historical events in an ancient world prior to investigating whether or not those events actually took place if they want to be taken seriously.[28]

With regard to the *Reformed Epistemology*, Alvin Plantinga seeks to show Christians can be entirely rational in having a "full-blooded Christian belief"[29] in "the great truths of the gospel."[30] But his conclusion is only correct if his Christian God exists. That's a big *IF!* All he's doing is arguing it's reasonable to believe in God, *if God exists*. Don't think so? Then listen to Richard Swinburne, who correctly argues that Plantinga's conclusion in his 500-page book in defense of reasonable Christian belief, *Warranted Christian Belief*, is "of little use." For Plantinga

---

[27] *Five Views on Apologetics*, p. 242.
[28] The most hard-hitting and persuasive critique of presuppositionialism is still the book by R.C. Sproul, John Gerstner and Arthur Lindsley, Classical *Apologetics: A Rational Defense of the Christians Faith and a Critique of Presuppositional Apologetics* (Grand Rapids: Zondervan, 1984), section III, pp. 183-338.
[29] Alvin Plantinga, *Warranted Christian Belief* (New York: Oxford, 2000), p. 200.
[30] Alvin Plantinga, *Warranted Christian Belief*, pp. 245, 262.

works up to the conclusion that 'if Christian belief is true, it very likely does have warrant.' But this conditional is of little use to anyone without some information about the truth of the antecedent (whether Christian belief is true); and on that, Plantinga explicitly acknowledges in his final paragraph, he cannot help us. For he writes there that on the really important question of 'is Christian belief true,' 'we pass beyond the competence of philosophy.'[31]

Plantinga challenges the idea that belief in God needs any evidence at all. He says

[T]he believer is entirely within his epistemic rights in believing, for example, that God has created the world, even if he has no argument at all for that conclusion. His belief in God can be perfectly rational even if he knows of no cogent argument, deductive or inductive, for the existence of God—indeed, even if there is no such argument.[32]

He argues there are countless things we believe (and do so properly) without proof or evidence, such as the existence of other persons (or minds); that the world continues to exist even when we don't perceive it; that we have been alive for more than twenty-four hours; that the past really happened; that we aren't just brains in a vat; that we live in an ordered universe; that we can trust our minds and our senses about the universe; that cause and effect are universal laws of nature; that nature is uniform and intelligible; and so on. He further argues by analogy that people can also believe in God (and do so properly) without proof or evidence. In particular, since believing there are other persons is rational without evidential support, so also is belief in God.

I have concluded that all of these scenarios are disanalogous to believing in God. For with God there is no empirical experiential evidence he exists—such as gained from seeing hearing or touching him—since

---

[31] Richard Swinburne, *Faith and Reason*, 2nd ed. (Oxford: Oxford University Press, 2005), pp. 74–75.
[32] Plantinga, "Reason and Belief in God," in *Faith and Rationality: Reason and Belief in God* ed. Alvin Plantinga and Nicholas Wolterstorff (Notre Dame: University of Notre Dame Press, 1983), p. 65.

he's conceived as a spiritual being. Nor does anyone see God do a miracle either. Even if an extremely rare unexplainable event took place we don't see him doing it.[33] By contrast, when it comes to experiencing life 24-hours ago we have the artifacts of yesterday, like a photograph, a dirty pair of pants, a friend who remembers what we talked about during lunch, and perhaps a future paycheck showing we worked that day, etc. So these scenarios do not apply to God. Other hypothetical scenarios that are far-fetched, including the possibility there isn't a material world, or that we're living in a Matrix, or the Cartesian demon hypothesis, are not good defeaters of the demand for sufficient evidence either, as I've argued at some length.[34] The major problem with them is that possibilities don't count. Only probabilities do if we're thinking like scientists. It may be remotely possible that we're living in the Matrix right now, or dreaming, or being deceived by an evil demon. But I'm not changing anything I do or anything I think based on a possibility. We must think exclusively in terms of the probabilities.

Now I unwittingly accept some things without objective evidence for them, like my own subjective experience of being me. However, I can easily offer concrete examples where it would be irrational not to have the needed objective evidence for them. Consider the nature of nature and the workings of nature, studied in the disciplines like geology, chemistry, astronomy, neurology, biology, zoology and so forth. In these concrete examples rational people need sufficient objective evidence before coming to any conclusions. They are the kinds of examples mathematician W.K. Clifford (1845–1879) surely had in mind when discussing the ethics of a shipowner who had stifled his doubts about a ship's seaworthiness by trusting in God's providence, rather than in patiently investigating the evidence for himself. Clifford may have claimed too much though when he stated, "it is wrong always, everywhere, and for

---

[33] David J. Hand explains how unexplainable rare events happen all of the time in his book, *The Improbability Principle: Why Coincidences, Miracles, and Rare Events Happen Every Day* (Scientific American / Farrar, Straus and Giroux, 2014).
[34] John W. Loftus, *The Outsider Test for Faith* (Amherst, NY: Prometheus Books, 2013), pp. 70-72, 134-144, and *Why I Became an Atheist*, pp. 43-47.

anyone, to believe anything upon insufficient evidence."[35] Does this apply to beauty, tastes, hunches, and subjective feelings? Most probably not. So Plantinga failed to properly and charitably understand him, for he focused on Clifford's *statement* rather than on his *concrete examples*. We most certainly do need sufficient objective evidence for everything when it comes to the nature of nature and its workings, studied in the above mentioned disciplines. So his ship of arguments sailed right past Clifford's ship in the middle of the night without a good skirmish.

The most I could grant for the sake of argument—as loathe as I am to do even this—is that it might be rational to believe in a supreme being without objective evidence. But even if I grant *that*, the belief in a particular triune God who created the universe from nothing, who tested Adam and Eve in the Garden, rescued the Israelites from Egyptian slavery, sent an incarnation of himself to earth, who was born of a virgin in Bethlehem, who did and said the things we read about in the canonical Gospels, who was crucified as a substitutionary sacrifice for our sins, who bodily arose from the dead and who ascended into the sky with the promise of coming again to judge the world *is simply not a god-belief it's rational to believe without sufficient objective evidence!* There's just way too much belief going on there.

Plantinga surely believes there is historical evidence for his fundamentalist "full-blooded Christian belief" even though bizarrely he argues it's reasonable to believe without any of it. Speaking for 16th century reformer John Calvin—and agreeing with him—Plantinga says the great truths of the gospel found in a self-authenticating Scripture are evident in themselves:

> [W]e don't require argument from, for example, historically established premises about the authorship and reliability of the bit of Scripture in question to the conclusion that the bit in question is in fact true; for belief in the great things of the gospel to be justified, rational, and warranted, no historical evidence and

---

[35] W.K. Clifford, "Ethics of Belief" 1877, found online: http://infidels.org/library/historical/w_k_clifford/ethics_of_belief.html

argument for the teaching in question, or for the veracity or reliability or divine character of Scripture are necessary.[36]

Upon what basis does Plantinga say this? He believes we all have a sense of divinity (or *sensus divinitatis*, if you prefer the Latin) within us, and a (holy) *Spirit Guide* who guides us to know "the great truths of the gospel" when reading the Scripture. This is the same kind of thing psychics claim they can do by reading tea leaves and tarot cards. He's effectively saying the spirit world gives Christians these same kinds of psychic abilities! This is something I already criticized at the end of my chapter 3 on the ECREE principle.

Lest anyone think I'm too harsh on Plantinga, I assure you I'm not trying to be, although in describing and criticizing such a large body of work in such a small space my descriptions contain within them my criticisms. I just disagree, strongly. Pay close attention to what Plantinga says: "Faith involves an explicitly cognitive element; it is, says Calvin, knowledge…and it is revealed to our minds. To have faith, therefore, is to know and hence believe something or other." And Christian beliefs come "by way of the work of the Holy Spirit, who gets us to accept, causes us to believe, these great truths of the gospel. These beliefs don't come just by way of the normal operation of our natural faculties, they are a supernatural gift."[37] If this is not claiming to have psychic abilities then I don't know what is. And if anyone thinks psychic abilities are incompatible with Christianity then just think of the Christians in Haiti who embrace both Catholicism and voodoo.

It is one thing to have a warranted belief that we are reading the Bible, so long as we're reading it with cognitive faculties functioning properly in the right kind of cognitive environment. It is something entirely different to be reading the Bible and claim "God is speaking to me." That additional claim is miles and miles away from what any rational person can conclude from the actual experience of reading the Bible itself. For that additional claim depends on the rationality of

---

[36] Alvin Plantinga, *Warranted Christian Belief*, p. 262.
[37] Ibid., pp. 245-246.

believing that all the ancient documents in the Bible are truly God's word, that what they say about God, the nature of nature, and its workings are true, and that how one interprets them when reading them is correct. Since the rationality of claiming "God is speaking to me" depends on the rationality of accepting these other claims, it should be shown that it's rational to accept these other claims before one can rationally claim, "God is speaking to me." Until then the rational conclusion when reading the Bible is "I am reading the Bible," not "God is speaking to me."

Old Testament scholar and philosopher of religion Jaco Gericke has written a devastating criticism of Plantinga's epistemology based on these concerns:

> [P]ast critiques of Plantinga have tended to focus almost exclusively on problems in the philosophical "superstructure" of Reformed Epistemology with little real attention being paid to the biblical-theological "base structure" of his arguments. And yet it cannot be disputed that the latter is ultimately foundational to the former—its raison d'être, if you will. But if this is indeed the case, it means that whatever the merits of Plantinga's sophisticated philosophical rhetoric, if it can be shown that his biblical foundations are both mistaken and/or nothing of the sort, the entire modus operandi of Reformed Epistemology will have been fatally compromised.[38]

One of Gericke's main criticisms concerns the particular belief in God that Plantinga thinks is properly basic. Plantinga's view of Yahweh, the God of the Bible, is

---

[38] Jaco Gericke, "Fundamentalism on Stilts: A Response to Alvin Plantinga's Reformed Epistemology," *Verbum et Ecclesia* 30, no. 2 (2009), http://www.up.ac.za/dspace/bitstream/2263/12356/1/Gericke_Fundamentalism%282009%29.pdf. See also his chapter, "Can God Exist If Yahweh Doesn't?" in the anthology I edited, *The End of Christianity* (Amherst, NY: Prometheus Books, 2011), pp. 131–54. For another great response see Graham Oppy's essay "Natural Theology" in *Alvin Plantinga*, ed., Deane-Peter Baker (Cambridge, Cambridge University Press, 2007.

radically anachronistic and conform[s] more to the proverbial "God of the Philosophers" (Aquinas in particular) than to any version of Yahweh as depicted in ancient Israelite religion. This means that the pre-philosophical "biblical" conceptions of Yahweh, the belief in whom is supposed to be properly basic, [are] not even believed by Plantinga himself. His lofty notions of God in terms of "Divine Simplicity," "Maximal Greatness," and "Perfect-Being Theology" are utterly alien with reference to many of the characterizations of Yahweh in biblical narrative (e.g., Genesis 18).[39]

In sum, presuppositionalists, including Plantinga, simply assume what needs to be proved. This is not an acceptable way for reasonable people to argue on behalf of Christianity, at all. Just think if all other religionists did this. Then we would be at a standstill with nothing but swords, shotguns and ships of war deciding which religion we should believe. It's the result of rejecting the requirement for sufficient objective evidence for one's faith.

4. APOLOGETICS BASED ON PRIVATE SUBJECTIVE EXPERIENCES

Soren Kierkeegaard, Karl Barth, John G. Stackhouse, Myron B. Penner, and others are roughly all representatives of this, uh, apologetical strategy as I'm loathed to call it. This is not a reasonable method for convincing nonbelievers at all. It's also called *Fideism*, or faithism since this "method" concedes the whole argument, that there just isn't sufficient evidence to believe.

Myron B. Penner, author of the book, *The End of Apologetics*, says his book is "against apologetics,"[40] that is modern rationalistic apologetics, saying it "is no longer valid. It tends toward an unbiblical and unchristian form of Christian witness and does not have the ability to attest

---

[39] Gericke, "Can God Exist If Yahweh Doesn't?" p. 150.
[40] Myron B. Penner *The End of Apologetics: Christian Witness in a Postmodern Context* (Grand Rapids: Baker Academic, 2013), p. 4.

truthfully to Christ in our postmodern context." Of course it doesn't, as we've seen. The reason is because apologists have simply not found the sufficient evidence to believe. Penner and his cohorts stand with the others who all agree there isn't a sufficient amount of evidence to believe. In its place Penner proposes the biblical concept of faithful witness. "Our task as Christians" he says, "is not to know the truth intellectually but to become the truth."[41] James K. Beilby tries to explain by saying, "Proponents do not hold that the truth of Christianity must be presupposed, but rather that it must be experienced."[42]

Okay then, not to be too blunt, but how does someone experience the story of the Israelite Exodus out of Egypt? How do we experience the story of Jesus turning water into wine in Cana of Galilee? Even if someone were to magically experience biblical stories in a dream-like state, what difference does it make if there is no evidence for their truth? The same would go for the resurrection of Jesus. How is a private subjective experience of Jesus' resurrection any indicator of the truth of that story? *A private subjective experience is only evidence of a private subjective experience and nothing more.* How does an experience of love in a Christian community mean anything either? A lot of people within other religious and non-religious communities, communes and social clubs experience love and acceptance.

There cannot be an apologetical method based on private subjective experiences, if we want to know the truth about the world we live in. The only thing that can be done with subjective experiences is to place oneself in a position whereby these experiences can be had to produce faith, presumably through prayer, saying the rosary, going to church, becoming under the influence of a Christian friend's "witness" and/or

---

[41] Myron B. Penner, ed., *Christianity and the Postmodern Turn: Six Views* (Grand Rapids: Brazos Press, 2005), p. 127. See Myron Bradley Penner and Hunter Barnes, eds., *A New Kind of Conversation: Blogging Toward a Postmodern Faith* (Downers Grove: IVP Books, 2007); and Robert C. Greer, *Mapping Postmodernism: A Survey of Christian Options* (Downers Grove: IVP Academic, 2003). See also John B. Cobb, Jr., *Living Options in Protestant Theology* (Westminster, 1962).
[42] James K. Beilby, "Varieties of Apologetics" in Khaldoun A. Sweis and Chad V. Meister, *Christian Apologetics: An Anthology of Primary Sources*, p. 34.

reading the Bible. One doesn't need apologetics or a method to do this. Basing one's apologetics on subjective experiences that supposedly lead to faith is to adopt a non-method, since it can produce many irreconcilable different and bizarre conclusions. To test whether subjective experiences can produce religious truth all we have to do is ask why Catholics, Fundamentalists, Hindus, Muslims, Orthodox Jews and/or Mormons perform similar religious activities from their perspectives, to see if they come away with the same or similar conclusions and faiths afterward. Hint: They won't. Then too, if people accept subjective experiences as objective truths then every crackpot purveyor of a dubious new religion who wants to sleep with your daughter and take all your money would have an extremely easy day of it. So this is a non-method. I should have excluded a discussion of this *cough* method from the outset since I'm focusing on a discussion of reasons to believe. None are offered here, just lots of hugs and kisses, and warm fuzzies. It abandons rational apologetics and is proud of it, which is absolutely bizarre.

5. ECLECTIC APOLOGETICS BASED ON PRIOR CONCLUSIONS

Representatives of this approach include Edward Carnell, Basil Mitchell, C.S. Lewis, Richard Swinburne, Paul Feinberg, John S. Feinberg, Kenneth Boa, Robert M. Bowman Jr., Douglas Groothuis, and others. Usually it's called the *Cumulative Case Method*, or the *Integrative Approach to Apologetics*. This eclectic apologetical method supposedly takes the best of each of the other methods by combining them all together into one. The reason apologists are being forced into this approach is because they realize none of the other approaches can be justified. This is their last hope in defending that which cannot be defended at all.

They rightly reject Evidentialism because it leads people away from Christianity. They rightly reject Classical Apologetics because they recognize it's nothing more than a dressed up evidentialism dependent on theistic arguments that themselves are not be justifiable. They rightly reject presuppositionalism because one cannot reason in a circular fashion by presupposing that which is being disputed. They rightly reject Fideism due to the abandonment of apologetics itself. Kenneth Boa and Robert M. Bowman Jr. even exclude Fideism from their own eclectic approach because it abandons rational apologetics, which means theirs is a selective eclecticism from the get-go.

Cumulative or integrative apologetics is what apologists eventually get when they reject evidentialism. It's the final stop on a journey with an evidential beginning. It's the slippery slope they eventually slide into. This method is best described as eclectic. An eclectic method is one where the conclusion largely dictates the method. Christianity is the conclusion. Now use whatever method needed to reach that conclusion. Their motto is this: "We'll use whatever works." If the available evidence doesn't work, then first use the theistic proofs. If the theistic proofs don't work, then presuppose what needs to be proved. If presuppositionalism asks way more than any reasonable person should accept, then switch to the need for private subjective experiences of God somehow someway someday. If none of these methods work separately, then choose to use something, anything that has the persuasive power to convince non-believers of the correct conclusion. Such a method is no method at all, but rather an adoption of ineffective and eclectically chosen methods which themselves have gaping holes in them.[43]

The interesting part is we see this same type of eclecticism among other apologists who claim that they accept a different apologetic method! Just carefully read through the debate book edited by Steven B. Cowan, *Five Views of Apologetics*, where five Christian apologists debate each other over the proper apologetical method. After debating each other William Lane Craig notes in his closing remarks that, "What we are seeing in the present volume is a remarkable convergence of views, which is cause for rejoicing."[44] Craig, a defender of *Classical Apologetics*

---

[43] I no longer think as I did in *Why I Became an Atheist* about cumulative type apologetics. While I still think a cumulative case is effective in debunking Christianity, I don't think it's a consistent way to defend Christianity at all.

[44] *Five Views of Apologetics* edited by Steven B. Cowan, p. 317. Cowan can be seen to concur on pages 380-81.

astoundingly admitted he and presuppositionalist John Frame "do not have any substantive disagreements."[45] Craig said this even though he had just accused Frame of arguing in a viciously circular manner. Craig also astoundingly admitted that he and evidentialist Gary Habermas are in agreement "on virtually everything."[46]

So, if we take Craig at his word then his views are in substantial agreement with two opposing views represented by Frame and Habermas. Habermas chides Craig for admitting this, saying Craig must now include himself "among the evidentialists" because "he does not take the classical position of the classical apologist!"[47] Habermas adds, "I have no problems with Bill Craig. I simply welcome him back to the evidentialist fold!"[48] John Frame acknowledged in the book that other presuppositionalists would not consider him to be "a pure presuppositionalist," for what he defends "is not clearly distinct from the other methodologies."[49] So okay then. Neither Craig nor Frame are true representatives of the positions they purport to defend. But Habermas the evidentialist doesn't have a position different than the eclectic *Cumulative Case Method*, for he says, "I have said repeatedly, evidentialists are eclectic in their methodology."[50] So Habermas says he "has no major disagreements with Paul Feinberg"[51] who in turn also admitted his approach was "eclectic"[52] in nature.

Whew! Did you get that? From reading that book it's confusing to know where these apologists stand. John S. Feinberg's discussion of these issues is also confusing. In his own apologetics book he discusses just two apologetic methods in two long separate chapters, *Presuppositionalism*,

---

[45] Ibid p. 314.
[46] Ibid p. 316.
[47] Ibid p. 336
[48] Ibid p. 343.
[49] Ibid p. 357.
[50] Ibid p. 343.
[51] Ibid p. 344
[52] Ibid p. 347

and *Evidentialism*.[53] Feinberg tells us in the one chapter that many current presuppositionalists "have so modified some of its main ideas that at times it is hard to detect much difference between their form of presuppositionalism and some forms of Christian evidentialism."[54] Right that! Then in the other chapter he defends the merits of "three varieties of evidentialism," which include *Evidentialism*, the *Classical Apologetics*, and the *Cumulative Case Method*. Feinberg ends up defending an eclectic integrated approach, except that he calls it "evidentialism."[55] Apparently you can describe something differently than what you call it. His kind of evidentialism is one where he's "most drawn to a cumulative case approach to defending Christianity."[56] But how can Feinberg adopt a cumulative case approach that in turn adopts the classical approach? He's already admitted the classical approach fails since the traditional arguments to God's existence fail. If we take the apologetic methods at face value in their purest forms, it should be clear they cannot be integrated without changing what each one stresses. It's like mixing oil with water.

The important point is that the eclectic method is a clear indicator, all on its own, that Christian apologists themselves don't think there is sufficient evidence for their faith. Either apologists think the evidence alone will lead a non-believer to Christianity or they don't. Only one method outlined above says yes, that Christianity stands or falls on the evidence. And that position has historically led to a rejection of Christianity. All of the other methods try to fix the problems with evidentialism because sufficient evidence simply is not there. They cannot sugar coat this inside the good ole boys bakery before dishing out their half-baked treats to the hungry crowds.

When we put it all together there are roughly five major apologetics methods. If we grant that an equal number of Christian apologists defend these respective approaches, then each one has the support of 20%

---

[53] John Feinberg thinks *Reformed Epistemology* "isn't a method for defending the Christians worldview as truth" in *Can You Believe It's True?: Christian Apologetics in a Postmodern Era*, p. 248.
[54] Ibid p. 249.
[55] Ibid p. 320.
[56] Ibid p. 321.

of them. Since evidentialism is the only method that accepts the need for reasoning based on sufficient evidence, and since it only has 20% support among apologists, then 80% of all apologists don't think there is sufficient objective evidence to believe. Let that sink in. Eighty percent of the very people who defend Christianity don't think there is sufficient evidence for their faith.

At the present time James Beilby acknowledges there are no clear lines to be drawn between apologetical methods. Instead there is "a dizzying diversity of approaches to apologetics."[57] And "there are many contemporary apologetic methodologies whose work is best labeled 'Eclectic.'"[58] True that! In their apologetics book, *Reasons for Our Hope*, H. Wayne House and Dennis W. Jowers unwittingly admit the eclecticism of their integrated approach to apologetics, and conclude:

> Several approaches are available to apologists, from classical to evidential to presuppositional to fideist. Each has strengths and weaknesses, and each presents valid and useful apologetics. The Christian apologist, then, needs to understand each approach thoroughly and glean the best from each of them. Further, the apologist needs to be able to employ different approaches in different contexts. Every person will react and be reached differently, so there is *no one approach that will work every time*. [Emphasis mine][59]

The rejection of evidentialism as an apologetical method by most Christian apologists should be seen as a big flashing bright red light and heard as a loud annoying buzzer to warn Christians that sufficient objective evidence does not exist for their faith. For if sufficient evidence existed evidentialism would not lead to the abandonment of Christianity and there would be no other alternative method of apologetics. Since it's

---

[57] James K. Beilby, "Varieties of Apologetics" in Khaldoun A. Sweis and Chad V. Meister, *Christian Apologetics: An Anthology of Primary Sources*, p. 37.
[58] Ibid.
[59] H. Wayne House and Dennis W. Jowers, *Reasons for Our Hope: An Introduction to Christian Apologetics* (Nashville, TN: B&H Academic, 2011), p. 47.

unreasonable to believe in a particular religion—or anything else about the objective world—without the requirement for sufficient objective evidence, it's unreasonable to believe in Christianity. It's not just me saying this. Christian apologists do.

7| WHY DO CHRISTIANS BELIEVE IN MIRACLES?

BY VALERIE TARICO

CHRISTIAN BELIEF IN MIRACLES—IT'S ONLY NATURAL

MIRACLES ARE MAGIC BY ANOTHER NAME

If it looks like a duck, and quacks like a duck, we have at least to consider the possibility that we have a small aquatic bird of the family Anatidae on our hands.
– Douglas Adams

Why do Christians believe in miracles?

One obvious answer is that Christians believe because our ancestors did. Handed-down religious beliefs are remarkably powerful and change-resistant, and the Christian belief in miracles dates all the way back to the beginnings of Jesus worship. In fact, it dates back even further, back into the beginnings of the Hebrew religion and the earlier religions of the Ancient Near East from which the Hebrew stories and beliefs emerged.

Christianity was born at a time in history when *every* religion included a belief in magic or miracles. Miraculous healings, natural "signs and wonders," good things magically happening to good people and (even more satisfying) bad people magically getting what they deserve…

Belief in all of these was the norm, along with the conviction that we humans can draw magic to ourselves by talking to supernatural beings, engaging in certain rituals, eating or drinking special foods, touching objects with talismanic powers, and more. What would have been truly miraculous would have been the emergence of Christian texts and traditions that *didn't* include magical thinking.

That would have been a real wonder.

From the beginning, the traditional Christian worldview has included all manner of supernatural beings and objects with special powers. In the Bible itself, this includes disembodied spirits, angels, devils, unicorns, dragons, seers, human sorcerers and witches, enchanted animals, and a whole pantheon of deities.[1]

Even today in the 21st century, Christian fundamentalists continue to inhabit this wonderland. They believe that an invisible ethereal plane underlies the physical world, and that our lives are part of a cosmic battle between the forces of good and evil which spills from the otherworldly plane into this one. In their minds, we all live in the magical world mapped out by our Iron Age ancestors.

Christian belief in miracles is a subset of Christianity's magical worldview, which is part of humanity's broader tendency to believe in magic. That said, many Christians vigorously deny this. Miracles, they say, are not magic! On the website, *Got Answers*, one miracle believer tried to clarify[2] the difference. His answer reflects the thinking of many biblical Christians:

> Basically, magic and miracles differ in their source: magic has either a human or demonic source, but miracles are a supernatural work of God.. . ." Miracles and magic sometimes look the same, but their goals are different. Magic and illusion distract the eye

---

[1] Gerald McDermott, (14, January 24). First Things | America's Most Influential Journal of Religion & Public Life. *The Bible's Many Gods. Retrieved* October 12, 2018, from http://www.firstthings.com/web-exclusives/2014/01/the-bibles-many-gods

[2] (n.d.). Got Questions? Bible Questions Answered. *What is the difference between miracles and magic?* Retrieved October 12, 2018, from http://www.gotquestions.org/difference-miracles-magic.html

from reality, while miracles draw the eye to reality. Miracles reveal; magic hides. Miracles are an expression of creative power; magic uses what already exists. Miracles are a gift; magic is a studied skill. Miracles do not glorify men; magic seeks to be noticed and bring glory to the magician. Jesus was not a magician. He was the Son of God, known for His many miracles.

Got that? Miracles are the magical stuff done by the Christian God or his proxies. Magic is the magical stuff done by the competition. The latter is bad, bad, bad, because it might trick you into worshiping someone or something else. And it's real! The Occult. The Dark Arts. Keep your kids away from Harry Potter.

To many outsiders, the distinction is little more than a cloud of smoke from an illusionist's mist-making machine. It is just one of many tedious ways that Christianity claims to be different—not a religion but a relationship, not polytheistic like Hinduism, not antiquated like the fairy tales of Pagan Europe, and definitely not a bundle of superstitious woo like New Age wonders involving crystals and incantations. Christian exceptionalism of this sort—philosophers call it *special pleading*—is a tiresome form of arrogance. Miracles are a subset of magic, and any discussion of Christian miracles must consider the long Christian love affair with magic more broadly.

BIBLE STORIES FIT COMMON PATTERNS OF MAGIC AND WIZARDRY

One person's religion is another person's magic and vice versa.
– Unknown

The Bible is full of magic. In the centuries after the biblical texts were written, Christianity refined the view that all supernatural events are part of a divine contest between God and the devil, with the miraculous on one side and the occult on the other. But during the formative years of the Hebrew religion and even Christianity, things weren't so crystalized.

Hebrew beliefs evolved from polytheism to monotheism, with a layer in between of monolatry—belief in many gods but worship of one. As monotheism displaced prior forms of worship, traditional folk magic became associated with earlier and competing religious traditions. It was replaced gradually by more encompassing theologies and condemned by an increasingly powerful priesthood.

But despite the best efforts of the priestly class, some ancient practices had staying power.

In the earliest texts of the Old Testament (the Torah), folk magic coexists with grand supernatural events attributed to the God of Abraham, Yahweh. In the New Testament nativity stories, the signs and wonders surrounding the birth of Jesus are of a sort that would have been familiar to people of the time. Similarly, the miracles attributed to the adult Jesus in the gospels are mostly of a sort commonly attributed to priests, sorcerers, god-men, and minor deities.

The Bible, as I said, is full of magic. Divination, astrology and fortunetelling, potions, conjuring, numerology, transmutation or alchemy, spellcasting and incantations, curses, healings, charms and talismans, conjuring…each of these can be found in the Bible—including in stories about people and events that have God's approval.

Mind you, some Bible writers also warn repeatedly against many of these practices, which are associated with competing gods and cultures (see, for example, Deuteronomy 18:10–11). But even as the writers seek to purge their religion of outside influences, they can't help but fall into the pre-scientific view of their age, which is woven through with folk magic and wizardry.

Here are just a few examples.

Divination—In Genesis (44:5), Joseph has a silver drinking cup, which he uses for divining. The passage likely refers to the practice of scrying, in which a vessel is filled with water and the fortuneteller gazes into it, similar to the technique reportedly used by Nostradamus. Exodus (28:30) refers to two divining objects, the Urim and Thummim, perhaps two flat stones, that the High Priest consults to determine the will of

God. In other passages, lots, meaning marked pieces of wood or stone like dice, are used by more ordinary people for a similar purpose (Numbers 26:55, Proverbs 16:33, Proverbs 18:18). In the book of Daniel, the protagonist—a Hebrew prophet—is employed for a number of years by the King of Babylon as the manager of his "magicians, enchanters, astrologers and diviners" (Daniel 5:11).

Jumping ahead to the New Testament book of Matthew, a visit from three foreign astrologers known as the three magi or wise men gives credence to the divinity of Jesus. They bring gifts that portend later events in his life. Today, some Christians engage in a form of divination known as bibliomancy—seeking messages from God by opening the Bible to a random page and putting a finger on a random verse. Bibliomancy dates back[3] at least to the 11th Century.

Potions—In Genesis, Rachel, the wife of Jacob, acquires magical mandrake roots to assist her in getting pregnant (Genesis 30:14–22). These may have been eaten in small bits or ground into a potion. The book of Numbers tells how a priest can make a magic potion that will cause a woman to abort any fetus she is carrying, but only if she has been unfaithful to her husband (Numbers 5:12–31). The potion is to be administered while the priest pronounces a curse.

Conjuring—When King Saul finds himself floundering in a war with the Philistines and can't get God's advice through his priests and prophets, he disguises himself, visits a witch and asks her to call up the spirit of Samuel, which she does. The spirit appears. (1 Samuel 28:11–15).

Numerology—Ancient peoples often attributed special meaning or significance to some numbers, and this pattern can be seen in the Bible. The number 12 (also significant[4] in Babylonian, Zoroastrian and

---

[3] (2010, February 23). NPR: National Public Radio. *Do You Believe in Miracles? Most Americans Do: Talk of the Nation*. Retrieved October 12, 2018, from http://www.npr.org/templates/story/story.php?storyId=124007551

[4] Karen Louise Jolly, John F.M. Middleton, Robert Andrew Gilbert, (n.d.). Encyclopedia Britannica. Britannica.com. Magic. Supernatural Phenomenon. Retrieved October 12, 2018 from http://www.britannica.com/topic/magic-supernatural-phenomenon

classical Greek religions) stands out. Think of the 12 tribes of Israel and 12 apostles of Jesus. The book of Revelation speaks of 12 pearls, 12 angels, 12x12 (144) righteous virgin men who will reach paradise, and 12 foundations of the heavenly Jerusalem, which has walls that are 12x12 stadia, 12 gates, and a size of 12,000 furlongs. Still today, some Jews and Christians analyze the numbers in the Bible for special hidden meanings.

Spellcasting and curses—In the book of Genesis (30:31–43), Jacob gets his father-in-law to agree that he can keep any spotted sheep and goats, which are uncommon. He then puts spotted sticks in front of the animals whenever they are breeding, causing them to have spotted offspring—ultimately building great flocks and becoming wealthy. In modern times, a breed of piebald sheep in England are called Jacob sheep, after the story.

Although the Bible specifically prohibits sorcery—casting spells to harm people (see, especially, Deuteronomy 18:10–11)—some of God's messengers do just that, and they seem to do so with God's approval. In the Hebrew book of 2 Kings (2:23–25), for example, the Prophet Elisha calls down a black magic curse on 42 boys who are taunting him, and they are killed by a bear. In the New Testament book of Acts, Peter similarly kills two people by cursing them (Acts 5:9–10) and, in another story, Paul makes one go blind (Acts 13:6–12). Jesus himself curses a fig tree so that it withers and dies (Mark 11:12–25).

Magical healings—Miracle healings performed by Jesus are an integral part of the gospel stories. Like many other kinds of magic in the Bible, these would have fit patterns familiar at the time. From the standpoint of modern trinitarian theology in which Jesus is an avatar of God almighty, he could have eradicated an entire category of malaise like leprosy or blindness. Instead, the Jesus of the gospel writers performs healings on people in front of him. Often, he cures with words or touch. One time he makes mud out of dirt and spit and then pastes it onto the eyes of a blind man (John 9:6).

Transmutation, alchemy—Turning one substance into another is another common form of magic, which Jesus performs by turning water into wine (John 2:1–11). The Roman Catholic Church will later claim that the ritual of Eucharist turns wine and bread into flesh and blood.

FROM EARLY CHRISTIANITY TO THE PRESENT

In the Middle Ages, chards of the Gethsemane cross and bits of foreskin from the baby Jesus were bought and sold in European markets and sometimes ensconced in elaborate reliquaries of silver and gold. Believers wore amulets bearing protective symbols like embossed images of patron saints or the cross.

Some medieval Christian beliefs blended the supernatural worldview of the Ancient Near East with local superstitions, as when a believer would make the sign of the cross after seeing a black cat or use holly and mistletoe to celebrate the birth of Christ. Statues of Jesus, Mary and saints became pilgrimage destinations—places of particular spiritual power and locations for miraculous healings akin to more ancient temples and oracles. Echoes of these beliefs and behaviors continue to the present, even though the significance of some has faded. The domain of the miraculous has shrunk, but it has not gone away.

Why not? Why do so many people still believe in miracles? Specific Christian beliefs about miracles may be products of a handed-down tradition, kept alive by the Church through the flow of history. But that can't be the whole answer, because Christians are not alone in their miracle belief. Nearly 8 in 10^5 Americans say they believe in miracles, including—get this—almost 20 percent of nonbelievers!

The fact is, most all of us find ourselves attracted to magic, even if we are firmly convinced it isn't real. Audiences flock by the thousands to marvel at tricks performed by illusionists. Viewers flock by the millions to watch movies about super-villains and superheroes with superpowers. Fiction, especially for young adults, is dominated by genres like

---

[5] Crabtree, V. (2010). Human Religions. *The Divine Number 12: 12 Gods, 12 Disciples, 12 Tribes and the Zodiac.* Retrieved October 12, 2018 from http://www.humanreligions.info/twelve.html

fantasy and science fiction and even paranormal romance. We humans love us some magic!

So, to answer the question, *Why do Christians believe in miracles?* we really have to ask—*Why do we all love magic so much, child and adult, believer and skeptic alike?* Why does magic so appeal to us that it emerges in myriad forms when we build worlds from the raw material of the human imagination? What are the habits of mind that make us so prone not only to create magical stories but to believe the ones that have been handed down by our parents, and their parents, and their parents before them all the way back into the shadowy mists of pre-history?

FROM ANGELS TO IPHONES

Any sufficiently advanced technology is indistinguishable from magic.
– Arthur C. Clarke

Human beings have told stories about miracles and other kinds of magic for as long as we have been telling stories. They are present in every human culture at every point in history. Here is one reason. We humans are inventors. We have taken over this planet by innovating. But in order to invent new technologies or come up with innovative solutions to challenging problems, we must first be able to want something that doesn't exist and then imagine that it does.

My writing desk is built into a cupboard with metal knobs on the doors, and stuck to four of those knobs are four magnets. They say: Wish It, Dream It, Believe It, Do It. The magnets are, of course, meant to inspire bold creativity on my part: Take the first step, then the next, then the next. Come on, Valerie, just do it! But the sequence also says something interesting about our belief in miracles and magic.

What if we want something that simply isn't possible given how the world works? What if we won't even know whether it's possible until science makes a few more centuries of progress? What if our wishes get fulfilled sometimes but not others, and we can't figure out the pattern of when and why? In other words, what if we make it through steps one through three and then get stuck?

How frustrating! Our wishes and dreams don't go away just because we don't know how to fulfill them. That's where superstitious beliefs and behaviors come in, and mythic stories about magic and miracles, and fairy tales and fantasies and science fiction stories that we find delectable and soothing even when we know them to be just that.

Let me illustrate by focusing for a moment on instantaneous long-distance communication.

Last year, I traveled with my family to Newfoundland. During one of our meandering excursions along the coast, we stopped in Heart's Content, a small town that 160 years ago became the western end of the first transatlantic cable. Today, an honor-system museum is all that remains of the once state-of-the-art telegraph station, which at its peak employed 200 people. We wandered around the old work rooms, basking in the nostalgic feeling evoked by the high windows, wooden tables, intricate switchboards, and clusters of heavy wires and plugs. We awkwardly tapped out silly messages on a makeshift telegraph machine and laughed at the slow, clumsy process.

Mostly, though, we marveled at the ingenuity of the scrappy human beings, who, in 1858—before penicillin or birth control, before even the American Civil War—somehow manufactured a copper cable as long as the Atlantic is wide, then loaded it onto ships, and then unrolled it across an ocean floor as deep as two miles down from Ireland to Canada. Their cable allowed the first tappity tap of instantaneous communication from one side of the planet to the other. It was game-changing.

Yesterday, I spent an hour curled up on the sofa in my study with my daughter Brynn next to me and a laptop propped on the table in front of us. We were video chatting with my other daughter, Marley, in her Boston dorm room and with my husband, Brian, who is on a business trip in New Delhi. And when the audio gave us problems, cutting out intermittently, we were positively indignant. We expected better!

Between the astounding feat of laying that first transatlantic cable and the astounding creation of the laptops, internet, data centers and communications satellites that let my family enjoy instantaneous video chat from the other side of the planet, lie 150 years of intermediate steps. Each required ingenuity and hard work on the part of countless scientists, mathematicians, engineers, laborers, and technicians. Even the incremental difference between the technology that my family used yesterday and the tech we would have used last year for the same purpose, took a colossal effort on the part of strangers we will never meet.

Our Iron Age ancestors who wrote the Bible lacked even the crudest form of instantaneous long-distance communications, the fastest messengers of their time being carrier pigeons. They would have been mind-boggled by the sophistication of the telegraph to the point that most would have thought it some form of magic.

But that didn't stop them from *wanting* instantaneous communications or being able to imagine such a possibility. What they couldn't imagine was all the steps in between the wish and the actuality. So, they left them out. Unable to invent iPhones, they invented stories in which winged celestial messengers—beautiful human carrier pigeons—bore messages from the distant realm of the gods, and stories in which gods and loved ones crossed great distances by appearing in dreams.

They also invented special beings that could hear and respond to human supplications wherever we were—even beings that could hear our thoughts but preferred for some reason that we speak them out loud. With no need to get electrons and sound waves moving in just the right pattern, prayer covered more ground faster than Skype or Hangouts. It offered instantaneous communication to the other side of the universe. From your lips to God's ears, as Jewish well-wishers used to say.

This history of instantaneous communication illustrates how magic, broadly, plays its role in the human psyche. Innovation require that we have the capacity to visualize and want something so that we can figure out the path to make it happen. Efficiency requires that we want that journey to be as short and easy as possible. (For survival reasons, all animals are programmed to get their needs and wants met as efficiently as possible.) Take this to the extreme and voilà, magic!

In sum, one key to understanding the power of magical thinking in the human psyche is recognizing that inventiveness—Wish It, Dream It, Believe It, Do It—defines our species. We are innovators and discoverers. We are explorers who boldly go where no one has gone before. We launch ourselves into uncharted landscapes, seeking hazy destinations visible only to the mind's eye. Some of us die in the quest, but the rest of us thrive because of it. Magic gave us wings three millennia before we could fly. But fly, we can, because the very same fantastical thinking that attracts us to magic also helps us make some of our wild dreams come true.

THE HUMAN MIND IS WIRED FOR MAGICAL THINKING

Nothing is so alien to the human mind as the idea of randomness.
– John Cohen

Magic may allow us to flesh out our dreams unfettered by the laws of physics and biology, but when it comes time to roll up our sleeves and turn those dreams into realities, we need to recognize fantasy for what it is. That's where things get tough, because some ordinary, adaptive aspects of human information processing predispose us to superstition and magical thinking.

That goes for all of us. Are you human? Then at some level you believe in magic. At least that's what psychological research suggests.

In the social sciences, magical thinking is defined as thinking (either consciously or subconsciously) that one event causes another even when there isn't any plausible evidence or explanation for how this would happen. In carefully structured experiments, people who don't consciously believe in magic behave as if they unconsciously do.

Why? Because kinds of thinking that help us survive and thrive— like pattern matching, seeking cause-and effect-relationships, and attending to unusual events—also incline us to specific glitches in rationality. Understanding human information processing makes it easier to understand why so many people see miracles and other kinds of magic in the world around us.

Snap judgments about cause and effect—When two things happen close in time or space without an obvious external cause, we tend to assume that one caused the other, instinctively equating correlation with causation. Our brains are constantly scanning for causes and effects, so we pair them up quickly, often before conscious processing can take place.

If aphids infest your rose bush and the leaves curl up, it is useful to suspect that one likely caused the other. But the same associative process is not so helpful when your brain tells you that a rabbit appeared from a hat because a magician waved his wand or that your headache went away because you prayed.

Paranoia (also known as agenticity, hyperactive agency detection or hyperactive intentionality detection)—The human mind puts inanimate objects and active agents in two very different categories. While inanimate objects are just objects, we treat agency as if it comes from an internal essence, a unique living force. Sometimes, though we get these categories crossed. We rarely treat humans as if they were inanimate objects, but the opposite is not true. For example, young children are quick to treat a stuffed animal or doll as if it were a living being.

We also tend by default to think that events were caused intentionally by a conscious actor. Research shows that infants assume the presence of an active agent when they see non-inertial movement. This would have had survival value for our ancestors. In the words of neurologist Steven Novella,

> We are descended from hominids who were more paranoid and had hyperactive agency detection, because they were less likely to be eaten by predators...
> When [Hyperactive Agency Detection] is triggered we tend to see a hidden agent working behind the scenes, making events unfold

the way they do, and perhaps even deliberately hiding its own tracks.[6]

Since we humans are social animals, it was natural for our ancestors to interpret the events in social terms. It is still natural for us to do so today.

Patternicity (also known as apophenia)—Our relentless search for patterns is one of humanity's greatest cognitive strengths. It is fundamental to survival and innovation. But it also means we have a tendency to see connections in events that are actually unrelated. Patternicity or apophenia underlies conspiracy theories and many kinds of parapsychology. Taken to an extreme it plagues people with schizophrenia who sometimes can't get away from the feeling that unrelated events around them are acutely meaningful. Even when we are willing to live with uncertainty and mystery, our brains keep pulling to fill in the unknowns. "Our greatest challenge may be learning to bear incoherence," says[7] psychologist Bruce Poulsen.

Pareidolia—One common type of patternicity is pareidolia, perceiving nonexistent patterns in visual and auditory input. We see and hear meaningful patterns even in white noise or random forms like ink blots.

One former meth addict describes[8] how drug use gradually turned background noise into intelligible messages. When neurotransmitters go awry, as in schizophrenia, the same progression can happen to people who don't use drugs. But nothing has to be wrong with biochemistry for us to see meaningful patterns where they don't actually exist. Every child has seen a rabbit in a cloud or a monster in the shadow cast by moonlight through a bedroom window.

---

[6] Novella, S. (2010, March 22). Skepticblog. *Hyperactive Agency Detection*. Retrieved October 12, 2018 from http://www.skepticblog.org/2010/03/22/hyperactive-agency-detection/

[7] Bruce Poulsen (2012, July 31). Psychology Today. *Being Amused by Apophenia*. Retrieved October 12, 2018, from http://www.psychologytoday.com/us/blog/reality-play/201207/being-amused-apophenia

[8] J. (2015, August 20). Skeptical Exaddict | The adventures of a godless skeptic and former addict in a credulous world. *Meth-induced voices in your head start with pareidolia | Skeptical Exaddict*. Retrieved October 12, 2018, from http://skepticalexaddict.wordpress.com/2015/08/20/meth-induced-voices-in-your-head-start-with-pareidolia/

The most common kind of pareidolia is the tendency to see faces in inanimate objects. Infants respond to two black dots and a slash as a human face, suggesting that parts of our brain are pre-programmed for facial information. It should come as no surprise, then, that on occasion people see the faces of Jesus, Mary and devils in objects as disparate as a Cheeto, a banana skin, an ancient shroud, or even a dog's bum.

Attraction to unusual or counter-intuitive events—We habituate to the familiar, but the unexpected captures our attention. This thought pattern is highly efficient, because it keeps us from squandering mental energy on things that stay the same. Instead, we can attend to whatever is moving or changing, new or puzzling. This tendency helps us stay safe (to avoid getting run over one needs to focus on the one moving car in an otherwise static landscape), and it helps us make discoveries. As Isaac Asimov famously said, "The most exciting phrase to hear in science, the one that heralds new discoveries, is not "Eureka!" (I found it!) but "That's funny..." Unfortunately, we glom onto stories that violate the expected, stories about the exception rather than the rule even when the opposite might be wiser.

Poor statistical intuition and reasoning—We humans are terrible at predicting the likelihood of rare events, which can make common occurrences seem miraculous. Most events that people experience as "miraculous" are predictably common given real-world base rates and population sizes, but that is not how they seem. To do this topic justice, I will dive in later. Suffice for now to say that people who believe in paranormal phenomena appear to do even worse[9] than average at statistical analysis.

Glitches like these lay the foundation for seemingly supernatural and paranormal experiences. Christians may see miracles in recovery from cancer or empty parking spots. New Agers may turn quantum

---

[9] Susan Blackmore, Tom Troscianko (1985, November). Wiley Online Library. Scientific research articles, journals, books, and reference works. *Belief in the paranormal: Probability judgements, illusory control, and the chance baseline shift.* Blackmore, 1985. *British Journal of Psychology.* Wiley Online Library. Retrieved October 12, 2018 from:
http://onlinelibrary.wiley.com/doi/abs/10.1111/j.20448295.1985.tb01969.

theory into woo. Psychics and paranormal aficionados may convince themselves that they're onto something. But don't get too smug. Really, when it comes to the mental glitches that cause magical thinking, we're all in this together.

SEVEN KINDS OF MAGICAL THINKING THAT EVEN SKEPTICS CAN'T ESCAPE

Here you leave today and enter the world of yesterday, tomorrow, and fantasy.
– Walt Disney

Skeptics like to believe, when we enter the realm of magic, that we are there by choice, knowingly drinking from the well of fantasy. This is often true, but it doesn't tell the whole story, because some kinds of magical thinking are subconscious and largely involuntary. Matthew Hutson, in his book The Seven Laws of Magical Thinking,[10] discusses seven magical assumptions that flow naturally from the structure of human information processing. Hutson summarizes these assumptions in a series of short sentences: Objects carry essences. Symbols have power. Actions have distant consequences. The mind knows no bounds. The soul lives on. The world is alive. Everything happens for a reason.

Each of these provides the foundation for a common kind of magical thinking.

Contagion—Acting as if the essence of something spreads by contact. Perhaps because of contagious diseases, people often have a deep intuition that psychological or moral qualities can pass from one person to another via contact. The word "cooties" used to mean lice; now, among grade school children it is some form of distasteful social failing that passes from one child to another by touching. But this isn't just a kid thing. Most adults don't want to own a shirt once worn by a

---

[10] Matthew Hutson, *The 7 laws of magical thinking: How irrational beliefs keep us happy, healthy, and sane*, (New York: Plume Book, 2013).

murderer; an old handkerchief that belonged to Gandhi, though, might be a treasure.

In the Old Testament, a menstruating woman was both physically and spiritually unclean, and anyone who touched her, or sat where she had sat, also became unclean. On the other hand, handkerchiefs and aprons brought "from Paul's body" have his power to heal the sick (Acts 19: 11–12).

Similarity—Confounding images or symbols with whatever they represent. Our brains can't completely separate images from objects. If people are throwing darts, they have more difficulty hitting a picture of a baby than a more neutral target. Scientists recently measured[11] perspiration while experimental subjects cut up pictures of either neutral objects or cherished objects from their childhood. Not surprisingly, the latter caused more nervous sweating. Or consider religious icons. Heaven forbid someone should throw out a Gideon's Bible or burn a cheap copy of the Quran no matter how many millions are in print.

Superstitious ritual—Engaging in repeated behaviors to avert bad luck or bring good luck. Some shared rituals like crossing your fingers, knocking on wood, or rubbing a rabbit foot trace back to the Middle Ages. Others are highly idiosyncratic, like the athlete who insists on wearing his lucky number. Religions are full of shared rituals. Catholic Christians cross themselves with holy water as they enter and leave a church building. Children kneel beside their beds, clasp their hands just so, and chant "Now I lay me down to sleep." Adherents of the prosperity gospel are told that filling offering baskets will make their remaining money multiply, and some report that it miraculously works.

Mind power—Seeking to control physical matter with thoughts or words alone. Does anyone you know wish friends luck, mutter over shaken dice, or send "thoughts and prayers" after a disaster? Some people readily admit a belief in telekinesis or telepathy; most of us live as if we

---

[11] Natalie Wolchover (2012, April 12). *Live Science: The Most Interesting Articles, Mysteries & Discoveries. Why Everyone Believes in Magic (Even You).* Retrieved October 12, 2018, from http://www.livescience.com/19665-belief-magic.html

did, at least a little. Word magic is big in Christianity. *In the beginning was the word*, says the book of Genesis, and throughout the Bible words affect the physical world, calling down fire and food from heaven, bringing healing, pregnancy, wealth and death. Disappointing research on prayer has done little to shake Christian belief in the power of words to invoke or channel supernatural power. The largest prayer study[12] to date spanned three years, six medical centers and thousands of prayers at a cost of 2.5 million dollars, only to find that heart attack patients who were prayed for did no better than control subjects. God, it would appear, operates at the margins of statistical significance if at all. But that hasn't stopped faith healers from earning millions by facilitating miraculous healings through chanting, shouting and praying.

Immortality—Denying or trying to avert the reality of death. Fantasy and science fiction allow us to play with the idea of immortality, but more seriously almost half of Americans believe in ghosts and far more believe in life after death. That includes almost a third[13] of people who say they are not religious or even spiritual. Among modern Christians, miracle stories often involve healing terminal illness or even—among less educated believers in places like rural Africa—resurrecting the dead. And, of course, the whole afterlife construct offers believers a get-out-of-death-free card.

Animism—Treating inanimate objects as if they had thoughts and powers and could be morally good or bad. We modern secular types may not think trees and rocks have spirits, but we still talk to objects around us. Who hasn't verbally coaxed an ailing houseplant or muttered, "Come on!" at a car that wouldn't start? Although the Bible writers rejected animism, they couldn't get away from it completely. Jesus, in the New Testament books of Matthew and Mark, curses a fig tree that

---

[12] Denise Gellene and Thomas H. Maugh II, (2006, March 31). Los Angeles Times. *Largest Study of Prayer to Date Finds It Has No Power to Heal*. Retrieved October 12, 2018, from http://articles.latimes.com/2006/mar/31/science/sci-prayer31

[13] (n.d.). Relationships in America. *Do people still believe in life after death? The Austin Institute for the Study of Family and Culture*. Retrieved October 12, 2018, from http://relationshipsinamerica.com/religion/do-people-still-believe-in-life-after-death

lacks fruit so that it withers and dies. In another story, he "rebukes" the wind and waves during a storm, and they "obey" him (Matthew 8:24–27 NIV).

Synchronicity—Perceiving meaning in coincidences and rare events. "In life, pure coincidences are statistically common, so a remarkable day is one where no coincidences occur at all," so tweeted physicist Neil deGrasse Tyson. But coincidence and the unexpected grab our attention and grip the imagination. When a rare event happens we often jump to concurrent events to explain the "miraculous." Religious believers often see coincidences as miraculous—even something as basic as "Just as I drove up, someone pulled out!" Underestimating the normalcy of "rare" events is such a common pattern that I will come back to address it at length in the next segment.

These types of magical thinking come so naturally that fantasy writers exploit them to create stories that our minds will accept. Like the writer of Genesis, Ursula Le Guin in her beloved Earthsea trilogy taps[14] our ready belief in the power of words: "No man, no power, can bind the action of wizardry or still the words of power. For they are the very words of Making, and one who could silence them could unmake the world." Patrick Rothfuss, in *The Name of the Wind*,[15] has one magician explain the magic of similarity: "The law of sympathy is one of the most basic parts of magic. It states that the more similar two objects are, the greater the sympathetic link. The greater the link, the more easily they influence each other." Many stories, needless to say, play with our yearning for immortality.

Besides providing the basis for satisfying fiction, magical thinking has other benefits according to Hutson.

Magical thinking provides a sense of control. The value of an illusory sense of control is that it reduces anxiety and increases a feeling of agency, which can spur you to seize real control. Second, magical thinking provides meaning. There's meaning as in

---
[14] Ursula Le Guin, *The farthest shore*, (New York: Pocket Books, 2004)
[15] Patrick Rothfuss, *The name of the wind*. London: Gollancz, 2017)

comprehension—understanding how things happen or how to do things—which allows for control. But there's also meaning as in a sense of purpose—grasping why things happen or why anything is worth doing. This is the stuff that gets you out of bed in the morning and lets you sleep at night…These habits of mind guide us through the world every day. In very basic ways they provide a sense of control, of purpose, of connection, and of meaning, and without them we couldn't function. (pp. 239-240)

Magic works its magic even when we know it's not real in part because of automatic processing and in part because our brains are remarkably good at getting us to suspend disbelief. Even when we watch or read fantasy, we mostly go along with the story, only occasionally being triggered by something that reminds us the whole thing is impossible. Unless we are actively erecting barriers against magical thinking—as when researchers apply the scientific method—magic wins.

HOW UNUSUAL EVENTS TRICK US INTO BELIEVING IN MIRACLES

"The really unusual day would be where nothing unusual happens."
– Persi Diaconis

One reason belief in miracles persists is that when it comes to big numbers we are really, really bad at math.[16]

Consider: The odds of your getting killed by lightning this year are around one in three million (slightly more if you are an avid mountain biker and slightly less if you spend most of your time playing video games). With over 500 million people in North America, about 150 will die this year from lightning strikes.

Around the world, as many as 24,000[17] people get killed by lightning each year and ten times that many get struck and injured, with even

---

[16] John Allen Paulos, *Innumeracy: Mathematical Illiteracy and Its Consequences*. (London: Penguin, 2014)
[17] Ronald L Holle, (2008, April 21). Vaisala - a global leader in environmental and industrial measurement. *Annual Rates of Lightning Fatalities by Country*. Retrieved October 12, 2018, from

more having close calls. There are over 7 billion people on planet earth. Over the course of a decade over 2 million of them will have been hit by lightning and millions more will have seen it happen. It is not hard to imagine that one unlucky victim said something about being hit by lightning before it happened. Nor is it hard to imagine that one of them took the name of the Lord in vain right before being struck down.

When you think seriously about the numbers the likelihood of *not* being able to find such a story on the internet might be more miraculous than finding one. After writing those words I opened my search engine and sure enough. The paradox is that such stories get written because we instinctively think them unlikely and, consequently, fascinating.

The internet abounds with lists of inexplicable coincidences. Here is a sampling:

Mark Twain was born on November 30, 1835, the first day that Halley's Comet appeared that year. He died when it reappeared in 1910. In 1909 he predicted his own death, saying, "I came in with Halley's Comet in 1835. It is coming again next year, and I expect to go out with it."

In 1898, 14 years before the sinking of the Titanic, novelist Morgan Robertson wrote a book called *Futility* about an unsinkable ship called the Titan. Just like the Titanic, it struck an iceberg and sank during the month of April.

Rosie Davies, who was given up for adoption wanted to meet her brother Chris but couldn't locate him. It turned out he was living across the street from her. They had known each other for months before discovering that they were siblings.

Stephen Hawking was born on the 300th anniversary of Galileo's death. He died on the anniversary of Einstein's birth.

---

http://www.vaisala.com/sites/default/files/documents/Annual_rates_of_lightning_fatalities_by_country.pdf

Senator John McCain died of a brain tumor on August 25. Nine years earlier, on August 25, Senator Ted Kennedy died from the same kind of cancer.

In 1930s Detroit a baby fell out of a window but was saved from harm by landing on the shoulders of a passerby, Joseph Figlock. A year later, the same baby fell out of the same window and landed on the same man.

In 2002, 70-year-old Finnish twin brothers died within hours of each other. The first was killed by a truck while riding his bicycle on Highway 8. The same is true for the second, who didn't yet know that is brother was dead.

Random? Probably, but our gut feeling tells us something more is going on. As I searched for examples to include in this list, several stories that I read gave me chills, and a faint eerie feeling lingered. Half of people say they get chills sometimes listening to music. Others find that looking at particular piece of art or landscape can trigger the same spontaneous response. Why is this reaction so involuntary and delectable?

Scientists suggest that emotional chills are related to the experience of expectations violated and satisfied. The mechanism appears to be a burst of dopamine, which can be intensified by anticipation and delay. For this reason, some people call emotional chills "skin orgasms," and as with sexual orgasms humans have refined techniques that aim to heighten the experience. Music may climb to a crescendo. The viral story genre called "glurge" exaggerates the heartwarming to the point of acuity. Poetry often builds up to a particularly powerful image or word.

Surprise appears to play a central role in triggering the rush and goosebumps. Some scholars believe that the dopamine rush is a "prediction error signal." That means it gets generated when we expect something to happen that doesn't or we don't expect something to happen that does. Correcting mistaken predictions is key to learning—so the theory goes—and learning is key to survival, so getting a prediction error signal may trigger a gush of pleasure.

If surprise is key when it comes to coincidences, better statistical reasoning might spoil some of the fun, because—as the lightning example illustrates—most surprising events aren't actually all that surprising. Consider the birthday paradox: With only 23 people in a room, the odds are 50-50 that two share a birthday. Like other statistical paradoxes, most of us find this counterintuitive.

If our intuitive sense of probabilities were better, would a tumor that disappears after prayer, or a hurricane that spares a statue of the Virgin Mary, or a bolt of lightning that strikes a van fleeing from a church robbery seem so improbable as to be deemed miraculous? Probably not.

In his book, *The Improbability Principle*,[18] statistician David Hand makes five key points about why coincidences seem incredible when they shouldn't.

Law of Truly Large Numbers—As lightning strikes illustrate, when the population of opportunities is large enough, virtually anything can happen. Somebody somewhere has just discovered a stash of gold. Another person has met their doppelganger. Another has been killed by their toaster.

Law of Selection—Out of all the bits of information coming at us, we selectively hone in on surprising coincidences. We are more likely to notice them, find them interesting, remember them, and tell others about them. (We don't talk about the woman who *didn't* find her long-lost brother living across the street.) And when we recount stories about eerie coincidences, we make them even more compelling by leaving out the parts that don't line up and emphasizing the parts that do.

Law of the Probability Lever—Two things may seem like they are unrelated or one caused the other, but if outside circumstances or prior events influenced both, the coincidence may not be so unlikely. If we hear that three siblings all died on the same day in three different cities, the coincidence strikes us. If we learn that they were triplets, aged 93,

---

[18] Hand, D. (2015). *The Improbability Principle*. Transworld.

who had just been to a family reunion where a relative gave them all influenza, it hits us in a different way.

Law of Near Enough—For the purpose of finding meaning in coincidences, we tend to treat things that are similar as if they were equivalent. It's cool to meet someone who shares our birthdate, but we get a little bit of the same surge if we learn a person was born on the day before or the day after. Prophecies are more likely to be fulfilled if there's a little wiggle room around their meaning.

Law of Inevitability—Something has to happen. Someone has to win the lottery. Lightning has to discharge somewhere. Albert Einstein had to have the same birthday as someone, because there aren't enough to go around.

Psychiatrists Stephanie Coleman and Bernard Beitman conducted research[19] examining how personality traits relate to the experience of meaningful coincidence. They found that people who self-describe as religious or spiritual report noticing coincidences more frequently.

People who believe in miracles often say that the events in question are so unlikely that the only possible explanation must be that something supernatural happened. Improbability serves as evidence that miraculous events—miraculous in the sense of surprising and wonderful—must be miracles—meaning cosmic wizardry of some sort.

They are wrong. Rationally, we should be incredulous about miracle stories for many reasons, but especially because of what we know about human nature. Human beings revise and adapt histories to support specific points of view. Stories evolve over time to fit tropes and scripts that are shaped by culture and biology. Scribes "correct" or omit awkward passages thinking they are simply clarifying the original intent. We all make stuff up, sometimes without even realizing what we are doing.

In evaluating the deity of Jesus, Anglican apologist C.S. Lewis looked at the gospel stories, assumed them accurate, and pronounced a

---

[19] Stephanie Coleman, MD; and Bernard D. Beitman, MD, (2009, April 24). Psychiatric Annals Online. *Characterizing High Frequency Coincidence Detectors*. Retrieved October 12, 2018, from http://coincider.com/wp-content/uploads/2014/10/PSYCH0509BeitmanColeman.pdf

famous trilemma often paraphrased as *Jesus must be liar, lunatic or lord.* His trilemma conveniently leaves out a fourth option: *legend*. Modern-day miracle stories are less subject to embellishment, but they aren't completely immune. People are still motivated to see what they want to see. And some people, as Lewis points out, are outright liars—religious leaders included.

But a more powerful fount of miracle-belief in the modern era is simply bad statistical reasoning. Christians make fewer and fewer claims for the impossible. (See the website, *Why Won't God Heal Amputees*.) But in the hazy realm of possibility and probability, believers continue to mistake probable for improbable, and improbable for miraculous, and miraculous for evidence of the biblical God.

PEOPLE LOVE MIRACLES. WHY NOT PLAY ALONG?

So why not live with the magic? Be a kid again and believe in the fantastical. Life is more fun with a little smoke and mirrors.
– L.H. Cosway, Six of Hearts

Superhero comics, Arthurian legends, fantasy, fairy tales, fables, folklore, science fiction, horror films, paranormal romance, ghost stories, trick-or-treating, haunted house tours, video games, cosplay, costume parties, themed amusement parks, illusionist stage shows…life is definitely more fun with a little smoke and mirrors.

Almost 80 percent of Americans, including young adults, believe in miracles; and if anything, this belief is on the increase as organized religion declines. In the Baylor Religion Survey of 2007,[20] over 70 percent of respondents said that God "often performs miracles which defy the laws of nature." Twenty-three percent said that they had witnessed a miraculous healing, and 16 percent said they had received one. Television

---

[20] Rodney Stark, *What Americans really believe*. (Waco, TX: Baylor Institute for Studies of Religion, 2008) percent Baylor University. 2007. *The Baylor Religion Survey, Wave II*.

talk shows like *Oprah* and dramas like *Touched by an Angel* seem to affirm that such occurrences are normal.

Doctor Eben Alexander has made a full-time career out of talking about the near-death experience described in his bestselling book, *Proof of Heaven*. He once made[21] a revealing comment about his mindset: "I'd always believed that when you're under the burden of a potentially fatal illness, softening the truth is fine. To prevent a terminal patient from trying to grab on to a little fantasy to help them deal with the possibility of death is like withholding painkilling medication."

We desperately want to believe that our lives have some transcendent meaning. We want to believe that every coincidence hints at some current of supernatural power rippling just beneath the surface of spacetime and that this power occasionally—miraculously—breaks through. In the words[22] of writer Cody Delistraty, "Longwinding, Dickensian stories of interconnected coincidences leading to a cathartic conclusion can provide us with a sense of meaning, of life holding subtler, unseen mysteries that make even our suffering worthwhile—as if our lives were really a series of sophisticated, interconnecting puzzle pieces."

Miracles are the proof that it's all real!

For many people this brings wonder into the world, and grounds for faith in every sense of the word. Brandon Sanderson expresses this beautifully in his novel, *Hero of the Ages*. "Why did they believe? Because they saw miracles. Things one man took as chance, a man of faith took as a sign. A loved one recovering from disease, a fortunate business deal, a chance meeting with a long-lost friend. It wasn't the grand doctrines or the sweeping ideals that seemed to make believers out of men. It was the simple magic in the world around them."[23]

---

[21] Mark Martin, (2012, November 26). Salon.com.*Dr. Eben Alexander's so-called afterlife*.Retrieved October 12, 2018, from http://www.salon.com/2012/11/26/dr_eben_alexanders_so_called_after_life/

[22] Cody Delistrati, (2018, July 10). Aeon. On *Coincidence. Retrieved* October 12, 2018, from http://aeon.co/essays/just-how-meaningful-is-coincidence-beyond-the-statistics

[23] Sanderson, B. (2008). *The hero of the ages: A Mistborn novel*. New York: Tor Book.

Besides which, magic is delightful. The power to do, effect, or create is a pleasure, and magic takes that pleasure to its logical extremes. We humans don't just seek pleasure, we play with it. We refine sugar into candy and ferment grain into hard liquor. We write orchestral music to delight parts of our brain that were designed to process the sounds of language. We paint pictures and pen poetry so poignant that they bring us to tears. We bungie jump and quiver deliciously at horror films. We have turned sexual arousal into an art form—from the crumbling pages of the Kama Sutra to the billions of bits that make up modern porn. The thrill of magic, including miracles, fits this pattern.

So why not simply go along with miracle stories? Why expose the man behind the curtain by talking about how magical thinking emerges from the structure of human information thinking and social dynamics?

Matthew Hutson, in explaining why he wrote *Seven Rules of Magical Thinking*, says it better than I can.

> I'm dissecting the sacred because the same magical thinking that leads to sentimentality, altruism, and self-efficacy can also lead to vilification, fatalism, irrational exuberance, or even depression, obsessive-compulsive disorder, and psychosis. By tearing down everything holy and pointing out the sand it was built on, I'm hoping we can learn how to build meaning back up in constructive ways. I don't want to eradicate magical thinking. I want to harness it.

One of the most fundamental things I learned in my years as a therapist is that understanding why you think, feel, and behave the way you do can be wonderfully freeing. It opens up choices. *Saber es poder.* Knowledge is power, and magical thinking plays such a huge part in our lives that understanding what's going on has the potential to be hugely powerful. Freed from the constraints imposed by dogma and tradition—freed from the assumption that magic comes from somewhere out there instead of somewhere in here—who knows where the human imagination may take us.

PART 2

PROPERLY INVESTIGATING THE MIRACLE OF BIBLICAL REVELATION

8| WHY THE ROMANS BELIEVED THE GOSPELS

By R. G. Price

One of the great magic tricks of the ancient world wasn't something that was performed in front of an audience, it was a trick performed by storytellers. The trick was writing stories about prophets who predicted things that had already occurred. This simple trick was actually extremely effective and had profound impacts on how people viewed the world—indeed on the course of civilization.

You see, this trick has a lot to do with why many Romans believed in the divinity of Jesus and adopted Christianity. A key reason that many Romans, especially Roman elites, adopted Christianity was because they believed that the Gospels were literally true reliable accounts. An important question that is raised about the Gospels is: Why would the Romans have believed the Gospels if they didn't contain at least some element of truth? Answering this question requires understanding Roman beliefs and the types of prophetic literature popular in the Roman empire.

Prophecy and oracles played important roles in Mediterranean cultures for centuries. Prophecy took many forms in these ancient cultures. The word prophecy comes down to us through Christian tradition. We use this word because this is the singular Greek word that Jews used to describe all acts of divine communication. The Greeks, however, had developed many fields and types of what we would call prophecy and had classified what we would simply call "prophets" into many different categories.

That some people had special gifts for divine communication was a given assumption in essentially all ancient Mediterranean cultures. But not all knowledge of the divine was thought to be inspired, some forms of divination could be learned with study, such as astrology and various other forms of sign reading. What's important to understand is that all of this was taken quite seriously. Prophets, or oracles, were viewed in these ancient cultures very similarly to how we view scientists and economists today. It was understood that these people were not always right, but they were nevertheless looked to as experts on predicting the future and understanding the designs and intentions of the gods.

There were several important legendary Greek and Roman prophets, though all of them were widely believed to have been real people. Orpheus is one of the oldest legendary prophets of the ancient Greeks. The mythology of Orpheus dates back to around the sixth century BCE. Orpheus was credited with various miracles and gifts to mankind, such as music and poetry. He was a heroic figure, similar to Hercules, credited with having traveled to the underworld. Greeks and Romans largely considered Orpheus to be a real historical figure. Orpheus is credited with writing many Orphic hymns, which were prophetic poems written in hexameter. Orphic hymns were widely believed to be genuine works of Orpheus, though Aristotle expressed doubts that they were authentic.[1] In *On the Nature of the Gods*, Cicero even states that Aristotle claimed Orpheus never existed at all, though such a position is not found in the extant works of Aristotle.[2]

We now know that many Orphic hymns continued to be written over time, with various works attributed to Orpheus having been written up through first century.

Two other important mythic prophets were Bakis and Sibyl. Both Bakis and Sibyl were described as real mortals, but there were in fact said

---

[1] Huxley, George. 1974. "Aristotle's Interest in Biography." *Duke University Library*. Accessed 2019. https://grbs.library.duke.edu/article/viewFile/8921/4637.
[2] Cicero. 1896. Book II – XXXVIII. *On the Nature of the Gods* translated by Francis Brooks. London: Methuen & Co.

to be many different incarnations of them throughout history and from many different cultures. Bakis was male and Sibyl was female. Works known as the Sibylline oracles gained significant prominence in Rome and were widely regarded as the premier works of prophecy. The earliest account of a Sibyl comes from a 5th century BCE fragment, which states, "the Sibyl, with frenzied mouth uttering things not to be laughed at, unadorned and unperfumed, yet reaching to a thousand years with her voice by aid of the god."[3]

In all there were said to be dozens of different Sybils from different places in different times. There was even a supposed Jewish Sybil. Various texts were produced over the centuries that claimed to be the records of Sibylline oracles. These works were deemed of great importance by the Romans, who collected them into the Sibylline Books. The books were entrusted to the care of an elite counsel of priests known as the *quindecimviri sacris faciundis*, under the order of the Roman Senate. The priests consulted the oracles at the behest of the Senate to offer direction on matters of policy and rule.

Unfortunately, the original Sibylline Books were destroyed in 83 BCE, when the temple they were stored in burned down. After the loss of the Sibylline Books, the Roman Senate sought to replace them with similar works. They sent scholars out to search for other writings deemed to be of a similar nature—thought to be genuine works of Sibyls. These works were then evaluated by the *quindecimviri* for authenticity. Ultimately, however, this new compilation was intentionally destroyed by the Christian general Flavius Stilicho during the reign of Theodosius I in the late 4th century.

A separate set of supposed Sibylline texts was composed by Jews and Christians starting in the first century known as the Sibylline Oracles. The Jewish historian Josephus mentioned one of these texts in his first

---

[3] Heraclitus. 5th century. Frag. 92. *The Fragments of Heraclitus*. Accessed 2019. http://www.heraclitusfragments.com/files/ge.html.

century work *Jewish Antiquities*.[4] The Sibylline Oracles were largely an attempt to convince pagans, who respected the Sibyls, of the virtues of their faiths by having Sibyls testify to the antiquity and authority of their religions. Indeed, when Josephus "quoted" from a Sibyl he did so in order to support the truth of the story of Babel, citing a passage from the Sibylline Oracles in which a Sibyl supposedly confirms the authenticity of the Jewish story. This is also an example of how these works, despite their dubious provenance, were treated as authoritative sources, even by supposed historians.

Yet, during the period leading up to the rise of Christianity, there was a widespread belief that the power of prophecy was in decline. This was true among Greeks, Romans and Jews. Literary prophecy played a key role in this perception. During this time there was strong admiration for the past. There was a belief that the gods no longer communicated with people as they used to. This was especially true among Jews but was true among Greeks and Romans as well. The reason for this view was that stories about ancient prophets clearly showed that ancient prophets had wonderous powers and were able to correctly predict major events with extreme accuracy. Compared to the prophets of the past, the prophets of the present were clearly inferior. This contributed to the view that people were falling out of favor of the gods.

The prophets of the past had a very special advantage however—the people writing their stories already knew their future. It seems almost unbelievable that people didn't understand that stories about ancient prophets had been contrived, yet it is very much the case that they did not. In fact, modern scholars still haven't been able to come to grips with how we should view ancient stories about prophecy and divine intervention. Were the writers simply recording popular legends, or were the writers themselves creating these narratives? Were these acts of intentional deception? What was the purpose behind many such stories? Why did so many people believe such stories, including highly educated

---

[4] Josephus and Winston. 94; 1737. *The Works of Flavius Josephus.* Accessed 2018. http://sacred-texts.com/jud/josephus/index.htm#aoj.

scholars? These are all questions that we still don't fully know how to answer and may never know. But nevertheless, it is clear that stories about prophets and divine intervention were widely believed and played a huge role in shaping public perceptions about how the world worked.

In *Prophets and Emperors*, David Potter notes that in ancient times prophecy was actually primarily about the framing and interpreting of the past.[5] As Potter states, this is because establishing that a prophet was credible required demonstrating that a prophet had been able to accurately predict the future. The best way to prove that a prophet had been able to accurately predict the future was for the prophet to "predict" things that everyone already knew had happened. Thus, most ancient prophetic stories follow a fairly standard formula. In ancient prophetic stories we typically find a prophet who: 1) predicts events that will happen within the story itself, 2) predicts events in the future relative to the time of the story, but which are in the past relative to the audience's present, and 3) prognosticates the ultimate fate of the world or delivers some message about what the gods ultimately want people to do (or something along those lines).

So essentially, the storyteller uses prophecy about the past as a means of establishing the credibility of the prophet, and thus assuring the reader that the prophet's ultimate message is true. We can know that these prophets were right and conveyed legitimate messages from the gods because we have proof that their other predictions had come true. Literary prophecy was also often highly political in nature. Prophecies about the past were often used to legitimize or delegitimize various political factions. Stories may portray the establishment of a ruling dynasty as being favored by the gods by showing that a ruler's reign had been foretold by a prophet, or they may cast rulers as illegitimate and prophecy their downfall, etc.

Some indication of the political significance of prophecy is indicated by the fact that toward the end of the first century BCE Augustus Caesar

---

[5] Potter, David. 1994. *Prophets and Emperors: Human and Divine Authority from Augustus to Theodosius.* pp. 2. Harvard University Press.

had over two thousand works of prophecy destroyed according to Suetonius.

> [H]e collected whatever prophetic writings of Greek or Latin origin were in circulation anonymously or under the names of authors of little repute, and burned more than two thousand of them, retaining only the Sibylline books and making a choice even among those; and he deposited them in two gilded cases under the pedestal of the Palatine Apollo.[6]

That Augustus would have gone to these lengths tells us something of the import of such works. The reason that Augustus would have bothered with this is because prophetic literature was very powerful politically. Anonymous works, in particular, were a way of influencing public perceptions at relatively little risk to the writer.

But where would such works have been rounded up from? The targets of Augustus' roundup wouldn't have been held in libraries, they would largely have been in the hands of private "oracle mongers," known as *chresmologi*.[7] *Chresmologi* were not prophets, but they played an important role in the dissemination of prophesies in the Greek and Roman world. *Chresmologi* were collectors and purveyors of prophetic literature, and in some cases produced their own writings that purported to convey the oracles of others.

In Rome at this time there was a substantial market for prophetic literature, much of it anonymously produced. The *chresmologi* were at the heart of this market. They would acquire prophetic works from various sources, make copies of them, and then sell such works to their clientele. Their clientele were often wealthy individuals who studied such works or had them studied by hired scholars. These stories sometimes made it into the public arena or were sometimes held for long periods in private libraries for purely personal use.

---

[6] Suetonius. (n.d.). *The Lives of the Twelve Caesars*. 120. Accessed 2018.
https://classics.mit.edu/Virgil/eclogue.4.iv.html.
[7] Potter, David. 1994. *Prophets and Emperors: Human and Divine Authority from Augustus to Theodosius*. Harvard University Press.

As Suetonius notes, some assessment was made as to the quality of these works, and those that were deemed of ill repute were destroyed, with the primary books that were retained being those of the famous Sibylline oracles. We'll get to the Sibylline oracles later, but first we must understand the process of evaluating the quality of prophetic literature.

The evaluation of prophetic legitimacy was carried out by individuals known as the *quindecimviri sacris faciundis*, "the fifteen men in charge of sacred rituals." The *quindecimviri* were a special group of Roman priests who were charged with the study and stewardship of prophetic literature, primarily the Sibylline oracles. The *quindecimviri* were regarded as authorities on the evaluation of prophets and prophecies to determine which prophecies were legitimate and which were false. The *quindecimviri sacris faciundis* were a special group of priests who held this role, but methods for evaluating the legitimacy of oracles were employed by a number of scholars and were somewhat uniform in the Roman world at this time.

So, what exactly were the methods used to determine the "authenticity" of oracles? They were surprisingly crude and unsophisticated. Indeed, when we look at examples of prophetic assessment, they seem almost juvenile in their credulity. Oracular texts were generally deemed to be "true" and "authentic" if they were of "high moral character," they contained oracles written in poetic verse, and the texts contained evidence of prophecies that were claimed to have come true. In addition, Greek was the favored language of prophetic stories and oracles, as opposed to Latin. Overall, the evaluation of literary oracles was highly subjective and naïve, as we will further explore.

What we do know about Augustus' efforts regarding prophetic literature, however, is that they were largely in vain. While Augustus may have sought some level of control over the role of prophecy during his reign, there is little evidence that he was successful. Indeed, prophetic literature flourished between the reign of Augustus and the rise of Christianity. So, let's now take a look at an example of prophetic literature that was popular in Hellenistic culture.

A classic example of prophetic literature comes to us from Phlegon of Tralles via a compilation he had assembled known as the *Book of Wonders,* which was composed in the second century. In this work Phlegon had compiled several older accounts of wonders that he considered to be "authentic" and true. Of particular note is the story of a Roman officer named Publius. I will provide a summary from David Potter:

> After receiving the Delphic oracle, the Romans were withdrawing toward Naupactus when an officer names Publius fell into a prophetic fit and predicted that the Romans would suffer disaster on their way home from the conquest of Asia. When asked to explain what this meant, Publius described, in reasonable detail, what would occur during the rest of the war with Antiochus. He also said that the returning army would be attacked by Thracians and lose some of its booty. He then fell into another prophetic fit and predicted, in verse, the destruction of Rome at the hands of an invading army; then, speaking in prose, that a large red wolf would come to devour him, thus proving that he had spoken the truth. The wolf duly arrived and ate Publius, leaving only the head, which once against burst into prophetic song, telling the Romans that Athena hated them, and that she would destroy Italy and drag its people off into slavery. The account ends with the statement that "hearing these words, they [the Romans] were deeply upset and established a temple and altar of Apollo Lyceus where the head had lain and got onto their ships and each one went to his own land. All these things that Publius predicted have come true."[8]

We can see in this account several tropes of prophetic literature. The "prophet" in this example predicts his own death, which then occurs within the story as a means of demonstrating the validity of the "predictions" made by the prophet. Several of the prophecies are delivered in verse, which was the expected format for oracles among Greeks and

---

[8] Potter, David. 1994. pp. 65-66.

Romans and was also common in Jewish literature as well. Some "predictions" were clearly written from a perspective long after they occurred. These were used to establish the validity of the later predictions of events in the actual future. Of this tale, classicist J. R. Morgan notes, "close analysis of the passage demonstrates that the whole thing is a farrago put together by a redactor during the Mithridatic War, adapting and combining narrative and prophetic material from several earlier contexts. From the perspective of 88 B.C. the piece is clear propaganda of resistance to Rome, using earlier oracles to demonstrate its own validity but also pointing to future defeats for the Romans which never in fact occurred."[9]

Phlegon also provides us with one of the very few remaining accounts of a supposed prophecy from the Sibylline Books. This is an account of a prophecy from an Erythraean Sibyl:

> But why indeed all-sorrowful do I sing divine oracles about other people's suffering, holding to my fated madness? Why do I taste its painful sting, retaining my grievous old age into the tenth century, raging in my heart and speaking things that are not believed, having foreseen in a vision all the unendurable griefs of mankind? Then, envious of my prophetic gift, the son of famous Leto, filling his destructive heart with passion, will loose my spirit, chained in its miserable body, when he will have shot through my frame with a flesh-piercing arrow. Then straightaway, my spirit, having flown through the air, sends to the ears of mortals audible omens mingled with the breeze [and] wrapped in complex riddles. My body will lie shamefully unburied on mother earth. No mortal will cover it with earth or hide it in a tomb. My black blood will trickle down through the broad pathways of the earth, dried by time. From there thick grass will shoot up, which, when the herds have grazed on it, will sink into their livers and show the purposes of

---

[9] Morgan, J. R. 1999. "Morgan, Review of Hansen." *Histos: The Online Journal of Ancient Historiography*. Accessed 2019. https://research.ncl.ac.uk/histos/documents/1998.RD02MorganReviewofHansen3027.pdf.

the immortal gods by prophecies; and birds in their feathered robes, if they taste my flesh, will give true prophecy to mortals.[10]

This account appears to be attested to by several other ancient writers, such as Plutarch and Lucian. Yet outside of this small fragment, we have little knowledge of what exactly the Sibylline Books contained.

Literary prophecy was not always direct either. In addition to accounts of explicit prophecies, it was a common practice in Hellenistic times to reinterpret older writings as hidden prophecies about recent or future events. It is likely that this was one of the major ways that the Sibylline works were used. According to this practice, diviners would scour works that were thought to contain prophetic material and look for passages that seemed to correspond to various known events. They would then identify these passages as having been hidden prophecies that confirmed the divine nature of various events, which could perhaps lead to other passages that may be able to predict the future.

This type of literary divination was also heavily used by the Jews who wrote many of the works found at Qumran, known as the Dead Sea Scrolls. A straight-forward example of this type of divination can be seen in 4Q177, a commentary on the "Last Days." In this text the writer is interpreting various passages from the Jewish scriptures as prophecies of future events:

> Fragments 12–13 Col 1: "Instruction [will not perish] from the [priest, or advice from the sage, or oracles] from the prophet" (Jeremiah 18:18).
>
> [This refers to] the Last Days, of which David said, "O LORD, do not [rebuke me] in Your anger. [Have mercy on me, for] I am fading. [Heal me, O LORD, for my innermost being is tormented.] Yes, my soul is in great torment. But now, O LORD, how long? Have mercy, deliver [my] soul [...]" (Psalm 6:1–4)

---

[10] Jacoby, Felix. 1959. Book II (257 fr. 37). *Die Fragmente der griechischen Historiker*. Brill.

[This refers to] the Last Days, about [the righteous, when] Belial [planned] to destroy them in his fury, so that none would remain of [...God will not allow] Belial [...]

Fragments 5–6: ["To the master singer,] to David. In the LORD [I have taken refuge, so how can You say to me, Flee] [to your mountain, little bird, for now the wicked are bending their bow,] and fitting arrows to [the string to shoot in the night at the honest in mind"] (Psalm 11:1–2)

[This means that] the men of [the *Yahad*] shall flee[...] [...like] a bird from its place and be exiled [from their land...they are written about] in the book of the [prophet Micah: "Rise and go, this is not the right place to stay, impurity has marred it, it is completely ruined.] It belongs to the one who walks [in lies and tells untruths..."] (Micah 2:10–11)[11]

There are abundant examples of this type from the Qurman writings, which show how older writings were being reinterpreted in new contexts. Robert J. Miller explores this issue in great detail in his 2015 book, *Helping Jesus Fulfill Prophecy*. We know that the Romans did this as well. Indeed, the emperor Constantine fancied himself a scholar of this type of literary divination. Constantine purportedly claimed that Virgil's *Fourth Eclogue* contained a prophecy that predicted the coming of Jesus.

> Now the last age by Cumae's Sibyl sung
> Has come and gone, and the majestic roll
> Of circling centuries begins anew:
> Justice returns, returns old Saturn's reign,
> With a new breed of men sent down from heaven.
> Only do thou, at the boy's birth in whom

---

[11] Wise, Michale, Marthin Abegg Jr., and Edward Cook. 1996. *The Dead Sea Scrolls A New Translation*. pp. 264-265. New York: Harper One.

The iron shall cease, the golden race arise,
Befriend him, chaste Lucina;[12]

Starting in the second century Christian apologists made frequent appeals to the Sibylline Oracles as further confirmation of Jesus' divinity. A classic example of this comes from the church father Eusebius. Writing in the fourth century Eusebius appealed to multiple supposed Sibylline prophecies, such as the following example:

> My desire, however, is to derive even from foreign sources a testimony to the Divine nature of Christ. For on such testimony it is evident that even those who blaspheme his name must acknowledge that he is God, and the Son of God if indeed they will accredit the words of those whose sentiments coincided with their own. The Erythræan Sibyl, then, who herself assures us that she lived in the sixth generation after the flood, was a priestess of Apollo, who wore the sacred fillet in imitation of the God she served, who guarded also the tripod encompassed with the serpent's folds, and returned prophetic answers to those who approached her shrine; having been devoted by the folly of her parents to this service, a service productive of nothing good or noble, but only of indecent fury, such as we find recorded in the case of Daphne. On one occasion, however, having rushed into the sanctuary of her vain superstition, she became really filled with inspiration from above, and declared in prophetic verses the future purposes of God; plainly indicating the advent of Jesus by the initial letters of these verses, forming an acrostic in these words: Jesus Christ, Son of God, Saviour, Cross.[13]

Eusebius went on to provide the text of the supposed prophecy. As you can see Eusebius took pains to both try and discredit the Sibyl, and also claim that she confirmed the divinity of Jesus. Following this

---

[12] Virgil. 37 BCE. "The Eclogues." *Internet Classics Archive*. Accessed 2019. http://classics.mit.edu/Virgil/eclogue.4.iv.html.
[13] Eusebius, translated by Ernest Cushing Richardson. 1890. *Oration of Constantine via Nicene and Post-Nicene Fathers*, Second Series, Vol. 1. Buffalo, NY: Christian Literature Publishing Co.

Eusebius went on to defend against the charge that the prophecy had been forged by Christians by noting that other pagan writers had cited the prophecy previously.

With all this we have some idea about the role of prophecy in Hellenistic life and how prophetic stories were interpreted by Romans. We know that Romans believed strongly in the power of prophecy, but they were also concerned with how to determine "real" prophecies from false. One of the key methods for evaluating prophets and prophecies was determining if a source of prophecy could be demonstrated to have correctly predicted future events. Yet, Jewish, Greek and Roman scholars alike all naively accepted written accounts of prophecy at face value, often believing that accounts of prophets were actually much older than they really were. For them the question was not whether these things really happened, it was whether or not the accounts contained "truth"—as in ideas that "rang true" or as in predictions that came to pass. But the whole concept of going out into the field and confirming whether any of these things really happened is just not something that the Romans engaged in. For them, confirmation of these types of prophetic accounts was to be found within the literature itself.

We now come to the Gospels themselves. The way that the Gospels were written led many Roman scholars to view them as among the most credible accounts of the strongest examples of prophecy ever seen. Justin Martyr, writing in the second century, is one our earliest examples of Roman assessment of the prophetic nature of the Gospels. Other prime examples come from Eusebius and Lactantius writing in the fourth century. Roman scholars were impressed by the fact that not only did the Gospels contain a multitude of "confirmed" prophecies, but that these prophecies were attested to in what they believed to be four separate, independently written, eyewitness accounts that corroborated each other.

So, what exactly are these prophecies that the Romans were so impressed by? There are basically four types of "prophecies" cited in the Gospels. There are cases where Jesus makes predictions that come true within the story, prime examples of which are Jesus' prediction of his own death as well as his prediction that Peter will betray him. There are cases where a scripture is explicitly cited, and it is claimed that an event in the story fulfills this prophetic scripture. There are scenes in which the events of the scene exactly parallel passages from the Jewish scriptures. And finally, there is Jesus' prophecy of the destruction of the Temple, which occurred in 70 CE during the First Jewish–Roman War.

All of these examples of prophecy fulfillment led various Roman scholars to conclude that, indeed, Jesus was an extremely significant individual. Add to that the fact that they had not just one account of these events, but at least four "distinct" accounts, all written by different people, all of which corroborated the same basic events and examples of prophecy fulfillment.

Of these examples of prophecy fulfillment, perhaps the most interesting are the cases where events from the story perfectly align with passages from the Jewish scriptures. These were particularly impressive to Roman scholars because they appeared mysterious and because they seemed like cases where perhaps the writers themselves didn't even realize that they were recording the fulfillment of prophecy. The classic example of this is the Crucifixion scene, which is based primarily on Psalm 22, as well as various other scriptures.

To understand the Crucifixion scene, we first have to understand a few things about how the Gospels were written. The first Gospel that was written is what we now call the Gospel of Mark, which was likely written shortly after the First Jewish–Roman War. Virtually every scene in the Gospel of Mark is based on literary references to the Jewish scriptures. Each of the other three Gospel writers copied from the Gospel of Mark in some fashion, and in so doing they also copied many of the literary references that are found in the Gospel of Mark, though they are often less clear than they are in Mark due to minor rewording.

So, let's look at the Crucifixion scene to get a basic understanding of these types of scriptural references.

Mark 15:
And they offered him wine mixed with myrrh; but he did not take it. And they crucified him, and **divided his clothes among them, casting lots to decide what each should take.**
It was nine o'clock in the morning when they crucified him. The inscription of the charge against him read, 'The King of the Jews.' And with him they crucified two bandits, one on his right and one on his left. **Those who passed by mocked him, shaking their heads** and saying, 'Aha! You who would destroy the temple and build it in three days, save yourself, and come down from the cross!' **In the same way the chief priests, along with the scribes, were also mocking him** among themselves and saying, 'He saved others; he cannot save himself. Let the Messiah, the King of Israel, come down from the cross now, so that we may see and believe.' **Those who were crucified with him also taunted him.**
When it was noon, darkness came over the whole land until three in the afternoon. At three o'clock **Jesus cried out with a loud voice, 'Eloi, Eloi, lama sabachthani?' which means, 'My God, my God, why have you forsaken me?'** When some of the bystanders heard it, they said, 'Listen, he is calling for Elijah.' And someone ran, filled a sponge with sour wine, put it on a stick, and gave it to him to drink, saying, 'Wait, let us see whether Elijah will come to take him down.' Then Jesus gave a loud cry and breathed his last. And the curtain of the temple was torn in two, from top to bottom. Now when the centurion, who stood facing him, saw that in this way he breathed his last, he said, 'Truly this man was the son of God!'[14]

This, as we can see, pulls heavily from Psalm 22, referencing lines from Psalm 22 in reverse order.

Psalm 22:
My God, my God, why have you forsaken me? Why are you so

---

[14] Society of Biblical Literature. 2006. *Harper Collins Study Bible*, (New Revised Standard Version). San Francisco: HarperCollins.

far from helping me, from the words of my groaning?
O my God, I cry by day, but you do not answer; and by night, but find no rest.

...

But I am a worm, and not human; scorned by others, and despised by the people.
All who see me mock at me; they make mouths at me, they shake their heads;
'Commit your cause to the Lord; let him deliver—let him rescue the one in whom he delights!'

...

I can count all my bones. They stare and gloat over me; **they divide my clothes among themselves, and for my clothing they cast lots.**[15]

This is just one example of the types of literary references used in the Gospel of Mark. The vast majority of scriptural refences like this in the Gospel of Mark are to passages from the Jewish prophets, such as Isaiah, Hosea, Malachi, Daniel, etc., or they are to Psalms like this example. The Psalms were believed to be prophetic because they were written in verse and were believed to have been authored by king David. In my book *Deciphering the Gospels Proves Jesus Never Existed* (2018), I analyze the scriptural references used in the Gospel of Mark in detail and explore the implications of those references.

The details about mocking and casting lots for clothing are contained in all three of the other canonical Gospels as well, and indeed even in non-canonical accounts of the Crucifixion. In the Gospel of John, the writer called out scriptural references explicitly, for example:

So they said to one another, "Let us not tear it, but cast lots for it to see who will get it." *This was to fulfill what the scripture says,*

---

[15] Society of Biblical Literature, 2006.

"They divided my clothes among themselves, and for my clothing they cast lots."[16] [Emphasis mine.]

The Gospels are literally filled with hundreds of parallels to the Jewish scriptures like this. Not all of these parallels were recognized by early Christian scholars, indeed new parallels are still being discovered. But early Roman scholars did recognize many of these parallels, and they saw in these parallels overwhelming evidence that the events of Jesus' life and death had been foretold by the Jewish scriptures in ways that surpassed any prior examples of prophecy they had ever seen.

In his second century work *First Apology*, Justin Martyr provided an extensive evaluation of the supposed prophetic evidence found within the Gospels. Martyr discussed many different "modes" of prophecy for which there is evidence in the Gospels and provided examples of various prophetic passages. Parallels between the Crucifixion scene and Psalm 22 were among his key proofs. Martyr also noted the relationship between the Gospels, the Jewish scriptures and the First Jewish–Roman War: "That the land of the Jews, then, was to be laid waste, hear what was said by the Spirit of prophecy."[17]

Martyr concluded his assessment of the "prophetic evidence" for Jesus with the following:

CHAPTER 52 – Certain fulfilment of prophecy
Since, then, we prove that all things which have already happened had been predicted by the prophets before they came to pass, we must necessarily believe also that those things which are in like manner predicted, but are yet to come to pass, shall certainly happen. For as the things which have already taken place came to pass when foretold, and even though unknown, so shall the things that remain, even though they be unknown and disbelieved, yet come to pass. For the prophets have proclaimed two advents of His: the one, that

---

[16] Society of Biblical Literature, 2006. John 19:24.
[17] Martyr, Justin, and Reith translated by Marcus. 2nd century translated 1885. *First Apology from Ante-Nicene Fathers*, Vol. 1. Christian Literature Publishing Co. Accessed 2018. http://www.newadvent.org/fathers/0126.htm.

which is already past, when He came as a dishonoured and suffering Man; but the second, when, according to prophecy, He shall come from heaven with glory, accompanied by His angelic host, when also He shall raise the bodies of all men who have lived, and shall clothe those of the worthy with immortality, and shall send those of the wicked, endued with eternal sensibility, into everlasting fire with the wicked devils. And that these things also have been foretold as yet to be, we will prove.

...

CHAPTER 53 – Summary of the prophecies
Though we could bring forward many other prophecies, we forbear, judging these sufficient for the persuasion of those who have ears to hear and understand; and considering also that those persons are able to see that *we do not make mere assertions without being able to produce proof, like those fables that are told of the so-called sons of Jupiter. For with what reason should we believe of a crucified man that He is the first-born of the unbegotten God, and Himself will pass judgment on the whole human race, unless we had found testimonies concerning Him published before He came and was born as man, and unless we saw that things had happened accordingly...* So many things therefore, as these, when they are seen with the eye, are enough to produce conviction and belief in those who embrace the truth, and are not bigoted in their opinions, nor are governed by their passions.[18] (emphasis mine)

It is apparent from Martyr's work that the prophecies, and the abundant literary parallels between the Gospels and the Jewish scriptures, played a key role in convincing Martyr (and other early Roman scholars) of the "truth" of the Gospel accounts and the divinity of Jesus.

But perhaps the most important Roman scholar to address this topic was Lactantius, because Lactantius was a close advisor to the emperor Constantine. It was likely Lactantius who convinced Constantine of the

---

[18] Martyr, Justin, and Reith translated by Marcus, 1885.

merits of Christianity, leading Constantine to embrace the religion—setting in motion events that would lead to adoption of Christianity as the exclusive religion of the Roman empire.

Around the turn of the fourth century Lactantius produced a seminal treatise in defense of Christianity called *Institutiones Divinae*, or The Divine Institutes. The Divine Institutes covers many topics—among them, the antiquity and authenticity of the Jewish scriptures, the folly of pagan religion, prophecies for Jesus among the Sibyls, and of course the "evidence" from the Gospels which "proved" that the events of Jesus had been foretold by ancient Jewish prophecies.

CHAPTER 46 – It is Proved from the Prophets that the Passion and Death of Christ Had Been Foretold
And the prophets had predicted that all these things would thus come to pass. Isaiah thus speaks: (Isaiah 50:5) I am not rebellious, nor do I oppose: I gave my back to the scourge, and my cheeks to the hand: I turned not away my face from the foulness of spitting. The same prophet says respecting His silence: (Isaiah 53:7) I was brought as a sheep to the slaughter, and as a lamb before its shearers is dumb, so He opened not His mouth. *David also, in the xxxivth Psalm: The abjects were gathered together against me, and they knew me not: they were scattered, yet felt no remorse: they tempted me, and gnashed upon me with their teeth. The same also says respecting food and drink in the lxviiith Psalm: They gave me also gall for my meat, and in my thirst they gave me vinegar to drink. Also respecting the cross of Christ: And they pierced my hands and my feet, they numbered all my bones: they themselves have looked and stared upon me; they parted my garments among them, and cast lots upon my vesture.* Moses also says in Deuteronomy: (Deuteronomy 28:66) And your life shall hang in doubt before your eyes, and you shall fear day and night, and shall have none assurance of your life. Also in Numbers: (Numbers 23:19) God is not in doubt as a man, nor does He suffer threats as the son of man. Also Zechariah says: (Zechariah 12:10) And they shall look on me whom they

pierced. *Amos (Amos 8:9–10) thus speaks of the obscuring of the sun: In that day, says the Lord, the sun shall go down at noon, and the clear day shall be dark*; and I will turn your feasts into mourning, and your songs into lamentation. Jeremiah (Jeremiah 15:9) also speaks of the city of Jerusalem, in which He suffered: Her sun is gone down while it was yet day; she has been confounded and reviled, and the residue of them will I deliver to the sword. *Nor were these things spoken in vain. For after a short time the Emperor Vespasian subdued the Jews, and laid waste their lands with the sword and fire, besieged and reduced them by famine, overthrew Jerusalem, led the captives in triumph, and prohibited the others who were left from ever returning to their native land. And these things were done by God on account of that crucifixion of Christ, as He before declared this to Solomon in their Scriptures,* saying, (1 Kings 9:7–9) And Israel shall be for perdition and a reproach to the people, and this house shall be desolate; and every one that shall pass by shall be astonished, and shall say, Why has God done these evils to this land, and to this house? And they shall say, Because they forsook the Lord their God, and persecuted their King, who was dearly beloved by God, and crucified Him with great degradation, therefore has God brought upon them these evils. For what would they not deserve who put to death their Lord, who had come for their salvation?[19] [Emphasis mine.]

    From this passage we again see examples of how the relationships between the Gospel narratives and the Jewish scriptures were interpreted. Lactantius points out many examples where the Gospel accounts align perfectly with passages from the Jewish scriptures—the example of Psalm 22 and the Crucifixion among them. These examples are pointed to as proof that the events of Jesus' life and death had been foretold by ancient Jewish prophets.

---

[19] Lactantius and William translated by Fletcher, 4th century translated 1886. *Divine Institutes from Ante-Nicene Fathers*, Vol. 7. Christian Literature Publishing Co. Accessed 2018. http://www.newadvent.org/fathers/0702.htm.

Beyond that Lactantius claimed, as many Christian scholars did, that the Gospel accounts foretold the destruction that befell the Jews during the First Jewish–Roman War. What I show in *Deciphering the Gospels*, however, is that the first Gospel was written as a commentary on the war after it had taken place. The other Gospels all copy the basic narrative from the first, making this a feature of all the Gospels. That the account of Jesus' Crucifixion at the demand of the Jews legitimized the Roman conquest of Jerusalem certainly appealed to Roman scholars and elites.

What is important to understand is that the Gospels really were the one and only source of information that anyone ever had about the life of Jesus. The earliest accounts that we have of real known people discussing the life of Jesus come from the mid-second century, and all of those accounts rely entirely on the Gospels. It is clear from the works of early Christian scholars that they had no information about Jesus the man from any sources other than the Gospels.

When Christian scholars began debating the doctrines of Christianity in the second century, there were many sects who claimed that Jesus was not a man, rather he was purely spiritual, or that he came to earth only in an immaterial form and never "took the form of flesh"—never became incarnate. Those who believed that Jesus had in fact been born and "become flesh" relied entirely on the Gospels and interpretations of the Jewish scriptures to support their position. No real evidence was ever put forward. Justin Martyr even records a dialog with a Greek philosopher named Trypho in which Trypho proposed that Jesus never existed at all. Martyr's rebuttal relied entirely on appeals to scripture and prophecies.

> But Christ—if He has indeed been born, and exists anywhere—is unknown, and does not even know Himself, and has no power until Elias [Elijah] come to anoint Him, and make Him manifest to all. And you, *having accepted a groundless report, invent a Christ for yourselves*, and for his sake are inconsiderately perishing."

"I excuse and forgive you, my friend," I said. "For you know not what you say, but have been persuaded by teachers who do not understand the Scriptures; and you speak, like a diviner whatever comes into your mind. But if you are willing to listen to an account of Him, how we have not been deceived, and shall not cease to confess Him,—although men's reproaches be heaped upon us, although the most terrible tyrant compel us to deny Him,—*I shall prove to you as you stand here that we have not believed empty fables*, or words without any foundation but words filled with the Spirit of God, and big with power, and flourishing with grace."[20]

Martyr then goes on to recount tale after tale of prophecy, citing scriptures and Gospels.

Again and again in the works of the early Christian apologists we find nothing but appeals to the Gospel accounts. Writing in the second century Irenaeus recounted several claims of various Christian sects who believed that Jesus was either purely human and not divine at all or that Jesus was purely divine and not human at all.

> *But, according to these men, neither was the Word made flesh, nor Christ, nor the Savior, who was produced from [the joint contributions of] all [the Æons].* For they will have it, that the Word and Christ never came into this world; that the Savior, too, never became incarnate, nor suffered, but that He descended like a dove upon the dispensational Jesus; and that, as soon as He had declared the unknown Father, He did again ascend into the Pleroma. Some, however, make the assertion, that this dispensational Jesus did become incarnate, and suffered, whom they represent as having passed through Mary just as water through a tube; but others allege him to be the Son of the Demiurge, upon whom the dispensational Jesus descended; while others, again, say that Jesus was born from Joseph and Mary, and that the Christ from above

---

[20] Martyr, Justin. 2nd century. "ST. JUSTIN MARTYR DIALOGUE WITH TRYPHO." *Early Christian Writings.* Accessed 2019.
http://www.earlychristianwritings.com/text/justinmartyr-dialoguetrypho.html.

descended upon him, being without flesh, and impassible. But according to the opinion of no one of the heretics was the Word of God made flesh. For if anyone carefully examines the systems of them all, he will find that the Word of God is brought in by all of them as not having become incarnate (sine carne) and impassible, as is also the Christ from above. Others consider Him to have been manifested as a transfigured man; but they maintain Him to have been neither born nor to have become incarnate; while others [hold] that He did not assume a human form at all, but that, as a dove, He did descend upon that Jesus who was born from Mary. *Therefore the Lord's disciple, pointing them all out as false witnesses, says, "And the Word was made flesh, and dwelt among us."*[21]

To refute the claim that Jesus had never become incarnate did Irenaeus point to clear evidence of his life on earth? No; he appealed to the Gospel of John's theological opening.

It is clear that the Gospels really were the only source of information about Jesus that Greek and Roman scholars had and they believed that the Gospels were all they needed. The Gospels were four writings that were just different enough that it appeared they were independent works, and they were just similar enough that they appeared to corroborate each other. The Gospels employed many of the prophetic tropes that were widely believed in other forms of prophetic literature. The many layers of prophecy within the stories were seen as confirmation of the "truth" of the accounts and the claims of divinity. The scenes based on scriptural references appeared to be wonderous hidden messages of divine prophetic confirmation. Yet, of course, none of these so-called "prophecies" were real, they were all just literary fabrications.

So while many people would like to think that the Romans wouldn't have believed the Gospel stories if there weren't at least some element of truth to them, the reality is that the people of this time and culture, while sophisticated in many ways, were not discerning investigators of

---

[21] Irenaeus, Alexander Roberts and William Rambaut. 1885. *Ante-Nicene Fathers*, Vol. 1. Christian Literature Publishing Co. Accessed 2018. http://www.newadvent.org/fathers/0103.htm.

empirical truth. Centuries of ancient literature show us both that many writings misrepresented reality and that these misrepresentations were widely believed and fundamentally shaped people's understandings of the world.

Over the past few centuries scholars have become increasingly critical of many ancient errors of understanding. The concept of prophecy and stories of supernatural phenomena have largely fallen into disrepute among modern scholars, as topics not worthy of study because they are just ancient misconceptions. This is particularly true of biblical scholars, who, over the last two centuries, have looked on prophecy and miracles with increasing embarrassment and sought to discover the "reality" behind the Gospel accounts. Many scholars have looked for the "real reasons" that Christianity rose to power, understanding that the prophecies weren't real. But the truth is that prophecy is at the heart of the rise of Christianity. The perception that a multitude of prophecies had been confirmed to have so accurately predicted the life and death of Jesus was central to the rise and adoption of Christianity, and the Gospel writings were the primary drivers of that perception.

9| HOW NEW TESTAMENT WRITERS HELPED JESUS FULFILL PROPHECY[1]

By Robert J. Miller

The belief that Jesus fulfilled prophecy is one of the earliest beliefs of his followers. This belief was crucial to them because it enabled them to relate what was new (Jesus) to what was old (the scriptures of Israel). Making that connection was essential in a time and culture that regarded old sacred writings with reverence and anything new in religion with suspicion. The belief in the fulfillment of prophecy was thus an important way for the earliest Christians to assure themselves of their religious legitimacy. The early followers of Jesus thus cultivated an identity as the new people of God, the heirs of God's promises to Israel. The New Testament attests to an impressive accumulation of prophecies from the Jewish scriptures that Christians believed were fulfilled by Jesus. Christian intellectuals from the second century onward used those numerous examples, and many more of their own, to construct an apologetic argument in which these fulfillments were construed as proof of the divine origin of their new religion. Everyone knew of stories about non-Christian figures who had fulfilled prophecies that had originated outside the Jewish tradition, but Christian apologists argued that Jesus fulfilled the prophecies of the Old Testament in such numbers and with such specificity that they amounted to a *miracle* and thus were evidence

---

[1] This essay is excerpted and adapted from Robert J. Miller, Helping Jesus Fulfill Prophecy (Wipf & Stock, 2016). Used with permission.

of the unique truth of Christianity. This "argument from prophecy," developed in minute detail and at great length by early Christian theologians,[2] still exists today among Christians seeking proof of the truth of their version of Christianity. This mentality is on ample display on the Internet. Just type "300 prophecies" (a popular meme among Christian apologists) into your search engine and you will find a plethora of sites arguing that the odds against Jesus fulfilling all three hundred prophecies are astronomical,[3] i.e., it is a miracle. This essay argues that this miracle appears to be such only because of the creativity of some early Christian writers who developed a set of ingenious interpretations that transformed often cryptic scriptural prophecies into (what they believed were) recognizable predictions about Jesus and their church.

Numerous passages in the New Testament (NT) quote a prophecy from the Old Testament (OT) and then explain how that prediction was fulfilled in the life of Jesus, a format that makes it seem obvious that Jesus fulfilled many prophecies about the coming Messiah. However, some rudimentary critical study shows that the situation is more complicated than the NT writers make it seem. All you have to do is compare the NT quotations of the prophecies to their originals in the OT to see the problems. For example:

- the connection between a prophecy and its alleged fulfillment is often less than clear, and sometimes seems farfetched;
- the quotation of a prophecy by the Christian author does not always match the wording of the prophecy as it appears in the OT;
- even in cases in which the quotation is accurate, the meaning of a prophecy in its OT context is seldom the same as, and usually very different from, the meaning it acquires in its new Christian context.

---

[2] See *Helping Jesus Fulfill Prophecy*, 227–319.
[3] See *Helping Jesus Fulfill Prophecy*, 1–3 and 347–50.

Awareness of these complications draws our attention to how Christian writers "helped" Jesus fulfill prophecy,[4] which they did in two basic ways: (1) by the sometimes subtle, sometimes blatant, manipulation of the OT scriptures so that they could correspond to their fulfillments presented in the stories about Jesus, and (2) by the sometimes subtle, sometimes blatant, manipulation of stories about Jesus to fit the predictions from the OT. (The brevity of this chapter does not allow an analysis of the second process, but it is thoroughly discussed in my book.)

Scrutinizing how Christian texts present the fulfillment of prophecy also suggests an explanation of *how* Christians identified the numerous scriptural passages that they claim were fulfilled by Jesus. The evidence indicates that the process of pairing prophecies to events in the life of Jesus, was, in most cases, a *retrospective* process. That is, Christians worked backwards from events in the story of Jesus to the prophecies those events were believed to fulfill. It is *not* the case that there was a more-or-less standard list of prophecies that the messiah was supposed to fulfill, that Jesus came along and fulfilled them, and that his followers came to believe that Jesus was the messiah because he had fulfilled those prophecies. Rather, the process usually worked the other way around: Jesus' followers, believing that he was the messiah, used the story of his life to guide their search for the prophecies he had, in their view, fulfilled.

HOW NEW TESTAMENT WRITERS HELP JESUS FULFILL PROPHECY

Within the limits of this chapter, I will analyze four of the particular ways NT writers helped Jesus fulfill prophecy: (1) connecting prophecies to events that do not fulfill them in any obvious way, (2) quoting prophecies out of context, (3) fabricating prophecies, and (4) rewriting (retrofitting) prophecies so that Jesus can fulfill them. Although these

---

[4] During a recent visit to a school of theology, an earnest seminary student who had seen the title of my book eagerly asked me how Christians today could help Jesus fulfill prophecy. I felt like the Grinch at Christmas as I witnessed his confused disappointment when I explained what the book is really about.

techniques and the limited sample of examples analyzed in this essay are only part of the story of how Christian writers helped Jesus fulfill prophecy, they furnish more than enough evidence to demonstrate that the "miracle" of fulfilled prophecy is an artifact of the ingenuity of Christian writers.

AWKWARD PAIRINGS OF PROPHECY AND FULFILLMENT

Matthew's gospel is by far the one most interested in the fulfillment of prophecy, and so most of my examples are drawn from that gospel, which has sixteen scenes in which Matthew interrupts the narrative in order to quote prophecy and point out that it was fulfilled in that scene. Eight of these fulfillments are based on details in stories that circulated prior to Matthew's gospel but for which there is no evidence that anyone other than Matthew noticed that those details fulfilled prophecy.[5]

It is worthwhile asking *why* others had not noticed that prophecies were fulfilled in any of those eight scenes. After all, Matthew's intense interest in the fulfillment of prophecies gives the impression that pointing them out was a primary task of someone telling the story of Jesus' life. Once the New Testament became a fixture in Christianity, Matthew's position as the favored gospel set the tone for what readers expect in all the gospels, all the more so because Matthew loads five fulfillment scenes into his first two chapters. The opening pages of the New Testament are thus dense with prophecy. Christians who learn the life of Jesus starting with Matthew can easily get the impression that Jesus fulfilled so many prophecies that his fulfillments must have been obvious not only to his disciples, but to anyone who knew the scriptures, especially to the Jewish religious authorities.

Contrary to such an impression, however, Matthew was the only evangelist to notice that prophecies were fulfilled in those eight scenes.

---

[5] Five of those cases are discussed immediately below. The other three details about Jesus that Matthew alone sees as fulfillments are his birth in Bethlehem (2:6), his residence in Nazareth (2:23), and his use of parables (13:10–15).

Apparently, those fulfillments were not as obvious as Matthew makes them seem to be. Why not? In five of those cases the most likely reason why no one other than Matthew identified them as prophecy fulfillments is that the prophecies Matthew quotes have no clear connection to the stories that allegedly fulfill them.

1) **Matt 1:23 (Isa 7:14).** We should not be puzzled that no one besides Matthew would think that Jesus fulfilled a prophecy that a virgin[6] would give birth to a boy named Emmanuel. Not only was Emmanuel not Jesus' name, we have insufficient evidence prior to Luke's gospel that any Christians believed in the virgin birth.[7]

2) **Matt 4:13–16 (Isa 9:1).** Who could have possibly recognized that Jesus' move to Capernaum had fulfilled a prophecy that people who lived all over northern Palestine had seen a great light?

3) **Matt 8:17 (Isa 53:4).** It was surely not obvious that Jesus' healing the sick and casting out demons meant that he was the one who "took our infirmities and bore our diseases."

4) **Matt 12:15–21 (Isa 42:1–4).** It is counter-intuitive, to say the least, that when Jesus ordered those he healed not to tell others about him that he thereby fulfilled the prophecy about God's servant who "will not wrangle or cry aloud, nor will anyone hear his voice in the streets," especially since Jesus often taught and argued with opponents in public, presumably in a loud voice.

5) **Matt 13:35 (Ps 78:2).** When, in order to reveal hidden truths, Jesus speaks to the crowds *only* in parables,[8] it is puzzling how

---

[6] I am convinced that Matthew does not believe in the virgin birth (see Robert J. Miller, "Did Matthew Believe in the Virgin Birth?" *The Fourth R* 21-6 [Nov-Dec, 2008]: 3-8, 26, or *Born Divine: The Births of Jesus and Other Sons of God* [Polebridge Press, 2003], 195–206), but because Matthew's story has always been understood that way, I will not belabor my position here.

[7] See Miller, *Born Divine*, 207–8.

[8] Matthew contradicts himself on this point, for it is not true that Jesus teaches the crowds *only* in parables. Matthew tells of Jesus teaching them many things without using parables. For example, the entire speech in chapter 23 is addressed to "the crowds and the disciples" and none of it is in parables.

he fulfills a verse from a psalm about someone who tells parables in order to explain traditional wisdom (see Ps 78:2–4), especially since Jesus had earlier decided to tell parables as a means of *hiding* the truth (Matt 13:10–15).

We should note one additional case of an awkward fit between prophecy and event, this time in a story found only in Matthew. When Joseph takes Mary and their baby to Egypt to escape Herod's murderous plan, Matthew tells us that Jesus thereby fulfilled the prophecy "I called my son out of Egypt" (Hosea 11:1). But this is confusing because the family fled *toward* Egypt (Matt 2:15). There are other problems here. The half-verse from Hosea that Matthew quotes is not a prediction. It refers to the Exodus, an event that occurred (if at all) more than five hundred years in Hosea's past. Moreover, in Exodus Egypt is the place of slavery and death, whereas in Matthew's story Egypt is the place of safety. Matthew also distorts what Hosea plainly means by "my son" (see below).

In each of these above cases the prophecy fits its "fulfillment" only in a vague or tangential way, sometimes in contradiction to what Matthew elsewhere reports about Jesus and sometimes in contradiction to what the prophecy means in its own context (see below). Many of the connections Matthew draws between prophecy and fulfillment require a generous imagination. Matthew was well aware that he was pressing some of his prophecies into uses that contradicted their natural meanings, as we can see from the skillful ways in which he lifted them out of their original contexts.

QUOTING OUT OF CONTEXT

A number of the prophecies Matthew identifies as fulfilled in his narrative are quoted out of context in ways that distort their original meanings. By context here I do not mean *historical* context, which Matthew always ignores, as do all ancient authors interested in the hidden meanings of prophecy. Here I have in mind the immediate *literary* contexts of the lines Matthew quotes. What happens to the meanings Matthew sees in these prophecies when we take into account the lines just before or after the ones Matthew selects for quotation? See for yourself in this quick analysis of seven examples.

1) **Matthew 1:23** applies to Jesus the prediction that "the virgin will conceive and give birth to a son" from Isa 7:14. Matthew includes the next line about naming the boy Emmanuel, for although Jesus was not called by that name, Matthew nonetheless believes that Jesus fulfills its symbolism. However, the next lines of the prophecy (Isa 7:15–16) have no possible application to Jesus. The same is true for the verse preceding the one Matthew quotes (Isa 7:13).

[13]Isaiah said: 'Hear then, O house of David! Is it too little for you to weary mortals, that you weary my God also?[14] Therefore the Lord himself will give you a sign. *Look, the young woman is with child and shall bear a son, and shall name him Immanuel.*[15] He shall eat curds and honey by the time he knows how to refuse the evil and choose the good. [16]For before the child knows how to refuse the evil and choose the good, the land before whose two kings you are in dread will be deserted. (Isa 7:13–16)[9]

Matthew can read Jesus into Isa 7:14 only if he isolates it from the verses immediately before and after it.[10]

2) **Matthew 2:13–15** correlates "I called my son out of Egypt" (Hos 11:1) to the family's escape to and return from that country. Matthew quotes only the second half of Hos 11:1 and it's easy to see why.

When Israel was a child, I loved him,
and *out of Egypt I called my son.*

---

[9] All biblical quotations, except those from the gospels, are from the NRSV (New Revised Standard Version). Quotations from the gospels are from the SV (Scholars Version).

[10] For a detailed philological and literary analysis of Isa 7:14 in its original context in Isaiah and its reuse by Matthew, see Robert J. Miller, "The Wonder Baby: The Immanuel Prophecy in Isaiah and Matthew," *The Fourth R* 28-2 (Mar-Apr, 2015).

> The more I called them,
> the more they went from me;
> they kept sacrificing to the Baals,
> and offering incense to idols. (Hos 11:1–2)

Hos 11:1a makes it clear that "my son" in 11:1b is a collective reference to Israel. Quoting the whole verse would wreck the correlation to Jesus. This is doubly true for the next verse. Not only does that verse refer to the Israelites in the plural, it also speaks of their idolatry. Both features of that verse make it impossible for Matthew to read Jesus into it.

3) **Matthew 2:16–18** asserts that Jeremiah's poetry about "Rachel weeping for her children" because "they are no more" (Jer 31:15) was fulfilled in Herod's massacre of the babies in Bethlehem. However, the verses immediately following 31:15 comfort Rachel with the promise that her children will return to her (Jer 31:16–17). No wonder Matthew selects only 31:15.

4) **Matthew 8:17** quotes Isa 53:4a ("he bore our infirmities and carried our diseases"), which Matthew sees fulfilled in Jesus' healings and exorcisms. It is far from obvious how Jesus thereby fulfilled what Matthew quotes, which is not even a prediction, much less one about a messiah. Furthermore, the context from which Matthew lifted this line ruins the meaning he tries to give it. Isa 53:4b ("we accounted him stricken, struck down by God, and afflicted"), as well as the immediate context in 53:3–5, indicates that 53:4a means that God's servant is sick with diseases that are punishments for the sins of others. The meaning Matthew assigns to verse 4a would not work if he quoted all of verse 4.

5) In **Matt 26:31** Jesus tells his disciples after the Last Supper that they will all desert him, "for it is written, 'I will strike the shepherd and the sheep will be scattered'" (Matt 26:31, copied from Mark 14:27 quoting Zechariah 13:7). This one line is expertly quoted out of context, for in Zech 13:7–9, the sentence

expresses God's determination to punish a worthless shepherd and to kill most of his sheep,[11] a meaning completely contradictory to the one the gospels give it.

Matthew is by no means the only NT writer to repurpose prophecies by quoting them out of context. Here are two transparent examples from the Gospel of John, whose author was as equally judicious as Matthew was in selecting which bits of a scriptural passage to quote.

6) **John 2:17.** When Jesus disrupts the commerce in the temple, John relates that his disciples remembered a verse from the psalms: "Zeal for your house will consume me" (Ps 69:9). The verses immediately following this one in Psalm 69 are antithetical to John's interpretation of Jesus because they describe the speaker of the psalm doing public penance for sin:

> When I humbled my soul with fasting,
> > they insulted me for doing so.
> When I made sackcloth for my clothing,
> > I became a byword to them. (Ps 69:10–11)

7) **John 15:25.** As Jesus reflects on the hatred he has encountered among those to whom he was sent, he reveals that their animosity "was to fulfill the word that is written in their law, 'They hated me for no reason.'" This complaint is found in two psalms (Ps 69:4 and Ps 35:19). Perhaps John knew this and studied both of them in search for scriptures that were fulfilled in Jesus. However, since John quotes Psalm 69 earlier in his gospel (2:17) and clearly alludes to it later (19:29), Psalm 69 is the likely source for his quotation in John 15:25.

Psalm 69 is a prayer for deliverance and revenge (see Ps 69:22–28), but also an expression of confession and repentance. The very next verse after John's quotation of Ps 69:4 reads, "O God, you know my folly; the wrongs I have done are not hidden from you" (Ps 69:5). John not only

---

[11] See *Helping Jesus Fulfill Prophecy*, 159–61.

had to locate the right piece of the psalm; he also had to remove that piece from its context in order for it to find credible fulfillment in Jesus.

These seven cases—there are many more in the NT—quote the scriptures in such a way as to exclude integral elements in the prophecies that disallow or work against the meanings Matthew and John read into them. Their studied process of quoting shows that they are not quoting from memory, for their selective quotations are precise textual maneuvers. It is only because Matthew and John can consult written texts that they know exactly which words to include in their quotations and, what is equally important, which words *not* to include. Their deliberate selectivity suggests that they were aware that the prophets they quoted did not think they were prophesying about Jesus. The evangelists believe that they have discovered the deeper significance of the prophecies, meanings that God had hidden even from the prophets who uttered them.

FABRICATING PROPHECIES

Selective quotation is one technique by which gospel writers adopt and adapt the words of the prophets so that they can be fulfilled in their gospel. Analyzing the precision with which they lifted short scriptural statements out of their contexts shows that they knew what they needed their prophecies to say, which guided their careful choices about how they quoted from the biblical texts. In three unusual cases, however, Matthew and John take a bolder approach by writing prophecies themselves and attributing them to the prophets.

1) **Matthew 2:23.** "He will be called a Nazorean" is not a quotation from the scriptures and Matthew knows it. We can tell that he knows it because he presents this prophecy differently than all the other quotations in his gospel, in two ways. First, he does not introduce it as a quotation, but instead inserts it into his story in indirect discourse, as a paraphrase: "He [Joseph] settled in a town called Nazareth, in order to fulfill the prediction of the prophets that he will be called a Nazorean." Second,

Matthew ascribes the saying generically to "the prophets," rather than to "the prophet" (as in 2:15, for example) or to a named prophet.[12] There is no prophecy about Nazareth in the scriptures; the village is not mentioned anywhere in the OT. Either Matthew created this prophecy out of nothing or else he got the idea for it from a verse or verses focused on some word that reminded him of the word "Nazorean." If the latter is the case, scholars can only guess which passage(s) Matthew had in mind.[13]

Whether Matthew produced this prediction by redoing some verse(s) from the scriptures or directly from his imagination matters little, for the fact remains that there is no scripture predicting anything about Nazareth or one of its residents.

2) **Matthew 27:9–10.** After Jesus is condemned to death, Judas, devastated by remorse for his betrayal of his master, throws the money the priests had given him into the temple and then kills himself. The priests then use the money to buy a cemetery for foreigners (Matt 27:3–8). "Then the prediction spoken through the prophet Jeremiah was fulfilled:

They took the thirty silver coins, the price put on a man's head (this is the price they put on him among the Israelites), and they donated it for the potter's field, as my Lord commanded me. (Matt 27:9–10)

This prophecy is most unusual. It is loosely based on Zechariah 11:13 and yet, strangely, Matthew attributes the oracle to *Jeremiah*, to whose prophecy it indirectly alludes, but from which Matthew has taken not a single phrase.[14] A detailed comparison of the prophecy in Matthew

---

[12] Paul (e.g., in 1 Cor 15:3–4) refers to the fulfillments of "the scriptures," and Luke to the fulfillments of "the prophets" (Luke 24:25–26 and 44), but in those cases the authors are referring to multiple prophecies, and they do not quote any passages.

[13] See *Helping Jesus Fulfill Prophecy*, 126–28 and/or *Born Divine*, 117–18 for the details.

[14] There is no convincing explanation for this misattribution, which has perplexed scholars since the earliest centuries of Christianity. A few ancient copyists of Matthew's gospel noticed this mistake, for they corrected the reference, changing Jeremiah to Zechariah, or (strangely) to Isaiah. The fourth-century scholar Eusebius

and the text of Zechariah[15] demonstrates that the prophecy quoted in Matt 27:9–10 is neither copied nor paraphrased from any biblical text. It is Matthew's own construction, based on Zech 11:13 from which Matthew quotes a few words, paraphrases some others, and to which he adds some of his own. Crucially, however, the central action described in the prophecy, and the deed that Matthew narrates as its fulfillment—the purchase of a field from a potter—is found neither in Zechariah nor anywhere else in the Old Testament.

    3) **John 7:37**. The Gospel of John furnishes a third example of a fabricated prophecy.

Jesus stood up and shouted out, "Anyone who's thirsty must come to me and drink. The one who believes in me—as scripture puts it—'will be the source of rivers of life-giving water.'" (He was talking about the spirit that those who believed in him were about to receive. You realize, of course, that there was no spirit as yet, since Jesus hadn't been glorified.) (John 7:37–39)

It is difficult to determine whether to classify this as a fulfillment of scripture or a somewhat vague promise that a scripture will come true. However, there simply is no such quotation in the Old Testament nor in any extant ancient text. Even if John is paraphrasing rather than quoting, there is no verse on which it is clearly based; the best scholars can do is suggest a phrase in Zech 14:8 ("living waters shall flow out of Jerusalem") as a possibility.

---

defended Matthew's accuracy, asserting that either Matthew himself wrote "Zechariah" and a careless scribe was responsible for "Jeremiah" or that the prophecy originally was in the scroll of Jeremiah but was deleted by some evildoer. Eusebius offers no evidence for either theory and the second one is, frankly, unbelievable. What his lame attempt to exonerate Matthew proves is that Eusebius was unable to identify any text in Jeremiah from which the alleged prophecy might be even loosely paraphrased. No scholar since Eusebius has done any better.

[15] See *Helping Jesus Fulfill Prophecy*, 129–31.

FABRICATED?

The above three cases feature predictions that the NT authors identify as scriptural, but because those predictions do not actually exist in the Jewish Bible, I have called them "fabricated." In one example, Matthew's quotation of a prophecy erroneously attributed to Jeremiah, a plausible case can be made as to how Matthew constructed the prophecy. In the other two cases, scholars can only guess which scriptural passage, if any, the NT author mined for the raw material for his fabrication. However, it is possible that the authors quoted from memory something they honestly believed they knew from the scriptures.[16] If so, they were mistaken. In this case, their fabrications would be unconscious, but fabrications, nonetheless.

It is also possible that the authors quoted from a text unknown to us,[17] in which case the term "fabricated" might not seem fair. Although that possibility cannot be ruled out a priori, I stand by my terminology. If Matthew or John quoted from non-extant texts, those would have been either lost pieces of canonical books, or works that Matthew or John considered biblical but that were not accepted into the Jewish or Christian canon. The former possibility can only be a *mere* possibility, for it is unsupported by even a shred of evidence. The latter possibility is somewhat plausible because there were many ancient religious writings that are lost to us and there was some fluidity in nascent Judaism and Christianity as to which writings were considered scriptural.[18]

We should exclude the first possibility from consideration for the simple reason that a hypothesis for which there is absolutely no evidence

---

[16] This *might* be the case for Matt 6:43: "You have heard that it was said, 'You shall love your neighbor and hate your enemy.'" The Bible nowhere says, "You shall hate your enemy." A modern example of a saying many mistakenly attribute to the Bible is "The Lord helps those who help themselves." Another might be "A man who does not protect his family is worse than an unbeliever," which is quoted as biblical by some Christians who support the National Rifle Association. I have been unable to find either this saying or its gist anywhere in the Bible.

[17] This is highly unlikely in Matt 2:23, because Matthew presents the prophecy in indirect discourse rather than introduce it with his customary quotation formula.

[18] One such example is 1 Corinthians 2:9, which is remarkably similar to Gospel of Thomas 17.

cannot be weighed. The second possibility leaves us with a quotation from an unverifiable source that neither Jews nor Christians regard as biblical. A quotation like that should still be considered fabricated, though not by a NT author. In the end that really doesn't matter because, regardless of what one calls such a prophecy, it seems inappropriate, if only on theological grounds, for Christians to count the fulfillment of a non-extant non-biblical prophecy as a miracle.

Retrofitting Prophecy

Next we analyze four NT examples of the curious practice of rewriting biblical prophecies so that they will match more closely the phenomena that allegedly fulfill them. I call this particular process "retrofitting." The term comes from engineering and names a process in which an already built object is added to or modified so that it can perform a function for which it was not originally designed. For example, a house built in the mid-twentieth century can be retrofitted with solar panels to convert the house to solar power. Applied to the NT, retrofitting is an apt analogy for the manner in which OT passages that by themselves do not work well as predictions about Jesus have been rewritten so that they can more easily be correlated with beliefs or stories about Jesus. Sometimes that rewriting involves

- deleting parts of the OT passage that would ruin the correlation with Jesus
- changing key words in the passage or adding new ones
- stitching together parts of two or more different scriptures to produce a hybrid passage

Some retrofits show a fair amount of textual intervention, whereas others required just a bit of rewriting in just the right place.

(1) Jesus / Emmanuel (Matthew 1:23)

Perhaps the most familiar fulfillment of prophecy scene in the Bible is the one from the Christmas story in which an angel appears to Joseph in a dream and tells him,

Joseph, son of David, don't hesitate to take Mary as your wife, since the holy spirit is responsible for her pregnancy. She will give birth to a son and you will name him Jesus, because he will save his people from their sins. (Matt 1:20–21)

Matthew then tell us:

All of this happened in order to fulfill the prediction of the Lord spoken through the prophet:
"Look, the virgin will conceive and give birth to a son,
and they will name him Emmanuel."
(The name means "God is with us"). (Matt 1:22–23, SV modified)

A conspicuous and well-known difference between Matthew's quotation and the Hebrew original (Isa 7:14) is that Isaiah's prophecy concerns a young woman, while Matthew's version is (or at least is traditionally translated as if it were) about a virgin.[19] That change in vocabulary was not Matthew's doing. He found it already there in the Septuagint from which he copied. But that difference is not my interest here.[20] Instead, I want to draw attention to what might seem to be an insignificant difference: who it is who will give the baby boy the name Emmanuel. Compare:

Isaiah (Septuagint):

Look, the virgin shall conceive and give birth to a son,
and *you* shall name him Emmanuel.

Matthew

---

[19] Again, for the sake of the argument, I use the term "virgin," which I consider an erroneous translation. See note 6 above.

[20] The Septuagint is ancient Greek translation of the Hebrew Bible that was produced in Egypt in the late third or early second century BCE in order to make the scriptures available to Greek-speaking Jews who could not read Hebrew. In many places the Greek version differs, sometimes slightly, sometimes significantly, from the surviving Hebrew text. The Hebrew of Isaiah 7:14 refers to the mother-to-be of Immanuel as *'almah*, "young woman." The Greek translates that word with *parthenos*, which normally means a young woman who has not yet borne her first child but can in certain contexts mean "virgin." For a full discussion of all the interesting issues involved in interpreting both Isaiah 7:14 and Matthew 1:23, see "The Wonder Baby" (note 10 above).

Look, the virgin shall conceive and give birth to a son,
and *they* shall name him Emmanuel.

Isaiah spoke this prophecy to King Ahaz (see Isa 7:1), who is therefore the "you" who will name the boy. Matthew has changed "you" to "they." The change is small, smaller still in Greek than in English, because one can change the subject of a Greek verb just by changing its ending: "you shall name" is *kaleseis*; "they shall name" is *kalesousin*. Furthermore, Matthew's change does not affect the meaning of the prophecy. So why did he tweak Isaiah's verb? Look at what the angel tells Joseph: "you are to name him Jesus." Since Joseph did what the angel told him—"he named him Jesus" (Matt 1:25)—Matthew's own story does *not* fulfill this detail of Isaiah's prophecy: Joseph did not name the boy Emmanuel. Matthew knew what to do: rewrite Isaiah so that the prophecy can be fulfilled by others' ("they") calling Jesus by that theologically rich name. And who is "they"? Look again at Matthew's story. The grammatical antecedent for "they" is "his people" whom "he will save from their sins" (Matt 1:21). Matthew's grammatical design here is ingenious because it makes his Christian audience—who are not characters in the story—the ones who will refer to their savior by the name that means "God is with us." Matthew thus enlists his audience to do their part in the fulfillment of prophecy.

(2) Born in Bethlehem (Matthew 2:6)

Another example of Matthew's retrofitting of prophecy relates to his claim that Jesus' birth in Bethlehem fulfills this prophecy:

And you, Bethlehem, in the land of Judah
    in no way are you least among the leaders of Judah.
Out of you will come a leader
    who will shepherd my people, Israel. (Matt 2:6)

The second line of the prophecy, in its original wording, addresses Bethlehem as "you who are the smallest of the clans of Judah" (Micah 5:2). Matthew added one Greek word (*oudamōs*) that means "not at all" or "in no way" to the beginning of this line, emphatically contradicting

Micah's recognition of Bethlehem's insignificance. From Matthew's perspective, it seems, Jesus had changed the status of Bethlehem. Although it had been a small and unassuming town, it was now famous because it was the birthplace of the Messiah.

Matthew's alteration here is interesting because it was unnecessary. The prophecy would work fine without Matthew's retrofit, but with the new wording it works even better.

(3) The Death of Judas (Acts 1:18–20)

An example of retrofitting from the Acts of the Apostles gives us another chance to see how thorough NT writers could be in adapting prophecies to match their stories. In this example the author relates a quotation of scripture to the death of Judas and its effect on a particular plot of land. To explain the relevance of the prophecy, the author provides some background information about how Judas died, drawing on a quite different story than the better-known one from Matthew in which Judas hangs himself (Matt 27:3–8).

This man [Judas] acquired a field with the reward of his wickedness; and falling headlong, he burst open in the middle and all his bowels gushed out. This became known to all the residents of Jerusalem, so that the field was called in their language *Hakeldama*, that is, Field of Blood. For it is written in the Book of Psalms, "Let his habitation be made desolate, and let there be no inhabitant in it." (Acts 1:18–20a)

The quotation is from Psalm 69:25, which in the OT reads as follows: "Let their habitation be made desolate; and let there be no inhabitant in their tents." Since this original wording does not quite fit the story of Judas, the author has adapted it to his story with two careful revisions: (1) replacing "in their tents," a detail obviously inapplicable to Judas, with "in it," and (2) altering the plural word "their," which refers to many enemies, to the singular "his" so that it can refer to Judas as an individual.

This example provides strong evidence that the alterations we observe were made deliberately. The revision of seemingly minor details—in this case, converting plural nouns and pronouns to singulars—is not

271

a change that would happen inadvertently, as might occur if the author had quoted scripture from memory. The retrofit here is too precise for that, and is clearly the result of the author's careful, word-for-word study of the written text of the psalm.

(4) "He gave gifts to his people" (Ephesians 4:8)

Each of us was given grace according to the measure of Christ's gift. Therefore it is said,

"When he ascended on high he made captivity itself a captive; he gave gifts to his people."

(When it says, "He ascended," what does it mean but that he had also descended into the lower parts of the earth? He who descended is the same one who ascended far above all the heavens, so that he might fill all things.) The gifts he gave were that some would be apostles, some prophets, some evangelists, some pastors and teachers. (Eph 4:7–11)

The author of Ephesians quotes (or better, paraphrases) scripture in v. 8 in support of what he states in v. 7. Taking it for granted that the "he" in the quotation refers to Christ, the author then explains what "he ascended" both means and implies (vv. 9–10). The author then indicates that the "gifts" to which the quotation refers are the different authoritative offices of the Christian church (v. 11).

The quotation in Eph 4:8 is a free paraphrase of the first part of Ps 68:18. Here is Ps 68:17–18, with the lines used by Ephesians in italics.

With mighty charioty, twice ten thousand,
thousands upon thousands,
the Lord came from Sinai into his holy place.
You ascended the high mountain,
leading captives in your train
and receiving gifts from people,
even from those who rebel against Yahweh God's abiding there. (Ps 68:17–18)

Ps 68:17–18 imagines Yahweh's triumphal procession from Sinai to his temple ("his holy place") in Jerusalem, where he receives tribute from its inhabitants, even from those who oppose his presence in their midst. "High mountain" was originally a literal expression of the very ancient belief that gods lived on high mountain tops. In the context of Psalm 68, however, "high mountain" is a grandiose reference to the modest hill in Jerusalem, Mount Zion, on which the temple stood.

The author of Ephesians leaves out the word "mountain" in his paraphrase of Ps 68:18. Through that strategic omission, he transforms the psalm's celebration of Yahweh's ascent of Mount Zion ("ascended a high mountain") into Christ's ascension into heaven ("ascended on high"). That interpretation probably came naturally to the author, but it created a problem: how to interpret the next clause in the psalm, "he received gifts from people"? The author solved that problem by rewording that part of the psalm, in two ways. First, he replaced the verb, reversing its meaning so that Christ *gives*, not receives, gifts. Second, the author added a possessive adjective, so that the gifts are given not to people in general, but to *his* people, i.e., to the church. Ephesians' rewriting of Ps 68:18 is thus a textbook example of retrofitting scripture so that it can find its fulfillment in the experience of Christians.

RETROFITTING IN HISTORICAL CONTEXT

The above four/five cases highlight one particular way that NT authors helped Jesus fulfill prophecy. When the quoted prophecies are understood in their own words they do not easily—or at all—mesh with the events or circumstances they are alleged to fulfill, which is why Christian writers rewrote the prophecies, tailoring them to their fulfillments. Rewriting scripture in this fashion surely seems audacious to us today. We can tolerate a preacher's interpretation of a biblical passage that strikes us as fanciful, because we can dismiss that interpretation as merely his opinion. But few moderns would be so tolerant if a preacher deliberately altered the text of the Bible so that it would say what he wanted it to say.

Modern sensibilities, however, are often unhelpful when seeking to understand the ancients. When assessing ancient interpreters, we need to try to understand their treatment of prophecy within their historical and religious contexts. And here it is important to realize that the followers of Jesus were by no means the only Jews to claim that biblical prophecies had been fulfilled in the events of their recent past. Study of interpretations of scripture from the third century BCE to the first century CE show that Jewish authors used several techniques to manipulate the words of the prophets so that they would match what the interpreters claimed the prophecies had predicted. The NT authors thus inherited a set of interpretive methods used in a variety of Jewish writings that worked to relate prophecies to the times and places of their audiences.[21] When the NT authors manipulated prophecies in the ways they did, they were using hermeneutical techniques that were traditional in their day. Other Jewish scholars of their time would have been surprised by the interpretations of the Christian authors, but not by their interpretive methods. That is important to recognize because it confirms that the NT authors were playing by the rules, as it were, of their own time.

IMPLICATIONS

The fact that NT writers felt the need to change the OT verses shows two things. (1) The NT authors were well aware that the OT in its own words often would not be seen as predicting Jesus. They apparently figured that it was most unlikely that someone reading or hearing the OT text in question would think that it was a prophecy about Jesus. The connection the NT author saw between the OT and Jesus was seen *despite* the actual words of the original passage, which is why it needed to be retrofitted. (2) The textual retrofitting also shows that the "flow" of understanding in these cases is *from* Christian beliefs about Jesus *to* the

---

[21] See pp. 65–105 in *Helping Jesus Fulfill Prophecy* for analyses of examples from the Dead Sea Scrolls, the Septuagint, the Targum (Greek and Aramaic translations of the Hebrew Bible), and the writings of the historian Josephus.

OT, not the other way around. The Christian authors came to understand the OT as they did because they already believed in Jesus. It is, emphatically, not the case that they came to believe in Jesus because of what they read in the OT. If that had been the case, there would have been no need for the retrofits. Those textual manipulations betray the frustrations of Christian authors hunting for prophecies of Jesus but finding passages that did not really fit with what they wanted to show.

The *retro*fitting of prophecy is evidence that the belief that Jesus fulfilled prophecy was *retro*spective. Only after his followers came to believe that Jesus was the promised messiah did they draw the conclusion that he had fulfilled prophecy, for that is what the messiah was supposed to do. Only then did they go hunting in their Bible to discover which specific prophecies he had fulfilled. They could find Jesus in the OT only because they already knew they would find him there.

And find him they did, often in scriptures that at first did not seem to be about him. The meanings the followers of Jesus attributed to prophecies are rarely evident when they are considered in their own contexts in the books of the prophets. But Christians did not look to those contexts to help them discern the meanings of those prophecies; they meditated on them within the new context of their belief in Jesus as the Messiah. In cases where the wording of those prophecies resisted the new meanings Christians found in them, the prophecies could be retrofitted, rewritten to let their "real" meanings shine through more clearly.

Conclusion

The NT's impressive set of testimonies to Jesus' fulfilling a large number of specific prophecies has been understood by the Christian tradition to constitute miraculous proof of the truth of Christianity. The precise definition of what a miracle is can be elusive, but a commonsense notion of a miracle in our time and place includes the idea that a miracle is something that cannot be explained as the result of natural processes or human skill. When, for example, a nerd from tech support taps a few keys and restores order to the chaos I have wreaked on my computer, it certainly seems like a miracle to me. But it isn't, because even though it is beyond my comprehension how that magic was worked, we know that it can be explained by the physical laws of electronics, the esoterica of coding, and the expertise of the technician.

This essay has argued that the seeming miracle of Jesus' fulfillments of prophecy can be explained as the result of the ingenious literary labor of early Christian writers. Those authors utilized a number of traditional techniques for manipulating passages from the Jewish scriptures, of which four have been analyzed above. The NT writers

1) connected prophecies to events that do not fulfill them in any obvious way, sometimes creating correlations that objective readers might consider implausible or farfetched;
2) quoted prophecies out of context, often with surgical precision, so that new meanings could be read into them, meanings that those prophecies cannot possibly have in their original contexts;
3) quoted a few fabricated prophecies, predictions that the NT authors probably composed themselves or perhaps copied from non-extant non-biblical texts;
4) retrofitted prophecies, rewriting them so that they can match the events presented as their fulfillments.

Those techniques would not be acceptable today. Making farfetched connections between prophecies and their alleged fulfillments would simply not be persuasive and would raise questions about the strength of your evidence. Quoting out of context so that you can attribute meanings to quotations that are foreign to and often incompatible with their original ones would severely damage your credibility. And fabricating quotations or rewriting them to get them to mean what you want them to mean would rightly be condemned as intellectual dishonesty.

The question can thus arise whether the NT authors were trying to deceive by manipulating scripture in the ways we can see that they did. Here it is vital to keep in mind what I explained a few paragraphs above, that the textual techniques by which the NT writers helped Jesus fulfill prophecy were in common use among ancient Jewish intellectuals. I have long wondered whether those writers, either Jewish or Christian, used those techniques with the intention of tricking unsophisticated audiences. The honest truth is that we cannot know their inner motivations. But we can say—and on this I want to be very clear—that the Christian authors were not violating what we would call the professional standards of their day.

That was then, this is now. An argument today that was shown to employ the techniques used by NT authors for manipulating texts would fail to convince the open-minded. Anyone knowingly using those techniques today without fully disclosing them would be judged intellectually dishonest. When we learn how a magician performs a trick, we still might admire his skill, but we can see that no miracle occurred. The same should hold for the argument that Jesus' fulfillment of prophecy was a miracle. When we understand how the NT authors produced the scriptural evidence on which that argument relies, we might well admire their literary skill, but we can see the alleged miracle for what it really is, an *expression* of religious faith rather than *evidence* for it.

10| THE PROPHETIC FAILURE OF CHRIST'S RETURN

BY ROBERT CONNER

"I say this, brothers, the allotted time has grown short. From now on let those who have a wife be like those who don't...for the form of this world is passing away."[1]

Few passages in the letters of Paul convey the urgency of his End Times expectations more clearly than his advice on sexual relations and marriage. Convinced the "last trumpet" could blow at any moment, Paul urged his followers to keep themselves sexually pure—"from now on," in the time they have left, "It is good for a man not to have sex with a woman."[2] Although he makes concessions for those who lack self-control, Paul's clear preference is a Christian "household of brothers and sisters rather than husbands and wives, fathers and mothers."[3] Urging Christians to live celibate lives like his own does not presuppose Jesus' return would take place decades, much less centuries, in the future. As Tabor notes, "[Paul] advised his followers not to marry, begin a new business, or worry if they were slaves, since everything in the world was about to be turned upside down and all social relations were terminal."[4] Paul desired to present the Church as a

---

[1] 1 Corinthians 7:29, 31b.
[2] 1 Corinthians 7:1.
[3] Dale B. Martin, *Sex and the Single Savior: Gender and Sexuality in Biblical Interpretation* (Louisville: Westminster John Knox Press, 2006), 108.
[4] James Tabor, *Paul and Jesus: How the Apostle Transformed Christianity*, (New York: Simon & Schuster, 2012), 16.

chaste virgin to the coming Lord,[5] but the Lord left the anxious Church standing at the altar.

A sense of immediacy pervades Paul's authentic letters: "…as you eagerly wait for our Lord Jesus Christ to be revealed…These things happened as examples, written down for us on whom the end of the ages has arrived."[6] "Do this, understanding the allotted time: the hour has already arrived for you to awaken from sleep, for now our salvation is nearer than when we first believed…the night is nearly spent, the day is about to break."[7] Paul believed the majority of his converts would survive until the return of Jesus—"we the living who survive"—and that those who received his letter would be *physically*, corporeally, alive when Jesus returned: "may your whole spirit and soul *and body* be preserved blameless until our Lord Jesus comes back."[8] "Come, Lord!"[9] reflects "consciousness of living in the final period of time that had begun, as demonstrated in their expectation of the impending coming of the glorified Lord."[10] "*We the living who survive*" as well as "*We will not all sleep*, but we will all be changed"[11] make no sense unless addressed in letters *to living people who do not expect to die*.

Paul's expectation is plain—"Paul taught his converts that the Lord would return so soon that they would live to see the day…Death was not expected."[12] His letter to the house church in Thessalonica, widely regarded as the oldest surviving Christian document, offers the following false assurance to the flock:

> Brothers we don't want you to be ignorant concerning those who are sleeping so you don't grieve like the rest who have no hope. For if we believe that Jesus died and rose, so also through Jesus

---

[5] 2 Corinthians 11:2.
[6] 1 Corinthians 1:7, 10:11.
[7] Roman 13:11-12.
[8] 1 Thessalonians 5:23.
[9] 1 Corinthians 16:22.
[10] Werner Georg Kümmel, "Futuristic and Realized Eschatology in the Earliest Stages of Christianity," *Journal of Religion* 43.4 (1963) 310.
[11] 1 Corinthians 15:51.
[12] E. P. Sanders, *Paul: A Very Short Introduction* (New York: Oxford University Press, 1991), 32-33.

God will bring back those who are sleeping together with him. We tell you by the Lord's word that we the living who survive until the Lord's return will by no means precede those who are asleep because the Lord will descend from heaven with a resounding command, with an arch-angel's voice, the trumpet call of God, and the dead in Christ will rise first. Then we who are still alive and remain will be snatched up in the clouds and meet the Lord in the air and so we will be with the Lord forever. So comfort one another with these words.[13]

Paul clearly considered himself Jesus' chosen revelator of divine secrets, his mystagogue, the hierophant extraordinaire of the Jesus mysteries. "I don't want you to be ignorant brothers," a favorite phrase,[14] is a self-aggrandizing formula that signals Paul's intention to reveal more plum insider information about the Risen Lord. We can easily imagine his credulous converts, hovering on the edge of their seats, clutching their apocalyptic pearls, breathlessly awaiting some new pronunciamento from Jesus' chosen oracle, the chief of the "servants of Christ and dispensers of God's mysteries."[15]

The unexpected death of some Thessalonian believers was clearly a source of angst, hence Paul's repeated reassurance about the imminent Parousia: "*we* will glory…when our Lord Jesus comes…*you* will be blameless and holy…when our Lord Jesus comes…may *your whole spirit, soul and body* be kept blameless at the Coming of our Lord Jesus Christ."[16] Paul's promises were made to those expectantly awaiting Jesus' Return in *the first century house church "of the Thessalonians,"*[17] and not to evangelical mega-church pew sitters living nearly two millennia later.

In short, "the Second Coming of Jesus will occur in the immediate future…the vast majority of Christians would be living witnesses to Christ's

---

[13] 1 Thessalonians 4:13-18.
[14] Romans 1:13, 11:25, 1 Corinthians 10:1, 12:1, 2 Corinthians 1:8, 1 Thessalonians 4:13.
[15] 1 Corinthians 4:1.
[16] 1 Thessalonians 2:20, 3:13, 5:23.
[17] 1 Thessalonians 1:1.

return from heaven..."[18] Paul's teaching on the imminent return of Jesus "is uncharacteristically clear and consistent throughout his letters. Believers whether living or dead will receive a new, glorious body, like Christ's at his resurrection—and this will happen very, very soon...Paul and his communities are troubled by the death of believers before Christ's Second Coming: they did not expect this and do not know what to make of it."[19] Bornkamm even proposed that Paul's ad hoc, makeshift approach to theology was due to his "striving to complete his grandiose missionary program before Christ's imminent return."[20]

Given the clarity of his statements there is near consensus among mainstream New Testament specialists that Paul expected the End within his lifetime and taught his followers they would live to see it:

"The earliest Christians were Jews who believed that they were living at the end of the age and that Jesus himself was to return from heaven as a cosmic judge of the earth..."[21] [In Paul's letter to the Thessalonians] "we learn Paul's converts were shaken by the fact that some members of the congregation had died; they expected the Lord to return while they were all still alive. Paul assured them that the (few) dead Christians would be raised so that they could participate in the coming kingdom along with those who were still alive when the Lord returned."[22]

"[Paul] writes about the coming of the Lord Jesus, who will meet the saints in the clouds...the point for us is that 1 Thess[alonians] 4:13–18 does not readily lend itself to being understood as metaphorical language...Paul expected Jesus to come on the clouds."[23]

"The earliest document we have from Paul is his letter 1 Thessalonians. It is intensely apocalyptic, with its entire orientation on preparing his

---

[18] Gerd Lüdemann, *Paul: The Founder of Christianity* (Amherst, New York: Prometheus Books, 2002), 14, 49.
[19] Paula Fredriksen, *Jesus of Nazareth, King of Jews: A Jewish Life and the Emergence of Christianity* (New York: Vintage Books, 1999), 58.
[20] Günther Bornkamm, *Paul*, (Minneapolis: Fortress Press, 1971), xxii.
[21] Bart D. Ehrman, *Jesus: Apocalyptic Prophet of the New Millennium*, (New York: Oxford University Press, 1999), 139.
[22] E. P. Sanders, *The Historical Figure of Jesus*, (London: The Penguin Press, 1993), 179.
[23] Dale C. Allison, *Jesus of Nazareth: Millenarian Prophet*, (Minneapolis: Fortress Press, 1998) 159-160.

group for the imminent arrival of Jesus in the clouds of heaven…[Paul] expects to live to see Jesus appear visibly in the clouds."[24] "…the chief theological question [in 1 Thessalonians] seems to concern the recent death of someone in the church at Thessalonica; the members are worried about the eschatological implications…It is clear from their concern, as well as his own summary statement in 1:9–10, that in his earlier preaching Paul had stressed apocalyptic themes…"[25]

"[The Christians] are eagerly expecting the *immediate* return of their Master…[the Corinthians] were perplexed, like the Thessalonians, by the death of some of their fellow converts."[26]

It bears repeating that the first mention of Jesus that has survived till the present comes not from the gospels but from the occasional letters of Paul of Tarsus—the letters of Paul predate the gospel accounts by at least a generation. Paul's epistles have almost nothing in common with the gospels: he never mentions John the Baptist or Jesus' many miracles, his exorcisms, walking on water, or even raising the dead. Paul says nothing about Jesus' remarkable youth, his virgin birth, his precocious wisdom, or his family's miraculous escape from the murderous Herod the Great. More surprising still, Paul barely alludes to Jesus' sermons and sayings. For all practical purposes Paul's interest in Jesus appears to begin and end with his crucifixion: "For I determined not to know anything while I was among you except Jesus Christ and him crucified."[27]

Paul is the first to declare Jesus is the Son of God, but unlike the gospels, Paul connects Jesus' Sonship not with his birth[28] or his baptism,[29] but his resurrection: "[Jesus] was constituted the Son of God in power through the spirit of holiness by resurrection from the dead."[30] For Paul, Jesus gets

---

[24] Tabor, *Paul and Jesus*, 233-234, 115.
[25] L. Michael White, *From Jesus to Christianity: How Four Generations of Visionaries and Storytellers Created the New Testament and Christian Faith*, (New York: Harper Collins, 2004), 175-176.
[26] Charles Gore, *Jesus of Nazareth*, (London: Thornton Butterworth, 1930), 119, 215. (Emphasis in the original.)
[27] 1 Corinthians 2:2.
[28] Luke 1:35.
[29] Mark 1:11.
[30] Romans 1:4.

interesting only after he's dead, exalted, and due to arrive in glory at any moment to collect his saints. Paul's claim to have "seen" Jesus—"Have I not seen Jesus our Lord?"[31]—was not based on a face-to-face encounter with him during his lifetime, but one of a series of "subjective visionary experiences...involving verbal exchanges with Jesus as well as extraordinary revelations."[32] And as Tabor points out, Paul is the "earliest witness, chronologically speaking," to claim to have seen Jesus after his resurrection and "his is the *only* first-person claim we have."[33] Our knowledge of Paul is largely based on Acts, but it's worth mentioning "that not a single passage in Luke's whole book [Acts] shows either knowledge of [Paul's] own letters or use made of them."[34]

Schweitzer famously summarized the earliest Christian focus this way:

> Paul shows us with what complete indifference the earthly life of Jesus was regarded by primitive Christianity. The discourses in Acts show an equal indifference, since in them Jesus first becomes the Messiah by virtue of his exaltation...The fact is, if one reads through the early literature one becomes aware that so long as theology had an eschatological orientation and was dominated by the expectation of the parousia, the question of how Jesus of Nazareth 'had been' the Messiah not only did not exist, but was impossible. Primitive theology is simply a theology of the future, with no interest in history.[35]

Paul made no recorded attempt to explain Jesus' teaching, to prove from his words and deeds that he was the Messiah...he made no reference to...any salient incident in Jesus' ministry...Paul was an apocalypticist, believing the end was rapidly

---

[31] 1 Corinthians 9:1.
[32] Tabor, *Paul and Jesus*, 1.
[33] Ibid, 11. (Emphasis in original.)
[34] Bornkamm, *Paul*, xx.
[35] Albert Schweitzer, *The Quest of the Historical Jesus: A Critical Study of Its Progress from Reimarus to Wrede*, (Mineola, New York: Dover Publications, 2005), 344-345.

approaching. He imagined himself carrying the gospel as one of the messengers promised for the end times.[36]

"Never does [Paul] make the slightest effort to expound the teaching of the historical Jesus."[37] In fact, Bornkamm, like so many others,[38] notes that Paul's "complete shift...has exposed the apostle to the reproach of having falsified Christianity and thus of having rather shadily become its real 'founder'...[Jesus'] life has assumed dimensions it did not have on earth, and for Jesus' own words are substituted the word about Jesus Christ, his death, resurrection, and second coming at the end of the world...The Jesus of history is apparently dismissed. Paul never met him."[39]

It has long been recognized that Paul's gospel "did not conform to any [previously] existing tradition" and that "Paul became the protagonist of an interpretation of Christianity which had little interest in the career of the historical Jesus,"[40] the Jewish Jesus "according to the flesh."[41] As one writer recently put it, "What makes us think that there was such a thing as Christianity to which Saul/Paul could be converted? Merely to say that Paul was converted to Christianity begs more questions than it answers."[42]

Paul claims to have received his gospel directly from Jesus "by revelation"[43] and "[Paul's] own revelations directly from the heavenly Christ are more significant than anything Jesus taught in his earthly life." Of the seventy-two occurrences of "gospel" in the New Testament, "the letters of Paul account for sixty of the total...and it is clear that his usage is proprietary and exclusive."[44] As Wilson notes, "[Paul's] experience of the Risen

---

[36] William H. C. Frend, *The Rise of Christianity*, (Philadelphia: Fortress Press, 1984), 92-93, 97.
[37] Bornkamm, op.cit., 109-110.
[38] Notably, Barrie Wilson's *How Jesus Became Christian* (New York: St. Martin's Press, 2008) and R. Joseph Hoffman, *Jesus Outside the Gospels* (Amherst, New York: Prometheus Press, 1984) to cite but two of many.
[39] Ibid, 109-110.
[40] Samuel G.F. Brandon, "The Historical Element in Primitive Christianity," *Numen* 2 (1955) 160, 162.
[41] 2 Corinthians 5:16.
[42] Barrie Wilson, *How Jesus Became Christian* (New York: St. Martin's Press, 2008), 16.
[43] Galatians 1:12.
[44] Tabor, *Jesus and Paul*, 3-4.

Jesus owed nothing to the testimony of Peter, James or John" and his gospel "was never based, and never claimed to be based, on the traditions which...informed the teaching of Jesus' family and close intimates."[45] *Paul does not claim he is transmitting an apostolic tradition from the disciples who coalesced around Jesus during his lifetime*—Paul's gospel "is not from man," nor was he "taught it," nor did he "receive it" from men, but rather he received it right from the Savior's mouth, "by a revelation of Jesus Christ."[46] In short, "Paul says that he hears from Jesus."[47] "It is possible...that [Paul] wishes to imply that the Apostles who can claim to have known and touched Jesus have no claim to an apostolate superior to his own."[48]

It has long been recognized that the New Testament reflects various levels of emerging theological speculation but the "apocalyptic interpretation...was certainly the oldest, and remained a determinative view until near the end of the century."[49] That apocalyptic expectation was the bedrock of primitive Christian belief has been cogently argued by Ehrman, who notes that *apocalyptic preaching is the major point of continuity* between John the Baptist, "an apocalyptic prophet" and the "apocalyptic Christian church."[50] John warns, "The ax is already laid at the root of the tree!...The winnowing fork is in his hand, ready to clean out the threshing floor and gather the wheat into his barn, but the husks he will burn with fire that cannot be put out!"[51] In a seamless continuum, Jesus proclaims, "The time allotted has run out and the kingdom has almost arrived! Repent and believe in the good news!"[52] "God's rule over the world was imminent."[53]

---

[45] Andrew Wilson, *Paul: The Mind of the Apostle*, (New York: W.W. Norton, 1997), 68-69.
[46] Galatians 1:11-12.
[47] Tabor, op. cit., 146.
[48] Nock, *Early Gentile Christianity and Its Hellenistic Background* (New York: Harper & Row, 1964), 28.
[49] William Scott, *Journal of Bible and Religion* 12/1 (1944) 19.
[50] Bart D. Ehrman, *Jesus: Apocalyptic Prophet of the New Millennium* (New York: Oxford University Press, 1999), 139.
[51] Luke 3:7-9, 13.
[52] Mark 1:15.
[53] Géza Vermes, *Jesus the Jew: A Historian's Reading of the Gospels*, (Philadelphia: Fortress Press, 1973), 27.

The present order will end violently and end soon: family members will turn on one another,[54] the disciples must hate their families, their wives, children and parents,[55] and must not pause to say farewell to those left behind.[56] There is no time to gather possessions or pick up one's cloak.[57] The nearness of the end abrogates even the most basic filial responsibilities: "Follow me and let the dead bury their dead."[58] In a survey of scholarly opinion, Crawford notes, "the assumption that Jesus anticipated the arrival of the Kingdom in the very near future has lost little momentum. With but few exceptions, studies of Jesus' teaching continue to include a near expectation of the Kingdom as one of the primary ingredients of his message."[59] Regarding the texts attributed to Jesus that are typically cited as reflecting the imminent parousia, Mark 9:1, 13:30, and Matthew 10:23, Crawford further notes, "there can be no question as to the meaning of these texts. Each is a straightforward announcement of the imminently impending eschatological consummation."[60] "There are some standing here who will not taste death until they see the kingdom of God that has arrived in power"[61] is a belated admission "that some who originally heard the words would die."[62]

The notion that Jesus' prediction was "fulfilled" by the transfiguration is a favorite dodge of apologists wishing to avoid the clear implications of Mark 9:1, but as Brower among others observes, "Few scholars, if any, consider the connection between the logion of [Mark] 9.1 and the pericope of 9:2-13 to be the original context…nor is it likely that anyone could actually say with a solemn expression like ["truly I say to you"] that some people who are listening will actually be alive in six days'

---

[54] Matthew 10:34-37.
[55] Luke 14:26.
[56] Luke 9:61-62.
[57] Matthew 24:17-18.
[58] Matthew 8:22.
[59] Barry S. Crawford, "Near Expectation in the Sayings of Jesus," *Journal of Biblical Literature* 101 (1982) 226.
[60] Ibid, 227.
[61] Mark 9:1.
[62] Kent Brower, "Mark 9:1: Seeing the Kingdom in Power," *Journal for the Study of the New Testament*, 6 (1980) 20.

time...In sum, the crucial logion in Mk 9:1 can best be understood as a combination threat/promise that the [kingdom of God] would come in power in the lifetime of at least some of the hearers."[63] The prediction that some would not die before the kingdom arrived in power was addressed to "*the crowd together with his disciples,*"[64] whereas the transfiguration is witnessed by only three disciples, Peter, James, and John[65]— "Jesus' prediction in Mark 9:1 is a threat of judgment aimed at the out-group (antagonists), whoever they may be.[66] The transfiguration was not God's "kingdom arrived in power."

Two crucial questions now present themselves: *What* kingdom did the first followers of Jesus expect and *where* did they expect it? The gospels provide answers to both of these questions that are both historically probable and internally coherent.

Traces of Jesus' original kingdom message are still discernible in the gospels. Jesus will be called "son of the Most High," and God will give him "the throne of his father, David,"[67] a promise based on an Old Testament prediction: God will raise up a descendent of David, whose throne will be established forever, who will be God's son.[68] After the "restoration of all things," when Jesus is seated on his throne, the twelve disciples will also be enthroned, judging the twelve tribes of Israel.[69] Those who leave all to follow Jesus will receive "houses...and fields" in the present age and in the generation or era to come, eternal life.[70] Jesus followers quarrel over who will be greatest[71] and political maneuvering ensues—the mother of James and John comes to Jesus to ask, "Say that

---

[63] Ibid, 23, 41.
[64] Mark 8:34.
[65] Mark 9:2.
[66] Thomas R. Hatina, "Who Will See 'The Kingdom of God Coming with Power' in Mark 9.1—Protagonists or Antagonists?" *Biblica* 86.1 (2005) 34.
[67] Luke 1:32.
[68] 2 Samuel 7:12-14.
[69] Matthew 19:28.
[70] Mark 10:30.
[71] Luke 9:46, 22:24.

these, my two sons, may sit one on your right and one on your left in your kingdom."[72]

The crowds that followed Jesus expected the restoration of Jewish rule from Jerusalem, David's ancient capital of the united tribes:[73] "While they were listening to these things, Jesus told them a story as well *because he was near Jerusalem and they assumed the kingdom of God was going to appear at once.*"[74] The author of Luke/Acts reiterates this expectation. The disciples are not to leave Jerusalem,[75] but to wait in anticipation. "Those gathered around him began to ask, 'Lord, *are you restoring the kingdom to Israel at this time?*'"[76] In both these cases the writer immediately moves to defuse the expectation of his readers,[77] but as Fredriksen notes, "Luke's text also hints at an originally political understanding of Jesus' messiahship."[78] Commenting on contemporary messianic expectations, historian Vermes references the Psalms of Solomon: "…the Messiah…was expected to be a king of David's lineage, victor over the Gentiles, saviour and restorer of Israel."[79]

Fields and houses, thrones and tribes, anointing[80] and triumphal entry, to say nothing of Jerusalem and the acclamation of excited crowds— "Blessed is the one coming in the name of the Lord, *the king of Israel*"[81]— speak to the expectation of an *earthly* kingdom as does the titulus, "Jesus of Nazareth, *King of the Jews*," affixed to the cross above Jesus' head.[82] The Romans shared their understanding of Jesus with the authors of the gospels: "Where is he *born king of the Jews?*"[83] Or, to quote Micah,[84] "out of

---

[72] Matthew 20:21.
[73] 2 Samuel 5:4.
[74] Luke 19:11.
[75] Acts 1:4.
[76] Acts 1:6.
[77] Luke 19:12-27, Acts 1:7-8.
[78] Fredriksen, *From Jesus to Christ*, 35.
[79] Vermes, *Jesus the Jew*, 130-132.
[80] Mark 14:1-8.
[81] John 12:13.
[82] John 19:19-20.
[83] Matthew 2:2.
[84] Micah 5:2.

[Bethlehem] will come a prince *who governs my people Israel.*"[85] Although Jerusalem is the city most often identified as the "city of David,"[86] David, the future king, was born in Bethlehem.[87] The "kingdom *of* heaven," used 32 times in Matthew, *and only in Matthew,* does not indicate that the kingdom is *in* heaven[88]—David did not rule in heaven.

Jesus directed his kingdom message to the Jews and *only* to the Jews: "Do not approach the Gentiles and do not enter any Samaritan city. Go instead to the lost sheep of the house of Israel, and as you go, say 'The kingdom of heaven is almost here!'"[89] Gore spelled out the narrow focus of Jesus' mission: "cosmopolitan interests and foreign ideas and worships were near at hand to the home of Jesus as he grew. But he appears, like the devout Jews generally, to have been quite untouched by them. During his ministry he never seems to have entered one of the Greek cities…God had called Israel to be in a special sense His people…and through the prophets had given to it the assurance of the good time coming when God's reign on earth should be realized in Israel…It is quite impossible to interpret Jesus of Nazareth with any reality except on the basis of this assurance."[90] Regarding "the message of John [the Baptist]," Gore observed, "the blessed time promised—the Kingdom of God to be realized in Israel—was now at hand," and of the messianic promise made through the prophets, Gore continues, "What [the prophets] foresaw was the sovereignty of God realized in Israel and centering in Jerusalem…All that is contemplated is the destruction of the 'godless peoples' and the purging and glorifying of Israel."[91]

In 2000, psychiatrists at the Kfar Shaul Hospital in Jerusalem issued a groundbreaking report on a constellation of delusional beliefs they called the "Jerusalem Syndrome" after encountering over a thousand "tourists

---

[85] Matthew 2:6.
[86] 2 Samuel 5:7-10.
[87] 1 Samuel 17:12, 15.
[88] Thomas J. Ramsdell, "The Kingdom of Heaven in the Gospel of Matthew," *The Biblical World* 4.2 (1894), 124-125.
[89] Matthew 10:5-7.
[90] Charles Gore, *Jesus of Nazareth*, (Oxford: Oxford University Press, 1929), 43-45.
[91] Ibid, 53, 108-109.

with severe, Jerusalem-generated mental problems."[92] Based on the data accumulated while treating these patients, the doctors noted certain striking commonalities, patterns of deranged thinking and behaviors that to a skeptical reader of the New Testament sound like the thinking and behavior ascribed to Jesus. Evidence of the syndrome, "behavioral phenomena observed in eccentric and psychotic tourists with religious delusions,"[93] has been located in travel accounts dating back to the 19th century, but these days it "most often hits Americans," particularly "American Protestants."[94] As the turn of the millennium approached, mental health authorities in Jerusalem began to gird their loins, expecting to be "overwhelmed with 'Messiahs,'" mostly delusional Brits and Americans. The BBC asked, "But what happens if the real Messiah puts in an appearance? It would be highly likely he would be deemed insane."[95]

As a recent history of Jerusalem notes, "All three Abrahamic religions believe in the Apocalypse, but the details vary by faith and sect…In this age of Jewish, Christian and Muslim fundamentalism, the Apocalypse is a dynamic force in the world's febrile politics…Jerusalem defies sense, practical politics and strategy, existing in a realm of ravenous passions and invincible emotions, impermeable to reason."[96] Jerusalem, the seat of the Davidic kings, became the focus of the world's first recorded *religious* war during the Maccabean revolt and has remained a trigger of religious fighting and fantasy role-playing ever since.

Based on surviving sources we know that Roman-occupied Palestine pullulated charismatic figures that violently opposed both Rome's taxation and its inept administration—historian Michael White lists no fewer than fifteen such figures that are still known by name.[97] Passover in particular was evidently an occasion for popular uprisings—"for it is

---

[92] Bar-El, et al., "The Jerusalem Syndrome," *British Journal of Psychiatry* 176 (2000) 86.
[93] Witzum & Kalian, *The Israel Journal of Psychiatry and Related Sciences* 36 (1999), 260.
[94] Ilan, *Chicago Tribune*, May 4, 1987.
[95] BBC News, December 24, 1999.
[96] Simon S. Montefiore, *Jerusalem: The Biography*, (New York: Alfred A. Knopf, 2011), xxiii, xxv.
[97] White, *From Jesus to Christianity*, 37-39. See particularly his chapter, "Entering the World of Jesus, 11-39.

on these festive occasions that sedition is most apt to break out"[98]—and during the festivals, Sicarii, "knife-men" with daggers concealed in their robes, murdered Jewish collaborators before fading back into the crowds. Josephus described, "the insanity of the Sicarii" that spread "like a disease."[99] Palestine, then as now, was a steaming platter of murderous nationalistic lunacy with a heaping side order of religious crazy.

Provocations from would-be prophets and messianic pretenders could anticipate a decisive response from the Temple authorities and their Roman overlords. Reading Josephus' account, it is easy to imagine that many such characters were either sociopaths or religious madmen, clinically insane. A similar thought apparently crossed Josephus' mind as well:

> *Deceivers (planoi)*[100] and fraudsters, under the pretense of divine inspiration, instigated revolutionary changes and persuaded the multitude to act like madmen and led them into the desert under the belief that God would there display signs of their deliverance.[101]

Herod's son Archelaus, faced with revolt over the excesses of his father, attempted to appease the crowds but as in modern times the disgruntled and dispossessed responded with a volley of rocks. As Passover approached, "an endless mass of people from the country" entered Jerusalem and Archelaus "ordered in a tribune with a cohort commanded to subdue the leaders of the revolt by force."[102] Josephus recounts yet another episode of rebellion when a mob of people—including many from Galilee, "the most troublesome of all Jewish districts"[103]—surrounded the terrified Roman garrison in the Temple

---

[98] Josephus, *Jewish War*, I, 88.
[99] Ibid, VII, 437.
[100] The term *planos, deceiver*, is also applied to Jesus (Matt. 27:63).
[101] Josephus, *War*, II, 259-260.
[102] Ibid, II, 10-11.
[103] Vermes, *Jesus the Jew*, 46.

during the festival of Pentecost.[104] During the festivals, Jerusalem swarmed with "people from the country...the majority bearing arms."[105]

Put in the context of a restive population of immiserated rural subjects, a collaborationist ruling class very much on edge, and the nationalistic essence of Passover that celebrated the deliverance of Jewish slaves from the oppression of their Egyptian masters following manifold signs and wonders,[106] it comes as little surprise that a prophet up from Galilee who announced the restoration of the kingdom of David, created a disturbance in the Temple, and excited crowds with reports of his own amazing signs and wonders would be met with a violent reaction from the authorities. The Jesus the gospels describe is yet another in a series of kingdom preachers, a man who riled the masses, a type as familiar to the Roman authorities as delusional Bible thumpers are to the Israeli psychiatrists of today.

Those who went ahead of him and those who followed shouted, "Hosanna! Glory to the one coming in the name of the Lord and blessed be the coming kingdom of our father David! Hosanna in the Highest!"[107]

As he entered Jerusalem, the whole city was thrown into commotion. "Who is this?" they asked. The crowd replied, "This is the prophet Jesus, the one from Nazareth in Galilee."[108]

Luke's announcement of the end of the Galilean phase of Jesus' career is as much ominous as hopeful: "When the time drew near for Jesus to be taken up, he braced himself to depart for Jerusalem."[109] It is probable that Jesus and the crowds that welcomed him expected his confrontation with the Temple authorities to trigger an immediate cosmic event, the restoration of the kingdom of David and the defeat of the Gentile powers. Jesus "forged his followers into a committed community and prepared them for an eschatological miracle. The one they all expected when they went up to Jerusalem was, most

---

[104] Josephus, II, 42-44.
[105] Ibid, I, 253.
[106] Exodus 11:10, Deuteronomy 34:11.
[107] Mark 11:7-10.
[108] Matthew 21:10-11.
[109] Luke 9:51.

likely, the arrival of the Kingdom."[110] Jesus expects to celebrate Passover *in the kingdom* and *the whole Sanhedrin*[111] will see the son of man coming on the clouds:

> Truly I tell you that by no means will I drink of the product of the vine until those days when I drink it anew in the kingdom of God.[112]
>
> The High Priest questioned him again and said to him, "Are you the Anointed, the son of the Blessed One?"
>
> And Jesus said, "I am. And you *(plural)* will see the Son of Man seated at the right hand of power and coming with the clouds of heaven!"[113]

As Martinez points out, "renouncing food and drink until a goal is attained solemnizes one's commitment to that goal and sanctifies its accomplishment within the supernatural realm. Jesus consecrates himself to the necessary action, making himself the instrument through which God will establish the new order. [Jesus] seals his absolute commitment to the apocalyptic age with the vow that he will not partake of the sacred bread and wine until the age is ushered in."[114] Vows not to eat[115] or to sleep[116] do not presuppose the expectation of fulfillment is decades or centuries away and "Jesus' death was not only contrary to prophecy but contrary to the divine nature of the Son of man."[117] There are no prophecies of a crucified Messiah who ascends to heaven and subsequently returns.[118]

---

[110] Paula Fredriksen, "Jesus and the Temple, Mark and the War," *Society of Biblical Literature Seminar Papers* 29 (1990), 301.
[111] Mark 14:55.
[112] Mark 14:25.
[113] Mark 14:61-62.
[114] David Martinez, "'May She Neither Eat nor Drink': Love Magic and Vows of Abstinence," *Ancient Magic and Ritual Power*, (Leiden: Brill Academic Publishers, 2001), 338, 350, 351.
[115] Acts 23:12.
[116] Psalm 132:3-5.
[117] Howard M. Teeple, "The Origins of the Son of Man Christology, "*Journal of Biblical Literature* 84/3 (1965) 228.
[118] Psalm 110 concerned David, *not* the Messiah, regardless of how early Christians interpreted it (Acts 2:34-35, Hebrews 1:13, etc.).

The crowds that followed Jesus clearly expected the kingdom of David to magically appear and Luke, writing at least two generations later, invents a parable to explain the delay.[119] When the chief priests and scribes hear about Jesus causing a disturbance in the Temple precinct we are told, "they began seeking how they might kill him because they feared him since the whole crowd *was driven to madness* (*exeplēsseto*) by his teaching."[120] The crowd was not simply "amazed," but in a state of *ekplēxis*, moved to "violent passion, psychological disturbance, madness"[121] by Jesus' kingdom proclamations. Considering when they might safely arrest him, the Temple authorities conclude, "Not during the [Passover] festival, lest the people riot."[122]

Nashawaty noted, "Self-styled prophets have been journeying to Jerusalem on messianic vision quests for centuries. A certain Nazarene carpenter was merely the most charismatic and most written about."[123] Many who experience mental derangement in proximity to Jerusalem have a previous history of psychiatric symptoms. Perhaps not coincidentally the gospel of Mark reports, "Jesus entered a house and the crowd gathered so that it wasn't even possible for them to eat and when his family heard about it, they went to restrain him. They were saying, "He's out of his mind!"[124] Here is the earliest story of what happened when Jesus entered the holiest site that existed in his day:

> They came to Jerusalem and when he entered the Temple he began to throw out those who were selling and buying in the Temple and he overturned the tables of the money exchangers and the chairs of those selling doves and he kept anyone from carrying merchandise through the Temple courtyard."[125]

---

[119] Luke 19:11-27.
[120] Mark 11:18.
[121] Franco Montanari, *The Brill Dictionary of Ancient Greek*, (Leiden: Brill Academic Publishers, 2015), 642.
[122] Mark 14:2.
[123] Chris Nashawaty, "The Jerusalem Syndrome: Why Some Religious Tourists Believe They Are the Messiah," *Wired*, February 17, 2012.
[124] Mark 3:20-21.
[125] Mark 11:15-16.

Jesus' agitation began to spread to the crowds[126] and the Temple authorities decided Jesus was going to be a problem that required a response, a response that ordinarily involved arrest and execution for incitement to violence. The gospel accounts of Jesus' activity prior to his mission to Jerusalem and his actions once he arrived closely match modern reports of Jerusalem syndrome: a break with the family, a "procession or march to one of Jerusalem's holy places," the delivery of a sermon, and the conviction that one's actions will set in motion a momentous event of religious significance such as "the resurrection of the dead."[127]

Josephus reports several rabble-rousing, wonder-working, Kingdom-of-God types who authenticated their message by dramatic charismatic performance. Josephus describes Theudas, mentioned in Acts 5:36, as a *goēs*, a *sorcerer* or *impostor*, as well as a *prophētēs*, a *prophet* whose followers expected the river Jordan to part so they could cross on dry land.[128] The authorities brought Theudas' head back to Jerusalem and put it on display *pour encourager les autres*. Josephus also informs us about a mob deceived by "a magician...who proclaimed salvation and an end to their troubles,"[129] who was also quickly disposed of. Another figure, "the Egyptian," mentioned in Acts 21:38, "established a reputation as a prophet" who amassed a throng of 30,000 and attacked Jerusalem but was repulsed and escaped.[130] The gospel of Luke may contain a reference to the suppression of another local independence movement: "the Galileans whose blood Pilate mixed with their sacrifices."[131] Since the Temple was the only place Jews offered sacrifices, the report indicates the Galileans were slain in the Temple compound. It is probably not coincidental that at the time of Jesus' trial "there was a man called Barabbas in prison with the partisans who had committed murder during the uprising."[132]

---

[126] Mark 11:18.
[127] Bar-El, 87-88.
[128] Josephus, *Jewish Antiquities* XX, 97.
[129] Ibid, XX, 259.
[130] Josephus, *War* II, 259.
[131] Luke 13:1.
[132] Mark 15:7.

Origen acknowledged the existence of charismatic figures Celsus compared to Jesus—"deceivers of Jesus' type"—among them Theudas, "Judas of Galilee" whom the Romans executed, as well as Dositheus, a Samaritan who was supposedly "the one prophesied by Moses," and the infamous "Simon the Samaritan magician [who] beguiled some by magic."[133] Celsus recognized Jesus as belonging to a familiar category—from a skeptical Roman point of view, the miracle-working Jewish exorcist from Nazareth was basically a walking, talking banality, a Palestinian cliché. "Jesus preached that the kingdom of God was at hand, and he was executed by the Romans as a royal pretender. *Prima facie*, he invites comparison with the various prophets and messianic pretenders, such as Theudas and the Egyptian, described by Josephus."[134]

Preterism, the belief that Jesus' predictions were mostly or completely fulfilled by CE 70, is N.T. Wright's explanation for the missing Second Coming now making its rounds. One of Wright's more bizarre let's-pretend claims is "that Jesus ultimately fits no known pattern within the first century,"[135] a transparent piece of humbug utterly overturned by writers such as Celsus, Lucian, Porphyry and Julian. Lucian documented the Christian grifting of Peregrinus—"Lucian's [Peregrinus] is a shyster—the first example in literature of an anything-for-profit evangelist who bilks his congregation."[136] "[Lucian] leaves the impression that

---

[133] Origen, *Contra Celsum* I, 57, II, 8.
[134] Collins, *The Apocalyptic Imagination: An Introduction of Jewish Apocalyptic Literature*, 2nd ed, (Grand Rapids: Eerdmans, 1998), 256.
[135] N.T. Wright, *Jesus and the Victory of God*, (Minneapolis: Fortress Press, 1996), 144.
 Wright's eisegesis has been questioned and refuted by various writers. Clive Marsh, "Theological History? N.T. Wright's Jesus and the Victory of God," *Journal for the Study of the New Testament* 69 (1998) 87; Robert H. Stein, "N.T. Wright's Jesus and the Victory of God: A Review Article," *Journal of the Evangelical Theological Society* 44/2 (2001) 207218; Steve Walton, "Exit the Second Coming?" *Anvil* 16/4 (1999) 281-291; Maurice Casey, "Where Wright is Wrong: A Critical Review of N.T. Wright's *Jesus and the Victory of God*," *Journal for the Study of the New Testament* 69 (1998) 96; Thom Stark, *The Human Faces of God: What Scripture Reveals When It Gets God Wrong (And Why Inerrancy Tries to Hide It)*, (Eugene, OR: Wipf and Stock Publishers, 2011), 187-199; Carey C. Newman, ed, *Jesus and the Restoration of Israel: A Critical Assessment of N.T. Wright's Jesus and the Victory of God*, (Downers Grove, IL: InterVarsity Press, 1999); John W. Loftus, ed, *The Christian Delusion: Why Faith Fails*, (Amherst, NY: Prometheus Press, 2010, 316-345).
[136] Hoffman, *Porphyry's Against the Christians*, 146.

Christians are not so much generous as they are gullible, and not so much faithful as they are foolish."[137]

Lucian described the Christians as *idiōtais anthrōpois*, "ill-informed men,"[138] eager to believe and easily misled—"He does not scruple...to call the Christians *idiōtai*, a word which was then applied by the philosophers to those whom they regarded as incapable of elevated thought."[139] Lucian mocked the "half-baked philosophers drawn from cobblers and carpenters,"[140] likely a gibe aimed at Jesus himself, and probably had Jesus specifically in mind when he composed his story of the "Syrian" exorcist.[141]

Everyone knows of the Syrian from Palestine, the master of his art, and how he receives many struck down by the moon,[142] frothing at the mouth,[143] and eyes rolling, and he sets them aright and sends them away sound of mind...standing beside them as they lie there, he asks from whence [the demons] have come into the body. The madman himself is silent, but the demon answers in Greek or a barbarian tongue[144] from whence and how he entered the man. By adjuring, or if the spirit does not obey, threatening,[145] he drives the demon out.[146]

---

[137] Wayne C. Kannaday, *Apologetic Discourse and the Scribal Tradition: Evidence of the Influence of Apologetic Interests on the Text of the Canonical Gospels*, (Atlanta: Society of Biblical Literature, 2004), 144-145. "...there is significant evidence to suggest that we have here a fairly accurate picture of historical events. In particular the mention of widows visiting Peregrinus is striking...The visibility of widows in the story of Peregrinus will come as no surprise to anyone who has even the most basic knowledge of the involvement of women in early Christianity." (Margaret Y. MacDonald, *Early Christian Women and Pagan Opinion: The Power of the Hysterical Woman*, (Cambridge: Cambridge University Press, 2004), 74-75.)
[138] Lucian, *On the Death of Peregrinus*, 13.
[139] Mark Edwards, *Christians, Gnostics and Philosophers in Late Antiquity*, (London: Routledge, 2012), 95.
[140] Lucian, *The Double Indictment*, 6.
[141] Smith: "It is possible that this parody was inspired by some gospel story like Mk 5.1-19..." (Morton Smith, *Jesus the Magician: Charlatan Or Son of God?* (New York: Harper & Row, 1978), 57.)
[142] Compare Matthew 4:24: "possessed by demons and moonstruck" and Matthew 17:15: "...have mercy on my son because he's moonstruck...he often falls into the fire and often into the water."
[143] Compare Mark 9:18: "the spirit...throws him down and he foams at the mouth."
[144] Compare Mark 5:9: "our name is Legion..."
[145] Compare Mark 5:7: "I beg you, do not torture me..."
[146] Lucian, *The Lover of Lies*, 16.

His feigned ignorance aside, N.T. Wright knows perfectly well the Roman critics of Christianity recognized Jesus as belonging to a familiar species, had access to gospels as old or older than any currently extant, and witnessed early Christian belief and behavior firsthand. *Their assessment of Christianity, however hostile, was not speculative.* Wright's assertion that Jesus fits no known first-century pattern is laughable and his methodology generally is "not the result of his historical researches but rather an article of faith that has informed his scholarly work from its inception."[147]

In the sixth book of his *Wars of the Jews*, Josephus briefly relates the story of a certain Jesus son of Ananias, a rustic from the hinterlands, who began incessantly preaching a series of woes upon Jerusalem several years before the Romans attacked. Regarded by the Jewish leaders as demon possessed, this Jesus was hauled before the Roman governor Albinus and flogged with whips. Albinus eventually pronounced the wretched man insane and ordered him released. During the siege of Jerusalem, still preaching judgment on the city, a stone from a Roman catapult struck the unlucky Jesus, killing him instantly.

Jesus son of Ananias bears a striking similarity to Jesus of Nazareth, another rustic from the boondocks—"No prophet comes from Galilee!"[148]—who likewise pronounced a series of woes on Jerusalem: "Not one stone here will be left on another! Every one will be thrown down!"[149] Jesus was considered mentally unbalanced by his family and the lawyers who came from Jerusalem claimed he was in league with Beelzeboul.[150] The religious authorities also handed Jesus of Nazareth over to a Roman governor, Pilate, who had him flogged, but this Jesus *wasn't* released. The similarities between the two Jesuses are anything but coincidental—Jerusalem "was the eschatological centre of the world, the destination of the homecoming Diaspora and of the pilgrimages of the

---

[147] Dale Allison, "Explaining the Resurrection: Conflicting Convictions," *Journal for the Study of the Historical Jesus* 3.2 (2005) 133.
[148] John 7:52.
[149] Mark 13:2.
[150] Mark 3:20-22.

nations, the place of the coming of the messiah...the place of judgment in Gehinnom and the metropolis of his coming kingdom" and as Hengel noted, Jerusalem was also a permanent focus of "eschatologically motivated attempts at rebellion."[151] Jerusalem, in short, was a world-class crazy magnet long before the days of Jesus and has retained that dubious status ever since. Were Jesus to appear next Easter, accompanied by a gibbering mob of evangelical End Timers, his predictions and his predictable confrontation with the authorities would barely merit a paragraph in the psychiatric literature.

Needless to say, no kingdom of David appeared, and no reign of God miraculously commenced as a result of Jesus' foray into Jerusalem and the words written by the prophets remained just that, words. Paul's promises aside, no glorified Christ burst from the clouds to the sound of trumpets to "rapture" early Christians, and by the end of the first century, believers began to doubt and apologists began to spin the promise of the Parousia:

> They will say, "Where is this 'coming' he promised? Ever since our ancestors died, everything goes on as it has since the beginning of creation."[152]

The apologetic "answer" to this reality-based assessment has been parroted ad nauseam: "To the Lord a thousand years is like a day and a day like a thousand years."[153] Within a generation or two of his brief career, Jesus himself is made to explain away the failure of his central prophecy: "No man knows that day or hour, not the angels in heaven or even the Son. Only the Father knows."[154] Not even the Lord knew the "day or hour"—or, it turns out, the century or the millennium—of his own Return and yet his followers expected Jesus to be back so soon they sold off their property and lived communally.[155]

---

[151] Martin Hengel, *The Pre-Christian Paul*, (London: SCM Press, 1991), 55-56.
[152] 2 Peter 3:4.
[153] 2 Peter 3:8.
[154] Matthew 24:36.
[155] Acts 4:34-35.

At the end of the 1st century at least some still clung for dear life to the illusion of the Parousia. The Didache, a tract written around the end of the century, encouraged its listeners, "Don't let your lamps go out, nor your loins be ungirded!...The Lord will come with all his saints. Then the world will see the Lord coming on the clouds of heaven!"[156] The faithful waited, loins girded and lamps ablaze, scanning the clouds in vain while the world turned. That doubt about the Second Coming had spread is clear from the letter of 1 Clement to Christians in Corinth, probably composed about the same time as Revelation: "Those who are uncertain are miserable, those who doubt in their soul and say, 'We have heard these things since our father's time and look! We have grown old and none of these things has happened.'" The writer continues, "You have peered into the scriptures," and assures the faithful, "that nothing mistaken nor anything falsified has been written in them."[157]

The response of religious groups to radical disconfirmation of their expectations began to be mapped out in Festinger's classic, *When Prophecy Fails*,[158] and as the investigators noted, there is no end to the cleverness of believers in response to defeated expectations—hope unmoored from reality can drift far in any direction.

Since Festinger, similar insights have been applied to early Christian belief.[159] As the Second Coming threatened to become the grandest non-event of all time, the gospel writers "recontextualized" it. For Mark, writing a generation after Paul, the Roman invasion of Palestine was the latest 'sign of the times'—"when you see these things happening, know that he is near, right at the door."[160] "...the fundamental faith of early Christianity is to be found precisely in the strictly temporal expectation of an imminent end of the world, a view that obviously soon proved to be false

---

[156] Didache 16:1, 7-8.
[157] 1 Clement 23:3, 45:2-3.
[158] Leon Festinger, et al., *When Prophecy Fails: A Social and Psychological Study of a Modern Group That Predicted the Destruction of the World*, (Minneapolis: University of Minnesota Press, 1956).
[159] Uri Wernik, "Frustrated Beliefs and Early Christianity: A Psychological Inquiry in the Gospels of the New Testament," *Numen* 22 (1975) 96-130.
[160] Mark 13:29

and by so doing compelled the early church to put something else in its place."[161] Christian apocalyptic is "a paradigm case of great expectations followed by repeated disappointments."[162] "This nostalgic emphasis on prophets of the past was partially motivated by the desire to replace the dismal realities of the present with the idealized glories of Israel's past."[163]

---

[161] Kümmel, *The New Testament: The History of the Investigation of Its Problems* (Nashville: Abingdon Press, 1972), 283-284.
[162] John Gager, *Kingdom and Community: The Social World of Early Christianity*, (Upper Saddle River, NJ: Prentice Hall, 1975), 26-27.
[163] David E. Aune, *Prophecy in Early Christianity and the Ancient Mediterranean World*, (Grand Rapids: William B. Eerdmans, 1983), 154.

11| FIVE INCONVENIENT TRUTHS THAT FALSIFY BIBLICAL REVELATION

BY DAVID MADISON

James Randi's famous million-dollar prize was cancelled in 2015, after going unclaimed for fifty years. The cash was available to anyone who could demonstrate, under controlled conditions, supernatural or paranormal powers. If I had a bankroll like that, I would offer a similar prize, specifically for theism. After so many centuries of pretense by believers, inquiring minds want to know: *Exactly how* can we find out about God? This challenge can be worded precisely: "You get the million bucks when you show us where we can find *reliable, verifiable* data about God, and all theists must agree, *yes,* this is where the data can be found."

One apologist protested that theists disagree about so much, failing to see the irony. But he missed the point. We're not asking that all theists agree about the *interpretation* of God-data—and they certainly don't agree about what they consider data—we're asking *where we can find* the data. It's not even necessary for them to show it to us. Just tell us where we can find the *reliable, verifiable* data about God, and we'll take it from there.

The usual suspects according to theists—the sources of God-knowledge—include prayer, mediation, visions, personal revelations, and 'feeling God in my heart.' Billions of believers go forth into the world every day armed with their certainties about God, based on these channels to the divine. And this is exactly where the apologist got it right: they don't agree. The most devout Jews, Christians (thousands of different brands), Muslims, and Mormons cannot agree on what God is like, wants, or how he prefers to be worshipped. This is why their prayers, visions, and 'feelings in the heart' are highly suspect: they fail the test of being reliable and verifiable. What's going on inside their heads can't be trusted.

Thomas Paine, in *The Age of Reason*, spotted the problem a long time ago: "Revelation when applied to religion, means something communicated immediately from God to man. It is revelation to the first person only, and hearsay to every other, and, consequently, they are not obliged to believe it. It is a contradiction in terms and ideas to call anything a revelation that comes to us at second hand, either verbally or in writing. Revelation is necessarily limited to the first communication."

We are "not obligated to believe" what someone thinks about God, no matter how devout the person might be.

But, You See, We Have this Book.

Obviously, the argument that it's-all-in-your-head could be circumvented if god-data came in the form of a tangible artifact in the external world. Evangelicals are always on the hunt in Palestine for artifacts to prove the Jesus story, but they're pretty sure they already have one. What more could you want than a thousand-page book? Christians have never been shy about the authenticity of this document. The Gideons claim that they are dedicated to "making the Word of God available to everyone." The American Bible Society doesn't hesitate to call its product "God's Word." Why would they lie? Behind this positioning is a PR campaign that has endured for centuries, fueled, of course, by that famous text, 2 Timothy 3:16–17: "All scripture is inspired by God and is useful for teaching, for reproof, for correction, and for training in righteousness, so that everyone who belongs to God may be proficient, equipped for every good work."

In this text, the words "inspired by God" translate *God-breathed*. So, "God's Word" isn't far off the mark, in terms of nailing the concept. Many Christians assume that the matter is settled. What more could you want? The Bible itself tells us that it is inspired. So, has the request for reliable, verifiable data about God been met?

SORRY, 2 TIMOTHY 3:16–17 DOESN'T WORK

Of course, this text has authority for those who already believe in the Bible. But for those who don't, why does it matter—why would it carry any weight at all? Faith can't be used to prove faith. There's a parallel belief that illustrates the point.

Is the Roman Catholic Church right that the pope is infallible? I was raised on the Protestant side of a Catholic-Protestant divide in small-town Indiana. We ridiculed the Catholics for two things especially: all of those "idols" in their church (our stark churches had no statuary at all) and the claim that the pope was infallible. I'm pretty sure we had no idea, really, what that meant. Our idea was a caricature of the dogma—we did not know its history, the politics behind it, and the restrictions that apply.

But here's the point. If a Catholic pleaded with us, "It's true *because the Church says it true*," our response was, "Big deal! We think the Catholic Church is wrong about just about everything, it's fake Christianity!" It didn't matter what *that* church said. As Glenda the Good Witch told the Wicked Witch in the *Wizard of Oz*, "You have no power here! Begone!" Likewise, the argument for inspired scripture based *on the Bible itself* has no power. The Bible's authority is not established outside the circle of those who already believe it. As Peter Brancazio has stated,

"Needless to say, the assertion that the Bible is divinely inspired because it says so in the Bible is an egregious application of faulty logic."[1]

---

[1] Peter Brancazio, The Bible from Cover to Cover, p. 484.

OTHER SUSPICIONS ABOUT 2 TIMOTHY

This letter was probably a forgery; few mainstream New Testament scholars believe that it is one of the apostle Paul's authentic letters. But whether it was written by Paul or one of his followers really doesn't matter. Why would we trust whomever it was that wrote "all scripture is inspired by God"? How would he know that? It's a popular sentiment, suitable for embroidery and pious greeting cards, but does it stand up to scrutiny? It's one of a thousand religious claims that cannot be verified.

This author wrote long before the New Testament even existed, so would his claim about scripture apply to the new Christian canon? Apologists might claim that this text applies to the *concept*, so the New Testament deserves inclusion. But are they willing to extend the courtesy to the Qur'an and the Book of Mormon?—after all, the wording is "all scripture," and Muslims and Mormons fall within the Abrahamic faith tradition. Why not bind their holy books with the Old and New Testaments in the Bible on the church altar? I suspect most Christians would balk.

Of course, the author of 2 Timothy, whoever he was, had no clue that his letter would end up "in the Bible." What would his reaction have been, had he been told, "Hey, this letter you're writing will one day be considered scripture too"? Having such high regard for holy writ, he might have said, "How could that possibly happen?" We know, of course, that a lot of stuff in the Bible shouldn't be there—which helps to disqualify it as Word of God, and that will be considered shortly.

So, alas, we have to give up on 2 Timothy.

But that doesn't slow down the Gideons and the American Bible Society pushing their product. More power to them, actually. Randal Helms has said that the Bible is a "self-destructing artifact,"[2] and when it's read without priests and apologists hovering nearby, it's not the most convincing read in the world. There's a reason church folks are urged to

---

[2] Randal Helms, *The Bible Against Itself*, p. 1

try the Chapter-a-Day Plan to get through it—because more than that is hard to stomach. Over-dosing would not be a good thing.

FALSIFICATION OF THE MIRACLE CLAIM: FIVE INCONVENIENT TRUTHS

INCONVENIENT TRUTH, NUMBER ONE:

Unless we're offered a reliable, verifiable way to tell the difference between Bible verses that came from a god and those that came from the mind of the guy pushing the pen, the case for the Miracle of Divine Inspiration can't be made.

In Rembrandt's depiction of the inspiration of St. Matthew, an angel whispers the gospel in his right ear. In the real world without mythical creatures, we'll have to settle for the holy spirit whispering into his brain. I suppose that's how inspiration is imagined; the author receives the divine message—somehow—and writes it on the page.

But it's not as clear-cut as all that. On any given day, thousands of thoughts bounce around in our heads. The brain is the seat of thoughts, emotions, imaginings, dreams—and sometimes, hallucinations; it's all there, even though no one has a full grasp yet of the science of consciousness. We're asked to believe by religionists that revelation is also part of the brain-mix, e.g., answered prayers and the 'knowledge of Jesus' in their hearts, and on rare occasions in the distant past, messages that were turned into scripture.

Now the red flags are up, however. Is it really true that words in some brains have been sparked by the holy spirit? Consider the proposed scenario: A pious author wrote paragraphs that are now revered as scripture; we can imagine him, quill and parchment in hand, scrawling the sentences. What exactly was flowing from his brain to the fingers that moved the quill? Were the words coming *from* his brain or *through* his brain from a supposed higher source? Was it really, truly revelation…or, instead, were his words the product of his own imagination or even hallucination? We know that the apostle Paul was convinced by his hallucinations of Jesus; should we be as well? Non-fundamentalist believers concede that three possibilities are in the mix. Unless you can propose a way to *tell the difference* between revelation, imagination and hallucination, don't expect skeptics to take you seriously. We suspect smoke and mirrors, a con job.

This is the challenge for 'Bible-believing' Christians: you must tell us *how you know* that any particular verse or chapter of the Bible came from God, and not from the mind of the author. It's not wise to grant Word-of-God status to stuff that tumbled out of somebody's imagination; this would throw the entire theological enterprise into massive confusion. Which is precisely what has happened. Christian theologian Jack Nelson–Pallmeyer states the problem clearly:

> [The Bible] is also a dangerous book because we often ascribe divine will to the many human distortions it contains. We undermine the sacredness of the Bible and fuel its dangers whenever we fail to discern the difference between distortions and revelation, whenever we give its words and its writers too much authority, or whenever we abandon or fail critically to examine the contents of its pages. Simply stated, the Bible can inform our religious experience, but it is often wrong about God.[3]

This kind of candor is refreshing, and follows in the wake of a couple of centuries of critical Bible scholarship. No surprise there. But, also no surprise, Nelson-Pallmeyer fails to take the next step and *tell how to spot the difference* between distortion and revelation.

Of course, we all make our own value judgments; we are tempted to say, "Oh yes, this is God's word," when we come across the better verses in the Bible. We are guided by our own sensibilities and moral compasses. Thus we can appreciate the sentiment of Micah 6:8: "He has told you, O mortal, what is good; and what does the Lord require of you but to do justice, and to love kindness, and to walk humbly with your

---

[3] Jack Nelson-Pallmeyer, *Jesus Against Christianity: Reclaiming the Missing Jesus*, p. 140.

God?" This is actually pretty cool; it tells us *exactly* what the Lord requires of us. But the apostle Paul claimed that he had an update about what God expects: "...if you confess with your lips that Jesus is Lord and believe in your heart that God raised him from the dead, you will be saved." (Romans 10:9)

So, Micah had an idea; Paul had an idea. Did either of these pronouncements come from God—or were they just the opinions of their authors? Theologians have probably written thousands of pages trying to mesh these two points of view, because they can't let go of the idea that both texts were inspired. So far, theologians have failed to provide the criteria that we must have to take their pronouncements seriously: how can we tell what came from God and what didn't? *There is no way to tell.* It's theological bias and guesswork.

Many years ago, a therapist friend said to me, "Reality is what happens *outside* the patient's head." That comes to mind when we acknowledge that all scripture, revelation, answered prayers, and visions begin their journey to the external world in the human brain. Believers make the claim that brain matter is acted upon by God, but they fail to make a convincing case.

Once when a skeptic visited Lourdes, he was shown the grotto with hundreds of crutches that had been thrown away by people who had been 'cured.' He asked to see the room with *discarded wooden legs*. Just one limb that had been miraculously regrown would be far more convincing—yes, indeed, a miracle—than a hundred crutches. That's the kind of unambiguity we want when we're told, "Ah ha, here for sure is a verse or chapter that really did come from the holy spirit." Lacking that, we suspect we're being conned.

There's a very helpful tool, by the way, to guide those who are up for the task of wading through the Bible verse-by-verse to test its quality. Steve Wells has done the wading, and produced *The Skeptic's Annotated Bible*. He sorted Bible verses into several broad categories, and indicated how many verses there are in each category. Into "Conflicts with Science and History" he placed 428 errors. It's a common faith aphorism that

God doesn't make mistakes, but the Bible itself offers evidence otherwise.

INCONVENIENT TRUTH, NUMBER TWO:

God deserves an F as an author. Christian theologians bring considerable skill to the task of finessing the truly bad ideas in the Bible, but they have embraced mission impossible.

All books about theology—those written by pop-theology specialists as well as seminary professors—should come with a disclaimer, perhaps a sticker on the cover: "Readers should be aware that they won't actually learn about God by reading this book. They will learn this author's opinions about God." They will also learn what the author has to say about other theologians' opinions. But all these books come up empty on the 'ultimate reality' supposedly behind the endless speculation. Sam Harris made the correct call: "Theology is now little more than a branch of human ignorance. Indeed, it is ignorance with wings."[4] Theology doesn't deliver on what it promises, but instead offers endless discussion of what god-channelers and theologians have claimed.

Christian theologians have had to work especially hard at modifying ancient descriptions of their god; driven by cognitive dissonance, they specialize in cleaning up the Bible. Most of them, fully aware of the world revealed by science, have hunches about how a good, ethical god ought to behave. They know that the god depicted in scripture is impossible. None of the so-called arguments for the existence of God can be used in its defense. Yet the Bible is one of their primary anchors. Neil Carter, author of the Godless-in-Dixie blog, pokes fun at the Bible defenders: "…many theologians love to meet at pubs. They need the alcohol to dampen their critical thinking skills so they can forget about all the angst they live with as professional theologians."[5]

---

[4] Sam Harris, *The End of Faith*, p. 173.
[5] Neil Carter, 6 November 2016, http://www.patheos.com/blogs/godlessindixie/2016/11/06/paul-the-true-founder-of-christianity/

Those who are raised Christian—who have gone through the full drill of Sunday school or catechism, and years of Sunday worship—don't commonly notice the flaws. Usually because the bad theology has been *euphemized*. For example, what's not to love about John 3:16? "For God so loved the world that he gave his only Son, so that everyone who believes in him may not perish but may have eternal life." "Gave his only son" sounds so much better than "God required a human sacrifice…"

And that human sacrifice extolled in the New Testament is the culmination of a long series of bad ideas, not the least of which is that animal sacrifice was a way to get right with God—with ghastly detailed descriptions preserved in the holy text. God deserves the F moreover for 'inspiring' authors to come up with the concepts *Chosen People* and *Promised Land*, which are the bellicose ravings of an ancient tribe whose folklore is preserved in the Old Testament. This theological hubris had to conjure even more crazed imaginings when cognitive dissonance became too painful. After the Chosen People had been beaten down for centuries by one invading empire after another, and their Promised Land handed off endlessly to others, yet another bad idea gained traction: there would be a hero, a superman—maybe he would even rank as a son of God—who would intervene to restore their ranking as the Chosen People.

"Palestine in the first century CE was experiencing a rash of messianism," Richard Carrier has pointed out. "There was an evident clamoring of sects and individuals to announce that they had found the messiah. It is therefore no oddity or accident that this is exactly when Christianity arose. It was yet another messiah cult in the midst of a fad for just such cults."[6]

In the Christian version of messianism, God was out to get even. When his son brought the Kingdom of God to earth, most of humanity would be killed off; Jesus said that the precedent for this was Noah's flood, during which sinners were swept away. To his credit I suppose,

---

[6] Richard Carrier, *On the Historicity of Jesus*, p. 67.

the apostle Paul downplayed the most-favored-nation status of the Jews, but took magical thinking to new heights. His obsession was the resurrection of Jesus, and all that mattered for salvation was belief that it had happened. Jesus would someday soon descend through the clouds to welcome the remnant—those who believed in the resurrection—including those who would emerge from their graves to keep the appointment. And, by the way, this is not a caricature of Chosen People/Promised Land/Messiah-on-the-Verge/Human Sacrifice theology. It's starkly presented in the sacred text, with an overlay of folklore, fantasy literature, and fairy tale.

None of the charming parables and sentimental aphorisms can disguise the underlying foundation of bad theology. Yes, such texts as the parables of the Good Samaritan and the Prodigal Son resonate with decent people, but so many of the parables of Jesus are cryptic allusions to the imminent Kingdom of God that was about to happen, but failed to materialize. And yes, "love your neighbor as yourself" is a good principle to follow, but is hardly original to the Bible.

It is tempting to say that 'no one in his right mind' could believe the dysfunctional theologies found in the Bible, but that's not true at all. Millions of people in their right minds—they function perfectly well in the real world—give their assent to the crude theologies invented by the ancient seers. Christian theologians have done their job well; they disguised the bad theology—at least have diverted attention from it.

They perfected Novocain for the mind. How else to explain the easy acceptance by the laity of mindless barbaric rituals? I grew up in low-church Methodism in the American heartland—surely the last place to find crude cult ceremony. Yet somehow—how were our minds rendered numb?—on Communion Sundays we pretended to eat human flesh and drink human blood. How did that become part of dignified worship? Why was there no one to step up and ask, "What the hell are you playing at?" Meanwhile, the Catholics on the other side of town had succumbed to the even weirder mythology that it *really was* blood and flesh being consumed. This all derives, I suspect, from Bad Theology Exhibit A in the New Testament, John 6:54–57:

> Those who eat my flesh and drink my blood have eternal life, and I will raise them up on the last day. For my flesh is true food and my blood is true drink. Those who eat my flesh and drink my blood abide in me, and I in them. Just as the living Father sent me, and I live because of the Father, so whoever eats me will live because of me.

There is it. Stark, undisguised, blatant. How could anything this dreadful have been inspired by God? But when a priest presides, and officiates with music, costumes, gestures, and incense—dramatic showbiz accoutrements—well, isn't that just the way it's been done forever? It works because priests turned it into theatre.

It's easy to get away with myth—and disguise the mistakes—when you've mastered awesome production values.

Even after Martin Luther had shifted authority from the papacy to the Bible—and it was finally translated into the vernacular—there was little capacity or inclination to read the Bible *critically*. It was holy writ, a relic to be venerated, and apologists could be trusted to find the 'spiritual truth' lurking behind the most hideous parts of the canon. But the reckoning finally came. Eventually it occurred to serious thinkers that the Bible should not be exempt from critical scrutiny. For the better part of two centuries scholars have debated and studied every verse of the Bible, and, truly, its status as 'word of God' has been wiped out.

For readers who step outside the aura of holiness that protects the Bible—seeing it on the church alter every Sunday, for example—the disguises don't work.

When it is deprived of 'sacred artifact' status, its full horrors come into sharp focus, and apologists have to pray with all their might that laypeople will not study the Bible unsupervised. Otherwise nightmare scenarios emerge:

- Andrew Seidel: "The road to atheism is littered with bibles that have been read cover to cover."
- Isaac Asimov: "Properly read, the Bible is the most potent force for atheism ever conceived."
- Penn Jillette: "Reading the Bible is the fast track to atheism."

Yes, it's that bad. *God deserves an F* might be considered too flippant, not befitting a serious discussion. While stating the case bluntly, perhaps Valerie Tarico is less abrasive. In her article, "Why Is the Bible So Badly Written?" she states:

> Millions of Evangelicals and other Christian fundamentalists believe that the Bible was essentially dictated by God to men who acted as human channelers. Each phrase is considered so perfect that it merits careful linguistic analysis to determine His precise meaning. If that were the case, one would have to conclude that God is a terrible writer. Although some passages in the Bible are lyrical and gripping, many would get kicked back by any competent editor or writing professor—kicked back with a lot of red ink.[7]

Many mainstream Protestants, who distance themselves from evangelicals and fundamentalists, may protest that I'm attacking a straw man. They don't have such a rigid view of biblical inspiration, so thus have more leeway in seeing the Bible as a 'human' document. But even among high church Episcopalians, I doubt that the richly bound book on the altar will be tucked away in a closet anytime soon: "Oh, now we see that it can't be the Word of God."

---

[7] Valerie Tarico, "Why Is the Bible So Badly Written?" https://valerietarico.com/2018/01/28/why-is-the-bible-so-badly-written/

Inconvenient Fact, Number Three

How can we be sure what those 'words of God' mean? Even if we could manage to bypass all the terrible texts and bad theology, to focus on the better parts, we still are at a loss: whose interpretations can we trust?

It would take several lifetimes and legions of scholars to even count the different interpretations. Which ones are right? The miracle of divine inspiration turns out to be flawed miracle, just a fragment of a miracle—hardly worth the trouble. God dumped this massive document on the ancient world with a shrug: "Now, you figure it out—and good luck with that." Didn't God see this problem coming?

Scholars have indeed been hard at work for centuries counting the interpretations, but also creating them, 'gaining new insights' into God's will. The goal, supposedly, is to figure out what the original authors meant, with the hope of getting closer to what God meant. How has that worked out?

A Case Study: The Letters of Paul

Even as a teenager I was a Bible geek. I was curious about how the Bible *happened*, and I sensed it would take a lot of study to understand it. Little did I realize that this undermines the very concept that God opted for an ancient book as a teaching tool for everyone. Sometimes I find confirmation of this in the most unlikely places. The Gideons and the American Bible Society have scattered billions of copies around the world; they seem to assume that its message is not hard to grasp. Why else push it on anyone who will take it? Hence what a stunning admission by conservative Christian scholar, Ben Witherington, in his 400-page analysis of Paul's Letter to the Romans; he states on the very first page: "…the goal of understanding this formidable discourse is not reached for a considerable period of time."[8] Witherington feels the pain: "Now, you figure

---

[8] Ben Witherington III, *Paul's Letter to the Romans: A Socio-Rhetorical Commentary*, p. 1.

it out—and good luck with that?" Shouldn't we be able to open the Bible, and, right away, 'get it'?

"Oh, that was a such a fun read," said no Christian ever after making it through Paul's letters. But 'fun' is not the point, of course. Can we grasp the mind of God as we soldier on through these dense pages? This is the brick wall, just one aspect of the third inconvenient truth: The ancient text itself is a dead, static document—a useless miracle, actually—that has been used as a platform for countless theological speculators—popes, pastors, priests and preachers—to claim that it means what *they* want it to mean. Those who are suspicious of the 'inspiration miracle' are entitled to ask, "Who gets to decide what God meant?"

A widely respected scholar, Jesuit Joseph A. Fitzmyer, has described the problem in a careful, understated way (I have added italics):

> Rudolph Bultmann, the great German NT scholar of the early part of this century, maintained that *there was no presuppositionless exegesis* of the Bible. Every commentator somehow *manifests his or her confessional stance* in interpreting a biblical text. Yet there also exists a corporate exegetical endeavor engaged in by interpreters of different backgrounds, whether Jewish, Protestant, or Roman Catholic. This corporate endeavor tends to produce over a period of time a *less subjective approach* to a particular biblical writing and also brings to light the often subconscious presuppositions of the individual interpreter. *From such presuppositions no one fully escapes.*[9]

This is one way of saying that consensus can be achieved, but this is usually along denominational lines. And when one strays into other theistic traditions, e.g., Jewish and Muslim, consensus will be well out of reach—especially about the letters of Paul, who had succumbed to magical thinking about the resurrection of Jesus. In fact, it would be difficult to name any patch of scripture that better illustrates the problem of *what*

---

[9] Joseph A. Fitzmyer, Romans: A New Translation with Introduction and Commentary (The Anchor Bible), p. xiv.

God meant. Maybe Paul was selected to write part of the Bible because of his zeal—but God neglected to ask, "What are your weaknesses?"

Classical scholar Michael Grant has written candidly about the problem of understanding Paul. He has explained what we're up against; these excerpts are from his 2000 book, *St. Paul*.[10] I have italicized the words that illustrate Inconvenient Truth Three:

- The Letters are vividly varied and lively, but unrounded, unarranged and muddled, making their points not by any orderly procedure but by a series of hammer-blow contrasts and antitheses. Paul is far too impulsive and enthusiastic to standardize his terms or arrange his material. *He is often ambiguous*—with results that have reverberated down the centuries. And he commits flagrant self-contradictions, which caused Augustine, among many others, the deepest anxiety.

- His highly idiosyncratic ways of thinking and expressing himself already *make the problem of understanding him a daunting one.* And his blend of Jewish thought with Greek expression—a forcible bringing together of two alien cultures—merely serve to make it more daunting still. In consequence, *it has always been possible to take widely differing views of what he intended to say.*

- One feels sympathy for those who dined at the house of John Colet, Dean of St Paul's, early in the sixteenth century. While guests ate, 'a servant would read aloud in a clear, distinct voice' a chapter from Paul's Epistles or the Proverbs of Solomon—and then their host was accustomed to ask them what they believed the significance of the passage in question to be. Even Martin Luther would have found this an awkward predicament, for *he was not always at all sure what Paul really meant*, though he 'thirsted ardently to know.'

Grant's critique is a knockout blow to inspiration-miracle credibility. Paul's letters could be the most written about works in Western

---

[10] Michael Grant, St. Paul, pp. 6, 8-9, and 34.

history—except perhaps for the gospels. Witherington's book on Romans includes an 18-page bibliography, and he points out, "This list could go on for miles..."[11] Every syllable that Paul wrote—every word, phrase, and sentence—has been analyzed, over analyzed, super analyzed. Since devout scholars are sure God inspired Paul, they don't want to miss anything. But this leaves a big muddle.

For example, at the opening of Paul's Letter to the Romans, he says of Jesus Christ our Lord (v. 1:5): "...through whom we have received grace and apostleship to bring about the obedience of faith for the sake of his name among all the nations..." That doesn't seem too daunting, does it? Witherington points out, however: "Certainly one of the most debated of phrases in a document full of debatable points is 'obedience of faith.'"[12] Who knew? Millions of readers haven't given it a second thought. Witherington cites the work of C. E. B. Cranfield, who lists *seven possible meanings* for 'obedience of faith.' Surely this is overthinking Paul's mediocre ramblings, a consequence of God dropping the ancient book and walking away: "Now, you figure it out—and good luck with that."

This orgy of competitive interpretation followed the Protestant Reformation especially, which championed 'the priesthood of all believers.' Stephen Prothero describes the resulting chaos: "In the absence of a spiritual Supreme Court (or papacy) to adjudicate competing scriptural interpretations, all believers were free to interpret the Bible for themselves. This new Christian liberty resulted—as Catholics predicted it would—not in unity but in near-anarchy, an endless splintering of Protestantism into a Babel of competing beliefs and practices."[13]

Hence there is the prevalent assumption that anyone can read the Bible and decide what it means: "The Holy Spirit speaks the truth to me." This resembles the common bragging in other areas of life, "I'm

---

[11] Ibid., p. xvii.
[12] Ibid., p. 34.
[13] Prothero, S. R. (2006). *American Jesus how the Son of God became a national icon*. New York: Farrar, Straus and Giroux.

entitled to my opinion"—without bothering to check if it is an *informed* opinion. Which means that we have wandered far off course trying to identify *reliable, verifiable* data about God.

The problem has been compounded a thousand-fold as our understanding of world has moved beyond ancient superstitions. No: virgin births, water into wine, and resurrections don't happen. So enlightened Christians, who grasp the threat, struggle to salvage "God's meaning." It's almost as if God didn't see the Enlightenment or the scientific revolution coming; that there would one day be people who know that the magical thinking saturating the gospels must be dropped. Paul Tobin, in an essay in another Loftus anthology, describes the dilemma, the discomfort, of theologians who want to have *their* Jesus but not the Jesus encumbered by magical thinking:

> It is obvious that since the late nineteenth century these [liberal] theologians have ceased to believe that the main events of the Gospels are historical, especially the virgin birth, the associated nativity stories, the miracles, and the bodily resurrection of Jesus. The liberals trip all over themselves trying to avoid saying the actual truth: *if the bodily resurrection of Jesus is not historical then traditional Christianity, in any form, is no longer valid.* This is the skeptic's position, of course. But the liberals added that the resurrection is to be understood in a different sense, but just exactly what sense is not clear. Their writings contain so much garbled speech that it is difficult to even see if they agree with one another.[14]

The garbled speech of one sect of theologians rarely matches the garbled speech of others. They are off and running, speculating endlessly. But the ancient text itself is stranded and helpless, the feeble fragment of a miracle. A mirage.

---

[14] *The Christian Delusion: Why Faith Fails*, John W. Loftus, editor. P172

INCONVENIENT TRUTH, NUMBER 4:

The damage the Bible has done wipes out the claim that God planned it to be our guide for the ages. Too much that was swept into the canon hasn't stood the test of time—and too much was left out. A competent God wouldn't have screwed up so badly.

Holy books are popular because they hold the promise of certainty: The Bible is the place 'to look it up' to find out what God wants and expects of us. But the concept of *canon* is a distraction; it diverts people from seeing that there are other sources of wisdom. The concept is also dangerous, because *that one book* is considered binding in a way that others are not, and there are those who assume the role of enforcer. In 1993 an anti-abortion zealot murdered a doctor, because "he wanted him to stop doing things the Bible says is wrong, and start doing what the Bible says is right."[15] Bishop John Shelby Spong has commented on the long history of this murderous impulse:

> My understanding and knowledge of the history of religious systems convinces me that whenever a group of religious folk begin to believe that they possess God's truth, almost inevitably they become those who in the name of their version of that truth persecute, excommunicate, purge, burn at the stake, or justify cruel religious wars against any who will not salute their tradition or acknowledge their rightness in things religious.[16]

If such zeal is planted into human minds—we crave certainties and appreciate absolutes—the stage is set for bad outcomes. Couldn't the deity who gave us this thousand-page book have foreseen the consequences?

As many critics have pointed out, there are least five items that should be in the Bible that aren't: clear, unequivocal, easy-to-grasp prohibitions. With these missing, and with the quantities of human misery that ensued, it's hard to take the Bible seriously as the best that could

---

[15] Anthony Lewis column, *The New York Times*, 12 March 1993.
[16] John Shelby Spong, *Rescuing the Bible From Fundamentalism*, p. 170.

emerge from the divine mind. Why did God leave out these commandments?

- Thou shalt not engage in war. And if you do, don't pray to me for consolation, support or victory. Don't assume I'm on your side.
- Thou shalt not enslave other humans. Ever. Period.
- Thou shalt not despise and discriminate on the basis of skin color or location of birth. Ever. Period.
- Thou shalt not discriminate against women. Ever. Period. In any way.
- Thou shalt not discriminate against gay people. I made them that way, so get over it.

Not only does the Bible leave out these prohibitions, there are many passages that *encourage all of these sins* that should have been condemned. God missed his chance to nudge us in the best directions, and humanity has paid the price.

Earlier I mentioned Micah 6:8: "What does the Lord require of you, but to do justly, to love mercy, and to walk humbly with your God." The five missing commandments could have gone a long way in nailing down *exactly how* to "do justice and love mercy." In addition to these omissions, believers have to face head-on the Bible texts—and collections of texts—that have brought substantial harm. Instead of reciting the usual litany of wars and persecutions that zealous belief in the Bible has provoked, we can focus on just three of Jesus' obsessions that are no credit to him.

INCALCULABLE DAMAGE: JESUS GOT IT WRONG ON DIVORCE

According to Mark 10:6–12 (RSV), Jesus said this:

> But from the beginning of creation, God made them male and female. For this reason a man shall leave his father and mother and be joined to his wife, and the two shall become one flesh. So

they are no longer two but one flesh. What therefore God has joined together, let not man put asunder.
And in the house the disciples asked him again about this matter. And he said to them, Whoever divorces his wife and marries another, commits adultery against her. And if she divorces her husband and marries another, she commits adultery.

No one can fault Jesus—or any other believer—for assuming that God set things up for men and women to get together: God authorized this 'joining.' It's one thing, however, to argue that God intended men and women to "become one flesh," but quite another to claim that God had his hand in hooking up all the couples. It is a *monumental non sequitur* that God has arranged every marriage that ever was, which is Jesus' implication: 'what God has joined together.' Full stop: Jesus was wrong about this (or Mark, who wrote this script). Think of all the bad marriages that have taken place in the history of the world, across all the centuries and all the cultures. Consider all the bad reasons for which people have been married. But never mind, God has arranged all of them? Giving full credit to Jesus (or Mark), this text can be judged against the background of Old Testament provisions for divorce, which were based on the property status of women—and the whim of the husband (see Deuteronomy 24:1–4). It is an advance to see marriage as a 'holy' union—ordained by God—that should not be so easily cancelled.

But the resort to absolutism is not an advance; it descends into absurdity. No matter how much human happiness could be rescued by ending bad marriages, *it can't be allowed* because God did the 'joining' in every case. Jesus makes it worse by adding that people who remarry commit adultery by doing so. This text has consigned so many lives to unending misery.

INCALCULABLE DAMAGE: WAITING FOR GOD AND JESUS TO RESCUE THE WORLD

The gospels fall so far off the reliability scale that we have no way of knowing what Jesus actually taught. But the first three gospels pushed the idea that a 'kingdom of God' was about to be realized on earth, with Jesus as the 'Son of Man' playing the leading role.[17] This new kingdom was imminent, i.e., 'before this generation passes away.' But the apostle Paul deserves most of the blame for the end-is-near thinking that took deep root in Christian thought. He was obsessed with the idea that Jesus' descent through the clouds, to make everything better, could be only a matter of months away—or a few years at the very most. He fully expected to be alive to see it.

Because of these texts, so many Christians have wasted so much time and energy stoking the belief that Jesus 'won't delay much longer.' Devout Christians of some brands can't get enough of looking to the clouds for Jesus and warning the rest of us to 'get ready'—and woe to those who won't pay attention. What's worse, some evangelicals are cheering for the turmoil mentioned in Mark 13:7–8, the prelude to Jesus' arrival: "And when you hear of wars and rumors of wars, do not be alarmed; this must take place, but the end is not yet. For nation will rise against nation, and kingdom against kingdom; there will be earthquakes in various places, there will be famines; this is but the beginning of the birth-pangs." Such calamities have been happening for thousands of years, so Jesus must be just around the corner—so bring it on…or so the evangelists hope.

Moreover, this mindset can undermine commitment to making the world a better place. It's all out of our hands—human effort is worthless, even futile—if we can count on Jesus/God to make things better. There is real-world impact of this delusion. In 2017, Republican congressman Tim Walberg told a town hall meeting:

---

[17] See Bart Ehrman's 2001 book, *Jesus: Apocalyptic Prophet of the New Millennium*, and John Loftus' article, "At Best Jesus was a Failed Apocalyptic Prophet," in *The Christian Delusion: Why Faith Fails*.

I believe there's climate change. I believe there's been climate change since the beginning of time. Do I think man has some impact? Yeah, of course. Can man change the entire universe? No. Why do I believe that? Well, as a Christian, I believe that there is a creator in God who is much bigger than us. And I'm confident that, if there's a real problem, he can take care of it.[18]

If enough of these low-wattage thinkers are in positions of power, we can add climatic disaster to the roster of agonies listed in Mark 13—and Jesus still won't show up.

INCALCULABLE DAMAGE: DEVILS AND DEMONS SHOULD BE RETIRED

The resurrected Jesus, in Mark 16:17, proclaims that baptized Christians have the power to cast out demons. Given the preoccupation with demons in this first gospel, it's no surprise that the fake ending of the gospel (16:9–20) included this 'quote.' It's clear that demonology has been part of the mindset from the very beginning. No wonder belief in evil spirits continues to this day among Bible-believers; the Vatican has a staff of exorcists.

The failure of humans to understand causation, until recent eras of history, has impeded our grasp of how the world works. Even as seismologists measure volcanoes and lava flows, there are folks who offer gifts to the volcano gods. Belief in demons, however, has had far more grievous outcomes. On most lists of human suffering—plagues, millions of slow deaths from cancer every year, genetic diseases, natural disasters, famines—I rarely see 'treatment of the insane.' Severe afflictions of the mind are so little understood; it's no surprise that ravings and strange behavior have been traced to demons. And this colossal misreading of human pain is legitimatized by the gospels especially. By what kind of miracle were

---

[18] http://time.com/4800000/tim-walberg-god-climate-change/

stories of Jesus haggling with demons allowed into the canon?

It can be noted, moreover, that God shot himself in the foot with these stories. Monotheism is *compromised* by the belief that the spiritual realm includes many beings lesser than God—but sharing powers inherent in the status. In Mark 6:7 we read that Jesus gave his disciples "authority over the unclean spirits," which only begs the question: Why didn't God exercise *his* authority to get rid of them altogether? How does the 'inspiration miracle' make sense, if the story doesn't make sense? That famous division of spiritual labor—Father, Son and Holy Ghost—becomes a minor embarrassment.

INCONVENIENT TRUTH, NUMBER FIVE:

The original Bible no longer exists; all of it has vanished. Its restoration means we have highly processed the Word of God. The miracle of inspiration—as was the case with *figuring out its meaning*—has been at the mercy of sycophants who have a vested interest in making the Bible look good. They manipulate the miracle as they see fit.

From the outset, God bungled the job. He failed to take proper care of the original documents and make sure they were copied with dead accuracy. In the wake of this error, scholars have painstakingly compared thousands of ancient manuscripts to figure out the most likely wording of the original, lost texts. All this effort has been made to get the 'correct Bible' into the hands of believers; they little suspect, however, that their 'word of God' is highly processed. Thousands of scholars and theologians have had their say in what we see on the printed page of every Bible. But is this a case of 'many hands make light work' or 'too many cooks spoil the broth'?

We are accustomed to the division of the text into chapters and verses; we take the punctuation for granted. In some Bibles, headings and titles have been added; in the case of the gospels, for example, "…according to Matthew," "according to Mark," etc.—though we don't know who wrote them. In some versions, the words of Jesus are printed in red.[19] The versification, punctuation, titles, and red ink were added later, well after the 'miracle' of inspiration. And then, of course, along came the translators. Once the 'best' New Testament manuscripts have been identified, the various Christian brands hire translators to make the text available to ordinary readers. While Protestants have overwhelmingly favored the King James Version of 1611, Elizabethan English is an imperfect vessel if you're trying to make the meaning clear today. So, Bible translation has become an industry; overwhelmingly, however, translators are people of faith, and that has an impact on how texts are rendered.

They function as cosmeticians, doing their best to disguise the blemishes and banalities that cast doubt on a miraculous origin. One independent New Testament translator, David Bentley Hart (whose effort was published by Yale University Press in 2017) warns us about the translation business (italics added):

> Over the years, I had become disenchanted with almost all the standard translations available, and especially with modern versions produced by large committees of scholars, many of whom (it seems to me) have been predisposed by *inherited theological habits to see things in the text that are not really there, and to fail to notice other things that most definitely are.* Committees are bland affairs, and tend to reinforce our expectations; *but the world of late antiquity is so remote from our own* that it is almost never what we expect.[20]

Translators are guided by theology, and see things that aren't there—and ignore things that are there. Let's return to that infamous text that makes most Christians cringe, Luke 14:26; here are four

---

[19] Some editors have been guilty of egregious goofs, e.g., printing in red Mark 13:14, "let the reader understand," which could not have been spoken by Jesus; and parts of 1 Corinthians 11: 23-26, in which Paul quotes Jesus *as heard in his hallucinations.*

[20] www.Aeon.com, 8 January 2018.

translations, the first two of which translate the Greek word, *miseo* (hate) honestly.

- King James: "If any man come to me, and ***hate*** not his father, and mother, and wife, and children, and brethren, and sisters, yea, and his own life also, he cannot be my disciple."
- New Revised Standard Version: "Whoever comes to me and does not ***hate*** father and mother, wife and children, brothers and sisters, yes, and even life itself, cannot be my disciple." But then, two other top-selling versions—among many listed on the biblegateway.com website—paraphrase the text into *comforting* contemporary English:
- *The Message Bible*: "Anyone who comes to me but refuses to let go of father, mother, spouse, children, brothers, sisters—yes, even one's own self!—can't be my disciple. Anyone who won't shoulder his own cross and follow behind me can't be my disciple."
- *The Passion Bible*: "When you follow me as my disciple, you must put aside your father, your mother, your wife, your sisters, your brothers—yes, you will even seem as though you hate your own life. This is the price you'll pay to be considered one of my followers."

Presumably, God/Luke/Jesus used the word *miseo* for a reason, so the translators of the second two are lying. "Hate" is rendered "refuses to let go of" and "must put aside." In a footnote, *The Passion Bible* says that 'hate' is a metaphor, adding: "In this case, Jesus, the King of love is not saying to hate but to put aside every other relationship into second place."[21] These translators suffer from a pre-existing condition: *faith brain damage.*[22] Their idealized Jesus is the King of Love, but in fact Luke 14:26 helps make the case that Jesus was *not* the King of Love. Like a

---

[21] https://www.biblegateway.com/passage/?search=Luke+14%3A26&version=TPT
[22] *The Message Bible* was produced by Eugene H. Peterson, who served for 29 years as pastor of a church he founded in Maryland; *The Passion Bible* was written by Brian Simmons, whom the BibleGateway website describes as a "passionate lover of God."

mother soothing a toddler, the translators want to make it all better. But *is it* all that better? Put every other relationship into second place behind Jesus?[23] Thomas Bentley Hart is distrustful of bland translation committees—and rightly so—but best-selling paraphrases are blatantly dishonest.

Do lay readers commonly understand that the 'best' translation is not the one that strikes their fancy? Of course, most Christians don't know New Testament Greek, nor do they understand the challenges of rendering the correct *sense* of a text when translating from one language to another. But they should understand that translating Greek into English means that the word of God has been processed yet again, on top of many centuries of manuscript copying, altering and tampering. God's timing was off, if he intended a book appropriate for the ages; David Bentley Hart identified the problem: *the world of late antiquity is so remote from our own.* So, we see a very troubled history: how the documents of the New Testament made their way from their original authors in late antiquity to everyone's bookshelf today. At every step along the way something was lost, transformed, distorted.

Devout translators have tried *so many times* to get it right.[24] Why doesn't the good Lord put them out of their misery? God could keep the miracle alive by creating perfect translations of the Bible and depositing updated versions every 25 years in a Vatican Bank vault. Let the pope, with pomp and fanfare, celebrate the recurring miracle.

Except, of course, that the original inspiration miracle itself is a fraud.

---

[23] See Hector Avalos, *The Bad Jesus: the Ethics of New Testament* (2015), for his 39-page analysis of Luke 14:26; he makes the case that *miseo* in this verse means exactly what it seems to mean.
[24] Check out the options at https://www.biblegateway.com.

PART 3

PROPERLY INVESTIGATING KEY BIBLICAL MIRACLES

12| EVOLUTION IS A FACT!

By Abby Hafer

In the beginning, there was self-replication. That is how life began.

Certain molecules began to copy themselves. Then those copies made copies of themselves, and those copies made more. Some were not perfect copies, and those molecules became the first mutants. If they continued to copy their mutated selves, new genetic lines were born. Thus did the first two aspects of life come into being: Replication and mutation: that is, slight genetic changes.

Please note that cells had not yet evolved, much less multicellular organisms like humans. Vast numbers of mutations over nearly 4 billion years took place before humans evolved. So, if you are a human, you are a mutant many, many times over.

So, my fellow mutants, let's take a look at the evidence for evolution—the process that got us where we are today, and that continues throughout the world right now.

EVOLUTION FOLLOWS THE RULES OF SCIENCE

Let's start with the biggest, best piece of evidence for evolution. It's this: The theory of evolution follows the rules of science, especially the fact that it makes *testable predictions* that turn out to be correct.

WHAT IS A THEORY?

Now, to satisfy readers who may claim that evolution is "only" a theory, let's start with the basics: A *theory* in science is a big, broad, explanatory idea with lots of evidence for it, not somebody's tentative guess (that's a *hypothesis*, which is different). A theory in science is a large model that takes account of many different facts, including ones that have not been explained before, and explains them in a coherent fashion, using quantifiable evidence. And a theory must make predictions about things you don't know yet, but may be able to test.

For example, gravity. Gravity is "only" a theory. Specifically, the theory began with Isaac Newton's equation predicting what gravity would do anywhere, anytime, from an apple to the moon. If I drop a pencil, I can predict that it will behave just as Newton foretold in 1687, and also if I drop a pencil on Jupiter or let go of a pencil in the orbiting Space Station. We say the theory of gravity is true because it makes exact predictions that prove to be reliable. I learned the math to do that back in high school.

People knew that Newton's equation was only part of the picture. Here on Earth, for instance, you also have to take air drag into account. And wind direction. In certain weird or extreme places in the universe, we've discovered, you need to use Einstein's broadening of Newton's equation. A tiny apparent crack around the edge of Newton's theory opened the way to a wider, more all-pervasive theory of gravity, the General Theory of Relativity. This revealed not just how gravity works, but what gravity *is*.

That didn't make Newton's theory *wrong*. It still works as well as always for apples, the moon, and artillery shells. It's just that we've discovered and tested a broader, grander theory that *encompasses* Newton's version.

A simpler example: helium balloons float up instead of down. That does not make the law of gravity wrong, even though helium balloons appear to defy it. I have yet to hear any religious person claim that helium balloons "disprove" gravity. What helium balloons prove is that helium is less dense than air, so it floats up in air like a bubble in water.

So, we understand gravity, and these days we use it to make accurate predictions from black holes to quasars; and oddities like helium balloons don't "disprove" it.

The same is true of evolution. If anyone believes that they can safely dismiss a scientific reality because it is "just" a theory, then I invite them to test this belief by jumping out of a tenth-story window because, after all, gravity is just a theory.

Evolution *began* as a hypothesis in the minds of Charles Darwin and Alfred Russel Wallace almost 200 years ago. Massive data-gathering proved it to be a powerful a scientific reality, a fact that explains many other facts. It is the biggest, most important idea in all biology, the one that ties everything else together. Nothing in biology makes sense except through the lens of evolution, and we pretend it doesn't exist at our peril. In fact, the problem is worse than that. If someone is foolish enough to ignore the theory of gravity and jump out a high window, they only harm themselves. But people have ignored the predictions of evolution for decades and *other* people are dying as a result, as we shall see later in this chapter. This is often the problem with those who ignore scientific reality: It's *other* people who are harmed first.

WHAT SCIENCE IS

Science is the opposite of magic. Where magic (and the magical aspects of religion) demand the supernatural, science rejects any reliance on the supernatural. Science states that the world is material, and that it can be successfully investigated through material means.

Where magical knowledge is *occult,* meaning hidden, scientific knowledge is out in the open, published in journals, and subject to examination and retesting by anyone. Where magic is dramatic, science is quietly determined. It approaches reality in small, humble steps, making sure of each step, and slowly accumulates tiny bits of knowledge. On a day-to-day basis science is unimpressive. But the small bits of knowledge accumulate and add up. Like one snowflake, one tiny bit of scientific knowledge has no real impact and can seem trivial. But as with snowflakes, when enough gang up in a blizzard, they're a force that changes your world.

Put another way, science is a bulldozer that moves at the speed of a glacier. You may never see it progressing from year to year, but it is moving and changing everything in its path.

Science is a method of investigation. By using that method of investigation, we have gained huge bodies of knowledge. Sometimes people get confused, and think that science is only this large warehouse full of jumbled facts, instead of also being the method by which we find facts out, then see how they fit together to make coherent structures, and how these structures reveal deep principles underlying all.

Careful observation is its root. Science is really just the art of looking carefully. The origin of all science is systematic observation. The investigator works with things that are observed.

When a science is new, the observations are often just descriptive—catalog-making—as investigators get the lay of the land. But experience has shown that for a science to advance, the observations must become quantified in some useful way. That is, they must involve numbers. Numbers, it turns out, are essential to the art of looking carefully.

SHARING OF INFORMATION

When early microscope users observed, drew, and counted tiny animals too small to see with the naked eye in a drop of pond water, they shared this information widely so that anyone could look for themselves and see them too. And add new observations of their own. They also did this when they looked at samples of plant tissue, and samples of human tissue. This is how we learned about the many types of cells that make up the human body, for example, and how we discovered the germ theory of infectious disease.

Sharing information includes not only the information you obtained, but how you obtained it. If a scientist discovers a new microorganism, for example, it is not enough to draw pictures of it (or these days, photograph it). You must say *how* you found it. What magnification did you use? Where was the microorganism obtained? Did you wipe it from your skin or dig it out of mud? Where was the mud? What was the temperature of the mud? If you did an experiment, *exactly* how did you do it? What equipment did you use? If it can be found in an equipment catalog, what is its name and model number? What were your procedures?

All these matters of how you obtained your new information must be written up as a part of your work. This is the Methods section of a scientific paper. For an article to be published in a scientific journal, it must contain a complete description of all the methods used.

Why all this transparency about methods in scientific work? Because that way other scientists can scrutinize what you did, decide if your methods could actually result in the outcomes you say you found, and do it again themselves to see if they get the same result.

REPRODUCIBILITY

For your new claim to be accepted, other scientists must be able to reproduce your results. This is an absolutely crucial aspect of science. If results are not reproducible, the original finding is rejected. Many things that have looked at first like great breakthroughs have had to be rejected for this reason. A complaint that scientists constantly have against the news media is that they jump the gun, reporting preliminary findings as if they were discoveries.

Another key aspect of scientific work: It doesn't matter how much you wish something were true. If it fails the tests that would show it to be true, including the test of reproducibility, you have to give it up. This is where anti-evolutionists always fall down. They *wish* for some other explanation to be true, and they proceed with the goal of fulfilling this wish—not from wanting to find out whether it is true or false. They may, for camouflage, dress up their wishes in language that sounds like science, but their work does not follow the rules of science, including the rule of reproducibility.

MAKING PREDICTIONS

Another important rule of science is that a field must develop enough to make testable predictions. That is, a scientist must be able to make a prediction based on the facts already known and available. It must be possible, at least in principle, to *test* the prediction. To get back to the gravity example: This part of physics is so well developed that all kinds of predictions can be made that come true over and over again. If I drop a pencil in my living room, I can confidently predict how fast it will fall to the ground. But if laws of gravity are universal, I can also predict that it will fall just as fast in Japan or Australia, and at a slower speed on the moon, depending on the moon's size and mass. And I'll be right.

FALSIFIABILITY

Another important rule is falsifiability. This means that there must be, in principle, a way to prove that a given idea is incorrect. If I say, "*Tyrannosaurus* dinosaurs all died out long ago," that is a falsifiable statement. If someone were to find a live *Tyrannosaurus,* and anyone could examine it to see if that's really what it is, then my statement would be proven false.

But if someone says, "I saw a *T. rex* but it got away, really I did," that doesn't cut it—in part, believe it or not, because such a statement *is not falsifiable;* there's really no way to test it.

Experiments and Controls

One way of testing a prediction is by doing an experiment. You create specific, careful circumstances that will allow you to find out if the prediction comes true or not. This is an exacting procedure. First, you must remove all other possible influences from the experiment, to the best of your ability. For instance, if you are testing a prediction about how fast an object will fall based on gravity, you need to use objects heavy enough that air resistance will be negligible, you have to release them in a way that won't give them a little extra push, and so on.

If you wondered whether a large object would fall faster than a small one, for instance (as Galileo did), you would need to do the experiment exactly the same way for each. And the large and small objects would have to be as alike as possible in all other ways. That way, you could be reasonably sure that any effect that you saw depended on the size of the objects alone rather than on anything else.

Statistical Analysis

In order to really be sure of your results, it's necessary to do that same test many times. That's because, despite your best efforts to remove all external influences, you might not have succeeded every time. If you repeat an experiment many times, and then use statistical analysis on your results, an error is more likely to be found out. Moreover, an average of many measurements of something is likely to be more accurate than one measurement alone, *and* statistical analysis will tell you the measurements' average uncertainty. In many fields of science, if you don't do good statistical analysis on your results, people are justified in doubting them and your paper won't pass peer review.

PEER REVIEW

After you have done all your observations and experiments and analyses, you not only have to share your information, you have to do it in a specific way. You must write a paper that explains your methods, your results, your analyses, and all other important aspects of your research, and you must submit it to your fellow scientists and let them try to poke it apart. If they can't find irreparable holes in your research, then you get to publish your paper in a peer-reviewed journal or present it at a conference in front of your fellow scientists.

HOW DID ALL THIS PLAY OUT WITH EVOLUTION?

Evolution follows the rules of science. No other idea about how species originate does.

To begin with, the theory of evolution makes predictions. Lots of them. Let's look at some of my favorites.

SOME PREDICTIONS MADE BY EVOLUTION

New diseases

My favorite piece of evidence for evolution is that new diseases pop up on a routine basis. Evolution by natural selection predicts this. It says this is obvious and inevitable. New mutations will allow existing microorganisms to exploit new resources, enabling some of them to thrive and breed in new ways. That some of those mutations will allow microorganisms to exploit the resources of the human body in new ways, and thereby breed up and spread, is utterly predicted by evolution.

Among the new diseases that have made news in our lifetimes are AIDS and Zika. Let's have a look.

The *Zika* virus can cause microcephaly, a birth defect of the brain in infants, if the mother contracts the infection during pregnancy.[1] It was first identified in monkeys in 1947 in Uganda, and human cases were first reported in 1953.[2] The birth defects caused by Zika include a very small brain and partially collapsed skull, damage to the eyes, joint problems, and overly contracted muscles.[3]

AIDS (Acquired Immune Deficiency Syndrome) is caused by the Human Immunodeficiency Virus (HIV). The virus destroys cells in the body's immune system, leaving the body less capable of fending off other diseases. Left untreated, the AIDS sufferer will die of these other diseases. The HIV virus spreads by gaining access to a person's bloodstream. These means of contact include shared hypodermic needles, accidental pricks from infected hypodermic needles, and sexual contact where an infected person's bodily fluids get through a small tear in another's mucous membranes.

The Human Immunodeficiency Virus evolved from a similar virus that attacks chimpanzees, called Simian Immunodeficiency Virus or SIV. Hunters who kill chimpanzees for meat frequently contact chimpanzee blood, and this was most likely how the original jump from animals to humans took place.[4] Somewhere along the line, a small mutation resulted in a new version of the virus that could race through human populations.

AIDS became a global pandemic in the 1980s and 1990s, and tens of millions of people have died as a result.[5] At this point AIDS is

---

[1] "Zika Virus" *Centers for Disease Control and Prevention* (https://www.cdc.gov/zika/about/overview.html)
[2] "The history of Zika virus" World Health Organization (https://www.who.int/emergencies/zika-virus/timeline/en/)
[3] Cynthia A. Moore, MD, PhD; J. Erin Staples, MD, PhD; William B. Dobyns, MD; André Pessoa, MD; Camila V. Ventura, MD; Eduardo Borges da Fonseca, MD, PhD; Erlane Marques Ribeiro, MD, PhD; Liana O. Ventura, MD; Norberto Nogueira Neto, MD; J. Fernando Arena, MD, PhD; Sonja A. Rasmussen, MD, MS Characterizing the Pattern of Anomalies in Congenital Zika Syndrome for Pediatric Clinicians JAMA Pediatr. 2017;171(3):288-295. doi:10.1001/jamapediatrics.2016.3982, March 2017 (https://jamanetwork.com/journals/jamapediatrics/fullarticle/2579543)
[4] "About HIV/AIDS" *Centers for Disease Control and Prevention* (About HIV/AIDS https://www.cdc.gov/hiv/basics/whatishiv.html)
[5] "The Global HIV/AIDS Epidemic" *Henry J. Kaiser Family Foundation,* July 25, 2018

treatable, so that people infected with HIV can live for many years, but it is not yet curable. As of 2017, between 31 million and 44 million people globally were reported to be living with HIV.[6]

A few additional things about AIDS are worth noting. First, if diseases didn't evolve, we wouldn't get new diseases. Second, if we were not so similar biologically to chimpanzees, it is far less likely that humans would have gotten AIDS at all, since we appear to have originally contracted the disease from contact with diseased chimps. Further, if scientists had accepted some religious peoples' opinions that AIDS was a punishment from God, they never would have discovered that it's actually caused by a virus and developed the treatments we now have. It is yet another case in which people around the world should be grateful that scientists do not accept supernatural explanations. It should also be noted that microorganisms have very short generations (hours or days instead of years or decades), which is why we so often observe new microorganisms evolving.

HOW DOES THIS COMPARE TO OTHER IDEAS ABOUT BIOLOGICAL ORIGINS?

No other idea of creation predicts new diseases. In fact, creation stories (as well as Creationism and Intelligent Design, which are religious stories that pretend to be science) generally insist that the world was made not very long ago and hasn't changed since. This includes all the kinds of living things, great and small. So, in this view, there shouldn't be any new diseases, period.

Sometimes people claim that diseases are sent by some divinity to punish people for some sin or other. That, of course, is in conflict with the idea that all organisms were created by that same god long ago. It implies numerous separate and unpredictable acts of creation. But why would God suddenly choose to infect women with a disease that

---
https://www.kff.org/global-health-policy/fact-sheet/the-global-hivaids-epidemic/
[6] "Global HIV & AIDS statistics – 2018 fact sheet", UNAIDS http://www.unaids.org/en/resources/fact-sheet

damages fetuses in the womb and causes untold suffering in the children they become? Religious people frequently claim to care deeply about fetuses, and use this as an excuse for preventing women from getting abortions. Yet in this case, why would God separately create the *Zika* virus, long after He supposedly created everything else, and then visit it on the unborn? Why would God create a virus that specifically tortures infants, who, according to many religions, are incapable of sin? And finally, in the case of AIDS, why would God send a disease that specifically excuses lesbianism? Although AIDS is often transmitted through sex, the people who disproportionately do *not* get AIDS through sexual transmission are lesbians.

Further, if diseases are sent to humans as punishment for sins, then there shouldn't be new diseases (or diseases at all for that matter) among other animals or plants, which are considered unable to sin since they don't know about God and his rules. Yet new diseases arise in animals and plants all the time.

An example of a new disease in animals is **Tasmanian devil facial tumour disease (DFTD)**. It causes infectious tumors to grow on the faces of Tasmanian devils, an animal native to Australia's island of Tasmania. It first appeared in 1996 and it has killed up to 90% of the populations it has spread to. Tasmanian devils are now threatened with extinction.[7]

Wheat blast is a new disease of wheat caused by the fungus *Magneporthe oryzae*. It was first identified in Brazil in 1985, and it has significantly limited wheat production in that country. Since then it has cropped up in Bangladesh, and it could become devastating to world wheat production because fungicides have not been effective in controlling it.[8]

---

[7] Hamish McCallum "Disease and the dynamics of extinction" Philos Trans R Soc Lond B Biol Sci. 2012 Oct 19; 367(1604): 2828–2839. doi: 10.1098/rstb.2012.0224 PMCID: PMC3427566 PMID: 22966138 https://www.ncbi.nlm.nih.gov/pmc/articles/PMC3427566/

[8] "Wheat Blast" Plant Disease in the News http://www.pseudomonas-syringae.org/Outreach/EduOutreach-Vegevaders/EduOutreach-DiseaseInTheNews.html

Famously, another fungal disease of plants—"Late Blight," or *Phytophthera infestans*—caused the **Irish potato famine** that destroyed the Irish potato crop for several years in the 1840s and led to mass starvation.[9]

So, we ask ourselves—if plants and non-human animals are incapable of sin, then why do they get new diseases, or indeed any diseases? On the other hand, evolution predicts that plants and animals will get new diseases for the same reason humans do: because microorganisms continually evolve, just as big creatures do but faster, and some of those new microbes multiply successfully enough to make their hosts sick. This makes perfect sense in light of evolutionary theory, and no sense in light of any non-evolutionary story of biological origins.

NEWLY EVOLVED ANIMAL SPECIES

We witness large new species coming into existence too. Evolution predicts this will happen, since evolution is an ongoing process. A recent example is a new species of crayfish. The marbled crayfish (*Procambarus virginalis* is its proposed scientific name) evolved from slough crayfish (*Procambarus fallax*), which are found in Florida and Georgia. The new species is larger and all-female. That is, it reproduces without males. The slough crayfish is a popular home aquarium pet, and the new species appears to have evolved (by way of mutations) in aquaria. The new species became popular with aquarium pet dealers, but they have since escaped into the wild, where they are doing extremely well, to the point that they are threatening native species in several places around the world. Slough crayfish cannot successfully breed with marbled crayfish, which is a primary definition of a new species. In addition, the marbled crayfish is genetically different enough from slough crayfish to qualify as a different species. Thus, within the lifetime of this author (the marbled

---

[9] Schumann, G.L., D'Arcy, C. J., and Ristaino, J. 2000. Late blight of potato and tomato. The Plant Health Instructor. Updated 2018. DOI: 10.1094/PHI-I-2000-0724-01.
http://www.apsnet.org/edcenter/intropp/lessons/fungi/oomycetes/pages/lateblight.aspx

crayfish were first discovered by German pet traders in 1995), a sizable new critter has come into existence and spread all too successfully, with its appearance and lineage well documented.[10]

How Does This Compare to Other Ideas About Biological Origins?

No other story of biological origins predicts that new species will arise. Nor do any predict a species composed entirely of females.

Antimicrobial-Resistant Organisms

Evolution by natural selection fully predicts antibiotic-resistant bacteria. These now threaten human health worldwide. Had Darwin known about antibiotics and antifungal drugs, he would have readily predicted that bacteria and fungi could evolve defenses against them.

Antibiotic drugs have transformed medicine and have saved millions of lives. The first discovered was penicillin in 1928.[11] The first sulfanilamide (sulfa)-based antibiotic was discovered in 1932.[12] Since then antibiotics have radically transformed our lives. We can now expect to live to a ripe old age in large part because we can now live through bacterial infections that would have killed our great-grandparents. In 1920, Americans had an average life expectancy of 56.4 years. Today, the average life expectancy in the United States is nearly 80 years. We can expect to live through major surgery, and we can expect to defeat infections while undergoing chemotherapy.

---

[10] Elizabeth Pennisi "Crayfish create a new species of female 'superclones'" Science, 2015, Aug. 26, 2015, 1:00 PM https://www.sciencemag.org/news/2015/08/crayfish-create-new-species-female-superclones
[11] C. Lee Ventola "The Antibiotic Resistance Crisis" Part 1: Causes and Threats, P T. 2015 Apr; 40(4): 277–283. PMCID: PMC4378521 PMID: 25859123
https://www.ncbi.nlm.nih.gov/pmc/articles/PMC4378521/
[12] "Gerhard Domagk—Biographical" *The Nobel Prize* https://www.nobelprize.org/prizes/medicine/1939/domagk/biographical/

However, bacteria, like all organisms, evolve. All natural populations have genetic diversity. This means that some bacteria will naturally be slightly more resistant to antibiotics than others. When antibiotics are applied, some bacteria will live through the first day or two of treatment, simply because they are slightly more resistant. So, if the person then discontinues their antibiotics (because they feel better now that most of the bacteria are gone), the bacteria that remain are the ones with some natural resistance to the antibiotic. Those bacteria will breed back up, and this new population will not die off as quickly under another dose of the antibiotic. So the person who is sick will get sicker for longer, and may die.

On top of this, all natural populations have some members undergoing mutations, that is, slight genetic changes. Although mutations themselves are random, *a few* may lead to greater antibiotic resistance. In an environment without antibiotics, those mutations would not become important. But when a population of bacteria is exposed to antibiotics, the few with those mutations are the ones that will survive and breed up again. So, in the decades since we began prescribing antibiotics, disease bacteria have been slowly evolving resistance to these medicines. The theory of evolution predicts this perfectly.

The same goes for fungal diseases and anti-fungal medications.[13]

As these valuable medicines have been overprescribed, and especially with the long-term practice of putting antibiotics into animal feeds, bacteria and funguses have developed resistance, and people are now dying of diseases we used to be able to cure.

What has saved us thus far has been the development of new antimicrobial medicines as the old ones become less useful. Sadly, we have reached a point in which some bacteria are now resistant to all known antibiotics. This is predicted by evolution. The only ways for us to get around resistance is to develop new antimicrobial drugs and to put old

---

[13] "Fungal Diseases–Antifungal Resistance" *Centers for Disease Control and Prevention*
https://www.cdc.gov/fungal/antifungal-resistance.html

ones on a rotation, taking them out of use for a period of time so that resistance in bacterial populations decreases over time.

HOW DOES THIS COMPARE TO OTHER IDEAS ABOUT BIOLOGICAL ORIGINS?

No other story regarding our biological origins predicts or even imagines antibiotic- and antifungal-resistant organisms.

EVOLUTION OF RESISTANCE TO HERBICIDES IN PLANTS, AND OTHER LESSONS FROM GENETICALLY MODIFIED CROPS

Genetically modified (GM) agricultural crops have proven to be a fine laboratory for evolution by natural selection. For instance, glyphosates are a group of potent weed killers, but they can kill crop plants as well. Genetically modified versions of food crop plants have been created to be resistant to glyphosates. These were originally very successful, since farmers could spray large doses of glyphosates on their fields and kill all the weeds while allowing the crops to thrive. However, as was inevitable, we are now seeing weed populations that have evolved resistance to these powerful herbicides.[14] This is perfectly predicted by Darwin's idea of descent with modification.

With glyphosates as with antimicrobial drugs, a powerful, beneficial tool has been abused. Antimicrobials save lives, and appropriate use of glyphosates can boost crops that feed more people. But overuse of these tools—in direct defiance of the predictions of evolution by natural selection—have made these once-powerful tools less and less helpful over time.

---

[14] Robert Douglas Sammons and Todd A Gaines "Glyphosate resistance: state of knowledge" Pest Manag Sci. 2014 Sep; 70(9): 1367–1377. Published online 2014 Mar 12. doi: 10.1002/ps.3743
https://www.ncbi.nlm.nih.gov/pmc/articles/PMC4260172/

POWERFUL PREDICTIONS

However, when evolutionary theory is consulted, humans regain the advantage.

This is what happened with genetically modified cotton. We now have a type of GM cotton that produces its own insecticide. This enables farmers to grow a successful crop without having to spray. However, in time, the GM cotton would virtually guarantee that resistant strains of cotton pests would evolve. The solution supplied by evolutionary theory is to plant non-GM cotton varieties nearby even if they get eaten. This allows populations of the insect pest that have *not* evolved resistance to mate with those that have. The progeny of these matings are very unlikely to have resistance to the GM cotton's internal pesticide. This strategy, known as the *refuge strategy*,[15] has dramatically slowed or even stopped the development of resistance in insect populations.

In both agriculture and in public health, I fear having public health officials who do not believe in evolution. I fear having agricultural policy officials who do not believe in evolution. What's more, since ecosystems involve coevolved relationships between organisms, I fear having environmental officials who don't believe in evolution.

HOW DOES THIS COMPARE TO OTHER IDEAS ABOUT BIOLOGICAL ORIGINS?

I guarantee you that no religious story of biological origins gives us any help in how to predict the outcomes of evolved resistance.

---

[15] "Bacillus thuringiensis—Bt Crop Refuge Area" University of California at San Diego
http://www.bt.ucsd.edu/crop_refuge.html

SHARED GENOMES

Evolution predicts that we should share many genes with our close relatives, and fewer with our most distant relatives. And, with the recent invention of DNA sequencing, this is what we see.

For example, in looking at our ape relatives, we share 99%[16] of our genes with chimpanzees. We share about 98% with gorillas.[17] Looking at species that are less related to us, we have 90% of our DNA in common with cats,[18] and 60% with fruit flies.[19] We even have some DNA in common with plants.

This stands to reason from an evolutionary point of view, and only from an evolutionary point of view. Species that have evolved from a recent common ancestor should have lots of DNA in common. Species that diverged from one another longer ago should share less DNA in common, since more mutations will have slowly accumulated.

HOW DOES THIS COMPARE TO OTHER IDEAS ABOUT BIOLOGICAL ORIGINS?

Other stories of biological origins usually posit that humans were made separately from all other animals. If that were so, we would have no DNA heritage from them.

---

[16] Ann Gibbons "Bonobos Join Chimps as Closest Human Relatives" Science Jun. 13, 2012, 1:30 PM
https://www.sciencemag.org/news/2012/06/bonobos-join-chimps-closest-human-relatives
[17] Dave Mosher "Gorillas More Related to People Than Thought, Genome Says" *National Geographic News* PUBLISHED March 8, 2012
https://news.nationalgeographic.com/news/2012/03/120306-gorilla-genome-apes-humans-evolution-science/
[18] Joan U. Pontius, & James C. Mullikin, et al "Initial sequence and comparative analysis of the cat genome" Genome Res. 2007. 17: 1675-1689 doi: 10.1101/gr.6380007
https://genome.cshlp.org/content/17/11/1675.full
[19] "Background on Comparative Genomic Analysis" December 2002 *National Human Genome Research Institute* https://www.genome.gov/10005835/

Speaking of diseases and shared genomes, if humans aren't closely related to other primates, why do we share so many diseases?[20]

The fact that many new human diseases originate in other primates is predicted by evolution in two different ways.

First, evolution predicts that humans and other primates, being so closely related, will have genomes that overlap to a large degree. In general, evolution predicts that because mutations are ongoing, organisms should have more genes in common with their close relatives and fewer with those that diverged from their line earlier.

Second, most mutations amount to very small changes in genes. But even a relatively small genetic change in a bacterium may allow it to newly infect a *closely related* organism, because it's only a small jump. Our relatedness to other apes is why we share a number of diseases with apes but few with jellyfish. It is also why a disease-causing organism like HIV only has to mutate a little to make the jump to us.

HOW DOES THIS COMPARE TO OTHER IDEAS ABOUT BIOLOGICAL ORIGINS?

Other ideas about biological origins make no comments either about shared genetics, or about disease sharing. It's as if they didn't really want to know why people get sick.

"NYLONASE"—MORE MICROBIAL EVIDENCE FOR EVOLUTION

Microorganisms reproduce rapidly and go through many generations fast, which is why they can evolve rapidly. Evolution predicts that when a new but indigestible source of energy becomes available, some organism is likely to evolve to digest it. Such is the case with bacteria that are now capable of digesting artificial byproducts of nylon manufacturing.

---

[20] Pedersen AB, Davies TJ. "Cross-species pathogen transmission and disease emergence in primates." Ecohealth. 2009 Dec;6(4):496-508. doi: 10.1007/s10393-010-0284-3. Epub 2010 Mar 16. https://www.ncbi.nlm.nih.gov/pubmed/20232229

Nylon has only existed since its invention in 1935. Yet in 1975, a type of microbe was discovered living in wastewater sludge near nylon factories that could digest and use some of the byproducts of nylon manufacturing, which were in the water. These byproducts do not exist in nature, but they would be good food for anything that could digest them. It is said that nature abhors a vacuum, and in this case, after thousands of bacteria generations, the bacteria in the runoff areas evolved the ability to use these resources. The bacteria in these areas, which became *Flavobacterium sp. K171 and K172*[21,22,23] underwent various mutations because that's what organisms do. Any mutations that allowed bacteria to digest the new stuff would promote their reproduction, what with all the free food that nothing else was eating. Enough generations of bacteria lived and died in the soil around nylon factories from 1935 to 1975 for random mutations to hit on a biochemical pathway that digested the new material. Those lucky bugs then bred up freely.

HOW DOES THIS COMPARE TO OTHER IDEAS ABOUT BIOLOGICAL ORIGINS?

Other ideas about biological origins make no predictions about the eventual utilization of unnatural food sources provided by industrialization—among bacteria or anything else!

---

[21] Negoro S, Shinagawa H, Nakata A, Kinoshita S, Hatozaki T, Okada H. "Plasmid control of 6-aminohexanoic acid cyclic dimer degradation enzymes of Flavobacterium sp. KI72." J Bacteriol. 1980 Jul;143(1):238-45. https://www.ncbi.nlm.nih.gov/pubmed/7400094

[22] Shinichi Kinoshita, Sadao Kageyama, Kazuhiko Iba, Yasuhiro Yamada & Hirosuke Okada "Utilization of a Cyclic Dimer and Linear Oligomers of ε-Aminocaproic Acid by Achromobacter guttatus KI72" Agricultural and Biological Chemistry Volume 39, 1975 - Issue 6 Pages 1219-1223 | Received 18 Nov 1974, Published online: 09 Sep 2014

[23] Seiji Negoro, Hideo Shinagawa, Atsuo Nakata, Shinichi Kinoshita,'Tomoya Hatozaki,' And Hirosuke OKADA "Plasmid Control of 6-Aminohexanoic Acid Cyclic Dimer Degradation Enzymes of Flavobacterium sp. KI72" JOURNAL OF BACTERIOLOGY, July 1980, Vol. 143, No. 1 p. 238-245

VESTIGIAL STRUCTURES

Let's move away from microbes to bigger things you can see and sometimes experience for yourself—whether you like it or not!

Evolution predicts that, as organisms evolve, they will retain old structures even if those structures are no longer useful. If those now-useless structures don't cause death before reproduction too much of the time, they will tend to remain. However, if mutations result in the slow degeneration of these structures, that too will usually cause no harm—and may be a benefit by reducing useless baggage. So, in evolved organisms, we should see the remains, sometimes degraded, of structures that were once useful but no longer are. Occasionally, these older structures may even wind up being useful in new ways, simply because evolution uses whatever happens to be available.

Our bodies have quite a few of these *vestigial* structures. At the base of your spine you have a vestige of your primate ancestors' tails. You have feet with nearly useless toes, because your primate ancestors had strong, finger-like toes that helped them grasp tree branches.[24]

The thing to remember here is that evolution is incapable of planning. Species just stumble from one generation to the next, and as long as enough members of the species can breed before they die, the species keeps going. When a mutation benefits its owner, the owner may have a chance to breed more than others do, and the benefit spreads to a greater proportion of the population. When that goes on for long enough, you see measurable evolution. But if a now-useless structure meets the very low criterion of "not causing death before reproduction too much of the time," it will not be weeded out of the population.

However, a useless structure may shrink over many generations. Shrinkage will result in a slight energy saving for the animal, which no longer has to carry around something useless, however slight it may be. But the evolutionary pressure for this is weak, and becomes even weaker

---

[24] Brian Switek "Ancient human ancestor had feet like an ape" *NATURE* | NEWS 28 March 2012
https://www.nature.com/news/ancient-human-ancestor-had-feet-like-an-ape-1.10342

as the structure shrinks, so small vestigial structures tend to remain for a long time.

An example of this is whale hips. Whales evolved from land mammals that used to walk on four legs. However, they have lived in the sea for millions of years. As a result, they have evolved a streamlined "fishy" shape, their forelimbs have evolved into flippers, and their hind limbs have almost completely disappeared. But not quite. Whales still have hip bones inside their bodies, which are now small, and in some cases even tiny remains of hind legs.

Interestingly, those hip bones have been co-opted for a new purpose, as you see so often in evolved systems. The bones provide a place for a male whale's penis muscles to attach (yes, whales have penis muscles). These muscles are really important to reproduction, so those little hip bones persist, even though they are useless for their original purpose of walking. In case you're wondering if this makes them a good example of something that is truly vestigial, keep in mind that *female* whales have hip bones too—and don't need them for the sake of their penises![25]

Speaking of things that aren't of use to both sexes but appear in both sexes, men have nipples. These are mildly detrimental—they can chafe against clothing and become painful and bleed.

More detrimental is the human appendix. The appendix is a part of the digestive system that in humans doesn't digest anything. Animals that eat woody food have a much larger appendix/cecum that serves as an incubator for bacteria that digest the cellulose that makes wood so tough.[26] We can't digest wood, but we still have this small blind sac, much reduced from its incubator days, but still with us because it's not detrimental enough to kill us before childbearing too much of the time. However, it does kill us sometimes, because it is still a reservoir for

---

[25] Carl Zimmer, "The Erotic Endurance of Whale Hips," *National Geographic*, September 5, 2014. https://www.nationalgeographic.com/science/phenomena/2014/09/05/the-erotic-endurance-of-whale-hips/
[26] "Cecum" Encyclopaedia Britannica https://www.britannica.com/science/cecum

bacteria, and these bacteria can sometimes breed too aggressively and cause appendicitis.[27]

Another interesting vestigial structure you have is the tiny muscle that attaches to each one of our hairs—the arrector pili muscle. When these tiny muscles contract, they pull the hair into standing position and you get goose bumps. When do we get goose bumps? When we are cold, or frightened. Why? Because having our hair stand up did us some good back when we had real fur, rather than the largely vestigial fur that now covers most of our bodies. In an animal with lots of fur, standing your fur up when you are cold increases the thickness of your coat and makes you warmer. When you are frightened, standing your fur on end makes you look bigger when facing down an enemy. But we do not have real fur, and getting goose bumps from standing our hair on end doesn't make us any warmer or make us look any bigger. It is a vestigial response.[28]

Vestigial structures in other animals include blind eyes in cave-dwelling fish[29] and tiny legs inside some snakes. Although pythons and boa constrictors don't use legs, their lizard ancestors did.[30]

TRAGIC VESTIGES

Many vestigial structures are odd, like male nipples and arrector pili muscles in humans. Some occasionally kill us, like the appendix. But in some cases, the result is closer to tragic.

---

[27] Jerry Coyne "Is the appendix a vestigial organ??" *Why Evolution is True* https://whyevolutionistrue.wordpress.com/2016/05/15/is-the-appendix-a-vestigial-organ/
[28] Jerry Coyne "A vestigial trait in humans: the arrector pili"
Why Evolution is True https://whyevolutionistrue.wordpress.com/2011/02/22/vestigial-trait-the-arrector-pili/
[29] James Owen "How This Cave-Dwelling Fish Lost Its Eyes to Evolution"
National Geographic SEPTEMBER 11, 2015 https://news.nationalgeographic.com/2015/09/150911-blind-cavefish-animals-science-vision-evolution/
[30] "Vestigial Organs" *American Museum of Natural History*
https://www.amnh.org/exhibitions/darwin/evolution-today/how-do-we-know-living-things-are-related/vestigial-organs

Vitamin C

Such is the case with vitamin C. Vitamin C is necessary for animals to make a protein called collagen, which comprises a large portion of our bodies, especially the connective tissues that hold us together. When we lack vitamin C, these tissues do not get replaced as they wear out. So symptoms of vitamin C deficiency include gum inflammation, bleeding from the skin, skin hemorrhages, joint pain, poor wound healing, loosening of teeth, general weakness, anemia, and if untreated, death.[31] This is the condition known as scurvy, and it used to kill people on long sea voyages or, in northerly climates, who didn't get vegetables in the winter.

Most other animals make their own vitamin C. That's why carnivores like cats and wolves can live on meat alone. A long chain of biochemical reactions in most animals' bodies produces vitamin C from scratch. Yet we humans lack this biochemical pathway.

Evolution predicts that since we are related to animals that can make vitamin C and have ancestors in common with them, we should still have *some parts* of that biochemical pathway. And we do.

In fact, we have most of that vitamin C-making pathway. All we're missing is the ability to make one enzyme in the last step of the process. We carry a broken version of the crucial gene for this one enzyme. This is why we have to eat a diet with some vitamin C or get scurvy if we don't.[32]

Having nearly all of a biochemical pathway that most other animals have, but missing the ability to make one enzyme in the last step, is a classic case of a vestigial structure. It is precisely the kind of structure that is predicted by evolution.

---

[31] "Vitamin C–Fact Sheet for Health Professionals" *National Institutes of Health*
https://ods.od.nih.gov/factsheets/VitaminC-HealthProfessional/
[32] Yan Jiao, Jifei Zhang et al.
"Differential gene expression between wild-type and *Gulo*-deficient mice supplied with vitamin C" Genet Mol Biol. 2011 Jul-Sep; 34(3): 386–395. Published online 2011 Jul 1. PMCID: PMC3168176 PMID: 21931508 doi: 10.1590/S1415-47572011005000031
https://www.ncbi.nlm.nih.gov/pmc/articles/PMC3168176/

How did we get this way? Well, some of our monkey ancestors had the mutation that broke the gene for that last step. If the animals with the broken gene got next to no vitamin C in their diets, they would have died out quickly and that would have been the end of it. But our monkey ancestors ate a mixed diet including fruits and vegetables and some raw meat. So those ancestors with the broken gene survived.

This worked well enough for a long time, in warm areas with plenty of fresh fruits and vegetables and raw meats all year. But then we humans spread around the world, including into climates that didn't provide year-round fresh produce. We also developed cooking, which can reduce the vitamin C in foods. So, a primate with a body adapted to plenty of fresh produce could wind up getting scurvy, from which people used to die routinely.

So a vestigial, long-broken biochemical pathway became tragic and deadly—not because our bodies were diseased, but because our bodies could not do this one last step that we *eventually* needed. Remember, evolution is blind and cannot plan ahead.

Cancer

An even more tragic case of vestigiality is cancer. Way back when all life was single celled, those single cells reproduced as much as they possibly could, just like bacteria today. Evolution predicts that the cells that reproduced the most would take over. When cells started clustering and forming multicellular organisms, however, it became important for cells to regulate their reproduction, so that organisms would have only the correct kinds of cells in the correct amounts and places. So, mechanisms that regulated the speed of cellular reproduction evolved as organisms started to become multicellular.

A term for this kind of regulation is *contact inhibition*. Basically, when cells come into contact with each other, they don't reproduce themselves in such a way as to crowd out their neighbors. They may reproduce a bit more freely when they are near a wound that needs to be healed, but otherwise, they just replace themselves and then die.[33] The exact genetics of any one cancer are complicated, but the basics are that when contact inhibition is removed (due to a mutation), the cell reverts to the ancestral state and reproduces uncontrollably. That's what cancer is.

In a designed system, cells would be programmed to only reproduce as needed, as opposed to the evolved system that we have, in which cells are programmed to reproduce as much as possible and need suppression mechanisms to keep them from doing so.

HOW DOES THIS COMPARE TO OTHER IDEAS ABOUT BIOLOGICAL ORIGINS?

Vestigial structures are not predicted by any supernaturally based idea of creation.

UNNECESSARILY LONG ANATOMICAL ROUTES

As organisms evolve, the simplest way to change is to expand or shrink something in some direction. If two organs need to remain connected, evolution will lengthen the connections between them if they move farther apart. No matter how the body changes as it evolves, the connections will just keep lengthening—since evolution is incapable of planning or going back for a re-do. So you will not see connections being rewired to better fit the new body dimensions. You will just see the old wiring getting longer and longer.

So, in evolved organisms, we should expect to see some necessary connections between organs be unnecessarily long and complex, compared to what a planned connection would look like.

---

[33] Ribatti D "A revisited concept: Contact inhibition of growth. From cell biology to malignancy." Exp Cell Res. 2017 Oct 1;359(1):17-19. doi: 10.1016/j.yexcr.2017.06.012. Epub 2017 Jun 20.
https://www.ncbi.nlm.nih.gov/pubmed/28642051

THE RECURRENT LARYNGEAL NERVES

Such is the case with the recurrent laryngeal nerves. These are branches of the left and right vagus nerves. The vagus nerves run from the part of the brain called the medulla down the sides of the throat, and eventually the recurrent laryngeal nerves branch off. They attach to the muscles that control your larynx, the "voice box," located where your Adam's apple is.

You might think that those recurrent laryngeal nerves would take the direct route: branch from the vagus nerves right there at the voice box. But no. The right one goes all the way down to just above your heart, loops underneath one of the arteries that come out of the aortic arch, and then *goes back up your throat* to attach to your laryngeal area. The left recurrent laryngeal nerve goes even farther. It goes all the way down into your chest and loops underneath the aortic arch itself just barely above the heart. It then turns around and also goes all the way back up to the larynx.[34] Thus, in humans, these nerves go about six inches out of their way before turning back to the larynx.

In animals like giraffes, this unnecessary detour becomes a matter of several yards of extra nerve tissue. It doesn't do the individual any good, but doesn't do much harm either.

Why are those nerves arranged that way? Because our distant ancestors, and those of giraffes, had very short necks and the complicated plumbing around the heart was up close to the throat. The nerves threaded through the plumbing right there. As necks lengthened, evolution did not, of course, have the planning capability to snip the nerves and re-route them without the tangles. So the tangles remain, now awkwardly stretched out. Even in the extreme case of giraffes.

---

[34] Haller JM, Iwanik M, Shen FH. "Clinically relevant anatomy of recurrent laryngeal nerve." Spine (Phila Pa 1976). 2012 Jan 15;37(2):97-100. doi: 10.1097/BRS.0b013e31821f3e86. https://www.ncbi.nlm.nih.gov/pubmed/21540775

The Vas Deferens in Men

Likewise, in men, the tube that conducts sperm from the testes to where they exit the body at the end of the penis travels through an unnecessary long loop. This tube is called the *vas deferens*. It leads out of the testes and joins the *urethra* that empties the urinary bladder. The direct route would be from the testicles straight to the base of the penis. That would make sense. But what we see instead is the vas deferens going up into the front of the abdomen, turning to the back of the abdomen, going down, turning forward again, *going into the prostate gland*, and joining up there with the urethra.[35] This amounts to about a foot of tubing, though the direct route would be only couple inches.

Why? Just as with your voice box nerves, evolution was incapable of planning. Nerves and tubes develop with no thought to the future. As animals evolve, their bodies may elongate, or, in the case of men's testes, move from inside the body to outside it (in the scrotum). But the nerves and tubes won't be disconnected and rewired. They keep to their original topology, even when the results become bizarre.

How Does This Compare to Other Ideas About Biological Origins?

Other ideas about biological origins tend to insist that animals were created by a conscious deity, that is to say, they were planned out. These unnecessary routes, left over from earlier forms, show the lack of planning that is the hallmark of evolution.

Shared Anatomical Structures (Homologs)

Since evolution says that new organisms evolve from older ones, and that many new organisms may evolve from one common ancestor, it predicts that creatures that evolved away from each other will have many

---

[35] "Ductus deferens" *Encyclopaedia Britannica* https://www.britannica.com/science/ductus-deferens

structures in common. These common structures are known as *homologs*. We see them throughout the biological world.

For example, in the human body, our forearms have two bones parallel to one another—the radius and the ulna.[36] Turtles have those same two bones in their front feet.[37] Birds have them in their wings.[38] Whales have them in their flippers.[39] Squirrels have them in their front feet,[40] as do kangaroos, platypuses, crocodiles, dogs, cats, and salamanders.[41] So did dinosaurs.[42] So did archaeopteryx, the ancient feathered bird-reptile.[43]

Why should this be? Why, because they are all related! All are descended from ancient tetrapods, those original four-legged, backboned animals that first made their way from oceans onto land hundreds of millions of years ago.

We share lots of other things too. Our spinal cords go through many small bones called vertebrae, and the vertebrae of all those diverse animals have similar structure. We also have that same basic four-legged body map—a head at one end, a tail at the other, and four legs in between. There's no reason that is has to be that way! Insects have six legs,

---

[36] "Homologous tetrapod limbs (5 of 6)" Understanding Evolution University of California at Berkeley https://evolution.berkeley.edu/evolibrary/search/imagedetail.php?id=393&topic_id%3D%26keywords%3D

[37] "Pectoral Girdle and Appendage of the Turtle" http://campus.murraystate.edu/academic/faculty/tderting/anatomyatlas/turtappenskelamy-becky.html

[38] "Homologous tetrapod limbs (5 of 6)" Understanding Evolution University of California at Berkeley https://evolution.berkeley.edu/evolibrary/search/imagedetail.php?id=393&topic_id%3D%26keywords%3D

[39] Ibid
https://evolution.berkeley.edu/evolibrary/search/imagedetail.php?id=393&topic_id%3D%26keywords%3D

[40] Thorington RW Jr, Darrow K. "Anatomy of the squirrel wrist: bones, ligaments, and muscles." J Morphol. 2000 Nov;246(2):85-102. https://www.ncbi.nlm.nih.gov/pubmed/11074577

[41] "Tetrapod" George R. Zug *Encyclopaedia Britannica* https://www.britannica.com/animal/tetrapod-animal

[42] Collin S. VanBuren, and Matthew Bonnan "Forearm Posture and Mobility in Quadrupedal Dinosaurs" PLoS One. 2013; 8(9): e74842. Published online 2013 Sep 18. doi: 10.1371/journal.pone.0074842 PMCID: PMC3776758 PMID: 24058633 https://www.ncbi.nlm.nih.gov/pmc/articles/PMC3776758/

[43] "*Archaeopteryx*: An Early Bird" *University of California Museum of Paleontology (UCMP)* http://www.ucmp.berkeley.edu/diapsids/birds/archaeopteryx.html

and they are successful walkers. In fact, they colonized land long before vertebrates did. Arachnids like spiders have eight legs, decapods (like lobsters) have ten legs and some other appendages, and centipedes and millipedes have many pairs of legs. We have two arms and two legs because we are descended from the first tetrapods, rather than because that is the best or only body plan that works. Such shared structures are known as *homologs*, and they are evidence for evolution throughout the animal, plant, and fungal kingdoms.

HOW DOES THIS COMPARE TO OTHER IDEAS ABOUT BIOLOGICAL ORIGINS?

As can be seen in robots, there is no reason why a body must have four limbs plus a head and a tail, or two bones in the forelimb, or two eyes above a nose above a mouth. These are all results of our evolutionary history, rather than a special creation. A supernatural creator starting from scratch would have no reason to create so many animals with body parts so much in common.

EXTINCTION

Evolution predicts that species will go extinct. Evolution is an ongoing process, and just as new species will evolve into existence, other species will be unable to cope with some changing condition and go extinct. Or, in evolving as they meet new environmental challenges, an older species may evolve to the point of being recognized as a new species, or even several new species if adaptive radiation takes place.

Nearly every kid loves dinosaurs. The fact that we can only visit their fossilized skeletons, in museums, is a powerful lesson that extinction happens.

The phenomenon of extinction is massively useful evidence for evolution. And we see evidence of extinction throughout the geological record.

Extinction is a problem for any supernatural view of life, since it is strange that a God would carefully design organisms that are unfit to stay alive.

Even entire worldwide ecosystems have been wiped out, with few or no remnants living now. Since about 440 million years ago there have been five *mass* extinctions, when large fractions of all species on Earth were wiped out. The most famous one for most people is the most recent, the one that wiped out the dinosaurs (as well as half of all species in general) at the end of the Cretaceous period 65 million years ago. In all, over 90% of all species that ever existed are now extinct.[44]

HOW DOES THIS COMPARE TO OTHER IDEAS ABOUT BIOLOGICAL ORIGINS?

Although death is certainly present in all religious worldviews, and genocide is not uncommon in these tales, extinction is not discussed as a possibility. The plentitude of fascinating animals and plants we see in the fossil record are not even mentioned in supernatural creation stories. What a small, limited world they discuss!

FOSSILS AND WHOLE FOSSIL ECOLOGIES

Evolution predicts that when the environment changes, the species in it will either adapt or die. It therefore predicts that whole ecologies of plants and animals will rise and fall.

Fossils are fascinating. In some cases, it's clear how they are related to today's organisms, and sometimes they are so different looking that it is difficult to figure out what living relatives they have today if any. One fascinating aspect of ecology is that entire fossil ecologies are found together, in predictable assemblages.

---

[44] "Mass Extinctions" *National Geographic* https://www.nationalgeographic.com/science/prehistoric-world/mass-extinction/

This was first noticed in the early 1800s by a British canal engineer named William Smith. In his diggings and mine examinations, he saw that different layers of sedimentary rock had different types of fossils in them. Even more importantly, he found that the different layers of fossil deposits always occurred in the same order, from deepest to shallowest. He found that he could predict which fossils would appear in which layers, even when the rock beds were many miles apart.[45]

Crucially, he also found that groups of fossils co-occurred. In modern terms, what he was seeing was the remains not just of individual organisms, but of ecosystems of organisms that lived together.

What William Smith did *not* find was fossils of humans or farm animals, as one would expect in a world populated by human cultivators from the beginning. Nor were there fossils of wild animals familiar in that area today.

The fact that modern animals were missing from these layers, and that whole ecosystems of unfamiliar, often extinct animals were there instead—in predictable communities, in a predictable order—is powerful evidence, since it is predictive.

HOW DOES THIS COMPARE TO OTHER IDEAS ABOUT BIOLOGICAL ORIGINS?

No other way to explain this phenomenon makes any sense, and none can make any predictions.

TRANSITIONAL SPECIES

Evolution predicts that as species evolve, they will usually change through intermediate forms, not jump over the gap to become whole

---

[45] Michon Scott "William Smith (1769-1839)" May 8, 2008, https://earthobservatory.nasa.gov/features/WilliamSmith

new creatures full-blown. As they change, they will resemble their old ancestral stock less and less, until they are clearly something new.

People like to put things into categories. We may put the old, ancestral stock into one category and the new organisms into a different one. But life is not that simple. What evolution tells us is that as the organism evolved, every step along the way was alive in its own right and worked well enough to survive and reproduce. Those species that fall between the categories we have created are called *transitional species*.

The transition of some vertebrates from water to land was one example of a dramatic transition. So was the transition from walking to flying. But in both cases, we find the remains of successful species that were partway along through those transitions.

One of the most entertaining things about evolution is the weirdness of its results. Animals that no rational Creator would have come up with exist perfectly well in our evolved world.

Again, the reason is that evolution is incapable of long-term planning. All that organisms do is stumble from one generation to the next, and as long as enough of them live to reproduce, the species keeps going. So vast changes can happen, but they do so in tiny increments, leading eventually to jumbled messes of structures and systems whereas a good designer, working from scratch, would create something simpler.

One of the big problems that people have with evolution is that its results don't *seem* logical, and our minds like logic. We want neat categories. We like to sort things out and classify them once and for all.

But even though *we* like neat categories, the natural world doesn't care about them.

This brings me to another reason why many people have trouble accepting evolution.

Many animals seem to fit so perfectly into *one* category that people can't imagine them being in any other. Many animals seem so perfectly adapted to their environments that people can't imagine them living successfully in any other. So, the idea of a species slowly changing from one category into another, and from one environment and into another, seems wrong. We wonder how a species would survive while transitioning from being seemingly perfectly adapted to one way of life to something else. Why would it "try" to do that? It seems crazy.

This is why the existence of transitional species is so important to understanding evolution. Examples include flying ancient dinosaurs with feathers, beaks, *and* teeth, whose descendants became the modern birds; fish with four-lobed fins that started walking; and the entire slow transition that we see in the evolution of the modern horse.

Change is slow, but organisms do not care if they are leaving one human-defined category and moving towards another. They are simply living and reproducing in their own way in their own time. Thus, instead of perfect adaptation to a given environment, what we really see is organisms that are only adapted well enough not to die before reproduction too much of the time. If that means having the teeth of a "dinosaur" in the beak of a "bird," nature doesn't care. Remember—evolution is incapable of planning.

So let's look at those fun examples I mentioned.

ARCHAEOPTERYX, THE FLYING, TOOTHY DINOSAUR WITH FEATHERS

Well preserved *Archaeopteryx* fossils show an animal that is clearly transitional between small predatory flying dinosaurs and modern birds. It had feathers, wings, and a wishbone (furcula) like a bird. It also had a full set of teeth, a flat sternum (breastbone) instead of the deep-keeled one that birds do, a long bony tail like a dinosaur (or lizard for that matter), and rib-like bones called *gastralia* floating in the muscles of the abdomen, like many dinosaurs and modern crocodiles. As a transitional species, *Archaeopteryx* ranks among the most important ever discovered.[46]

---

[46] *"Archaeopteryx: An Early Bird" University of California Museum of Paleontology (UCMP)*
http://www.ucmp.berkeley.edu/diapsids/birds/archaeopteryx.html

TIKTAALIK, THE ANCIENT FISH THAT WALKED

The idea of fish walking out of the ocean onto land strikes many as ridiculous. Again, that's the old naive notion that creatures must jump suddenly from being one kind to a very different kind. Yet even today, there are many fish that occasionally visit land and some that spend most of their lives there. American eels, lungfish, and walking catfish can all spend time on land. Mudskipper fish spend most of their lives on land and even climb trees. So in general, fish being able to "walk" is not a huge surprise.

One line of ancient lobe-finned fishes fully transitioned to land and became the first fully land-dwelling vertebrates. *Tiktaalik* is a fossil of one of those ancient fishes involved in this process, and it has features of both fish and land animals. It had scales and gills like a fish, a flattened head like a crocodile, and a neck that allowed the head to move like a land animal's rather than a solid, unturnable head like a fish. It had four fins—two front fins and two back fins. There's that tetrapod body plan! The fins, which face the ground, contain bones that flare out for swimming, and interior bones sturdy enough to allow the animal to support its weight in shallow water. These and other characteristics show that *Tiktaalik* was a transitional species between swimming fish and those of its descendents who wound up walking as four-legged vertebrates—the group that includes you, me, our fellow mammals, amphibians, dinosaurs, turtles, and birds.[47]

THE EVOLUTION OF THE HORSE

We have really excellent specimens of many of the stages of horse evolution, starting with the small, dog-sized *Hyracotherium* about 55 million years ago. Through *Orohippus, Mesohippus, Miohippus, Parahippus,*

---

[47] "What has the head of a crocodile and the gills of a fish?" May 2006, updates added in June 2009 and June 2010 *Understanding Evolution* University of California at Berkeley, https://evolution.berkeley.edu/evolibrary/news/060501_tiktaalik

Merychippus, Pliohippus, and *Dinohippus,* we can see the slow evolutionary transitions that led to our modern genus called *Equus,* which includes zebras, donkeys, and domestic horses.

Tracing evolution through these fossil specimens, we see teeth that slowly became more high-crowned, legs and faces that became longer, and toes that diminished in number from four on the back and three in the front to one large central toe with two smaller side toes, to the one central toe (hoof) you see on modern horses. However, even modern horses still have tiny vestigial toes in the bones above their hoofs. In fact, modern horses are occasionally born with "extra" toes in addition to the central hoof. Such occasional genetic throwbacks are called *atavisms.*[48]

The fact that we see not one, but many transitional forms of ancestral horses leading to modern horses is stark evidence for evolution.

HOW DOES THIS COMPARE TO OTHER IDEAS ABOUT BIOLOGICAL ORIGINS?

If one posits a god or any other creative being who came up with this sequence of horse evolution, one must also posit that this Creator came up with all the intermediate species specifically with the idea of killing them off later, since they do not exist now. One must also posit that they were created and killed off *in just the right order,* and in the same sequence of geologic time that we see in the fossil record. But accepting evolution makes horse evolution simple and obvious.[49,50,51]

---

[48] Adams, J. & Shaw, K. (2008) Atavism: embryology, development and evolution. Nature Education 1(1):131 https://www.nature.com/scitable/topicpage/atavism-embryology-development-and-evolution-843
[49] "Horse Evolution Over 55 Million Years" Tufts University http://chem.tufts.edu/science/evolution/horseevolution.htm
[50] "*Hyracotherium* had 4 toes on the front foot, and 3 toes on the hind foot." *University of Florida* https://www.floridamuseum.ufl.edu/vertpaleo/fhc/hyraco4.htm
[51] "On Your Toes" *American Museum of Natural History* https://www.amnh.org/exhibitions/horse/the-evolution-of-horses/on-your-toes

ATAVISMS

Evolution, in combination with modern genetic knowledge, predicts that our genetic code will still retain the ability to make many older structures, but that those abilities will be suppressed genetically in modern species.

Sometimes a genetic fluke happens, and a suppressed trait reappears. An atavism is sometimes called a "throwback." The reason for atavism is that, as species evolve, it's often easier for a trait to be genetically suppressed rather than edited right out of the DNA as would be done by a deliberate editor. If the suppression fails for some reason, then those genes can be expressed. This is why we occasionally see a chicken with teeth, horses with additional toes, and, yes, humans with tails.[52]

HOW DOES THIS COMPARE TO OTHER IDEAS ABOUT BIOLOGICAL ORIGINS?

Other ideas about biological origins can only call these humans and animals inexplicable monsters.

BADLY "DESIGNED" BODY PARTS

Evolution predicts that many organisms will have structures with obvious design flaws. Remember, the only standard for an evolved system is "good enough not to cause death before reproduction too much of the time." Structures that meet this low criterion will crop up and continue to exist. This, or course, should not happen in an organism that was designed by an intelligent Creator. This is why human bodies have so many structures that work poorly even when at their best.

---

[52] Adams, J. & Shaw, K. (2008) Atavism: embryology, development and evolution. Nature Education 1(1):131, https://www.nature.com/scitable/topicpage/atavism-embryology-development-and-evolution-843

MEN'S TESTICLES

An obvious example is men's testicles. They hang outside the body in a sac of skin called the scrotum. This makes them far more vulnerable than if they were inside the body like all our other organs. Men's testicles hang outside the body because they need to be slightly cooler than body temperature in order to make sperm. However, many other warm-blooded animals have no such need for their testes to be cool. Mammals with internal testes include elephants, rhinoceroses, sloths, hyraxes, armadillos, echidnas, platypuses, manatees, seals, whales, and dolphins.[53] Birds have internal testes,[54] yet their body temperatures are higher than ours. So, it is clearly possible to have warm body temperature and internal testes, yet humans got an inferior kludge of a system that leaves a crucial part vulnerable. Such poor design can only be explained by evolution. This problematic setup does not kill us or prevent reproduction often enough to be weeded out, so it persists.

THE TWO TUBES IN THE HUMAN THROAT

Your throat has two tubes: the esophagus for eating and the trachea (windpipe) for breathing. However, they meet and join in the neck. So sometimes food gets inhaled into the windpipe and gets stuck there. We can suffocate and die as a result.[55] This would not happen if we simply had separate tubes for air and food. And indeed, mammals like whales and dolphins have this arrangement, showing that it's perfectly possible.[56] Here's another case of an obvious, sometimes fatal, and completely unnecessary design flaw in humans that fails reasonable criteria for a

---

[53] Werdelin, L, Nilsonne, A. *Journal of Theoretical Biology* 1999 Jan 7 196(1): 61-72
[54] Jacquie Jacob Avian Reproductive System—Male *eXtension—A Part of the Cooperative Extension System* May 05, 2015, https://articles.extension.org/pages/65373/avian-reproductive-systemmale
[55] Elaine N. Marieb *Human Anatomy & Physiology*, 6th Edition Benjamin Cummings May 2, 2003
[56] Dziak, Bob & Haxel, J & Lau, T.-K & Heimlich, Sara & Caplan-Auerbach, Jacqueline & Mellinger, David & Matsumoto, Haru & Mate, B. "A pulsed-air model of blue whale B call vocalizations" *Scientific Reports.* 7. 10.1038/s41598-017-09423-7 2017

competent designer. On the other hand, it does meet evolution's low standard: "good enough not to cause death before reproduction too much of the time."

Many, many other avoidable "design" flaws exist in the human body and in most other organisms as well.

HOW DOES THIS COMPARE TO OTHER IDEAS ABOUT BIOLOGICAL ORIGINS?

Other ideas about biological origins insist that humans and all other creatures were made by a designer so powerful and all-knowing that they could build the entire cosmos and everything in it, yet failed at simple, basic design tasks—in what we now know to be evolved systems.

EVIL ADAPTATIONS

Evolution is *amoral,* meaning it doesn't care. It has no mind with which to care. Therefore, it predicts, no ecological niche will be so disgusting, so cruel, that some organism will not occupy it. If food or necessary water, shelter, or temperature are available in some way, some organism will evolve to exploit it.

Some adaptations are so horrific that only the blind, amoral process of evolution really makes sense. For instance, there over 60,000 species of ichneumon wasps.[57] These wasps paralyze caterpillars, lay their eggs on them, and then the paralyzed caterpillar is eaten alive by the larvae that hatch out of the eggs. Charles Darwin wrote to the botanist Asa Gray in 1860, "I cannot persuade myself that a beneficent & omnipotent God would have designedly created the Ichneumonidæ with the express intention of their feeding within the living bodies of caterpillars, or that

---

[57] "Ichneumonidae" *New World Encyclopedia,* http://www.newworldencyclopedia.org/entry/Ichneumonidae

a cat should play with mice."⁵⁸ From Guinea worms to brain-eating bacteria, the examples are endless.

HOW DOES THIS COMPARE TO OTHER IDEAS ABOUT BIOLOGICAL ORIGINS?

Although other ideas about biological origins allow for the presence of evil, they do not posit a deliberately evil creator.

BIOGEOGRAPHIC DISTRIBUTION

Why are there kangaroos in Australia and nowhere else? Why do regions with similar climates have different plants and animals? If a supernatural Creator created animals and plants to be suited to their environments, then why do we see different animals and plants inhabiting places that have similar environments but that are separated physically?

Careful maps of where plant and animal species occur show that rivers and mountain ranges often form the edges of the plants' and animals' territories. Why should this be, if there is the same climate on the other side of the mountains or river?

Evolution predicts this—because evolution is random, not directed.

The answer is that species arise and diversify wherever their common ancestor happened to be. This is why you find not one species of kangaroo in Australia but four, and no species of kangaroos anywhere else

This field of study is called biogeography, and it was crucial to both Charles Darwin and Alfred Russel Wallace in their co-discovery of evolution by natural selection. Wallace even more than Darwin is the person who recognized it and developed it as a field.

---

⁵⁸ Darwin Correspondence Project, Letter no. 2814, accessed on 5 February 2019, http://www.darwinproject.ac.uk/DCP-LETT-2814

Here's how it works: As a species spreads out, it colonizes new areas that may contain new challenges. So, adaptations start to take place in that part of the population. However, the species can spread only where it can get to. So, for instance a wide river would be a barrier for animals that can't swim or fly very far. Such a species might spread far along the riverbank but not to the other side. Then, if the range of this continually spreading species is divided, let's say by a flood creating a new river or a tectonic shift that submerges some of the land, the one big population is divided into two or more isolated, smaller populations, and each evolves henceforth on its own.

Evolution and biogeography are inextricably mixed. To understand one, you must understand the other. To know where a species originated, you need to know its evolutionary history and the geological history of the region where it has lived.

HOW DOES THIS COMPARE TO OTHER IDEAS ABOUT BIOLOGICAL ORIGINS?

Other ideas about biological origins say nothing about how species will be distributed around the globe, except perhaps that some supernatural being placed them there, and replaced them at various times, and kept coming back to put different species in different places, in an ongoing and completely unpredictable basis. This lack of any hope of *prediction* about the natural world means that these ideas do not qualify as science, and no amount of dressing them up in scientific language will make them science.

OBSERVABLE EVOLUTIONARY CHANGES IN ANIMALS TODAY

Evolution predicts that selective changes in organisms should be happening right now. The emergence between 1935 and 1975 of bacteria that eat nylon-factory waste was one. Another has to do with the lengths of birds' wings.

THE WINGS OF CLIFF SWALLOWS THAT NEST OVER HIGHWAYS

Cliff swallows (*Petrochelidon pyrrhonota*) are sparrow-sized birds that plaster their cantaloupe-sized mud nests under overhangs on cliff faces. But when highway overpasses began to be built, cliff swallows moved right in. They can build hundreds of nests among the girders of one bridge. Thirty years ago, many of these highway-nesting swallows were killed by cars. Over the years, their deaths by oncoming car has decreased dramatically. Why? The lengths of these birds' wings have measurably decreased. Smaller wings allow these birds to maneuver more quickly, thereby avoiding cars better. The longer-winged individuals were more often killed. Over many generations (30 years is quite a few generations for these birds) individuals with slightly shorter wings managed to stay alive and breed more often and pass on their traits to the next generation.

This should not be considered a speciation event—the short-winged underpass birds and their long-winged country cousins are not so different yet that they can't interbreed—but it is a nice example of natural selection at work today.[59, 60]

HOW DOES THIS COMPARE TO OTHER IDEAS ABOUT BIOLOGICAL ORIGINS?

Other ideas about biological origins posit that species do not change, that all organisms are as they ever were.

---

[59] Meghan Rosen "Shorter-winged swallows evolve around highways." *Science News* 12:48pm, March 18, 2013 Vol. 183 #8, April 20, 2013, p. 17 https://www.sciencenews.org/article/shorter-winged-swallows-evolve-around-highways

[60] Mary Bomberger Brown and Charles R. Brown *"INTENSE NATURAL SELECTION ON MORPHOLOGY OF CLIFF SWALLOWS (PETROCHELIDON PYRRHONOTA) A DECADE LATER: DID THE POPULATION MOVE BETWEEN ADAPTIVE PEAKS?" The Auk* 128(1):69–77, 2011 The American Ornithologists' Union, 2011.

Mendelian Genetics

Evolutionary biology did not directly predict Gregor Mendel's discoveries in genetics. But it does predict that any genetics would have to work in a way that allows evolution to take place.

The founder of modern genetics, Mendel did not publish his findings about the basis of inheritance until 1866; seven years after Darwin published *On the Origin of Species*. Mendel's work was mostly ignored for almost 40 years. Once rediscovered, however, it became clear that genetics provides vast amounts of evidence for evolution and that mutation and natural selection makes sense as its mechanism. It is profound that although Darwin did not know genetics in the modern sense, his work on evolution predicted the basics of how it *would* work. Darwin's work and Mendel's work mesh so intensely that the integration of the two became known as the Modern Synthesis[61] of evolution.

How does this compare to other ideas about biological origins?

No other idea about biological origins makes any predictions about the properties that the mechanism for genetic inheritance would have and not have.

What's more, only evolution explains the existence of 24 pairs of chromosomes in our near relatives the great apes, but 23 pairs in humans. Why the difference? Because, it turns out, one pair of human chromosomes, those in position number 2, are actually fused chromosomes. They have basically the same information as the two original unfused chromosomes, and they even have the remains of the ends of the

---

[61] "The Modern Synthesis: A Historical Approach" *Science Education Resource Center, Carlton College* https://serc.carleton.edu/introgeo/earthhistory/modsyn.html

old chromosomes buried (vestigially) in their cores. No "alternate" idea about biological origins comes near to addressing such things.[62]

PREDICTIONS IN MEDICINE

Many medical breakthroughs are the direct result of using predictions made by evolution. This has helped medical researchers find new treatments for cancer.[63] A new hormone that suppressed appetite was also discovered by using predictions based on evolution by natural selection. "Darwin led us to this new hormone" said the researcher.[64]

HOW DOES THIS COMPARE TO OTHER IDEAS ABOUT BIOLOGICAL ORIGINS?

No other ideas about biological origins make any predictions that are useful to medical research.

PREDICTIONS IN OTHER FIELDS OF SCIENCE

Physics

One remarkable aspect of how powerful evolution is as a science is its ability to make predictions about other fields of science, and indeed, to correct them when they are wrong. For instance, the field of physics was corrected and pointed in the right direction by the publication of Darwin's *Origin*.

---

[62] Carl Zimmer "The Mystery of the Missing Chromosome (With A Special Guest Appearance from Facebook Creationists)" Discover July 19, 2012 12:13 pm
http://blogs.discovermagazine.com/loom/2012/07/19/the-mystery-of-the-missing-chromosome-with-a-special-guest-appearance-from-facebook-creationists/#.XE4ht817IOQ
[63] L.M. Merlo et al., "Cancer as an Evolutionary and Ecological Process" *Nature Reviews Cancer*, 2006, 6(12), 924-35.)
[64] "Stanford Scientists' Discovery of Hormone Offers Hope for Obesity Drug" Stanford University School of Medicine, news release, November 10, 2005

Lord Kelvin was the preeminent mathematical physicist during Darwin's time. He calculated the maximum age of the sun (and therefore the earth), based on incorrect assumptions about why the sun is so hot. The age he got was far too short for evolution to have produced the vast diversity of species on Earth, so he decided that Darwin had to be wrong. But Darwin was not wrong. Kelvin's problem was that nuclear fusion had not yet been discovered. In the end, Kelvin's tiny age estimates were shown to be wildly wrong, and physicists realized that the sun and the other stars must run on some unknown, super-powerful source of energy yet to be discovered.[65]

HOW DOES THIS COMPARE TO OTHER IDEAS ABOUT BIOLOGICAL ORIGINS?

No other ideas about biological origins make any predictions that are useful to the field of physics.

Geology

Alfred Russel Wallace, the co-discoverer of evolution with Darwin, was a biologist-explorer who made bold predictions about the geology of the area between Southeast Asia and Australia.

In 1856, while in that part of the world, Wallace journeyed from the island of Bali to the island of Lombok. They're only 15½ miles apart. However, on Lombok Wallace found animals very different from those on Bali. On Lombok there were *Australian* cockatoos and *Australian* birds called honeyeaters. But just across the strait on Bali, *and* on the

---

[65] S. Gavin, J. Conn, and S. P. Karrer "The Age of the Sun: Kelvin vs. Darwin" http://rhig.physics.wayne.edu/~sean/sean/course_information_files/kelvinsunf.pdf

island of Borneo, *and* in Malaysia, he had seen Asian birds such as woodpeckers, fruit thrushes, and oriental barbets.[66, 67]

The climates on these islands are very similar, the islands are very close, and yet the animals on them are different. So different, said Wallace, that the faunas of Japan and Great Britain were more similar to one another than were the faunas of these two islands![68]

Why was this so? Wallace figured it out. It turns out that Southeast Asia used to be one connected stretch of dry land all the way out to Bali when sea levels were lower during one of the Ice Ages. This means that Asian species were the starter populations for all the animals that lived on the islands remaining of this land after the Ice Age ended and the sea rose again.

Meanwhile, Australia was connected at the time to New Guinea. So Australian land animals extended all the way out to New Guinea. That continent then provided the jumping-off point for the species that came to inhabit the islands that were nearby. Once again, as sea levels rose, parts of the Australia-New Guinea continent were submerged. Today, the parts of this former continent that are underwater are called the Sahul Shelf. The parts still above water are Australia, and New Guinea. There are still some remains of those off-coast islands as well.

The islands (including Lombok) between Bali and New Guinea are now called Wallacea, after Wallace. The dividing line between them and the former parts of Southeast Asia (including Bali) is called the Wallace line.

So this is how it came to be that islands just 15½ miles apart, with very *similar* climates and terrains, have very *different* animals living on them. Wallace was able to peer into the deep geological past of this entire

---

[66] Penny van Oosterzee "Drawing the line at Bali"
http://www.abc.net.au/science/articles/2013/11/07/3885420.htm)
[67] Jared Diamond "Mr. Wallace's Line" *Discover* magazine Friday, August 01, 1997 http://discovermagazine.com/1997/aug/mrwallacesline1198)
[68] David Bressan "The Forgotten Naturalist: Alfred Russel Wallace" *Scientific American,* January 9, 2013
https://blogs.scientificamerican.com/history-of-geology/the-forgotten-naturalist-alfred-russel-wallace/

region, and he did it just by looking at the biology, and knowing that evolution is true.[69]

HOW DOES THIS COMPARE TO OTHER IDEAS ABOUT BIOLOGICAL ORIGINS?

No other ideas about biological origins make any predictions that are useful to the field of geology.

WRAP-UP

By definition, science is always learning more because science knows it doesn't know everything. If we did, nobody would do any more scientific research. Not knowing things is why scientists get out of bed in the morning! We want to find out, and we know that we often can, in time.

As a means of finding out material facts about the material world, science has an unsurpassed track record, and the material world is where we live. Others may posit other worlds, but so far there is no evidence that they are anything other than imaginary. Science works through careful investigation, by believing only what we can discover using our own senses and equipment that amplifies them, and by rejecting supernatural explanations. The latter would have stopped all science, every time.

In the 400 years since the invention of modern science, the knowledge gained through this method of investigation has improved the health, safety, longevity and well-being of humankind far beyond anything that our ancestors could have dreamed of. Let's not screw it up!

---

[69] Penny van Oosterzee "Drawing the line at Bali"
http://www.abc.net.au/science/articles/2013/11/07/3885420.htm

13| OLD TESTAMENT MIRACLE GENRES AS FOLKLORE AND LEGEND

By Randall Heskett

Bible Christians misconstrue the Bible as history and fail to read it in its historical development; that is, they do not use methods to isolate original traditions, to identify how editors combine traditions separated several hundred years, and they do not read it genre-specifically. Moreover, they are unaware of cross-cultural ancient Near Eastern vocabulary and mythological concepts. They also do not discern how ancient biblical descriptions of the natural world not only violate science but show serious historical and logical flaws. These Bible Christians are uninformed about how historical-critical methods function in solving some of these problems. Hence, this chapter will describe how methods can help determine original sources, oral settings, and the form and function of various miracle genres.

For Hermann Gunkel, history and historiography are not inborn traits of ours. They require intellectual development that isn't based on what we imagine the past to have been, but rather based on impartial findings. The concept of history and historical consciousness itself did not reside in the minds of ancient writers.[1] It came later with the development of civilization. Thus, Sunday School interpretations present

---

[1] Hermann Gunkel, *The Folktale in the Old Testament*, trans. Michael D. Rutter, et al. (Sheffield: The Almond Press, 1987).

otiose options that ignore the tradition history of each text but misconstrue biblical narratives as history.

One original method used in distinguishing original and conflicting traditions was source criticism. Even before the modern era, R. Ibn Ezra was able to identify that Moses could not have written the first five books of the Old Testament, known as the Pentateuch (or Torah). In early modernity, even conservative readers knew Moses could not have written about his death and so they ascribed this narrative to Joshua (their J source). Subsequently, readers came to detect bold anachronisms and duplications of the same stories with different consequences. The most striking anachronisms were, "When the Canaanite was still in the land" (Gen. 12:6); "when the Canaanites and Perizzites still were in the land" (Gen. 13:7); "Before there reigned a king over that children of Israel" (Gen. 36:31). If Moses were the writer of Genesis, he could not have known the Canaanites were thrust from the land or that a king eventually ruled the land. Genesis mentions the cities of Hebron and Dan, but Judges said that they were named much later (Gen. 13:18; 14:14; Judges 18). Some narratives recount laws given before Israel takes the land and others describe laws already operative in the land. Genesis refers to clean and unclean animals before this distinction was revealed to Moses. Domesticated Camels have no business in Genesis during the period of Abraham. Semites in Abraham's time herded sheep, goats, and donkeys but had no camels because they were not domesticated until 1100–1000 BCE.[2] Furthermore, "Joseph told the Pharaoh's chief butler, "I was stolen from the land of the Hebrew..." (Gen. 40:15) but Hebrews were wandering nomads who did not yet own their own land. Moreover, the storyteller uses the name Yahweh, which other sources did not use until later revealed to Moses (Exodus 3:14 and 6:1ff.) The Reed Sea episode seems to intertwine four different stories.

The most striking duplications of the same stories with different consequences were as follows: There are two different creation stories,

---

[2] See, Richard W. Bulliet, *The Camel and the Wheel* (New York: Columbia University Press, 1975), 36.

each using different divine names (Genesis 1:1–2:4a and 2:4b–3), and two flood accounts (Genesis 6–9). Abraham pawns off his wife Sarai, as his sister, to Pharaoh (Gen.12:10–20) and then to Abimelech (20:1–18). Isaac does the same thing, pawning Rebekah off to Abimelech (26:1–17). Later, the first story is whitewashed, but Sarai seems originally to conjugate a marriage with Pharaoh (Gen 12:19). Finally, Yahweh tells Moses in one version to hit the rock at Rephidim which he names Meribah (Exod. 17:1–11), but in another, he strikes the rock in anger, God punishes him and does not allow him to enter the promised land (Num 20:10–12).

Therefore, Abraham Kuenen and Julius Wellhausen simultaneously put forward a "documentary hypothesis" that claimed that the Pentateuch was composed from 4 sources, which they called J–E–D–P (see below). While the JEDP hypothesis is sophomoric at best, I will show in this first part how source criticism works well to interpret miracles in Creation, Flood, Abrahamic, and Yam Sûf (Reed Sea) narratives.

In the second part, I will show how the form that literary genres take reveal how miracles function in the Hebrew and Aramaic Bible. Writers of the Old Testament/Tanakh often use epic, legend, and folklore. Frank Cross's description of "Hebrew Epic" displays both commonality and departure from Aristotle's categories on Epic in his Poetics. For Aristotle, an epic has five main traits. 1) It has a plot but is different from historical writings in that it sets forth the events of a single period of time and casts one or more persons who are only incidentally related to each other (the J source fits this description).[3] 2) An epic must be lengthy poetry, which rules out the J source that is written in prose while the "Song of the Sea" in Exodus 15 is old poetry.[4] 3) Aristotle praises Homer for speaking little as the poet but remaining in the background in the way J does.[5] 4) The material should be full of wonder and surprise using the untrue to

---

[3] Frider Sylburgii, ed. *Aristotelis De Poetica Liber Graece Et Latine*, ed. and trans from Latin (Lipsiae: Impensis Siegfried Lebrecht, 1780), 176.
[4] Op. cit. 178.
[5] Op. cit. 184.

explain reality.[6] J's setting Yahweh walking on earth fits this category. 5) Finally, poets should choose probable impossibilities versus unconvincing possibilities.[7] Some genres exceed these limits. From this perspective, Epic has an extremely broad meaning.

However, Gunkel suggests that biblical narratives comprise folktales belonging together with myth, Saga, and legend. When conservative Bible readers fail to interpret genre-specifically, they confuse these genres with actual events. In his book, *Elijah, Yahweh, and Baal*, Gunkel explains that various folklore forms (*Gattung*) such as Saga and legend are history-like in that they are set in time and space but describe events that exceed human history such as axes floating on water or snakes talking. At most, the stories provide windows into history but reveal more about the history of Israelite religion than history itself.[8]

SOURCE-CRITICAL ASSESSMENT OF MIRACLE PASSAGES

Various sources in the Pentateuch describe miracles stories differently. A trained eye can discern how the secular academician (*Wissenschaftlicher*) divided the sources into the Jahwist (10th or 9th century in Judah), Elohist (8th century from Ephraim), Deuteronomist (7th century during Josiah's reform) and Priestly writer (6th to 5th century, liturgical, genealogical, legal and technical), what came to be known as JEDP. Each source designates God by different names (J =Yahweh ["LORD"and rarely "LORD God"], E= ElÇhîm God[s] until Exodus 3, D=Yahweh your God, P= Elhîm ["God" or "God almighty"]). They stress different locations (J=Judah, E=Israel, D=central shrine in Jerusalem, P=Judah).

Relationship with the divine varies. In J, Yahweh walks and talks with humans, in E God speaks in dreams, D is moralistic, and P takes a magical cultic approach to God. Divine communication in J happens in

---

[6] Op. cit. 183.
[7] Op. cit. 184.
[8] First published as *Elias, Jahve und Baal*, ReligionsgeschichtlicheVolksbücher, II. Reihe, 8. Heft (Tübingen, Mohr, 1906).

anthropomorphic speech, in E refined speech, in D speech recalling God's work, and P portrays majestic speech. Each diverge where Israel received the Torah (J=Sinai, E=Horeb, D=Horeb, P=Sinai). Human attitudes toward theophany differ; J is comfortable, E is anxious, D is afraid, and P describes the transcendent. Various sources specify when people started worshipping Yahweh; J depicts it "in the beginning," E when Yahweh revealed himself to Moses in Exodus 3:14, and for P at the time of Moses in Exodus 6:3. Each describes the performance of miraculous acts diversely, J through nature, D legendarily, and P in a miraculous acts of divinity.

In the creation, flood, Abraham, and reed sea episodes, multiple sources converge but the earlier sources describe the so-called miracles through natural phenomena. In its epical or legendary in nature; the J source boldly anthropomorphizes Yahweh as walking and talking with humans and snakes even talk. A characteristic of folklore, Genesis 3 portrays the snake as "the trickster."[9] Yet in P, God is transcendent.

CREATION MIRACLES

P and J show differences in creation. In J God is a peasant farmer, who plants his garden, functions like a potter/sculptor, and who "molds" the first human, *Adam*, breathes into his nostrils, and puts *him* in the midst of the garden full of fruit trees. Now God walks with him daily, but *Adam* has to till it. The miracle of creation for J is very anthropomorphized and involves the human art of sculpting, using a genre that describes a time when gods were men in a manner similar to myth and legend. This form attempts to domesticate the divine. (Genesis 2:4b–3:24)

P later elevates god as wholly other, using Mesopotamian cosmology. P claims *Elohîm* merely spoke and the world, or universe (i.e., the heavens and the earth) was formed and filled in six days. (Genesis 1:1–

---

[9] Susan Nidich, *Folklore and The Hebrew Bible* (Minneapolis: Fortress Press), 43, 44.

2:4a). Unlike J's god, *P's god* was not a local deity. Compare the Hebrew account with the Babylonian *Enuma Elish*. According to it, the great god Marduk created the Earth from the slain body of Tiamat.

A mother goddess Tiamat (who controls the saltwaters from below) collided with her husband Apsu (who controls the fresh waters from above) and created four generations of *Igigi* gods. To celebrate, the stars, moon, and sun gather to dance but the noise disturbs the rest of the inactive parental gods. Tiamat, the patient mother, placates her children. But her husband, Apsu, sets out to kill them in order to restore peace and quiet. They kill Apsu instead. After her children kill her lover, Momma Tiamat sets out to destroy her children for killing her husband who was trying to kill her children. Discovering her plans, they ask the supreme god Marduk to protect them. Marduk fights Tiamat with thunder and lightning:

> Face to face they came, Tiamat and Marduk, sage of the gods.
> They engaged in combat, they closed for battle.
> The Lord spread his net and made it encircle her,
> To her face he dispatched the wind, which had been behind.
> Tiamat opened her mouth to swallow it,
> And he forced the wind (imhullu) so that she could not close her lips.
> Fierce winds distend her belly;
> Her insides were constipated, and she stretched her mouth wide.
> He shot an Arrow which pierced her belly,
> Split her down the middle and slit her heart,
> Vanquished her and extinguished her life.
> He threw down her corpse and stood on top of her.

After the battle, Marduk builds a temple and places the stars, moon and sun over it so that they may indicate the days, months and years. He then approaches the corpse of Tiamat and takes her spit to form clouds and heaps up mountains on her head and breasts as pillars to hold up the roof of the sky. He bores through the mountains in order to release the Tigris and Euphrates from her eyes.

P polemically purports a Hebraic creation, which is based in this ancient Near Eastern war politic. Due to Babylonian dominance in the world, they claim Marduk was more powerful than the Hebrew god, Yahweh. So, Genesis 1 tells Israel they are a great nation because ʿElohîm is the creator, not Marduk, but he has the power to reach into the chaos of Israel as he reaches into the cosmic chaos where the waters from above and waters from below are at odds with each other. Genesis reacts to the mythology of Babylonian gods. In response to the *Enuma Elish*, P makes a monotheistic claim that ʿElohîm created the stars, moon and sun who were not gods, like the Babylonian sun god Šamaš, and their moon god Sin. Grounded in the same Mesopotamian cosmology, P says ʿElohîm separated the salt and fresh waters by pounding out the dome of the sky (*rakîa*). The word *rakîa*, which is often translated "firmament" or "dome," really is built on the verb that means to "pound out" bronze or iron. P suggests that this god distinguished light from darkness to rule day and night after "pounding out" the dome of the sky.

P's description of this dome (rakîa) separating the waters from above and below underline how the Old Testament portrays Yahweh in the sky with the stars making up the heavenly hosts. The Hebrew calls him "the rider of the clouds" in the same way that the Ugaritic Baal Epic describes the god Baal (Deut 33:16; 2 Sam 22:1, 12–15; Ps 68:4, 33; Psa 104:3; Isa 19:1). Like Baal, Yahweh, the storm god, rides the clouds as his chariot and opens the windows of heaven to let the waters from above through the dome. The Bible tells about an earth that is built on pillars and has four corners just like Babylonian cosmology. In Psalm 133, the windows of heaven are opened on the temple floor. The biblical writers describe a solar-centric universe where the sun moves above a flat earth just as the Akkadian Šamaš hymn portrays the sun going into the netherworld at night. That is why the sun itself stands still in Joshua 10:13. Analogously, conception begins when a man deposits his "seed" in a woman's fertile ground with no understanding whatsoever of a sperm and ovum, explaining why the man is credited for begetting throughout the Bible. This is the biblical description of the natural world, which is the same as the Babylonian conception of the world with the main difference being which god was the creator, Yahweh or Marduk. We know the answer. Neither of them.

In that mind-set, spirits and Gods rule the earth. A multitude of mythological beasts live just beyond their purview in the oceans and forests. In that world axe heads float, beasts talk, magic wands have power, and virgins and menopausal women have babies. At the very least, some people believed them. At least, the rank and file, the true believers did.

The king was adopted as a god at his accession to the throne; that is why Psalm 45:6 says of the king, "your throne O God is forever." So later traditions rest on the king being a god but explain that the broken promises to David, when the temporal kingdom is destroyed (2 Samuel 7, Psalm 89) will be fulfilled by an eschatological Messiah, who comes down from the sky with an army of angels to set the world right.

The tools of the Enlightenment, including the microscope, telescope, and historical-critical methods exposed how these pre-scientific notions of cosmology and conception are absurd. Science describes an entirely different cosmogony—namely the origins of the universe—pushing humankind out of the "dark ages" into new horizons. In light of science, a wise person, whether atheist or theist, cannot read the Bible verbatim nor accept the miracles of creation because they are based on a flawed cosmology. Those who have drunk from the well of modernity cannot fail to recall science when considering biblical miracle stories.

THE FLOOD MIRACLE

The Genesis 6–9 flood narrative serves as a textbook case for source criticism.[10] Two stories are being intertwined. J is the oldest flood source

---

[10] Some of the most salient writings on source critical problems within the flood narrative are as follows: Francis Anderson, *The Sentence in Biblical Hebrew*. Paris: The Hague, 1974. J. Bleinkensopp, *The Pentateuch: An Introduction to the First Five Books of the Bible*. New York: Doubleday, 1992; "The Structure of P," Catholic Biblical Quarterly, Vol. 38 (1976), 275-92. Frank Moore Cross, *Canaanite Myth and Hebrew Epic*. Cambridge, Massachusetts: Harvard University Press, 1976. J.A. Emerton, "*An Examination of Some Attempts to Defend the Unity of the Flood Narrative in Genesis—Part I,*" Vetus Testamentum. Vol. XXXVII, 4 (1987), 401-420; "An

while P is post-exilic (6th to 5th century BCE). Gunkel claims this narrative provides a textbook case of J and P: "The method of how source criticism is to function can best be understood for the beginner from this passage."[11] The flood narrative contains sources that are intertwined instead of side by side, making it a bit harder to see,[12] but it makes the most sense of the doublets, repetitions, and glaring contradictions.[13] Similarly, Abraham receives what appears to be two divine calls to leave Ur of the Chaldeans which did not yet exist (11:32–12:1; 12:4). The name Beersheba is explained in two distinct manners *(Gen* 21:31; 26:33). The husband passes his wife off as his sister *(Gen. 12:10–20, 20:1–18 & 26: 8–13)*; Sarah casts out Hagar twice *(Gen. 16:1–14 & 21:1–21)*; Moses striking the rock twice and two different etiologies appear for Meribah *(Ex. 17:1–9 & Numbers 20:1–13)*, etc. All these doublets and triplets appear to have common sources diverted through the process of oral transmission which took place in different regions and different times.

In addition, several inconsistencies make it improbable that a single writer composed such a dissonant narrative.[14] The use of divine appellations of Elohîm in P and Yahweh in J, at the opening (6:5–7:5) and the closing (8:15–9:17), provide the most striking evidence that these titles fit into the source pattern.[15] Yet the middle section (7:6–8:14) does not include divine titles. A good source critic can see several stylistic

---

Examination of Some Attempts to Defend the Unity of the Flood Narrative in Genesis," Part II. *Vetus Testamentum*, Vol. XXXVII, 1 (1991), 1-21. Hermann Gunkel, *Handkommentar zum Alten Testament: Genesis.* Gottingen: Vandenhoeck und Ruprecht, 1902. Habel, Norman. *Literary Criticism of the Old Testament.* Philadelphia: Fortress Press, 1986. Gordon J. Wenham, *"The Coherence of the Flood Narrative"* Vetus Testamentum, Vol. XXVIII (1978), 336-348; "Method in Pentateuchal Source Criticism" Vetus Testamentum, Vol. XLI, 1 (1991), 84-109.

[11] "My translation. Hermann Gunkel, *Handkommentar zum Alten Testament: Genesis* (Gottingen: Vandenhoeck und Ruprecht, 1902), 122.

[12] See James L. Crenshaw, *Story and Faith: A Guide to the Old Testament* (New York: Macmillan Publishing Company, 1986), 39. See also K. Koch, *The Ancestress of Israel in Danger: (in) the Growth of the Biblical Traditions* (New York: 1969), 122.

[13] See James L. Crenshaw, *Story and Faith: A Guide to the Old Testament* (New York: Macmillan Publishing Company, 1986), 39-40.

[14] Crenshaw, 39-40.

[15] Ibid.

peculiarities in passages where divine names do appear and then employ the same observations where they do not appear. First, P says one pair of each type of animal enters the ark (6:19, 20) but J says seven clean and two unclean enter it (7:2–3). P does not distinguish between clean and unclean because God had not yet revealed this to Moses.[16] P doesn't use the anachronism that Noah sacrificed after the flood, but J does (Gen. 7:15–16).[17]

Several duplications are not characteristic of a single narrative. Twice God sees the sin of humanity (6:5, 6:11,12), twice he announces the end of humankind by a flood (6:17, 7:4), and twice Noah enters the ark (7:7–9, 7:13–16). Then the flood comes twice (7:10, 7:11); water increases and the ark floats on water twice (7:17, 7:18); all living beings die twice (7:21–22); the flood ends twice (8:2a, 8:2b); Noah can leave the Ark twice (8:6–12 & 13b, 8:15–16); and God promises never to send a flood again twice (8:20–22, 9:8–17).

Various contradictions recur that indicate more than one solitary account:[18] The number of animals and when the deluge ends are depicted in two ways. The waters from above and below come together in P (7:11) but the deluge in J is also a 40-day shower (7:12). Noah uses his own brain to find out whether he can leave the ark in J by seeing that the mud was drying up (8:6–12) but in P God commands Noah to leave. In J, the ark is already present but in P they have to build one (6:14–16).

J alone opens telling of the offspring of the "sons of God" coming down from heaven and 'fucking' the daughters of humans. These were the heroes of old, warriors of renown. J also describes Yahweh repenting for his mistake of making humans but in P, God merely sees the

---

[16] Norman K. Gottwald, *The Hebrew Bible: A Socio-Literary Introduction* (Philadelphia: Fortress Press, 1985), 333. See also Joseph, Bleinkensopp, *The Pentateuch: An Introduction to the First Five Books of the Bible* (New York: Doubleday, 1992), 80.

[17] See Edwin Firmage, *The Biblical Dietary Laws in Studies in the Pentateuch*, ed. J.A. Emerton (Leiden: E.J. Brill, 1990), 178-208. See also Gunkel, *Genesis*, 122.

[18] See Gunkel, *Genesis*, 122-125.

corruption. Perhaps in J, Yahweh wipes out humankind because divine beings mingled with them.

Moreover, J and P employ different Hebrew expressions characteristic of individual sources. J writes "from upon the face of the ground" and "all existence" exclusively. P utilizes a more erudite word, gäwa`, to speak of the impending death of the wicked whereas J uses the common word môt "to die." P employs "these are the generations of Noah," which also appears in other P texts in standard tôledôt (genealogical) formulae (2:4, 5:1).[19] The term Bürît "covenant"—a favorite topic of P—may refer to Genesis 17 without citing it; the phrase "establish a covenant" appears both in 6:18, 9:9, 11, 17 and also Genesis 17.[20] J employs 'îšwü'išTô "man and his woman" but P uses zäkär/nüqëbâ "male and female."

P and J are very distinctive. J works out scenes with greater sympathy and artistic form than the P.[21] J composes for the common folk.[22] P piles up "priestly" data without considering aesthetics nor relevance for the community.[23] P writes in a sober spirit and an inflexible and solemn nature without feeling; Noah is no longer a concrete character but merely a type of a pious man.[24] P describes the past in static models of how the world relates to 'Elōhîm; the flood is not about the land covered with water for many weeks as in J. In P, Noah has to prove his faith by building an ark on dry land, but God magically closes the doors of the arc behind him (7:16). In Myers & Briggs descriptions, J is a P and P is a J.

P emphasizes the mythological *mabbul* (מבול), the cosmic waters released from chaos as creation is undone, engulfing the earth for an entire

---

[19] Gunkel, *Genesis*, 122.
[20] Gunkel, Genesis, 123.
[21] Von Rad, 121.
[22] Von Rad suggests that the very fact that "Yahweh himself shut up the Ark behind Noah is again one of those surprising statements of the Yahwist almost hybrid in its combination of near-childlike simplicity and theological profundity." Pg. 120.
[23] Gunkel, *Genesis*, 123.
[24] Gunkel, *Genesis*, 123.

year, rising over the mountain tops.²⁵ Possibly *mabbul* is a cognate with the Akkadian term for flood *"abubum"* that is also used in the Babylonian Flood Myth.²⁶ Its articular mode, *"the mabbul"* can imply "catastrophe." For the Hebrews, the *mabbul* was a well-known entity where water belonged and an ancient designation for the heavenly ocean (Psalm 29:10). Possibly, מבול (*mabbul*) derives from the Hebrew נבל (*nabal*) "water skin" (Job 38:37), fitting the concept of "heavenly storage" or "heavenly ocean" above. God, who is also called the "rider of the clouds," rides on them as his chariot while opening the "windows of heaven" and he lets these waters through the windows of the rakîa or dome in the sky (Gen 7:11, 8:2). The cosmology, upon which the whole marvel depends, squelches the miracle. If we cannot accept the Biblical description of the flood, we cannot accept the miracle based on it either.

A strong distinction can be seen between J and P; God tells Noah in J that God will destroy the earth with water, but *mabbul* alone is not mentioned. J uses the phrase "waters of the *mabbul*" once but P speaks solely about "the *mabbul*" in its mythological sense. Normally, J refers to the flood as "the waters."

J resolves human fate in the phrase, "Noah found favor" unlike P's ethereal version of divine intervention. J idealizes Noah, not as a figure of superior character, but resolves the conflict by his own human actions. J anthropomorphizes Yahweh smelling the aroma of the sacrifice. J couches the flood in hamartiology (sin narrative in Genesis 3–11) in universal terms of sin exemplified in standardized models. Creation and redemption merge into one act of dramatic divine saving action in the picture of the struggle with the dragon of chaos. The struggle between chaos, creation, and Yahweh's counterbalance of a flood illustrates Yahweh's anthropomorphic proximity in human existence. J epitomizes Yahweh as though he were a human, and so Yahweh repented that he

---

[25] See, J. Begrich, "Mabbul Eine exegetisch-lexikalische Studie," *Zeitschrift fur Semitistik*, 6 (1928), 135-53.
[26] Walter C. Kaiser, "נבל," *The Theological Wordbook of the Old Testament*. Eds. R. Laird Harris, Gleason Archer, Jr. and Bruce Waltke (Chicago: Moody Press, 1980), 489. See also Von Rad, *Genesis*, 128.

made the human on the earth. In the Babylonian creation and flood myths all the gods fight, but in J, Yahweh struggles with himself.

Although J is earlier, P uses older traditions learned from the Babylonians with new concepts such as the anthropomorphism of God needing a rainbow to remind him not to wipe out humankind (9:13). Just as Genesis 1 is creating a polemic against Babylonian myths, it does so by using the same Babylonian flood myths, for Marduk puts an undrawn bow in the heavens as a sign of victory against Tiamat and the cosmic chaos, and his propensity to punish.

Seldom has the case of the documentary hypothesis been stated so clearly and persuasively as in the Flood narrative. The legendary miracles are not new but cast in new settings. The Flood story depicts, 'if you do not understand it, blame it on God.' Hence, Hans Walter Wolff maintains that P has formulated the institution of capital punishment as an edict for humankind after the Flood. This decree provides unqualified protection for human life as opposed to the life of animals.

The flood narratives are grounded in ancient cosmological myths. The earlier J source attributes actions to some human or natural intervention while the later P source assigns the whole deluge to God. Even the five-Sumerian city laments assign the storm to god's actions.[27] This stands directly opposed to science which tells us cosmological disasters are due to atmospheric weather patterns and not superstitions. But if we accept science, we cannot accept the flood narratives as depicting a real flood.

MIRACLE OF SARAH'S IMPREGNATION

Yahweh is just a man according to J. He walks with Adam in the divine garden (Gen 3:8–10), a major motif in ancient cosmologies. In the story of Sarah's impregnation Yahweh is one of the three men who visit Abraham and implies a hidden visit to Sarah (Genesis 18). Does this mean,

---

[27] See the second chapter on Sumerian city laments in my, *Reading the Book of Isaiah: Destruction and Lament in the Holy Cities* (Macmillan, 2011), 7-30.

as both Philo and Paul claim, that Isaac was born from Yahweh's conception (Philo, *Allegorical Laws*, 3:219; Gal 4:22–23)?

In Gen 18:9, the word ʾēlāyw in the phrase, "they said unto him/them" has dots above called *puncta extraordinaria*, which communicate some sort of hesitation about whether the words or letters really belong in the text. R. Azariah assumes that the dots communicate a missing scene, namely that the three messengers entered the tent and spoke with Sarah directly. The change of the preterit verb in verse 9 from plural "they said" (ויאמרו) to the singular in verse 10 "he said" (ויאמר) implies that there is a new scene. In the first, all three angels are speaking with Abraham but in the next, only one messenger announces Sarah's pregnancy.

Between these two scenes, the messengers entered the tent to be with Sarah, but the one who comes out and announces the pregnancy is identified as Yahweh. Why would a text imply a scene with Sarah secluded with one or three messengers? It explains how Sarah, a woman in menopause, miraculously becomes pregnant. Genesis 21:1 tells that Yahweh visited Sarah as he had promised and did for Sarah as he had spoken. So, the miraculous impregnation of Sarah occurred when gods were men and walked the earth (Gen 18:2, 18:22–19:1). Interesting, Yahweh also impregnates Mary Mother of God.[28] Maybe they needed to start the "me too" movement back then!!!

THE YAM SÛF MIRACLES

I will use the transliterated Yam Sûf here—instead of Reed Sea or Red Sea—because no one really knows how to translate this phrase. The greater Yam Sûf episode comprises four sources, E, J, P, and one very old 13th-century poem in Exodus 15, according to Frank Moore Cross and David Noel Freedman (all four intertwined in Exodus 13–15).[29]

---

[28] See Mary Daly, *Gyn/ecology: The metaethics of radical feminism*. Boston: Beacon Press, 1978), 83-85.
[29] Frank Moore Cross and David Noel Freedman, Studies in Ancient Yahwistic Poetry (Grand Rapids: Eerdmans, 1975), 31-45.

Predictably, the older stories do not portray the event through miracles but through natural phenomena. As Miller reminds us:

> If the account is analyzed with an eye toward reconstructing its events...the reader is faced with several problems—historical, geographic and logistic—that many scholars have been forced to solve geographically.[30]

However, I do not think that scholars can pinpoint an exact dating nor historical circumstance for each tradent. Each tradition explains this story differently. For purpose of illustration, I have relied on Gottwald's source-critical distinctions though views differ on the limits of each source.[31]

J 13:20–22; 14:5–7, 10–14, 19b–20, 21b, 24–25, 27b, 30–31 (p. 182 # 18–20)

P 14:1–4, 8–9, 15–18, 21 ac, 22–23, 26, 27a, 28–29; 15:19 (p. 185 # 83)

E 13:17–19; and the "Song of Mariam" 15:20–21 (p. 183 #42–43). While the J source speaks of the Egyptians or Egypt, P speaks of Pharaoh or Pharaoh king of Egypt. Exodus 14:1–4 has no pillars of cloud and fire found in J. P tells about the hardening of Pharaoh's heart. The narrative shows successively a two-source switch back and forth from divine impact and human decision similar to the flood. J even depicts six hundred picked chariots and all the other chariots of Egypt with officers over all of them. In 14:10–14, the earlier J speaks about Moses' agency of taking the Israelites into the wilderness and Yahweh fights for them (14:10–14) using natural resources but P in 14:15–18 describes supernatural intervention and Yahweh takes the credit. In Exodus 14:21, the sources divide in P by Yahweh working directly through Moses and the Israelites walk on dry ground. In J, however, Yahweh drives "back the sea by a strong east wind of nature all night" (14:21b). This pattern continues and instead of mentioning dry ground, J describes in 14:24–25 Egyptian

---

[30] Robert Miller, Crossing the Sea: A Reassessment of Source Criticism of the Exodus, ZAR, 15 (2007) 187.
[31] Norman K. Gottwald, The Hebrew Bible: A Socio Literary Introduction (Philadelphia: Fortress Press, 1987), 182-87.

chariot wheels having problems turning because they are clogged from mud. J only mentions that Yahweh saved Israel, describes the dead on the seashore, and the people not only believe in Yahweh but in Moses (14:30–31). In P, the water stacks up and then returns on the Egyptians after Israel walked through on dry ground (14:28–29). J suggests that "the Angel of God" caused a "pillar of cloud," a natural phenomenon.

The sources even differ on where they cross the Yam Sûf and where they take their trip. E suggests that Elôhîm does not lead them by way of the land of the Philistines although that is nearer but Elôhîm himself reasons that they should not face war on the short trip because then they would change their minds and go back to Egypt (13:17–19). So Elôhîm leads them roundabout the way of the wilderness toward the Yam Sûf. For E, they most likely go from Goshen through Succoth into the wilderness. E adds that Moses takes the bones of Joseph to keep his promise (Gen. 50:24–26). P suggests that they camp in front of Pi-hahiroth, between Migdol and the sea, in front of Baal-zephon. J states they set out from Succoth and camp at Etham.

The earliest traditions did not include miracles beyond the forces of nature. The late post-exilic P, who seems influenced by Babylon, added the miracles to bolster Israelite power over the nations. The miracle then becomes a theme of ancient Near Eastern war politics against Babylon.

Moses the prophet is spirit possessed and God comes down to him in a cloud. Analogously, in Numbers 11, Yahweh comes down in the cloud and takes some of that spirit, which was on Moses, and puts it in 70 elders who prophesy. However, Eldad and Medat scandalously go out and prophesy without taking a portion of Moses' anointing that falls on the 70. Moses, however, affirms them. Similar to Pentecostal-miracle services today, there is always a curtain behind the curtain in the magic show.

Key to the performance, P describes Moses' staff like a magic wand that accompanies every sorcerer and magician. When he throws it on the ground, it turns into a snake (Ex 7:8ff). Moses, raising his staff with his outstretched arm, is indicative of the secret power of ancient sorcerers

(Ex 14:16 ff 26 ff). He raises his staff over the Reed Sea and the sea splits in two so that the Israelites could walk through on dry ground (Ex 14:16). Similarly, he strikes the rock with his rod and water gushes (Ex 17:5).

The P narrator claims, "you lift up your staff, and stretch out your hand over the sea and divide it, that the Israelites may go into the sea on dry ground." (14:16). We recall the event where Moses also uses his magic wand prevailing against the Amalekites and when his arm becomes tired and he can no longer hold up his staff, the Israelites begin to lose until two of his comrades hold up his arm. A similar occurrence appears in the "sun stood still in the sky" episode where Joshua the sorcerer seems to have power over the sun and moon (Jos 10:13), which betrays the fallacy of the legend purely on the basis of a solar-centric universe. Isaiah similarly causes the sundial to go backwards in the book of Hezekiah (Isa 38:7). Remember Aaron's staff that budded? The magic wand has power in folklore.

The expansion of miracles develops in successive traditions. Earlier sources do not set the tradition history in miracles but in acts of nature. Full-blown miracles in Genesis and Exodus seem to be later, post-exilic, priestly traditions still working on the ideas of folklore and legend, both in the description and the dating. Yet miracle genres also appear in the so-called Deuteronomistic History (DtrH), stories of which are later written down from oral traditions that seem to be added by either DtrH, DtrH 2 or a later editor.

FORM-CRITICAL EVALUATION OF MIRACLE GENRES

Hermann Gunkel shows interest in how unconscious rules of poetic beauty govern the oral discourse that operates within the Deuteronomistic History (the original core chapters of Deuteronomy and Joshua-Kings). As soon as a tradition is written down, it assumes a certain artificiality. It takes on self-conscious rules belonging to the scribal class and creating a new artistry that does not always have the same semantic import that it once had at the oral level.

While Julius Wellhausen thought legend was something that was not historical, Gunkel aimed to locate it not within history but within the history of the literature of ancient Israel via an oral story spoken on some occasions to an audience. Gunkel called this oral setting the *Sitzim Leben*. Only when the reader understood that form and function, could he or she do justice to the aesthetic critique of oral traditions, oral performance, pre-literary oral stages. So Gunkel aimed to describe the history of religions with a goal to discover the content or function in which he hoped to find through typical things in society that were retained at the unconscious level.

He asserts that everyone knows *Alice in Wonderland* is a fairytale, Goethe's *Sorrows of Werther* a novel, and Mommsen's *Roman History* a book of history. Yet the modern mind is not familiar with many ancient genres. Scholars disagree about the literary types (*Gattungen*) in DtrH narratives. Some considered DtrH to be history and others Legend (Sagé). Legend and history are similar in that narratives embody them, they both deal with historic personality types, and involve events set in time and space. They differ in that history is a learned-prosaic description when legend is a popular-poetic folklore type. History attempts to relate what really has occurred, but legend inspires, makes glad, and moves the heart. History was not the concern of ancient times. Yet the so-called "Deuteronomistic historian," who compiles mainly legends in First and Second Kings, constantly reminds the reader that if s/he wants to know what really happened, they need to refer to the annals of the kings.

Hence, Gunkel's aesthetic critique attempts to understand why some narratives are compelling and others are not. Legendary genres awaken the imaginative and describe miracles to create towering heroes. Early form critics tried to adopt the original oral folklore perspective before the redactors recontextualize it. When editors change the context, they alter the meaning but at the price of losing the unconscious aesthetic.

The Elijah narrative opens in 1 Kings 17 without a proper introduction. The original seems to be lost and replaced by 1 Kings 16 describing prophecy and fulfillment or claims about the word of God that are applied throughout the Elijah narratives. The chapter repeatedly lists Jeroboam as the worst of all Israelite kings until Ahab comes to the scene.

First Kings 17 presents the first miracle involving Elijah. The ravens feed the prophet bringing him bread and flesh, which is quite contrary to their nature but a common-folktale motif of helpful animals (1 Kgs 17:6–7); an angel also feeds him when he is hiding for his life in fear of Jezebel (1 Kgs 19:5).[32] Much later, Rev 8:13 portrays an eagle hovering in the sky crying out at the top of his voice a three-part lament for the world habitations.

Another miracle involves Elijah causing the widow of Zarephath's flower jar never to run out and later the oil vessel was never exhausted of oil (1 Kings 17). Similarly, Elisha causes a flow of oil that could fill many jars (2 Kings 4). Elisha feeds many people with a few loaves and has some leftover (2 Kgs 4:42–44), which creates a mimesis for Jesus feeding of the 5000 (Matt 14:14ff). Maybe these were the miracles of early potlucks!

Next, Elijah brings the widow's son back to life. His power is in his body like in other folktales describing the body of the magician. Elijah extends his body over the dead son of the widow of Zarephath three times before he brings him back to life (1 Kgs 17:21). Likewise, in a later account, Elisha lies on the child seven times, mouth on mouth, eyes on eyes, hands on hands (2 Kgs 4:4). A similar tale tells of laying a dead man's body in Elisha's grave and raising the dead man back to life when his body touches the prophet's bones. Part of miracles in ancient pagan sorcery takes place in private. Elisha, for example, shuts the door of the room beforehand (2 Kgs 4:3, 33). Therefore, no one can verify what

---

[32] Hermann Gunkel, *Religionsgeschichtliche Volksbücher*, Das Märchen im Alten Testament (Tübingen: J.C.B Mohr, 1917), 20, 34.

happens, that it happens, nor how it happens. The same occurs in Akkadian literature.[33] In the Elijah and Elisha episodes, the prophet's body and cloak seem to have more power contained in them than a staff.

Ordinarily, the staff serves as a magic wand. Both Moses and Elijah seem to have the secret power of a sorcerer though Moses' staff is his magic wand, especially in the P source, where he parts the Reed Sea by extending his staff over it and making the waters part and then come back together (Exod 14). Elijah, however, wears a hairy cloak over his naked body filling him with magic. Similar to Moses in P, Elijah divides the water, so he can pass through on dry ground. He uses his mantle, which for Elijah is like Moses's staff (see 2 Kings 2:8).

MT CARMEL

Gunkel says that even people today, who believe in miracles or the miraculous stories of Elisha, would have problems with iron swimming on water. However, if one tries to amend or resolve the miracle, one loses the legend. Legends are purposefully exaggerative. The Mt Carmel incident seems to have that same miraculous flare.

On Mt Carmel, Elijah kills 400 prophets of Baal single-handedly (like Samson killing the Philistines). This exaggerates beyond reality not to mention the narrative speaking of only 7000 Israelites true to Yahwism. First Kings overstates the conflict between Elijah and the king. The legend amplifies prophetic deeds, the fall of Ahab's dynasty, and the extermination of the prophets of Baal from the lesser man and it then attributes them to the greater, who was spirit possessed. This escalates Elijah's heroism. Therefore, Gunkel suggests that the Carmel story is not a real event in life but as the "dream" of the writer's ardent heart. Where history is silent, we meet legend. Legend makes the situation more dramatic and heroes more powerful.[34]

---

[33] Hermann Gunkel, ReligionsgeschichtlicheVolksbücher, 97.
[34] "Elias, Jahve und Baal," 100, 108.

The authenticity of the legend is the naïveté of Elijah pouring water on the sacrifice to such a degree that it overflows before fire from heaven supposedly consumed Ahaziah's messengers.[35] The legend relies on the miraculous to portray Yahweh's spirit taking hold of the prophet who resembles the typical legendary hero.[36]

Israel probably was not monotheistic at the time, at least not completely. Elijah is the protagonist and Ahab is the antagonist, who becomes the suppressor of Yahwism. Gunkel asserts that legend betrays an unconscious retention of the typical, which here is the movement from henodeism to monotheism. Miracles function to aggrandize Yahwism. Elijah taunts Baal saying in Hebrew that he is on a trip, he is asleep, or he is on the toilet. This does not claim that Yahweh is mightier than Baal but rather is God. Through the miracles, the widow of Zarephath converts to Yahwism. Elijah then becomes the milestone in the formation of monotheism.[37]

As a shaman, Elisha, who receives a double portion of Elijah's power, removes leprosy by his word (2 Kgs 5). Subsequently, he causes an axe iron to float on water (2Kgs 6). Ironically, the very sorcery that the narrator hates, he ascribes to the prophets. However, sorcery is not the problem here but that it is not done in Yahweh's name. Sorcery roots itself in the magic of primitive stories. Prophets who are spirit possessed (Isa 11:4) try to steer the heavenly powers with some mysterious actions.

Like the third law of Hammurabi speaking against sorcery to a culture that embraced it, biblical writers speak against this sort of magic (Ex 22:17; Lev 20:17; Deut 18:10; 1 Sam 15:23; 2 Sam 28:3; 2 Kgs 21:67; Isa 8:19). Yet the heart of biblical-miracle stories really is sorcery. This was endemic to the population of Israel (Isa 2:6). Numbers 22–23 does not condemn the sorcery of Balaam, who is not an Israelite, but

---

[35] "Elias, Jahve und Baal," 44.
[36] "Elias, Jahve und Baal," 148.
[37] "Elias, Jahve und Baal," 166-68.

condemns the fact that his prophecy is against Israel. The real issue is that they wanted these esoteric arts to be performed for Yahwism.[38]

Sunday school curriculum always touts Elijah's slaughtering the prophets of Baal as victory. Elijah's climb up Mount Horeb is reminiscent of the Mosaic hero. Yet why then does he end up in a cave for fear of his life? Elijah tells Yahweh that he killed them out of zeal. Ethically, Elijah's zeal could not bridge the gap between his word and what is purported as God's word.

The Elijah story ends with Elijah passing on the magician's mantle to Elisha, the tradition of the Mosaic prophets. Finally, he ascends to heaven. The concept of such an ascent is based itself on the ancient cosmology already described. Long before there were airplanes and spaceships, humans fantasized about flying into the heavens on magic chariots, magic horses, magic coats such as what Faustus flew on, magic carpets, and even the magic suit case as portrayed in Anderson's fairytale.[39] Hence, the concept of the chariot ascending to heaven arose out of this kind of setting. Elijah flies away to heaven on a chariot of fire pulled by magic horses, Enoch ascends to heaven as well (Enoch 70:2), and Yahweh flies on a cherub (Ps 28:11). Note that on the Magic Mountain or the heavenly palace is from where God's chariots come (Zech 6:1).

Probably first entertained by Bruce Malina, with whom I ate lunch every Wednesday in the late 80s and first heard orally of the following ideas long before they were published, John Pilch and Malina describe the sky journeys in the ancient world.[40] While still alive, the magical person ascends into the heavens and must return in order to complete the round trip (Enoch, Gen 5:24; Elijah, 2 Kings 2:1–12; Ezra, 2 Esdras 8:19b). Some never return, like Jesus whose return is still awaited. Malina and Pilch suggest that various biblical books mention an opening in

---

[38] Gunkel, *Folktales*, 112.
[39] Hermann Gunkel, *ReligionsgeschichtlicheVolksbücher*, 62, 63.
[40] Bruce Malina & John J. Pilch, *Social-science Commentary on the Book of Revelation* (Fortress Press, 2000), 74-75.

the sky (1 Kings 22:19; 2 Chron 18:18; Ezek 1:1; Mark 1:10; Matt 3:16; Rev 4:1). To enter God's real home in his celestial temple and attendant city, a holy person had to pass through this opening in the rakîa (the dome or firmament) that led to the other side of the vault of the sky where the god in question was enthroned. Mesopotamian lore inspired Israel to locate this opening directly over God's earthly temple. Acts depicts the sky opening above Jerusalem to allow the resurrected Jesus to ascend to God through that opening in the rakîa, the dome of the sky (Acts 1:2–7). Likewise, when this crack in the sky opened up for Stephen at his stoning in Jerusalem, he saw the exalted Jesus standing by the throne of God and the heavens opened up to receive him (Acts 7:56). Moreover, apocalyptic literature frequently mentions this opening and seeing the ark of the covenant in the center of the Temple. This is harmonic with Israel's tradition of people seeing God's presence in the sky from earthly Jerusalem. God's habitation is his dwelling place in the sky (Deut 26:15; 1 Kings 8:43; 2 Chron 30:27), high in the sky (Job 22:12); he walks on the vault of the sky (Job 22:14) but his throne is located above the stars beyond the vault near the magic mountain (Isa 14:13–14; 2 Chron 18:18). Concepts of humans reaching to heaven are also seen in Jacob's ladder and where humans build a tower of Babel so high that it touches heaven (Gen 11:1–9). The prophet Micaiah saw Yahweh sitting on his throne, and all the host of heaven standing on his right and left hand (1 Kings 22:19; 2 Chron 18:18). God's throne is in the sky (Ps 11:4) although he does have a house in Jerusalem (2 Chron 36:23; Ezra 1:2).[41] This is where Elijah's fiery chariot was headed.

People who believe these tales today fail to explain that we have already sent modern chariots into outer space only to find a conflicting cosmology and no dome. Never did a modern spaceship ever collide into the rakîa, nor crash through a window, nor encounter water from above, nor a heavenly palace. Neither do they explain why this opening does

---

[41] John J. Pilch, The Ascension of Jesus: A social scientific perspective (Hong Kong: Studium Biblicum, 2007).

not allow the celestial waters from above through this opening in the rakîa, the dome of the sky.

CONCLUSIONS

Ever since I was a child, I cringed when people said things like, "in the latest hurricane all the houses in my neighborhood were destroyed but not mine because God was with me." In the great 1989 earthquake, Bethany College sent out a publication about the destruction of downtown Santa Cruz, which devastated buildings at University of California Santa Cruz, but God miraculously took care of them leaving no damage. They rose to the level of the J source. I immediately wrote the president using rhetorical questions such as, "was God not looking out for the people of Santa Cruz, and UCSC but only Bethany?" Even in the scientific age people still want to believe the absurd. A guy with one leg two inches longer than the other used to come to Intervarsity Christian Fellowship and told everybody that he went to a healing service and God healed him. He continued to walk with a huge limp, coming back weekly to repeat the same story. He finally left Christianity because he felt deceived. Some biblical literalists want to believe that such miracles of epic proportions exist today. For many of them God is a Genie in the bottle.

Rudolph Bultmann demythologizes the teachings of Jesus by stripping away the miraculous. Yet his teacher, Hermann Gunkel, suggests that legend relies on the miraculous. A quest for history loses the value of folklore. Spinoza held that God's understanding and will are one and the same, both are unchanging and eternal, and laws of nature flow out from these. Thus, miracles defy the laws of nature, indicating some essential change in the nature of God, which is impossible. For Hume, evidence of the unchangeability of natural is absolute so that even if, for argument sake, one had absolute proof for the occurrence of a miracle, this would equal the opposing evidence and imply that a miracle could not be asserted with any certainty. Christianity requires faith that none can prove based on reason.

Before one addresses miracles in the Hebrew and Aramaic Bible, she or he must address science in relation to the narrative. Primitive beliefs that Elôhîm pounds out a dome in the sky called the *raqîa* with windows attached to it for Yahweh to open manually for fresh waters to enter the earth, bind themselves to miracle stories. J attributed natural phenomena to Yahweh and then the traditions grew to a level of direct intervention which the P source anchored in the cosmology. Natural traditions originating in J later developed into miraculous tradition histories in Deuteronomistic and Priestly sources.

While there is no proof outside of the Bible that the Hebrews were enslaved in Egypt or that Moses, Elijah or Elisha figures ever lived, Bible-believing Christians cannot fathom legendary genres in the Bible because they fail to embrace how the ancient mythical mind explained the workings of the natural world. Gunkel's explanation that oral traditions betray a self-conscious retention of the typical, illustrates that miracle genres tell more about the history of religions than history itself.

Christians embracing biblical miracles cannot honestly rule out claims of other religious literature. Ugaritic and Hebrew legends of Yahweh and Baal riding on the clouds leverage the event about Baal and Yahweh on Mount Carmel from one bias. Hermeneutical honesty would entertain that the Iliad and other myths carry the same historical weight.

Liberal Christians suggest that biblical legends are not meant to be taken literally but that only when the scientific mind and the rise of a historical consciousness arose (via Herodotus, the father of history) could readers distinguish real historical claims from the mythical ones. However, ancient cosmology explains how belief in miracles imbeds itself in prescientific ways to explain the natural order. A world where spirits and gods rule, gods and humans walk together, snakes talk, and a multitude of wild beasts lived just beyond their purview in the oceans and forests can entertain how axe heads float, magic wands create miracles, and both virgins and menopausal women can have babies. Whether superstitious or pious frauds as De Wette suggested, ancient writers failed to satisfy the appetite for modern science and history.[42] In light of cosmological beliefs, some ancient people believe in such miracles. The rank and file of the true believers embraced what the Reed Sea and Elijah stories described.

Belief that biblical miracles are historical events overlooks how various literary genres in the Bible—such as legend, folklore, and myth—do not make ostensive reference to historical events. These genres depend on the miraculous to elevate heroes and gods within ancient Near Eastern war politics, and to jockey for power.

Failure to read Old Testament "texts" genre-specifically, creates a major epistemological shift that nullifies faith claims, whether Jewish or Christian, whether conservative or liberal. Historical, logical, literary, and scientific categories deem it impossible to make such claims. Ignoring methodology leads to false assumptions. On these grounds, the whole house of cards comes crashing down.

---

[42] Wilhelm M. L. de Wette, Beiträge zur Einleitung in das Alte Testament, vol 1 (Halle: Schimmelpfenig & Compagnie), 292, 293, 295.

14| SCIENCE, MIRACLES AND NOAH'S FLOOD

BY CLAY FARRIS NAFF

FROM THE INTRODUCTION

Why would anyone presume to apply science to Bible stories? Isn't it enough to say that by faith alone we know they are true? Or to say that we're sure they are nothing more than folklore? In this book, we're going to do something amazing: We are going to apply scientific methods of inquiry, explanation, and, yes, speculation to the sprawling narrative known as the Bible—more particularly, to many of the miracles appearing in the tale. That means we need to know what counts as scientific knowledge, and what counts as a miracle. To take the last first, the *Stanford Dictionary of Philosophy* tells us that a miracle is "an event that is not explicable by natural causes alone." Taken at face value, that would seem to deflate the tires on this project before it moves out of the driveway. However, we don't have to give up yet.

There are several interesting possibilities. One is that there is an overlooked natural explanation for the event, and that people have been fooled or have deceived themselves into accepting a supernatural explanation. For the most part, we will focus on such circumstances. Of course, they will be inadequate to explain every aspect of the biblical miracles we examine. But, for sake of better understanding, it is worth teasing out the core of the story—the strange event—and assuming that the rest is embroidery or apologetics (rationales intended to bolster a religious claim).

These are not wild assumptions. The tendency to embroider is as natural as storytelling itself. Every culture has its tall tales and legends, and ours is no exception. From Paul Bunyan to Bigfoot and from the Bermuda Triangle to Area 51, the brief span of American history is replete with mysterious and wildly exaggerated tales. Other cultures offer myths as comprehensive as those from the Bible. They include creation stories utterly different from the Bible's twin accounts, such as the magic reed story of the Navajo, the Shinto island-creation story, and the Hindu story of cyclical creation. So, peering inside biblical miracles for a natural event that may have prompted the story is an entirely reasonable undertaking.

A second interesting possibility is that some miracles were simply frauds—products of the illusionist's art, presented as magic. Again, we know that illusionists have been a part of human culture for millennia, and we know that even today they sometimes commit frauds on the gullible. The illusionist known as The Amazing Randi has dedicated a large part of his career to unmasking such frauds. But there was no Amazing Randi in the ancient Near East, and no one had a grasp of inviolable scientific principles that give rise to skepticism about extraordinary claims. Indeed, even today if you ask anyone who believes in ghosts about the conservation laws of physics, you invariably draw blank stares. No one who understands those laws, their basis, and the overwhelming evidence that supports them spends any time worrying about ghosts.

A third possibility is that the Bible's miracle stories are literal accounts of actual happenings. Apologists exert a great deal of effort to promote this possibility, but all too often they get the science wrong or invoke magic. That's too bad. Magic is actually the most boring of all explanations. "God willed it" tells us nothing of interest. Miracles aren't even instructive. No one seeking to find moral guidance from God's miracles can avoid picking and choosing among their implications. (See bears—children below.) Ambiguity in Scripture may be why you find

Christians passionately for and against the death penalty, for example. (Incidentally, Muslims face the same dilemma. Some read the Quran as an injunction for mercy and compassion, others see it as a license for murder.) But what if God chose to perform miracles via natural means? Or plausible but as yet untested natural means, such as teleporting technology back through time? Now that could make for some interesting scenarios!

Showing *how* leaves a deeper point unaddressed: if a miracle is an event that defies normal explanation, then *why* attempt to use science to explain it? Fair question. Fortunately, for the sake of reader and writer alike, there are at least three good answers.

First, if miracles are, as many believers claim, signs from God, then it is critically important to distinguish the authentic from the phony. If science can provide a plausible explanation for an event, then it's not truly a miracle. For example, sightings of the Madonna are a commonly claimed miracle. Since we now know things the ancients did not—that hallucinations can be prompted by many things, from sleep or oxygen deprivation to peyote to a powerful magnetic field, and that moreover group delusion is easy to induce—should we include such claims in the roster of miracles? If God wanted to send a sign, mightn't we expect one that is unmistakable? If dispatched by the deity, shouldn't the Madonna appear, say, as a guest on the Late Show on CBS rather than as a ghostly apparition perched in a tree in Cameroon?

Second, it is epistemically important to maintain the coherence of science by explaining away mysteries in natural terms—where we can. Science is only as reliable as nature is consistent. If spectacular miracles occur, why not trivial ones? Indeed, sporting events often give rise to claims of a minor miracle, with winning players giving credit for their victories to God. If the deity chooses winners of baseball and football games and tennis matches, how can we assume that he does not alter the results of a pharmaceutical trial to favor one drug over another? Indeed, what scientific result could be considered reliable in a world where any sort of miracle takes place?

Third, if miracles are authentic, it is theologically important to clarify through them what kind of deity stands behind them. If God created both the Universe we inhabit and the laws that govern them, then how and why would he violate those laws? Indeed, can a supremely perfect God be a lawbreaker? If not supremely perfect, what's he like?

For example, in 2 Kings 2:23–24, the prophet Elisha, who has been wandering about the Holy Land invoking miracles for pay, approaches the gates of Bethel. Before he can enter, a large group of children come pouring out and mock him for his bald head. Elisha curses them and, hey, presto, a pair of bears comes loping along and mauls 42 children to death. It's hard to see why anyone would want to claim this as a miracle on behalf of a just, loving, and perfect God. Not even in Texas does corporal punishment go that far.

In any event, a ready explanation springs to mind: coincidence. There are bears in the Middle East. They are Syrian brown bears, which happen to be among the smaller and shyer of the species. They live in the mountains, not in the plains, and they rarely attack humans. But even shy bears will wander if food runs short, and hungry or nervous bears may attack—especially if their young are nearby.

It's notable, then, that the Bible describes the attackers as "she-bears." A group of youngsters calling out, "Ha, ha, check out old baldy!" from the wooded side of the road might provoke bears to attack. What's utterly implausible, however, is that two bears could maul 42 children. Even if the kids had been paralyzed with fear—not a likely conjecture—the bears surely would have lost interest less than halfway through the job. On the whole, Syrian brown bears would rather snack on pine nuts than brats. So, along with coincidence, to explain this we have to include a large dollop of exaggeration.

In suchlike fashion, we will explore the miracles recorded in the Bible. Not every miracle, of course. Some are trivial, some are repetitive, and some are incoherent. But most, like the unfortunate lads of Bethel, are fair game.

Speaking of fair game, though, before we go further, we must specify what counts as science. For starters, must it be natural? The consensus view is that it must, although a lively argument exists as to whether this expresses a worldview—naturalism—or is merely a method of science.

This problem existed long before the emergence of modern science. People everywhere have a naive and largely instinctive sense of what is natural (as well as an agency instinct that promotes belief in the supernatural). As we will see, the ancients who wrote the Bible sometimes described as miracles things that we take to be quite natural. Earthquakes, for instance, can be much more easily and consistently explained by plate tectonics than God's wrath. But there are plenty of other stories in the Bible that defy easy scientific explanation. That's where the fun comes in.

So, what is a scientific explanation? Dictionary definitions of science are generally dry, abstract, and deeply inadequate. Here, for example, is Merriam–Webster's primary definition: "Science 1: knowledge about the natural world that is based on facts learned through experiments and observation." What most of us learned in the public-school classroom is hardly any better. This is changing for the better, but in too many instances American pedagogy ranges from the good old science-fair model (observation- hypothesis-experiment-conclusion) to "shut up and learn these facts for the quiz on Friday."

As a science writer I've had many opportunities to watch scientists at work and to listen to them think out loud. I know that Nobel prize-winning physicist Max Born was right when he said: "There is no philosophical high-road in science…No, we are in a jungle and find our way by trial and error, building our roads behind us as we proceed." Yet, as it hacks through the jungle of the unknown, science leaves in its trail a lawful, coherent, and reliable description of the world.

By lawful I mean that certain simple statements about the world prove reliable again and again, whether put to the test in one culture or another, or at one time or another. An example you can rely on in all but the most extreme conditions is this: with any two magnets, like poles repel and unlike poles attract. It may yet be that under some never-yet-seen conditions, there is a bizarre phenomenon called a magnetic monopole, but even if this proves to be the case, in ordinary conditions the usual rules will still apply. You can rely on that.

By coherent, I mean that one area of science meshes with all the other established areas of science. Roughly speaking, there is a nested hierarchy of sciences. Physics is the most fundamental, dealing with the elementary particles (or fields) and forces of nature. Every other science must, therefore, cohere with physics. If a conflict arises, it may mean that an unknown mechanism of reconciliation has yet to be discovered (as in the quarrelsome cousins, general relativity and quantum physics), or it may mean that we are faced with a pseudoscience.

Astrology is a stellar example of the latter. We know this not only because reading the stars fails to consistently predict human affairs, but because the stars are simply too distant to coordinate their influence. The stars of the Big Dipper, that most familiar of constellations to those of us in the West, are not only far too distant from us to have real-time effects. They are far too distant from each other. They may appear to lie together on the inner surface of a dome, but in reality, the closest is 63 light years away, while the furthest is 210 light years distant. Just to coordinate a single event would take the stars of the Big Dipper a minimum of 147 years, plus another 63 to deliver the message to Earth. Anything less would violate a fundamental law of physics: information cannot travel faster than the speed of light. Unlike the fussy rule about ending a sentence with a preposition, the speed-of-light limit is a law upon which you can rely.

By reliable I do not mean that science is guaranteed to be The Truth, but that it provides the best available explanation of a given observation that is consistent with the evidence. Tomorrow, better data or better interpretation may give us an even better explanation. In most cases that won't render the old explanation useless, but will simply give us a more refined picture of nature. A nice example is Newton's law of gravity. In 1687, he described it as an attractive force between any two massive objects that is directly proportional to the product of their masses and inversely proportional to the square of the distance between them. Put as an equation, it works exquisitely well to predict the behavior of objects. Just ask NASA, which uses Newtonian methods to plot the paths of its planetary probes.

But Newton didn't have the last word. In 1915, Einstein published his general theory of relativity, which describes gravity as a warping of spacetime that bends the path of objects, and in 1919 observations of starlight bent by the sun validated the theory. So, Newton didn't get it all right. But neither did Einstein. Neither one offers a perfect description of gravity. Instead, Newton's laws work just fine for nearly every human endeavor. When extremely high speeds and/or strong gravity is involved, we have to make use of Einstein's more accurate equations. When gravity becomes so extreme that a black hole forms, Einstein's equations stumble over quantum mechanics.

One more characteristic needs to be taken into account. Science is more than laws or equations. It is also a theoretical explanation of the natural world. The explanatory side of science can be found in theory. It is an irritating quirk of the English language that in popular usage the word "theory" means a hunch. A hunch is like Sherlock Holmes's best guess about who killed the lord of the manor. In science "theory" means something quite different. It is the end of the road, after the jungle has been cleared. Theory gathers all the available data about a particular phenomenon and embeds them in a consistent explanatory tale. Germ theory, for example, is not a wild guess about what makes people sick (look up the history of chiropractic for that), but rather a comprehensively tested explanation for how microbes cause infectious disease.

With all this in mind, what counts as a scientific explanation is a tale that fits the facts—or a reasonable restatement of the facts—and is consistent with the relevant branches of science. These will range from physics, astronomy, and geology to biology, psychology and neuroscience. As for kinds of explanation, you can look forward to weather, volcanism, cometary impact, chance, and a host of other natural phenomena, including human frailties such as delusion, misinterpretation, beguilement, and confabulation. Just to stretch the boundaries of the possible, we'll consider what would happen if God or his surrogate were all-knowing but constrained to perform miracles by natural means. Borrowing from fantasy novelist Terry Pratchett, we'll call this kind of explanation "technomancy." We'll indulge in some science-based speculation as well.

Will all those explanations be true? Will any? Not necessarily. Just because something can be described in natural terms consistent with science doesn't mean it's true. Claiming that our universe is a simulation running on a computer is (so far) consistent with science. That doesn't make it necessarily true.

What's more, while the findings of science make an airtight case for naturalism, that in itself does not rule out the involvement of an external agency. Say, you buy a lottery ticket and pray that your number wins. The next day you check and find that you have indeed won millions. How can we explain this? It might be mere chance. Nothing unnatural about that. Even though the odds against scooping the jackpot are typically close to 300 million to 1, with enough tickets in circulation a winner will come up, just by chance. But we cannot prove thereby that God never puts a finger on the spinning wheel. The deeper question is this: why would God listen to your prayer and brush aside those of all the other poor believers who bought a ticket?

If you allow God the power to be arbitrary, unjust, or unintelligible, then anything logically possible may indeed be. Curiously enough, science has its counterpart: In quantum physics there arises what is known as the Totalitarian Principle: whatever is not forbidden is mandatory, or to put it a bit more elegantly, anything that can be must be. With all the foregoing in mind, read on at ease, knowing that nothing in pages that follow can either destroy a well-founded faith or turn skepticism into credulity. But I hope you will learn a thing or two, have a little fun, and stretch your imagination.

WATER, WATER, EVERYWHERE

Ancient tales of a great deluge abound, but there's none quite so influential as the Noachian Flood. People still produce photos of rills and humps on Mount Ararat that they breathlessly proclaim to be the remains of Noah's Ark. A creationist museum in Kentucky is building what it claims to be a reproduction of the original seagoing zoo. What was the Ark *really* like? Here's how the Bible describes it:

Genesis 7:6–16, NRSV

Noah was six hundred years old when the flood of waters came on the earth. And Noah with his sons and his wife and his sons' wives went into the ark to escape the waters of the flood. Of clean animals, and of animals that are not clean, and of birds, and of everything that creeps on the ground, two and two, male and female, went into the ark with Noah, as God had commanded Noah. And after seven days the waters of the flood came on the earth.

In the six hundredth year of Noah's life, in the second month, on the seventeenth day of the month, on that day all the fountains of the great deep burst forth, and the windows of the heavens were opened. The rain fell on the earth forty days and forty nights. On the very same day Noah with his sons, Shem and Ham and Japheth, and Noah's wife and the three wives of his sons entered the ark, they and every wild animal of every kind, and all domestic animals of every kind, and every creeping thing that creeps on the earth, and every bird of every kind—every bird, every winged creature. They went into the ark with Noah, two and two of all flesh in which there was the breath of life. And those that entered, male and female of all flesh, went in as God had commanded him; and the Lord shut him in.

No wonder the Lord slammed the cabin door, for by now the ark must stink to high heaven. Things can only get worse as millions of corpses bob in the waters. Perhaps to tamp down the stench, God keeps spigots open for months.

Genesis 7: 19–24, NRSV

The waters swelled so mightily on the earth that all the high mountains under the whole heaven were covered; the waters swelled above the mountains, covering them fifteen cubits deep. And all flesh died that moved on the earth, birds, domestic animals, wild animals, all swarming creatures that swarm on the earth, and all human beings; everything on dry land in whose nostrils was the breath of life died. He blotted out every living thing that was on the face of the ground, human beings and animals and creeping things and birds of the air; they were blotted out from the earth. Only Noah was left, and those that were with him in the ark. And the waters swelled on the earth for one hundred fifty days.

Okay, so now the entire planet is covered in water to a depth of about 29,000 feet (5.5 miles or 8.8 km). We know this, because Mt. Everest currently stands at 29,029 feet above sea level, and 15 cubits more adds another 22 feet, but as we'll explain below, Everest has grown a bit since Noah took to sea. How could this scenario possibly take place without a "magic wand"? Let's see how far we can get.

First, could Noah really be six hundred years old? Senescence is not fully understood, but much of what we know suggests that he could not live to that age in years as we understand them. Normal human cells can only divide between 40 and 60 times. This is known as the Hayflick Limit. At that point the telomere—a kind of doomsday clock on a cell—reaches its end and the cell undergoes apoptosis, or programmed cell death. There are some cells that avoid this fate, but they are not welcome in our bodies. Such cells multiply for their own benefit. We call them cancer.

So, rather than revise normal human biology, let's assume that the Earth was both spinning faster and orbiting the Sun faster—by a factor of about ten. This turns out to be a somewhat useful assumption for what will follow.

Now, we are confronted with a big problem: What would it take to cover every bit of land mass on the Earth, and how might that be achieved?

If we idealize the Earth as a sphere, we can approximate how much water would be needed. First, let's get a measure of the volume of the Earth. (For simplicity's sake, we'll work in metric units. Keep in mind that a kilometer is a little more than half a mile. We could make the calculations even simpler by starting with the Earth's area, but to keep a feel for the process we'll work with volumes.) The tried-and-true formula for finding the volume of a sphere, which we all have forgotten from our schooldays, is 4/ 3 r^3. Now, the Earth's radius is 6,371 kilometers. So, plugging numbers into the formula: [(4 x 3.14159) / 3] x (6371 x 6371 x 6371)] equals…wait for it…okay, that gives us 1,080,000,000,000 or 1.08 trillion cubic kilometers. Now, we must figure out how much bigger a sphere would be created if the surface of the Earth were one big ocean overtopping the highest mountains. Here, we run into several tricky points, starting with the highest mountain. Is it really Mt. Everest?

That depends. From sea level, yes, but taking into account the bulge of the Earth at its middle, Mt. Chimborazo in Ecuador has a claim to being taller. If you were on the moon bouncing a laser beam off the surface of the Earth at various points, the summit of Chimborazo would appear closer than the summit of Everest. If the Earth were spinning faster in those days, the bulge would have been even greater. Anyway, if you got caught shining a laser beam that could put out someone's eye, God would surely have punished you. So, let's put that aside mighty Chimborazo, because what we want to know is how much extra water it would take to cover all the mountains. Under the centrifugal force of the Earth's rotation, water will bulge just like land, so sea level should be the relevant measure. In those terms, Everest remains the champ, standing 29,029 feet above sea level. However, as I mentioned above, we can't assume that it was precisely that height some six to ten thousand years ago, when the Great Flood presumably happened.

Geologists say that the Himalayan Range, including Everest, was thrust up at least 30 million years ago, when the Eurasian plate collided with the Indian subcontinent plate. In recent years, two opposing forces have been manipulating Everest's height. Lingering upthrust pushing the mountain higher by a few millimeters each year, while erosion caused by the snows that perpetually fall on its peak files it down ever so slightly. Call it a wash.

Even so, in converting from feet to the metric system, we'll round up from 8.85 km to 9 km to account for those extra cubits the Bible mentions and to make sure the peak doesn't pop up during low tide. How much difference do 9 additional kilometers make? We need to run the numbers again. (Skip the formula if numbers make your brain hurt.)

Let's see: [(4 x 3.14159) / 3] x (6380 x 6380 x 6380)] equals...here it comes now...1.09 trillion cubic kilometers (rounding up a bit). Subtract the 1.08 trillion cubic kilometers of the Earth's interior volume and we have our answer: We'd need roughly 10 billion cubic kilometers of extra water to flood the Earth so as to cover all the mountains.

That's a colossal amount of water. A really, really huge quantity. It's more than all the water on Earth. A lot more. Roughly five times as much. At present, the oceans hold about one and a third billion cubic kilometers of water, and the remaining 7 million or so cubic kilometers of water are in clouds, ice, lakes, rivers, aquifers, etc.

Even though the difference between the surface of the Earth versus the enveloping sphere of extra water is tiny (about 0.3 percent), it makes a significant difference in volume. That's because volume grows much faster than surface area as you scale up—by the cube versus the square. (It's why hummingbirds can fly, and pigs cannot.)

We do get a little break, however. The protruding mountains and land masses themselves displace some of the volume in question, so we can trim our water budget. Not by much, though. Land above sea level only occupies about a third of the Earth's surface, and of that most lies in plains. Let's be generous, though, and give ourselves a 20 percent discount on the amount of water needed.

So, where are we going to find 8 billion cubic kilometers of water? That figure represents nearly six times the amount of water known to exist on Earth. The Moon is big enough to hold that quantity, but transferring such a volume (representing well over 10 percent of the satellite's mass) to the Earth would have sent the Moon spiraling away from us. If it had been closer to begin with the tides would have swamped the Holy Land long before Noah laid a single cubit of timber down.

Some have argued that we don't need more water at all. The continents, they say, simply lowered beneath the waterline for 150 days and then popped back up. There are a few problems with this idea. First, rock is denser than water (that's why it doesn't float). Therefore, if you were to lower the continents, you would cause the Earth to spin faster, like a spinning skater who pulls in her arms. Then, when you pushed them back up, it would slow again. Since everything on the surface of the Earth shares the rotational momentum of the planet, this would be like a cargo plane taking off and landing with a plastic swimming pool in its hold. To say the water would slosh around is understating it. Then there is the unimaginable displacement of all that water as the continents rise and fall. Think of a fat man doing a cannonball into a child's pool. Noah's Ark would have been swamped by the largest waves ever seen. Surf's up, dude.

The idea of continents sinking and then rising again in a matter of months is a nonstarter, anyway. No natural process could account for such antics. That being so, we're still in the market for water. There is a plentiful source, way out in the Oort Cloud. There, beyond Pluto, in the inky depths of space, lurk innumerable comets, largely composed of water. Comets are like dirty snowballs floating in space. Suppose, then, that two of them were perturbed in such a way that they came streaking toward the Sun and collided with each other just ahead of our planet? Their collision would cause their water content to vaporize and then flash freeze in a beautiful cloud of ice crystals. If the respective momenta were just right, the Earth might overtake the cloud and experience forty days and forty nights of worldwide rain.

There are at least two problems with this idea. First, if we were to dump that much fresh water into the ocean, its salinity would vanish. Ocean life is adapted to living in saltwater; ocean-dwelling fish, marine mammals, plants and crustaceans can no more live in freshwater than you could in a nitrogen-only atmosphere. Yet, we know that the ocean waters gained their saltiness from interaction with the Earth's minerals. Finding a pre-salted comet might be like expecting a hen's egg to come with its own seasoning in the shell.

Yet, we have to assume that the rainwater of the Great Flood had the same salinity as the oceans; otherwise, Noah would have had to take aboard all kinds of whales, sharks and every other kind of marine creature that depends on saltwater for life. A single blue whale would be nearly a fifth of the length of the Ark (30 meters versus 158 meters).

Assuming Noah could install a tank for the pair of them, a third of the Ark's storage capacity would be gone. As for stocking enough krill to feed the blue whales…fuhgeddaboudit. Noah's got troubles enough keeping the crocodiles from polishing off the pigs. As for the Komodo dragons…Don't get me started. We have to go with the saline hypothesis.

There may yet be a way to boil up a salt solution. It was long thought that comets delivered the water that today covers two-thirds of the Earth's surface and makes up the clouds, ice caps and other features of the hydrological cycle. We know the Earth could not have formed with all that water intact. Its early days were hellishly hot, and (as the Moon's pockmarked surface attests) under constant bombardment. Nearly all the primordial waters would have been blasted away into space.

Later, when cooler volcanic heads prevailed, water returned to the Earth. But how? It's long been thought that comets delivered it. However, in 2014 a close-up inspection of a comet by the Rosetta Spacecraft threw, er, cold water on that idea. The hitch is this: there are different kinds of water. Most water is made of an oxygen atom plus two ordinary atoms of hydrogen. But a tiny fraction of it is made of oxygen and deuterium, or heavy hydrogen. What makes the deuterium heavy is the addition of a neutron to the proton at the atom's core. The ratio of regular hydrogen to deuterium in the water on comet that Rosetta inspected differed a lot from the ratio we find on Earth.

That led scientists to think again. Maybe asteroids rather than comets delivered the water we find on Earth. Asteroids are largely made up of rocks and minerals. So, could they deliver salt along with water? This is at least conceivable. Would we then be able to turn that cloud into 40 days' and 40 nights' worth of rain, amounting to 10 billion cubic km of water? Improbable, to say the least. Friction is a major problem. That much mass traveling through our atmosphere in such a short period would surely overheat and turn the world into a deadly steambath. There is a period early in our planet's history when huge volumes of rain fell as the nascent Earth cooled. It rained and it rained and it rained, filling the oceans to the brim. It took a while, though. The deluge evidently went on for thousands of years. Even the most dedicated YMCA fan would have quit the steambath by then.

Let's suppose that by a *nearly* miraculous coincidence the saltwater crystals left by some deuterium-laden comets required exactly as much heat to melt as they generated by falling through the Earth's atmosphere, and that they went from ice to liquid water in a single step, bypassing the usual vapor path to rain. Let's also suppose that in doing so they came in at an angle that slowed the Earth's orbit and rotation just enough to allow for Noah's age. That would raise still more problems, mentioned above, about friction and rotational momentum, but we'll let them go. We'll assume that it was an almost miraculous gentle braking action—one that gives more time for the rain to fall, as each day becomes longer than the last.

Of course, in saving the ocean's creatures, we raise the necessity of a huge number of on-board aquariums to accommodate all the freshwater fish, otters, turtles, and other river dwellers that would die in a deluge of saltwater. It's not clear how Noah would have built aquariums, but maybe he assigned that task to his sons.

That's only the beginning of the troubles. Boarding is one thing; feeding pairs of every kind of animal on Earth for a little more than a year is quite another. A single elephant, for example, eats up to 600 pounds of fodder a day. For a pair of elephants, Noah would have needed to stow around 10,000 bales of hay on the ark, or risk them going hungry. You really don't want a hungry bull elephant rampaging on your ark.

But let's skip past the on-board agricultural challenges to face up to the biggest of them all: how do we get rid of a volume of water greater than all the world's oceans in a matter of months? Here's what the Bible tells us happened:

Genesis 8:1-5, NRSV
But God remembered Noah and all the wild animals and all the domestic animals that were with him in the ark. And God made a wind blow over the earth, and the waters subsided; the fountains of the deep and the windows of the heavens were closed, the rain from the heavens was restrained, and the waters gradually receded from the earth. At the end of one hundred fifty days the waters had abated; and in the seventh month, on the seventeenth day of the month, the ark came to rest on the mountains of Ararat. The waters continued to abate until the tenth month; in the tenth month, on the first day of the month, the tops of the mountains appeared.

You might think that after all that time on board, with a cacophony of shrieking peacocks, howler monkeys, roaring lions, trumpeting elephants, not to mention the flies, everybody would be good and ready for some shore leave. But no. According to Noah, it's still too soggy outside. The old hydrophobe makes them all wait another forty days before he even tests for dry land...ever so cautiously:

Genesis 8:6-10, NRSV

Noah opened the window of the ark that he had made and sent out the raven; and it went to and fro until the waters were dried up from the earth. Then he sent out the dove from him, to see if the waters had subsided from the face of the ground; but the dove found no place to set its foot, and it returned to him to the ark, for the waters were still on the face of the whole earth. So he put out his hand and took it and brought it into the ark with him. He waited another seven days...

They're on a mountain, fer chrissakes. Can't they at least get out and stretch their legs?

Genesis 8:10-16, NRSV

...and again he sent out the dove from the ark; and the dove came back to him in the evening, and there in its beak was a freshly plucked olive leaf; so Noah knew that the waters had subsided from the earth. Then he waited another seven days, and sent out the dove; and it did not return to him any more.

Finally! I lost track of how many days and nights this took, but relying on the good apologists at DefendingGenesis.org, I believe it was no less than 335 days from the end of the flood to day of disembarkation. That's a hellishly long time for anyone to be cooped up on the Ark. But is it truly enough time for all that water to recede?

Problem. The mutual attraction law of gravity creates a one-way street. Anything can fall onto the planet, but without the force of a rocket, nothing can get off. To leave the planet, an object has to exceed the minimum escape velocity, which is just over 25,000 mph (or 11 kilometers per second). At that speed, you could travel from New York to Los Angeles in about seven minutes. Don't count on being served a drink along the way.

It takes enormous power to accelerate objects for long enough to get out of the clutches of Earth's gravity. The Saturn V rocket, the most powerful in NASA's fleet, needed to generate nearly 30 kilos of thrust for every kilo of cargo it put into low-Earth orbit. Keep that in mind as we click through some staggering numbers: a cubic meter of water weighs a metric ton. Now, you might think that a cubic kilometer has a thousand cubic meters in it, but that would be wrong. A cubic kilometer runs to a thousand meters per side, but within the box that forms are a million cubic meters. So, to shift 8 billion cubic kilometers off the surface of the Earth, we'd need at least 30 x 1,000,000 x 8,000,000,000 kilos of force. That's 2.4 x 10^{17}, a number so big that it doesn't have its own name. We call it a hundred quadrillion. It's, uh, ten times a million times a billion. In other words, it's abso-freakin'-lootely huge.

Yet, there are forces in the universe capable of the job. The solar wind, for example, has blown most of the atmosphere and water off the surface of Mars. Of course, that's taken billions of years, and the gravity of Mars was only about 40 percent of Earth's to begin with.

There is a least one cosmic tool that can get the job done on time. A gamma ray burst could flash-vaporize and blow the water away in a jiffy. Gamma ray bursts are somewhat mysterious cosmic lightning bolts, carried by high-energy photons streaking across space. They are thought to emanate from stars with nearby massive planets that wind up their magnetic fields until they snap.

The trouble is that a gamma ray burst with the power to blow away that much water would sterilize the planet like God's own autoclave. The laws of thermodynamics say that you just can't heat up water that fast and blow it away without the heat spreading. The energies required for the job would be globally catastrophic. Mount Ararat, where Noah's Ark supposedly came to rest, would be the scene of a flash-fry barbeque of every living creature left on Earth. Pass the Famous Dave's…

Could the water have drained into vast caverns under the sea? That idea has been kicked around, but its no-hoper. The Earth's gravity draws everything toward its center of mass. Only the interposition of something denser prevents an object from continuing its journey to the center of the Earth. You've probably known this since childhood days in the bath. If you press a rubber ducky to the bottom, it will pop up when you release it, because the air inside it is much less dense than the water in the bath.

It's true that electromagnetic forces, being far stronger than gravity, can temporarily offset gravity's pull for some objects. A steel truss bridge, held together by electromagnetic force between its atoms, can keep a roadway suspended above the air for a lifetime or more. But even the best bridge has a load limit. Any attempt to hide a vast ocean of boiling water (it's hot down there!) under a crust of rock would eventually give way. The first volcanic eruption would spurt all that water back up the surface as the rock pressed downward, and it would be steambath time all over again.

In any case, we know that there isn't a second ocean hidden under the Earth's crust. Even though no one has ever drilled into our planet's interior (the crust is just too thick), scientists have mapped it in detail. How? The same way that an expectant mother can get an image of her fetus: by sonogram.

When earthquakes occur, seismic waves rattle through the Earth, and seismologists can read the information they carry to the surface to create a portrait of the Earth's core.

The only other natural solution would be a black-hole vacuum cleaner. Black holes can, in principle, absorb a limitless amount of stuff. (In practice, astrodynamics limits them to gobbling up a decent chunk of a galaxy before the stellar winds and rotational forces put other stars out of reach.) So, in principle, a black hole could soak up all the excess water and leave Noah high and dry. The trouble is that, unlike a Hoover, black holes don't have an off switch. Any black hole that started to feast on the Earth's bounty just wouldn't quit. It would consume the entire planet like a fat man getting out of the child's pool to slurp up a plate of spaghetti. Black holes are a dead end.

But here's the weirdest thing of all. In a passage that never seems to get quoted, the Bible tells us that at the end of the voyage, Noah roasted at least one of every kind of animal:

Genesis 8:20–21, NRSV

Then Noah built an altar to the Lord, and took of every clean animal and of every clean bird, and offered burnt offerings on the altar. And when the Lord smelled the pleasing odor, the Lord said in his heart, "I will never again curse the ground because of humankind...

This makes it is highly improbable that we should have any elephants, pandas, polar bears, or orangutans. These slow-reproducing animals are quite unlikely to have become impregnated or given birth during the voyage.

So, in the end, we are stumped. What a wild and pointless ride. After all that, the world is still full of sin and cockroaches. No wonder Noah got blind drunk when it was all over.

The sober truth is this: either Noah's Flood is a tall tale gone wild, or God is a magician after all.

15| JESUS CHRIST: DOCETIC DEMIGOD

BY ROBERT M. PRICE

Central, crucial, to Christianity is the doctrine of the Incarnation of God in Jesus Christ. One might consider the doctrine of the Atonement as of greater importance, but that tenet depends on the prior question of Christology: was Jesus Christ a created being who proved himself worthy of divine honors (as Arians taught) or was he of the identical nature with the Father (as per Athanasius)? If the former, Jesus was basically an ideal encouraging efforts of believers to work for their salvation. If the latter, he was the divine source of saving grace for sinners.[1] In any case, the question to be considered here is whether the Incarnation doctrine makes any sense: is it even meaningful, intelligible? Because if it is not, one cannot go on to ask whether it is true.

An associated doctrine is that of the Virginal Conception of Jesus. Is it integral to, even consistent with, the Incarnation doctrine? Some theologians have maintained you can't have one without the other.[2] Others insist the Virgin Birth doctrine contradicts Incarnationism. Gordon Kaufmann says,

> The doctrine of the so-called virgin birth... intends to affirm that it is God himself who is here in this man, truly and actually present in his very being. However, it says this crudely, offering a

---

[1] Robert C. Gregg and Dennis E. Groh, *Early Arianism: A View of Salvation* (Philadelphia: Fortress Press, 1981).
[2] Robert Glenn Gromacki, *The Virgin Birth: Doctrine of Deity* (Grand Rapids: Baker Book House, 1981).

quasi-explanatory account of the matter... it turns Jesus into a kind of demi-god—half human, half-divine.[3]

Paul Tillich writes similarly that the symbol of the Virgin Birth "is theologically quasi-heretical. It takes away one of the fundamental doctrines of Chalcedon... A human being who has no human father has no full humanity."[4] This, too, we must consider, for it is perhaps surprisingly relevant to our main question.

IS THE LOGOS LOGICAL?

Is the Incarnation even *supposed* to make sense (to us mortals)? Historically, theologians have (in my opinion) made virtue of necessity, throwing up their hands (ostensibly in worship) and declaring the doctrine a "divine mystery" and warning that any attempt to reduce it to rational sense is reductionism, a whittling down or, better, dumbing down, of a truth that passes understanding for the simple reason that the human mind may discern only "the edges of his ways" (Job 26:14). That sounds pious and even Socratically humble, even reasonable in that we are supposedly inadequate to grasp something so deep and profound. The great heresies were all oversimplifications and thus *reductionistic*. But what if the shoe is on the other foot? What if the very notion of the unfathomable mystery is instead a case of *mystification*, obfuscation of something that will dissolve under unwelcome close scrutiny? The great and powerful Oz may turn out to be no more than a fraud behind a curtain in a special effects booth.

But there have been Rationalist theologians who were not satisfied with mysteries. Protestant Rationalists in the eighteenth and early nineteenth centuries insisted that things make sense. Under the influence of Newtonian mechanism, these Rationalists repudiated all notions of divine violations of the clockwork system of natural laws. If the Creator

---

[3] Gordon Kaufmann, *Systematic Theology: A Historicist Perspective* (NY: Scribners, 1968), p. 203.
[4] Paul Tillich, *Theology of Culture* (Chicago: University of Chicago Press, 1959), p. 66.

had got it right to begin with, why would he need to make mid-course corrections?

To put it another way, can you believe what you cannot understand? Is belief merely the signing of a document you haven't read? Or *can't* read? I suggest you can't and you don't. The problem emerges with especial clarity in the case of the Trinity: what is it you say you are believing? No one can understand it, nor is anyone *supposed* to: another mystery. But not so fast! You are not permitted to believe there are three Gods, or that a unitary God merely reveals himself in different forms. Those are heresies, Tritheism and Modalism respectively. But the supposed alternative is too slippery to hold onto. I submit that Trinitarian Christians, in prayer and worship, cannot but default to either of these "heretical" conceptions since they cannot grasp, mentally represent, the orthodox model—because there isn't one. Trinitarianism is no more than a shibboleth, a required slogan. What if the "belief" in the Incarnation is cut from the same cloth, the cloth of which the Emperor's new clothes were woven?

To put it yet another way, isn't a "revelation" supposed to *tell* us something? To *clarify* things? If it leaves us deeper in the dark, under a cloud of unknowing, how is it revealing anything? "To reveal, is to make known, but for a mystery to compose any part of a revelation, is absurd; for it is the same as to reveal and not reveal at the same time; for was it revealed, it would cease to be mysterious" (Ethan Allen).[5]

Nineteenth-century theologian Friedrich Schleiermacher was in important aspects a Protestant Rationalist. He insisted that a viable doctrine of the Incarnation of God in Christ must not violate what we know of genuine humanity.[6] If it does, then we are discarding the orthodox belief that, though also True God ("Very God," i.e., "Veritable God"), Jesus Christ must also have been True Man—or the whole thing is a

---

[5] Ethan Allen, Reason the Only Oracle of Man Or A Compendious System of Natural Religion (Bennington, VT: Haswell & Russell, 1784), p. 207.
[6] Friedrich Schleiermacher, The Life of Jesus. Trans. S. Maclean Gilmour. Lives of Jesus Series (Philadelphia: Fortress Press, 1975), p. 34.

charade. The Incarnation must be more than a god zipping himself into a scuba suit of human flesh. Schleiermacher's proposal was that for God to be incarnated in Jesus meant that the man Jesus was completely "God-conscious" at every moment, as everyone should be but is not.[7] Thus Jesus is quantitatively, not qualitatively, different from the rest of us. David Friedrich Strauss called Schleiermacher's bluff: "the very fact that he calls it a real existence [of God in Jesus] shows that he rather senses that it is an unreal one."[8]

It is not surprising, then, that Schleiermacher[9] dismissed the notion of the Virginal Conception of Jesus as inimical to the Incarnation, since real human beings are not born that way. Instead, he proposed, God had prevented the transmission of sin from Mary and Joseph to their son Jesus. This is to transfer the Immaculate Conception from Mary to Jesus. And it would seem to have entailed just as much of a divine intervention (interference) as the traditional biological miracle of a Virgin Birth. Did Schleiermacher succeed in framing a rational theory of the Incarnation? I think not. Perhaps ironically, his attempt vindicates the warning of the old theologians: it was indeed an exercise in anticlimactic reductionism. But did the orthodox have anything better to offer?

It strikes me as rather ironic that theologians should disparage the competence of the human mind to comprehend the divine, since they have never hesitated to claim to do just that, stopping only when their (presumptuous) reasonings hit a wall, at which point they might better have heeded the wisdom of theologian Bugs Bunny and admitted to themselves that they must have "made a wrong turn in Albuquerque" and go back to the drawing board. If for a moment one steps outside of the theological mind game, it becomes apparent that all the claims to know that the incarnate Christ must have had this many "natures" and that many "persons," and all the precise formulas defining the extent and

---

[7] Friedrich Schleiermacher, The Christian Faith. (Harper Torchbooks, Cloister Library (NY: Harper & Row, 1963), Volume 2, pp. 385-389.
[8] David Friedrich Strauss, The Christ of Faith and the Jesus of History: A Critique of Schleiermacher's The Life of Jesus. Trans. Leander E. Keck. Life of Jesus Series (Philadelphia: Fortress Press, 1977), pp. 24-25.
[9] Friedrich Schleiermacher, Christian Faith, p. 405.

relations of the natures, persons, and what all, are not the metaphysical autopsies they are supposed to be. In fact, I think, what we witness going on in all the decades of the Christological debates (to be discussed presently) are rather attempts to *design*, to *create*, a suitable object of worship, in principle no different from Ptolemy I Soter's fusing together the gods Apis and Osiris to manufacture the new deity Serapis.[10]

OLD TESTAMENT ROOTS

By my reckoning, the DNA of both the doctrines of Incarnation and Virgin Birth may be found in the Hebrew scriptures. The Israelite precedent for divine Incarnation on earth is clearly the *theophany*, an appearance of Yahweh ("Jehovah") on earth on particular occasions. Examples include the appearance of Yahweh to Abram (Gen. 17:1-6); to the rechristened Abraham with two retainers preliminary to the reconnaissance of Sodom and Gomorrah (Gen. 18:1-2), to Hagar in the wilderness (Gen. 16:7-14; 21:17-21), to Gideon, recruiting him to defeat the Midianites (Judg. 6:12-23), and to the parents of Samson (Judg. 13:2-25). There is a crucial element of striking ambiguity in these tales. The characterization of the celestial visitor vacillates between Yahweh and the Angel of Yahweh (or Angel of God [= Elohim]).

This ambiguity vanishes in later writings such as Tobit and the Gospel of Luke (1:26-28 ff). There the messenger is clearly an angel, not God himself, Raphael appearing to Tobias, Gabriel to Mary. The ambiguity has been resolved. But the earlier ambivalence was not simple inconsistency or sloppy writing. It was, I think, quite intentional. Was the "angel" (= "messenger") supposed to be Yahweh himself, or only his representative speaking with his Master's authority? ("Whoever hears you hears me," Luke 10:16a). It would make sense if an earlier version unselfconsciously had God himself appear, as he still does in Genesis

---

[10] I am reminded of Bob Dole's quip during the chaotic aftermath of the 2000 election when Florida's disputed votes were being recounted, "hanging chads" and all. Dole said, "They're not *counting* votes in there; they're *casting* votes in there!"

Chapter 18, while subsequent redactors altered this to "the *Angel of* Yahweh/Elohim" in order to safeguard the transcendence of God. And yet even in the cases of Hagar, Gideon, and Samson's parents the recipient of the visitation exclaims that he or she has surprisingly survived seeing God himself ("Man shall not see me and live," Exod. 33:20). If the redactor wanted simply to substitute Yahweh's servant for Yahweh himself, it would have been easy enough to do it, but he didn't.

This is part of a larger trend occurring throughout the Deuteronomic writings[11], in which earlier mythic materials depicting the Deity in anthropomorphic terms are altered to reflect a more sophisticated understanding of God. For instance, it is no longer God himself who dwells in the Temple, enthroned upon the Ark of the Covenant. Rather it is the *Name* of God or the *Shekinah* (glory cloud) of God that dwells there. All talk about the Finger of God, the Word of God, and the Spirit of Yahweh denotes a distancing from raw mythology to divine transcendence. The trick is this: one must not remove divine involvement, delegating the task to someone else, but neither can one any longer imagine God himself stooping to get his "hands" dirty giving the Torah, creating a man from muddy clay, standing amid the flames of the burning bush, etc. Not God himself but not someone else. The "solution" was a retreat into strategic vagueness. Here is the origin of the "Divine Mystery" (mystification). We will see it again, rest assured.

Did the theophanic visitor have a body of flesh? No, if we're talking about eating food. When Samson's parents and Gideon offer food to the Angel of Yahweh, he disappears in a jet of flame, which also consumes the food, implicitly, as a sacrifice to the god who has just disappeared. Raphael explains that, while he travelled with Tobias he only pretended to eat with him (Tob. 12:19). One may speculate that an earlier version of the stories allowed that the theophany could and did eat, as when Yahweh sits down to a tasty repast in Abraham's camp (Gen. 18:4-8).

---

[11] Deuteronomy, Joshua, Judges, Samuel, and Kings.

The Greek myths offer a compromise: the gods ate, yes, but it was "the bread of angels" (Psalm 78:25), nectar and ambrosia.

How about sex? If the Sons of God (Gen. 6:1-4) are relevant here, a theophanic entity could indeed grow lustful and do something about it. When Jesus says (Luke 20:34-36) that the angels in heaven neither marry nor give in marriage (implying the existence of female angels?) he may mean that the ones still living in heaven, unlike the fallen Sons of God, were committed to celibacy, not that they couldn't get frisky if they wanted to. I am spending time on this because it relates to the purpose and nature of these Old Testament theophany stories. Most of them introduce the miraculous conception and/or divine destiny of various biblical heroes: Ishmael, Isaac, Samson, and the Shunammite's son. The Angel/Yahweh announces the coming birth of the child of promise.[12] I feel sure that these are rewrites of originals in which Yahweh was depicted as *sexually impregnating* the women to whom he appears. The stories would have been just like the Greek myths in which Apollo impregnates Coronis, begetting Asclepius; Theseus is Poseidon's son by the mortal Aethra; Perseus was begotten by Zeus upon Danaë; and Hercules was the mighty son of Zeus and the mortal Alcmene.

I have suggested that the theophany stories began with Yahweh appearing on earth in human(oid) form, able to eat and drink and to have sex, just like the gods of ancient Greece, but that the Deuteronomic redactors had altered them in order to put ontological distance between the older anthropomorphism and the more abstract transcendence they preferred.

MIRACULOUS (MIS)CONCEPTIONS

Before going on to apply these insights to the Christian doctrines of Incarnation and Virgin Birth, I want to pull back the historical curtain a bit further. The whole notion of a divine hero as the offspring of a god

---

[12] A derivative version had the theophanic agent involved at an earlier point, helping to arrange God-ordained marriages, as in the Book of Tobit and in Genesis Chapters 28-29.

and a mortal woman ("the daughters of men," Gen. 6:2) very likely had its origin from an ancient type of surrogate paternity practiced even today in Arabia and Africa.[13] When a woman proved unable to bear children, the husband might take on a second wife or a concubine (as Abraham does with Hagar). But what if he could not afford it?[14] An alternative was to turn to one of the circuit-riding shamans, sometimes called "angels." This man would seclude himself with the "barren" woman, miraculously enabling her to bear children. The truth was that it was not the wife who was at fault but rather the husband, being sterile, but this must not be admitted, to save face for him. It *must* be the female's fault, right? No one was fooled: of course, the resulting offspring had been sired by the shaman ("angel"), but you had to keep up appearances. Such liaisons did not count as adultery. It was more analogous to a woman visiting a male gynecologist today.

The "official" story of the visit of the angel/man of God to announce the birth of a child to a woman hitherto unable to conceive continued to circulate, and to grow in the telling. The character of the itinerant shaman came to be understood in literal, mythical terms, and his activity was restricted to the conception of biblical (and other mythic) heroes. These characters were esteemed so highly that their exceptional gifts had to be ascribed to superhuman parentage. Even in what might be deemed the prototype biblical case, that of the Sons of God and the daughters of men (Gen. 6:1-4), the original point, imputing no impropriety to the godlings, was to explain the great stature of the (non-mythical) Canaanite and Philistine Nephilim (Gen. 6:4; 14:5; Deut. 2:10, 20-21; 1 Sam. 21:18-22), who, like Goliath of Gath, towered to the amazing height (then rare) of *six feet* (cf, the Dinkas of Sudan today). They must have possessed divine DNA. These exceptional traits grew to the proportion

---

[13] M.J. Field, *Angels and Ministers of Grace: An Ethno-Psychiatrist's Contribution to Biblical Criticism* (NY: Hill and Wang, 1971).
[14] William Sargent, *The Mind Possessed: A Physiology of Possession, Mysticism and Faith Healing* (Baltimore: Penguin Books, 1975), pp. 137-138, tells how African women prevent their husbands from taking on a second wife by claiming to be possessed by *zar* spirits who demand all kinds of expensive presents or they will raise hell. This strategy breaks the budget so that hubby can no longer afford to support a second wife!

of divine superpowers. Demigods like Hercules, Samson, Gilgamesh and Nimrod were the result.

Miraculous conception produced two types of offspring. To borrow a Hindu term, there were *avatars* ("descents," i.e., from heaven),[15] gods who visited the earth by way of a woman's womb. Krishna was an avatar of Vishnu. Apollonius of Tyana was Proteus in (illusory) human form.[16] Gautama Buddha (in Mahayana belief) descended from the Tushita Heaven through the womb of his "mother," Maya (hint, hint). Avatars were the same beings on earth they had been in heaven. When they appeared among mortals it was exactly analogous to Kal-el (Superman) arriving on earth in a rocket from the planet Krypton, the rocket being equivalent to the womb of the avatar's mother. As in the case of the Buddha, the avatar's seemingly physical form was an illusion, a Nirmankya ("Transformation Body"). The spiritually enlightened could see through to the Sambogkya ("Enjoyment Body"), the celestial, superhuman body.[17] Similarly, Krishna reveals his true form to Arjuna:

Behold My forms, son of Prtha,
By hundreds and by thousands,
Of various sorts, marvelous,
Of various colors and shapes…

Here the whole world united
Behold today, with moving and unmoving things,
In My body, Gudakesa,
And whatsoever else thou wishest to see.

---

[15] Geoffrey Parrinder, Avatar and Incarnation: The Wilde Lectures in Natural and Comparative Religion in the University of Oxford (London: Faber and Faber, 1970), Chapter 16, "Theophany: Differences Between Krishna and Christ," pp. 223-239; Chapter 17, "Docetism, in Buddhology and Christology," pp. 240-250.
[16] Philostratus, The Life of Apollonius of Tyana. Trans. F.C. Conybeare. Loeb Classical Library (rpt Forgotten Books, 2008) Book 1, Chapter IV; Book 8, Chapter XXXVIII. See Robert M. Price, "Was There a Historical Apollonius of Tyana?" Journal of Higher Criticism. Vol. 13, No. 1, Spring 2018, pp. 4-40.
[17] Paul J. Griffiths, On Being Buddha: The Classical Doctrine of Buddhahood. SUNY Series, Toward a Comparative Philosophy of Religions (Albany: State University of New York Press, 1994), pp. 90-101.

> But thou canst not see Me
> With this same eye of thine own;
> I give thee a supernatural eye:
> Behold My mystic power as God![18]

This would add up, I think, to a type of theophany, just a longer-lasting one, decades in duration. That is why avatars can be depicted, even as children (like Jesus in the Infancy Gospels of Matthew and Thomas), as possessing more wisdom and knowledge than the dull-witted adults among whom they are temporarily stranded. ("How long am I to be with you? How long must I put up with you?" Mark 9:19). Jesus in the Gospel of John is an avatar.

The other variety of divinely conceived hero is a *demigod* ("half-god"). The demigod is half-human. Though a virginal conception is usually contrasted with adoptionism (the bestowal of divine power and dignity upon a worthy adult), I venture to suggest that the demigod is a variation on the theme of adoptionism. Adoptionism is directly derived from the ancient Royal Ideology of Israel and Judah and the adjacent Middle Eastern monarchies. Upon enthronement, each new king became the Anointed Son of God (Psalm 2:1, 7) and could even be addressed as "God" (Psalm 45:6). He was not supposed to have descended to earth from heaven. He received divine honors by virtue of his position. Likewise, Jesus is adopted Son of God at his baptism (Mark 1:9-11; Luke 3:21-22 mg: "You are my Son; today I have begotten you."). Some supposed he had received adoptive Sonship at his resurrection (Acts 2:36; Rom. 1:3-4). Again, it is pretty much irrelevant when the divine adoption occurs. In the case of a miraculously conceived demigod, it happens in the womb. The child is an augmented human, augmented to the same degree as Jesus at the Jordan baptism. For Matthew and Luke, with their virgin birth stories, Jesus was an "adopted" demigod.

---

[18] Franklin Edgerton, trans. and ed., *The Bhagavad Gita*. Harper Torchbooks, Cloister Library (NY: Harper & Row, 1964), p. 55.

Upon even closer examination, the differences between an avatar and a demigod seem to vanish, as, at bottom, the two categories would seem to converge. Where do demigods enter the evolutionary process of religion? They appear once a religion approaches monotheism. Previously, people worshipped natural forces and heavenly bodies, who were personified to the extent that they were believed to possess mind and will. Thus mere mortals could beseech their aid, pray for rain, etc. Rupert Sheldrake asks, "Does the sun *think*?" The ancients answered yes. The next stage of personification assigned them bodies and humanoid personalities. The sun was, e.g., Apollo driving his flaming chariot across the sky. But once monotheism arrived, what was one to do with the old gods? People were reluctant to cast them aside, as in the *Star Trek* episode "Who Mourns for Adonis."[19] So the gods are demoted to human superheroes. But there is a penultimate stage in which the old gods become demigods, fathered by full-fledged gods but living on earth among men and women.[20] Hercules and his counterpart Samson are perfect examples. Both were the sun, then the sun god, then the son of a god (a demigod on earth), and finally a supposed historical figure.[21] The upshot here is that the demigod is ultimately an avatar, too. The difference is that ancient believers in Hercules, Samson, etc., lacked the historical perspective to understand that their heroes began as gods but had been, by their time, watered down into half-mortal demigods. It was a *literary* process of incarnation, not a tale depicting the demotion of a god to the status of a demigod. The latter is a scholarly theory, not a myth in its own right.

What does this information tell us about Jesus and how the categories of Incarnation and Virgin Birth apply to him? I take very seriously

---

[19] Gilbert Ralston, "Who Mourns for Adonis?" *Star Trek*, September 22, 1967.
[20] "This transposition of myth to heroic saga is a notable mechanism in ancient Indo-European traditions, wherever a certain cultic system has been supplanted in living religion and the superannuated former apparatus falls prey to literary manipulation." Jaan Puhvel, *Comparative Mythology* (Baltimore: Johns Hopkins University Press, 1987), p. 39.
[21] For Samson, see Ignaz Goldziher, *Mythology Among the Hebrews and Its Historical Development* (1877, rpt NY: Cooper Square Publishers, 1967), pp. 392-446.

Margaret Barker's[22] theory that Jesus was first (or very early) understood to have been an Old Testament-style theophany of Yahweh. Barker demonstrates to my satisfaction that early Christians (including Gnostics) never accepted the Deuteronomic revisionist theology which had sought to merge the ancient Father and Son deities El Elyon ("God Most High," i.e., ruler of a pantheon) and Yahweh (see Deut, 32:8-9, which differentiates them) into a single God. When Jesus spoke of (and to) his Father, he was Yahweh addressing El Elyon. Note that Jesus is called the "Son of God" (Elohim) but never "Son of the Lord" (i.e., of Yahweh) – because he *was* Yahweh.

Would this make Jesus Christ a divine incarnation? Not as Christian tradition defines it. Remember, I have suggested that the older conception of theophanies assumed Yahweh took on a bodily form capable of eating and sexual intercourse, but it looks to me as if Jesus was understood, on the secondary model, as a docetic[23] theophany.

The Gospel of John preserves both sides of a Christological debate. On one side[24] we read that the Word became flesh (John 1:14), that Jesus became hungry (4:8) and thirsty (4:7; 19:28). The Roman spear thrust released water and blood from his chest cavity (19:34). Jesus invited Thomas to touch his crucifixion wounds (20:27). On the other side,[25] Jesus is said to have "tabernacled" (1:14), i.e., pitched his nomadic tent for the night, among us, which certainly seems to minimize Jesus' fleshly sojourn. Once Jesus' disciples bring him food, he turns it down, requiring no nourishment save for obedience to God (4:32). On the

---

[22] Margaret Barker, *The Great Angel: A Study of Israel's Second God* (Louisville: Westminster/John Knox Press, 1992), Chapter One, "The Son of God," pp. 4-11.

[23] "Docetism" comes from the Greek *dokeo*, "to seem." Theologically it refers to the belief that Jesus (or Buddha or Ali, etc.) only *seemed* to have a body of flesh but instead was something like a hologram.

[24] Udo Schnelle, *Anti-Docetic Christology in the Gospel of John*. Trans. Linda M. Maloney (Minneapolis: Fortress Press, 1992).

[25] Ernst Käsemann, *The Testament of Jesus: A Study of the Gospel of John in the Light of Chapter 17*. Trans. Gerhard Krodel (Philadelphia: Fortress Press, 1968), pp. 26, 66, 70. Cf, Schleiermacher, *Life of Jesus*, p. 31: "when we consider the kinds of concepts which prevail even today among Christians, as they are presented in conversations in everyday life, we find very frequent traces of this hidden docetism; and the stronger the faith in the divinity, the more the faith in the humanity is transformed into a mere appearance."

cross Jesus says "I thirst" only because scripture decreed that he must mouth the line (19:28). Yes, he invites Thomas to touch him, but we do not read that he did.

An only slightly later work, The Preaching of John (a self-contained portion embedded in the Apocryphal Acts of John) is overtly docetic. John son of Zebedee reminisces about the old days with Jesus.

> I will recount another glory, brothers. Sometimes when I would take hold of him, I encountered a solid, material body, while other times when I touched him, the substance was immaterial, as if it did not even exist. And on any occasion he was invited by one of the Pharisees and attended the dinner, we went with him, and our hosts set a roll before each one of us, and he received one as well, and he would bless his own and divide it between us, and everyone was satisfied with so small a morsel, and our own rolls were left over untouched, which amazed our hosts. And often, as I walked beside him, I wanted to see the impression of his foot, whether his foot left any print on the ground, for it appeared to me that he walked just above the ground, and I never saw a footprint.[26]

This Jesus is a phantom theodicy. We need not regard this docetism as some secondary theological aberration. It is easy to understand it as the original version. If a virginally conceived Jesus was a divine avatar like Apollonius, the Buddha, and Lord Krishna, again, we are dealing with a docetic deity.

If anything is an aberration, it is traditional Christology. It sought to formulate a Jesus Christ perfectly balanced between Jesus' perfect divine nature and his perfect human nature: not half man plus half God but rather 100% human and 100% God. The repeated Christological Councils (Nicea in 325 CE; Constantinople in 381; Ephesus in 431; Chalcedon in 451) tried to stop the pendulum swinging from divine to

---

[26] Robert M. Price, ed., *The Pre-Nicene New Testament: Fifty-Four Formative Texts* (Salt Lake City: Signature Books, 2006), p. 725.

human and back again, correcting any encroachment of docetism on the one side, adoptionism on the other.

Athanasius held that Jesus Christ was the Word made flesh (John 1:14). The Word (Logos, the creative reason of God, a notion derived from Heraclitus, the Stoics, and Philo) was a separate person sharing the divine nature. The Word is also the Son. The Father begat or generated the Son, but this is a logical, not a chronological priority. They have always been in a relationship of loving interdependence: the Son is "eternally begotten" by the Father, as Origen said. The Word is God's own wisdom through which he created all things (Prov. 8; John 1). The Son took on human flesh (not yet understood as a full human nature, just a human body, which will later be considered heresy) in order to save humanity.

Arius held that Jesus Christ was the incarnation of a heavenly being who had been the very first creature, and through whom as an agent or assistant God had created the rest of the creation (Wis. 8:22; Sir. 1:4; Col. 1:15-16). But he did not share divine nature, the nature of the Father. Both before and during his earthly sojourn he learned wisdom and virtue through discipline and suffering. At the resurrection he was given divine honor and dignity. He was adopted *by grace* as "Son," "Word," "Lord," "Wisdom," even "God," because by his perfection in virtue he had come to participate in these qualities which *by nature* belong to God alone. God's foreknowledge told him from the beginning that Christ would successfully attain this perfection, and so scripture calls Christ "Son," "Word," "God," etc., by anticipation even before his earthly life (e.g., John 1:1; Gal. 4:4).

The Arian theologians made three *scriptural* points. The outline of this schema of Christ being pre-existent in heaven, yet later receiving even greater glory as a reward, is certainly to be found in Philippians 2:5-11 and in the Epistle to the Hebrews. The idea that the pre-existent Word as an agent of creation was himself created can easily be inferred from John 1:1 ("and the Word was divine" or "the Word was a god.") since the created status of Wisdom is explicit in the texts that clearly form the background of John 1. The notion of Christ's being perfected through endurance and suffering and of growing in wisdom is certainly found in Luke 2:52 and in Hebrews 2:10.

Likewise, they made three *theological* points. The idea of the Father begetting the Word smacked of Gnostic emanationism. Even worse, if the Word were eternal, he must be unbegotten, and this would seem to make Christ into God's brother, not his Son![27] "Eternal generation" is a piece of incoherent sophistry, like a "square circle." And if God is Father *by nature*, and if the Son is Son *by nature*, then God was *forced* to beget the Son, and this is to reject God's sovereignty and freedom. The bishops assembled at the ecumenical Council of Nicea voted in favor of Athanasius' view. The Nicene Creed was drafted to resolve the Christological controversy between the Arians (Arius, Asterius, Eusebius of Nicomedia) and the Alexandrians (Bishops Alexander and Athanasius). Arianism survived and spread especially among the Goths converted through the missionary efforts of Ulfilas. But neither of these Christological positions was identical with what would later emerge as "orthodoxy."

Not long afterward, Apollinaris, a disciple of Athanasius, raised the question of the genuine humanity of Christ. He posited that the divine Logos replaced a human soul/spirit in the humanity of Jesus so that he was fully divine but not quite fully human.[28] The Three Cappadocians, Gregory of Nyssa, Gregory of Nazianzus, and Basil of Caesarea, replied that, if Jesus was only two-thirds human, he could not have won salvation for genuine humans. Apollinarianism was rejected at the Council of Constantinople.

Nestorius was affronted by the popular veneration of the Virgin Mary as "Mother of God," thinking that it implied Mary was a goddess. His opponents contended that the point was not to deify Mary but rather to affirm that, even as a newborn, Christ was already fully God. This Nestorius could not brook, and he declared that "God is not a baby two

---

[27] We think of the mighty Thor as the son of All-Father Odin, but some ancient Norsemen regarded the two deities as brothers.
[28] "It had a greater share of the outsideness in it." H.P. Lovecraft, "The Dunwich Horror."

or three months old!" Cyril of Alexandria protested that Nestorius was driving a wedge between Christ's full humanity and full divinity. In effect, Nestorius' Jesus Christ was somehow two persons in the one body: two natures, two persons. The Council of Ephesus sided with Cyril, condemning Nestorianism as heresy. Nestorian churches still exist today, though they seem to have dropped Nestorius' central doctrine. At any rate, the orthodox position that emerged, made Christ one person with two natures.

But how were those two natures related to one another? Eutyches taught that Christ's divine nature had absorbed his human nature. His Christology is called Monophysitism ("one-nature-ism") because it makes Jesus Christ one person possessing a single nature. Pope Leo argued, in *Leo's Tome*, that Christ's divine and human natures remain distinct, not melded together, yet inseparable. Monophysitism was finally voted down at the Council of Chalcedon. But the Coptic, Ethiopian, and Armenian ("Oriental Orthodox") churches remain Monophysites today.

In the years that followed, theologians began to debate whether the divine Logos had taken on a man who would have existed anyway, incarnation or no incarnation, or whether the fully human nature of Jesus was brought into being for the sake of the incarnation. The ecclesiastical thumb came down on the divine side of the scale. Theologians decided that, yes, Jesus was one person with two distinct natures, divine and human, but that this single "person" was divine. For my money, that's still docetism. The much-vaunted "true humanity" is reduced to that fleshly scuba suit, there's just more tech to it.

Is it not obvious by now that these learned savants were not so much debating the implications of data but rather simply negotiating a paper agreement? Like a theological policy statement. Or like a cabal of screen writers trying to hammer out the defining traits of the main character. They're making it up as they go along.

GOD OF THE PHILOSOPHERS

Theologians have both celebrated and bemoaned the Hellenization of Christianity (though Judaism was Hellenized first). Adolf Harnack[29] in particular thought Hellenization was essentially a corruption and distortion of the pure, primitive Galilean gospel of Jesus. But you don't have to go as far as Harnack did to judge the feeding of Christianity through the filter (the meat-grinder?) of Greek philosophy a source of endless theological mischief. Principally, the problem is the opening of a vast chasm (Luke 16:26) between, as Pascal put it, the God of the philosophers and the God of Abraham, Isaac, and Jacob. At issue was the viability of what is now called "biblical personalism."

Already Philo of Alexandria and Saint Augustine, under the influence of Platonism and Stoicism, had compromised the individual personhood of God by virtue of making God the same as Infinite Being, outside the conditions of time and space, omnipresent and occupying an eternal Now. In my opinion, this move amounted to a leap into Non-dualist Hinduism. It is pretty simple, really. If God does not experience the passage of time, "he" cannot act or even have serial thoughts. If "he" is infinite, "he" cannot be a person, since persons are rendered definite, a person like this or a person like that, when defined by a specific combination of traits, features, characteristics, resulting in this kind of personality, not that. But to de*fin*e is to impose "*fin*ish lines," limits, something utterly incompatible with being in*fin*ite.

God is Perfect Act, as per Aristotle. That is, God is already fully realized with no unactualized potential. This is why God does not and cannot change ("with whom there is no shadow of turning," James 1:7). God by definition cannot move in space for the simple reason that, if "he" is *actually* at point A, "he" is only potentially at point B. And that cannot be. This is why "he" is said to be omnipresent. He cannot create

---

[29] Adolph Harnack, *What Is Christianity?* Trans. Thomas Bailey Saunders. Harper Torchbooks, Cloister Library (NY: Harper & Row, 1957), pp. 199-207.

because that would entail his moving from being potentially a Creator to being actually a Creator.

If God possesses "aseity" (self-sufficiency, invulnerability to harm or influence by anything outside him, if we can even say anything could *be* outside "him"), "he" can't and won't listen to prayers, be offended by sin, or become angry at human evil.

In view of all this, what is the status of the time-space world that we experience? It cannot be real, can it? It must be exactly what Nondualism says it is: Samsara, *maya*, an illusory world produced by the refraction of Nirguna Brahman ("Brahman without qualities") through the *upadhis* ("limiting-conditions"). Our "knowledge" of this world of seeming is "lower knowledge," which amounts to "nescience," ignorance of the realm of higher Reality, which is Brahman. Samsara "exists" by virtue of *maya*, "magic,"[30] the stage illusion performed by the demiurge Saguna Brahman ("Brahman with qualities"), who is a Samsaric (illusory) version of or counterpart to Nirguna Brahman or *Sat-chit-ananda* ("Being-Consciousness-Bliss"), the One with which the mystic realizes his or her identity in the moment of *Samadhi* or *Moksha* (Enlightenment). To "explain" this distinction between the Real world of Brahman and the illusory world of Samsara by chalking it up to *maya*, i.e., part of the illusion from which you need to be delivered, is to retreat to the same theological dodge we found in Deuteronomic theology as well as the Christian claims of impenetrable Mystery. Rationality here is abandoned in favor of butt-covering mystification. Again.

When Hindu theologians posit a Samsaric Creator of Samsara, which is somehow a reflection of the impersonal Brahman,[31] are they not talking about just what both Philo and the Gospel of John call the Logos?[32] Here is more theology of equivocation: what is the ontological

---

[30] L. Thomas O'Neil, *Maya in Sankara: Measuring the Immeasurable* (Delhi: Motilal Banarsidass, 1980), p. 31.
[31] God "is a person and the negation of himself as a person." Paul Tillich, *Biblical Religion and the Search for Ultimate Reality*. James W. Richard Lectures in the Christian Religion, University of Virginia, 1951-52 (Chicago: University of Chicago Press, 1955), p. 85.
[32] Raymond Panikkar, in his The Unknown Christ of Hinduism (London: Darton, Longman & Todd, 1964), does make this very identification: "Further, the dogma of the Trinity would appear as the unsought for...

status of the Logos? Philo (whose conceptuality closely parallels John's and probably underlies it) says that the Logos is an aspect of God, his reason, which projects itself from the Godhead to become/provide the blueprint for the creation, initiating a series of emanations which eventually become the (Stoic) *spermatikoi logoi* ("seeds of reason") which translate the divine order into material objects.[33] So where along the line does the Logos stop being God and start being part of the creation? Better not to ask. We wouldn't want to dispel the cloud of opportune ambiguity. Again, this is the very issue in dispute between the Arians and Athanasians: was the Logos the highest created being or a slippery (autonomous? Semi-autonomous?) aspect of the One God? The Council of Nicea decided in favor of strategic ambiguity. The Logos was God, but a distinct person within the Godhead yet not a second G/god. With Athanasian Christology came Trinitarianism which only multiplied the difficulty and required yet more equivocation. Is there anything here to believe?

IS GOD-TALK JUST GLOSSOLALIA?

Given the way the hybridization of Christianity with Greek philosophy produced a divine Abstraction, Thomas Aquinas had to wrestle with a question that did not trouble pre-philosophical believers: how can we speak meaningfully of God? In other words, how can we bridge the chasm between the God of the philosophers and the God of the biblical patriarchs? Because it doesn't look like they have much in common. Aquinas decided there were three options. The first, *univocal* speech

---

answer to the inevitable question of an ontic mediator between the one and the manifold, the absolute and the relative, Brahman and this world. This is in my opinion not just a Vedantic problem; in the final analysis, the amr of the Koran, the Logos of Plotinus and the Tathagata of Buddhism, for example, spring from a similar view as to the necessity for an ontological link between those two apparently irreconcilable poles: the absolute and the relative" (p. 120). "That from which all things proceed and to which all things return and by which all things are (sustained in their own being) that 'that' is God, but primo et per se not a silent Godhead, not an inaccessible Brahman, not God the Father and source of the whole Divinity, but the true Isvara, God the Son, the Logos, the Christ" (p. 126).

[33] If you cannot help thinking of Spinoza, Gnosticism, and the Kabbalah, it's no accident.

about God, Aquinas ruled out: given the surpassing, indeed mind-blowing, superiority of God (Isa. 55:9), any mental image we tried to make of him would have to be a dumbed-down idol. The second, *equivocal* speech about God, is equally useless. The point here would be totally opposite to the first. God is so different from us that no word we employ referring to God could have the same meaning it has in reference to us. An example familiar from theology would be saying that, for God, "good" does not mean what it means for humans, so that if God could have stopped Hitler in his tracks but didn't, we must still consider him "good," even though any human who did not do what he or she could would be barely less wicked than Adolf himself. But if "good" is so different for God and for us—heck, why use the same word at all?

Aquinas chose Door Number Three: we may and must speak of God *by analogy*. What God does and is, is not very much like what we are and what we do, but there is a parallel or analogy between them such that we *can* use the same words for both, albeit metaphorically. We are not describing God, but neither are we speaking in a misleading way. As I understand it, we can say my dog loves me, even though Prissy doesn't have the brain capacity to experience the emotion we call "love." But a dog is a pack animal whose safety lies in sticking with its fellow dogs, and the dog feels happy when Fido, Spot, Rover and the rest are all accounted for. A domesticated dog has transferred her loyalty to her owners. When the whole family assembles in the evening, the dog wags her tail and yips excitedly. When we comment on how the dog loves us, we are speaking meaningfully because we are speaking analogically, and a good analogy does exist.

But if God is Wholly Other,[34] can there really be any true analogy between God and us? I think of a Buddhist parable in which a young tadpole asks his froggy father to describe what he has to look forward to when he grows up and lives on dry land. Poppa Frog has to disappoint him: every word Tad knows is predicated upon living under water. No

---

[34] Rudolf Otto, The Idea of the Holy: An Inquiry into the Non-Rational Factor in the Idea of the Divine and Its Relation to the Rational. Trans. John W. Harvey (London: Oxford University Press, 1924).

word he knows can convey what life in the surface world is like. In the same way, no word informed by Samsaric existence can even begin to describe Nirvana.

Not surprisingly, Muslims have faced the same dilemma. The Koran often speaks anthropomorphically of Allah. Traditionally, Muslims took these references literally and insisted that Allah possesses humanoid body parts, despite the fact that scripture teaches total incompatibility between God and man. How to "resolve" this dilemma? It seemed satisfactory to hold that Allah does possess body parts but "without how" (*bila kayfa*).[35] There we go again! At the crucial point we claim a Mulligan, a freebie. We cop out. It's like that great cartoon by Sidney Harris in which two scientists are scrutinizing a blackboard filled with chalked mathematical formulae. Right in the middle is a note: "Then a miracle occurs."

---

[35] Ignaz Goldziher, Introduction to Islamic Theology and Law. Trans. Andras and Ruth Hamori. Modern Classics in Near Eastern Studies (Princeton: Princeton University Press, 1981), p. 92.

"I think you should be more explicit here in step two."

This question of whether human words can mean anything in reference to God is fundamental to our inquiry. What possible sense can it make to say that an inconceivable God whose existence is antipodal and contradictory to human existence in every way has become human? To say that "though he was in the form of God, he emptied himself and assumed the form of a servant" (Phil. 2:6)? Kierkegaard admitted there was an infinite qualitative distinction between God and man, but, by a leap of faith, he affirmed the paradox of the Incarnation anyway. But that is to wittingly abandon any attempt to have it make sense. And then you have to ask what it is you are believing.

ARE MIRACLE BIRTHS AND DIVINE INCARNATIONS POSSIBLE?

It doesn't even get that far. There has to be some intelligible meaning before we can tell if a claim is even *possibly* true. In conclusion, let me suggest that the real Incarnation of Jesus Christ was his *historicization*. Like all the other demigods and theophanies of mythology, he became as historical as he ever will be when his worshippers came to believe he had once been a historical figure.

16| MIRACLES OF THE CHRISTIAN MAGICIANS

BY ROBERT CONNER

In the first reported case of Christian book burning we are informed that the newly converted in Ephesus, a city infamous for superstition and sorcery, gathered up their magical works and consigned them to the flames. The story begins with a clearly magical claim followed by a comically failed exorcism in which a single demon drives out seven exorcists:

God did uncommonly powerful works through Paul's hands so that when clothes and aprons that touched his skin were laid upon the sick, they were set free from their diseases and the evil spirits came out of them:

Some of the itinerant Jewish exorcists attempted to invoke the name of the Lord Jesus over those who had evil spirits, saying, "I conjure you in the name of Jesus that Paul preaches!" Seven sons of Sceva, a Jewish high priest, were some of those doing this.

The evil spirit answered them, "I know of Jesus and I am acquainted with Paul, but who are you?" And the man in whom the evil spirit was assaulted and overpowered them so that they were forced to flee, bleeding and injured, from that house.

After all the Jews and Greeks living in Ephesus learned of this, they were all overcome with fear and the name of the Lord Jesus gained in fame. Many of those who had believed came forward and openly confessed their deeds and a great many of those dabbling in the magical arts gathered up their books and burned them publicly. When their value was calculated it came to fifty thousand silver coins. Just like that the word of the Lord grew in fame and spread.[1]

The fictitious nature of this pious story is widely acknowledged—there was no High Priest named Sceva, a name probably concocted from the Latin *scaeva, ill-omened*,[2] and the number seven had magical connotations associated with exorcism as evidenced by the apocryphal tale of Mary Magdalene, from whom seven demons were expelled,[3] as well as this bit of demonic folklore attributed to Jesus:

> Whenever the unclean spirit comes out of the man, it travels through desert places seeking a place to rest and not finding one. Then it says, "I'll go back to my house from which I was cast out," and finds it has been swept out and put in order. Then it leaves and recruits seven other spirits more wicked than itself and when they break into the place and it sets up residence, the man's final plight is worse than at first.[4]

Magical sevens abound in the spell books of the era[5] as well as in the text of the gospels—there are seven signs in the gospel of John,[6] seven witnesses who say Jesus is the Son of God or sent from God,[7] and seven

---

[1] Acts 19:11-20.
[2] Rick Strelan, *Strange Acts: Studies in the Cultural World of the Acts of the Apostles*, (Berlin: Walter de Gruyter, 2004), 2, 109-110.
[3] Mark 16:9.
[4] Luke 11:24-26.
[5] Robert Conner, *Magic in the New Testament: A Survey and Appraisal of the Evidence*, (Oxford: Mandrake of Oxford, 2010), 137, 140, 189, 237, 263-264, 295-297.
   "Take water from seven springs on the seventh day of the month, in the seventh hour of the day, in seven unfired pottery vessels...Expose them beneath the stars for seven nights; and on the seventh night take a glass vial, *etc*." (Michael A. Morgan, *Sepher HaRazim: The Book of the Mysteries* (Chico, CA: Scholars Press, 1983), 26.
[6] Water into wine (2:1-11), dispelling a fever (4:46-54), a healing at Bethzatha (5:1-48), feeding the multitude (6:1-14), the translocation of a boat (6:15-21), curing a blind man (9:1-41) and the raising of Lazarus (11:1-57).
[7] John the Baptist (1:34), Nathanael (1:49), Peter (6:69), Jesus himself (10:36), Martha (11:27), Thomas (20:28), and the author of gospel (20:31).

"I am" sayings.[8] As Roy David Kotansky points out in connection with the "seven sons of Skeva" tale, the Hebrew *shaba* means both *seven* and *to adjure* or *imprecate*. In short, "to adjure" is "to seven."[9]

A naïve reading of Acts might suggest that the newly converted in Ephesus left magic behind as a result of Christian preaching, but an attentive reading of Paul's letter to the Ephesians quickly corrects such a misinterpretation. That the Ephesians had merely traded up, exchanged one magical system for a more potent one, is confirmed by Paul's impressive string of magical power words: "the surpassing greatness of his power for the use of us believers, according to the operation of the power of his might that he put into effect when he raised Christ up from the dead...far above all rulership and authority and power and lordship and every name named..."[10] Regarding Paul's terminology, Clinton E. Arnold notes identical use in the magical papyri as well as Ephesian inscriptions, and of "every name named," observes, "This particular phrase is loaded with significance for exorcism and magical incantation both in Judaism and the pagan world...In fact, the very term [name] is so important in the magical papyri that in the index to his collection, Karl Preisendanz lists close to 400 occurrences of it."[11]

Paul's aprons and sweat cloths are magical; Roy Kotansky has proposed that "once used effectively, [they] would have been deployed again and again. These magically charged reliquaries would have no doubt been reapplied with the necessary prayers or incantations: the young Christian community at Ephesus, it seems, adhered tenaciously to their

---

[8] "I am the bread of life" (6:35), "the light of the world" (8:12), "the good shepherd" (10:11), "the resurrection and the life" (11:25), "the way, the truth, and the life" (14:6), "the true vine," (15:1), and "before Abraham, I am." (8:58)
[9] Roy Kotansky, "Greek Exorcistic Amulets," *Ancient Magic and Ritual Power* (Leiden: Brill, 2001), 243.
[10] Ephesians 1:19-20.
[11] Clinton E. Arnold, *Ephesians: Power and Magic: The Concept of Power in Ephesians*, (Grand Rapids, MI: Baker Book House, 1989), 54, 72-73. See Karl Preisendanz, *Papyri Graecae Magicae: Die Griechischen Zauberpapiri I*, (Munich: K.G. Saur Verlag, 1973).

magical beliefs."¹² "The cloths take on the function of amulets and talismans which were so common in the magic of antiquity."¹³

The function of such magical cloths is similar to the "Isis bands" mentioned in the spell books, strips of black cloth torn from Isis' robes of mourning—"while wearing a completely black Isis band"¹⁴—that induced dream revelations when placed over the eyes, or the enigmatic Anubis cord,¹⁵ possibly "thread used in mummification."¹⁶ Clothing or body parts serve as material conductors that carry the power of enchantment between the magician and those on whom he casts his spell. Describing the items needed by a "Syrian" witch, the courtesan Bakchis tells her girlfriend Melitta, "You'll also need something belonging to the man himself, like clothes or boots or a few hairs, or something of that sort," to which Melitta replies, "I have his boots."¹⁷

According to its earliest documents, signs and wonders, not the message of Christianity, were the primary driving force behind Christian conversion—"My speech and my preaching were not persuasive words of wisdom but a demonstration of the spirit's power so that your faith is not in the wisdom of men, but the power of God."¹⁸ "…bringing the Gentiles into submission to God by my word and deed, by powerful works, by signs and wonders…"¹⁹ "Now, Lord, behold their threats and give your servants complete freedom to speak and stretch forth your hand to heal and perform signs and wonders through the name of your holy servant, Jesus!"²⁰ Although the Christian miracle mongers were of "rude speech" as the church historian Eusebius freely admits, they

---

[12] Kotansky, *Ancient Magic and Ritual Power*, 244.
[13] Hans Josef Klauck, *Magic and Paganism in Early Christianity: The World of the Acts of the Apostles*, (Edinburgh: T&T Clark Ltd, 2000), 98.
[14] Karl Preisendanz, *Papyri Graecae Magicae: Die Griechischen Zauberpapiri I*, (Munich: K.G. Saur Verlag, 1973), I, 58, IV, 176.
[15] Ibid, I, 147.
[16] Hans Dieter Betz, *The Greek Magical Papyri in Translation Including the Demotic Spells*, 2nd ed. (Chicago: University of Chicago Press, 1986), 7.
[17] Lucian, *Lucian: Volume VII, Dialogues of the Courtesans*, 4 (Cambridge: Harvard University Press, 1961).
[18] 1 Corinthians 2:4-5.
[19] Romans 15:18.
[20] Acts 4:29-30.

"proclaimed the knowledge of the kingdom of heaven only by the display of the divine spirit working in them and by what the wonder-working power of Christ accomplished through them."[21] In short, Eusebius confirms the success of Christian preaching depended on thaumaturgy, not doctrine.

Given the cultural context of Paul's letter, it is significant that Paul's expression "the breadth and length and height and depth"[22] "never occur in succession except for their appearance in Greek Magical Papyri (or Papyri Graecae Magicae, IV.965, ff).) The expression occurs in the context of a magical formula for the obtaining of a vision while awake."[23]

The magical text referenced by Arnold reads, "I conjure you, holy light, holy radiance, breadth, depth, length, height, radiance, *by the holy names…*"[24] The newly converted are assured that Jesus' name is "above every name that is named,"[25] and therefore of superior magical power. The names of spirits are central to magical working; they are "the reservoir of heavenly power,"[26] hence the question, "By what power or what name did you do this?"[27]

Paul's work clothes may have worked magic, but Peter's magical ability was nothing less than a public spectacle:

Many signs and wonders occurred among the people at the hands of the apostles and they all gathered at Solomon's Portico. None of the others dared associate with them, but the people esteemed them. A multitude of men and women began joining those who believed in the Lord with the result that the sick were carried into the streets on litters and cots so that as Peter passed by at least his shadow might overshadow some of them.[28] Crowds from the

---

[21] Eusebius, *Ecclesiastical History: Books I-IV*, (Cambridge: Harvard University Press, 1926), III, 24, 3.
[22] Ephesians 3:18.
[23] Arnold, *Ephesians: Power and Magic*, 91-92.
[24] Preisendanz, *Papyri Graecae Magicae* IV, 978-979.
[25] Ephesians 1:21. Compare Philippians 2:9, Hebrews 1:4.
[26] Rebecca Lesses, "Speaking with Angels: Jewish and Greco-Egyptian Revelatory Adjurations," *Harvard Theological Review* 89.1 (1996) 52.
[27] Acts 4:7.
[28] Although clumsy, this is the literal translation.

towns around Jerusalem congregated, bringing the sick and those afflicted with unclean spirits and all were healed.[29]

Peter's shadow functioned as a *paredros*, a magical assistant.[30] The grimoires of the age included this procedure for turning a magician's shadow into his personal assistant:

> You will create your own shadow so that it will be your servant. Go at the sixth hour of the day, face east in a solitary place...Standing in the place, kneel while raising your hands and say this spell: "Make my shadow serve me now because I know your holy names and the signs and the passwords and who you are each hour and what your name is...Therefore, Lord, make my shadow serve me." At the seventh hour it will come to you, face to face, and you say, "Follow me everywhere."[31]

It would appear from the magical spells that the shadow could be considered a spirit entity: "Protect me from every demon of the air and on the earth and under the earth, and every phantasm and shadow and visitation..."[32] "...the *skiasmos* [shadow] is the Semitic *tinyth*, a shadow spirit..."[33] Rick Strelan points out that Peter's shadow had the same magical power as his hand or voice;[34] as an extension of Peter's person, his shadow is his double. Based in part on the stories of Paul's "aprons and handkerchiefs" and "the mere falling of St. Peter's shadow on the sick as they lay in the streets," Harry Magoulias concluded, "magic

---

[29] Acts 5:12-16.
[30] See particularly Leda Jean Ciraolo's "Supernatural Assistants in the Greek Magical Papyri" in *Ancient Magic and Ritual Power*, (Leiden: Brill Academic Publishers, 2001), 279-295, and Anna Scibilia, "Supernatural Assistance in the Greek Magical Papyri: The Figure of the *Paredros*," in *The Metamorphosis of Magic from Late Antiquity to the Early Modern Period* (Leuven: Peeters Publishers, 2002), 71-86. The role of familiar and tutelary spirits in shamanism is described by Mircea Eliade, *Shamanism: Archaic Techniques of Ecstasy*, (Princeton: Princeton University Press, 2002), 88-99.
[31] Preisendanz, op. cit., III, 612-632
[32] Preisendanz, *Papyri Graecae Magicae*, IV, 2700-2702.
[33] Kotansky, *Greek Magical Amulets*, 385.
[34] Rick Strelan, *Strange Acts*, 194.

indeed lies at the very heart of Christianity."[35] To the dismay of Christian apologists, the cloven hoof prints of magic can be traced throughout the gospels, Acts, and letters of Paul.

The book of Acts is a compendium of Christian magic using the formula "in the name of Jesus." Walter Stuermann identified "thirty direct or indirect references to the use of the name of Jesus Christ in order to effect startling events" and noted, "The insistent repetition of the formula, 'in the name of Jesus,' suggests a practice of word magic."[36] Commenting on the use of powerful names by Egyptian magicians and Christian exorcists, Miroslav Šedina notes, "Christian preachers...use an identical method to address divine or daimonic powers and the only difference consists in the extent of their effect" and of Origen's theory of names observes, "magic incantations dispose of a certain natural power which take effect even in the cases when the one who pronounces them is not aware of the meaning of the words."[37] "In Origen's theory of effective language, divine names do not 'represent'; they manifest divine power...The power of a divine name is automatic and not based on the intention of the speaker,"[38] a conclusion supported by the language of the gospels: "Lord, Lord, did we not prophesy in your name and drive out demons in your name and in your name perform many powerful works?"[39]

That religion is magic and religious ritual is magical ritual has been recognized in some quarters for well over a century: "Magic...consist[s] especially in the art of compelling spirits or deities to do the will of him who performs the requisite acts or speaks the needful words...All magic is a kind of religion...incantations are prayers...magic has to do more or

---

[35] Harry J. Magoulias, "The Lives of Byzantine Saints as Sources of Data for the History of Magic in the Sixth and Seventh Centuries A.D.: Sorcery, Relics and Icons," *Byzantion* 37 (1967) 228.
[36] Walter E. Stuermann, "The Name of Jesus: Word-Magic in the Book of Acts," *ETC: A Review of General Semantics* 14.4 (1957) 263-264.
[37] Miroslav, Sedina, "Magical Power of Names in Origen's Polemic Against Celsus," *Listy filologicke/Folia philological* 136 1/2 (2013) 22-23.
[38] Naomi Janowitz, "Theories of Divine Names in Origen and Pseudo-Dionysius," *History of Religions* 30/4 (1991) 360, 362.
[39] Matthew 7:22.

less with all stages of religion."⁴⁰ Christian use of the name of Jesus shares the *pars pro toto* conception of ancient magic generally: the name carries within it the power of the one named. "In pagan opinion Christians seemed to use the name of Christ or other Christian signs and symbols, e.g., relics, for magical purposes like exorcisms, healing, divination and magical protection."⁴¹

Although Peter's shadow could heal on contact, his words could kill, "a typical feature of magic,"⁴² or as one writer terms it, "faith-killing."⁴³ Ananias, confronted with his dishonesty by Peter, drops dead on the spot. Three hours later, his wife Sapphira arrives, reiterates their lie, and is told, "Why did you conspire to test the spirit of the Lord? Now look! The feet of the men who buried your husband are at the door and they will carry you out!"⁴⁴ Sapphira instantly drops dead at Peter's feet.

In a masterful analysis of the curse speeches in Acts, Kent draws attention to various features that allow us "to see a greater degree of similarity between the apostles' speeches and 'magical' curse spells than has previously been appreciated," including elements of vocabulary as well as the succession of sibilants that give Peter's denunciation the hissing quality employed in magical spells. That Sapphira instantly dies also marks the speech as magical: "Such emphasis on immediacy characterizes Peter's speech as words of power that cause Sapphira's death."⁴⁵

The earliest gospel describes how Jesus secured his regional fame as a master manipulator of spirits. Jesus teaches "as one who has authority and not like the scribes"⁴⁶ and lest any doubt remain about what Jesus'

---

⁴⁰ T. Witton Davies, "Magic, Divination, and Demonology Among the Semites," *The American Journal of Semitic Languages and Literature* 14.4 (1898) 241-242.
⁴¹ Andrzej Wypustek, "Magic, Montanism, Perpetua, and the Severan Persecution," *Vigiliae Christianae* 51.3 (1997), 282.
⁴² Howard Clark Kee, *Medicine, Miracle and Magic in New Testament Times*, (Cambridge: Cambridge University Press, 1986), 118.
⁴³ Joshua C. Gregory, "Magic, Fascination, and Suggestion," *Folklore* 63.3 (1952), 143.
⁴⁴ Acts 5:9-10.
⁴⁵ Benedict H.M. Kent, "Curses in Acts: Hearing the Apostles' Words of Judgment Alongside 'Magical' Spell Texts," *Journal for the Study of the New Testament* 39 (2017) 427, 431-432, 434.
⁴⁶ Mark 1:22.

authority encompassed, Mark has his Jewish contemporaries answer: "A new teaching based on authority—*he gives orders to the unclean spirits and they obey him*! And instantly the report about him spread out in every direction into the whole region of Galilee."[47] Or as François Lenormant has it, "the sorcerer…subjected the demons to his orders."[48]

The fame of "the Teacher" is not based on his superior knowledge of Jewish law—his authority is "*not like the scribes.*" Bookish knowledge was hardly the kind of news that would spread like wildfire among the mostly illiterate country folk of Galilee, "this accursed mob that knows nothing of the law."[49] In short, "it is therefore misleading to compare [Jesus'] style of instruction to that of later rabbinic academies. It is more probable that people saw the exorcisms and cures as confirmation of Jesus' teaching."[50] Hull noted that of the ten occurrences of *exousia, authority*, in Mark, only one is *not* connected with exorcism or healing, and concluded, "The people do not admire Jesus for his learning but for his power over the demons."[51]

After the initial report from Capernaum,[52] news that Jesus has returned home causes a dense crowd to gather[53] and when Jesus leaves, a mob of Galileans follows, joined by the curious from Judea, Jerusalem, Idumea and villages across the Jordan, and from Tyre and Sidon.[54] By now Jesus' renown is such that he can no longer openly enter a town,[55] and at this point Jesus chooses twelve disciples and sends them out "to preach and *have authority to cast out demons.*"[56] Jesus and his troupe, the

---

[47] Mark 1:27-28.
[48] François Lenormant, *Chaldean Magic: Its Origin and Development*, (London: Samuel Bagster & Sons, 1877), 60.
[49] John 7:49.
[50] Géza Vermes, *Jesus the Jew: A Historian's Reading of the Gospels*, (Philadelphia: Fortress Press, 1981), 27.
[51] John Hull, *Hellenistic Magic and the Synoptic Tradition*, (London: SCM-Canterbury Press, 1974), 165.
[52] Mark 1:21.
[53] Mark 2:1-2.
[54] Mark 3:7-8.
[55] Mark 1:45.
[56] Mark 3:14-15.

Ghostbusters of Galilee, hit the Podunks of Palestine,[57] spinning the heads of the yokels. Spirits fled, paralytics picked up their cots, and the people declared, "We've never seen anything like this!"[58] The rural populace "from the whole region of Galilee...brought him all the sick and the demon-possessed"[59] in the hope of being healed, not to be entertained with parables.

Jesus' fame as an exorcist continued to spread; soon other exorcists began to invoke the power of his name—"for his name became known."[60] Jesus' name was literally a name to conjure with:

'Teacher,' said John, "we saw someone driving out demons in your name and we told him to stop because he was not one of us.[61]

The use of Jesus' name by other exorcists is "clearly an example of professional magical use,"[62] a practice that continued even after Jesus' death. The use of Jesus' name "had nothing to do with believing in Jesus...the magical use of the name of Jesus worked automatically, no matter whether or not the magician believed in Jesus."[63] The Christian apologist Origen expresses just that understanding, common throughout the Mediterranean world: demons "are spellbound, constrained by the magical arts" and therefore "forced to obey magicians."[64] Christian exorcists prevail by the name of Jesus: "demons and other unseen powers...fear the name of Jesus as superior" and the demons fly away "at the recitation of his name."[65] Words attributed to Jesus express this belief in the

---

[57] On Jesus' avoidance of Galilean cities such as Sepphoris and Tiberias, see Bart Ehrman, *The New Testament: A Historical Introduction to the Early Christian Writings*, 6th ed., (Oxford: Oxford University Press, 2015), 254, John D. Crossan, *The Historical Jesus: The Life of a Mediterranean Jewish Peasant*,(New York: Harper Collins, 1992), 193, and Seán Freyne, *Galilee, Jesus and the Gospels: Literary Approaches and Historical Investigations*, (Minneapolis, MI: Fortress Press, 1988), 173.
[58] Mark 2:12.
[59] Mark 1:28, 32.
[60] Mark 6:14.
[61] Mark 9:38.
[62] Hull, Hellenistic Magic and the Synoptic Tradition, 72.
[63] Peter Schäfer, *Jesus in the Talmud*, (Princeton University Press, 2007), 60.
[64] Origen, *Contra Celsum* II, 51.
[65] Ibid, III, 36.

magical power of his name: "Did we not cast out demons in your name and in your name perform many wonders?"[66]

Early Christian faith in the magical power of a name coincides exactly with the nonsense derided by Lucian: "the fever or the swelling *is in fear of a divine name or barbarous invocation* and because of this flees from the inflamed gland."[67] Mark is therefore careful to include Jesus' Aramaic invocations, *talitha koum*, "get up, little girl," and *ephphatha*, "be opened."[68] Morton Smith suspected the formula used by Peter to raise Dorcas—*Tabitha anastēthi*, "Tabitha rise"—"is a mispronunciation of *talitha*, which the storyteller mistook for a proper name."[69] The magical formulae of Mark are carefully edited out of Matthew and Luke lest Jesus be implicated in the practice of magic, but there was a motive for their retention in the oldest gospel: "In view of the importance attributed to preserving adjurations and incantations in their original languages, these formulas were probably preserved for the purpose of guiding Christian thaumaturges in exorcistic and healing activities. In early Christianity, therefore, these Aramaic phrases may have functioned as magic formulas."[70] Support for this comes from none other than the Christian apologist Origen: "And on the topic of names, we have mentioned that those who are experts in the use of incantations relate that the spell pronounced in the appropriate dialect achieves the very thing commanded, but said in another tongue becomes weak and capable of nothing."[71]

The Christian confessions of faith that Celsus regards as "vulgar words," are for Origen "just like spells that have been filled with power."[72] This understanding of the efficacy of word magic will eventually flow seamlessly into what E.G. Weltin describes as "Augustine's pseudo-magical theological speculations on the *ex-opere-operato* virtue of

---

[66] Matthew 7:22.
[67] Lucian, The Lover of Lies, 9.
[68] Mark 5:41, 7:34.
[69] Morton Smith, *Jesus the Magician: Charlatan of Son of God?*, (New York: Harper Collins, 1978), 95.
[70] David E. Aune, "Magic in Early Christianity," *Aufstieg und Niedergang der Römischen Welt*, II.23.2, 1535.
[71] Origen, *Contra Celsum*, I, 25.
[72] Ibid, III, 68.

the sacraments."⁷³ Christianity's Roman critics, who lived in an era that pullulated seers and sorcerers, prophets and exorcists, demons and ghosts, quickly pegged Jesus and his followers as magicians and frauds. Celsus charged that Jesus was "a worthless sorcerer, hated by God"⁷⁴ and claimed that "after being brought up in obscurity, he hired himself out in Egypt and having become experienced in certain magical arts, he made his way back"⁷⁵ to Galilee, and as Samson Eitrem noted, "common Jewish people considered Jesus a [magician]..."⁷⁶

Fifteen centuries later, as ecclesiastical thought control eroded, Western scholars began to catch up with Christianity's Roman critics. Particularly notable was David Friedrich Strauss' work, *The Life of Jesus*, that appeared in 1835. Regarding the demon folklore of the age, Strauss noted, "Jesus gives a description quite accordant with the idea of his cotemporaries of the departure of the unclean spirit, his wandering in the wilderness, and his return with a reinforcement" and observed, "the main instrument against demoniacal possession was conjuration."⁷⁷ Strauss did not fail to note the marked similarities between the exorcisms described by Josephus, those attributed to Apollonius, and the exorcisms performed by Jesus and his apostles,⁷⁸ nor did he neglect Paul's enchanted laundry and Peter's magical shadow: "In reading these last histories, every one knows he is in the realm of fiction and legend."⁷⁹ Although Strauss carefully avoided the M-word, even the casual reader knew the topic under review was *magic in its most primitive form*, a comparison of Judeo-Christian magical folklore to Greco-Roman magical folklore. As the noted scholar F. C. Conybeare observed—in 1896—

---

[73] E.G. Weltin, "The Concept of *Ex-Opere-Operato*: Efficacy in the Fathers as an Evidence of Magic in Early Christianity," *Greek, Roman, and Byzantine Studies* 3, 2/3 (1960), 78.
[74] Origen, op. cit., 1:71.
[75] Ibid, I, 38.
[76] Samson Eitrem, *Some Notes on the Demonology in the New Testament*, 2ⁿᵈ ed, (Oslo: Symbolae Osloenses, 1966), 41.
[77] David Friedrich Strauss, *The Life of Jesus, Critically Examined*, (New York: Cosimo Classics, 2009), 416, 422.
[78] Ibid, 430.
[79] Ibid, 461.

"the demonological beliefs of the New Testament are absolutely the same as those of prior and subsequent ages."[80]

During the late 19th century various magical papyri collected by antiquarians were published, and in 1928 and 1931 Preisendanz issued the first edition of his well-known two-volume collection of the papyri, *Papyri Graecae Magicae*, a trove of documents that opened a window on the religio-magical lore of Jesus' era. However, scholars had already begun to detail the connections between "conventional thaumaturgic techniques" in the wider culture and Jesus' healing techniques, actions "considered as a conventional feature of the wonder-worker's behavior."[81] That Jesus conformed in both word and deed to the magical praxis of his day became increasingly well recognized: P. Samain summarized the evidence in a forty-page article as early as 1938.[82] Carl Kraeling, a respected scholar at Yale, proposed that Jesus had been accused of necromancy,[83] a thesis I have defended in detail.[84]

Book length examinations of the evidence for magic in the New Testament followed. John Hull's classic, *Hellenistic Magic and the Synoptic Tradition*, already mentioned, appeared in 1974, followed in 1978 by Morton Smith's *Jesus the Magician*, a work aimed at a general readership and still in print, a book that earned its author the everlasting animus of biblical literalists. That Jesus practiced magic, now nearly a consensus in New Testament studies, is acknowledged by Crossan:

> The title *magician* is not used here [of Jesus] as a pejorative word but describes one who can make divine power present *directly through personal miracle* rather than *indirectly through communal ritual*. Despite an extremely labile continuum between the twin

---

[80] F. C. Conybeare, "Christian Demonology II," *The Jewish Quarterly Review* 9.1 (1896), 70.
[81] Campbell Bonner, "Traces of Thaumaturgic Technique in the Miracles," *Harvard Theological Review* 20 (1927), 171172.
[82] P. Samain, "L'accusation de magie contre le Christ dans les évangiles," *Ephemerides Theologicae Lovanienses* 15 (1938), 449-490.
[83] Carl H. Kraeling, "Was Jesus Accused of Necromancy?" *Journal of Biblical Literature* 59.2 (1940), 147-157.
[84] Robert Conner, "The Ghost of John the Baptist," *Apparitions of Jesus: The Resurrection as Ghost Story*, (Valley, WA: Tellectual Press, 2018), 31-51.

concepts, magic renders transcendental power present concretely, physically, sensibly, tangibly, whereas ritual renders it present abstractly, ceremonially, liturgically, symbolically.[85]

"Jesus' opponents accused him of black magic, an accusation which stands as one of the most firmly established facts of the Gospel Tradition."[86] In short, starting with Strauss, scholars began to recognize the essentially folkloric magical character of "the Judeo-Christian tradition." Jacob, for example, places multi-colored branches before the watering holes of Laban's sheep and goats and when the animals mate in front of the branches they produce multi-colored offspring,[87] *similia similibus evocantur*, a classic example of sympathetic magic. When Moses appears before Pharaoh, his staff becomes a serpent, a "miracle" the Egyptian magicians are quick to duplicate,[88] i.e., "the reality of the magical power of the Egyptians is acknowledged."[89] The edifice of Christian folklore rises upon the foundations of Jewish "folk story themes"[90]—the scarlet rope by which the Israelite spies escape[91] becomes a symbol for the saving blood of Christ. Folk tales with "a magico-religious content and purpose" are "handed down...from one person to another, repeated as it has been received, remembered and retold" and eventually written down.[92] The "strong man" of Mark's exorcism story[93] is based on a yet more primitive stratum of folklore,[94] and as Frank W. Beare noted, "we can hardly fail to see that [the gospel tradition] had been enlarged by the admission of both sayings and incidents which derived from other sources."[95] In short, the gospels follow a general rule enunciated by

---

[85] John D. Crossan, *The Historical Jesus: The Life of a Mediterranean Jewish Peasant*, (New York: Harper Collins, 1992), 138. (Emphasis in original.)
[86] Eric Plumer, "The Absence of Exorcisms in the Fourth Gospel," *Biblica* 78.3 (1997), 357.
[87] Genesis 30:37-43.
[88] Exodus 7:8-13.
[89] Davies, op. cit., 246.
[90] Frank W. Beare, "Concerning Jesus of Nazareth," *Journal of Biblical Literature* 87.2 (1968), 129.
[91] Joshua 2:18.
[92] Edwin O. James, "The Influence of Folklore on the History of Religion," *Numen* 9.1 (1962), 4.
[93] Mark 3:27.
[94] S. Legasse, "'L'Homme fort' de Luc XI 21-22," *Novum Testamentum* 5.1 (1962) 5-9.
[95] Beare, op. cit., 126.

Campbell Bonner: "What the hearer has learned to expect, the teller will not fail to provide; and it would be strange if the recorders of the life and works of Jesus had not woven into the accounts of his miracles some bits of conventional thaumaturgic technique."[96]

Debate in Jesus Studies about whether Jesus was really, truly a magician—to the extent that the topic is still debated at all—amounts to little more than pedantics about semantics. Commenting on Jesus' command, "Ephphatha!"[97] Howard C. Kee declares it a "prayer consisting of a single word" and contrasts it to the "extended invocations" of the magical books.[98] However Mark nowhere says that Jesus prayed, but does tell us that Jesus groaned, looked up into the sky, put his fingers into the man's ears and touched his tongue, all consistent with magical techniques. Writing in the same volume, Susan R. Garrett notes, "Matthew excised not only the more blatant thaumaturgical traits but even whole incidents, such as the stories of the healing of the deaf mute (Mark 7:31–37) and of the blind man near Bethsaida (Mark 8:22–26), both of which might lend themselves to magical interpretation.[99] Kee's quibble over the brevity of the formula is feeble apologetics: "the holy man of the Greco-Roman period…can accomplish his object with one wonder-working word."[100] "…the older the magical forms, the shorter and more precise are the formulas…The short authoritative commands of Jesus to demons in the gospel narratives are formulas of magical adjuration."[101]

There was little aside from religious belief to distinguish Jewish and Christian wonder workers from their pagan counterparts, holy men with

---

[96] Campbell Bonner, Harvard Theological Review 20 (1927), 171.
[97] Mark 7:34.
[98] Howard C. Kee, "Magic and Messiah," *Religion, Science, and Magic: In Concert and in Conflict* (Oxford: Oxford University Press, 1989), 136.
[99] Susan R. Garrett, "Light on a Dark Subject and Vice Versa: Magic and Magicians in the New Testament," *Religion, Science, and Magic: In Concert and in Conflict*, (Oxford: Oxford University Press, 1989), 143.
[100] Frederick E. Brenk, "In the Light of the Moon," *Aufstieg und Niedergang der Römischen Welt*, II, 16.3, 2113.
[101] Aune, Aufstieg und Niedergang der Römischen Welt, II, 23.2, 1531-1532.
For a more detailed discussion of apologetic ploys see Robert Conner, Magic in the New Testament: A Survey and Appraisal of the Evidence (Mandrake of Oxford, 2010), 176-182.

"supernatural powers, possessed of penetrating insights into the thoughts of others, and able to work miracles, summon spirits," men such as Plotinus who "had an inner circle of about a dozen."[102] Reading across the ever-expanding literature on ancient magical arts it's clear that Jewish magical folklore, based in large part on Babylonian and Canaanite folklore, forms the basis of Christian magical folklore, which in turn incorporates elements of Greco-Egyptian magical belief. Comparing the gospels with similar material from contemporaneous Mediterranean cultures, the distinction between prayer and incantation, miracle and magic, dissipates like an early morning fog. As Conybeare, taking a rationalist approach, said, "there is really nothing about the history of the early Church which justifies us in lifting it out of general history and claiming for its documents a right to be tested by other tests of probability than those which we apply to secular narratives."[103]

The cultural substrate of magical belief surfaces repeatedly in Paul's letters: "Who has *bewitched* (*ebaskanen*) you?"[104] Paul is employing "the common practice of accusing one's enemies and rivals of sorcery,"[105] specifically *baskania*, to "blight by the evil eye, to fascinate, bewitch."[106] Paul both accepts and participates in the folklore common to the ancient Middle East: "the evil eye was associated with witchcraft and sorcery...and other evils caused by malevolent human beings."[107] The *baskanos* is a *sorcerer* who casts a spell based on malevolence or envy, a person who possessed an *ophthalmos ponēros*,[108] an *evil eye*, linked by Jesus to murder, greed, adultery and theft.[109] "Biblical texts, like all texts,

---

[102] Garth Fowden, "The Pagan Holy Man in Late Antique Society," *Journal of Hellenic Studies* 102 (1982), 37, 39.
[103] Fredrick C. Conybeare, "Demonology of the New Testament, I," *The Jewish Quarterly Review* 8.4 (1896), 576.
[104] Galatians 3:1.
[105] Jerome H. Neyrey, "Bewitched in Galatia: Paul and Cultural Anthropology," *Catholic Biblical Quarterly* 50.1 (1988), 73.
[106] George Abbott-Smith, *A Manual Greek Lexicon of the New Testament*, (Edinburgh: T&T Clark, 1937), 78.
[107] Marie-Louise Thomsen, "The Evil Eye in Mesopotamia," *Journal of Near Eastern Studies* 51.1 (1992), 22.
[108] As in Matthew 6:23, Luke 11:34.
[109] Mark 7:22-23.

embed, encode and presume elements of the social and cultural systems in which they are produced, which means that the genre, content, structure and meaning of these texts are all socially and culturally determined."[110] Belief in the evil eye "is probably one of the oldest continuous religious constructs in the Mediterranean basin."[111] The short answer to Paul's question, "Who has bewitched you?" is *other Christian preachers who, according to Paul, engaged in magic.*

That no ritual of the Christian liturgy is more overtly magical than the Eucharist has long been recognized. "The Sacraments especially come within the definition of magical functions" and to emphasize his point Herbert Chatley quotes the text of the 18th century *Grimoire of Pope Honorius*: "I conjure thee by virtue of the blood of Jesus Christ contained daily in the chalice."[112] S.G.F. Brandon named "ritual magic" as the means by which early man sought "to preserve or re-create the efficacy of events which he believed to be beneficial" and offered "the Eucharist, as set forth by Paul" as a prime example.[113] Conybeare noted, "Whether, therefore, Christ himself instituted this sacrament, or whether Paul, under influence of his ecstatic revelations, merely fathered it on Christ, in either case ideas and conceptions which to-day we call magical underlay and motivated it...It would be against all analogy that an institution so tainted with magic from the first as was the Eucharist, should not, as the ages rolled by, gather about it ever fresh accretions of superstition."[114] Indeed, such were the "accretions of superstition" surrounding the Eucharist that the elements required constant surveillance

---

[110] John H. Elliott, "Social-scientific criticism: Perspective, process and payoff. Evil eye accusation at Galatia as illustration of the method," *HTS Theological Studies* 67.1 (2011), accessed 24 September 2018.
[111] Leonard W. Moss & S.C. Cappannari, "Mal'occhio, Ayin ha ra, Oculus fascinus, Judenblick: The Evil Eye Hovers Above," *The Evil Eye*, (New York: Columbia University Press, 1976), 12.
[112] Herbert Chatley, "Mediæval Occultism," *The Monist* 18.4 (1908), 511, 513.
[113] S.G.F. Brandon, "The Historical Element in Primitive Christianity," Numen 2.3 (1955), 166-167.
[114] Fredrick C. Conybeare, *Myth, Magic and Morals: A Study of Christian Origins*, 2nd ed, (London: Watts & Company, 1910), 264-265.

and security measures to prevent theft of the Host so it could be used for sorcery.[115]

Paul's understanding of the Eucharist was basically magical, likely reflecting widespread assumptions about the basis for the efficacy of sacrificial ritual:

> The cup of blessing that we bless, is it not sharing in the blood of Christ? The bread we break, is it not sharing in the body of Christ?...but what [the Gentiles] sacrifice, they sacrifice to demons and not to God and I don't want you to be partakers with demons! You cannot drink the cup of the Lord and the cup of demons! You cannot sit at the table of the Lord and the table of demons!...For he who eats and drinks without discerning the body eats and drinks judgment on himself. That is why many among you are weak and sick and a number have died.[116]

Even those who argue for a "spiritual" understanding of being weak, sick, and dying, acknowledge that the majority of interpreters believe Paul is speaking literally.[117] "Paul argues that participation in sacrificial meals brings about communion with demons...[Paul] does not dispute a quasi magical view of the sacraments."[118] "In both the Christian and the pagan rites there seems to be a formal correlation between sacrifice and the release of Spirit or spirits. Somehow the violent killing of a sacrificial victim led to the release of spirits/Spirit that took possession of the communicants in both traditions."[119]

---

[115] Thomas M. Izbicki, *The Eucharist in Medieval Canon Law*, (Cambridge: Cambridge University Press, 2015), 182-188.

[116] 1 Corinthians 10:16, 20-21, 11:29-30.

[117] Ilaria L.E. Ramelli, "Spiritual Weakness, Illness, and Death in 1 Corinthians 11:30," *Journal of Biblical Literature* 130.1 (2011), 146-148.

[118] J. Smit, "'Do Not Be Idolaters': Paul's Rhetoric in First Corinthians 10:1-22," *Novum Testamentum* 39.1 (1997), 46, 48. "They have an 'enthusiast's' or a 'magical' view of the sacraments...The Corinthians really thought they were secure because of a somewhat magical view of baptism and the Lord's Supper." (Gordan D. Fee, "Eidwloqusa Once Again: An Interpretation of 1 Corinthians 8-10," *Biblica* 61.2 (1980), 180, 192-193.

[119] J. A. Loubser, "Possession and Sacrifice in the NT and African Traditional Religion: The Oral Forms and Conventions Behind the Literary Genres," *Neotestamentica* 37.2 (2003), 232.

The use of food to transmit demonic forces is attested in the gospels. The piece of bread Jesus dips in the bowl and hands Judas is the equivalent of Judas' kiss of betrayal: "and after *the morsel* (*psōmion*), then Satan entered [Judas]."[120] It comes as little surprise to find a close parallel to Jesus' action recorded in the magical papyri, in this case an attraction spell to call up the gods of the underworld using morsels of bread:

> Leave a little of the bread you did not eat, and breaking it apart, make seven morsels and go to where the heroes and gladiators and men who died violently were slain. Say the spell *into the morsels* (*eis tous psōmous*) and toss them. This is the spell to be pronounced into the morsels...[121]

The bread forms a magical conduit for the entry of the spirits: "The notion that a demon can be sent into food so as to enter anyone who eats the food is common."[122] An ancient Christian amulet offers a textbook summary of the belief that magical transmission could occur through food, clothing, contact, or a mere glance:

> God of Abraham, God of Isaac and God of Jacob, protect Alexandra, daughter of Zoē, from demons and enchantments...flee from Alexandra, Zoē's daughter...lest you use potions on her, either by a kiss...or by food, or by drink...or by the [evil] eye, or by an article of cloth-ing...One God and his Christ, help Alexandra.[123]

Perhaps no single text more perfectly captures the fuzzy boundary between early Christian sacrament and magic than Ignatius' well-known reference to the bread of the Eucharist as "the medicine (*pharmakon*) of immortality, the antidote that [we] not die, but live forever in Jesus Christ."[124] The term pharmakon, which could mean either medicine or poison, retained a strong connotation of malevolent sorcery—the related

---

[120] John 13:27.
[121] Preisendanz, *Papyri Graecae Magicae* IV, 1992-1395.
[122] Smith, Jesus the Magician, 110.
[123] Kotansky, *Greek Magical Amulets*, 278-281.
[124] Ignatius, Ephesians 20.

term pharmakeus meant poisoner or sorcerer. Like many early Christians, Ignatius took the words attributed to Jesus—"unless you eat the flesh of the Son of Man and drink his blood you have no life in yourselves"[125]—in their most literal sense. Christians "are revitalized by the blood of God"[126] and true Christians confessed, "that the Eucharist is the flesh of our Savior Jesus Christ."[127] Ignatius thought of the Eucharist "as charged with a magical quality for keeping both body and soul deathless."[128]

For many Christians, eating Christ's flesh and drinking his blood was neither metaphor nor symbol: "The teaching of the [orthodox] Church is explicit on this point. The body eaten is the same as that once born of a virgin and now seated at the right hand of the Father; the sacrifice of the mass is one and the same as that of the cross."[129] In any case, it is clear from Christianity's beginnings that the *hoi polloi* (i.e., the common people) considered both the cross and Eucharist magical; the Host was buried with the dead, "taken as a test of innocence or guilt," and used as an amulet or protective talisman.[130] Indeed, as a recent writer points out, "Were it not for magical thinking it would be difficult to make sense of the representations which people ascribe to their participation even in the rituals of doctrinarian modes of religion such as, for example, the Eucharist of the Roman Catholic mass or the Lord's Supper as celebrated in the Evangelical-Lutheran Church of Denmark."[131]

---

[125] John 6:53.
It is, of course, impossible that these words originated with an observant Jew who followed the prohibition against eating blood (Leviticus 17:13-14) or from the first followers of Jesus (Acts 15:20). "The material alleged to be from oral tradition contains language and points of view that are improbable on the lips of Jesus. The content often indicates that the material originated with the problems and issues in the church." (Howard M. Teeple, "The Oral Tradition That Never Existed," *Journal of Biblical Literature* 89.1 (1970), 61).
[126] Ignatius, Ephesians 1:1.
[127] Ignatius, Smyrnaeans 6:2.
[128] Preserved Smith, "Christian Theophagy: An Historical Sketch," *The Monist* 28.2 (1918), 203.
[129] Ibid, 161.
[130] Valerie I.J. Flint, *The Rise of Magic in Early Medieval Europe*, (Princeton, NJ: Princeton University Press, 1991), 178, 214, 282, 285.
[131] Anders K. Petersen, "Paul and Magic: Complementary or Incongruent Entities," *Studies on Magic and Divination in the Biblical World*, (Piscataway, NJ: Gorgias Press, 2013), 198.

A summary of the evidence for magical praxis in the career of Jesus and for magical belief in the early Church would hardly fit within a work of a thousand pages in length. It would necessarily encompass relevant primary material in Hebrew, Aramaic, Greek, Latin and Coptic, hundreds of secondary sources in all the modern European languages spanning at least a century, as well as insights into magical belief in the literatures of anthropology, psychology, and comparative religion. The biblical world is magical throughout, top to bottom, end to end, and the few examples given in this chapter barely skim the surface of the cumulative evidence. The conclusion is incontrovertible: to enter into the world of Jesus and primitive Christianity is to enter fully into the world of magic.

17| CREDULITY AT CANA?

BY EVAN FALES

John's Gospel relates a marriage celebration in the town of Cana, to which Jesus and his disciples were invited. When the wedding party runs out of wine, Jesus' mother, also present, goes to inform him of the problem. After responding to Mary with a brusque rebuff, he orders the servants to fill ten stone storage jars with water; and when they had so done, he changes the water into a wine that is judged by the steward, unaware of the miracle, to be better than the previous supply.

This famous story, of the first miracle attributed to Jesus by John, has been accepted by a multitude of people although, in so doing, these individuals believe that something incredible happened—that is, literally, something impossible to believe. How can this be? Are those who accept the story gullible, irrational, or deeply ignorant of natural processes? While human nature falls prey to all of these failings, second thoughts seem to be in order when a story has won so much affirmation for so long by so many individuals. Is a skeptic forced to conclude that credulity runs that rampant through the annals of human attempts to understand the workings of nature?

On closer reflection, we find a number of mitigating factors that make it considerably less clear how irrational someone must be to believe that Jesus, with God's help, changed water to wine. For starters, it is easy to underestimate the extent to which the acquisition of new beliefs is a process in which the testimony of others plays a pervasive role. It plays a significant role, either directly or indirectly, in a vast range of the belief-formation events that build our understanding of the world. A vivid illustration of this is provided by the ease with which a class of elementary physics students can be befuddled by a challenge to prove that the earth is spherical and not a flat plane, or that the earth orbits the sun rather than vice versa. It does not take much sophistication to be able to explain away, in scientific terms, all of the "data" (mostly acquired by way of testimony) that are offered to defeat the rogue claims, and to get members of the class to realize that their heliocentric conception of the solar system stems from, and is maintained by, the testimony of teachers and others whose claims are accepted as authoritative. It is a reasonable conjecture that testimony-acceptance is a deeply embedded social instinct in humans, one that is surely instrumental in the early stages of simply learning one's native tongue.[1]

But testimony-based learning does not confer on us simply a hodgepodge of factual information. It is deeply implicated in the development of our theoretical understanding of things, and a great deal of what we are taught from early childhood consists in more or less systematic congeries of explanations for phenomena: what we call theories. There is indeed a strong drive to achieve a tightly knit, coherent theoretical understanding of things that we might call a worldview. I bring this up for two reasons. First, the evidential grounds, gained both by direct experience and from testimony, that support such a worldview are extremely complex and often impossible to reconstruct. Second, the resulting beliefs are intertwined in ways that make them mutually supporting—and mutually vulnerable, in the sense that a challenge to one belief can have, to a greater or lesser degree, an impact upon the security of other beliefs. Rejecting one belief typically threatens other beliefs, and some reconstruction of the belief system, beyond replacement of the delinquent belief, is generally in order. So, on the one hand, systematic interconnectedness provides one with flexible resources for explaining away recalcitrant data, while on the other, the admission of empirical failure

---

[1] That does not entail, obviously, that it is not subject to critical scrutiny as cognitive abilities develop.

or theoretical inconsistency is often cognitively expensive. It can generate cognitive dissonance, and potentially the overthrow of a wide range of views one had taken for granted.

That explains, I think, a major dialectical pressure that impels fundamentalists in the direction of scriptural literalism. To claim that some scriptural passages, even if quite peripheral, are false or meant non-literally can seem to threaten the rest of the corpus, including passages whose literal understanding is central to the faith. (That consideration is coupled with the familiar finding that fundamentalism—of all stripes—is associated with a psychological intolerance for ambiguity, shades of gray, and an aversion to wrestling with hard dilemmas, both ethical and intellectual. That personality trait and fundamentalism are, arguably, mutually reinforcing.) Under such circumstances, it is arguably not rational to sacrifice an embracing, coherent world-view on the altar of a few troublesome data.[2] So maybe those who take the Cana story on-board as (literally) true aren't mad; but neither are they, as I shall argue, correct.

It is worth noting that much of what I have said by way of an apologia for Biblical literalists applies to most contemporary believers, who have bearing down on them both the *gravitas* of long tradition and recognized authority, and the multi-dimensional pressure to preserve communion with a social peer group. But it is *harder* to afford the same apologetic maneuvers as we move back in time to the origins of the story. For back then—certainly when Jesus began preaching—there was no Christian community, there were no organized Christian institutions, and there was no established hierarchy of doctrinal authority (including no canonical scripture). All of that was in the earliest stages of formation, a process in which precisely the acceptance of such stories as the ones relating Jesus' miracles played a significant role, and occurred in the face of accepted wisdom, tradition, and religious authority. In short, rational acceptance in the First Century CE would have been largely an uphill battle for the Christian movement, whereas it is in contemporary

---

[2] As Thomas Kuhn articulately pointed out in *The Structure of Scientific Revolutions*.

Christian environments a downhill glissade. Or, to bring the issue squarely before us in thinking about John 2: What did the disciples at Cana experience? Did they experience *anything* that would have fomented such a miracle story; and if so, what? Does, indeed, the entirety of the narrative in Jn. 2 have any historical basis? Whose record of the event would have provided the source-material for the author of John? Would that have been the author himself? In any case, what motivated him to include it, and what reason did he have for thinking that it would be believed and would promote his aims in composing the Gospel?

We cannot, unfortunately, give definitive answers to any of these questions—but we can nevertheless think about them, and perhaps offer reasonable conjectures. I will proceed by considering at least a good sample of the major options on offer for explaining the story of Cana and, indeed, other Biblical miracle stories. I will attempt, in so doing, to separate wheat from chaff, so far as possible. I should begin by noting that my aim is to understand the Cana narrative in the way in which "John" (as I will call the author) intended it, and presumably intended (with reason) for his readers to understand it. These two things—authorial meaning and intended/expected reception by the target audience—are for my purposes the touchstones of interpretation.

These aims naturally have and will raise epistemological challenges. How can we ever know authorial intent or expected reader message-uptake? Those are fair questions into which I cannot now digress,[3] but it may serve the present purpose to point out that it is these aims that constitute the fundamental teloi of acts of communication (whether linguistic or not) in the first place. Moreover, reflection brings into relief just what the necessary conditions are for communicative success; these become evident when one considers the requirements that attend the teaching of a first language to children. The assignment of semantic content to conventionalized verbal or other signs presupposed, inter alia, that there pre-exist non-conventionalized means of conveying semantic

---

[3] I have argued at some length for their hermeneutical primacy elsewhere; see Fales, "Truth, Tradition, and Rationality," *Philosophy of the Social Sciences* 6 (1976): 97-113.

content between communicators. That, in turn, demands that an audience (A) be able, independently of being told, (a) to discern an intention on the part of the speaker (S) to convey some message (which requires some natural, perhaps innate, ability to read off S's purpose from nonconventional aspects of S's behavior, some implicit understanding of S's natural interests, and surrounding circumstances), (b) to engage in inductive and deductive reasoning competently, and (c) to work from sensory inputs that give A rational grounds for inferences concerning which aspects of a perceived environment will also be perceived by or known to S and judged relevant to the occasion.

All of that, in turn, underwrites an epistemological principle which, though variously formulated, we can call a Principle of (Interpretive) Charity. For our purposes here, we give the following (somewhat rough) formulation of this principle:

PC: Given that the normal adult members of every human society have a shared means of linguistic communication, and that all such human beings share profound biological similarities of the relevant sorts, there is, between competing interpretations of a communication—especially when it is widely shared, accepted, and preserved—a presumption in favor of an interpretation that ascribes to the communicants a universally normal capacity for rational, critical norms of acceptance over interpretations that ascribe content that would not be rationally held by those communicants.

Two observations are in order. First, human individuals range widely in cognitive capacity, sagacity, and education. Second, human cultures vary widely in what they collectively know, and of what they are non-culpably ignorant. The variations in human intelligence have the consequence that communications can vary in intellectual sophistication, and members of an audience can vary, commensurately, in their competence in understanding communications. Communicators, for their part, can knowingly construct texts that have easily accessible surface-meanings and deeper levels of meaning that will convey messages only to the cognoscenti. The second caveat makes allowance for the fact that, while it may be irrational for the members of one culture with certain common knowledge to accept a proposition, it may be rational for the members of another culture which lacks that knowledge to accept that belief.

With these considerations in hand, let's return to Cana and see what can be said about John's narrative of the first miracle of Jesus. How are we to understand the presence and significance of this story? Why has John given it a prominent position near the beginning of his gospel? Here are some of the options:

1) *Orthodoxy*: God is in his heaven, and enabled Jesus to perform this miracle as a sign of his preeminent prophetic status as divinely chosen; John's description is on the whole historically faithful to an event that marked the initiation of Jesus' calling, and its preservation by the early Christian community and evident significance as a harbinger of Jesus' historical destiny led to its inclusion by John.

2) *Dark Ages*: Nothing of the kind actually happened, but the scientific ignorance of John's day, human fascination with wonders, and especially the absence, in those times, of scientific critical reasoning and reflection provided fertile ground for the confabulation of all manner of superstitions and wonder-tales, especially ones that could be placed in the service of some cause or social movement.

3) *Creeping Hyperbole*: Something very surprising did occur in connection with Jesus' presence at the Cana wedding—unprecedented, perhaps, or with deep emotional impact, but not literally a miracle. It was memorable enough to be re-told; and retellings spawned distortions and exaggerations that, over time, grew wilder and more wondrous. By the time John heard the tale, its content was extraordinary—and he may have contributed further to the history of embellishment.

4) *Prevarication*: John's tale is simply a crude (or perhaps not so crude) fabrication, perhaps composed by him, perhaps rooted

in early Christian lore, and fobbed off on a credulous population with the aim of gaining Christian converts.

5) *Amazing Nature, or Weird Stuff Happens*: The actual transformation of water into wine through the operation of natural processes is astronomically unlikely, but not literally impossible; and such things do on occasion occur: so here.

6) *Amazing Grace*: The transformation of the water cannot be understood by rational or scientific means; understanding it lies beyond the purview of human intellectual powers; nevertheless by God's grace one can come to know—as John did—that Jesus performed such a miracle.

7) *Parable*: This wonder-tale was composed by John (or his sources) as a parable whose content is meant to be fictional, and whose pedagogical purpose, perhaps quite insightful, is conveyed by means of a vocabulary of symbols and a figurative use of language.

This list, by no means compendious, does, I think, cover many of the more prominent understandings of the Cana story, not all mutually exclusive but roughly mapping the dialectical terrain I mean to explore. Are there good reasons to judge any one of these options superior to—more likely to be true—than the rest? I shall proceed by discussing them in turn.

I. ORTHODOXY

The orthodox view provides a natural explanation for John's inclusion of the Cana episode in his Gospel; and, if it had ample attestation available to John, it satisfies, perhaps as any other option, the Charity criterion—at least at first blush. For, whatever John's larger purposes might have been in the Gospel, it is patent that the Cana miracle would serve to single Jesus out as a man with divine powers, something John surely intended. The explanation in question is simply: John relates the story because he knows, or has good reason to believe, that it's true (reasons deriving from the fact that it did occur); and it intimates Jesus' power and celebratory mission.

What about second blush? Let's suppose that God is indeed in His heaven, and that he empowered Jesus to perform the miracle. How likely is it that John would have had credible and adequate attestation to the latter? It is rather striking, for example, that we have no independent attestation to the miracle elsewhere: not in the other Gospels, not in such other potential sources as are to be had. Because the miracle itself is so striking, and its position at the onset of Jesus' ministry is distinctive, it is striking that episode did not find its way into the other, earlier Christian sources we have.

Unfortunately, the early Christian materials that could provide such evidence comprise a slender portfolio. And so, the absence of a plurality of records of a particular biographical detail concerning Jesus does not provide anything like conclusive reason to think that such records did not exist in the First Century CE. And, of course, many of Jesus' miracles can boast multiple attestation in existing records. (Whether these come from independent sources remains a further, unsettled, issue.)

A different line of argument cites passages such as, e.g., Lk 1:1–4 in support of the view that the Evangelists meant to adhere to the historical record in their biographies of Jesus. That John himself shared that intention is at least suggested by the remark with which he concludes his Gospel: "But there are also many other things that Jesus did; were every one of them to be written, I suppose that the world itself could not contain the books that would be written." Setting aside the obvious hyperbole, this may sound like the testimony of a man who had extensive familiarity with the noteworthy events that attended Jesus' ministry.

Appearances, however, may be deceiving, and it is a matter under dispute whether even Luke so much as intended to convey to his friend Theophilus an unvarnished account of (some of) those events. It has, for example, been pointed out that not even Luke adheres—as was already normal practice among historians at that time—to the scholarly imperative to cite one's sources of information; none of the canonical Gospels gives proper citations of that sort.⁴ Luke, for one, quite clearly puts on display his penchant for symbolic narrative in a chronological discrepancy between the conclusion of his Gospel and the opening claims of the Book of Acts. For the narrative of the former, while not chronologically explicit, quite clearly implies that the period of time the post-mortem (risen) Jesus spent communing with his disciples before leaving them lasted a day or possibly a couple of days, whereas the opening of Acts explicitly speaks of a period of 40 days. What accounts for the disparity? Was Luke so careless or forgetful as not to have noticed the inconsistency? If so, how much trust can we repose in his supposed history of Jesus? An exonerating explanation is, of course, ready to hand: the 40-day reference is meant to evoke the 40 days Jesus spent in the wilderness, fasting and resisting the devil, at the inauguration of his ministry (as per Lk. 3:23), which is in turn meant to evoke the 40 years of rulership attributed to Israel's greatest leaders, Moses, David, and Solomon. But this explanation concedes that Luke was quite willing to allow history to subserve pedagogical ends presented through symbolical narrative not intended as literal history—which raises the question how permeated Luke's Gospel (and Acts) might be by other such exercises. Indeed they are not hard to identify elsewhere in Luke and across the miracle narratives in the other Gospels.

Thus far, we have considered just a few of the textual particulars found in Jn 2 that bear on literal historicity. We shall return to others. There are, however, two lines of argument against historicity that present not just hurdles for the Cana story, but challenge the evidential value of miracle stories generally. One, whose *locus classicus* is Hume's "Of Miracles," offers an epistemological challenge. The other, which is a matter of current debate, raises a metaphysical objection.

Hume's epistemological claim is that when testimony providing reports of the miraculous is offered to support a religious agenda, it should always be discounted because it is at least counterbalanced by (and

---

⁴ See, e.g., Richard Carrier, *On the Historicity of Jesus: Why We Might Have Reason for Doubt*. Sheffield, UK: Sheffield Phoenix Press, pp 21-26, 396-399, *et passim*.

almost always outweighed by) non-supernatural explanations for the events testified to or for the existence of the (false) testimony itself. Hume's argument, *very* roughly, is that, in order for a miracle story to provide sound evidence of the supernatural, it must first be established that the laws of nature are such as to preclude the production of the reported event by natural processes—a determination that presupposes a uniformity of wide experience regarding the operations of nature—and a showing that there is no better naturalistic explanation for the occurrence of the testimony (e.g., human ignorance, credulity, or deception).

Many objections to Hume's argument have been offered, from his day to the present. For my part, I shall say that I think the argument, a bit modified to take account of developments in probability and confirmation theory, stands. But here I shall not enter into the rather technical matters of how the argument is best formulated in light of contemporary work in probability theory. Rather, my strategy will be to concede, arguendo (as Hume himself comes close to doing), that testimony, buttressed by certain other evidentially relevant considerations, might in principle commend, as reasonable, a verdict in favor of accrediting the miracle. I shall however argue, though not along Humean lines, that in point of fact, the evidence surrounding John's witness to Cana, and indeed that surrounding the Biblical miracle stories generally, provides a new line of explanation that outdistances the fundamentalist readings of these texts.

The metaphysical objection to which I alluded argues for the claim that a deity who is immaterial, non-spatial, and (optionally, but also in many theologies) atemporal, cannot stand in causal relations to physical events, and that the miracles in question always involve some creation, disappearance, or alteration in material objects. The required causal relations are, so the objection contends, metaphysically impossible—and so impossible even for an omnipotent God to initiate. As above, this argument hinges on certain technical, and contested, positions—here, on the ontology of causation, the modality of laws of nature, and an argument that divine/world causation would violate certain conservation laws. And, as above, I shall set aside these matters and allow, for the sake of argument, that some coherent account can be given of the supernatural/natural causal relations that would have to obtain to account for genuine miracles. Again, my strategy is to argue, in connection with Cana and Biblical miracle stories generally, that a better explanation— more plausible, richer in explanatory potential, and more parsimonious, can be had that makes no appeal to supernatural tinkering with nature.

II. DARK AGES

In a large number of discussions of the sources of religious belief, a major role is played by the claim that believers are the victims of pervasive ignorance and/or a kind of naiveté that produces irrational thought, superstition, or a failure to develop the sophisticated methodological tools that guide scientific discovery and the production of bona fide knowledge. Credulous religious convictions and their propagation are then explained as the products of these primitive, unsophisticated thought-patterns working upon various of the exigencies and contingencies of human life.

As regards the miraculous, suggestions have been made ranging from confusions about dreams and reality (Tylor) or utterances and reality (Fraser on magical beliefs) to failures in inductive or causal reasoning, failures that may occur naturally but that can also be used by impostors and charlatans to advantage. Perhaps, for example, Galilean fishermen, ignorant of Archimedes' Principle (that a floating object displaces a volume of water equal in weight to its own weight in air), could have readily accepted a story that some among their number had seen Jesus strolling across the waves of a stormy Sea of Galilee. Or, not understanding the limited power of words or the organic chemistry of vinification, Jewish peasants could have swallowed a rumor that Jesus had turned six jars of water into good wine at a wedding. All of that would easily enough make a kind of sense if it was promulgated within a populace that had already been convinced, by a long history of similar stories and errors of judgment, that the universe and all its operations were governed by a deity who sponsored certain special individuals whom he selected to be his apprentices. Could God summon up a strong east wind to part the waters of the Red Sea and thus ensure the leadership of Moses? Why not?

It is worthy of note that this line of line of explanation, which trades on the ignorance of "pre-scientific" cultures, is hospitable to the notion that sometimes genuinely unusual natural events may have been misconstrued as signs of special supernatural intervention (see options 3 and 5). But option 2 seems even less charitable to non-industrialized societies, in explicitly ascribing to them a collective ignorance or intellectual incompetence. One does not have to be familiar with Archimedes' Principle, or with a scientific notion of laws of nature, to understand that someone's walking on water, or effectively commanding water to transform to wine are just not the sorts of things that Mother Nature can conjure up. Nor need one have mastered sophisticated inductive methods to learn this sort of thing from quotidian observation. Fishermen in particular will be well versed in the limitations on buoyancy. Why wouldn't they judge the gospel mastery-of-the-sea tales as a bill of goods?

III. Creeping Hyperbole

Fishy fish stories are no stranger to the human imagination or oral traditions. Normal human beings learn to be on guard against them, when anything serious is at stake. Even a fisherman might believe, on sufficient evidence, that someone caught a 24-pound largemouth bass. But only a fool would take the bait if some old salt bragged of a 100-pound catch. Large-mouth bass just don't get that big...but could that old salt's credibility be sufficiently improved if he'd begun with a 24-pound story that gained weight in the retelling—by him and then others? Perhaps: but at some point, and well before we reach a 100-pound bass, the story simply gets too far out of line with what bass fishermen know of their quarry and of animal growth limits generally. So, too, with human hydroperambulation, or wine from water.

Studies such as those by Sherwin-White[5] of the rate of embellishment-accretion by ANE wonder-tales have supposedly shown that the process is quite slow, and that, as concerns the canonical Gospels in particular, insufficient time had elapsed since Jesus' ministry for such "unembellished" traditions as those of Jesus' miracles (e.g. his Resurrection appearances) to have been created from whole cloth. (Ergo they must have originated in events such as those they describe. It is admitted that later, apocryphal gospels do display such accretions.)

This should strike us as a dubious inference indeed. Is it because human credulity can be stretched only at a certain rate? Or that really out-of-the-blue reconstructions of recent history, when sufficiently bizarre, will provoke convincing counterwitness? Everyday experience plainly demonstrates that consequential fabrications, even in the era of instant mass communication, even blatant ones, even blatant ones that have been subjected to sound public refutation, often acquire a life of their own among certain sub-populations. It is hard for me to judge how many people who consume yellow journalism of the National Enquirer ilk engage for the sake of entertainment, and how many take such stories at face value. But recent US history leaves no room for doubt that political lies can immediately become received wisdom among the initiated.

All this creates difficulties for my announced principle of charity. On the one hand, it suggests that modern cultures belie the notion that it takes some kind of primitive mentality to absorb the astonishing, in the face of good evidence to the contrary. On the other hand, it seems to leave one with the conclusion that our Principle of Charity is much too charitable after all—that human nature, both past and present, is permeated by emotional and cognitive mechanisms that cast good sense adrift.

---

[5] A. N. Sherwin-White, Roman Society and Roman Law: The Sarum Lectures 1960 – 1961, (Torrance, CA, 2000).

A certain sobering realism is in order. It is important to recognize, and take into account, human cognitive vulnerabilities. At the same time, there are mitigating circumstances that argue in favor of taking the Bible stories more seriously than those that are peddled, to whatever ends, by the yellow press and by so-called conspiracy theorists. There is no special pleading here. We know that the texts preserved in the canon won their status in heated debates with partisans of competing documents. It would be too much to suppose—and the evidence does not support—the idyllic presumption that these debates were all conducted with level-headed good sense and truth-seeking intentions by disinterested parties, or parties willing and able to quarantine their truth-irrelevant interests.[6]

Nevertheless, it cannot be denied that these early debates during the first few centuries of the emergence of Christianity subjected both ideological claims and texts to rigorous scrutiny by some of the most acute and well-educated minds of the ancient world. In those debates, philosophical acumen, adherence to canons of reason, and theoretical cogency certainly did not count for nothing. Political clout aside, good reasons can be given for granting more intellectual weight (we might venture) to, say, St. Augustine's theological arguments than to those of Faustus of Mileve, and why more literary skill and intellectual penetration should be ascribed to, say, the Gospel of John than to Philostratus's biography of Apollonius or to the Gospel of Peter. It behooves us, then, to consider seriously whether the early Church's beliefs and textual deposits do not contain, at their core and when polemical posturing is set aside, some sort of astute assessment of the existential conditions and challenges of the day, and efforts to propose sensible approaches to addressing these. If early Christian views fall lamentably short of that, our PC makes allowance for such failings, but with the proviso that, in the presence of

---

[6] See, e.g. Athanasius' *Contra Arius* for a sobering example of the kind of vitriol that found its way into (in this case) the early debates over Christian orthodoxy. That sort of animus was not infrequently backed by efforts to destroy or incapacitate ideological opponents.

failure to adduce good reasons *for* a belief, we must seek some other explanation for the *holding* of the belief.

IV. PREVARICATION

"...it is nothing strange, I hope, that men should lie in all ages," Hume laconically observed,[7] and it might be added (as Hume himself does) that sometimes men deceive not only others, but also themselves. Often enough there are, or may easily seem to be, good prudential reasons for mendacity. When there are, we have a ready explanation for why it could be rational for someone to truck in tall-tale-telling; and Hume surveys the many circumstances in which deception is a strong temptation.

One of the circumstances that improves the attractiveness of a lie noted by Hume is that the liar has reason to believe that he or she can escape detection of the falsehood. And herein lies the rub. Although many a mundane falsehood may not so much as arouse suspicion, we generally account prevarication to be foolish when the burden of the lie is in itself bizarre and—literally—incredible. To tell such a lie, especially when the stakes are high, is a fool's errand; and to believe such a lie is foolishness twice over. Now there are circumstances (as Hume astutely notes) under which the very wonderousness of a tale attracts credulity. But even then, caution and reason must go on holiday. So again, there's extra labor to be faced in understanding the successful propagation of such a story. Thus prevarication is, other things being equal, a less attractive explanation than one that preserves the truth or at least the reasonableness of accepting a story, given the available evidence.

V. WEIRD STUFF HAPPENS

Nature does not always live up to our well-founded expectations. Astonishing things occur; by their means, Nature teaches us to hedge our bets,

---

[7] David Hume, *An Inquiry Concerning Human Understanding*, Section II, p. 127 of the Charles W. Hendel edition (New York: Bobbs-Merrill, 1955).

even on near-certainties. Might it not be the case that the Red Sea really *did* part, in response to an easterly gale, in perfect synchrony with Moses' travel itinerary?[8] Might the surface of the Sea of Galilee have frosted over with ice, unnoticed (it was night) by Jesus' disciples, floating nearby in a rowboat beset by heavy winds?[9] Might the host's servants at Cana have unthinkingly poured about 150 gallons of the best wine—now we're reaching—into the stone jars, thinking all the while that they were dipping water from the well?

If you think those are stretchers, what about the suggestion that Jesus' walk on the surface of the Sea was engineered by a secret order, who surreptitiously built a raft that floats Jesus across the Sea, hidden just under the surface of the waves? That suggestion, actually floated by a 19th-Century scholar (Bahrdt),[10] demonstrates how easily such efforts at naturalistic explanation devolve from the sublime to the ridiculous.[11]

The entire maneuver, enduring from the early 19th Century to this day, to provide "naturalistic" explanation for the miracles in the Bible suffers from a kind of dialectical malaise. It is motivated by an attempt to "save" the historicity of the miracle stories in the Bible, but it does so, not only at the repeated cost of implausibility, but by robbing God of

---

[8] As proposed by Drews C, Han W (2010) Dynamics of Wind Setdown at Suez and the Eastern Nile Delta. PLoS ONE 5(8): e12481. https://doi.org/10.1371/journal.pone.0012481

[9] See Nof, D., I. McKeague, N. Paldor 2006 Is There a Paleolimnological Explanation for "Walking on Water" in the Sea of Galilee? J. of Paleolimnology. Vol. 35: 417 - 439

[10] See Albert Schweitzer , *Quest for the Historical Jesus*. W. Montgomery, transl. 2nd ed. London: Adam and Charles Black, 1911: 63.

[11] I have mapped out some of the difficulties with the Red Sea crossing elsewhere (See Fales, "It is Not Reasonable to Believe in Miracles" Chapter 22, sec. 3 in J. P. Moreland, Chad Meister, and Khaldoun Sweis, eds., *Debating Christian Theism*. Oxford: Oxford University Press, 2013). As for the frozen-surface suggestion, one might just quickly note that (a) the strong wind would have caused new ice to creak and crack – something hard to ignore if you're fighting the waves in the freezing cold; (b) the ice would have had to have been thick enough to support a man's weight (though not visible) up to within a few yards of the boat, yet have vanished across the remaining distance; (c) in which case Jesus would have had to swim that distance; and (d) even if he got away with it, Jesus would have had to hoodwink his disciples in allowing them to believe he had supernatural powers. Of course, maybe God saw to it that the 3 or 4-inch-thick ice formed silently in the storm and abruptly ended just shy of the ship, and that Jesus was able, with icy footing, to jump the gap over open water to the boat. But why bother with such tinker-toy miracles? If you're going to invoke the supernatural, why not just go whole-hog and have God provide Jesus with an airlift from shore?

either His power or His willingness to intervene in the regular course of nature. Following out that line of reasoning does not lead one into theological Elysian Fields, both because divine intervention lies at the heart of Judeo–Christian chosenness and eschatological hopes, but because we know anyway that much Biblical narrative is ahistorical, even when not miracle-suffused.

VI. Amazing Grace

Within Christian history, there is a perennial current of thought that devalues the products of human reasoning and is deeply skeptical about the capacity of human cognitive abilities to understand our situation, especially of the power of human rational inquiry to plumb the depths of the divine. Something like this anti-intellectual attitude can at least seem to be expressed in the famous Pauline diatribe against the wisdom of the "world" (I Cor. 1:17 – 4:1).[12] In its more extreme forms, such a suspicion of human faculties can be used to justify an insistence that Scripture takes precedence over the deliverances of both scientific investigation and common sense. It has moderate forms, among which one might number versions of Presuppositionalism and Reformed Epistemology that give reasoning some legitimate role, but still accept the alleged leadings of the Holy Spirit in warranting the acceptance of Biblical veracity and of the miracle stories as historical.

Such maneuvers may be reassuring to some; to the common-sense evidentialist, it is apparent that they throw caution to the winds. For if human reason is that frail, how is faith supposed to serve inquiry? The blind may blunder down the correct path and arrive safely home, or perhaps be led by the mysterious guidings of a providential force of some sort; but neither of these cures their ignorance of the lay of the land or reveals what a genuine understanding of the human condition demands. As Locke astutely noted, the testimony of another (even God) can give

---

[12] In my view, that way of reading Paul is a misunderstanding, but it has long encouraged Christian anti-intellectualism.

only so strong an assurance as our assurance that the witness is honest and someone in the know—and for that assurance, we have no further recourse than reliance upon our own total evidence and capacity for astute judgment. Suppose you are at the gaming table, about to bet on the roulette wheel. Muggsy, the stranger sitting to your left, happens to know that the wheel is rigged, and in a fit of generosity whispers the winning number in your ear. In one sense, it isn't pure chance that you win the play. But in another sense, you owe thanks to your lucky stars: for even though Muggsy was a sure guide, you had no business relying on his intentions, nor any recognition of whether or how he came to be in the know.

A deeply convincing faith has undeniably led many an honest person astray, even though they be generous of heart. What proper assurance can such faith provide, when it must row upstream against a flood of conflicting evidence?

VII. Parables

The effectiveness of the parable as a teaching device was well appreciated by the Biblical authors. And of course they understood that pedagogical punch did not depend upon an audience's mistaking the parable for factual narrative. The intent of a parable is to illuminate, not deceive. What if the stories of Genesis and Exodus, or each of the canonical Gospels, fell under that genre?

It is one thing for the narration of some "biographical" episode in Jesus' ministry given by an ancient author to have a didactic, rather than historical or merely historical purpose; it is another for purposes of the former kind to shape the entirety of a larger work in which that narrative is embedded. In the Cana story—and quite pervasively throughout the Gospels, we find narratives that are not only presented as integral to Jesus' teaching mission, as items in a larger corpus, but that can more profoundly be seen to be pieces of a larger puzzle: pieces the proper understanding of which requires scrutiny of the work as a whole, and of references to themes that shape the cultural traditions that form the conceptual space within which the author writes. Let us examine how, for the Cana episode, this plays out. In doing so, we can address a methodological demand. It is one thing to propose that the meaning of a narrative might be symbolic; it is another to make good on that suggestion by showing, on the basis of textual and other evidence, what that content might be, with a de-coding procedure that produces an interpretation that meshes with, and enhances, the broader pedagogical themes of the gospel (or other larger textual unit).

And there is a further methodological demand: that the suggested interpretation "make sense" within the larger cultural context in which it was produced. That is, we have a right to concern ourselves with the question why a treasured text was revered and preserved by some community of persons. Satisfaction of that demand provides an alternative explanation for the high standing of a text to the usual explanation that the text preserves a record of the working of God's providential care in human history. If both of the above demands can be met, then the parabolic/symbolic understanding of a miracle story stands to score better on the criterion of charity than the supposition that the tale presents a historical record.

In pursuing this kind of reading of Jn. 2, I will make use of the notion of a *symbolism alert* (SA). By a symbolism alert I mean a vignette, phrase, or word in the text that, in context, resonates with similar phrasings in the tradition and/or likely known to the author and his/her audience in such a way as to evoke some symbolic content. The terms 'resonate' and 'evoke' defy definition, but a rough and ready practical test for them is the question: Would alert readers who are familiar with the tradition and possibly relevant texts be put in mind of similar passages from those texts that, in *their* contexts, seem to convey some common message or idea? Obviously, judging the presence and significance of an SA is something of an art—but then, textual interpretation quite generally is an art.

Here, then, are—by my lights—some of the SAs (though not by any means all) we find in the story of Cana and its textual environment:
1) Asked by emissaries from the Pharisees who he is and why he baptizes, John the Baptist replies, cryptically, that he is *a voice crying in the wilderness*, and announces the advent of one who will offer *a deeper baptism of the Spirit*, and who is *the Son of God* (Jn.1:24–34).
2) The Son of God is also *the Lamb of God* (Jn, 1:36) and the *Son of Man* (Jn.1:51).
3) There was a wedding in Cana *on the third day* (Jn. 2:1)
4) Jesus' mother tells him the party has run out of wine. Jesus seems to rebuff her: "*Oh woman, what have you to do with me? My hour has not yet come.*" (Jn.2:3–4)
5) Jesus orders the servants to fill to the brim *six stone jars* with water, each holding two or three metretae (= 120—180 gallons), which Jesus *changes to wine* (Jn. 2:6–8). It is perhaps worth noting that this amount of wine (I am assuming that the water was converted to wine gallon-for-gallon) would be enough to inebriate a small army of soldiers—even if they had not already exhausted the *vin ordinaire* provided by the host. Cana was a small town. The invitation list must have extended to a much larger population.
6) The steward (who is in the dark about the miracle) samples the wine and comments to the groom that, contrary to usual practice, *he has saved the best wine for last* (Jn.2:9–10).
7) This, the *first of Jesus' signs*, manifested his glory and caused his disciples to have faith (Jn 2:11).
8) Having scourged the Jerusalem Temple merchants and moneychangers on the Passover feast, he has—unsurprisingly—provoked the Jews to question by *what sign* he has presumed to do this. He replies that if they destroy the Temple *he will raise it up again in three days*. And lest the significance of this be lost on John's readers, he notes that Jesus is referring to his

Resurrection—which will be a sign that *his body* is the new Temple (Jn. 2:13–22).

I proceed with some comments on what the narrative is trying to achieve in providing these passages, matched by number.

1) In the first chapter, John introduces the figure of John the Baptist, identifying him as a divinely inspired seer. It is Jesus' encounter with John that initiates his ministry. John announces his authority, and catalyzes the process of discipleship. Jesus acquires five disciples over the course of three days.

2) "On the third day" Jesus and his supporters attend a wedding in Cana. There is considerable controversy over John's chronology here, and how the "three days" are to be related to the preceding narrative. I shall not enter into that discussion here, but take note of an intriguing suggestion by Greg Witherow[13], to the effect that the chronology in the first two chapters of John parallels the six days of creation (and seventh day of rest, in Capernaum) in Gen. 1. Though not without difficulties, this suggestion is plausible, given that John explicitly evokes the creation motif in his opening verses, introducing an identification of the Christ with the Logos, or Word, of God.[14] Jesus is, in effect, claiming in Jn. 2 to be the mediator through which a "new earth" (cp. Is. 65:17, 66:22 and Rev. 21:1) is formed.[15]

---

[13] Witherow *The Gospel of John, Creation and Liturgy*, p. 1. http://www.holytrinityparish.net/wp-content/uploads/2014/11/The_Gospel_of_John2.pdf (accessed 12/7/18).

[14] John by no means invented the theme of a personified Word of God with creative power; it is broadly present in the Jewish Wisdom literature. Note that to be a Christ (Hebrew 'messiah') – God's anointed – is to assume a social role, viz. that of King. To say that Jesus is the Christ is just to say that he is God's designated king. Qua natural human being, Jesus is just a private person; qua Christ, he has proper claim to leadership as the royal ruler of a nation. The personage, the *Christos,* is not mortal; the natural person who assumes the royal mantle is. They are not literally identical, but intimately connected by a relation I call embodiment (see Fales, "The Ontology of Social Roles" Philosophy of the Social Sciences 7, 1977: 139-161.) for details.

[15] It is also suggestive that 'Cana,' the name of the town, is associated with a Hebrew root verb, qana:
The root-verb קנה (qana) means to acquire or create. It's the regular verb for a commercial purchase, which extends into the financed redemption of slaves (Nehemiah 5:8). It's probably this line of thought that describes God as redeeming Israel from Egypt (Exodus 15:13). In a small minority of instances this verb may mean to create: Psalm 139:13, Deuteronomy 32:6, Genesis 14:19. Our verb is also the one exclaimed

In any event, 'on the third day' in Jn. 2:1 is quite clearly meant to echo the death and resurrection of Jesus (of which more anon); and in John's chronology, my guess is that it refers to the two days during which Jesus begins to build his following, and the next day on which they embark for Cana.

3) There are various translations of the Greek into English that attempt to soften the apparent insolence of this reply from Jesus. I have given the RSV translation which, on its face, portrays Jesus as bereft of normal respect for his mother. It might be tempting to read Jesus' insolence through the lens of his repeated invective, in the Synoptic Gospels, against family loyalties.[16] But this animus against kinship ties is not evident in John.

It seems rather more likely that Jesus is reprimanding Mary for straying from a kind of choreographed script in which she is to play a prescribed role in the events that mark "his hour."

4) What Jesus means by his "hour" is not in doubt; he explicitly announces its arrival at Jn. 12: 23–24 (cp. Lk. 22:53). His hour comes, through his Passion, when he is crucified and then raised. Significantly, his mother, Mary, is present (Jn. 19:25). Significant how? Mothers are the givers of life; and not insignificantly in ancient lore, were also the mediators of death. In his Passion, Jesus is undergoing a rite of passage to a new status ("glorification"); his mother stands at the threshold, a symbol of parturition.

5) Here we arrive at the heart of Cana's symbolism: blood, wine, and water. Because of limited space, it is not possible for me to expand here on the large topic of the symbolic and ritual significance of blood, water, and wine in ancient Jewish lore and the Hebrew Bible, or the soteriological work those substances were

---

by Eve when she says, "I have gotten/made a man-child with the Lord," after giving birth to Cain (Genesis 4:1)." See Abarim Publications, Hebrew Bible Dictionary, quoted at http://www.abarim-publications.com/Meaning/Cana.html#.XArKJttKj4Y(accessed 12/7/2018).

[16] See, inter alia, Mt. 8: 22/Lk. 6:60; Mt. 12: 46-50; Mk. 3: 31-35; Lk. 14: 26-27.

symbolically charged with in early Christian thought. The textual sources are abundant. Jewish law strictly forbade the consumption of blood; when an animal is slaughtered, the blood must be ritually poured into the ground. When Moses consecrated the binding of Israel to the law, he sprinkled the blood of sacrificial oxen upon the people. That reminds us, of course, of baptism and the role of water in Jewish ritual purification and in rites of passage. It makes its first appearance in Gen. 1:2 in the form of the primal chaos waters, which God repeatedly thereafter parts, confines, and controls (e.g. the Noachic deluge, in parting the Red Sea—a rite of passage—the parting of the Jordan, and literally hundreds of passages in the Psalms, the book of Jonah, and elsewhere). Water is also the source of life. It makes workable the clay from which God formed Adam; it flows from Eden in the four life-giving rivers, and so forth. And wine, of course, plays no minor role in Jewish sacrificial law and lore—e.g. the accounts of Noah and Lot. Their significance was not confined to Jewish tradition: nearby pagans in Tyre and Sidon worshipped at temples to Bacchus where water was annually changed to wine.[17]

Is the changing of water to wine a miracle? There are, after all, natural processes that regularly achieve it: the vine-roots take in water, from which the vine produces grapes; the fermentation of their juice yields wine. That's not "the same" as wine-to-water resulting from the mere imperative of man or God. It does, however, reflect the cycle of life—as does the flow of blood, from female menstruation to the sacrifice of a lamb. And a blood/water connection is firmly intimated at Jn. 19: 23–24, which directly associates the death of Jesus with the sacrificial consumption of the Passover lamb.

Even though I must shelve further discussion of these topics, what I have said is sufficient, I think, to make the point I am arguing here—

---

[17] See Morton Smith, "On the Wine God in Palestine," in *Salo Wittmayer Baron, Jubilee Volume*, vol. II. (Jerusalem: American Academy for Jewish Research and New York: Columbia University Press), 1974: 815–829.

viz., that the symbolic content of the Cana narrative is virtually undeniable. A Christian might deny it—at the price of a wooden literalist reading of Jn. 2, stripped of all its symbolic significance, and the task of staring down a mass of evidence to the contrary; or she might concede, even insist upon, symbolic content, while pointing out that such content is quite compatible with a theistic understanding, one that attributes to God the intention to communicate with Israel through a providential history rich with events that signify beyond themselves.

But such a theistic hermeneutics also comes at a price. We may parse the matter as follows. There are (roughly) three alternatives: that stuff just happened by sheer chance; it happened as part of a divine soteriological plan carefully choreographed by God, or creative human authors fashioned the texts as powerful ways of poetically communicating their insights into their human and cultural condition and solutions to the challenges those pose. The first alternative is extraordinarily unlikely on any accounting of probabilities; the second not only requires the existence of a deity who can do such things and wants to, but an extraordinarily long and detailed manipulation of historical events (think of how much stage-setting just the miracle at Cana involves). The third requires nothing more than the familiar facts of human creativity, love of narrative, and deep concern with both fundamental and quotidian dimensions of human existence. I claim that the third option wins this contest hands-down. Of course, it does leave us with the extraordinarily intriguing question just what, at such a great distance in time, space, and culture, an author might have meant when they spoke of a God, Yahweh, performing these particular miracles. To put flesh and bones on the third hypothesis (as must be done to give it bite), one must show how the SAs in a miracle (or other) narrative encode a message that would have found a ready audience, would have impressed them with its proper significance, and, in the context of a millenarian movement, would have moved them to act on behalf of a proposed solution to some pressing problem(s). Just how *that* story goes for the Cana episode—and for the other Biblical miracle narratives—must be deferred for another occasion.

18| THE RESURRECTION OF JESUS NEVER TOOK PLACE

BY JOHN W. LOFTUS

Skeptics Society founder and President Michael Shermer informs us what we're dealing with here:

The principle of proportionality demands extraordinary evidence for extraordinary claims. Of the approximately 100 billion people who have lived before us, all have died and none have returned, so the claim that one (or more) of them rose from the dead is about as extraordinary as one will ever find.[1]

In this chapter I'm going to argue that the case for the bodily resurrection of Jesus fails to meet the reasonable standard of extraordinary evidence required.[2] There are too many problems with it, which has nothing to do with a skeptical presumption or anti-superstitious bias. The texts themselves produce this doubt. When additionally coupled with the other chapters in this anthology, rejecting the resurrection miracle is something every informed reasonable person should do.

The first hurdle apologists must leap over is whether Jesus existed, for the probability that he didn't exist significantly reduces the case for

---

[1] Michael Shermer, "What Would It Take to Prove the Resurrection?" Scientific American, URL: https://www.scientificamerican.com/article/what-would-it-take-to-prove-the-resurrection/
[2] This chapter is a significant revision of Chapter 21 "On the Resurrection of Jesus" found in my book, *Why I became an Atheist*, 2nd ed., (Amherst, NY: Prometheus Books, 2012). Unfortunately, the word count is cut by half.

491

his resurrection. On this see the writings of Jesus mythicists like Richard Carrier, Earl Doherty, David Fitzgerald, Raphael Lataster, Robert M. Price, R.G. Price, Frank Zindler, and others. In what follows I'll grant for the sake of discussion that the gospel traditions go back to a failed Jewish apocalyptic prophet we'll call Jesus.[3]

WHAT WE DO AND DON'T HAVE

When it comes to the evidence Jesus rose from the dead let's first consider what we don't have, but would like to, most of which even Christian apologist Michael R. Licona admits.[4] We don't have anything written directly by Jesus or any of his original disciples. We have no written responses to Jesus from the Pharisees, Sadducees, scribes, or teachers of the law either. Jesus always had the last word in the disputes in the gospels—something I have never seen in any *real* religious debate. This shows us the anonymous gospel writers were spreading propaganda rather than producing the results of a disinterested investigation, despite what they claim (i.e., Luke 1:1–4). We don't have anything written by the apostle Paul before he converted, which would tell us about the church he was persecuting, nor anything written by the Jewish leaders in response to Paul's preaching. We have nothing written by the Romans about Jesus, the content of his preaching, why he was killed, or what they thought about claims that he had been resurrected.

We have no collaborating objective evidence for this extraordinary miraculous claim. We have no independent corroboration of the Star of Bethlehem at the birth of Jesus,[5] nor that the veil of the temple was torn in two at Jesus' death (Mark 15:38), nor that darkness came "over the whole land" from noon until three in the afternoon (Mark 15:33), nor that "the sun stopped shining" (Luke 23:45), nor that there was an

---

[3] On this see my chapter 12 in *The Christian Delusion* (2010), "At Best Jesus was a Failed Apocalyptic Prophet," pp. 316-344.
[4] Michael R. Licona, *The Resurrection of Jesus: A New Historiographical Approach* (Downers Grove, IL: IVP Academic, 2010), pp. 275, 587–88.
[5] On this see Aaron Adair's chapter 13 in my anthology *Christianity in the Light of Science* (2016).

earthquake at his death (Matt. 27:51, 54), with another "violent" one the day he arose from the grave (Matt. 28:2). Could these events really have occurred without any corroborating evidence? Even though there's some archaeological evidence *consistent* with the biblical tales, there is nothing that *confirms* any miracle.[6]

There's no corroborating evidence that Old Testament saints were raised to life at the death of Jesus who subsequently "went into the holy city and appeared to many people" (Matt. 27:52–53) but were never heard from again. Why is there no record of these zombies apart from what we find in Matthew's gospel? How were they identified? What stories did they tell? Why did no one write them down? How did they die? Where are their tombs? Why didn't Jewish philosopher Philo of Alexandria (20 BCE–50 CE) or Jewish historian Flavius Josephus (37–100 CE) mention them? They were both contemporaries of the time period. These silences are telling. Neither is there any objective corroborating evidence that Jesus was raised from the dead, since the Shroud of Turin is now considered a fake.[7]

All we have is ancient second- third- fourth-handed testimonial evidence as told to us by four authors in four Gospels, plus Paul. None of these gospels were written by eyewitnesses to the resurrection of Jesus since there were no actual eyewitnesses to his rising up from the dead on the first Sunday Morning. We don't have the actual testimonies of Peter or John or "doubting Thomas" or the women at Jesus' tomb or the two men on the road to Emmaus, or the more than five hundred brethren Paul claimed saw the risen Jesus at the same time. We don't have any post-Easter words from Jesus either. With the exception of Paul, who claimed to have seen the resurrected Jesus but tells us nothing much at all about the Jesus who walked the earth, everything we're told comes from someone who was not an eyewitness. This is hearsay evidence as filtered through decades of oral story-telling and re-telling that

---

[6] See Part 4, "Science and the Bible," in my anthology *Christianity in the Light of Science,* (2016).
[7] The best resource for this is Joe Nickell's chapter 15 on "The Turin Shroud: A Postmortem" for my anthology, *Christianity in the Light of Science* (2016).

presumably went from Aramaic to Greek, then compiled together in the four gospels, traditionally known as the Four Evangelists, who in turn sought to convince their targeted audiences by painting different portraits of Jesus. In other words, everything we read in the Gospels *depends entirely on authors who were not there and did not see any of it for themselves,* who had selected their oral stories then edited them to fit into their specific portraits of Jesus in mind. Despite these facts, Licona says "what we do have is good."[8] I think not. Not by a long shot.

THE EARLIEST TESTIMONIES

The earliest testimonies about Jesus are purportedly found in a few of Paul's letters, in Q (German for "source"), the Gospel of Mark, and the Gospel of Thomas. Paul's early letters are our earliest sources, which include I Thessalonians, Galatians and I Corinthians, written between 50 CE to about 54 CE. The Gospel of Mark is our earliest gospel source, written about 66–70 CE. Most scholars think this gospel was based in part on a conjectured source they call Q, from which later gospels sometimes plagiarized word for word—and embellished. But there is no evidence it actually existed, argues Mark Goodacre who makes a very strong case against its existence.[9] Richard Carrier argues the Gospel of Matthew is Q. "In fact all the evidence for Q is 100% consistent with Q being a redaction (a later edition) of Mark...And that means Q sounds pretty much exactly like Matthew. In fact, it's almost certainly Matthew."[10] Then finally there's the Gospel of Thomas, discovered near Nag Hammadi, Egypt, in December 1945. Although scholars generally date Gospel of Thomas in the mid- to late-2nd century CE, a few of them think it was written in the 80's, fifty years after the death of Jesus.

---

[8] Licona, *The Resurrection of Jesus*, p. 275.
[9] Mark Goodacre, *The Case Against Q: Studies in Markan Priority and the Synoptic Problem* (Trinity Press International, 2002).
[10] See "Richard Carrier On the Non-Existence of Q" on my blog, URL: http://www.debunking-christianity.com/2018/12/richard-carrier-on-non-existence-of-q.html

Given that the earliest testimony in the earliest documents should be the best testimony, what do we have? We can quickly eliminate two of these sources as being nonexistent, irrelevant and/or late testimony. Q probably never existed prior to the Gospel of Mark in the first place, but even if it did, there's no resurrection claim to be found in it. The Gospel of Thomas was probably written too late to be reliable, but even if it's early, there's no resurrection claim to be found in it either. This means we can reduce the earliest testimony of the resurrection of Jesus to just two authors, Paul and the anonymous author of Mark's Gospel. So the extraordinary resurrection miracle claim hangs on just two early testimonies, from two ancient authors, neither of whom actually saw Jesus rise up from the dead, and neither of whom touched him, or sat down with him for a face to face interview.

Before turning to Paul's testimony let's first consider what Mark's Gospel tells us. In Mark's Gospel Jesus doesn't appear to anyone after his death. All we have is an announcement by "a young man dressed in a white robe" that he had risen (Mark 16:5), and an implausible story about women who went to the tomb without any means to roll back the stone, who left it afraid to tell anyone what they had seen, inexplicably disobeying the very command of the young man who told them to "tell his disciples and Peter" (Mark 16:6–8). In Mark, Jesus never reappears before the final curtain is dropped. The play ends abruptly. We don't know whether we should offer any applause. We sit in shocked silence, not knowing if the play is really over. There are no sightings or visions of the risen Jesus. The last time Jesus was seen was when the stone was purportedly put in front of the tomb. The women were told Jesus had risen from the grave but were not given any evidence that he had, because he never appeared to them. The rest of the Gospel of Mark from 16:9 onward, was added a century or more later in order to supply the missing appearances, which never took place in the original gospel.[11]

---

[11] The longer ending of Mark (16:9–20) is now universally rejected as a forgery that was added later to the original Gospel. Bruce Metzger, *A Textual Commentary on the Greek New Testament* (London: United Bible

When it comes to the earliest complete Greek manuscripts of the gospel of Mark, and the New Testament as a whole, we have two full manuscripts, the Codex Vaticanus and the Codex Sinaiticus, both dated to the fourth century CE, after three centuries of being copied by hand, and edited, which allowed for many variants. So not only do we not have any actual eyewitness testimonies, or eyewitness writings, we don't have any original writings either. What were the original documents like before being copied and edited by the scribes for their own doctrinal purposes?[12] We just can't say for sure.

Before moving on too quickly, we should note there are two other early testimonies that should be taken into consideration. They undercut the earliest Christian testimonies to the resurrection. There is the early testimony coming from the Jews, which most apologists ignore or forget. They lived in Palestine during the ministry of Jesus. They were beloved of their god, we're told. They believed in their god Yahweh and that he does miracles, and they knew their Old Testament prophecies. Yet the overwhelming majority of them did not believe Jesus raised up from the dead. How many Jews? This is hard to specify since numbers are generally exaggerated. The most plausible estimate of the first century Jewish population comes from a census of the Roman Empire during the reign of Claudius (48 CE) that counted nearly 7 million Jews. If we add in the Jews outside the Roman Empire in places like Babylon, the total first century Jewish population could have been 8 million. Jews living in Palestine during the ministry of Jesus are estimated to have been as many as 2.5 million. But as Catholic New Testament scholar David C. Sim argues, "Throughout the first century the total number of Jews in the Christian movement probably never exceeded 1,000 and by the end of

---

Societies, 1971), pp. 122–26. See also Richard Carrier's debate on that subject, URL: https://www.richard-carrier.info/archives/14921

[12] See Bart Ehrman, *Misquoting Jesus: The Story Behind Who Changed the Bible and Why* (NY: HarperOne, 2007) and his more scholarly treatment in *The Orthodox Corruption of Scripture: The Effect of Early Christological Controversies on the Text of the New Testament* (Oxford University Press, 2011).

the century the Christian church was largely Gentile."[13] So the Jews overwhelmingly rejected the resurrection of Jesus and the earliest form of Christianity. That explains why early Christian missionary gravitated to the Gentiles outside Palestine, most notably by the Apostle Paul.

The Christian response is that these Jews didn't want to believe because Jesus was not their kind of Messiah, a king who would throw off Roman rule. But then, where did they get that idea in the first place? They got it from their own Scriptures. And who supposedly inspired them? Their god. This means that even though their god loved them over all others, he purposely misled them, thereby condemning them to hell along with centuries of persecution as "Christ killers" *for correctly getting Old Testament prophecy right!*[14] Why should we believe if they didn't? I see no reason to do so.

There is also the type of testimony that David Hume argued cancels out Christian testimonies, which is his fourth supplement argument seen earlier in my ECREE chapter. Other similar kinds of virgin born dying and rising gods were floating around in the first century. The prolific apologist N. T. Wright acknowledges this when writing about these dying and rising gods that have "too many variations even to list."[15] Wright goes on to say these dying and rising gods were "intertwined, combined, separated out again and recombined." In fact, this is what the early church father Justin Martyr (103–165 CE) said when defending what

---

[13] David C. Sim, "How Many Jews Became Christians in the First Century: The Failure of the Christian Mission to the Jews *Hervormde Teologiese Studies* 61 (1/2) 2005): 417-440, which can be read online at http://www.hts.org.za/index.php/HTS/article/view/430/329
On the Jewish population of the first century see "Population," in *Encyclopedia Judaica*, vol. 13, and Magen Broshi, "Estimating the Population of Ancient Jerusalem," *Biblical Archaeological Review* 4, No. 2 (June 1978). Josephus estimates that at the fall of Jerusalem in 70 CE there were over one million Jewish fatalities (*The Jewish War* 6.9.3), whereas in northern Galilee, if we add up his figures, there were somewhere around three million Jews (*The Jewish War* 3.3.2). Alexandria, according to Philo, had a Jewish population of over one million (*Contra Flacum* 43).
To see why Jews didn't convert to Christianity one can look no further than Michael Alter's excellent book *The Resurrection: A Critical Inquiry* published by Xlibris in 2015, for it surely contains many of the same arguments.
[14] On prophecy see Part 2 of this book.
[15] N. T. Wright, *The Resurrection of the Son of God* (Minneapolis, MN: Fortress Press, 2003), p. 80.

he believed about Jesus to the Romans, and it's simply inconceivable he would have said this if it wasn't true: "When we say that the Word, who is our teacher, Jesus Christ the firstborn of God, was produced without sexual union, and that he was crucified and died, and rose again, and ascended to heaven, we propound *nothing new or different from what you believe* regarding those whom you consider sons of Jupiter [i.e., the supreme Roman deity]."[16]

Justin Martyr also insisted that "the Devil" introduced "Asclepius as the raiser of the dead" in order to undermine the Christian message in advance.[17] Yep, before it was claimed Jesus resurrected. Where did the idea of resurrection come from? Richard Carrier explains, "The idea of a future resurrection for all the saved actually derives from pagan Zoroastrianism, then the Persian state religion, which had influenced many popular cults in the Roman Empire (including Mithraism and religious Stoicism). And indeed it's from them that the Jews got the idea in the first place, having picked it up when they were in captivity in Persia several centuries before Christianity began."[18]

THE TESTIMONY OF PAUL

This leaves Paul, the only known author to testify he had seen the risen Jesus. In the earliest written account we have of the resurrection, dated around 55 CE Paul writes:

> For I delivered to you as of first importance what I also received, that Christ died for our sins in accordance with the scriptures, that he was buried, that he was raised on the third day in accordance with the scriptures, and that he appeared to Cephas, then to the twelve. Then he appeared to more than five hundred brethren at

---

[16] Justin Martyr, *Apology* 1.21. Richard C. Miller defends Justin Martyr's statement with a plethora of tales and stories of that era in his scholarly book, *Resurrection and Reception in Early Christianity* (Routledge; 2017).
[17] Justin Martyr, *Dialogue of Justin and Trypho the Jew* 69. See also Origen, *Contra Celsum* 3.24.
[18] See Richard Carrier's chapter 2, "Christianity's Success Was Not Incredible," in my anthology, *The End of Christianity* (2011), pp. 53–74.

one time, most of whom are still alive, though some have fallen asleep. Then he appeared to James, then to all the apostles. Last of all, as to one untimely born, he appeared also to me (1 Corinthians. 15:3–8).

Again, let's note what we don't find here. There are no angels or women eyewitnesses, nor is Joseph of Arimathea one of them, people who would all be important to mention in an over-all case for the resurrection of Jesus. Let's take a closer look.

"For I delivered to you as of first importance what I also received…"

Paul is handing down to the Corinthians an earlier church tradition or creed. The major problem with his statement is that in his letter to the Galatians Paul denies he ever received his gospel from anyone else, for he says, "The gospel I preached is not of human origin. I did not receive it from any man, nor was I taught it; rather, I received it by revelation from Jesus Christ" (Gal. 1:11–12). So, either he received his gospel from earlier church tradition, or from private revelation. Which is it?

I think we can figure it out. Elsewhere Paul says he received it from visions. In 2 Corinthians 12:1–7 Paul is clearly talking about himself and claiming he had a plurality of visions and surpassing revelations. That's why he rhetorically asks, "Have I not seen Jesus our Lord?" (1 Cor. 9:1) Whether or not he's describing his experience on the Damascus road is beside the point. When people in the Corinthian church disagreed with his first letter and denied he was a legitimate apostle, Paul responded by asserting he had received a number of revelations from Jesus himself that were supposed to legitimize the gospel he preached. Who can dispute him if that's the case, right?

Paul and the Corinthian believers were visionaries, based on the prophecy of Joel 2:28, as quoted in Acts 2:17: "your young men shall see visions." They were convinced they were receiving divine messages from Jesus and expressed these revelations in church worship through the "spiritual gifts" of divine "wisdom," "knowledge," "prophecy," or "tongues" (1 Cor. 12:7–10). The book of Acts describes several of Paul's visions in 16:9–10; 18:9; 22:17–18; and 23:11. We also hear of another one in Galatians 2:2. Paul repeatedly speaks of "revelations" that he passed down to the church (1 Cor. 2:13; 7:40; 14:37). He even says he learned about the Lord's Supper from "the Lord" himself (1 Cor. 11:23). G. A. Wells comments, "According, then, to Paul, the risen Jesus personally told him that he, Jesus, had, during his earthly life, instituted the Eucharist in this way,"[19] and says: "One can easily envisage how all manner of rulings and doctrines could have emerged on such a basis, and in time be ascribed not to the risen Jesus but to the earthly Jesus."[20] In this Paul was following the example of Jesus, who was a visionary himself, who's quoted as saying he saw "Satan fall from heaven like a flash of lightning" (Luke 10:18). The author of Revelation additionally claimed to have a vision during which the glorified Jesus dictated seven letters to seven early churches taking up two whole chapters (2–3). Anyone could claim such things. Why should we believe anyone who claims such things?

"that Christ died for our sins in accordance with the scriptures..."

I have found nothing in the Old Testament that can legitimately be considered a specific prophecy about Jesus dying on the cross for our sins. It's just not there in the original contexts. In fact, given the way the Gospel writers misused prophecy it's more likely that they constructed many of the details of his death from Old Testament passages, and they did so in part to exonerate the Romans and to blame the Jews.[21]

In Luke 24:25–27 we find Jesus admonishing his two doubting companions on the road to Emmaus. There we read: "And beginning with Moses and all the Prophets, he explained to them what was said in all the Scriptures concerning himself." What passages? The Psalms? Which ones? They are basically prayers in times of suffering and praises

---

[19] G. A. Wells, *Cutting Jesus Down to Size: What Higher Criticism Has Achieved and Where It Leaves Christianity* (Chicago: Open Court, 2009), p. 9.
[20] Ibid., p. 8.
[21] On this, see John Dominic Crossan, *Who Killed Jesus: Exposing the Roots of Anti-Semitism in the Gospel Story of the Death of Jesus* (New York, HarperSanFrancisco, 1995).

to God. They also include condemnations of enemies. But there is literally nothing about Psalms 22 or 69 that have anything to do with the sufferings of a Messiah, much less about Jesus. Contextually these two Psalms are prayers of someone who is suffering and asking for God's help, even though they are misapplied in the Gospel stories of the trial and crucifixion of Jesus (Matt. 27:34, 35, 43, 46). The way they are used looks exactly as if the details about the death of Jesus were created from them. The same thing goes for the suffering servant of Isaiah 53, which describes the sufferings of Israel, god's servant (see Isaiah 49:3 for the context). There's nothing in the Old Testament about a suffering Messiah. It cannot be found. That's why the Jews rightly rejected Jesus as their Messiah.

"that he was buried..."

These words have drawn a lot of attention. As the earliest writer of the gospel Paul simply says Christ was buried. He doesn't tell us where Jesus was buried because he didn't know. So much for the empty tomb! It would've been a great addition to the apologist's case had Paul mentioned it. For if there was a verifiable empty tomb it would need an explanation. Yet, Paul failed to mention the most important fact used by Christian apologists. Apologists today stress there was early testimony of tomb, that Jesus was laid in it, and that he was raised out of it. Paul didn't think much of this apologetic because he didn't need it for his faith. Paul's Christianity probably didn't need a bodily resurrection.

Byron McCane has argued that Jesus was given a dishonorable burial based upon Jewish customs of that day, not the kind of honorable burial in a special tomb described in later gospels. McCane goes on to argue the body of Jesus was placed in "the Jewish graveyard of the condemned, in disgrace."[22] Richard Carrier cites the Jewish Mishna tractate (*Sanhedrin* 6.5e–f) the Talmud (*Sanhedrin* 47a) and other sources that indicate criminals should not be buried with the righteous. They are to be buried in the graveyard of the condemned, and there "were no

---

[22] Byron McCane, *Roll Back the Stone: Death and Burial in the World of Jesus* (Harrisburg, PA: Trinity Press International, 2003), pp. 89–108.

apparent exceptions made for a just execution by a Gentile government, particularly when the Sanhedrin had already condemned the man, since that meant his death was 'merited' in the eyes of Jewish law."[23]

"that he was raised on the third day..."

If Christ "was raised," as Paul says, then what did he think he was talking about? He writes more about it later in the chapter:

> But someone will ask, 'How are the dead raised? With what kind of body will they come?' How foolish! What you sow does not come to life unless it dies. When you sow, you do not plant the body that will be, but just a seed, perhaps of wheat or of something else. But God gives it a body as he has determined, and to each kind of seed he gives its own body. (15:35–37).

David Edwards reminds us "in the ancient world it was believed that a seed dies in the ground (cf. John 12:24)."[24] Then out of the ground comes a *spiritual body*, Paul says (v. 44). "There are heavenly bodies and there are earthly bodies" (v. 40). "Flesh and blood cannot inherit the kingdom of God, nor does the perishable inherit the imperishable" (v. 50). Elsewhere Paul wrote that "if the earthly tent we live in is destroyed, we have a building from God, an eternal house in heaven, not built by human hands (2 Cor. 5:1–8). In Philippians (3:20–21) Paul tells us that someday Christ will "transform our lowly bodies so that they will be like his glorious body."

The Gospel writers don't help much. What little Jesus purportedly said about the resurrection leads us to think both he and Paul shared the same view. Jesus said there is no marriage in heaven because believers "will be like the angels in heaven" from which they "will shine like stars" (Mark 12:24–27; Matt. 13:43). What's it like to be an angel anyway? The resurrection body of Jesus was a very strange one. In later gospels Jesus' body was one that could be touched (Luke 24:39, John 20:27) and could eat fish (Luke 24:42–43). But it could also pass through walls

---

[23] Richard Carrier, "The Burial of Jesus in Light of Jewish Law," in Robert Price and Jeffery Jay Lowder (Amherst, NY: Prometheus Books, 2005), p. 381.

[24] David Edwards (with John R.W. Stott) *Evangelical Essentials* (Downers Grove, IVP, 1989), p. 207.

(John 20:19, 26), or appear out of thin air (Luke 24:36), then disappear at will (Luke 24:31, 51). What kind of body was this? Who really knows?

Who can really make any sense of this? No wonder there is such a debate over it. Evangelicals are sure as sure can be that the resurrection of Jesus was a bodily one despite this debate, and despite the massive philosophical objections to a bodily resurrection itself.[25]

Historian Robert Grant is sure: "No word in this account [1 Corinthians 15:3–8] suggests that the appearances of Jesus were other than 'spiritual': it was not the 'flesh and blood' of Jesus which the witnesses saw...what [Paul] saw, and what he believes other Christians saw was the 'spiritual body' of Jesus."[26] Of course, there is no measurable difference between a spiritual body and no body at all.

Liberals like Bishop John Shelby Spong argue,

> There is no sense at all in Paul of a physical resurrection of Jesus back into the life of this world. God did not, for this apostle, raise Jesus from the grave to life on this earth. Rather, for Paul, God raised Jesus from death into God's presence; from the grave to God's right hand...The essential thing to note about Paul's understanding of the appearances to him is that it was identical with every other appearance on his list. That is, it was not a physical, historical encounter but a revelatory manifestation of the living Christ from heaven."[27]

Atheists like Richard Carrier concur, that Paul's understanding of Jesus' resurrection didn't require a resurrected body, but that independent from Paul and later in time, the author of Mark invented the story of the empty tomb. Mark did this, as other biblical authors did, making

---

[25] Which I summed up in my chapter 21 on the resurrection, in *Why I Became an Atheist*, 2nd edition.
[26] *Journal of Religion* 28 (1948), 125.
[27] John Shelby Spong, *Resurrection: Myth or Reality* (HarperOne, 1995), pp. 50, 53, said:
There is no sense at all in Paul of a physical resurrection of Jesus back into the life of this world. God did not, for this apostle, raise Jesus from the grave to life on this earth. Rather, for Paul, God raised Jesus from death into God's presence; from the grave to God's right hand...The essential thing to note about Paul's understanding of the appearances to him is that it was identical with every other appearance on his list. That is, it was not a physical, historical encounter but a revelatory manifestation of the living Christ from heaven.

the empty tomb a metaphor symbolizing either the corpse of Jesus or the ascension of Jesus. He writes,

> the empty tomb story originated as a symbol, not a historical fact. It then became the subject of legendary embellishment over the ensuing generations, eventually becoming an essential element in the doctrine of a particular sect of Christians, who spurned Paul's original teachings, and insisted on a resurrection of the flesh instead.[28]

Others like Robert Conner have argued that the resurrection tale is a ghost story. We know the New Testament authors believed in ghost stories (Matt. 14:25–26; Luke 24:37). Was the resurrection tale of Jesus one of them? Conner:

> When it came time to tell the central story of Christianity, to explain how and why a man came back from the grave, the New Testament writers used the only resources available to them: the language and frames of reference current in their culture—the culture of Judaism and the Old Testament, and the wider Greco–Roman culture in which Judaism was embedded. So it's hardly surprising that we've encountered visions in the New Testament similar to stories of visions from Greco–Roman sources, or that terms from the nearly ubiquitous mystery cults find their way into the letters of Paul and his imitators. That common elements of ghost lore should also appear in stories of Jesus, returned from the grave to make a brief appearance to his disciples, is less surprising still.[29]

Conner goes on to say,

> Every essential feature of the resurrection stories–sudden appearance and disappearance, the fear and confusion of witnesses, the empty tomb and tokens found within it, speaking, eating, and drinking as proof of life, tangible presence, the brevity of the

---

[28] "The Spiritual Body of Christ" in Price and Lowder, *The Empty Tomb*, pp. 158–59.
[29] Conner, *Apparitions of Jesus: The Resurrection as Ghost Story*, (Tellectual LLC, 2018), p. 153.

appearances, the display of pre-mortem wounds, encouraging and admonishing—is also found in contemporary Greco–Roman ghost stories.[30]

At the very least, as David Edwards admits, "the long dispute of the scholars shows that it is uncertain whether or not Paul believed in the physical resurrection of Jesus."[31] How uncertain Edwards didn't say, but reasonable people must always think exclusively in terms of the probabilities here, never in terms of certainties. Since the resurrection apologetic depends on Jesus having a resurrected body, then given the philosophical objections and these alternative views, the resurrection apologetic cannot be sufficiently probable. For nothing less than testimony considered to be 100% probable can make the resurrection of Jesus' body *equally probable* given the regularities of the laws of nature where dead people stay dead..

"in accordance with the scriptures…"

Just as there are no prophecies about a suffering Messiah in the Old Testament, there are also no prophecies about him being resurrected from the grave, none. Just try to find one in the original context in the Old Testament. None exist. There is Psalm 16:8–10, which in Acts 2:25–28 and again in Acts 13:35 is interpreted as being fulfilled in Jesus' resurrection. There we read King David's prayer that he will not die from a sickness. We read of him saying:

Therefore my heart is glad and my tongue rejoices;
my body also will rest secure,
because you will not abandon me to the realm of the dead,
nor will you let your faithful one see decay.

If this is a genuine Psalm of King David, he's not talking about his death and resurrection at all. The original meaning of this passage was King David's prayer for recovery from sickness. He's praying that his God will not let him die. The very first verse of this Psalm is a prayer for

---

[30] Ibid.
[31] Edwards (with Stott), *Evangelical Essentials*, p. 202.

safety: "Keep me safe, my God, for in you I take refuge." This is the context: his health and being kept safely away from death. It's not about a hope in resurrection after death, and it's emphatically not about a future Messiah when read in its context. For if David had died then God did not keep him safe.

We are told Jesus himself repeatedly predicted he would die and be resurrected (in Mark 8:31; 9:31, 10:32b–34). But as fellow blogger Franz Kiekeben asks, if Jesus really did predict his resurrection then,

> There would have been quite a few people hanging around the tomb waiting to see what would happen. Even the disciples would most likely have come out of hiding for a chance to see the wondrous event—the single most important one of their entire lives—especially if they could have done so by blending into the crowd...Instead, according to the scriptures, no one went to see if he would come out as he supposedly predicted. Not a single person could be bothered to do so.

The point Kiekeben makes is the shocking truth that these prophecies were made up after the fact, that some of what we read in the gospels is not true.[32] Don't be so shocked, there's plenty of evidence of these kind of redactions, like the description of church discipline before there was a church (Matthew 16:17–20), the command of the Great Commission to evangelize the world before the Holy Spirit was given on Pentecost to help them (Matthew 28:18–20, see Acts 2), and the prediction

---

[32] "Did Jesus Predict the Resurrection?" By Franz Kiekeben at 1/30/2019, URL: http://www.debunking-christianity.com/2019/01/did-jesus-predict-resurrection.html. Robert Conner's take on this is characteristically interesting:

According to the gospels, the apostles witness the very public resurrection of the son of the widow of Nain (Luke 7:11-17), the more private raising of Jairus' daughter (Luke 8:49-57), the dramatic resurrection of Lazarus after three days in the tomb (John 11:1-44), and the crowds that subsequently gathered hoping to see Lazarus who Jesus has raised from the dead (John 12:9). Before calling Lazarus forth from the grave, Jesus declares, "I am the resurrection and the life." (John 11:25)

In spite of all this alleged first-hand, eyewitness experience, the apostles remain the Twelve Stooges, the dumbest yokels in all of yokeldom—they can't understand what Jesus means by 'rising from the dead' (Mark 9:32) even after the Master calls them aside and Jesus explains it all (Mark 10:32). See his series "So Just How Dumb Were the Disciples", at exchristian.net, URL: https://new.exchristian.net/search/label/Robert%20Conner

of Jesus that Peter would be martyred, which was written after he was dead and after it was clear Jesus had not come back in his generation as predicted (John 21:18–19).

"and that he appeared to Cephas, then to the twelve."

Cephas here is probably the apostle Peter. Paul claims Christ appeared to "the twelve." Something is definitely wrong since the twelve would have included Judas, who was dead by the time of this appearance by Jesus (Matt. 27:3–5; cf. Acts 1:18–19), and they had not yet picked a successor to replace him (Acts 1:21–26). The best understanding is that the person who betrayed Jesus was not one of the twelve apostles, which goes to the heart of the trustworthiness of the testimonial evidence of the gospels.[33]

"Then he appeared to more than five hundred brethren at one time..."

This statement of an even number of witnesses seems oddly out of place, claims G. A. Wells, "in a list which otherwise names only notable personages of Christian communities."[34] Because of this he suggests it could well be "post-Pauline," "for an appearance to five hundred was surely too good a piece of evidence to be ignored, and had it been early tradition it would presumably have surfaced in some form in the gospels, even though they, as later documents embodying later traditions, present a quite different account of the appearances from Paul's."[35] Should they have believed Paul just because he said so? Should we? After all we're talking about an extraordinary type of extraordinary claim here, which requires sufficient objective corroborating evidence.

"Then he appeared to James..."

This is probably James, the brother of Jesus (Mark 6:3; Gal. 1:19) who was a "pillar" of the Jerusalem church (Gal. 2:9), a participant in

---

[33] On this issue I recommend Bart D. Ehrman, *The Lost Gospel of Judas Iscariot: A New Look at Betrayer and Betrayed* (Oxford: Oxford University Press, 2006), and John Shelby Spong, *The Sins of Scripture* (New York: HarperCollins, 2005), pp. 183–210.

[34] G. A. Wells, *Cutting Jesus Down to Size*, p. 149.

[35] Ibid.

the first church council (or councils) at Jerusalem (Gal. 2:1–10; cf. Acts 15:1–20), and the same man referred to in Acts 12:17, 15:13, and 21:18. But I cannot grant he was a nonbeliever prior to this appearance Paul speaks of, since the only place he is described as a nonbeliever is in John 7:5, which is a late and unreliable Gospel. People who are already believers are the most likely candidates for being visited by an appearance of Jesus anyway. That's what makes Paul's conversion the exception. If Paul thought for one moment this appearance to James converted him then he would have said so. However, if James was a nonbeliever prior to seeing the risen Jesus, then Jesus can convert people without abrogating their free will. If he can do this once with James (or twice, when Paul is included—or God with Moses or Gibeon), then he can do it a number of times, again and again. So why doesn't he do this?

"then to all the apostles."

The concept of "apostles" in the New Testament included the original twelve disciples, whom Paul mentioned earlier, but it also included several others, perhaps many others, probably missionaries. Who these apostles were we simply do not know.

So let's sum up so far. If this list of eyewitnesses is supposed to be considered evidence Jesus had been raised from the grave it just does not work, especially in those cases where he doesn't give us names. When it comes to the people Paul named, it seems highly improbable the Corinthians had personally met any of them. So why would the Corinthians believe Paul? Why should we do so today? I would have wanted to talk with a few or all of these so-called witnesses so that I could ask them some questions. I might even have wanted to withhold judgment because I had not personally seen the risen Jesus myself. Such a stance would be no more unreasonable than it would be to doubt Balaam's tale until he made his ass talk in front of us. When it comes to such a claim as this, we should all be doubting Thomases who would also doubt the story of doubting Thomas (John 20:24–29).

A parallel case might be the golden plates Joseph Smith claimed the angel Moroni led him to discover, which he "translated," producing the

Book of Mormon. Smith carefully chose eleven men beside himself who became "eyewitnesses" to these plates, and their "testimonies" are found in the front of modern editions of the Book of Mormon. Their testimony is that they "beheld and saw the plates and the engravings thereon" and that they "know of a surety that the said Smith has got the plates of which we have spoken." Let's say this is all we know. Is it enough to believe? Wouldn't we want to know more about who these men were and why they claimed what they did, rather than simply trust their testimony? We would simply want to investigate it for ourselves. We would want to know what they knew and how they knew it, if they knew anything at all. Surely it would be important to know, if we could, that all the witnesses were family, close friends, or financial backers of Joseph Smith, which was the case. It would also be important to know, if we could, that they didn't actually physically see these plates but rather saw them in visions, since they were visionaries, some of whom recanted because of this, which is also the case.[36]

This is what we would want to know when it comes to Paul's eyewitnesses to the risen Jesus. But we cannot know the answers to our questions because we are separated in time from them. Even if we grant these people were eyewitnesses, how do we know they were not duped? How do we know they really saw Jesus and not just a vision of him that did not correspond to objective reality? How do we know they all told the same story of what they had seen? Would their testimonies be inconsistent with the others? Did any of them recant? How do we know they didn't go along with what others were saying just to belong within the evolving church community? People do this all the time. People can convince themselves of many things just to belong. Without independent corroborating evidence to believe them we must remain doubtful.

"Last of all, as to one untimely born, he appeared also to me."

The only record we have of Jesus' appearance to Paul is the incident on the Damascus Road that is recounted in Galatians 1 and probably

---

[36] On this, see David Persuitte, *Joseph Smith and the Origins of the Book of Mormon*, 2nd ed. (Jefferson, NC: McFarland, 2000).

fictionalized later in Acts 9, 22, and 26.[37] Paul says the appearance of Jesus to him was the same as Jesus' appearance to the others he mentions in this list. What did he see? There are discrepancies in these three accounts,[38] but Paul never claimed to have actually seen or touched Jesus in any of them. Perhaps at best he saw a bright light and heard a voice identifying itself as Jesus, and that's it. What scholars lead us to believe is that the word for "appeared" (*ophthē*) used in these accounts is an important clue for understanding what happened. According to Willi Marxsen, "What is being spoken of is a vision."[39] The texts in Acts even say as much, for after Saul (Paul's name before becoming a Christian) described his experience on the Damascus Road, Ananias said to Saul afterward that Jesus "appeared [*ophthē*] to you on the road as you were coming here " (Acts 9:17). In Acts 26:19, after recounting his experience to King Agrippa, Paul says: "So, King Agrippa, I did not prove disobedient to the heavenly vision" (*optasia*, the noun form of *ophthē*). Given that Paul was a visionary, the visionary understanding of the word is a given. This word, *ophthē*, is also used in the Greek Septuagint translation of the Hebrew Old Testament to describe appearances of god and angels (Gen. 12:7; Exod. 3:2; 6:2–3). It is also used in Luke's Gospel about Zechariah's vision of the angel Gabriel (Luke 1:22), Abraham's vision of God (Acts 7:2), and several times in the epistles to describe Jesus' appearances (1 Cor. 9:1, 2 Cor. 12:1–4).

Paul's experience of Jesus at best was a vision, like other visions he claimed to have. So it can be understood the witnesses he lists in 1 Corinthians 15 had "a vision" of Jesus too. These types of things, if they happened, are *private subjective experiences*. Why should anyone who did

---

[37] Richard Carrier argues, successfully I might add, that much of what we find in the book of Acts is fictionalized history. See his lecture "Richard Carrier's Lecture On 'Acts as Historical Fiction'" on my blog: http://www.debunking-christianity.com/2015/12/richard-carriers-lecture-on-acts-as.html

[38] On this, see Dan Barker, *Godless: How an Evangelical Preacher Became One of America's Leading Atheists* (Berkeley, CA: Ulysses Press, 2008), pp. 243–50.

[39] Willi Marxsen, *The Resurrection of Jesus of Nazareth*, trans. Margaret Kohl (Philadelphia: Fortress Press, 1970), p. 69.

not have such an experience accept the testimony of another? I see no reason why we should.

What doesn't count as evidence for the truth of the resurrection are believers who were transformed by their visions and willing to die for their beliefs. Many people who weren't eyewitnesses of Jesus were willing to die for their beliefs too. Christian heretics were also willing to die for their beliefs. It just means they were sincere, but plenty of people have died for sincerely held beliefs that were wrong, like the 911 suicide mission of nine Muslims. Nonetheless, the supposed martyrdom of the early Christians was a fabrication according to Candida Moss in her book, *The Myth of Persecution: How Early Christians Invented a Story of Martyrdom*, which goes toward the trustworthiness of the early church as a whole.[40]

THE GOSPEL TESTIMONIES COMPARED

When we compare the four Gospel accounts there are many discrepancies. There are incompatibilities with how many women came to the tomb (1, 2, or 3 plus "others"), when they came ("while it was still dark" or "just after sunrise"), why they came ("to look at the tomb" or "to anoint the body with spices"), who they saw (one angel, two angels, a man dressed in white, or Jesus himself), what was said, who said what, who else came (Peter, or both Peter and John), who saw the resurrected Jesus first (Peter or Mary Magdalene), and what they did as they left the tomb ("they said nothing to anyone" or "they ran to tell his disciples"). Matthew seems to imply the stone was rolled away in the presence of the women who came to the tomb, while Mark, Luke, and John say the women arrived to discover the stone had already been rolled away. Matthew and Mark have Jesus on his way to Galilee by the time the women arrive at the tomb, while Luke and John have Jesus in Jerusalem on the night of the first Easter Sunday. Luke's Gospel says the disciples "stayed

---

[40] Published by HarperOne, 2013.

continually in the temple" because Jesus had told them to wait in Jerusalem until they had been "clothed with power from on high," whereas Matthew has Jesus appearing and commissioning the eleven in Galilee. John's Gospel simply says the disciples returned to their fishing trade in Galilee. It mentions an appearance of Jesus in Galilee and says: "This was now the third time Jesus appeared to his disciples" (John 21:14). But Paul's list and order of appearances (1 Cor. 15:5–8) doesn't square with John's order of appearances. Matthew and Luke have women visiting the tomb, encountering angels, and telling the others what they had seen, while John has the women encountering no angels on their first visit and relaying no message. Luke mentions that Jesus appeared on the first Easter Sunday to eleven men (Luke 24:13, 36), which would include "doubting Thomas" (minus Judas), although John denies Thomas was there (John 20:19–24).

It's worth noting that even among those who it's claimed saw the risen Jesus, "some doubted" (literally "they doubted", Matt. 28:17). How is that really possible? What is it that made them doubt? And if John's Gospel is correct that Jesus was given a proper Jewish burial (John 19:40), it is inexplicable why the women came on Sunday morning to finish the job (Mark 16:1), since they had supposedly watched this burial in the first place (Mark 15:47).

One would think the gospel testimonies should be reasonable and consistent if we are to believe a resurrection miracle took place. But they aren't, by a long shot. David Edwards concludes: "It has proved impossible to construct a fully harmonized version of the resurrection stories, despite many attempts to do so . . . the stories as given constitute not a jigsaw puzzle but an insoluble mystery."[41] Willi Marxsen agrees: "The conclusion is inescapable: a synchronizing harmony of the different accounts of the resurrection proves to be impossible."[42] Bishop John Shelby Spong adds: "When we embrace all of their versions in our minds at one

---

[41] Edwards and Stott, *Evangelical Essentials*, p. 205.
[42] Willi Marxsen, *The Resurrection of Jesus of Nazareth*, p. 74.

time, we discover that all we have in the Bible about Easter is an inconsistent, contradictory, mutually exclusive witness."[43]

NATURAL EXPLANATIONS OF THE RESURRECTION

There is just no good reason to think Jesus arose from the dead. The testimony we find in the New Testament is of poor quality to think nature gave a dead man up from the dead. It didn't come directly to us from the eyewitnesses, nor authors who were eyewitnesses or documents we can say were the originals. Etcetera. One does not have to embrace a skeptical presumption to think this. Given that there is no corroborative objective evidence it's a slam dunk case for reasonable people to reject it, given the arguments of David Hume.

So, if a miracle didn't occur, what happened? There are several natural theories about what happened. If any of them has a degree of improbability, they are still more probable than that Jesus was bodily raised from the dead by God. Perhaps there just isn't enough evidence to say what happened. After all, just because historians can tell us what did not happen at *Custer's Last Stand* does not mean they must tell us what did happen. Again, there just may not be enough evidence to say for sure. Bart Ehrman explains one possible scenario if the tomb of Jesus was empty:

> Our very first reference to Jesus' tomb being empty is in the Gospel of Mark, written forty years later by someone living in a different country who had heard it was empty. How would he know?...Suppose...that Jesus was buried by Joseph of Arimathea...and then a couple of Jesus' followers, not among the twelve, decided that night to move the body somewhere more appropriate...But a couple of Roman legionnaires are passing by, and catch these followers carrying the shrouded corpse through the streets. They suspect foul play and confront the followers, who pull their

---

[43] Spong, *Resurrection: Myth or Reality?* p. 105.

swords as the disciples did in Gethsemane. The soldiers, experts in swordplay, kill them on the spot. They now have three bodies, and no idea where the first one came from. Not knowing what to do with them, they commandeer a cart and take the corpses out to Gehenna, outside town, and dump them. Within three or four days the bodies have deteriorated beyond recognition. Jesus' original tomb is empty, and no one seems to know why.

Is this scenario likely? Not at all. Am I proposing this is what really happened? Absolutely not. Is it more probable that something like this happened than that a miracle happened and Jesus left the tomb to ascend to heaven? Absolutely! From a purely historical point of view, a highly unlikely event is far more probable than a virtually impossible one..."[44]

One theory has recently been defended by Kris Komarnitsky, author of *Doubting Jesus' Resurrection: What Happened in the Black Box?*[45] He has done an excellent job of showing what could have happened in an online post on Mathew Ferguson's blog titled, *The Rationalization Hypothesis: Is a Vision of Jesus Necessary for the Rise of the Resurrection Belief?*[46] I find it to be the most detailed defense of this theory, making it worth considering, complete with four real-life examples of it in history. He takes issue with the bereavement visionary hypothesis of the disciples, widely regarded as a plausible naturalistic explanation for the data, and argues instead for what he calls the cognitive-dissonance-induced rationalization hypothesis. The question he discusses is whether bereavement visions produced the belief that Jesus arose from the dead, or whether the resurrection belief came *first* due to cognitive dissonance reducing

---

[44] Bart Ehrman, *Jesus, Interrupted: Revealing the Hidden Contradictions in the Bible* (NY: HarperOne, 2009), pages 171-179. For some more plausible conjectures, see the following books: John Hick, *The Metaphor of God Incarnate* (Louisville, KY: Westminster, 1993), pp. 23–26; Marcus Borg and N. T. White, *The Meaning of Jesus: Two Visions* (New York: HarperSanFrancisco, 1999), pp. 130–35; Gerd Lüdemann, *What Really Happened to Jesus?* (Philadelphia: Westminster, 1995); Price and Lowder, *The Empty Tomb*; and Spong, *Resurrection: Myth or Reality?* pp. 233–60, to mention a few.
[45] Published by Stone Arrow Books; 2 edition (February 1, 2014).
[46] URL: https://celsus.blog/2019/01/04/the-rationalization-hypothesis-is-a-vision-of-jesus-necessary-for-the-rise-of-the-resurrection-belief/

rationalizations, favoring the later. Go read it. Now! Forget the swoon theory that Jesus didn't actually die, the conspiracy theory that the disciples purportedly concocted to perpetrate a hoax, the impersonation theory that someone impersonated Jesus, or the unknown tomb theory where the disciples went to the wrong tomb.

CHRISTIAN PROCLAMATION AND THE AFTERMATH

When early Christians got the courage up, they would have gone into Jerusalem to announce what they had come to believe about Jesus—that he had risen from the dead. But the people in Jerusalem had some counterarguments. I think the best explanation for the textual evidence is that the theology of the church evolved as it responded to Jewish arguments against the resurrection of Jesus. We do not have any evidence to tell us about the controversies early believers had with the Jewish and Roman authorities and how they responded to them. That they had them is easy to imagine. In what order they came is harder to determine. Perhaps they came in a flurry of counterarguments that were continually being responded to with better arguments from the early Christians. We can only guess at the earliest counterarguments, since we don't know what the earliest Christians believed. One of the first ones was to ask where Jesus was buried. They didn't know. So, the anonymous Gospel of Mark was written to provide the answer. There was a tomb with a "very large" stone that covered the entrance (presumably to keep a dead body from being stolen?). It was a stone so large the women could not roll it away themselves (which is overkill)—that was found by them rolled away with the tomb empty (16:1–5). This is clearly a contrived tale since it sounds exactly like an apologetic for an empty tomb, and an explanation for why the initial readers hadn't heard of the empty tomb before. They hadn't heard of it because the women who saw it ran away, and "said nothing to anyone" (16:8). Ahhh, now we understand!

Mark's gospel accomplished its task to show there was an empty tomb. Apparently though, either real or imagined, the counterargument that the disciples stole the body did not go away. To counter this accusation Matthew's later gospel concocted an implausible story where Pilate was so concerned about an itinerant doomsday preacher Jesus arising from the dead that he placed guards at the tomb *a day later* (Matthew 27:62), who were there on Sunday to see Jesus arise from the dead. However, they were persuaded with money to tell Pilate a lie that the Jews, whom they generally hated, stole the body, not the disciples. Of course, the lie would be a cause for their deaths (Matthew 27:62–66; 28:11–15). Even the author of Luke didn't think that was a good tale. For though he says he researched thoroughly into the life of Jesus (Luke 1:1–4), he did not include it.

Another major Jewish argument was that Jesus did not fulfill Old Testament prophecy so he couldn't have been the coming Messiah. So Christians went in search of validation by grabbing any text, even if way out of context, to support their preaching. This is something already addressed by Robert Miller in an earlier chapter.[47]

Somewhere along the line, one Jewish counterargument was this: Either Jesus did not rise from the dead or he should be found walking around somewhere and should have to die again. As the Gospels kept making more and more corporeal claims about Jesus after his resurrection, they had to deal with this objection. So, Luke's Gospel came up with the answer, probably first seen in a dream or a vision. Jesus isn't walking around somewhere, nor has he died. Jesus ascended directly into heaven (Luke 24:50–53; Acts 1:9–11). This leads the whole trail of arguments and counterarguments to their logical conclusion. Unfortunately for Christians, at this point, the jig is up. For if Jesus bodily ascended back into heaven, then as Scott McKellar tells us, "In the course of his ascension, at around 15,000 feet, Jesus began to wish he had brought a sweater. At 30,000 feet he felt weak from lack of oxygen. By 100,000 his bodily fluids were boiling away from every orifice. If he ever

---

[47] See Robert Miller's chapter on helping Jesus fulfill prophecy in this book, along with my chapter 21 on the resurrection for *Why I Became an Atheist*, 2nd, ed.

did return, it would be as a fifty-pound lump of bone and frozen jerky."[48] This assumes an ancient three-tiered universe no one can believe today, with heaven above the earth and hell below. Such a view has been utterly shattered by cosmology and geology. Since the bodily resurrection of Jesus and his ascension into heaven hang together, modern science makes both claims exceedingly improbable to the point of refutation.

Conclusion

At every juncture of this study of the resurrection, there is some strong doubt about the ancient testimony we have of Jesus bodily raising from the dead. Apologists have become so desperate they have resorted to arguing that by selecting a set of minimal facts that skeptics and Christians both agree on can lead one to believe Jesus arose out of the grave. But it's precisely because of the multitude of issues they disagree with believers about that lead skeptics to reject that case. It would be like an anti-vaccination conspiracy theorist sweeping off the table everything reasonable then proclaim, "See, you should agree not to vaccinate your children." Professor Stephen Law states it succinctly and truthfully: "Anything based on faith, no matter how ludicrous, can be made to be consistent with the available evidence, given a little patience and ingenuity."[49]

It would seem if our eternal destiny were at stake god should've made the evidence rock solid for those of us who hear about it centuries later. But there isn't a god so he couldn't do this, because it's not the

---

[48] David Madison comments: "Digging for the spiritual meaning, apologists may say that the ascension is a metaphor for Christ's unity with the Father, or his full participation in the Holy Trinity—whatever. But that doesn't eliminate a big problem. If Jesus really existed, and really did resurrect bodily—his dead body started breathing again, blood flowed again, he walked out of the tomb—then what happened to that body? Whether it was active again for four or forty days—but it didn't leave Planet Earth—then Jesus died again. The 'spiritual' meaning of the ascension be damned: Christians have a dead-again Jesus on their hands. So his victory over death was...what, temporary? This theology fails to make any sense at all. On this key point alone, Christianity is falsified." ["What to Do about Your Dead-Again Jesus?" at http://www.debunking-christianity.com/2019/08/what-to-do-about-your-dead-again-jesus.html.
[49] Stephen Law, *Believing Bullshit* (Amherst: New York, Prometheus Books, 2011), p. 75.

case Jesus arose from the dead. What we have is a nearly airtight case against this faith-based miraculous claim. Jesus died on the cross. He did not bodily arise from the grave. His body has rotted away.

19| PAUL'S CHRISTIANITY

BY ROBERT CONNER

Generally speaking, I wouldn't advocate psychoanalyzing figures from the remote past—those sufficiently motivated to write their stories were often motivated to glorify or vilify their subjects as well, so the accounts must be read with caution. That said, given the self-revelation in his letters, Paul of Tarsus has proven an inviting target for armchair psychoanalysis. Without gratuitously speculating about the mental state of a person none of us ever met, it's worth looking at *what Paul said about himself* as well as what our secondary sources say about him. To use a term of art from psychology, Paul's letters can be considered an example of "self-reporting." That Paul's sanity had been called into question is strongly implied by his own letters: "for if we went crazy, [it was] for God, if we are sane, [it is] for you. For the love of Christ compels us…" Indeed, Paul often defends himself from accusations of mental defect and counters with ad hominem attacks against his opponents:

If only you would allow me some small *folly* (*aphrosunēs*)…I do not regard myself as inferior to the crackerjack apostles, for if I am ordinary in speech I am not inferior in knowledge as is clearly apparent to you in every way…for men like that are false apostles, dishonest workers, masquerading as apostles of Christ and no wonder for Satan transforms himself into an angel of light. It is no great thing therefore if his servants disguise themselves as servants of righteousness…Again I say let no one think me *of unsound mind* (*aphrona einai*), but if so, bear with me so I may brag about myself a little...Even if I am inclined to brag, I will not be *a fool* (*aphrōn*) because I will be speaking the truth but I refrain lest anyone think more of me than justified by what he sees in me or what he hears from me and on account of the transcendence of [my] revelations...I have become *a fool* (*aphrōn*). You compelled me. I ought to have been esteemed by you—I was not inferior to the crackerjack apostles even if I am nothing. To the contrary, I constantly performed the signs of an apostle in your midst, signs and wonders and powerful works.[1]

Paul's opponents are "false apostles...masquerading as apostles of Christ" and in case there is any doubt about who these minions of Satan are, Paul asks, "Are they Hebrews? So am I! Are they Israelites? So am I! Are they the seed of Abraham? So am I! Are they ministers of Christ? *I speak like a man deranged* (*paraphronōn lalō*)—I am even more so!"[2] His use of the verbal form of *paraphronesis*, "madness, delirium,"[3] could easily lead a skeptic to suspect that Paul was responding obliquely to claims by the "false apostles" that he'd lost his mind.

Evidently something about his demeanor made him a figure of ridicule and given the intensity of Paul's response it seems unlikely that his opponents merely claimed that he was "ordinary in speech." After all, Paul claimed to bear the "the marks of Jesus" (*ta stigmata tou Iēsou*),[4] to have received transcendent revelations, and performed "signs and wonders and powerful works," i.e., miracles.

"Am I not an apostle?" Paul asks, "Have I not seen Jesus our Lord?"[5] The term *aphrōn*, "fool," may include something more serious than inelegant speech or being socially inept—one lexicon offers, "want of

---

[1] 2 Corinthians 11:1, 5-6, 13-14, 16, 12:6-7, 11-12
[2] 2 Corinthians 11:13-14, 22-23.
[3] Franco Montanari, The Brill Dictionary of Ancient Greek, (Leiden: Brill, 2015), 1572.
[4] Galatians 6:17.
[5] 1 Corinthians 9:1.

mental sanity"[6] as a possible meaning and another, "unreasonable, senseless, crazed."[7] *Aphrōn* literally means *lacking reason* or *good sense*.

Paul's first ever encounter with Jesus appears to have been his visionary experience on the road to Damascus. Although Paul never directly mentions the episode in his letters, the assertion that he had "seen Jesus our Lord" is generally understood as referring to his vision on the road, retold three times in Acts. According to the "road account," which varies in the detail with each retelling, Paul saw a bright *light*,[8] heard the *voice* of Jesus,[9] *fell* to the ground,[10] remained *blind* for a period of three days,[11] and afterward remained convinced he was *God's chosen spokesman*.[12] We will skip the tedious and tendentious apologetic debate over the conflicting details of the stories—whether *phonē* means "voice" or just "sound," or whether *akouō* means "understand" or merely "hear." The episode is generally understood to describe Paul's conversion if "converted" is really the appropriate term since it assumes something like the Christianity Paul preached already existed.

At this point I must insert a few words of caution. The writer of Luke/Acts never identifies himself by name and there is no intrinsic evidence in his history to suggest that he ever met Jesus. All of the gospels are anonymous compositions—none of their authors are self-identified—and the attribution of the gospel to Luke, whoever he was, likely did not take place before the 2nd century. Whether "Luke" ever met Paul is open to question. A person named Luke is mentioned in Colossians,[13] but it is nearly certain that Paul didn't write Colossians. Luke is again mentioned in 2 Timothy,[14] but Paul did not write the letters to Timothy. The only mention of

---

[6] George Abbott-Smith, A Manual Greek Lexicon of the New Testament, 3rd ed, (Edinburgh: T&T Clark, 1950), 72.
[7] Montanari, op.cit., 360.
[8] Acts 9:3, 22:6, 26:13.
[9] Acts 9:4, 22:7, 26:13.
[10] Acts 9:4, 22:7, 26:14.
[11] Acts 9:8-9, 22:11.
[12] Acts 9:15, 22:14, 26:16.
[13] Colossians 4:14.
[14] 2 Timothy 4:11.

a person named Luke that comes from a genuine letter of Paul[15] is found in Philemon[16] where Luke is named along with Mark, Aristarchos, and Demas as one of Paul's "coworkers."

Paul's speeches in Acts are the compositions of the author of Luke/Acts, whoever he was, *not verbatim reports*, i.e., they are hardly history. In short, we cannot determine if the road-to-Damascus account attributed to Paul could, at least in theory, be traced back to a first-person account or if it was all simply a pious invention. Luke's reports about Paul are therefore not primary evidence. Indeed, the facticity of the whole trip-to-Damascus story, like so much of the rest of Acts, is suspect. In his widely-read study of Paul, Bornkamm concluded that he could "hardly have been present at the stoning of Stephen" and noted as well that Paul's authority "to drag the Christians in bonds before the Sanhedrin" is patently fictitious "because under the Roman administration the supreme [Sanhedrin] never possessed such a sphere of jurisdiction—Damascus is far beyond the frontiers of Judaea!"[17] It must be acknowledged that if the setting of the story is dubious, the core of the story is suspect as well. It is also worth mentioning, "that not a single passage in Luke's whole book [Acts] shows either knowledge of [Paul's] own letters or use made of them."[18] As one writer expressed it, "Like Tolkien's fairy-stories, the mythic narrative at the center of Christian belief concerns a 'secondary world'. This secondary world is constructed in the reader's imagination from her experience of the ordinary, everyday 'primary world', but it is believed to be even more real than the primary world is."[19]

Historical accuracy aside, based on the accounts in Acts several authors have suggested that Paul's conversion experience resulted from an epileptic

---

[15] Seven of the New Testament documents were indisputably written by Paul: Romans, 1 and 2 Corinthians, Galatians, Philippians, 1 Thessalonians and Philemon. Textual "breaks" in 2 Corinthians suggest that it may be a composite that preserves parts of two or as many as four original letters.
Ephesians, Colossians, and 2 Thessalonians, attributed to Paul, are of doubtful authenticity. The "pastoral" epistles, 1 Timothy, 2 Timothy, and Titus, were not written by Paul.
[16] Philemon 1:24.
[17] Güther Bornkamm, Paul, (New York: Harper & Row, 1971), 15.
[18] Ibid, xx.
[19] G. Aichele, "Two Fantasies on the Death of Jesus," Neotestamentica 26.2 (1992), 486.

seizure and a review of the literature shows that the connections between "religious sentiment," sudden religious conversion, and epilepsy have been recognized for at least two centuries,[20] particularly by William James in his landmark *The Varieties of Religious Experience*.[21] Recent studies have concluded that "the association between religiosity and [temporal lobe epilepsy] is supported by anatomic and functional bases."[22] Landsborough famously cited Paul's "ecstasy...[his] sense of unreality in relation to his body"—"in the body or out of the body, I do not know"[23]—as well as "[his] elaborate auditory sensations whose details cannot be recollected" as evidence of seizures. Landsborough regarded Paul's "ineffable" or "mysterious words" (*arrhēta rhēmata*)[24] as favoring a diagnosis of a temporal lobe seizure as well. Additionally, Paul's "increased concern with philosophical, moral and religious issues" and his "temporary blindness"[25] are also suggestive of temporal lobe seizures.

Ecstatic seizures or "ictal religious experiences" in the setting of epilepsy are known to include "autoscopic phenomena," or depersonalization, the sense of "leaving one's own body." In one documented case of persistent depersonalization it "took three days for [the patient's] body to be reunited with its soul."[26] In a study of ecstatic prophecy in the Old Testament, André notes, "inducement of the vision is not mentioned nor do we know in what state the prophet was when he saw his vision," but concludes, based on Ezekiel 3:22–27, "that the prophet was mute and paralyzed after a vision" and based on the description in Jeremiah 4:19 and 23:9 adds, "more extensive study of the material proves the dominance of paralytic reactions over vigorous movement of the

---

[20] Orrin Devinsky, "Religious experiences and epilepsy," Epilepsy and Behavior 4 (2003), 76.
[21] James, William, The Varieties of Religious Experience: A Study in Human Nature, (New York: Longman, Green & Company, 1902).
The emerging literature on "neurotheology" is large, complex, and rapidly expanding. Interested readers are referred to the articles cited for comprehensive bibliographies.
[22] Souza Tedrus, Gloria Maria de Almeida, et al., "Religiosity aspects in patients with epilepsy," Epilepsy and Behavior 50 (2015), 69.
[23] 2 Corinthians 12:3.
[24] 2 Corinthians 12:4.
[25] D. Landsborough, "St Paul and temporal lobe epilepsy," Journal of Neurology, Neurosurgery, and Psychiatry 50 (1987), 660-662.
[26] Orrin Devinsky & George Lai, "Spirituality and Religion in Epilepsy," Epilepsy and Behavior 12 (2008), 638.

body."[27] Even to a casual observer, being left mute or paralyzed suggests a neuro-psychiatric basis for "prophetic" visions and the fact that the outlandish predictions of Christian "prophets" predictably fail to come true can only reinforce that impression. Whatever the case, there is a growing suspicion that micro-seizures could be "the biological basis for ecstatic and mystical states." As well, a growing recognition that "methods for altering consciousness are embedded in religion."[28]

Between seizures, "religiosity usually takes the form of a heightened state of religious conviction"[29] that may include a powerful sense of religious mission. Temporal lobe seizures or "electrical ectopics" are known to cause "flying or floating sensations…the presence of sacred or malefic ghosts or apparitions…voices and visual experiences of heavenly as well as hellish kinds" and as a result "the individual ends up defining oneself as a unique persona with a special meaning"[30] all of which are consistent with Paul's self-reported experiences. Temporary blindness following seizures, while not common, is well documented and the appearance of supernatural figures who speak to Paul, Jesus as well as an angel, is reported on several occasions in Acts. In a now classic article that first appeared in the *British Journal of Psychiatry*,[31] Dewhurst and Beard described abrupt religious conversions following temporal lobe seizures. One subject "felt he was literally in Heaven" and gave "a somewhat incoherent account of his celestial experience"[32] and another "saw a flash of light" and "had a series of visions," remained completely convinced of "the validity of everything he had seen and heard" and felt he'd been

---

[27] Gunnel André, "Ecstatic Prophecy in the Old Testament," Scripta Instituti Donneriani Aboensis 11 (1982), 192-193. On the role of culture in shaping delusional belief, see Frank Larøi, et al., "Culture and Hallucinations: Overview and Future Directions," Schizophrenia Bulletin 40, Supplement 4, 2014, S213-S220.
[28] Dieter Vaitl, et al., "Psychobiology of Altered States of Consciousness," Psychological Bulletin 131.1 (2005), 99, 105.
[29] Ibid, 640.
[30] Samantha Shukla, et al. "Neurotheology: Matters of the Mind or Matters that Mind?" Journal of Clinical and Diagnostic Research 7 (2013), 1488.
[31] Kenneth Dewhurst & A.W. Beard, "Sudden Religious Conversion in Temporal Lobe Epilepsy," British Journal of Psychiatry 117 (1970), 497-507.
[32] Kenneth Dewhurst & A.W. Beard, "Sudden religious conversions in temporal lobe epilepsy," Epilepsy and Behavior 4 (2003), 79.

"singled out" as "God's chosen instrument."[33] Others had a range of experiences that included "a very vivid dream of the Crucifixion" or a sudden realization "that he was the Son of God" with "special powers of healing."[34]

Although Murray is unconvinced that Paul's Damascus road experience is attributable to epilepsy, he noted Festus' negative impression of Paul, and applying "a modern neurobehavioral paradigm," observes that if Paul's experiences "occurred as narrated" they could represent "psychotic auditory-visual phenomena."[35] That said, a recently published report documents a "messianic revelation" in a subject during a real-time EEG recording that positively correlated his delusional state with a complex partial temporal lobe seizure.[36] Whether attributable to complex seizures or other mechanisms of psychosis, Paul's self-reports do not inspire confidence in the reality of his experiences regardless of how real his close encounters of the religious kind seemed to him. After noting that Paul's writing is suggestive of auditory and visual hallucinations, hyper-religiosity, grandiosity, delusions, and paranoid thinking, Murray and his co-authors conclude, "productive writing tends to be more strongly

---

[33] Ibid, 80.
[34] Ibid, 81.
[35] Evan D. Murray, et al. "The Role of Psychotic Disor-ders in Religious History Considered," Journal of Neuropsychiatry and Clinical Neurosciences 24 (2012), 421.

A growing body of literature examines the potential role of seizure and other disorders in the generation of transcendent experience: Michael Persinger, "Religious and Mystical Experiences as Artifacts of Temporal Lobe Function: A General Hypothesis," Perceptual and Motor Skills 57 (1983), 1255-1262; Emmanuelle Peters, et al., "Delusional ideation in religious and psychotic popula-tions," British Journal of Clinical Psychology 38 (1999), 83-96; Harry T. Hunt, "Experiences of Radical Personal Transformation in Mysticism, Religious Conversion, and Psychosis: A Review of the Varieties, Processes, and Con-sequences of the Numinous," The Journal of Mind and Behavior 21.4 (2000), 353-397; Alexander Moreira-Almeida, "Religion, Spirituality, and Psychosis," Current Psychiatry Reports 12 (2010), 174-179; Marjaana Lindeman & Annika M. Svedholm, " What's in a Term? Paranormal, Superstitious, Magical and Super¬natural Beliefs by Any Other Name Would Mean the Same," Review of General Psychology 16 (2012), 241-255.

[36] Shahar Arzy & Roey Schurr, "God has sent me to you": Right temporal lobe epilepsy, left prefrontal psychosis," Epilepsy and Behavior 60 (2016), 7-10.

Recent articles on hallucinations and delusions related to seizures include Brent Elliott, Eileen Joyce & Simon Shorvon, "Delusions, illusions and hallucinations in epi-lepsy: 1. Elementary phenomena," Epilepsy Research 85, 2/3 (2009), 162-171 and "Delusions, illusions and halluci-nations in epilepsy: 2. Complex phenomena and psycho-sis," Epilepsy Research 85, 2/3 (2009), 172-186.

associated with mood disorders than psychosis or epilepsy. This is persuasive toward Paul having a mood disorder, rather than schizophrenia or epilepsy."[37]

The intransigence of Paul's belief is well documented—perhaps the most notable example is the persistence of his conviction of an imminent Parousia despite the failure of Jesus to return as predicted.[38] Given the psychological implications of his writing, his declaration, "I am convinced that neither death nor life, neither angels nor rulers, neither things present or things to come, or powers, or height or depth, or anything created will be able to separate us from the love of God that is in Christ Jesus our Lord"[39] can be read as an example of the suppression of countervailing evidence, thinking "that eschews deliberation in favor of rigid conviction."[40] As noted in a recent article, "Empirical beliefs are indications of how the world appears to us and are updated according to accumulated evidence. Fundamentalist religious beliefs, in comparison, do not track and predict variation in the world. Rather, they appear to track and predict social group-level commitments."[41] Various psychometric studies demonstrate the "religiosity effect," the finding that "religiosity and intelligence negatively correlate" because "religious individuals are less likely to engage logical processes and be less efficient at detecting reasoning conflicts; therefore, they are more likely to take intuitive answers at face value…a cognitive-behavioral tendency to forgo logical problem solving when an intuitive answer is available."[42]

What clearly emerges from the larger context of Acts is that following his trip to Damascus Paul became a man known for visions—while

---

[37] Evan D. Murray, Miles G. Cunningham & Bruce H. Price, "The Role of Psychiatric Disorders in Religious History Considered," Neuropsychiatry and Clinical Neurosci-ences 24.4 (2012), 415-417.
[38] 1 Thessalonians 4:17.
[39] Romans 8:38-39.
[40] Zhong, Wanting, et al. "Biological and cognitive un-derpinnings of religious fundamentalism," Neuropsycholigia 100 (2017), 24.
[41] Ibid, 19.
[42] Daws, Richard E. & Adam Hampshire, "The Negative Relationship between Reasoning and Religiosity Is Under-pinned by a Bias for Intuitive Responses Specifically When Intuition and Logic Are in Conflict," Frontiers in Psycholo-gy 8, Article 2191 (December, 2017), 2, 10.

still blind Paul has a vision of Ananias,[43] and after recovering his sight another vision of "a man from Macedonia,"[44] and another in Jerusalem in which Jesus speaks to him while "in a trance" (*en ekstasei*),[45] and yet another in which Jesus speaks,[46] and another of an angel during a storm at sea.[47] Paul also decided to visit Jerusalem in response to a vision.[48] Ever a man of furious conviction,[49] Paul is now convinced of his divine calling—God "set me apart from my mother's womb"[50]—"Paul believed he had been set apart and called *before he was even born.*"[51] In short, Paul's commission is in no way inferior to the prophet Jeremiah's: "before you were born I set you apart; I appointed you as a prophet to the nations."[52] "It seems plain enough that Paul thought of his calling as analogous with those of Jeremiah and the servant of Deutero-Isaiah."[53] The observation that religiously fixated epileptics "reported their first significant religious experience at an earlier age"[54] may explain Paul's belief. Based on current research in neurology it is probable that Paul's frequent transports influenced his thinking generally and in reference to Paul specifically, Shantz notes, "even when a trance state has ended, ecstatic experience continues to have measurable effects."[55] In Paul's case the continued effect appears to have been a sense of overweening grandiosity. Paul's mental state fits the picture of delusion generally: "those

---

[43] Acts 9:12.
[44] Acts 16:9.
[45] Acts 22:17-18.
[46] Acts 23:11.
[47] Acts 27.23.
[48] Galatians 2:2.
[49] Acts 9:1.
[50] Galatians 1:15.
[51] James D. Tabor, Paul and Jesus: How the Apostle Transformed Christianity, (New York: Simon & Schuster, 2012), 18. (Emphasis in original.)
[52] Jeremiah 1:5.
[53] Dale C. Allison, Resurrecting Jesus: The Earliest Christian Tradition and its Interpreters, (London: T&T Clark, 2005), 264.
[54] Trimble, Michael & Anthony Freeman, "An investigation of religiosity and the Gestaut-Geschwind syndrome in patients with temporal lobe epilepsy," Epilepsy and Behavior 9 (2006), 413.
[55] Colleen Shantz, Paul in Ecstasy: The Neurobiology of the Apostle's Life and Thought, (Cambridge: Cambridge University Press, 2009), 116.
See particularly "Paul's Voice: Parsing Paul's Ecstatic Discourse," 110-142.

with mental disorders report unusually strong convictions about supernatural phenomena" as well as "intense religious experiences."[56] As already noted, Paul's experience of hearing "ineffable words"[57] also fits some descriptions of seizures. "The ineffability of the experience would suggest that there are insufficient verbal concepts or words to characterize it...the absence of categories and words for the experiences could suggest that the right hemisphere plays a leading role."[58]

Paul's unhinged mentality did not go unnoticed by the Romans who encountered him. During his court appearance before Agrippa and Festus, his sanity became an issue: "As he was saying these things in his defense, Festus said in a loud voice, "Paul, *your many scriptures* (*ta polla se grammata*) are driving you insane!"[59] Many if not most English translations render the text in italics "your great learning,"[60] implying that his extensive education *in general* drove him mad, but these clumsy renditions avoid Festus' clear reference to *Paul's constant appeal to scripture*, to his understanding of "the prophets and Moses"[61]—like thousands of Christians in the centuries to follow, it would appear that Paul was basically rummaging around in the Old Testament in search of texts that could be construed as supporting his fantasies.

This observation by historian Lane Fox regarding the interpretive techniques current in Paul's day merits close attention:

Among the Jews, in the century or so before Jesus, ["enthusiasts and keen believers"] played havoc with authors' meanings. They took their texts word by word and read them for the oddest senses; they over-interpreted words, ignored their context and general gist. Nobody put critical, historical questions to the texts which

---

[56] Simon Dein, "Mental Health and the Paranormal," International Journal of Transpersonal Studies 31 (2012) 63, 66.
[57] 2 Corinthians 12:4.
[58] Peter Fenwick, Psychosis and Spirituality: Consolidating the New Paradigm, 2nd ed. (Hoboken, NJ: Wiley-Blackwell, 2010), 13.
[59] Acts 26:24.
[60] The New International Version, English Standard Version, and the New American Standard Bible, for instance.
[61] Acts 26:22.

they had inherited, and, as a result, they raped them. They also avoided the fundamental question: how much, if anything, was true?[62]

Paul's use of scripture fully confirms this grim assessment. Quoting what appears to be an established formula, Paul says, "that [Jesus] was buried and that he was raised *according to the scriptures*."[63] A very similar claim appears in Luke: "*So it is written*: the Messiah is to suffer and rise from the dead on the third day."[64] Even an apologetic writer concedes, "The problem is obvious—where do Israel's Scriptures speak of a suffering Messiah? Attempts to identify where 'it is written' have been unconvincing. Likewise, scholarly efforts to find the concept of a suffering Messiah in the Second Temple Jewish literature have proved fruitless."[65] Regarding Paul's reference specifically, another apologist admits, "Paul apparently views the timing of the resurrection 'on the third day' as a fulfillment of Scripture, but nowhere in the Old Testament is the resurrection of an individual associated with a third day. The relation of the words 'according to the Scriptures (v.4) to the words 'raised on the third day' has been a longstanding problem, as there is no explicit reference in the Old Testament to the resurrection of an individual 'on the third day.'"[66] Nineteen centuries later, no one in Christendom has been able to identify "the Scriptures" to which Luke and Paul referred, but that is not to say no attempt in that direction has been made by ripping Old Testament verses out of any possible historical or logical context.

It is quite unlikely that Jesus or any other Jew believed God's Messiah would at long last appear—"coming with the clouds of heaven"[67]—only to be arrested and crucified by Gentiles. Matthew attempted to

---

[62] Robin Lane Fox, The Unauthorized Version: Truth and Fiction in the Bible, (New York: Alfred A. Knopf, 1992), 107-108.
[63] 1 Corinthians 15:4.
[64] Luke 24:46.
[65] Joshua W. Jipp, "Luke's Scriptural Messiah: A Search for Precedent, A Search for Identity," Catholic Biblical Quarterly 72.2 (2010), 255.
[66] John C. Poirier, "Psalm 16:10 and the Resurrection of Jesus 'on the Third Day' (1 Corinthians 15:4)," Journal for the Study of Paul and His Letters 4.1 (2014), 149.
[67] Daniel 7:13.

overcome this inconvenience by attributing the "sign of Jonah the prophet" saying to Jesus: "For just as Jonah was in the belly of the sea monster three days and three nights, so will the Son of Man be in the heart of the earth for three days and three nights."[68] However for Jonah to serve as a "type" of Jesus' resurrection, one must assume both that Jonah was a real person and that a giant fish obligingly swallowed him and barfed him up on dry land, breathing, undigested, and none the worse for wear, after spending three days in its guts.[69]

The same ludicrous interpretive tactics pervade the letters of Paul. Referring to the "rock of Horeb" that Moses struck to produce water for the thirsty Israelites,[70] Paul speaks of a "spiritual rock that followed" the Israelites and concludes, "the rock was Christ."[71] Not only did Paul believe in spiritual rocks, he accepted "a rather pedestrian Jewish legend" about a water-bearing rock that followed the Jews through the desert like a movable water fountain,[72] and identified the itinerant rock with Jesus. Anyone who takes the New Testament at face value is necessarily left with the question posed by Enns: "After all, if at the very climax of redemptive history, the Holy Spirit can do no better than communicate the supreme Good News through pedestrian and uninspired Jewish legends, in what sense can we claim that the New Testament revelation is special, distinct, and unique?"[73] Paul also claimed the Law of Moses was given through angels[74] despite there being no mention of angels giving the Law anywhere in the Old Testament. In point of fact, Paul regularly changes word order and vocabulary, disregards the "historical setting" of

---

[68] Matthew 12:40.
[69] Jonah 2:10.
[70] Exodus 17:6.
[71] 1 Corinthians 10:4.
[72] Peter E. Enns, "The 'Moveable Well' in 1 Cor. 10:4: An Extrabiblical Tradition in an Apostolic Text," Bulletin for Biblical Research 6 (1996), 25.
[73] Ibid, 34.
[74] Galatians 3:19.

prophecies, inserts terms to suit his purpose, and disregards the context of his citations.[75]

Portius Festus may have been among the first to suspect Paul of Tarsus was mad, but he would hardly be the last. In any case Festus' response raised an important issue that has only recently been resuscitated, namely "it is the way in which psychosis and spirituality have been kept so distinct that demands explanation."[76] Or as Devinsky puts it, "how can we distinguish the physiology or validity of a religious experience in someone with epilepsy or psychosis from that of a religious sage? We can't."[77] Based on sheer probability, who bears the greater burden of proof, the Christian apologist who claims *as a historical fact* that Jesus repeatedly appeared and spoke to Paul from beyond the grave or the skeptic who points out that Paul's self reporting coheres with known symptoms of neurological disorders and that at least one pagan as well as some in his Christian audience considered Paul to be out of his mind?

It is instructive to reframe the history of early Christianity by looking at it through the lens of its Roman critics who charged "both the believers and the scriptures they read and trusted lacked intellectual integrity…Constituting a third facet of this [pagan] literary barrage, followers of Jesus were ridiculed as ignorant, gullible fools, and for mainly consisting of women and fanatics."[78] The house churches Paul established "can be characterized as a spirit-possession cult. Paul establishes communities of those possessed by the spirit of Jesus."[79] "The worshippers and the attending spirits form a double assembly"[80] even as Paul acknowledged: "because you are *zealous devotees of spirits*" (*humeis epei*

---

[75] F. S. Malen, "The Use of the Old Testament in 1 Corinthians," Neotestimentica 14 (1980), 138, 141, 156, 159.
[76] Isabel Clarke, Psychosis and Spirituality: Exploring the new frontier, (London: Whurr Publishers, 2001), 1.
[77] Orrin Devinsky & George Lai, "Spirituality and Religion in Epilepsy," Epilepsy and Behavior 12 (2008), 637.
[78] Wayne C. Kannaday, Apologetic Discourse and the Scribal Tradition: Evidence of the Influence of Apologetic Interests on the Text of the Canonical Gospels, (Atlanta: Society of Biblical Literature, 2004), 35.
[79] Christopher Mount, "1 Corinthians 11:3-16: Spirit Possession and Authority in a Non-Pauline Interpolation," Journal of Biblical Literature 124 (2005) 316.
[80] Francis C. Thee, Julius Africanus and the Early Christian View of Magic, (Heidelberg: Mohr Siebeck, 1984), 382.

zēlōtai este pneumatōn).[81] Speech altered by spirit possession is a common cross-cultural phenomenon: "the language of the diviner hovers on the brink of incomprehensibility because he garbles his words and uses unusual intonation...after the Chinese shaman (*tang-ki*) becomes possessed he speaks an unintelligible, loud and high pitched 'gods' language..."[82]

Paul recognized that a pagan entering a house church full of raving Christians would encounter a pandemonium of the spirit possessed—"if the whole church comes together and all speak in tongues and strangers or unbelievers enter, will they not say *you are possessed (mainesthe)*?"[83] He also clearly attempted to rein in the cacophony of the jabbering Christians at least for the sake of appearances—"The one speaking in tongues speaks not to men but to God. No one understands for he is speaking mysteries by the spirit...if anyone speaks in a tongue, do so two at a time, or three at most, and in turns."[84] Yet Paul affirms, "I thank God I speak in tongues more than all of you!"[85] What would "strangers or unbelievers" have thought of Paul's incomprehensible speech? Very likely what the Roman historian Livy thought of the spirit possessed followers of Dionysus: "Men, as if their minds had been taken from them, prophesied with frenzied tossings of their bodies..."[86]

Ancient authors often noted the correlation between madness and spirit possession:

Whenever [the light of the mind] dims, ecstasy and possession naturally assail us, divine seizure and *madness (mania)*. For whenever the light of God shines upon us, human light is extinguished and when the divine sun sets, the human dawns and rises. This is

---

[81] 1 Corinthians 12:3.
[82] Lisa Maurizio, "Anthropology and Spirit Possession: A Reconsideration of the Pythia's Role at Delphi," Journal of Hellenic Studies 115 (1995), 81.
[83] 1 Corinthians 14:23.
[84] 1 Corinthians 12:2, 27.
[85] 1 Corinthians 14:18.
[86] David G. Rice & John E. Stambaugh, Sources for the Study of Greek Religion, corrected edition, (Atlanta: Society of Biblical Literature, 2009), 150.

what is apt to happen to the guild of the prophets. When the divine spirit arrives, our mind is evicted. When the spirit departs, the wandering mind returns home, for it is well established that that which is subject to death may not share a home with that which is deathless. Therefore the eclipse of the power of reason and the darkness that envelops it begets *ecstasy (ekstasin)* and *inspired madness (theophorēton manian)*.[87]

Paul's gentile converts would have been familiar with mania as a religious phenomenon—"that religious trances and ecstasy were the manifestations of possession by a god was one of wide currency in Greek and Eastern religions"[88] The common notion that only those possessed by the gods are in their right mind has been noted by Kraemer among others: "Those who yield to the divine madness of Dionysiac possession are the truly sane, while those who resist the holy insanity are truly insane…It is insane to be sane, sane to be insane." Kraemer also observed that "abstinence from marital sexual obligations" was "attributed to the worshippers of Dionysus,"[89] which is remarkably like Paul's advice to the possessed in Corinth: "The time left is reduced. Henceforth let those who have wives live as those who don't."[90]

Paul's possession cult had many points in common with other ecstatic religions. Dionysus, Son of Zeus, was born from the mortal woman Semele as Jesus, Son of God, was born from the mortal woman Mary. Dionysus is borne to earth in a "fiery bolt of lightning"[91] much as Mary conceives because "holy spirit *will fall upon you (epeleusetai epi se)* and the power of the Most High will overshadow you."[92]—the verb *eperchomai, to fall upon,* is used in the papyri for magical attacks: "defend me

---

[87] Philo, Quis rerum divinarum heres. I have used the Greek text of the Loeb Philo IV (Cambridge: Harvard University Press, 1932), 264-265.
[88] Philip S. Esler, The First Christians in Their Social Worlds: Social-scientific approaches to New Testament Interpretation, (London: Routledge, 1994), 46.
[89] Ross S. Kraemer, "Ecstasy and Possession: The Attraction of Women to the Cult of Dionysus," Harvard Theological Review 72 (1979), 67.
[90] 1 Corinthians 7:29.
[91] Euripedes, Bacchae, 3.
[92] Luke 1:35.

from all troubles *befalling me* (*eperchomenou mou*)."[93] Dionysus "exchanged [his] *divine form* (*morphēn..ek theou*) for a mortal one,"[94] just as Jesus, "who existed in *the form of God* (*en morphē theou*), "assumed human likeness and was found in the appearance of a man."[95] The similarity has been noted before: "Dionysus assumes human form, a grim predecessor of Christ."[96] It's worth pointing out that the double nature of Jesus celebrated in Philippians almost certainly derives verbatim from an early doxology, a hymn that with little modification could have been addressed to Dionysus or any one of several other Greco–Roman deities.

The prominence of women in the ecstatic cult of Dionysus is well attested, and the similarities between spirit possession during Bacchic and Christian ritual are also worth pointing out—similarities that extended beyond the mere mechanics of ecstatic ritual to the theology of both religions. Euripedes' *Bacchae* is "our earliest substantial witness"[97] to the mania that accompanied Dionysian ecstasy, as 1 Corinthians is the earliest witness to Christian spirit possession. Just as Christians gathered for worship in an *ekklēsia*, a *meeting* or *gathering*, worshippers of Bacchus gathered in a *thiasos*, a *guild* or *company*. Other reported features of the cult of Jesus resemble the cult of Bacchus: of the maenads in the throes of possession it is reported, "fire flickered on their curls but did not burn them."[98] Similarly "tongues of fire" signal the presence of the spirit in the ecstatic Christian assembly.[99]

Classical scholar Catherine Kroeger addresses the cult from the vantage point of "the socio-religious world of [Greco-Roman] women."[100]

---

[93] Karl Preisendanz, Papyri Graecae Magicae: Die Griechischen Zauberpapyri, 2, (Munich: K.G. Sauer Verlag, 2002), XXXVI, 176.
[94] Bacchae, 4.
[95] Philippians 2:6-8.
[96] Richard Rutherford, Classical Literature: A Concise History, (London: Blackwell, 2005), 61.
[97] David Kovacs, Euripedes: Bacchae, Iphigenia at Aulis, Rhesus, (Cambridge: Harvard University Press, 2002), 2.
[98] Bacchae 757-758.
[99] Acts 2:3.
[100] Catherine Kroeger, "The Apostle Paul and Greco-Roman Cults of Women," Journal of the Evangelical Theological Society 30 (1987), 25.

It is of particular relevance that Paul's congregations in Asia Minor, particularly in Antioch, "lay in the very heart of Anatolia, where religious expression—particularly that of women—took on an extremely noisy, wild and orgiastic aspect...Ancient women, as disadvantaged, neglected and repressed members of society, often turned to religion as a release and escape. In it they vented violent emotions that were not able to be expressed through any other channel...Neither is it surprising that women who lacked any sort of formal education flocked to cults that were despised by the intellectuals."[101] As Lisa Maurizio observes, "women can exercise considerable power in political and religious spheres, as long as they are believed to be possessed and to speak with the authority of the spirits or god(s) possessing them."[102] This was likely the case with women in primitive Christianity as well.

As noted by Julian, the healing god Asclepius also appeared "in the form of a man."[103] Just as Dionysus is "the son of God,"[104] Jesus is "the Son of God."[105] The maenads of Bacchus take up serpents;[106] early Christians were promised they would also pick up serpents without harm.[107] Bacchus causes the ground to "run with wine"[108] and "fountains of milk and wine" were supposedly produced during Bacchic rites;[109] Jesus turns water into wine as the first of his miracles.[110] Dionysus' enemies berate him, claiming, "some stranger has come in, *a sorcerer, a spell caster.*"[111] "Jesus' opponents accused him of black magic, an accusation which stands as one of the most firmly established facts of the Gospel

---

[101] Bacchae, 26, 28.
[102] Maurizio, op. cit., 75.
[103] Julian, Against the Galileans, 200A. (Wilmer C. Wright, tr, Julian III, (Cambridge: Harvard University Press, 1923).
[104] Bacchae, 84.
[105] John 3:16.
[106] Bacchae, 103-104.
[107] Mark 16:9-20, while ancient, is not widely regarded as part of the original text.
[108] Bacchae, 142.
[109] Frederick C. Conybearse, Philostratus: The Life of Apollonius VI (Cambridge: Harvard University Press, 1989), 11.
[110] John 2:9-11.
[111] Bacchae, 233-234.

Tradition."[112] The enemies of Dionysus accuse him of being "a new divinity."[113] Jesus introduces "a new teaching, with authority."[114] Of Dionysus it is claimed, "*The god is a prophet...he makes those possessed foretell the future.*"[115] Jesus is also a god[116] as well as a prophet[117] and Philip the evangelist had no less than four virgin daughters who prophesied.[118] Without endlessly prolonging this list of comparisons it might fairly be asked why women with little education, once "enslaved to those who by nature are not gods,"[119] women who previously may have regarded an "altered state of consciousness as a gift from Dionysus,"[120] would not naturally bring their understanding of religious ecstasy to their new Christian faith. "The figure of Dionysus who walked the earth concealing his own divinity [is replaced by] the actual or folk-memory of the Galilean preacher..."[121]

We should be completely clear that *when Paul wrote and preached there were no "gospels" as currently understood*—Mark, the first gospel composed, was not written until well after Paul, James, and Peter had died. At that early stage there is no evidence that "the gospel" was anything other than an individual's oral version of the meaning of Jesus' life; there were as yet no authoritative "New Testament" gospels waiting on bookshelves to be consulted, no "proof texts" that could be cited to bolster an argument. The "gospel" was whatever a preacher said it was, and Paul's gospel, his version of events, "owed its *origin*...not to the historical Jesus who was a teacher and Messiah claimant, but to Paul's personal experience of the mystical Christ."[122] As Paul's own letters make clear,

---

[112] Eric Plumer, "The Absence of Exorcisms in the Fourth Gospel," Biblica 78 (1997), 357.
[113] Bacchae, 273.
[114] Mark 1:27.
[115] Bacchae, 300-301.
[116] John 1:1, 20:28.
[117] Matthew 21:11.
[118] Acts 21:9.
[119] Galatians 4:8.
[120] Kroeger, op. cit., 33.
[121] Barrie Wilson, How Jesus Became Christian, (New York: St. Martin's Press, 2009), 114.
[122] Ibid, 113. (Emphasis in original.)

there were competing, contradictory "gospels" being preached in the first house churches—Paul complains that some of the Galatians had turned to "a different gospel."[123] Paul did not mean a different *written* gospel like the now-familiar Gospel of Thomas or Gospel of Judas, but *a different preaching* of Jesus' message, an interpretation that often formed the basis of competing factions: "I follow Apollos," or "I follow Cephas," or "I follow Paul,"[124] or a splinter movement like the current "prosperity gospel" in which the prosperity is more likely to refer to the preacher's sprawling mansion, private jet, or fleet of luxury cars than to the personal finances of his flock.

In short, in the mid-1st century a "gospel" was whatever an authority figure *said* it was. Hence Paul's anxiety to establish the basis of *his* authority—Paul has "seen" the Lord,[125] and the Lord speaks to him in visions,[126] visions and revelations just too wonderful for words,[127] but Paul also backs up his words with "signs and wonders,"[128] demonstrations of "the spirit's power."[129] Adopting essentially the same shtick, generations of televangelists talk like they've just gotten off the phone with Jesus His Own Damn Self.

Then as now, God's spokesmen were expected to look and sound the part. Alexander of Abonoteichus, to cite an easy example, is described by Lucian as tall, handsome, fair, and "touched by the divine," with "eyes like the Gorgon and *shining as if possessed by a god*," as well a "most gentle manner of speaking"[130] by which he ingratiated himself with those he duped. Paul's critics correspondingly noted that his "physical presence is weak and his speech contemptible."[131] In many ways the world has

---

[123] Galatians 1:6.
[124] 1 Corinthians 1:12.
[125] 1 Corinthians 9:1.
[126] Acts 18:9.
[127] 2 Corinthians 12:1-6.
[128] Romans 15:19.
[129] 1 Corinthians 2:4.
[130] Lucian, Alexander the False Prophet, 3. I have used the Greek text of the Loeb edition (Lucian IV, A.M. Harmon (tr), Cambridge: Harvard University Press, 1921).
[131] 2 Corinthians 10:10.

changed beyond recognition since the days of Paul and in others it is exactly the same; religious advocacy is more often than not a matter of star power, of showmanship and, in Alexander's case, marvelous hair.

While the Romans slaughtered, enslaved, and scattered the Jewish populace in Christianity's homeland during the First Jewish–Roman War, the new cult, profoundly changed in character, progressed apace among Gentiles. As a lasting result of this change in fortune the New Testament canon, finalized in the 3rd and 4th centuries, over-represented the importance of Paul among his 1st century rivals—"because he figures so prominently in the New Testament, Paul's significance in early Christian history has tended to be grossly overrated."[132] A case has been made on the basis of early manuscript evidence that Paul's letters to his churches had already been collected into a "Pauline epistolary" that widely circulated by the middle of the 2nd century,[133] and a late 1st century reference to "all [Paul's] letters"[134] would certainly support that view.

"The disciples were first called Christians"[135] in Antioch following Paul's arrival—in short, a Jewish faction that followed Paul's Christ just as some identified themselves by allegiance to particular preachers as described by Paul himself: "One of you says, 'I follow Paul,' another, 'I follow Apollos,' another, 'I follow Cephas,' yet another, 'I follow Christ.'"[136] Antioch, a city "infamous for its sense of humor," did not mean *Christian* as a compliment—"it was the Antiochenes who dubbed followers of Christ 'Christians' or 'Christ-groupies.'"[137] "Christian," as Bornkamm points out, was "a designation they would hardly have

---

[132] John G. Gager, Kingdom and Community: The Social World of Early Christianity, (Upper Saddle River, NJ: Prentice Hall, 1975), 4.
[133] Jerome D. Quinn, "P46—The Pauline Canon?" Catholic Biblical Quarterly 36 (1974) 379, 383.
[134] 2 Peter 3:16.
[135] Acts 11:26.
[136] 1 Corinthians 1:12.
[137] Adrian Murdock, The Last Pagan: Julian the Apostate and the Death of the Ancient World, (Rochester, VT: Inner Traditions, 2008), 120.

assumed of their own free will; it must have been conferred on them by their pagan neighbors."¹³⁸

Seen from the viewpoint of the founding family in Jerusalem, defeated as much by demographics and the vicissitudes of history as by theology, Paul's ethnophilic Christianity was the first of many heresies. Starting with Paul, the trajectories of Judaism and Christianity radically diverged: "Although [Christianity] has its roots in Judaism, those roots are both shallow and distributed across a diverse and divided first-century Judaism that was itself deeply marked by Greco–Roman culture."¹³⁹ After 70 CE an invocation, the *Birkat ha-Minim*, the "Blessing on the Heretics," began to be recited in synagogues to distinguish Jews from Jewish Christians. The recitation is probably the basis for the apologist Justin's claim that the Jews cursed Christ in their worship.¹⁴⁰

In any case it is abundantly clear that the gospel preached by Paul—"my gospel" as he repeatedly calls it¹⁴¹—would have amazed and appalled Jesus the Jew. Yet Paul claims to have received his gospel directly from Jesus "by revelation,"¹⁴² and "[Paul's] own revelations directly from the heavenly Christ are more significant than anything Jesus taught in his earthly life." Of the seventy-two occurrences of "gospel" in the New Testament, "the letters of Paul account for sixty of the total…and it is clear that his usage is proprietary and exclusive."¹⁴³ As a recent biographer notes, "[Paul's] experience of the Risen Jesus owed nothing to the testimony of Peter, James or John" and his gospel "was never based, and never claimed to be based, on the traditions which…informed the teaching of Jesus' family and close intimates."¹⁴⁴ It is worth reiterating that *Paul does not claim he is transmitting an apostolic tradition from the*

---

¹³⁸ Bornkamm, Paul, 29.
¹³⁹ Luke T. Johnson, Among the Gentiles: Greco-Roman Religion and Christianity, (New Haven: Yale University Press, 2009), 131.
¹⁴⁰ Paul McKechnie, The First Christian Centuries: Perspectives on the Early Church, (Downers Grove, IL: InterVarsity Press, 2001), 86.
¹⁴¹ Romans 2:16, 16:25.
¹⁴² Galatians 1:12.
¹⁴³ Tabor, op. cit., 3-4.
¹⁴⁴ Wilson, op. cit., 68-69.

disciples who coalesced around Jesus during his lifetime. To the contrary, he plainly states his gospel "is not from man", nor was he "taught it," nor did he "receive it" from men, but rather he received it direct, "by a revelation of Jesus Christ."[145] In short, "Paul says that he hears from Jesus."[146] Even a scholar of distinctly apologetic bent, writing two generations ago, acknowledged, "It is possible...that [Paul] wishes to imply that the Apostles who can claim to have known and touched Jesus have no claim to an apostolate superior to his own."[147] Noting the evidence of "concerted opposition to Paul's gospel and apostolic authority," Harrison remarks, "It is an irony of history that by late antiquity Paul had become the authority figure he never was during his lifetime. Paul's letters provide ample evidence that his gospel and apostolic authority were under serious challenge while he was alive."[148]

The skeptic might ask what makes Paul's private revelations from Jesus any more trustworthy than the revelations given Zarathushtra by Vohu Manah, or Muhammad's revelations from the angel Gabriel, or Moroni's private revelations to Joseph Smith, or for that matter the "mahatma" Koot Hoomi's disclosures of divine secrets to Helena Blavatsky. After all, by the time of Paul, spirits had been whispering secrets to mediums for millennia as evidenced by the Old Testament tale of Saul and the medium of En Dor[149] and according to its own history, early Christianity pullulated prophets with their revelations—"your sons and your daughters will prophesy and your young men will see visions and your old men will receive visions in dreams."[150]

Paul shows scant interest in the "historical Jesus" who has so exercised the ingenuity of modern scholars, the Jesus "according to the flesh." Paul is clear on this point: "even if we have known Christ

---

[145] Galatians 1:11-12.
[146] Tabor, op. cit., 146.
[147] Nock, Early Gentile Christianity, 28.
[148] J.R. Harrison, "In Quest of the Third Heaven: Paul and His Apocalyptic Imitators," Vigiliae Christianae 58.1 (2004), 24.
[149] 1 Samuel 28:1-20.
[150] Acts 2:17.

according to the flesh, henceforth we know him so no longer."[151] For Paul the story of Jesus truly begins with his death and resurrection and will continue at his imminent return—"Paul, an apostle not from men or through men but through Jesus Christ and God the Father *who raised him from the dead*."[152] "Paul lifts the [crucifixion] completely out of its contemporary context and treats it as a supernatural happening, and the Eucharist, as set forth by Paul, in effect lifts the historical event of the death of Jesus completely out of its setting in time and space and confers upon it that transcendental significance of the *Heilsereignis* [salvation, *my note*] of the *mythoi* of the various mystery cults."[153] For the typical pew sitter who assumes a seamless continuity of Christian teaching, the implications of Paul's claim are hard to absorb. Be that as it may, if we take Paul at his word it emerges that "Paul does in fact stubbornly assert his independence of all human authorities" and claims he "had no relation whatsoever" with the mother church in Jerusalem.[154] So where might Paul have picked up his ideas?

Christianity found itself in competition with "a whole host of mystery cults and doctrines of salvation"[155] and Paul's dying-and-rising-together imagery[156] likely "arose in the Hellenistic churches under the influence of pagan mystery cults in which the initiates were given a share in the fortunes of their deity and, by means of a ritual dying and rising along with him, attained salvation."[157] Tarsus, Paul's native city, was a center of Mithraic and other mystery cults[158] and the term *mystery* (*mustērion*), secret knowledge available only to religious initiates, is virtually confined to the writings of Paul and the forgeries produced in his name. The notion of *initiation* was central to the mysteries as pointed out by Johnson: "why would adult males seek to undergo a painful and

---

[151] 2 Corinthians 5:16.
[152] Galatians 1:1.
[153] Brandon, op. cit., 159, 167.
[154] Bornkamm, op. cit., 18-19.
[155] Ibid, 7.
[156] Romans 6:3-4.
[157] Ibid, 190.
[158] A.N. Wilson, Paul: The Mind of the Apostle, (New York: W.W. Norton, 1997), 24-28.

even dangerous genital mutilation within a short time of an easy and painless initiation by water?" The answer is almost certainly due to the analogy between the cult of Jesus and other mystery cults—"the cult of the Messiah...can be thought of as a Mystery—especially if it proclaimed as Lord a human being who had died and was raised." Besides that, Paul's churches in Asia Minor were located in a region where "sexual mutilation would have been familiar as a sign of advanced status within a cult."[159] Paul's incessant mystery talk could only have encouraged such an understanding.

Mystery occurs only once in Mark—"The mystery (*mustērion*) of the kingdom has been given to you"[160]—and it is dutifully reproduced in Matthew[161] and Luke[162] but not in John. Aside from four occurrences in Revelation,[163] all the remaining references are in writings ascribed to Paul: "we declare the wisdom of God *in mystery (en mustēriō)*, [the wisdom] that has been hidden, that God foreordained before the ages for our glory...but God revealed [them] to us by his spirit."[164] *Mystery* is used of everything imaginable: the recalcitrance of Israel,[165] the resurrection of believers,[166] Christ's will,[167] Christ and the church,[168] and naturally "the mystery of the gospel."[169]

Paul clearly considered himself Jesus' chosen revelator: "You heard about the mission of God's grace entrusted *to me* on your behalf, the mystery revealed *to me* by revelation, just as I've written briefly. When you read this, you will be able to understand *my insight* into the mystery of Christ that in previous generations was not made known to the sons

---

[159] Johnson, op. cit., 146.
[160] Mark 4:11.
[161] Matthew 13:11.
[162] Luke 8:10.
[163] Revelation 1:20, 10:7, 17:5, 7.
[164] 1 Corinthians 2:7, 10.
[165] Romans 11:25.
[166] 1 Corinthians 15:51.
[167] Ephesians 1:9.
[168] Ephesians 5:32.
[169] Ephesians 6:19.

of men as it has now been revealed in spirit to his holy apostles and prophets."[170] Paul claimed God was pleased "to reveal his Son *in me* so I might preach him among the Gentiles."[171] Accordingly Paul tells his congregation, "Become imitators of me as I [am] of Christ."[172]

As a religious term *hupēretēs* could refer to a messenger of Zeus or of Apollo, the god of prophecy, or in Paul's case,[173] a messenger of Jesus. Paul's correspondence is riddled with mystery talk and his gospel is "the proclamation of Jesus Christ according to the *revelation of a mystery* that has been concealed for ages past but is now brought to light through the prophetic writings."[174] Paul's forays into scripture set a tiresome precedent for two millennia of hollow Christian "revelations" of mysteries, typically brought to light by uninspired rummaging through the "prophetic writings." In fact, technical terms from the mystery cults, likely due to the influence of Paul, crop up in later New Testament writings: "For we revealed the coming of our Lord Jesus Christ in power to you not by following cleverly devised stories, but by becoming *eyewitnesses* (*epoptai*) of that magnificence."[175] The *epopteia*, ascent to the level of an *epoptēs*, "one who has seen,"[176] indicated that the person had been initiated into the highest grade of the mysteries after preliminary ceremonies.[177]

It seems to be *de rigueur* among biographers of Paul to characterize him as a genius. A.N. Wilson, for example, while acknowledging that Paul's beliefs are "bizarre…within the context of Jewish hopes" nevertheless refers to him in the same breath as "a sublime religious genius."[178] To his credit Wilson is clear that Paul's predictions were an utter failure

---

[170] Ephesians 3:2-5.
[171] Galatians 1:15-16.
[172] 1 Corinthians 11:1.
[173] 1 Corinthians 4:1.
[174] Romans 16:25-26.
[175] 2 Peter 1:16.
[176] Nock, op. cit., 6.
[177] Everette Ferguson, Backgrounds of Early Christianity, 3rd ed, (Grand Rapids, MI: William B. Eerdmans Publishing Company, 2003), 257-258.
[178] Wilson, op. cit., 177.

and his view of the world completely mistaken— "the plans of God as they have been specially revealed to Paul just don't work out" and a generation after Paul "it must be obvious that the Lord has not come and that all Paul's immediate prophecies and predictions about the nature of the world and God's purpose for it, have not been just slightly off beam, not open to interpretation, but plumb wrong."[179] So let's propose a different definition of genius, a definition that doesn't involve being mistaken about literally everything.

Isaac Newton was clearly a genius. Besides being the co-discoverer of calculus, Newton's math combined with Johannes Kepler's astronomical data (and the advance of rocket technology) finally put a man on the moon—not half bad for two men born in the 17th and 16th centuries respectively. Using these men as two of many possible examples, let's agree that to qualify as a real genius a person has to say something real about the world and that something real must eventually follow as a result. Clearly a genius doesn't have to be right one hundred percent of the time—Newton was famously fascinated by alchemy and eventually gave up math to ponder prophecy. Before the codification of the scientific method, there was virtually no possibility that Paul or any of his contemporaries could be right about anything. "Without the instruments and accumulated knowledge of the natural sciences—physics, chemistry, and biology—humans are trapped in a cognitive prison…they are wrong, always wrong, because the world is too remote from ordinary experience to be merely imagined…Still encumbered by precepts based on Iron Age folk knowledge, [theology] is unable to assimilate the great sweep of the real world now open for examination. Western philosophy offers no promising substitute. Its involuted exercises and professional timidity have left modern culture bankrupt of meaning."[180]

In recent years many of the social strictures governing how religion may be discussed have at least partially lifted with the result that religious

---

[179] Ibid, 208-209.
[180] Edward O. Wilson, Consilience: The Unity of Knowledge, (New York: Random House, 1999), 49, 294.

belief is increasingly interrogated from the psychiatric point of view—essentially picking up where Festus left off. "The plasticity of religious delusions argues for the status of religious themes as 'epiphenomena' of an underlying disease process. However, recent research suggests that religious delusions, beyond being merely evidence of a religious outlook, have genuine clinical significance...Societies in which single texts are imbued with authority, such as the Koran and the Bible, could produce more religious delusions because of the stability of the referents contained therein."[181] A more mature modern psychology with superior investigative techniques and tools can now question whether Paul of Tarsus was functionally, if not clinically, insane—and whether the religion he championed is based on delusion.

---

[181] Vishal Bhavsar & Dinesh Bhugra, "Religious Delusions: Finding Meaning in Psychosis," Psychology 41 (2008), 166, 169.

EPILOGUE

To see the sheer number of miracle claims in the Bible, I would have liked to reproduce the longest chapter I ever wrote, titled, "The Strange and Superstitious World of the Bible," from my book *Why I Became an Atheist* (2nd edition, 2012). Instead, I'll just rehearse a few of the strange and superstitious things found in that world.

What we find in the Bible is a world in which gods lived in the sky just above the mountains, and people who died actually went to live in the dark recesses of the earth (*Sheol*). Gods, goddesses and their sons ruled over specific lands and met in divine councils to decide human fate. In that world snakes and donkeys could talk, giants lived in the land, and people could live to be more than nine hundred years old. In that world a god brought fire down from the sky, created a pillar of fire that directed people by night, kept three men safe when thrown into a fiery furnace, and threatened sinners with everlasting torment in an eternal fire. In it a woman turned into a pillar of salt, the sun stopped moving across the sky, a star pointed down to a specific place, people instantly spoke in unlearned foreign languages, the evil eye could hurt people, and someone's shadow or handkerchief could heal them, as could bathing in a pool. In it the gods sent diseases, famines, plagues of locusts, and droughts. It was one where a world-wide flood was divinely sent to punish people, a man could be swallowed by a "great fish" and live to tell about it, and an axe head could float. In that world a demigod was born of a virgin, walked on water, calmed a turbulent sea, changed water into wine, and rose up from the dead. In the biblical world dead saints of old levitated with Jesus and talked with two of his disciples, were raised from the dead with Jesus and walked around Jerusalem, never to be heard from again. That world was populated by invisible demons that could wreak havoc on earth and who made people very sick. It was a world where human and animal sacrifices pleased god, and victory in war was due to their god.

That ancient world was one full of miracle workers, magicians, diviners, sorcerers, and oh yes, ancient psychics who were called prophets. The story of Aaron's staff turning into a snake before Pharaoh, whereupon his sorcerers did likewise by turning their staffs into snakes, makes no sense *unless Pharaoh's sorcerers did likewise with their magic arts* (Exod. 7:10–12). Daniel was appointed by King Nebuchadnezzar to be in charge of his "wise men" (Daniel 2:48), which included magicians, enchanters, astrologers, and diviners (Dan. 5:11). This can only mean Daniel successfully performed these arts, especially since we read he could interpret dreams, which is what these "wise men" were called upon to do. The people inhabiting this world made important decisions by throwing stones (Urim and Thummim), casting lots, and by threatening to cut a baby in half (yep, wise 'ole Solomon). They sought guidance from dreams and their interpretations, visions, divination, and any prophecy that turned out to be correct based on hindsight.

None of these extraordinary miraculous beliefs had any objective evidence for them as literally understood. Yet a few billion people today believe what they read in the Bible based on ancient pre-scientific oral testimony, as handed down by word of mouth from generation to generation, and from century to century, until written down by mostly anonymous authors we can no longer interrogate, who in turn added their own tales—some plagiarized, and others forged—which were then transcribed for a few centuries by scribes who had agendas of their own, and who made mistakes and even admitted inserting lies into these sacred texts (Jeremiah 8:8).

There is something clearly wrong here. Reasonable people should require objective evidence before accepting any extraordinary tales like these. Who, for instance, would take the word of ancient pre-scientific sorcerers or diviners or psychics or prophets *or any ancient person for that matter*, over the consensus of scientists working in any given field? On this point, think evolutionary biology, climate change, and the effectiveness of vaccinations.

David Hume challenged believers to do something very important if they want to be honest with their faith. Using words indicative of my argument in *The Outsider Test for Faith*, Hume asked them to consider the Pentateuch (i.e., the first five books in the Bible) "not as the word or testimony of God himself, but as the production of a mere human writer and historian."[1] In other words, examine it as they examine other holy books, without any double-standards, without any special pleading.

> Here then we are first to consider a book, presented to us by a barbarous and ignorant people, written in an age when they were still more barbarous, and in all probability long after the facts which it relates, corroborated by no concurring testimony, and resembling those fabulous accounts, which every nation gives of its origin. Upon reading this book, we find it full of prodigies and miracles. It gives an account of a state of the world and of human nature entirely different from the present: Of our fall from that state: Of the age of man, extended to near a thousand years: Of the destruction of the world by a deluge: Of the arbitrary choice of one people, as the favourites of heaven; and that people the countrymen of the author: Of their deliverance from bondage by prodigies the most astonishing imaginable: I desire any one to lay his hand upon his heart, and after a serious consideration declare, whether he thinks that the falsehood of such a book, supported by such a testimony, would be more extraordinary and miraculous than all the miracles it relates; which is, however, necessary to make it be received, according to the measures of probability above established.[2]

It's a rhetorical question. Hume already knew the answer based on the reasonable measures of probability he previously established.

---

[1] Hume, *Of Miracles* #100.
[2] Ibid.

Reasonable nonbelievers would not accept these extraordinary miraculous tales. That's because an honest investigator would require more than mere ancient pre-scientific testimonial evidence. An honest investigator would require sufficient objective evidence.

New Testament scholar Rudolph Bultmann made a similar point: The cosmology of the N.T. [New Testament] is essentially mythical in character. The world is viewed as a three-storied structure, with the earth in the center, the heaven above, and the underworld beneath. Heaven is the abode of God and of celestial beings—angels. The underworld is hell, the place of torment. Man is not in control of his life. Evil spirits may take possession of him. Satan may inspire him with evil thoughts. It is simply the cosmology of a pre-scientific age...It is no longer possible for anyone seriously to hold the N.T. view of the world. We no longer believe in the three-storied universe. No one who is old enough to think for himself supposes that God lives in a local heaven. There is no longer any heaven in the traditional sense. The same applies to hell in the sense of a mythical underworld beneath our feet. And if this is so...we can no longer look for the return of the Son of Man on the clouds of heaven. It is impossible to use the electric light and the wireless and to avail ourselves of modern medical and surgical discoveries, and at the same time to believe in the N.T. world of spirits and miracles.[3]

What is there not to understand? No reasonable person accepts this view of the world because there's no objective evidence for it, and lots of objective evidence against it.

While Bultmann was appealing to conservative fundamentalists, I only can wish believers of a more liberal mind would be consistent with where this leaves their own faith. Why hold on to a faith that has its roots in ignorance and superstition, fear and hatred, censorship and

---

[3] Rudolph Bultmann, *Kerygma & Myth: A Theological Debate*, ed. Hans Werner Bartsch (New York: Harper & Row, 1961), pp. 1–7.

oppression? Why stay in an organization that has a history of killing anyone who disagrees, misogyny, racism, homophobia, slavery, pederasty, rape and a multitude of wars?[4] One might as well join the hate-filled Ku Klux Klan version of Christianity and seek to reform it from the inside.

---

[4] I've argued for some of these things elsewhere in my book, *Christianity is Not Great* (2014).

APPENDIX: HUME ON PROOF AND MATHEMATICAL PROBABILITY

BY JOHN W. LOFTUS

As mentioned in my chapter 3, a major defense of Hume on miracles was to be published in 2019, written by Humean scholar William L. Vanderburgh, titled, *David Hume On Miracles, Evidence, and Probability* (Lanham: Lexington, 2019). This present anthology on miracles was already in the production stages when I received a copy of it. So, I'm thankful my publisher allowed me to add this Appendix where I'll briefly review what Vanderburgh writes, since after reading it I think he gets Hume right.

It's easy to criticize Hume if one seeks to do so. Just nitpick, for one thing. Or uncharitably foster upon his one lone chapter on miracles—of about 8700 words—a worst possible interpretation. With so many uncharitable criticisms of Hume out there, the hard part is to buck the trend by trying to understand Hume.

As I mentioned in my chapter 3 there are some atheists who have agreed with the unfair Christian criticisms of Hume. In my book *Unapologetic* I mention one possible atheist motive, which is to placate Christian apologists into thinking well of them. By agreeing with the Christian criticisms of Hume, Christians in turn will reward them by quoting from them, asking them to write for their anthologies, and even debate them, which brings them a bigger audience and more respect. But if atheists treat the Christian faith as it deserves, with no more respect than any other delusional faith, or if they defend Hume, Christians will ignore you if they can. That's the strategy of William Lane Craig, my former professor at Trinity Evangelical Divinity School. He won't acknowledge my work as important, or debate me. He dislikes the fact that I'm blunt about his faith, by saying it's delusional. He is embarrassed that I exist, hoping others will follow his example by ignoring me. To do so, he has to ignore my work and the fact that other Christian scholars have acknowledged its importance, like Norman Geisler, Chad Meister, Dale Allison, Gary Habermas, Karl Giberson, James Sennett, Victor Reppert, Randal Rauser, David Marshall, and several others.

Since Christians are convinced Hume's arguments against miracles have been "refuted" (per William Lane Craig in a personal conversation), some atheists are trying to reach out to Christians by avoiding Hume entirely. Benjamin Blake Speed Watkins, who Hosts and Produces Real Atheology – A Philosophy of Religion Podcast, is one of them. He said, "I see arguments against miracles as separate from Hume. We can have substantive discussion without ever appealing to him." Now this can be done, I don't doubt. But I don't see the need to do it. I also think we should give credit where credit is due. I can't imagine ignoring David Hume, the philosopher who originally put the issue of miracles up for discussion, like no other had done before. That would be an injustice. I understand that Christians identify the best arguments against miracles with Hume's arguments. I also understand they think Hume's arguments fail. So I'm not oblivious they conclude that with Hume's demise so also goes the case against miracles. Just the same, it makes sense to defend Hume if he can be defended, and I think he can. When we do so successfully it doubly undercuts Christian apologetics. For not only do we show Hume's arguments defeat the believability of miracles. By showing Christians are wrong about Hume, it also shows how badly they argue their case on behalf of miracles.

With so much at stake, I'm going to argue that Vanderburgh's book is indispensable reading for understanding why Hume's case against miracles succeeds. His book is a treasure trove of arguments in Hume's defense. He argues that "Hume's account of evidential probability is solid and that when it is understood on its own terms instead of being reinterpreted in a way that Hume did not intend, his conclusion about the incredibility of miracles will be seen to be correct" (p. 4). One specific hope of his is that after considering what he says, "commentators will now stop trying to give Bayesian or other mathematical analyses of Hume on probability, which cannot possibly correctly represent Hume's own view" (p. 167).

First things first. Hume's critics object that by defining a miracle as a "violation of the laws of nature" he begged the question of whether a miracle could occur by setting up an impossible standard to overcome. Such an objection gets Hume wrong, Vanderburgh tells us. Hume did not consider it impossible that the laws of nature could be violated by a miracle, since for him the "laws of nature are at most probable, never certain." When we put miracle claims in the same context of questions about the existence of cause and effect, or the existence of the self, or the existence of god, they are all "epistemological rather than ontological categories." This means the real question for Hume "is not what sorts of events do and don't occur, but rather what events it is rational, given the available evidence, to believe to have occurred." (p. 56) So Vanderburg answers this mistaken objection as follows: "For Hume's purposes, only miracles conceived as violations of laws of nature deserve the name, since only miracles in that sense could possibly provide an additional, independent kind of evidence for religious hypotheses" (p. 24). That is, if miracles were events that could be completely explained within the world of nature without any supernatural interference, then they lose their capability to provide any reasonable support for religious hypotheses. This would leave the appearance of design to do all the supportive work by itself, something Hume excoriates in his *Dialogues concerning Natural Religion.*

Vanderburgh sums up Hume's main argument against miracles in several places. The briefest summations are in his Prologue, where he says, "Some stories are too improbable to be believed, no matter the source of the testimony" (p. 1). Then being more specific, "there is never sufficient evidence for rational belief in the occurrence of miracles" (p. 3). His most detailed summation is as follows:

> Hume's argument here is relatively straightforward. A miracle is a violation of the laws of nature. We construct laws of nature on the dual basis of 'a firm and unalterable experience'—that is, from an observed constant conjunction of event types, an exceptionless regularity—plus an expectation of the mind that the future resembles the past. The depth and breadth of the exceptionless regularity of past experience gives the strongest kind of warrant possible to the belief that the law will continue to hold in the same way in the future. It is not that the evidence demonstrates with certainty that the law is true, it is just that no empirical claim can possibly have stronger evidence than what we have with regard to those things we call laws of nature. Testimony, the evidence offered in opposition to the exceptionless regularity, is known to be fallible and is especially suspect in cases of reports of miracles because of the likelihood of deception or misperception. Thus, the weight of evidence derived from testimony about a purported exception to a law of nature in fact will *never* come close to the weight of evidence from experience that the law will be regular in all cases (italics mine, p. 50).

On this point Vanderburgh offers a helpful analogy to answer John Earman's claim that Hume's argument is an *a priori* one (i.e., independent of experience, as opposed to *a posteriori*, dependent on experience), by arguing that *never* doesn't mean *logically never*. He asks us to consider the claim that, "A human will never bench press 1,500 pounds." The current record, as he tells us, is 735.5 pounds set by Kirill Sarychev in 2015.

> Given what we know about ...human physiology, and the laws of physics (breaking strength of bones, etc.), it is utterly unbelievable that a human (as we currently understand the reference class) could complete a 1,500-pound raw bench press. It isn't logically impossible, just impossible-given-what-we-know. There is a sense

in which it is possible that this claim is wrong, but you still should not believe a report that someone has raw benched 1,500 pounds if you hear one. (p. 50).

Of course, an extraordinary claim that someone bench pressed 1,500 pounds would still be more likely than the miraculous claim that someone walked on water or rose from the dead. So he goes on to say, "If you would not believe the bench press claim, then on pain of inconsistency you should not believe the miracle claim either." (p. 50–51).

Let me turn now to what I consider the main thrust of Vanderburgh's defense of Hume, having to do with what Hume means by "proof" and Hume's non-mathematical kind of probability.

ON PROOF

Hume makes a key distinction between what he calls *matters of fact* and *relations of ideas*. Relations of ideas are things that are known to be certain, because we see that their contraries contain logical contradictions. So, for example, "All bachelors are unmarried" and "2+5=7" are relations of ideas since statements like "some bachelor is married" and "2+5=6" are contradictory. Matters of fact, by contrast, are about factual matters whereby if we conceive of their opposites we do not thereby conceive a contradiction, like "this is a chair" and "the sun rises every 24 hours." Although direct sensation and induction are typically reliable, we can make mistakes about them: this means that matters of fact cannot be certain. They have "higher and lower degrees of probability, depending on the kind and strength of the evidence available," Vanderburgh explains. But relations of ideas, according to Hume, "provide us with certainty, effectively because they are analytic" (p. 27). For Hume, it's a kind of category mistake to put certainty and probability on the same scale, since they apply to different kinds of ideas.

So far this is pretty much standard stuff with Hume. As I see this, it seems that most all of his critics just aren't paying attention, for if they understood Hume's distinction between these two categories of ideas, they could pretty much derive everything important to correctly understand what he says about miracles.

Take for instance Hume's claim to have produced a "full proof" against miracles. Vanderburgh informs us, "[W]hether or not a miracle has occurred is a question regarding a matter of fact, and for Hume a degree of belief for or against a matter of fact can never reach the level of perfect certainty or logical necessity (demonstration), only moral certainty (proof)" (p. 106). For Hume, "a proof is a category of probability and not a certainty of the sort we have in the case of relations of ideas" (pp. 87–88). So Hume cannot be properly understood to mean that "there is *zero* chance that miracles can happen" (italics his, p. 87). "A *proof against the existence of any miracle* is still an *epistemic* rather than an *ontological* claim for Hume, because *proof* is an epistemic category" (italics his, p. 88). So "Contrary to what many of his critics have suggested, Hume does not think that his *proof* against miracles establishes the *impossibility* of the existence of miracles. Rather, Hume thinks that the available evidence gives us such a high degree of probability to the laws of nature that belief in the existence of miracles can never be rational—that is, sufficiently well-grounded epistemically" (italics his, p. 7).

Vanderburgh: [T]he whole structure of Hume's argument against miracles is a posteriori (and hence cannot lead to logically necessary propositions). Hume argues that *as a matter of fact*, and *given what we know* about human psychology and the facts of history there has never been and probably never will be an instance in which the probability that a miracle has occurred rises to the level greater than the probability that the reporter is mistaken, has been deceived, or is a deceiver. It is true that Hume puts this point very strongly but, in the context of Hume's thought, it is easy to see that despite his rhetoric he does not really mean anything stronger than this" (italics his, p. 106).

On Mathematical Probability

Vanderburgh shows us that Hume stood in a long tradition of non-mathematical reasoning stretching back through Francis Bacon to the Roman world. The fact that so many of Hume's critics have misunderstood and objected to Hume's case against miracles is because they have interpreted him as if he was arguing for a mathematical probability.

To see this as a mistake in action take a closer look at Hume's general maxim: "That no testimony is sufficient to establish a miracle, unless the testimony be of such a kind, that its falsehood would be more miraculous, than the fact, which it endeavours to establish; and even in that case there is a mutual destruction of arguments, and the superior only gives us an assurance suitable to that degree of force, which remains, after *deducting* the inferior." [italics mine, Hume, "Of Miracles" #91] It looks like Hume is using mathematical reasoning at the very end. But if this were the case then as John Earman easily objects, Hume is "double counting." For as Vanderburgh explains, the "degree to which one should believe that the next roll of a die will come up six is not calculated by subtracting the probabilities that the event will not occur from the probability it will occur: 5/6th minus 1/6th = 4/6th against, or 2/6th in favor. Clearly the correct degree of belief is 1/6th in favor" (p. 67).

In my view Hume surely would not make such a huge math mistake, so he was not making a mathematical argument! It should be that simple. Hume was trained in law though, and such an argument does make good sense in a criminal trial. Vanderburgh suggests we think instead of a "balance beam" where we pile evidence on one side or another to see which side has the weight of evidence for it. Vanderburgh concludes that mathematical means of understanding Hume "are not appropriately analogous to Hume's reasoning about evidential probability" (p. 68). Vanderburgh: "In Hume's epistemology, mathematical calculations are *relations of ideas*, things that can be known with absolute certainty, whereas empirical *matters of fact* are not the sorts of things that can be known with certainty" (italics his, p. 29).

When it comes to Bayes' Theorem, I've already discussed it in chapter 3 of this volume, where I also put a link in footnote #61 expressing some reservations on using it to investigate miracles. I stand by what I said. It's nice Vanderburgh seems to share my reservations about it. I'll not repeat myself here. Vanderburgh makes two claims about it. Firstly, using precise numbers to express probabilities (including but not limited to Bayes Theorem) is not the proper way to understand Hume. We've already seen this to be the case, and Vanderburgh has a lot more interesting things to say on that topic. Secondly, Hume's non-mathematical approach to evidential probability is "perfectly adequate" (p. 163) and "might even be correct" (p. 112). Vanderburgh argues that "mathematical probability is not the only viable approach to problems regarding weight of evidence." Furthermore, "in many situations the numerical approach to probability is simply inappropriate" (p. 114).

Vanderburgh argues that subjective values are not always (or easily) quantifiable (p. 127), especially when the issues are deeply complex (pp. 113–114, 126, 164). "Bayesianism," he notes, "does not solve the problem of induction" either, "it just sidesteps or ignores that problem" (p. 165). Furthermore, Bayesianism "has not shown itself to be able to improve upon the conclusions of the non-numerical tradition in many spheres of analysis" (p. 166). On this he notes the many different conflicting Bayesian interpretations of Hume's argument itself (pp. 122, 124 & 128). He informs us that "the central problem of determining the probability of propositions supported by exceptionless past experience has resisted all attempts at mathematical analysis" (p. 114).

There is a time to use math and a time not to use it though: "Mathematical probability applies perfectly in stochastic setups with known alternatives; in other contexts, it is an artificial tool that does not accurately reflect how humans do or should reason about evidence; using it can mislead us" (p.127). Too often however, "The appearance of precision is nothing but an illusion." So, "it can be potentially misleading, and is even positively harmful" (p. 163). "Numbers are impressively powerful in a great many contexts" he says. But "We should expect only the degree of precision appropriate to the subject matter" (p. 127).

We've already seen an instance of this dangerous illusion in my chapter 3, where I quote William Lane Craig in a debate with Bart Ehrman, saying that his arguments against miracles are "mathematically fallacious." *cough*

Non-mathematical reasoning isn't as precise, but some issues don't lead to precision. It's good enough in those cases. It's even better when evaluating miracle claims according to the strength of the evidence. Sound non-mathematical reasoning, Baconian reasoning, legal reasoning according to the standard of reasonable doubt, reasoning on a continuum from an extremely high degree of probability to an extremely low degree of probability, and every point in between, can be described without mathematical precision. What's the difference in saying x is highly probable or saying x is 92% or 93% or 94% or 95% or 96% or 97% or 98% probable? Very little if anything. We're not counting spoons here. We're weighing evidence. One can even translate Bayes' Theorem into language and use it without the math, by asking and answering the same kinds of questions it demands. We can start by putting off all mathematical reasoning as little more than pure guesswork and conjecture, until there is some objective evidence for an extraordinary miraculous claim. On this point Christopher Hitchens is dead on when he said, "What can be asserted without evidence can also be dismissed without evidence." (*God Is Not Great*, p. 150).

Like myself and many others, Vanderburgh agrees with the ECREE principle I defended earlier in this book, saying "The more extraordinary the claim, the more extraordinary must be the evidence that would be required in order to establish belief in the claim as reasonable" (p. 109). As Hume, Vanderburgh and I argue, there is no escaping this reasonable requirement, which just happens to be the demise of all miracles. It didn't have to turn out this way. It's just that miracles never meet this reasonable requirement. The very fact that believing apologists must reject the ECREE principle is evidence, all on its own, that they're trying to defend that which cannot be defended by reason.

ABOUT THE CONTRIBUTING AUTHORS

Edward T. Babinski is an assistant librarian, and editor of the book, *Leaving the Fold: Testimonies of Former Fundamentalists* (2003). His writings appear on the Secular Web, Talk Origins, Debunking Christianity, and at www.edwardtbabinski.us/

Robert Conner studied Greek, Hebrew, some Aramaic and even Coptic back in the mid-70s at Western Kentucky University. He's written nine books, including *Jesus the Sorcerer, The Secret Gospel of Mark* and *Magic in Christianity*, as well as a number of articles and essays.

David Corner received his PhD from the University of California at Santa Barbara. He's a Senior Lecturer in the Department of Philosophy of California State University, Sacramento. He's the author of *The Philosophy of Miracles*. (Corner died in October 2019.)

Evan Fales earned his doctorate from Temple University and is an Associate Professor of Philosophy at The University of Iowa. He has written numerous articles and works including *Divine Intervention* (2010).

Abby Hafer has a doctorate in zoology from Oxford University and teaches human anatomy and physiology at Curry College. She has worked on many different human physiology research projects, including ones at Harvard School of Public Health. She is the author of the book *The Not-So-Intelligent Designer--Why Evolution Explains the Human Body and Intelligent Design Does Not*.

Randall Heskett earned a PhD in Hebrew Bible/Old Testament from the University of Toronto, where he has served as a lecturer in his expertise. He has written/edited a number of publications including *Messianism Within the Scriptural Scroll of Isaiah* (2007).

John W. Loftus earned MA, MDiv, and ThM degrees in philosophy of religion, the last of which was under William Lane Craig. John also studied in a PhD program at Marquette University. He is the author of *Why I Became An Atheist, The Outsider Test for Faith, How to Defend the Christian Faith: Advice from an Atheist, Unapologetic,* and co-wrote *God or Godless* with Randal Rauser. He's also the editor of *The Christian Delusion, The End of Christianity, Christianity is Not Great* and *Christianity in the Light of Science.*

David Madison is the author of *Ten Tough Problems in Christian Thought and Belief: a Minister-Turned-Atheist Shows Why You Should Ditch the Faith* (2016), and has been a contributing writer to the Debunking Christianity Blog for two years. He has a PhD in Biblical Studies from Boston University, and was a pastor in the Methodist Church for nine years.

Matthew McCormick (Sacramento, CA) is professor of philosophy at California State University, Sacramento. He wrote the book *Atheism and the Case against Christ* (2012) and has contributed chapters to *The Impossibility of God*, edited by Michael Martin and Ricki Monnier, and to *The End of Christianity*, edited by John Loftus. He has published widely in philosophy, particularly on atheism.

Robert J. Miller is Rosenberger Chair of Christian and Religious Studies at Juniata College in Pennsylvania. A Fellow of the Jesus Seminar since 1986, he was Scholar-in-Residence at Westar Institute in 2001. He is the author of numerous books, including *Born Divine: The Births of Jesus and Other Sons of God*; *The Jesus Seminar and Its Critics*; editor of *The Apocalyptic Jesus: A Debate* and *The Complete Gospels*, and *Helping Jesus Fulfill Prophecy.*

Clay Farris Naff is a science journalist and the Humanist magazine's science and religion correspondent. He is the author/editor of numerous books,including *Free God Now!* and *It's a Miracle?: What Modern Science Tells Us about Popular Bible Stories.*

R. G. Price is a software engineer and data analyst by profession, with a Bachelor of Science in biology. He's the author of the book, *Deciphering the Gospels Proves Jesus Never Existed* (2018), which was good enough to merit a foreword written by Robert M. Price. For the book, he used his expertise in systematic data analysis to go through the Gospel called Mark line by line, searching for related passages in the Old Testament and Pauline letters using various translations, including the Septuagint (the ancient Greek translation of the Hebrew Scriptures), something that could only be done recently thanks to computers and the internet.

Robert M. Price is a member of the Jesus Seminar and author of several books including *Deconstructing Jesus* (2000), *The Incredible Shrinking Son of Man: How Reliable is the Gospel Tradition?* (2003), co-editor of *The Empty Tomb: Jesus Beyond the Grave* (2005), *The Paperback Apocalypse: How the Christian Church Was Left Behind* (2007), *Inerrant the Wind: The Evangelical Crisis of Biblical Authority* (2009), and a chapter in *The Christian Delusion: Why Faith Fails*, edited by John W. Loftus.

Darren M. Slade earned a PhD in theology and church history from the Rawlings School of Divinity (Liberty University), and specializes in historic-speculative theology, theoretical metaphysics, and the socio-political development of religious belief systems. His academic publications include investigations into Islamic history, church history, ancient Near-Eastern textual interpretations, and the academic study of the philosophy, sociology, and psychology of religion. Darren is currently the Research Director of the FaithX Project and Founding Editor of the peer-reviewed academic journal, *Socio-Historical Examination of Religion and Ministry* (SHERM Journal).

Valerie Tarico earned a doctorate degree in Counseling Psychology from the University of Iowa and completed postdoctoral studies at the University of Washington. She is the author of the book *Trusting Doubt: A Former Evangelical Looks at Old Beliefs in a New Light* (2010), and chapters in *The Christian Delusion: Why Faith Fails* (2010), *The End of Christianity* (2011), *Christianity is Not Great* (2014) and *Christianity in the*

Light of Science, all edited by John Loftus. She founded WisdomCommons.org and writes regularly for online news and opinion sites including AlterNet and *The Huffington Post*. Her articles can be found at AwayPoint.Wordpress.com.

www.ingramcontent.com/pod-product-compliance
Lightning Source LLC
Chambersburg PA
CBHW020321170426
43200CB00006B/230